EAST ASIA: A BIBLIOGRAPHY FOR UNDERGRADUATE LIBRARIES

Donald Gillin
History Department, Vassar College
Area Editor

Edith Ehrman
Manager, Foreign Area Materials Center
Project Editor

Ward Morehouse
Director, Center for International
Programs and Comparative Studies
Project Director

Occasional Publication No. 10
Foreign Area Materials Center
University of the State of New York,
State Education Department
and
National Council of Associations for International Studies
New York, 1969

BRO-DART PUBLISHING COMPANY
WILLIAMSPORT, PENNSYLVANIA · 1970

The research reported herein was performed pursuant to a contract with the Office of Education, U.S. Department of Health, Education, and Welfare. Contractors undertaking such projects under Government sponsorship are encouraged to express freely their professional judgment in the conduct of the project. Points of view or opinions stated do not, therefore, necessarily represent official Office of Education position or policy.

EAST ASIA: A BIBLIOGRAPHY FOR UNDERGRADUATE LIBRARIANS

To HAL (IBM-1),
an intricate piece of machinery,
which has been most helpful
except when he tried
to think for himself.

CONTENTS

CONTENTS

CONTENTS

CONTENTS

CONTENTS

Foreword

If libraries are the cornerstone of academic endeavor, it follows that no language and area study program can be effective without adequate library resources for student reading and faculty research. Undergraduate library collections on "neglected" foreign areas are woefully inadequate - a circumstance amply reflected in recent studies and surveys. The Association of American Colleges study, <u>Non-Western Studies in the Liberal Arts College</u> (1964), for example, concluded that:

> After faculty, if not before, the most essential resource of a college is teaching materials. For the humanities and the social sciences, which embrace all courses normally embodied in a non-Western program, this means, above all, books and periodicals. Our inquiry shows that library facilities reveal as serious deficiencies as do faculties for the purpose of non-Western studies. With a few exceptions, even among the colleges that have already made a start on a non-Western program, libraries are woefully inadequate for student reading, let alone further study on the part of the faculty. The cost of filling the gaps will be high...at the same time economy dictates careful discrimination in the choice of items. This may well be beyond the capacity of the average college librarian with no training in non-Western fields. Outside advice will almost always be needed....

In addition, as the interest in foreign area studies grows, more libraries are buying the same basic works and even recently published books tend to go out-of-print fairly rapidly. In discussing the acquisitions program of the Trevor Arnett Library of the Atlanta University Center for the year 1963-64, the same survey states:

> These figures reflect another difficulty, which is that many important works, including some published fairly recently, are out-of-print and hard to obtain. For example, even in the case of books on China, which in turn are probably more plentiful than those on India, which in turn are probably more numerous than those on Africa, the Atlanta program ordered over 700 publications but actually acquired just over 400....

The Center for International Programs and Comparative Studies of the State Education Department, University of the State of New York, under the auspices of which this bibliography was compiled, has a special concern with the problems of library resources on foreign areas. The need for such resources in New York State has been accentuated by recent activities of the Center. A number of modest matching grants to colleges have been made out of funds received from private foundations in support of different aspects of the Center's programs in undergraduate education to secure basic library materials in Asian and African studies, but frequently the desired works have not been available. There are, furthermore, more than 125 institutions in New York, faculty of which have participated in various seminars, faculty research, and fellowship programs organized by the Center for International programs and Comparative Studies. The faculty members involved in such programs - over 1,000 in the past half dozen years - customarily request library acquisitions on the basis of bibliographic guidance offered in the programs, only again to be disappointed because the books are not in print or cannot be found.

But these problems are not confined to colleges in New York State. Recent discussions within the National Council of Associations for International Studies make it clear that similar problems exist in undergraduate institutions throughout the country. The National Council, a consortium of regional associations of over 400 colleges in some 20 states, has since 1967 also sponsored the work of the Foreign Area Materials Center where this bibliography was compiled.

This bibliography and similar ones on South Asia, Africa south of the Sahara, and a guide to reference works on non-European areas are one step in meeting the needs described in the preceding paragraphs. The compilation of these bibliographies was supported by a contract with the U.S. Office of Education, Department of Health, Education, and Welfare, which has an active concern with encouraging international studies in American colleges and universities. Similar bibliographies on Southeast Asia and the Middle East and North Africa are being compiled under another office of Education contract and will be published in early 1970.

Each entry in this bibliography has been graded as to degree of essentiality for undergraduate collections and keyed to annotations in existing bibliographies and reviews in selected journals. The entries have been graded on the following scale:

A: Books that should be in all undergraduate libraries whether or not any courses on the area are taught

B: Books that should be in a library collection if a few courses or parts of courses on the area are offered

C: Books necessary for an undergraduate area studies program or equivalent concentration of advanced undergraduate courses on the area

The last line of each entry contains a list of annotations and reviews. The list of reviews is based on the Book Review Digest and the tables of contents of journals such as The Journal of Asian Studies which are not indexed in the Book Review Digest. A Listing of abbreviations used appears at the end of the Introduction.

Out-of-print titles, reprints, and material in microform are also indicated. Reprints are denoted by (R) at the end of the publication information; in most cases, the original publisher and date have been given. Material in microform is indicated by (M) followed by the microfilmer's name. A list of microfilm companies and their addresses appears at the end of the bibliography. Any titled not followed by "o.p." is in print; entries have been checked against Books in Print, 1968, British Books in Print, The Publishers' Trade List Annual, 1968, and other available sources. All entries have also been checked against the National Union Catalogue, and some for which there is no card number will be found in the NUC.

The Foreign Area Materials Center has been attempting to interest publishers in reprinting out-of-print titles included in this bibliography with the result that the status of many entries is continuously changing. Librarians and others wishing to determine the present availability of out-of-print titles may write to the Foreign Area Materials Center.

Prices of the books have not been included because they are subject to change. They are, however, indicated in many of the annotations and reviews cited. For budgetary purposes, many librarians now calculate the average cost per title at $8.40.

This bibliography was produced by computer, using a combination of the IBM Call/360 Datatext system for data entry and updating and Honeywell 200 for sorting and indexing. The programs written for the project are in the public domain. Copies of the bibliographies on magnetic tape are also available at a cost of around $5.00-$10.00. It should be noted, however, that a conversion program would have to be written to make these tapes compatible with the Library of Congress Machine Readable Catalog (MARC) system.

Without the generous assistance of numerous individuals, compilation of the bibliography would not have been possible. A list of consultants follows the Foreward. The library panel of advisers for the project consisting of Anne C. Edmonds, Mt. Holyoke College; Nancy Devine, Mt. Holyoke College; Dorothy Drake, Scripps College; Evan Ira Farber, Earlham College has provided invaluable counsel. Donald Gillin, Vassar College, has served as area editor for this bibliography and has given much needed guidance. Advice on the computerized aspects of the project was provided by Stephen Mitchell, Syracuse University; Mrs. Lynda Sloan, Project URBANDOC; Barbara Gill, Robert S. Tucker, and Edward C. Barasch of IBM Datatext; and Gary Brown of Commercial Programming Unlimited. The day-to-day operations of the project were greatly assisted by the patience and understanding of Les Flynn and others at Datatext Operations who spent many hours over the past few months in assisting with any problem, large or small, that arose. Christopher Samuels and other staff members of the Reference and Orientalia Divisions of the New York Public Library and Evan Farber and his staff at the Earlham College Library helped enormously in checking for book reviews and verifying publication information.

Lois Brown, Joan Ells, and Kathleen Hale of the Foreign Area Materials Center staff played a large role in typing most of the material, checking for out-of-print books, and other tedious and time-consuming tasks. Their involvement went well beyond the call of duty.

Edith Ehrman, Manager of the Center, supervised the day-to-day operations of the project and was responsible for the editing, as well as arrangements for the use of the computers and seeing the final manuscript through the press. She more than anyone else is responsible for whatever accomplishment this undertaking represents.

The entire project is being carried out by the Foreign Area Materials Center, an undertaking of the Center for International Programs and Comparative Studies which is concerned with strengthening teaching about foreign areas, mainly at the undergraduate level. The activities of the Foreign Area Materials Center are also sponsored by the National Council of Associations for International Studies, a group of eleven regional college associations and consortia. The work of the Foreign Area Materials Center is described in a brief note which appears at the conclusion of this bibliography.

Ward Morehouse
Project Director

April, 1969

List of Consultants

Faubion Bowers
New York City

Robert Brower
University of Michigan

Ardath Burks
Rutgers University

Chu-yuan Cheng
University of Michigan

Wm. Theodore De Bary
Columbia University

Ronald P. Dore
University of London

Donald Gillin
Vassar College

C. T. Hu
Teachers College,
Columbia University

C. T. Li
University of Kansas

William Lockwood
Princeton University

Robert Marsh
Brown University

Shannon McCune
American Geographical
Society

Fred G. Notehelfer
Princeton University

Herbert Passin
Teachers College,
Columbia University

Marleigh Ryan
Columbia University

William Schultz
University of Arizona

Harold P. Stern
Freer Gallery of Art

Library Panel of Advisors

Nancy Devine
Mt. Holyoke College

Dorothy Drake
Scripps College

Anne C. Edmonds
Mt. Holyoke College

Evan Ira Farber
Earlham College

Introduction

Compiling this bibliography has involved certain tasks which merit discussion and explanation, namely: periodization, categorization, and classification or "rating" of the materials listed. The periodization employed here more or less conforms to that used in generally accepted texts on East Asia, such as <u>A History of East Asian Civilization</u> written by Fairbank, Reischauer, and Craig. In the case of China, we have divided the time span of Chinese history into four parts: 1) Early, which includes most of the period before the coming of the West, 2) Ming and Manchu, which might be called "early modern," 3) Revolution and Republic or "late modern," and 4) Communist or contemporary. Japan's history has been divided into four comparable parts: 1) Early History, meaning the period before the advent of Chinese influence, 2) Pre-modern or through the Meiji Restoration, 3) Modern to 1945, meaning from the Meiji Restoration to the end of World War II, and 4) Post-war or contemporary. A comparable method of periodization has been employed with respect to Korean history. Although many scholars favor other ways of periodizing East Asian history, we feel that the method used here is the most widely accepted.

As for categorization, books dealing with more than one country in the area - e.g., Japan and China - have been listed under East Asia general to avoid duplicate entries. Besides grouping works under History, we have also employed the following categories: Bibliographies, Reference Books, General Books, Geography, Government and Politics, Economics, Sociology, Anthropology, and Linguistics, Language and Literature, Philosophy and Religion, Fine Art and Architecture, Performing Arts, Education and Mass Communication, and Science and Technology. Users of this bibliography should be warned, however, that many of the works included in it can, with almost equal justification, be fitted into more than one of these categories; frequently a book having much to do with one discipline nevertheless will show up in a different category. This especially is true in the case of books dealing with what might be called "contemporary history" inasmuch as teachers in disciplines like economics, sociology, and political science generally make use of modern systems; works dealing with these subjects in periods earlier than modern will generally be found under History. Our aim has been to make this bibliography as useful as possible not only to librarians but also to college and university teachers.

With respect to classification, it should be emphasized that many of the books classified here as B or even C are in no way inferior to those labeled A. Our object in the first instance is to meet the needs of colleges and smaller universities, having very limited funds available for the purchase of books dealing with East Asia and generally offering only survey or similarly non-specialized courses on the area. We have excluded from the A category many otherwise excellent books which, at least in our opinion, are too specialized to be of significant value to those users although such titles are clearly important for more advanced students. We hope, however, that those titles in the B and C categories will be useful to institutions offering more advanced undergraduate work on East Asia.

Donald Gillin
Vassar College

Sample Entry

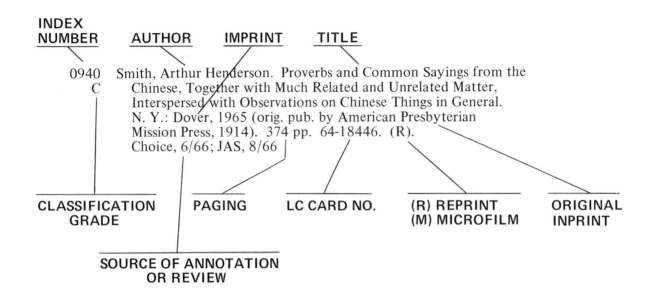

INDEX
NUMBER   AUTHOR   IMPRINT   TITLE

0940   Smith, Arthur Henderson. Proverbs and Common Sayings from the
C   Chinese, Together with Much Related and Unrelated Matter,
        Interspersed with Observations on Chinese Things in General.
        N. Y.: Dover, 1965 (orig. pub. by American Presbyterian
        Mission Press, 1914). 374 pp. 64-18446. (R).
        Choice, 6/66; JAS, 8/66

CLASSIFICATION   PAGING   LC CARD NO.   (R) REPRINT   ORIGINAL
GRADE   (M) MICROFILM   INPRINT

SOURCE OF ANNOTATION
OR REVIEW

Key to Abbreviations for Annotation and Review

AUFS: American Universities Field Staff. A Select Bibliography: Asia, Africa Eastern Europe, Latin America.

Sup. 61: 1961 Supplement to the American Universities Field Staff Bibliography.

Sup. 63: 1963 Supplement to the American Universities Field Staff Bibliography.

Sup. 65: 1965 Supplement to the American Universities Field Staff Bibliography.

Sup. 67: 1967 Supplement to the American Universities Field Staff Bibliography.

Hucker: Charles O. Hucker. China: A Critical Bibliography.

Silberman: Bernard S. Silberman. Japan and Korea: A Critical Bibliography.

Choice: Choice.

JAS: Journal of Asian Studies.

FEQ: Far Eastern Quarterly.

Am. Anthropologist: American Anthropologist.

Am. Econ. R.: American Economic Review.

AHR: American Historical Review.

Am. J. Pub. Health: American Journal of Public Health and the Nation's Health.

Am. J. Soc.: American Journal of Sociology.

Am. Pol. Sci. R.: American Political Science Review.

Am. Soc. R.: American Sociological Review.

Ann. Am. Acad.: Annals, the American Academy of Political and Social Science.

Arch. Forum: Architectural Forum.

Art Bul.: Art Bulletin.

China Q.: China Quarterly.

Japan Q.: Japan Quarterly

Geog. R.: Geographical Review

J. Am. Hist.: Journal of American History.

JAOS: Journal of the American Oriental Society.

J. Philosophy: Journal of Philosophy.

J. Pol. Econ.: Journal of Political Economics.

J. Religion: Journal of Religion.

Library Journal: Library Journal.

Mod. Lang. J.: Modern Language Journal.

Music Lib. Assn. Notes: Music Library Association Notes.

Pacific Affairs: Pacific Affairs.

Pol. Sci. Q.: Political Science Quarterly.

Science: Science.

TLS: Times (London) Literary Supplement.

Bibliography
by Country and Subject

BIBLIOGRAPHIES

0001 American Universities Field Staff. Select Bibliography: Asia,
A   Africa, Eastern Europe, Latin America. N.Y.: American
    Universities Field Staff, 1960. 534 pp. Supplement,
    1961; Supplement, 1963; Supplement, 1965; Supplement, 1967.
    60-10482.
    Silberman, 13

0002 Bibliography of Asian Studies. Ann Arbor: Association for
A   Asian Studies, 1956- 43-14717 rev. 2.
    Hucker, 16

0003 Bulletin of Far Eastern Bibliography. Washington: American
A   Council of Learned Societies, 1936-1940. 5 v. 42-6022 rev.

0004 Johns, Francis A. A Bibliography of Arthur Waley. New
B   Brunswick, N.J.: Rutgers University Press, 1968.
    187 pp. 67-20388.
    Choice, 9/68; Library Journal, 5/1/68; TLS, 5/2/68

0005 Kerner, Robert Joseph. Northeastern Asia, a Select Bibliog-
C   raphy. Berkeley: University of California Press, 1939.
    2 v. 39-33136.
    AUFS, 4599; Silberman, 10; AHR, 7/40; JAOS, 9/40; Pacific
    Affairs, 3/40

0006 London. University. School of Oriental and African Studies.
B   Library. Monthly List of Periodical Articles on the Far
    East and South East Asia. London: 1954- 56-16909.
    (R-Kraus).
    Silberman, 26

0007 Pearson, James Douglas. Oriental and Asian Bibliography, an
B   Introduction with Some Reference to Africa. Hamden, Conn.:
    Archon, 1966. 261 pp. 66-1006.
    Choice, 11/66; JAS, 2/67; Library Journal, 6/1/66

0008 Quarterly Check-list of Oriental Studies. v.1- Darien,
C   Conn.: American Bibliographic Service, 1959- 65-45222.
    Hucker, 21; Silberman, 25

0009 Silberman, Bernard S. Japan and Korea, a Critical Bibliogra-
A   phy. Tucson: University of Arizona Press, 1962. 120 pp.
    62-11821.
    JAS, 5/63

REFERENCE BOOKS

0010 Asia Society. American Institutions and Organizations Interested
A   in Asia: a Reference Directory. ed. by Ward Morehouse. 2d
    ed. N.Y.: Taplinger for Asia Society, 1961. 581 pp.
    61-11435.
    Sup. 63, 2873; JAS, 5/62; Library Journal, 9/1/61

0011 Beasley, William Gerald and E. G. Pullyblank, eds. Histor-
A   ians of China and Japan. N.Y.: Oxford, 1961. 351 pp.
    (University of London, Historical Writing on the Peoples
    of Asia, Vol. 3). Hand catalog.
    Sup. 63, 2876; Hucker, 1620a; JAS, 5/62; Japan Q., 1-3/62

0012 Columbia University. Columbia College. A Guide to the Oriental
A   Classics, Prepared by the Staff of the Oriental Studies
    Program, Columbia College, and Edited by Wm. Theodore De Bary.
    N.Y.: Columbia University Press, 1964. 199 pp. 63-20463.
    Sup. 65, 3045; Choice, 9/64

0013 De Bary, William Theodore, ed. Approaches to Asian Civiliza-
A   tions. N.Y.: Columbia University Press, 1964. 293 pp.
    63-20226.
    JAS, 2/65

0014 Hinton, Harold C., ed. Major Topics on China and Japan; A Hand-
B   book for Teachers. ed. by Harold C. Hinton and Marius B.
    Jansen. N.Y.: Institute of Pacific Relations, 1957. 326 pp.
    57-4216. o.p. (M-University).
    AUFS, 91; Hucker, 5; JAS, 8/58

0015 London. University. School of Oriental and African Studies.
A   Handbook of Oriental History, by Members of the Dept. of
    Oriental History, School of Oriental and African Studies,
    University of London. London: Offices of the Royal Histori-
    cal Society, 1963 (orig. pub. in 1951). 265 pp. 51-4902.
    (R).
    AUFS, 38

0016 Maki, John McGilvrey, comp. Selected Documents, Far Eastern
B   International Relations (1689-1951). Seattle: University
    of Washington Press, 1951. 333 pp. A52-9869. o.p.
    Sup. 61, 2752; Hucker, 656; Silberman, 332

0017 Sellman, Roger Raymond. An Outline Atlas of Eastern History.
A   London: Arnold, 1954. 63 pp. Map 54-1526. o.p.
    AUFS, 54; Hucker, 96

0018 Stucki, Curtis W. American Doctoral Dissertations on Asia,
A   1933-June, 1966, Including Appendix of Master's Theses at
    Cornell University, 1933-June, 1968. Ithaca, N.Y.: South-
    east Asia Program, Dept. of Far Eastern Studies, Cornell
    University, 1968. 304 pp. (Data Paper No. 71). 64-2901.
    (M-University).
    Hucker, 23

0019 Wint, Guy, ed. Asia; A Handbook. N.Y.: Praeger, 1966.
B   856 pp. 65-13263.
    Sup. 67, 3207; Library Journal, 6/15/66; Pacific Affairs,
    Fall-Winter/66-67; TLS, 7/7/66

JOURNALS

0020 Amerasia. v.1-11. 1937-1947.
C

0021 American Oriental Society. Journal, v.1- 1843/49-
A   (R-Kraus).
    AUFS, 2; Hucker, 38

0022 Ars Asiatica, v.1-18. 1914-35.
B

0023 Ars Orientalis. v.1- 1954-
B   Sup. 61, 2749

0024 Artibus Asiae, v.1- 1925- (R-Johnson).
A

0025 Asia and the Americas. v.1-46. 1898-1946.
C

0026 Asia Major, v.1-10. 1924-35. n.s.v.1- 1949- (R-Johnson).
B   Hucker, 31; Silberman, 39

0027 Asian Recorder. v.1- 1955-
C   Sup. 61, 2750

0028 Asian Survey, v.1- 1961- (1932-61 as Far Eastern Sur-
A   vey, v.1-30). (R-Kraus).
    AUFS, 86; Hucker, 27

0029 Far East Digest. nos. 1-135. 1947-1958.
C

0030 Far Eastern Ceramic Bulletin, v.1-12. 1948-60.
C

0031 Far Eastern Economic Review, v.1- 1946- (M-Microphoto).
B   Hucker, 2158

0032 Harvard Journal of Asiatic Studies, v.1- 1936- (R-Micro-
A   photo, M-IDC).
    AUFS, 25; Hucker, 28; Silberman, 31

0033 Journal of Asian Studies, v.1- 1941- (1941-56 as Far
A   Eastern Quarterly). (R-AMS).
    AUFS, 30; Hucker, 24; Silberman, 30

0034 Journal of Oriental Studies, v.1- 1954- (M-IDC).
B   Hucker, 32

0035 Literature East and West. v.1- 1954-
B

0036 London. University. School of Oriental and African Studies.
C   Bulletin, v.1- 1917- (R-Kraus, M-IDC).
    Hucker, 30

0037 Modern Asian Studies. v.1- 1967-
A

0038 Oriens, v.1- 1948-
C   Hucker, 37

0039 Oriens Extremus; Zeitschrift fur Sprache, Kunst und Kulture
C   der Laender des Fernen Ostens, v.1- 1954-
    Hucker, 36; Silberman, 38

0040 Oriental Art. v.1-3. 1948-1951. n.s.v.1- 1955-
C

0041 Oriental Ceramic Society. Transactions. London: 1921-
C

0042 Pacific Affairs, v.1- 1926- (1926-28 as Institute of
A   Pacific Relations News Bulletin).
     AUFS, 44; Hucker, 26; Silberman, 33

0043 Pacific Historical Review. v.1- 1932-
B

0044 Philosophy East and West. v.1- 1951- (R-Johnson).
B   FEQ, 5/45

0045 Revue des Arts Asiatiques, v.1-13. 1924-42.
B

0046 Royal Asiatic Society of Great Britain and Ireland. Journal.
B   v.1-20. 1834-1863. n.s.v.1-21. 1864-1889. s.3 v.1-
     1889- (R-Kraus).
     Hucker, 44

0047 Stockholm. Ostasiatiska Samlingarna Bulletin, v.1-
C   1929-
     Hucker, 42

0048 Tokyo. Oriental Library (Toyo Bunko). Publications. Series B.
C   Research Department Memoirs. no.1- 1926- (M-IDC).
     Hucker, 43

0049 United Asia, v.1- 1948-
C   AUFS, 61

0050 United Nations. Economic Commission for Asia and the Far
C   East. Economic Bulletin for Asia and the Far East. v.1-
     1950- (R-Johnson).
     FEQ, 11/52

GENERAL BOOKS

0051 Chicago. University. Committee for the Comparative Study of
B   New Nations. Old Societies and New States, the Quest for
     Modernity in Asia and Africa. ed. by Clifford Geertz.
     N.Y.: Free Press of Glencoe, 1963. 310 pp. 63-8416.
     Sup. 65, 3046; JAS, 2/64; Am. Anthropologist, 8/64; Am. J.
     Soc., 3/64; Am. Pol. Sci. R., 3/64

0052 The Developing World; AUFS Readings - Vol. I- N.Y.: American
C   Universities Field Staff, 1966- 66-29570.
     Sup. 67, 3204

0053 Eastern and Western World; Selected Readings. ed. by S. Hofstra.
B   The Hague: W. van Hoeve for Netherlands Universities Founda-
     tion for International Co-operation, 1953. 181 pp. 53-40444.

0054 Greene, Fred. U.S. Policy and the Security of Asia. N.Y.:
C   McGraw-Hill for Council on Foreign Relations, 1968. 429 pp.
     (Council on Foreign Relations/United States and China in
     World Affairs). 68-11606.
     Choice, 7-8/68

0055 Grousset, Rene. The Civilizations of the East. tr. from French
A   by Catherine Alison Phillips. N.Y.: Cooper Square, 1967
     (orig. pub. by Knopf, 1931-34). 4 v. 66-30807. (R).
     (M-University).
     AUFS, 24; Choice, 3/69; FEQ, 8/42; TLS, 11/1/34

0056 Grousset, Rene. Histoire de l'Extreme-Orient. Paris:
B   Geuthner, 1929. 2 v. 30-9378.
     AUFS, 89

0057 Isaacs, Harold Robert. No Peace for Asia. Cambridge, Mass.:
C   M.I.T. Press, 1967 (orig. pub. by Macmillan, 1947). 295 pp.
     67-15237. (R).
     Choice, 1/68

0058 Jackson, Barbara (Ward). The Interplay of East and West,
B   Points of Conflict and Co-Operation. N.Y.: Norton, 1957.
     152 pp. 57-8337.
     AUFS, 29; JAS, 2/58; TLS, 6/21/57

0059 Lattimore, Owen. The Situation in Asia. Boston: Little,
C   Brown, 1949. 244 pp. 49-2218. o.p.
     AUFS, 34; Am. Pol. Sci. R., 10/49

0060 Lattimore, Owen. Solution in Asia. Boston: Little, Brown,
C   1945. 214 pp. 45-1566. o.p.
     FEQ, 8/45; Pacific Affairs, 12/45

0061 Low, Sir Francis. Struggle for Asia. N.Y.: Praeger, 1955.
C   239 pp. 55-11624. o.p.
     JAS, 11/57

0062 Moraes, Francis Robert. Yonder One World; A Study of Asia and
C   the West. N.Y.: Macmillan, 1958. 209 pp. 58-6962.
     JAS, 5/59; Library Journal, 4/15/58

0063 Peterson, Alexander Duncan Campbell. The Far East, a Social
C   Geography. London: Duckworth, 1949. 336 pp. 50-717.

0064 Reischauer, Edwin Oldfather. Beyond Vietnam: the United States
B   and Asia. N.Y.: Knopf, 1967. 242 pp. 67-25614.
     Choice, 4/68; Library Journal, 10/15/67; TLS, 11/17/67

0065 Romein, Jan Marius. The Asian Century, a History of Modern
A   Nationalism in Asia. tr. by R. T. Clark. Berkeley:
     University of California Press, 1962. 448 pp. 62-51755.
     Sup. 63, 2874; JAS, 5/65; AHR, 10/63; Ann. Am. Acad., 11/63;
     Pacific Affairs, Fall/63; Pol. Sci. Q., 12/63

0066 Rosinger, Lawrence Kaelter. The State of Asia, a Contemporary
C   Survey. N.Y.: Knopf, 1951. 522 pp. 51-11245. o.p.
     AUFS, 51; FEQ, 2/52; Library Journal, 7/51

0067 Strausz-Hupe, Robert. American-Asian Tensions. N.Y.: Praeger,
C   1956. 239 pp. 56-10497 rev. o.p.
     JAS, 8/57; Am. Pol. Sci. R., 6/57; Am. Soc. R., 4/57;
     Ann. Am. Acad., 7/57; Library Journal, 6/15/56

0068 Studies on Asia. Lincoln: University of Nebraska Press, Vol.
B   I- 1960- 60-15432.
     Sup. 63, 2875; Choice, 6/66

0069 Thomson, Ian. The Rise of Modern Asia. N.Y.: Pitman, 1958.
B   265 pp. 58-6406. o.p.
     Library Journal, 4/1/58; TLS, 2/7/58

0070 Toynbee, Arnold J. The World and the West. N.Y.: Oxford,
A   1953. 99 pp. 53-5911.
     AUFS, 60; AHR, 10/53; Am. Soc. R., 8/53; Ann. Am. Acad.,
     5/53; Library Journal, 5/15/53

0071 Wint, Guy. Spotlight on Asia. Baltimore: Penguin, 1955.
B   221 pp. 59-7728. o.p.
     Pacific Affairs, 12/60; TLS, 4/17/59

0072 Wittfogel, Karl August. Oriental Despotism, a Comparative Study
A   of Total Power. New Haven, Conn.: Yale University Press,
     1957. 556 pp. 56-10873.
     AUFS, 65; Hucker, 1791; Am. Anthropologist, 6/57; JAOS,
     1-3/61; Library Journal, 4/1/57

0073 Zinkin, Maurice. Asia and the West. new and rev. ed. N.Y.:
B   International Secretariat, Institute of Pacific Relations,
     1953. 304 pp. A54-8866. o.p.
     FEQ, 11/52; Am. Pol. Sci. R., 9/53; Am. Soc. R., 8/52;
     Ann. Am. Acad., 11/53; J. Pol. Econ., 8/52; Pacific Affairs,
     6/52

GEOGRAPHY

0074 Cressey, George Babcock. Asia's Lands and Peoples, a Geog-
A   raphy of One-third of the Earth and Two-thirds of Its
     People. 3d ed. N.Y.: McGraw-Hill, 1963. 663 pp. 62-22087.
     AUFS, 19; Sup. 65, 3044; Hucker, 50; Silberman, 81; FEQ,
     5/45; Am. Anthropologist, 6/64; Library Journal, 3/15/64

0075 East, William Gordon, ed. The Changing Map of Asia, a Political
A   Geography. rev. ed. London: Methuen, dist. by Barnes &
     Noble, 1966 (orig. pub. in 1950). 434 pp. 59-1411. (R).
     Silberman, 85

0076 Ginsburg, Norton Sydney. Pattern of Asia. Englewood Cliffs,
A   N.J.: Prentice-Hall, 1958. 929 pp. 58-8513.
     AUFS, 23; Hucker, 49; JAS, 11/58

0077 Robinson, Harry. Monsoon Asia; A Geographical Survey. N.Y.:
B   Praeger, 1967. 561 pp. 67-24687.
     Choice, 11/68; JAS, 8/68; Library Journal, 2/1/68; Pacific
     Affairs, Fall/68

0078 Stamp, Laurence Dudley. Asia; A Regional and Economic Geog-
B   raphy. 11th ed. N.Y.: Dutton, 1962. 730 pp. 62-5766.
     AUFS, 56; Hucker, 51; Silberman, 83

HISTORY
GENERAL

0079 Griswold, Alfred Whitney. The Far Eastern Policy of the United
B   States. New Haven, Conn.: Yale University Press, 1964
      (orig. pub. by Harcourt, Brace, 1938). 530 pp. 62-809.
      (R).
      AUFS, 88; Hucker, 808; Silberman, 431; Choice, 2/65

0080 Hall, Daniel George Edward. A History of South-East Asia.
B   3d ed. N.Y.: St. Martin's, 1968. 807 pp. 68-15302.
      AUFS, 1279; Hucker, 117; FEQ, 5/56; Ann. Am. Acad., 5/56;
      Library Journal, 12/1/55; Pol. Sci. Q., 6/56; TLS, 11/18/55

0081 Iriye, Akira. Across the Pacific; An Inner History of
B   American-East Asian Relations. intro. by John K. Fairbank.
      N.Y.: Harcourt, Brace & World, 1967. 361 pp. 67-19202.
      Choice, 10/68; JAS, 11/68; Library Journal, 10/15/67

0082 Lach, Donald Frederick. Asia in the Making of Europe. Chicago:
A   University of Chicago Press, 1965- 985 pp. 64-19848.
      Sup. 65, 3048; JAS, 2/68; Library Journal, 1/15/65; TLS,
      8/26/65

0083 Latourette, Kenneth Scott. A Short History of the Far East.
C   4th ed. N.Y.: Macmillan, 1964. 776 pp. 64-14965.
      AUFS, 99; Choice, 9/64; FEQ, 2/47; Ann. Am. Acad., 9/46;
      Library Journal, 4/15/46

0084 MacNair, Harley Farnsworth. Modern Far Eastern International
B   Relations. 2d ed. Princeton, N.J.: Van Nostrand, 1955.
      777 pp. 55-8831.
      AUFS, 104; Silberman, 330; FEQ, 8/51

0085 Maki, John McGilvrey, ed. Conflict and Tension in the Far East:
B   Key Documents, 1894-1960. Seattle: University of Washington
      Press, 1961. 245 pp. 61-17709.
      Sup. 63, 2872; JAS, 8/62

0086 Michael, Franz H. The Far East in the Modern World. N.Y.:
B   Holt, 1956. 724 pp. 55-6036.
      AUFS, 105; Silberman, 324; JAS, 2/57; Pacific Affairs,
      6/57; TLS, 4/5/57

0087 Peffer, Nathaniel. The Far East, a Modern History. Ann
B   Arbor: University of Michigan Press, 1958. 489 pp.
      58-62522.
      AUFS, 109; Silberman, 325; JAS, 8/59; AHR, 4/59; Ann. Am.
      Acad., 5/59; Library Journal, 10/1/58; Pacific Affairs,
      12/59; TLS, 7/10/59

0088 Reischauer, Edwin Oldfather. A History of East Asian Civili-
A   zation. Boston: Houghton Mifflin, 1960- 2 v. 60-4269.
      Sup. 61, 2753; Sup. 65, 3054; Hucker, 98; Silberman, 156;
      Choice, 5/65; JAS, 8/61, 11/65; AHR, 1/61; Ann. Am. Acad.,
      11/61; JAOS, 1-3/63, 4-6/66; Library Journal, 6/15/65;
      TLS, 8/18/61

HISTORY
ANCIENT HISTORY

0089 Collis, Maurice. The Grand Peregrination, Being the Life and
C   Adventures of Fernao Mendes Pinto. N.Y.: Macmillan, 1949.
      313 pp. 50-233. o.p.
      Hucker, 592

HISTORY
EARLY HISTORY

0090 Wang, I-t'ung. Official Relations between China and Japan,
B   1368-1549, by Wang Yi-t'ung. Cambridge, Mass.: Harvard
      University Press, 1953. 128 pp. (Harvard-Yenching Insti-
      tute Studies, IX). 53-5062. o.p.
      Hucker, 490; Silberman, 228; FEQ, 5/54; JAOS, 7-9/64

HISTORY
MODERN HISTORY

0091 Battistini, Lawrence Henry. The Rise of American Influence in
B   Asia and the Pacific. East Lansing: Michigan State Uni-
      versity Press, 1960. 241 pp. 59-15833. o.p.
      Silberman, 432; JAS, 2/61

0092 Bisson, Thomas Arthur. America's Far Eastern Policy. N.Y.:
C   Institute of Pacific Relations, dist. by Macmillan, 1945.
      235 pp. 45-1072. o.p.
      Silberman, 507; FEQ, 8/45; Am. Pol. Sci. R., 8/45; Pacific

Affairs, 9/45

0093 Bisson, Thomas Arthur. Japan in China. N.Y.: Macmillan, 1938.
B   417 pp. 38-27434. o.p.
      AUFS, 777; Hucker, 797; Am. Pol. Sci. R., 10/38; Pacific
      Affairs, 9/38

0094 Borg, Dorothy. The United States and the Far Eastern Crisis
A   of 1933-1938; From the Manchurian Incident through the
      Initial State of the Undeclared Sino-Japanese War. Cam-
      bridge, Mass.: Harvard University Press, 1964. (Harvard
      East Asian Series, 14). 674 pp. 64-13421.
      Sup. 65, 3085; Choice, 7-8/64; JAS, 11/64; AHR, 1/65;
      Library Journal, 5/15/64; Pacific Affairs, Winter/64-65;
      Pol. Sci. Q., 12/64

0095 Carnegie Endowment for International Peace. Division of Inter-
C   national Law. The Sino-Japanese Negotiations of 1915,
      Japanese and Chinese Documents and Chinese Official State-
      ment. Washington: Carnegie Endowment, 1921. 76 pp.
      21-21869. o.p.
      Hucker, 750

0096 China. Assessor to the Commission of Enquiry into Sino-Japa-
C   nese Dispute. Memoranda Presented to the Lytton Commission,
      by V. K. Wellington Koo, assessor. N.Y.: The Chinese Cul-
      tural Society, 1932-33. 3 v. 33-7709 rev. 2. o.p.
      Hucker, 789

0097 Clyde, Paul Hibbert. The Far East, a History of the Western
A   Impact and the Eastern Response, 1830-1965. 4th ed.
      Englewood Cliffs, N.J.: Prentice-Hall, 1966. 511 pp.
      66-10814.
      Sup. 67, 3208; Choice, 5/66; JAS, 2/67

0098 Curry, Roy Watson. Woodrow Wilson and Far Eastern Policy,
B   1913-1921. N.Y.: Octagon, 1968 (orig. pub. by Bookman,
      1957). 411 pp. 68-22300. (R).
      Hucker, 814; Silberman, 517

0099 Dallin, David J. The Rise of Russia in Asia. New Haven,
B   Conn.: Yale University Press, 1949. 293 pp. 49-9059. o.p.
      AUFS, 20; Hucker, 702; Silberman, 417; FEQ, 5/50; Library
      Journal, 4/15/49; Pol. Sci. Q., 9/49

0100 Dallin, David J. Soviet Russia and the Far East. New Haven,
B   Conn.: Yale University Press, 1948. 398 pp. 48-9035 rev.
      o.p.
      AUFS, 80; Hucker, 834; Silberman, 491; FEQ, 5/49; AHR, 4/49;
      Am. Pol. Sci. R., 6/49; Ann. Am. Acad., 5/49; Library
      Journal, 10/15/48; Pacific Affairs, 6/49

0101 Dennett, Tyler. Americans in Eastern Asia; A Critical Study of
A   the United States' Policy in the Far East in the 19th Century.
      N.Y.: Barnes & Noble, 1963 (orig. pub. in 1922). 725 pp.
      NUC 64-38454. (R).
      AUFS, 81; Hucker, 689; Silberman, 314; JAS, 2/64; FEQ, 5/42;
      AHR, 4/23

0102 Eudin, Xenia Joukoff. Soviet Russia and the East, 1920-1927,
B   a Documentary Survey. Stanford, Calif.: Stanford Uni-
      versity Press, 1957. 478 pp. 56-8690.
      Hucker, 883; JAS, 2/58; AHR, 4/58; Pacific Affairs, 9/58;
      Pol. Sci. Q., 3/58; TLS, 1/3/58

0103 Holcombe, Arthur Norman. The Spirit of the Chinese Revolution;
C   Lowell Institute Lectures, 1930. N.Y.: Knopf, 1930. 185 pp.
      30-25102. o.p.
      Hucker, 731; Am. Pol. Sci. R., 2/31

0104 Hull, Cordell. The Memoirs of Cordell Hull. N.Y.: Macmillan,
B   1948. 2 v. 48-6761. o.p.
      Hucker, 815; Am. Pol. Sci. R., 10/48; Ann. Am. Acad.,
      7/48; Library Journal, 7/15/48

0105 Iriye, Akira. After Imperialism, the Search for a New Order
A   in the Far East, 1921-1931. Cambridge, Mass.: Harvard
      University Press, 1965. 375 pp. (Harvard East Asian
      Series, 22). 65-22052.
      Sup. 67, 3209; Choice, 6/66; JAS, 8/66; AHR, 7/66

0106 Kawakami, Kiyoshi Karl. Manchoukuo, Child of Conflict. N.Y.:
C   Macmillan, 1933. 311 pp. 33-8957. o.p.
      Hucker, 790; Am. Pol. Sci. R., 6/33; Ann. Am. Acad.,
      9/33; J. Religion, 10/33

0107 Kim, Young Hum. East Asia's Turbulent Century, with American
B   Diplomatic Documents. N.Y.: Appleton-Century-Crofts, 1966.

386 pp. 66-10328.
Choice, 9/66; Ann. Am. Acad., 9/66

0108 Malonzemoff, Andrew. Russian Far Eastern Policy, 1881-1904,
B   With Special Emphasis on the Causes of the Russo-Japanese
     War. Berkeley: University of California Press, 1958.
     358 pp. 58-12831. o.p.
     Hucker, 701; Silberman, 415; JAS, 5/59

0109 Moore, Harriet Lucy. Soviet Far Eastern Policy, 1931-1945.
B   Princeton, N.J.: Princeton University Press, 1945.
     284 pp. A45-5523. o.p. (M-University).
     AUFS, 4989; Silberman, 489; FEQ, 5/46; Library Journal,
     9/15/45

0110 Morse, Hosea Ballou. Far Eastern International Relations. N.Y.:
A   Russell & Russell, 1967 (orig. pub. by Houghton Mifflin,
     1931). 2 v. 67-15998. (R).
     AUFS, 107; AHR, 1/32

0111 Quigley, Harold Scott. Far Eastern War, 1937-1941. Boston:
C   World Peace Foundation, 1942. 369 pp. 42-14269. o.p.
     (M-University).
     Hucker, 795; Silberman, 498; FEQ, 2/43; Am. Pol. Sci. R.,
     10/42; Ann. Am. Acad., 11/42; Pacific Affairs, 9/42

0112 Satow, Sir Ernest Mason. Korea and Manchuria Between Russia
C   and Japan, 1895-1904; The Observations of Sir Ernest Satow,
     British Minister to Japan (1895-1900) and China (1900-
     1906). sel. and ed. with an historical intro. by George
     A. Lensen. Tallahassee, Fla.: Diplomatic Press, 1966.
     296 pp. 66-17316.
     Choice, 11/66; JAS, 8/66; AHR, 1/67; Japan Q., 10-12/66;
     Pacific Affairs, Spring-Summer/66

0113 Shepherd, Jack. Australia's Interests and Policies in the
C   Far East. N.Y.: Institute of Pacific Relations, 1939.
     212 pp. 39-33667. o.p. (M-University).
     AUFS, 112

0114 Stimson, Henry Lewis. The Far Eastern Crisis; Recollections and
B   Observations. N.Y.: Harper for Council on Foreign Rela-
     tions, 1936. 293 pp. 36-20072. o.p. (M-University).
     Silberman, 521; TLS, 9/26/36

0115 Tompkins, Pauline. American-Russian Relations in the Far
C   East. N.Y.: Macmillan, 1949. 426 pp. 49-48919. o.p.
     FEQ, 2/51; AHR, 7/50; Am. Pol. Sci. R., 9/50; Ann. Am.
     Acad., 3/50; Pacific Affairs, 6/50

0116 Treat, Payson Jackson. The Far East, a Political and Dip-
C   lomatic History. rev. ed. N.Y.: Harper, 1935. 563 pp.
     35-13968. o.p.
     AUFS, 120

0117 Wint, Guy. The British in Asia. rev. ed. N.Y.: Institute
B   of Pacific Relations, 1954. 244 pp. 56-32415. o.p.
     AUFS, 63

HISTORY
POST-WAR

0118 American Assembly. The United States and the Far East. ed. by
B   Willard L. Thorp. 2d ed. Englewood Cliffs, N.J.: Pren-
     tice-Hall, 1962. 188 pp. 62-3632.
     AUFS, 70

0119 Angus, Henry Forbes. Canada and the Far East, 1940-1953.
B   Toronto: University of Toronto Press, 1953. 129 pp.
     53-13495.
     AUFS, 73; FEQ, 11/54; AHR, 10/54; Am. Pol. Sci. R., 6/54;
     Ann. Am. Acad., 11/54; Library Journal, 3/15/54

0120 Beloff, Max. Soviet Policy in the Far East, 1944-1951. N.Y.:
A   Oxford, 1953. 278 pp. 53-12887. o.p.
     AUFS, 75; Hucker, 835; FEQ, 11/54

0121 Buss, Claude Albert. The Far East; A History of Recent and
B   Contemporary International Relations in East Asia. N.Y.:
     Macmillan, 1955. 738 pp. 55-2617. o.p.
     AUFS, 77; Silberman, 331; FEQ, 11/55; TLS, 11/18/55

0122 Cameron, Meribeth Elliot. China, Japan and the Powers. N.Y.:
B   Ronald, 1952. 682 pp. 52-6194.
     AUFS, 78; Silberman, 326; FEQ, 2/53; Library Journal,
     7/52

0123 Clune, Frank. Ashes of Hiroshima; A Post-war Trip to Japan
C   and China. Sydney: Angus & Robertson, 1950. 299 pp.
     51-10012.

0124 Isaacs, Harold Robert, ed. New Cycle in Asia; Selected
B   Documents on Major International Developments in the
     Far East, 1943-1947. N.Y.: Macmillan for Institute of
     Pacific Relations, 1947. 212 pp. 47-12404. o.p.
     AUFS, 94; FEQ, 11/48; Ann. Am. Acad., 5/48; Library Journal,
     11/1/47; Pacific Affairs, 9/48

0125 Kennedy, Malcolm Duncan. A History of Communism in East
C   Asia. N.Y.: Praeger, 1957. 556 pp. 56-5139. o.p.
     AUFS, 32; JAS, 2/58; Library Journal, 6/15/57; Pol. Sci.
     Q., 12/57; TLS, 8/2/57

0126 Latourette, Kenneth Scott. The American Record in the Far
C   East, 1945-1951. N.Y.: Macmillan, 1952. 208 pp.
     52-12394. o.p.
     Hucker, 821; AHR, 4/53; Am. Pol. Sci. R., 4/53; Ann. Am.
     Acad., 4/53; Library Journal, 6/1/52; Pacific Affairs,
     4/53; Pol. Sci. Q., 6/53

0127 Massachusetts Institute of Technology. Center for Inter-
C   national Studies. Essays on Communism in Asia, Papers
     from the CENIS China Project. Cambridge, Mass.: M.I.T.,
     1955. 56-46285. o.p.

0128 Morley, James William. Japan and Korea: America's Allies in the
A   Pacific. N.Y.: Walker, 1965. 152 pp. 64-23055.
     Choice, 4/66; JAS, 8/66; Ann. Am. Acad., 9/66; Library
     Journal, 11/15/65

0129 Payne, Pierre Stephen Robert. Red Storm over Asia. N.Y.:
B   Macmillan, 1951. 309 pp. 51-2375. o.p.
     FEQ, 5/52; Library Journal, 3/15/51

0130 Payne, Pierre Stephen Robert. The Revolt of Asia. N.Y.:
C   John Day, 1947. 305 pp. 47-31380. o.p.
     Library Journal, 9/15/47

0131 Tai, Sheng-yu. Peking, Moscow, and the Communist Parties of
B   Colonial Asia. Cambridge, Mass.: Center for International
     Studies, M.I.T., 1954. 167 pp. 55-32094. o.p.

0132 Vinacke, Harold Monk. A History of the Far East in Modern
B   Times. 6th ed. N.Y.: Appleton-Century-Crofts, 1959.
     877 pp. 59-7077.
     AUFS, 122; Silberman, 328; FEQ, 5/42

0133 Vinacke, Harold Monk. The United States and the Far East,
B   1945-1951. Stanford, Calif.: Stanford University Press,
     1952. 144 pp. 52-1172. o.p. (M-University).
     AUFS, 123; AHR, 10/52; Am. Pol. Sci. R., 6/52; Ann.
     Am. Acad., 7/52

GOVERNMENT AND POLITICS

0134 American Universities Field Staff. Expectant Peoples, Nation-
B   alism and Development. ed. by K. H. Silvert. pref. by
     Kenneth W. Thompson. N.Y.: Random House for American
     Universities Field Staff, 1963. 489 pp. 63-19716.
     Sup. 65, 3052; Choice, 3/64; Am. Anthropologist, 8/64;
     Am. J. Soc., 11/64; Am. Soc. R., 10/64; Ann. Am. Acad.,
     9/64; Library Journal, 4/15/64

0135 Ball, William Macmahon. Nationalism and Communism in East
B   Asia. 2d ed. rev. Carlton: Melbourne University Press,
     1956. 220 pp. 56-4246. (M-University).
     AUFS, 74; JAS, 8/57; FEQ, 8/53

0136 Barnett, A. Doak, ed. Communist Strategies in Asia: a Comparative
A   Analysis of Governments and Parties. N.Y.: Praeger, 1963.
     293 pp. 63-10823.
     Library Journal, 1/15/64

0137 Brecher, Michael. The New States of Asia, a Political Analysis.
B   N.Y.: Oxford, 1963. 226 pp. 64-549.
     Sup. 65, 3043; Choice, 9/64; Ann. Am. Acad., 9/64; JAOS,
     4-6/65; TLS, 7/9/64

0138 Kahin, George McTurnan, ed. Major Governments of Asia. 2d ed.
B   Ithaca, N.Y.: Cornell University Press, 1963. 719 pp.
     63-15940.
     AUFS, 31; JAS, 5/59, 5/64

0139 Kebschull, Harvey G., comp. Politics in Transitional Societies;
C   The Challenge of Change in Asia, Africa, and Latin
     America. N.Y.: Appleton-Century-Crofts, 1968. 435 pp.

GENERAL - GOVERNMENT AND POLITICS

68-13149.
Choice, 11/68

0140   Linebarger, Paul Myron Anthony. Far Eastern Government and
C   Politics: China and Japan. 2d ed. Princeton, N.J.:
       Van Nostrand, 1956. 643 pp. 56-12290.
       AUFS, 101; Hucker, 622; Silberman, 564; FEQ, 5/55

0141   Macridis, Roy C., ed. Modern Political Systems. Vol. II,
A   Asia. ed. by R. E. Ward and R. C. Macridis. Englewood
       Cliffs, N.J.: Prentice-Hall, 1963. 482 pp. 63-11095 rev.
       Sup. 65, 3053; JAS, 5/64

0142   Silvert, Kalman H., ed. Discussion at Bellagio; The Political
B   Alternatives of Development. N.Y.: American Universities
       Field Staff, 1964. 191 pp. 64-25830.
       Sup. 65, 4566; Choice, 5/65

0143   Tewksbury, Donald George, ed. Source Book on Far Eastern
C   Political Ideologies. N.Y.: Institute of Pacific Relations,
       1952- 53-24605. o.p.
       AUFS, 116

0144   Tinker, Hugh. Ballot Box and Bayonet; People and Government
B   in Emergent Asian Countries. N.Y.: Oxford, 1964. 126 pp.
       (Chatham House Essays, 5). 64-5587.
       Choice, 11/64; JAS, 5/65

0145   Vinacke, Harold Monk. Far Eastern Politics in the Postwar
C   Period. N.Y.: Appleton-Century-Crofts, 1956. 497 pp.
       55-10400.
       AUFS, 121; AHR, 10/56; Ann. Am. Acad., 7/56

ECONOMICS

0146   Allen, George Cyril. Western Enterprise in Far Eastern Eco-
A   nomic Development, China and Japan. N.Y.: Macmillan, 1954.
       291 pp. 54-2001.
       AUFS, 69; Hucker, 663; Silberman, 1561; Ann. Am. Acad.,
       7/54; Pacific Affairs, 9/54; TLS, 3/26/54

0147   Bellah, Robert Neelly, ed. Religion and Progress in Modern
A   Asia. N.Y.: Free Press of Glencoe, 1965. 246 pp.
       65-16267.
       Sup. 67, 3351; Choice, 1/67; JAS, 5/66; Am. Anthropologist,
       6/66; Am. Soc. R., 10/66; Ann. Am. Acad., 5/66; Library
       Journal, 9/1/65; Pol. Sci. Q., 12/66

0148   Belshaw, Horace. Population Growth and Levels of Consumption,
B   with Special Reference to Countries in Asia. N.Y.: Insti-
       tute of Pacific Relations, 1956. 223 pp. 56-4881. o.p.
       AUFS, 10; Am. Econ. R., 6/57; Am. Pol. Sci. R., 9/57; Ann.
       Am. Acad., 1/57; TLS, 8/3/56

0149   Benham, Frederic Charles. The Colombo Plan, and Other Essays.
C   N.Y.: Royal Institute of International Affairs, 1956. 89 pp.
       56-14552.
       AUFS, 11; JAS, 8/57

0150   Chandrasekhar, Sripati, ed. Asia's Population Problems; With
B   a Discussion of Population and Immigration in Australia.
       N.Y.: Praeger, 1967. 311 pp. 66-21773.
       Choice, 10/67; JAS, 2/68; Library Journal, 5/1/67

0151   Cowan, Charles Donald, ed. The Economic Development of China
B   and Japan; Studies in Economic History and Political
       Economy. N.Y.: Humanities, 1964. 255 pp. (Praeger
       Studies on Modern Asia and Africa, 4). 64-14125.
       Choice, 7-8/64; Ann. Am. Acad., 3/65; Pacific Affairs,
       Spring/65; TLS, 3/26/64

0152   Field, Frederick Vanderbilt, ed. An Economic Survey of the
C   Pacific Area. N.Y.: International Secretariat, Institute
       of Pacific Relations, 1941- 42-8899. o.p.
       Silberman, 1497

0153   Froelich, Walter, ed. Land Tenure, Industrialization and
C   Social Stability: Experience and Prospects in Asia.
       Milwaukee, Wis.: Marquette University Press, 1961.
       301 pp. (Marquette Asian Studies, 2). 61-10914.
       Sup. 63, 2871

0154   Ho, Alfred Kuo-liang. The Far East in World Trade; Develop-
C   ments and Growth since 1945. N.Y.: Praeger, 1967. 388 pp.
       (Praeger Special Studies in International Economics and
       Development). 68-14159.

GENERAL - ECONOMICS

Choice, 7-8/68; Pacific Affairs, Fall/68

0155   International Labor Office. The Economic Background of Social
C   Policy Including Problems of Industrialization. New Delhi:
       International Labor Office, 1947. 221 pp. 48-104.

0156   Jacobs, Norman. The Origin of Modern Capitalism and Eastern
B   Asia. Hong Kong: Hong Kong University Press, 1958. 243 pp.
       58-59961.
       Hucker, 2028; Silberman, 1506; JAS, 2/60

0157   Kirby, E. Stuart. Economic Development in East Asia. N.Y.:
B   Praeger, 1967. 253 pp. 67-26565.
       JAS, 8/68; Library Journal, 12/15/67; TLS, 6/6/68

0158   Klein, Sidney. The Pattern of Land Tenure Reform in East Asia
B   after World War II. N.Y.: Bookman, 1958. 260 pp. 58-2808.
       Hucker, 2183

0159   Kuznets, Simon Smith, ed. Economic Growth: Brazil, India,
C   Japan. Durham, N.C.: Duke University Press, 1955. 613 pp.
       55-9491.
       Silberman, 384; FEQ, 5/56; Am. Econ. R., 6/56; Am. Soc. R.,
       8/56; Ann. Am. Acad., 11/56; Pacific Affairs, 9/56; TLS,
       10/5/56

0160   Thompson, Warren Simpson. Population and Progress in the Far
C   East. Chicago: University of Chicago Press, 1959. 443 pp.
       59-10428.
       Hucker, 2192; Silberman, 1611; JAS, 2/60; Am. Anthropologist,
       6/60; Am. Econ. R., 3/60; Am. Soc. R., 2/60; Ann. Am. Acad.,
       11/59; Library Journal, 5/15/59; Pol. Sci. Q., 12/60

0161   United Nations. Bureau of Social Affairs. The Population of
B   Asia and the Far East, 1950-1980. N.Y.: United Nations
       Dept. of Economic and Social Affairs, 1959. 110 pp.
       (Population Studies, No. 31). 60-1676. o.p.
       Hucker, 2189; JAS, 11/60

0162   United Nations. Economic Commission for Asia and the Far
C   East. Economic Survey of Asia and the Far East. N.Y.:
       United Nations, 1947- 49-48996 rev. 2.
       AUFS, 62; Hucker, 2157; FEQ, 2/52, 5/52, 11/53, 11/54

0163   Wickizer, Vernon Dale. The Rice Economy of Monsoon Asia.
C   Stanford, Calif.: Food Research Institute in cooperation
       with the International Secretariat, Institute of Pacific
       Relations, 1941. 358 pp. (Grain Economics Series, 3).
       42-355. o.p.
       Hucker, 2203; FEQ, 8/42

SOCIOLOGY, ANTHROPOLOGY AND LINGUISTICS

0164   Moore, Barrington. Social Origins of Dictatorship and Democ-
A   racy; Lord and Peasant in the Making of the Modern World.
       Boston: Beacon, 1966. 559 pp. 66-23782.
       Choice, 1/67; JAS, 2/67; AHR, 7/67; Am. Pol. Sci. R., 9/67;
       Am. Soc. R., 10/67; Library Journal, 10/15/66; Pol. Sci. Q.,
       12/67; TLS, 12/21/67

0165   Swarup, Ram. Communism and Peasantry, Implications of Col-
C   lectivist Agriculture for Asian Countries. Calcutta:
       Prachi Prakashan, 1954. 194 pp. 55-31858. o.p.
       Sup. 61, 2754

LANGUAGE AND LITERATURE
LITERATURE

0166   Ceadel, Eric B., ed. Literatures of the East, an Appreciation.
C   London: Murray, 1953. 194 pp. 54-1444.
       AUFS, 14; Hucker, 1523

LANGUAGE AND LITERATURE
LITERATURE
EARLY PERIOD
PROSE

0167   The Mythology of All Races. Vol. 8: Chinese and Japanese. ed.
C   by Louis Herbert Gray and George Foot Moore. Boston:
       Marshall Jones, 1916-32. 17-26477. o.p.
       Hucker, 150

GENERAL - LANGUAGE AND LITERATURE

**LANGUAGE AND LITERATURE
LITERATURE
EARLY PERIOD
HISTORY AND CRITICISM**

0168 Bowers, Faubion. Theatre in the East; A Survey of Asian Dance
C   and Drama. N.Y.: Grove, 1960 (orig. pub. by Nelson, 1956).
     374 pp. NUC 63-6677. (R). o.p.
     Hucker, 1672; JAS, 11/56; Library Journal, 7/56; TLS,
     8/10/56

0169 Conference on Oriental Classics in General Education, Columbia
A   University, 1958. Approaches to the Oriental Classics; Asian
     Literature and Thought in General Education. ed. by Wm.
     Theodore De Bary. N.Y.: Columbia University Press, 1959.
     262 pp. 59-9905.
     JAS, 5/60; Library Journal, 5/15/59; Pacific Affairs, 12/59

0170 Wells, Henry Willis. The Classical Drama of the Orient. N.Y.:
B   Asia Publishing House, 1965. 348 pp. 66-75404.

**LANGUAGE AND LITERATURE
LITERATURE
MODERN PERIOD
PROSE**

0171 Milton, Daniel L., ed. A Treasury of Modern Asian Stories.
B   N.Y.: New American Library, 1961. 237 pp. 61-9137.
     Hucker, 1744

**PHILOSOPHY AND RELIGION
GENERAL**

0172 The Bible of the World. ed. by Robert O. Ballou. N.Y.: Vik-
C   ing, 1939. 1415 pp. 39-27953.
     Hucker, 1060

0173 Grousset, Rene. Histoire de La Philosophie Orientale. Paris:
C   Nouvelle Librairie Nationale, 1923. 376 pp.

0174 Kitagawa, Joseph Mitsuo. Religions of the East. rev. and enl.
B   ed. Philadelphia: Westminster Press, 1968. 351 pp.
     68-7174.

0175 Lin, Yutang, ed. The Wisdom of China and India. N.Y.:
C   Random House, 1942. 1104 pp. 42-50902. o.p.
     AUFS, 36; Hucker, 1057; FEQ, 5/43

0176 Muller, F. Max, ed. Sacred Books of the East. Varanasi:
C   Chowkhamba Sanskrit Studies Office, dist. by Lawrence Verry,
     1965-66 (orig. pub. by Clarendon, 1879). 50 v. (R).
     Hucker, 1112

0177 Nakamura, Hajime. Ways of Thinking of Eastern Peoples,
C   India, China, Tibet, Japan. rev., tr., and ed. by Philip
     P. Wiener. Honolulu: East-West Center Press, 1964.
     712 pp. 64-63438.
     Sup. 65, 3049; Choice, 9/65

**PHILOSOPHY AND RELIGION
BUDDHISM**

0178 Asanga. La Somme du Grand Vehicule d'Asanga (Mahayanasamgraha)
C   par Etienne Lamotte. Louvain: Bureaux du Museon, 1938-39.
     2 v. 42-46855.

0179 Berry, Thomas Mary. Buddhism. N.Y.: Hawthorne Books, 1967.
A   187 pp. 66-15226.

0180 Dumoulin, Heinrich. A History of Zen Buddhism. N.Y.: Pantheon,
A   1963. 335 pp. 62-17386. o.p.
     Japan Q., 10-12/63; JAOS, 7-9/65

0181 Khantipalo, Phra. What is Buddhism; An Introduction to the
C   Teaching of Lord Buddha, with Reference to the Belief In
     and Practice of Those Teachings and Their Realization.
     Bangkok: Social Science Association Press of Thailand, 1965.
     150 pp. NUC 66-16102.
     JAS, 5/66

0182 Shcherbatskoi, Fedor Ippolitovich. The Conception of Buddhist
C   Nirvana, by Th. Stcherbatsky. The Hague: Mouton, 1965
     (orig. pub. by Publishing Office of the Academy of Science
     of the U.S.S.R., 1927). 246 pp. 65-6423. (R). (M-Uni-
     versity).

GENERAL - PHILOSOPHY AND RELIGION

**PHILOSOPHY AND RELIGION
OTHER RELIGIONS**

0183 Latourette, Kenneth Scott. The Great Century: In Africa
C   and Asia, A.D. 1800-A.D. 1914. N.Y.: Harper, 1940.
     (A History of the Expansion of Christianity, Vol. VI).
     37-20993. o.p.
     FEQ, 2/45; J. Religion, 7/41

**FINE ARTS AND ARCHITECTURE
GENERAL**

0184 Buhot, Jean. Chinese and Japanese Art; With Sections on Korea
C   and Vietnam. tr. from French by Remy Inglis Hall. ed. by
     Charles McCurdy. Garden City, N.Y.: Anchor Books, 1967.
     428 pp. 67-10368.
     Choice, 2/68; JAS, 5/68; Library Journal, 12/1/67

0185 Eumorfopoulos, George. The George Eumorfopoulos Collection;
C   Catalogue of the Chinese and Corean Bronzes, Sculpture,
     Jades, Jewellery and Miscellaneous Objects. by W. Per-
     ceval Yetts. London: Benn, 1929- 30-16020. o.p.
     Hucker, 1426

0186 Getty, Alice. The Gods of Northern Buddhism; Their History,
B   Iconography, and Progressive Evolution through the
     Northern Buddhist Countries. Rutland, Vt.: Tuttle, 1962
     (orig. pub. by Oxford, 1914). 220 pp. 62-13617. (R).
     JAS, 8/63

0187 Lee, Sherman E. A History of Far Eastern Art. N.Y.: Abrams,
A   1964. 527 pp. 64-9319/CD.
     Choice, 12/64; JAS, 5/66

0188 Munsterberg, Hugo. Zen & Oriental Art. Rutland, Vt.:
B   Tuttle, 1965. 158 pp. 65-17589.
     Choice, 12/65; JAS, 5/66

0189 Rowland, Benjamin. The Harvard Outline and Reading Lists
C   for Oriental Art. rev. ed. Cambridge, Mass.: Harvard
     University Press, 1958. 74 pp. 58-13770.
     Silberman, 711; JAOS, 4-6/53

0190 Seckel, Dietrich. The Art of Buddhism. tr. by Ann E. Kemp.
C   N.Y.: Crown, 1964. 331 pp. (Art of the World). 64-23800.
     Choice, 4/65; JAS, 5/67; Library Journal, 2/15/65; TLS,
     6/10/65

**FINE ARTS AND ARCHITECTURE
FINE ARTS**

0191 Bossert, Helmuth Theodor, ed. Decorative Art of Asia and
C   Egypt; Four Hundred Decorative Motifs in Color, Forming a
     Survey of the Applied Art of Egypt, China, Japan, Siam,
     Tibet, of the Lapps and Siberian and Islamic Peoples.
     N.Y.: Praeger, 1956. 13 pp. 56-9928. o.p.

0192 Eumorfopoulos, George. The George Eumorfopoulos Collection;
C   Catalogue of the Chinese, Corean and Persian Pottery and
     Porcelain. London: Benn, 1925-28. 6 v. 26-5494. o.p.
     Hucker, 1443

0193 Fenollosa, Ernest Francisco. Epochs of Chinese and Japanese
A   Art, an Outline History of East Asiatic Design. new and
     rev. ed. N.Y.: Dover, 1963 (orig. pub. in 1913). 2 v.
     63-5655. (R).
     Hucker, 1411; Silberman, 716; JAS, 5/65

**FINE ARTS AND ARCHITECTURE
FINE ARTS
PAINTING**

0194 Binyon, Laurence. The Spirit of Man in Asian Art. N.Y.:
C   Dover, 1965 (orig. pub. by Harvard University Press,
     1935). 217 pp. 65-24017. (R).
     AUFS, 12; JAOS, 9/35

0195 Munsterberg, Hugo. The Landscape Painting of China and Japan.
A   Rutland, Vt.: Tuttle, 1955. 144 pp. 55-10622 rev.
     Silberman, 753; FEQ, 5/56

0196 Rowland, Benjamin. Art in East and West; An Introduction Through
B   Comparisons. Cambridge, Mass.: Harvard University Press,
     1954. 144 pp. 54-9777.
     Hucker, 1479; Library Journal, 4/1/55

SCIENCE AND TECHNOLOGY

0197   Winter, Henry James Jacques. Eastern Science; An Outline of
B   Its Scope and Contribution. London: Murray, dist. by
     Paragon, 1952. (Wisdom of the East Series). 52-10111.
     Hucker, 1367

BIBLIOGRAPHIES

0198   British Museum. Dept. of Oriental Printed Books and Manuscripts.
B   Descriptive Catalogue of the Chinese Manuscripts from Tun-
     huang in the British Museum, by Lionel Giles. London:
     Trustees of the British Museum, 1957. 334 pp. 58-31979.
     Hucker, 263; JAS, 8/58; JAOS, 4-6/58

0199   Chan, Wing-tsit. Chinese Philosophy, 1949-1963; An Annotated
C   Bibliography of Mainland China Publications. Honolulu:
     East-West Center Press, 1967. 290 pp. 65-20582.
     Choice, 6/67; JAS, 8/68

0200   Chan, Wing-tsit. An Outline and Annotated Bibliography of
A   Chinese Philosophy. New Haven, Conn.: Far Eastern Pub-
     lications, Yale University, 1959. 127 pp. Supplement,
     1961; Supplement, 1965. 60-9.
     Hucker, 1022

0201   Chao, Kuo-chun. Selected Works in English for a Topical Study
B   of Modern China, 1840-1952. Cambridge, Mass.: Regional
     Studies Program on East Asia, Harvard University, 1952.
     38 pp. o.p.

0202   Cordier, Henri. Bibliotheca Sinica. Dictionnaire Bibliogra-
A   phiques des Ouvrages Relatifs a l'Empire Chonois. Taipei:
     Ch'eng-wen Publishing Co., dist. by Chinese Materials and
     Research Aids Service Center, 1966 (orig. pub. by Guil-
     moto, 1904-24). 5 v. (R). (M-IDC).
     Hucker, 19

0203   Davidson, Martha. A List of Published Translations from Chinese
C   into English, French, and German. tentative ed. Ann Arbor,
     Mich.: J. W. Edwards for American Council of Learned Soci-
     eties, 1952-57. 2 pts. 52-4721 rev. o.p.
     AUFS, 1039; Hucker, 1520; JAS, 8/59; FEQ, 5/54; JAOS,
     10-12/58

0204   Fairbank, John King. Japanese Studies of Modern China; A Biblio-
C   graphical Guide to Historical and Social-Science Research
     on the 19th and 20th Centuries. Rutland, Vt.: Tuttle for
     Harvard-Yenching Institute, 1955. 331 pp. A55-7749.
     FEQ, 2/56

0205   Fairbank, John King. Modern China; A Bibliographical Guide to
B   Chinese Works, 1898-1937. Cambridge, Mass.: Harvard Uni-
     versity Press, 1950. 608 pp. (Harvard-Yenching Institute
     Studies, I). 50-5236.
     Hucker, 717; FEQ, 8/51; AHR, 7/50; Pacific Affairs, 6/50

0206   Franke, Herbert. Sinologie. Bern: A. Francke, 1953.
B   216 pp. A55-7033.
     Hucker, 21

0207   Gardner, Charles Sidney, ed. A Union List of Selected Western
B   Books on China in American Libraries. 2d ed. N.Y.:
     Burt Franklin, 1967 (orig. pub. by American Council of
     Learned Societies, 1932). 111 pp. 32-5871. (R).
     JAOS, 6/32

0208   Hightower, James Robert. Topics in Chinese Literature; Out-
A   lines and Bibliographies. rev. ed. Cambridge, Mass.:
     Harvard University Press, 1953. 141 pp. 53-5058.
     AUFS, 1041; Hucker, 1518; FEQ, 2/51; JAOS, 1-3/51

0209   Hsueh, Chun-tu. The Chinese Communist Movement, 1921-1937;
C   An Annotated Bibliography of Selected Materials in the
     Chinese Collection of the Hoover Institution on War,
     Revolution, and Peace. Stanford, Calif.: Stanford Uni-
     versity Press, 1960. 131 pp. 61-625 rev.
     JAS, 11/68

0210   Hsueh, Chun-tu. The Chinese Communist Movement, 1937-1949;
C   An Annotated Bibliography of Selected Materials in the
     Chinese Collection of the Hoover Institution on War,
     Revolution, and Peace. Stanford, Calif.: Stanford Uni-
     versity Press, 1962. 312 pp. 61-625 rev.
     JAS, 11/68

0211   Hucker, Charles O. China; A Critical Bibliography. Tucson:
A   University of Arizona Press, 1962. 125 pp. 62-10624.
     Sup. 63, 2916; JAS, 5/63

0212   Hucker, Charles O. Chinese History; A Bibliographic Review.
A   Washington: Service Center for Teachers of History,
     1958. 42 pp. 58-59931. o.p.
     AUFS, 685; Hucker, 14

0213 Kuo, T'ing-i, comp. Sino-Japanese Relations 1862-1927, a Check-
C list of the Chinese Foreign Ministry Archives. N.Y.: East
Asian Institute, Columbia University, 1965. 228 pp.
65-26953.

0214 Li, Tien-yi. Chinese Fiction: a Bibliography of Books and Arti-
C cles in Chinese and English. New Haven, Conn.: Far Eastern
Publications, Yale University, 1968. 356 pp. 68-7553.

0215 Li, Tien-yi. The History of Chinese Literature: a Selected Bib-
A liography. New Haven, Conn.: Far Eastern Publications, Yale
University, 1968. 24 pp. NUC 69-2096.

0216 Lust, John. Index Sinicus; A Catalogue of Articles Relating
A to China in Periodicals and Other Collective Publications,
1920-1955. Cambridge: Heffer, 1964. 663 pp. 64-7164.
JAS, 8/65

0217 Mote, Frederick W. Japanese Sponsored Governments in China,
C 1937-1945: an Annotated Bibliography Compiled from Materials
in the Chinese Collection of the Hoover Library. Stanford,
Calif.: Stanford University Press, 1954. 68 pp. (Bibliographical Series, 3). 55-854. o.p. (M-University).

0218 Revue Bibliographique de Sinologie. 1- Paris: Mouton, 1955-
B 58-23000.
Hucker, 20

0219 Rhoads, Edward J. M. The Chinese Red Army, 1927-1963; An Anno-
A tated Bibliography. Cambridge, Mass.: Harvard University
Press, 1964. 188 pp. (Harvard East Asian Monographs, No.
16). 65-1422.
Choice, 7-8/65; JAS, 11/65

0220 Skachkov, P. E., comp. Bibliografia Kitain. Moscow: Isda-
C tel'stvo Vostochnoi Literatury, 1960. 691 pp.

0221 Sun, I-tu (Jen). Bibliography on Chinese Social History; A
B Selected and Critical List of Chinese Periodical Sources, by
E-tu Zen Sun and John de Francis. New Haven, Conn.: Institute
of Far Eastern Languages, Yale University, 1952. 150 pp.
53-780. o.p.
Hucker, 116; FEQ, 2/54; JAOS, 10-12/53

0222 Teng, Ssu-Yu. An Annotated Bibliography of Selected Chinese
B Reference Works. rev. ed. Cambridge, Mass.: Harvard Uni-
versity Press, 1950. 326 pp. (Harvard-Yenching Institute
Studies, II). 50-11027.
Sup. 61, 2805; Hucker, 1616

0223 U.S. Department of the Army. Office of Military History. Guide
B to Japanese Monographs and Japanese Studies on Manchuria,
1945-1960. Washington: Office of Chief of Military History,
Dept. of the Army, 1962. 282 pp. o.p.

0224 U.S. Library of Congress. Science and Technology Division.
A Chinese Scientific and Technical Serials Publications in
the Collections of the Library of Congress. rev. ed. Washington: Library of Congress, 1961. 107 pp. 62-60011. o.p.

0225 Walker, Richard Louis. Western Language Periodicals on China; A
B Selective List. New Haven, Conn.: Institute of Far Eastern
Languages, Yale University, 1949. 3030 pp. 49-3650. o.p.

0226 Wu, Wen-chin. Leaders of Twentieth Century China; An Annotated
C Bibliography of Selected Chinese Biographical Works in
the Hoover Library. Stanford, Calif.: Stanford University
Press, 1956. 106 pp. (Bibliographical Series, 4).
56-13811. o.p.

0227 Yang, Winston L. Y. A Bibliography of the Chinese Language.
A N.Y.: American Association of Teachers of Chinese Language and Culture, dist. by Paragon, 1966. 171 pp.
66-27975.
JAS, 5/67

0228 Yuan, T'ung-li. China in Western Literature; A Continuation of
B Cordier's Bibliotheca Sinica. New Haven, Conn.: Far East-
ern Publications, Yale University, 1958. 802 pp. 58-59833.
Hucker, 15; JAS, 8/59

0229 Yuan, T'ung-li. Economic and Social Development of Modern
B China: a Bibliographical Guide. New Haven, Conn.: Human
Relations Area Files, 1956. 130 pp. 57-92. o.p.
Hucker, 1972

0230 Yuan, T'ung-li. Russian Works on China, 1918-1958; A Selected
B Bibliography. Tokyo: 1959. 388-430 pp. (Monumenta Serica,
Vol. 18). 60-4119. o.p.

REFERENCE BOOKS

0231 Berton, Peter Alexander Menquez. Contemporary China; A Research
A Guide. Stanford, Calif.: Hoover Institution on War, Revolu-
tion and Peace, 1967. (Hoover Institution Bibliographical
Series, Vol. XXXI). 695 pp. 67-14235.
JAS, 11/68; Library Journal, 7/68

0232 Biographical Dictionary of Republican China. ed. by Howard L.
A Boorman and Richard C. Howard. N.Y.: Columbia University
Press, 1967- 67-12006.
Choice, 6/67, 9/68; AHR, 12/67; Am. Pol. Sci. R., 3/68;
Library Journal, 3/1/67, 8/68

0233 Carnegie Endowment for International Peace. Treaties and
B Agreements with and Concerning China, 1919-29. Wash-
ington: Carnegie Endowment, 1957. o.p.
Hucker, 828

0234 Chan, Wing-tsit, comp. and tr. A Source Book of Chinese Phi-
A losophy. Princeton, N.J.: Princeton University Press,
1963. 856 pp. 62-7398.
JAS, 5/64; JAOS, 1-3/64; Library Journal, 10/1/63; TLS,
4/9/64

0235 Ch'en, Shou-j'ung. A Concise English-Chinese Dictionary, with
B Romanized Standard Pronunciation. 2d ed. Stanford, Calif.:
Stanford University Press, 1955. 416 pp. 55-9693.
Hucker, 85

0236 China Handbook. 1937/43- comp. by Chinese Ministry of Infor-
C mation. Taipei: China Publishing Co., 1937- 43-14605.
Am. Pol. Sci. R., 4/44; Pacific Affairs, 6/44

0237 The China Year Book. 1912-39. ed. by H. G. W. Woodhead.
C Shanghai: North China Daily News and Herald. 20 v.
12-20762 rev. (R-Kraus).
Hucker, 718

0238 China Yearbook, 1937/43- Taipei: China Publishing Co.
C 43-14605.
Hucker, 849

0239 Ch'ing Administrative Terms; A Translation of the Terminology
C of the Six Boards with Explanatory Notes. tr. and ed. by
E-tu Zen Sun. Cambridge, Mass.: Harvard University Press,
1961. 421 pp. 61-15279.
Sup. 63, 2927; JAS, 5/62

0240 Chou, Ts'e-tsung. Research Guide to the May Fourth Movement:
B Intellectual Revolution in Modern China, 1915-1924.
Cambridge, Mass.: Harvard University Press, 1963. 297 pp.
(Harvard East Asian Series, 13). 63-22745.
JAS, 8/64

0241 Commercial Press. A Comprehensive English-Chinese Dictionary.
B 2d rev. ed. Shanghai: Commercial Press, 1948. 1502 pp.
46-44900. o.p.

0242 Contemporary China; Economic and Social Studies, Documents,
B Bibliography, Chronology, 1955-. ed. by E. Stuart Kirby.
Hong Kong: Hong Kong University Press, 1955- 57-22028.
Hucker, 1974; JAS, 11/57, 8/59, 8/64; China Q., 4-6/62

0243 Creel, Herrlee Glessner. Chinese Writing. Washington: Amer-
A ican Council on Education, 1943. 16 pp. 43-10984.
Hucker, 72

0244 Cressy, Earl Herbert. Understanding China; A Handbook of
C Background Information on Changing China. N.Y.: Nelson,
1957. 278 pp. 57-11898. o.p.
JAS, 8/58

0245 Fenn, Courtenay Hughes. Chinese-English Pocket Dictionary.
B rev. Amer. ed. Cambridge, Mass.: Harvard University Press,
1944. 694 pp. 50-49251.
Hucker, 86

0246 Forrest, Robert Andrew Dermod. The Chinese Language. London:
C Faber & Faber, 1948. 352 pp. 48-21629.
AUFS, 1029; Hucker, 66; FEQ, 8/50

0247 Gentzler, J. Mason. A Syllabus of Chinese Civilization. N.Y.:
B Columbia University Press, 1968. 107 pp. (Companion to
Asian Studies/Committee on Oriental Studies). 68-55814.

Choice, 4/69

0248 Gibert, Lucien. Dictionnaire Historique et Geographique
C   de la Mandchourie. Hong Kong: La Societe des Missions-
    Etrangeres, 1934. 1040 pp. AC35-2634.
    Hucker, 127

0249 Giles, Herbert Allen. A Chinese Biographical Dictionary. N.Y.:
C   Burt Franklin, 1966 (orig. pub. by Kelly & Walsh, 1898).
    Hand catalog. (R).
    Hucker, 91

0250 Giles, Herbert Allen. A Chinese-English Dictionary. 2d ed.
C   rev. and enl. N.Y.: Paragon, 1964 (orig. pub. by Kelly &
    Walsh, 1912). 2 v. 64-8885. (R).
    Hucker, 87

0251 Herrmann, Albert. An Historical Atlas of China. new ed.
A   Chicago: Aldine, 1966 (orig. pub. by Harvard, 1935 as
    Historical and Commercial Atlas of China). 88 pp. Map
    65-13. (R).
    Hucker, 95; Choice, 12/67; JAS, 8/67; AHR, 1/37; JAOS, 6/37;
    TLS, 8/29/36

0252 Hsia, Tao-t'ai. China's Language Reforms. New Haven, Conn.:
A   Institute of Far Eastern Languages, Yale University, 1956.
    200 pp. 57-871.
    Hucker, 77; JAS, 5/57

0253 Irick, Robert L. American-Chinese Relations, 1784-1941; A Survey
B   of Chinese-language Materials at Harvard. Cambridge, Mass.:
    Harvard University Press, 1960. 296 pp. (Dept. of History,
    American Far Eastern Policy Studies: Research Aids, No. 3).
    60-4930. o.p.
    JAS, 5/62

0254 Karlgren, Bernhard. The Chinese Language, an Essay on Its
A   Nature and History. N.Y.: Ronald, 1949. 122 pp. 49-11524.
    Hucker, 64; FEQ, 2/51; JAOS, 4-6/50; Pacific Affairs, 3/50

0255 Karlgren, Bernhard. Sound and Symbol in Chinese. London:
B   Oxford, 1923. 112 pp. 23-11701.
    AUFS, 1032

0256 Kennedy, George Alexander. ZH Guide, an Introduction to Sinology.
B   New Haven, Conn.: Sinological Seminar, Yale University, 1953.
    171 pp. 53-1408.
    FEQ, 11/53

0257 King, Frank H. H. A Research Guide to China Coast Newspapers,
B   1822-1911. Cambridge, Mass.: East Asian Research Center,
    Harvard University, 1965. 235 pp. (Harvard East Asian
    Monograph, 18). 65-5287.

0258 Kuang, Ju-ssu. Chinese Written Characters; Their Wit and Wisdom.
C   N.Y.: Cobble Hill, dist. by Hill & Wang, 1968 (orig. pub.
    by Pantheon, 1944 under title Chinese Wit, Wisdom, and
    Written Characters). 72 pp. 45-2993. (R).
    Hucker, 73

0259 MacMurray, John Van Antwerp, ed. Treaties and Agreements With
C   and Concerning China. N.Y.: Oxford, 1921. 2 v. 21-8012.
    o.p.
    Hucker, 659, 827

0260 Mathews, Robert Henry. Mathews' Chinese-English Dictionary. rev.
A   ed. Cambridge, Mass.: Harvard University Press for Harvard-
    Yenching Institute, 1944. 186 pp. A43-2019 rev. 2.
    Hucker, 84

0261 Moule, Arthur Christopher. The Rulers of China, 221 B.C.-A.D.
B   1949; Chronological Tables. With an Introductory Section
    on the Earlier Rulers c. 2100-249 B.C. by W. Perceval
    Yetts. N.Y.: Praeger, 1957. 131 pp. 57-11146. o.p.
    Hucker, 93; JAS, 11/58

0262 Perleberg, Max. Who's Who in Modern China. Hong Kong: Ye
B   Olde Printerie, 1954. 428 pp. 54-19583.
    Hucker, 716

0263 Teng, Ssu-yu. Research Guide for China's Response to the
B   West; A Documentary Survey, 1839-1923. by Teng Ssu-yu
    and John K. Fairbank. N.Y.: Atheneum, 1963 (orig. pub.
    by Harvard University Press, 1954). 84 pp. NUC 63-59347.
    (R).
    FEQ, 8/55

0264 U.S. Library of Congress. Orientalia Division. Eminent Chinese
A   of the Ch'ing Period (1644-1912). Taipei: Chinese Materials
    and Research Aids Service Center, 1966 (orig. pub. by
    Government Printing Office, 1943-44). 2 v. 64-53640. (R).
    Hucker, 508; FEQ, 8/44

0265 Werner, Edward Theodore Chalmers. A Dictionary of Chinese
B   Mythology. Shanghai: Kelly & Walsh, 1932. 627 pp.
    33-18090. o.p.
    Hucker, 1086

0266 Who's Who in China. 6th ed. Shanghai: 1919-1951. 51-1089.
B

0267 Williams, Charles Alfred Speed. Encyclopedia of Chinese Sym-
B   bolism and Art Motives; An Alphabetical Compendium of Leg-
    ends and Beliefs as Reflected in the Manners and Customs
    of the Chinese Throughout History. intro. by Kazimitsu
    W. Kato. N.Y.: Julian Press, 1960 (orig. pub. by Kelly &
    Walsh, 1932 under the title Outlines of Chinese Symbolism
    and Art Motives). 468 pp. 60-15987. (R).
    Hucker, 1508

JOURNALS

0268 The Broadsheet. v.1- 1964-
C

0269 China Monthly Review. v.1-124. 1917-1953. (1917-21 as
B   Millard's Review; 1921-23 as Weekly Review of the Far
    East; 1923-50 as China Weekly Review). (M-Microphoto).

0270 China Pictorial. v.1- 1951- (M-IDC).
C

0271 The China Post. Taiwan. 1952-
C

0272 The China Quarterly, v.1- 1960- (M-IDC).
A   Hucker, 25

0273 China Reconstructs. v.1- 1952- (M-IDC).
C   Hucker, 2159

0274 China Report. v.1- 1964-
C

0275 China Review. v.1-25. 1872-1901. (M-Research Publications).
C

0276 Chinese Art Society of America, Inc. Archives, 1- 1945-
C   (M-IDC).
    JAS, 2/58; FEQ, 2/52, 8/56

0277 Chinese Communist Affairs. v.1- 1964-
C

0278 Chinese Culture, v.1- 1957-
C   Hucker, 39

0279 Chinese Economic Bulletin. v.1-27. 1921-1935.
C

0280 Chinese Economic Journal and Bulletin. v.1-20. 1927-1937.
C

0281 Chinese Economic Studies. v.1- 1967-
C

0282 Chinese Education. v.1- 1968-
C

0283 Chinese Law and Government. v.1- 1968-
C

0284 Chinese Literature. v.1- 1951-
C   Hucker, 1757

0285 Chinese Repository. v.1-20. 1832-51. (R-Kraus, M-Microphoto,
C   M-Research Publications).
    Hucker, 616

0286 Chinese Social and Political Science Review. v.1-24. 1916-41.
B   (M-Research Publications).
    Hucker, 40

0287 Chinese Studies in History and Philosophy. v.1- 1967-
C

0288 Chinese Studies in Sociology and Anthropology. v.1- 1966-
A

0289 Ch'ing Hua Hsueh Pao. v.1-15. 1924-1948. n.s.v.1- 1956-
C   Hucker, 35

0290 Contemporary China, v.1- 1955-
B   Hucker, 909

0291 Current Scene; Developments in Mainland China. v.1- 1961-
C

0292 Geological Society of China. Bulletin. v.1- 1922-
B   Hucker, 53

0293 Monumenta Serica; Journal of Oriental Studies. v.1- 1935-
C   (R-Johnson, M-IDC).
   Hucker, 33

0294 National Palace Museum Quarterly. v.1- 1966-
C

0295 North China Herald. 1850-1941. (M-Microphoto).
C

0296 Peking Review. v.1- 1958-
B

0297 Royal Asiatic Society of Great Britain and Ireland. North
B   China Branch Journal, v.1-2. 1858-1860. n.s.v.1-
   1864- (R-Kraus, M-IDC, M-Research Publications).
   Hucker, 41

0298 Shanghai Evening Post and Mercury. 1931-35-
C

0299 Sinologica, v.1- 1947-
B   Hucker, 34

0300 The South China Morning Post. Hong Kong. 1881-
C   (M-Microphoto).

0301 T'oung Pao ou Archives Concernant l'Histoire, les Langues, la
B   Geographie et l'Ethnographie de l'Asie Orientale. v.1-10.
   1890-1899. Series 2., v.1- 1900- (M-IDC).
   Hucker, 29

0302 Union Research Institute, Hong Kong. Communist China Prob-
B   lem Research Series. no. 1- 1953-

0303 U.S. Consulate General. Hong Kong. Current Background, v.1-
B   1950-
   Hucker, 906

0304 U.S. Consulate General. Hong Kong. Index to Survey of Mainland
A   Magazines. no. 1- 1956-

0305 U.S. Consulate General. Hong Kong. Review of the Hong Kong
A   Chinese Press. no. 1-53/1961. 1947-1961.

0306 U.S. Consulate General. Hong Kong. Selections from China
A   Mainland Magazines. no. 1- 1955-

0307 U.S. Consulate General. Hong Kong. Survey of China Main-
A   land Press. no. 1- 1950-

GENERAL BOOKS

0308 American Academy of Political and Social Science. Contemporary
B   China and the Chinese. ed. by Howard L. Boorman. Philadelphia: American Academy of Political and Social Science,
   1959. 220 pp. 59-1059. o.p.

0309 Bagchi, Prabodh Chandra. India and China; A Thousand Years
A   of Cultural Relations. 2d ed., rev. N.Y.: Philosophical
   Library, 1951. 234 pp. A52-8492. o.p.
   Hucker, 119; FEQ, 11/52

0310 Balazs, Etienne. Chinese Civilization and Bureaucracy;
A   Variations on a Theme. tr. by H. Wright. ed. by
   Arthur F. Wright. New Haven, Conn.: Yale University Press
   for East Asian Research Center, Harvard University and
   Council on East Asian Studies, Yale University, 1964.
   309 pp. 64-20909.
   Sup. 65, 3083; Choice, 2/65; JAS, 5/65

0311 Bodde, Derk. China's Cultural Tradition, What and Whither?
B   N.Y.: Rinehart, 1957. 90 pp. 57-59558.
   AUFS, 673; Hucker, 9; JAS, 8/58; JAOS, 10-12/57

0312 Collis, Maurice. The Great Within. London: Faber & Faber,
C   1941. 349 pp. 42-2761
   Hucker, 482

0313 Dawson, Raymond Stanley, ed. The Legacy of China. N.Y.:
C   Oxford, 1964. 392 pp. 64-6757.
   Sup. 65, 3091; Choice, 12/64; JAS, 5/65

0314 De Bary, William Theodore, ed. Sources of Chinese Tradition.
A   contrib. by Yi-pao Mei and others. N.Y.: Columbia University Press, 1960. 976 pp. (Records of Civilization:
   Sources and Studies, 55, Introduction to Oriental Civilizations, 3). 60-9911.
   Sup. 61, 2794; Hucker, 1045; JAS, 5/61; Ann. Am. Acad.,
   1/61; Library Journal, 5/1/60; Pacific Affairs, Summer/61

0315 Fairbank, John King, ed. Chinese Thought and Institutions.
A   Chicago: University of Chicago Press, 1957. 438 pp. 57-5272.
   AUFS, 676; Hucker, 1063; JAS, 5/60; AHR, 4/58; Am. J. Soc.,
   1/59; Am. Pol. Sci. R., 9/58; Am. Soc. R., 6/58; Ann. Am.
   Acad., 9/58; JAOS, 10-12/58; TLS, 4/25/58

0316 Harvard University. East Asian Research Center. Papers on
A   China. Cambridge, Mass.: Harvard University Committee on
   Regional Studies (since 1957, Center for East Asian Studies),
   n.d. 56-2493 rev. 2.
   Hucker, 614

0317 Hu, Ch'ang-tu. China: Its People, Its Society, Its Culture.
B   ed. by Hsiao Hsia. New Haven, Conn.: Human Relations Area
   Files, 1960. 610 pp. 60-7382.
   Hucker, 3; Am. Anthropologist, 10/60; Am. J. Soc., 1/61;
   Am. Pol. Sci. R., 9/60; Am. Soc. R., 7/60; Ann. Am. Acad.,
   11/60; Library Journal, 3/1/60; Pol. Sci. Q., 3/61

0318 Latourette, Kenneth Scott. The Chinese; Their History and
C   Culture. 4th ed. rev. N.Y.: Macmillan, 1964. 714 pp.
   64-17372.
   AUFS, 688; Hucker, 4; Choice, 1/65; JAS, 2/65

0319 Li, Dun Jen, comp. The Essence of Chinese Civilization.
C   Princeton, N.J.: Van Nostrand, 1967. 476 pp.
   67-25328.
   Choice, 9/68; JAS, 5/68

0320 MacNair, Harley Farnsworth, ed. China. Berkeley: University
B   of California Press, 1946. 573 pp. A47-14. o.p.
   AUFS, 691; Hucker, 1; Library Journal, 10/15/46

0321 Maspero, Henri. Les Institutions de la Chine; Essai Historique.
B   Paris: Presses Universitaires, 1952. 174 pp. 54-2554.
   Hucker, 105; FEQ, 11/53

GEOGRAPHY

0322 Cressey, George Babcock. China's Geographic Foundations,
B   a Survey of the Land and Its People. N.Y.: McGraw-Hill,
   1934. 436 pp. 34-1104. o.p.
   Hucker, 48; Am. J. Soc., 11/34; Am. Pol. Sci. R., 6/34;
   Ann. Am. Acad., 5/34; J. Pol. Econ., 12/34; Pol. Sci. Q.,
   9/34

0323 Cressey, George Babcock. Land of the 500 Million; A Geography
B   of China. N.Y.: McGraw-Hill, 1955. 387 pp. 55-8895.
   Hucker, 46; FEQ, 8/56; Geog. R., 10/56; Library Journal,
   1/1/56; Pacific Affairs, 6/56

0324 Li, Ssu-Kuang. The Geology of China, by J. S. Lee. London:
C   Thomas Murby, 1939. 528 pp. 40-310. o.p.
   Hucker, 54

0325 Mallory, Walter Hampton. China: Land of Famine. N.Y.: American
B   Geographical Society, 1926. 199 pp. (Special Publication,
   6). 27-1575. o.p. (M-University).
   Hucker, 2201

0326 Shabad, Theodore. China's Changing Map; A Political and
B   Economic Geography of the Chinese People's Republic.
   N.Y.: Praeger, 1956. 295 pp. 55-11530. o.p.
   AUFS, 970; Hucker, 47; JAS, 11/57; Ann. Am. Acad., 9/56;
   Library Journal, 7/56; TLS, 11/2/56

0327 Tregear, Thomas R. A Geography of China. Chicago: Aldine, 1966.
A   342 pp. 65-26752/CD.
   Sup. 67, 3252; Choice, 5/67; JAS, 11/66; JAOS, 4-6/66;
   Library Journal, 4/15/66

HISTORY
GENERAL

0328　Aspects de la Chine: Langue, Histoire, Religions, Philosophie,
B　　Litterature, Arts; par E. Balazs et al. Paris: Presses
　　　Universitaires, 1959. 2 v. Hand catalog.
　　　Sup. 61, 2787; Hucker, 6; JAS, 2/61

0329　Bloodworth, Dennis. The Chinese Looking Glass. N.Y.: Farrar,
A　　Straus, & Giroux, 1967. 432 pp. 67-22047.
　　　Choice, 11/67; Library Journal, 6/15/67

0330　Chi, Ch'ao-ting. Key Economic Areas in Chinese History as
A　　Revealed in the Development of Public Works for Water-
　　　Control. 2d ed. N.Y.: Paragon, 1963 (orig. pub. by Allen &
　　　Unwin, 1936). 168 pp. 63-24179. (R).
　　　Hucker, 111; JAS, 5/64; AHR, 7/37; Pacific Affairs, 9/36;
　　　TLS, 2/22/36

0331　Chinese Dynastic Histories Translations. Berkeley: University
C　　of California Press, 1952-
　　　Hucker, 1641

0332　Eberhard, Wolfram. A History of China. tr. by E. W. Dickes.
B　　2d ed., rev. Berkeley: University of California Press, 1960.
　　　358 pp. A62-8636.
　　　Hucker, 103; FEQ, 8/51

0333　Fairbank, John King. The United States and China. new ed.
A　　rev. and enl. Cambridge, Mass.: Harvard University
　　　Press, 1958. 365 pp. 58-11552.
　　　AUFS, 806; Hucker, 2; JAS, 5/60; FEQ, 5/49; Library Journal,
　　　9/1/58

0334　Feuerwerker, Albert. Approaches to Modern Chinese History.
A　　Berkeley: University of California Press, 1967. 356 pp.
　　　67-15640.
　　　Choice, 2/68

0335　Franke, Otto. Geschichte des Chinesischen Reiches; Eine
B　　Darstellung Seiner Entstehung, Seines Wesens und Seiner
　　　Entwicklung bis zur Neuesten Zeit. Berlin: De Gruyter,
　　　1930- 31-2382.
　　　Hucker, 104; FEQ, 8/52, 8/53; JAOS, 10-12/62

0336　Frankel, Hans Hermann, comp. Catalogue of Translations from the
C　　Chinese Dynastic Histories for the Period 220-960. Berkeley:
　　　University of California Press, 1957. 295 pp. (Chinese
　　　Dynastic Histories Translations, Supplement No. 1). A58-9014.
　　　Hucker, 247; JAS, 11/58

0337　Gardner, Charles Sidney. Chinese Traditional Historiography.
A　　Cambridge, Mass.: Harvard University Press, 1961. 124 pp.
　　　(Harvard Historical Monographs, No. 11). Hand catalog.
　　　Sup. 63, 2912; Hucker, 1622; JAS, 5/62

0338　Goodrich, Luther Carrington. A Short History of the Chinese
C　　People. 3d ed. N.Y.: Harper, 1959. 295 pp. 59-7025.
　　　AUFS, 681; Hucker, 99; FEQ, 5/44

0339　Goodrich, Luther Carrington. A Syllabus of the History of Chinese
B　　Civilization and Culture. 6th ed. N.Y.: China Society of
　　　America, 1958. 59 pp. A60-3148. o.p.
　　　Sup. 61, 2796; Hucker, 13; FEQ, 2/42

0340　Grousset, Rene. The Rise and Splendour of the Chinese Empire.
A　　tr. from French by Anthony Watson-Gandy and Terence
　　　Gordon. Berkeley: University of California Press, 1953.
　　　312 pp. A53-9939.
　　　Hucker, 101; FEQ, 11/53; AHR, 10/53; Library Journal,
　　　5/15/53; Pacific Affairs, 6/53; TLS, 5/9/52

0341　Hsu, Francis L. K. Religion, Science, and Human Crises; A Study
B　　of China in Transition and Its Implications for the West.
　　　London: Routledge & Kegan Paul, 1952. 142 pp. 52-2962.
　　　Hucker, 1079

0342　Latourette, Kenneth Scott. The Development of China. 6th ed.,
C　　rev. Boston: Houghton Mifflin, 1946. 343 pp. 46-4889.
　　　o.p. (M-University).

0343　Li, Tieh-tseng. The Historical Status of Tibet. N.Y.: King's
C　　Crown, 1956. 312 pp. 55-10627. o.p.
　　　Hucker, 120; JAS, 5/57; AHR, 7/56; Ann. Am. Acad., 11/56;
　　　JAOS, 7-9/56; Library Journal, 11/1/56

0344　Marsh, Robert Mortimer. The Mandarins; The Circulation of Elites
A　　in China, 1600-1900. N.Y.: Free Press of Glencoe, 1961.
　　　300 pp. 60-10899.
　　　JAS, 8/62; JAOS, 4-6/62

0345　McAleavy, Henry. The Modern History of China. N.Y.:
B　　Praeger, 1967. 392 pp. (Praeger Asia-Africa
　　　Series). 66-18911.
　　　Choice, 5/68; Library Journal, 10/15/67; TLS, 11/9/67

0346　Meskill, John Thomas, ed. The Pattern of Chinese History;
A　　Cycles, Development, or Stagnation? Boston: Heath, 1965.
　　　108 pp. (Problems in Asian Civilization). 65-17466.
　　　Choice, 1/68

0347　Needham, Joseph. Time and Eastern Man. London: Royal Anthro-
B　　pological Institute of Great Britain and Ireland, 1965.
　　　52 pp. 65-29667.
　　　JAS, 2/66

0348　Quigley, Harold Scott. China's Politics in Perspective. Minne-
B　　apolis: University of Minnesota Press, 1962. 266 pp.
　　　62-13606. o.p.
　　　Sup. 63, 2926; JAS, 11/62; China Q., 4-6/63; Library Journal,
　　　4/1/62

0349　Silverberg, Robert. The Great Wall of China. Philadelphia:
C　　Chilton, 1965. 232 pp. 65-15940.
　　　Choice, 1/66; Library Journal, 7/65

0350　Yang, Lien-sheng. Studies in Chinese Institutional History.
B　　Cambridge, Mass.: Harvard University Press, 1961. 299 pp.
　　　(Harvard-Yenching Institute Studies, XX). 61-8844.
　　　Hucker, 107; JAS, 2/62

0351　Yang, Lien-sheng. Topics in Chinese History. Cambridge,
B　　Mass.: Harvard University Press, 1950. 57 pp. (Harvard-
　　　Yenching Institute Studies, IV). 50-10183. o.p. (M-Uni-
　　　versity).
　　　Hucker, 97; JAOS, 1-3/51

HISTORY
EARLY HISTORY

0352　Andersson, Johan Gunnar. Children of the Yellow Earth; Studies
A　　in Prehistoric China. N.Y.: Macmillan, 1934. 345 pp.
　　　35-2425. o.p.
　　　Hucker, 142

0353　Bielenstein, Hans. The Restoration of the Han Dynasty; With
B　　Prolegomena on the Historiography of the Hou Han Shu.
　　　Stockholm: 1953- 209 pp. 55-21208.
　　　Hucker, 1624

0354　Bodde, Derk. China's First Unifier; A Study of the Ch'in Dynasty
B　　As Seen in the Life of Li Ssu, 280?-208 B.C. London: Oxford,
　　　1967 (orig. pub. by Brill, 1938). 270 pp. 67-108881. (R).
　　　AUFS, 698; Hucker, 183; JAOS, 9/38

0355　Carter, Thomas Francis. The Invention of Printing in China
A　　and Its Spread Westward. rev. by L. Carrington Goodrich.
　　　2d ed. N.Y.: Ronald, 1955. 293 pp. 55-5418.
　　　AUFS, 699; Hucker, 335; FEQ, 2/56; TLS, 8/27/55

0356　Chang, Kwang-chih. The Archaeology of Ancient China. rev. ed.
B　　New Haven, Conn.: Yale University Press, 1968. 483 pp.
　　　68-24780.
　　　Choice, 3/69; JAS, 2/64, 5/69; Am. Anthropologist, 2/64;
　　　JAOS, 4-6/62, 1-3/66; Library Journal, 5/1/63; TLS, 4/2/64

0357　Chau Ju-kua: His Work on the Chinese and Arab Trade in the Twelfth
C　　and Thirteenth Centuries, Entitled Chu-fan-chi. tr. from
　　　Chinese and annotated by Friedrich Hirth and W. W. Rockhill.
　　　N.Y.: Paragon, 1966 (orig. pub. by Imperial Academy of Sci-
　　　ences, 1911). 2 v. 66-30339. (R). (M-University).
　　　Hucker, 344

0358　Chavannes, Edouard. Documents sur Les Tou-kiue (Turcs) Occi-
C　　dentaux. St. Petersbourg: Commissionaires de l'Academie
　　　Imperiale des Sciences, 1903. 378 pp. 6-24267.
　　　Hucker, 286

0359　Cheng, Te-k'un. Archaeology in China. Cambridge: Heffer,
B　　1959- 59-1455.
　　　Hucker, 137, 152; Choice, 5/67; JAOS, 9-12/63

0360　Chin shu. English. Selections. Account of the T'u-yu-hun in
C　　the History of the Chin Dynasty. tr. and annotated by Thomas
　　　D. Carroll. Berkeley: University of California Press, 1953.

47 pp. (Chinese Dynastic Histories Translations, No. 4).
A54-5210. o.p.
Hucker, 267; FEQ, 11/54; JAOS, 7-9/55

0361 Chiu T'ang shu. Biography of An Lu-shan. tr. and annotated
C   by Howard S. Levy. Berkeley: University of California Press,
     1960. 122 pp. (Chinese Dynastic Histories Translations,
     No. 8). 61-63071. o.p.
     Hucker, 319; JAS, 2/62

0362 Collis, Maurice. Marco Polo. N.Y.: New Directions, 1960.
B   190 pp. 60-14665. o.p.
     Hucker, 403

0363 Creel, Herrlee Glessner. The Birth of China; A Study of the
A   Formative Period of Chinese Civilization. N.Y.: Ungar,
     1954. 402 pp. 54-5633.
     AUFS, 700; Hucker, 153; JAOS, 9/37

0364 Crump, James Irving. Intrigues; Studies of the Chan-kuo ts'e.
B   Ann Arbor: University of Michigan Press, 1964. 212 pp.
     64-17440.
     JAS, 2/66; JAOS, 1-3/66

0365 Debnicki, Aleksy. The Chu-shu-chi-nien as a Source to the Social
C   History of Ancient China. Warszawa: Panstwowe Wydawnictwo
     Naukowe, 1956. Hand catalog.
     Hucker, 174

0366 Eberhard, Wolfram. Conquerors and Rulers; Social Forces in
B   Medieval China. 2d ed. N.Y.: Heinman, 1956. 129 pp.
     52-11731.
     AUFS, 703; Hucker, 328

0367 Ennin. Diary; The Record of a Pilgrimage to China in Search
A   of the Law. tr. from Chinese by Edwin O. Reischauer. N.Y.:
     Ronald, 1955. 454 pp. 55-5553.
     Hucker, 281; Silberman, 634; FEQ, 11/55; Ann. Am. Acad.,
     11/55; Library Journal, 6/15/55; Pacific Affairs, 12/55

0368 Fitzgerald, Charles Patrick. The Empress Wu. Melbourne: Cheshire
B   for Australian National University, 1955. 252 pp. 58-27599.
     Hucker, 316; JAS, 8/58

0369 Fitzgerald, Charles Patrick. Son of Heaven, a Biography of Li
B   Shih-Min, Founder of the T'ang Dynasty. Cambridge: Uni-
     versity, 1933. 232 pp. 35-4016. o.p.
     Hucker, 314

0370 Frankel, Hans Hermann, ed. and tr. Biographies of Meng Hao-jan.
C   Berkeley: University of California Press, 1952. 25 pp.
     (Chinese Dynastic Histories Translations, No. 1). A52-9556.
     Hucker, 327; FEQ, 5/53

0371 Gernet, Jacques. Daily Life in China on the Eve of the Mongol
B   Invasion, 1250-1276. tr. by H. M. Wright. N.Y.: Macmillan,
     1962. 254 pp. 62-4325.
     Hucker, 339

0372 Granet, Marcel. Chinese Civilization. tr. by Kathleen E.
A   Innes and Mabel R. Brailsford. N.Y.: Meridian, 1958.
     444 pp. 58-8529. o.p.
     Hucker, 181; JAOS, 6/31

0373 Granet, Marcel. Festivals and Songs of Ancient China. N.Y.:
A   Dutton, 1932. 281 pp. 33-4631. o.p.
     Hucker, 2004; JAOS, 3/34; TLS, 4/28/32

0374 Grousset, Rene. L'Empire des Steppes: Attila, Gengis-Khan, Tam-
C   erlan. 4th ed. Paris: Payot, 1960. Hand catalog. o.p.
     Hucker, 123

0375 Han, Yu. The Veritable Record of the T'ang Emperor Shun-tsung,
B   February 28, 805 - August 31, 805: Han Yu's Shun-tsung shih-
     lu. tr. with intro. and notes by Bernard S. Soloman. Cam-
     bridge, Mass.: Harvard University Press, 1955. 82 pp.
     55-9441.
     Hucker, 307; FEQ, 2/56; JAOS, 1-3/56

0376 Hsu, Cho-yun. Ancient China in Transition; An Analysis of
A   Social Mobility, 722-222 B.C. Stanford, Calif.: Stanford
     University Press, 1969 (orig. pub. in 1965). 238 pp.
     (Studies in the Civilizations of Eastern Asia). 65-13110.
     (R).
     Choice, 12/65; JAS, 5/66; AHR, 4/66; Am. Soc. R., 6/66;
     JAOS, 7-9/66; Library Journal, 5/15/66

0377 Huan K'uan. Discourses on Salt and Iron; A Debate on State
B   Control of Commerce and Industry in Ancient China. chap-
     ters I-XIX, tr. by Esson M. Gale. Leiden: Brill, 1931.
     165 pp. 33-4201.
     Hucker, 204

0378 Hughes, Ernest Richard. Two Chinese Poets; Vignettes of Han Life
B   and Thought. Princeton, N.J.: Princeton University Press,
     1960. 266 pp. 59-11078.
     Hucker, 211; JAS, 2/61; JAOS, 4-6/62

0379 Komroff, Manuel, ed. Contemporaries of Marco Polo. N.Y.: Boni &
B   Liveright, 1928. 358 pp. 28-14790.
     Hucker, 393

0380 Kracke, Edward A. Civil Service in Early Sung China, 960-1067;
B   With Particular Emphasis on the Development of Controlled
     Sponsorship, to Foster Administrative Responsibility.
     Cambridge, Mass.: Harvard University Press, 1953. 262 pp.
     52-5399.
     AUFS, 706; Hucker, 333; FEQ, 2/54; JAOS, 10-12/53

0381 Lamb, Harold. Genghis Khan, the Emperor of All Men. N.Y.:
C   Doubleday, 1952 (orig. pub. by McBride, 1927). 270 pp.
     A58-9870. (R).
     Hucker, 369

0382 Li, Chi. The Beginnings of Chinese Civilization; Three Lec-
A   tures Illustrated with Finds at Anyang. Seattle: Uni-
     versity of Washington Press, 1957. 123 pp. 57-5285.
     Hucker, 159; JAS, 5/58; Am. Anthropologist, 4/58; JAOS,
     1-3/59; Library Journal, 6/15/57

0383 Li, Chi. The Formation of the Chinese People; An Anthropo-
A   logical Inquiry. Cambridge, Mass.: Harvard University
     Press, 1928. 283 pp. 28-22008.
     Hucker, 57

0384 Li, Chih-ch'ang. The Travels of an Alchemist; The Journey of
B   the Taoist, Ch'ang-ch'un, from China to the Hindukush at
     the Summons of Chingiz Khan, Recorded by his Disciple. tr.
     by Arthur Waley. London: Routledge, 1931. 166 pp. 31-31754.
     Hucker, 437

0385 Ling-hu, Te-fen. Accounts of Western Nations in the History
C   of the Northern Chou Dynasty. tr. and annotated by Roy
     Andrew Miller. Berkeley: University of California Press,
     1959. 83 pp. (Chinese Dynastic Histories Translations,
     No. 6). A59-9437.
     Hucker, 268; JAS, 8/60

0386 Ling-hu, Te-fen. Biography of Su Ch'o. tr. by Chauncy S. Good-
C   rich. 2d ed. rev. and enl. Berkeley: University of Cali-
     fornia Press, 1961. 116 pp. (Chinese Dynastic Histories
     Translations, No. 3). A53-9763 rev.
     Hucker, 266; FEQ, 5/54

0387 Liu, James Tzu-chien. Ou-yang Hsiu, an Eleventh Century Neo-
A   Confucianist. Stanford, Calif.: Stanford University Press,
     1967. 227 pp. 67-13660.

0388 Liu, Tzu-chien. Reform in Sung China; Wang An-shih (1021-
B   1086) and his New Policies. Cambridge, Mass.: Harvard
     University Press, 1959. 140 pp. (Harvard East Asian
     Series, 3). 59-9281.
     Sup. 63, 2922; Hucker, 348; JAS, 11/62

0389 Loewe, Michael. Records of Han Administration. N.Y.:
C   Cambridge, 1967. 2 v. (University of Cambridge Oriental
     Publications, 11 and 12). 67-28684.
     Choice, 7-8/68; JAS, 11/68; Pacific Affairs, Summer/68;
     TLS, 8/15/68

0390 Mahler, Jane Gaston. The Westerners Among the Figurines of
C   the T'ang Dynasty in China. Rome: Instituto Italiano
     per il Medio ed Estremo Oriente, 1959. 204 pp. A60-3049.
     Hucker, 310; JAS, 5/60; JAOS, 7-9/59

0391 Martin, Henry Desmond. The Rise of Chingis Khan and His Conquest
B   of North China. Baltimore: Johns Hopkins Press, 1950.
     360 pp. 51-444. o.p. (M-University).
     AUFS, 711; Hucker, 364; AHR, 7/51

0392 Maspero, Henri. La Chine Antique. new ed. Paris: Imprimerie
C   Nationale, 1955. 519 pp. 56-43490.
     Hucker, 167

0393 Maspero, Henri. Melanges Posthumes sur les Religions et
C   l'Histoire de la Chine. Paris: Civilisations du Sud,

S.A.E.P., 1950. 3 v. A51-4214.
Hucker, 202; FEQ, 8/52

0394   McGovern, William Montgomery. The Early Empires of Central Asia;
C   A Study of the Scythians and the Huns and the Part They Played
          in World History, with Special Reference to the Chinese
          Sources. Chapel Hill: University of North Carolina Press,
          1939. 529 pp. 39-6490.
          Hucker, 221; Am. Anthropologist, 1/40; AHR, 1/40

0395   Menzel, Johanna Margarete, ed. The Chinese Civil Service; Career
A   Open to Talent? Boston: Heath, 1963. 110 pp. 63-12327.
          JAS, 11/64

0396   Meskill, John Thomas. Wang An-shih, Practical Reformer? Bos-
A   ton: Heath, 1963. 99 pp. 63-12328.
          JAS, 11/64

0397   Olschki, Leonardo. Marco Polo's Asia; An Introduction to his
B   "Description of the World" called "Il Milione". Berkeley:
          University of California Press, 1960. 459 pp. 60-8315.
          Hucker, 410; AHR, 7/61; Ann. Am. Acad., 3/61; JAOS, 4-6/65;
          Pacific Affairs, Fall/61

0398   Olschki, Leonardo. Marco Polo's Precursors, with a Map of Asia.
B   Baltimore: Johns Hopkins Press, 1943. 100 pp. 43-8440. o.p.
          Hucker, 395; FEQ, 11/47; AHR, 1/44; Geog. R., 1/44

0399   Ou-yang, Hsiu. Biography of Huang Ch'ao. tr. and annotated
C   by Howard S. Levy. 2d ed. rev. and enl. Berkeley: Univer-
          sity of California Press, 1961. 153 pp. (Chinese Dynas-
          tic Histories Translations, No. 5). NUC 64-11480.
          Hucker, 322; FEQ, 8/55; JAOS, 7-9/55

0400   Pan, Ku. Food and Money in Ancient China. tr. and annotated
B   by Nancy Lee Swann. Princeton, N.J.: Princeton University
          Press, 1950. 482 pp. 50-7084. o.p. (M-University).
          Hucker, 172; FEQ, 5/51

0401   Pan, Ku. The History of the Former Han Dynasty: A Critical Trans-
C   lation with annotations by Homer H. Dubs. N.Y.: American
          Council of Learned Societies, dist. by Columbia University
          Press, 1964 (orig. pub. by Waverly, 1938-). 43-46839 rev.
          (R).
          Hucker, 187; JAS, 11/58; FEQ, 11/44

0402   Pan, Ku. Wang Mang; A Translation of the Official Account
B   of His Rise to Power as Given in the History of the
          Former Han Dynasty. intro. and notes by Clyde Bailey
          Sargent. Shanghai: Graphic Art Book Company, 1947. 206 pp.
          A49-7492. o.p.
          Hucker, 220; FEQ, 2/52

0403   Pulleyblank, E. G. The Background of the Rebellion of An Lu-shan.
B   N.Y.: Oxford, 1955. 264 pp. A58-1352.
          Hucker, 279; FEQ, 11/55; JAOS, 7-9/55

0404   Ratchnevsky, Paul. Essai sur la Codification et la Legislation
C   a l'Epoque des Yuan. Paris: Leroux, 1937. 41-36376.
          Hucker, 415

0405   Reischauer, Edwin Oldfather. Ennin's Travels in T'ang China.
A   N.Y.: Ronald, 1955. 341 pp. 55-6273.
          Hucker, 280; Silberman, 633; FEQ, 11/55; Ann. Am. Acad.,
          11/55; Library Journal, 6/15/55; Pacific Affairs, 12/55

0406   Ruysbroek, Willem Van, 13th Century. The Journey of William
B   of Rubruck to the Eastern Parts of the World, 1253-55, as
          Narrated by Himself, with Two Accounts of the Earlier Jour-
          ney of John of Pian de Carpine. tr. by William W. Rockhill.
          Lichtenstein: Kraus, 1966 (orig. pub. by Hakluyt Society,
          1900). 304 pp. 1-9024. (R).
          Hucker, 402

0407   Schafer, Edward H. Ancient China. by Edward H. Schafer and
C   the editors of Time-Life Books. N.Y.: Time-Life Books,
          dist. by Silver Burdett, 1967. 191 pp. (Great Ages of
          Man). 67-30847.
          Choice, 7-8/68; Library Journal, 4/15/68

0408   Schafer, Edward H. The Empire of Min. Rutland, Vt.: Tuttle
B   for Harvard-Yenching Institute, 1954. 146 pp. 59-34309.
          Hucker, 329; FEQ, 8/55; JAOS, 1-3/56

0409   Schafer, Edward H. Golden Peaches of Samarkand; A Study of
A   T'ang Exotics. Berkeley: University of California Press,
          1963. 399 pp. 63-8922.
          JAS, 2/64; JAOS, 4-6/65; Library Journal, 5/1/63; Pacific

Affairs, Fall/63

0410   Schafer, Edward H. The Vermillion Bird; T'ang Images of the
A   South. Berkeley: University of California Press, 1967.
          380 pp. 67-10463.
          Choice, 3/68; JAS, 5/68; Library Journal, 9/1/67

0411   Schurmann, Herbert Franz, comp. The China Reader: Imperial
B   China. N.Y.: Random House, 1967. 322 pp. 66-21489.
          Choice, 1/68; JAS, 2/68; Library Journal, 2/1/67, 11/15/67

0412   Sino-Iranica. Sino-Iranica; Chinese Contributions to the History
C   of Civilization in Ancient Iran, with Special Reference to
          the History of Cultivated Plants and Products. N.Y.: Kraus,
          1967 (orig. pub. in Chicago, 1919 as Field Museum of Nat-
          ural History Publication, 201). 445 pp. 68-4203. (R).
          Hucker, 2209

0413   Ssu-ma, Ch'ien. Les Memoires Historiques de Se-ma Ts'ien.
C   tr. and annotated by Edouard Chavannes. Paris: Leroux for
          Societe Asiatique, 1895-1905. 5 v. in 6. 21-17126 rev.
          Hucker, 196

0414   Ssu-ma, Ch'ien. Records of the Grand Historian of China. tr.
B   from the Shih chi of Ssu-ma Ch'ien by Burton Watson. N.Y.:
          Columbia University Press, 1961. 2 v. (Records of Civili-
          zation: Sources and Guides, No. 65). 60-13348.
          Hucker, 188; JAS, 2/63; AHR, 7/62; Ann. Am. Acad., 5/62

0415   Ssu-ma, Ch'ien. Statesman, Patriot, and General in Ancient
B   China; Three Shih Chi Biographies of the Ch'in Dynasty (255-
          206 B.C.). tr. by Derk Bodde. N.Y.: Kraus, 1957 (orig.
          pub. by American Oriental Society, 1940). 75 pp. 40-11696.
          (R). (M-University).
          Hucker, 184

0416   Ssu-ma, Kuang. The Chronicle of The Three Kingdoms (220-265).
C   Chapters 69-78 from the Tzu Chih T'ung Chien. Cambridge,
          Mass.: Harvard University Press, 1952- (Harvard-Yenching
          Institute Studies, VI). 52-677.
          JAS, 5/66; FEQ, 11/52; JAOS, 4-6/66

0417   Swann, Nancy Lee. Pan Chao: Foremost Woman Scholar of China,
B   1st Century A.D.; Background, Ancestry, Life and Writ-
          ings of the Most Celebrated Chinese Woman of Letters.
          N.Y.: Russell & Russell, 1968 (orig. pub. by Century, 1932).
          179 pp. 68-10946. (R).
          Hucker, 201

0418   Teggart, Frederick John. Rome and China; A Study of Correla-
A   tions in Historical Events. Berkeley: University of
          California Press, 1939. 283 pp. 40-86. o.p.
          Hucker, 235; FEQ, 8/42

0419   Twitchett, Denis Crispin. Financial Administration under the
B   T'ang Dynasty. Cambridge: University, 1963. 373 pp.
          63-3532.
          JAS, 2/64; JAOS, 1-3/64

0420   Vladimirtsov, Boris Iakovlevich. The Life of Chingis-Khan. tr.
B   from Russian by Prince D. S. Mirsky. London: Routledge,
          1930. 172 pp. 30-31732. o.p.
          Hucker, 366

0421   Vladimirtsov, Boris Iakovlevich. La Regime Social des Mongols;
C   La Feodalisme Nomade. tr. by Michel Carsow. Paris: Maison-
          neuve, 1948. 291 pp. 50-14455.
          Hucker, 370

0422   Walker, Richard Louis. The Multi-state System of Ancient China.
B   Hamden, Conn.: Shoe String Press, 1954. 135 pp. 54-7778.
          o.p.
          Hucker, 164; AHR, 10/54; Am. Pol. Sci. R., 6/54; JAOS,
          10-12/54

0423   Wang, Gungwu. The Structure of Power in North China during
B   the Five Dynasties. Stanford, Calif.: Stanford University
          Press, 1968 (orig. pub. by University of Malaya Press,
          1963). 257 pp. SA64-2651. (R).
          JAS, 5/65

0424   Watson, Burton. Ssu-ma Ch'ien, Grand Historian of China.
A   N.Y.: Columbia University Press, 1958. 276 pp. 57-13030.
          Hucker, 190; Library Journal, 5/15/58; TLS, 9/26/58

0425   Watson, William. Early Civilization in China. N.Y.: McGraw-
A   Hill, 1966. 143 pp. (Library of the Early Civilizations).
          66-16974.

Choice, 2/67; Library Journal, 9/15/66; Pacific Affairs,
Fall-Winter/66-67

0426 Williamson, Henry R. Wang An Shih...a Chinese Statesman and
C Educationalist of the Sung Dynasty. London: A. Probsthain,
1935-37. 2 v. 35-13711 rev. o.p.
Hucker, 347; FEQ, 11/41; JAOS, 12/37

0427 Wittfogel, Karl August. History of Chinese Society: Liao
B (907-1125). Philadelphia: American Philosophical Society,
1949. 725 pp. (Transactions of the American Philosophical
Society, n.s., XXXVI). 49-8472. o.p.
Hucker, 355; FEQ, 5/50

0428 Yang, Lien-sheng. Money and Credit in China; A Short History.
C Cambridge, Mass.: Harvard University Press, 1952. 143 pp.
52-5413.
Hucker, 2264; FEQ, 11/53; JAOS, 7-9/53; Pacific Affairs, 6/53

0429 Yu, Ying-shih. Trade and Expansion in Han China; A Study
C in the Structure of Sino-barbarian Economic Relations.
Berkeley: University of California Press, 1967. 251 pp.
67-12492.
Choice, 3/68; JAS, 5/68

HISTORY
MING AND MANCHU PERIODS

0430 Anderson, Flavia. The Rebel Emperor. London: Gollancz, 1958.
C 356 pp. 58-4562. o.p.
Hucker, 623

0431 Appleton, William Worthen. A Cycle of Cathay; The Chinese Vogue
B in England during the Seventeenth and Eighteenth Centuries.
N.Y.: Columbia University Press, 1951. 182 pp. 51-9335.
o.p.
Hucker, 575; FEQ, 2/52

0432 Backhouse, Sir Edmund Trelawny. Annals & Memoirs of the Court
B of Peking (from the 16th to the 20th Century). Boston:
Houghton Mifflin, 1914. 531 pp. 14-30273. o.p.
AUFS, 727; Hucker, 477; AHR, 7/14; Am. Pol. Sci. R., 8/14

0433 Bales, William Leslie. Tso Tsungt'ang, Soldier and Statesman
C of Old China. Shanghai: Kelly & Walsh, 1937. 436 pp.
38-5016. o.p. (M-University).
Hucker, 641

0434 Banno, Masataka. China and the West, 1858-1861; The Origins
A of the Tsungli Yamen. Cambridge, Mass.: Harvard Univer-
sity Press, 1964. 367 pp. (Harvard East Asian Series,
15). 64-13419.
Choice, 9/64; JAS, 11/64; AHR, 1/65; JAOS, 7-9/64; Pacific
Affairs, Winter/64-65; TLS, 4/8/65

0435 Bernard, Henri. Matteo Ricci's Scientific Contribution to China.
C tr. by Edward Chalmers Werner. Peiping: Vetch, 1935. 108 pp.
36-17357. o.p.
Hucker, 553; TLS, 9/26/36

0436 Bernard, Henri. Le Pere Matthieu Ricci et la Societe Chinoise de
C son Temps (1552-1610). Tientsin: Hautes Etudes, 1937. 2 v.
38-33085. o.p.

0437 Bland, John Otway Percy. China Under the Empress Dowager;
B Being the History of the Life and Times of Tzu Hsi. new
and rev. ed. Taipei: Chinese Materials and Research Aids
Service Center (orig. pub. by Houghton Mifflin, 1914).
322 pp. A17-407. (R). (M-University).
AUFS, 730; Hucker, 610; FEQ, 11/41

0438 Boardman, Eugene Powers. Christian Influence Upon the Ideology of
A the Taiping Rebellion, 1851-1864. Madison: University of
Wisconsin Press, 1952. 188 pp. 52-13339. o.p.
Hucker, 624; FEQ, 5/53

0439 Boxer, Charles Ralph. Fidalgos in the Far East, 1550-1770; Fact
B and Fancy in the History of Macao. The Hague: Nijhoff, 1948.
297 pp. 49-21659.
Hucker, 557; FEQ, 2/52

0440 Boxer, Charles Ralph, ed. South China in the Sixteenth Century,
C Being the Narratives of Galeote Pereira, Fr. Gaspar da
Cruz, and Fr. Martin de Rada (1550-1575). tr. by editor.
Lichtenstein: Kraus, 1967 (orig. pub. by Hakluyt Society,
1953). 388 pp. (Works issued by the Hakluyt Society, 2d
ser. No. 106). NUC 68-28970. (R).
Sup. 61, 2789; Hucker, 573; FEQ, 5/56

0441 Braga, Jose Maria. China Landfall, 1513. Hong Kong: K. Weiss,
C 1956.
Hucker, 584

0442 Braga, Jose Maria. The Western Pioneers and Their Discovery
B of Macao. Macao: Imprensa Nacional, 1949. 248 pp. 51-24246.
Hucker, 569

0443 Bunger, Karl. Quellen zur Rechtgeschichte der T'ang-zeit.
C Peking: Catholic University, 1946. (Monumenta Serica Mono-
graph, IX). o.p.
Hucker, 287

0444 Cahen, Gaston. History of the Relations of Russia and China
C under Peter the Great, 1689-1730. tr. and ed. by W.
Sheldon Ridge. Banger, Me.: University Prints-Reprints,
1967 (orig. pub. in Shanghai, 1914 under title Some Early
Russo-Chinese Relations). 128 pp. (Russian Series, 4).
67-23371. (R).
AUFS, 733; Choice, 5/68

0445 Cameron, Meribeth Elliot. The Reform Movement in China, 1898-
A 1912. Stanford, Calif.: Stanford University Press, 1931.
223 pp. 31-32244. o.p.
Hucker, 646; Am. J. Soc., 9/32; Am. Pol. Sci. R., 2/32;
Ann. Am. Acad., 5/32

0446 Campbell, Charles Soutter. Special Business Interests and the
B Open Door Policy. Hamden, Conn.: Shoe String Press, 1968
(orig. pub. by Yale University Press, 1951). 88 pp.
(Yale Historical Publications, 53). 68-21689. (R).
Hucker, 692

0447 Chang, Chung-li. The Chinese Gentry; Studies on Their Role in
A Nineteenth-Century Chinese Society. Seattle: University of
Washington Press, 1968 (orig. pub. in 1955). 250 pp.
NUC 69-7002. (R).
Hucker, 1831; FEQ, 2/56; AHR, 1/56; Am. J. Soc., 5/56; Ann.
Am. Acad., 1/56; Pacific Affairs, 3/56

0448 Chang, Hsin-pao. Commissioner Lin and the Opium War. Cam-
B bridge, Mass.: Harvard University Press, 1964. 319 pp.
(Harvard East Asian Series, 18). 64-21786.
Choice, 2/65; JAS, 5/65; AHR, 7/65; Library Journal, 11/15/64

0449 Ch'eng, T'ien-fang. A History of Sino-Russian Relations.
C Washington: Public Affairs Press, 1957. 389 pp. 57-6908.
o.p.
Hucker, 839; Library Journal, 8/57

0450 Chiang, Siang-tseh. The Nien Rebellion. Seattle: University of
A Washington Press, 1968 (orig. pub. in 1954). 159 pp.
54-3971. (R).
Hucker, 640; FEQ, 5/55; JAOS, 4-6/56

0451 China. Laws, Statutes, etc. Manuel du Code Chinois, par le P.
C Guy Boulais. Taipai: Ch'eng-wen Publishing Co., dist. by
Chinese Materials and Research Aids Service Center, 1966
(orig. pub. by Mission Catholique, 1923-24). 2 v. (Varietes
Sinologiques, 55). Hand catalog. (R).
Hucker, 1886

0452 Ch'oe, Pu. Diary: a Record of Drifting Across the Sea. tr.
C with intro. and notes by John Meskill. Tucson: University
of Arizona Press, 1965. 177 pp. (Association for Asian
Studies, Monographs and Papers, XVII). 64-19165.
Choice, 10/66; JAS, 11/65; JAOS, 10-12/65; Library Journal,
6/15/65

0453 Ch'ou pan i wu shih mo. China's Management of the American Bar-
B barians; A Study of Sino-American Relations, 1841-1861, with
Documents. by Earl Swisher. New Haven, Conn.: Yale Univer-
sity Press for the Far Eastern Association, 1953. 844 pp.
(Association for Asian Studies, Monographs and Papers, VI).
54-2170.
Hucker, 685; FEQ, 11/54

0454 Ch'u, T'ung-tsu. Local Government in China under the Ching.
A Stanford, Calif.: Stanford University Press, 1966 (orig.
pub. by Harvard University Press, 1962). 360 pp.
(Harvard East Asian Series, 9). 62-11396. (R).
JAS, 11/63; AHR, 1/63; Ann. Am. Acad., 1/63; Library Journal,
6/15/62; Pol. Sci. Q., 6/63

0455 Clyde, Paul Hibbert, ed. United States Policy Toward China;
B Diplomatic and Public Documents, 1839-1939. N.Y.:
Russell & Russell, 1964 (orig. pub. by Duke University

Press, 1940). 321 pp. 64-15018. (R). (M-University).
Choice, 4/65; Hucker, 690; FEQ, 2/42; Am. Pol. Sci. R.,
10/40; Ann. Am. Acad., 1/41; Pacific Affairs, 12/40

0456 Cohen, Paul A. China and Christianity; The Missionary Movement
A and the Growth of Chinese Anti-foreignism, 1860-1870.
Cambridge, Mass.: Harvard University Press, 1963. 392 pp.
(Harvard East Asian Series, 11). 63-19135.
JAS, 8/64; AHR, 10/64; Ann. Am. Acad., 3/64; Library Journal,
1/1/64

0457 Collis, Maurice. Foreign Mud, Being an Account of the Opium Im-
B broglio at Canton in the 1830's and the Anglo-Chinese War that
Followed. N.Y.: Norton, 1968 (orig. pub. by Knopf, 1947).
300 pp. 47-31165. (R). (M-University).
AUFS, 739; Hucker, 672; FEQ, 8/48

0458 Constant, Charles Samuel de. Les Memoires de Charles de Constant
C sur le Commerce a la Chine par Louis Dermigny. Paris:
S.E.V.P.E.N., 1964. 491 pp. (Ecole Pratique des Hautes
Etudes-VI Section-Centre de Recherches Historiques). NUC
66-5605.
JAS, 5/66

0459 Dawson, Raymond Stanley. The Chinese Chamelion: an Analysis of
B European Conceptions of Chinese Civilization. N.Y.: Oxford,
1967. 235 pp. 67-81516.
Choice, 11/67; JAS, 11/67; Library Journal, 8/67; TLS,
5/18/67

0460 Der Ling, Princess. Son of Heaven. N.Y.: Appleton-Century,
C 1935. 248 pp. 35-5894. o.p.
Hucker, 612

0461 Der Ling, Princess, "Mrs. Thaddeus G. White". Two Years in the
B Forbidden City. N.Y.: Moffat, Yard and Co., 1911. 383 pp.
11-29741. o.p.

0462 Eastman, Lloyd E. Throne and Mandarins: China's Search for a
A Policy during the Sino-French Controversy, 1880-1885.
Cambridge, Mass.: Harvard University Press, 1967. 254 pp.
(Harvard Historical Studies, Vol. XXIX). 67-12098.
Choice, 11/67; JAS, 11/67; AHR, 2/68

0463 Fairbank, John King. Ch'ing Administration; Three Studies.
C Cambridge, Mass.: Harvard University Press, 1960. 218 pp.
(Harvard-Yenching Institute Studies, XIX). 60-7991.
Hucker, 513

0464 Fairbank, John King, comp. Ch'ing Documents; An Introductory
C Syllabus. 2d ed. rev. Cambridge, Mass.: Harvard University
Press, 1959. 2 v. 60-3385.
Hucker, 520; FEQ, 5/53; JAOS, 1-3/53

0465 Fairbank, John King. Trade and Diplomacy on the China Coast; The
A Opening of the Treaty Ports, 1842-1854. Stanford, Calif.:
Stanford University Press, 1968 (orig. pub. by Harvard
University Press, 1953). 2 v. 65-100264. (R).
AUFS, 741; Hucker 660; AHR, 10/54; Am. Pol. Sci. R., 6/54;
Ann. Am. Acad., 4/54

0466 Feuerwerker, Albert. China's Early Industrialization; Sheng
A Hsuan-huai (1844-1916) and Mandarin Enterprise. Cambridge,
Mass.: Harvard University Press, 1958. 311 pp. 58-12967.
AUFS, 742; Hucker, 2219; JAS, 8/59

0467 Fitzgerald, Charles Patrick. China: a Short Cultural History.
B 4th rev. ed. N.Y.: Praeger, 1954. 621 pp. 54-6804.
AUFS, 678; Hucker, 102

0468 Fleming, Peter. Bayonets to Lhasa; The First Full Account of the
C British Invasion of Tibet in 1904. N.Y.: Harper, 1961.
319 pp. 61-6431. o.p.
Hucker, 680; Library Journal, 4/1/61; TLS, 2/3/61

0469 Fleming, Peter. The Siege at Peking. N.Y.: Harper, 1959.
B 273 pp. 59-10580.
Hucker, 654; JAS, 8/60; AHR, 10/60; Library Journal, 9/15/59;
TLS, 6/26/59

0470 Franke, Wolfgang. Preliminary Notes on the Important Chinese
C Literary Sources for the History of the Ming Dynasty (1368-
1644). Chengtu: Chinese Cultural Studies Research Institute,
West China Union University, 1948. 118 pp. (Studia Serica
Monographs, Series A, No. 2). o.p.
Hucker, 442

0471 Friese, Heinz. Das Dienstleistungs-Systen der Ming-zeit. Weis-
C baden: Otto Harrassowitz, 1959. 163 pp. (Mitteilungen der
Gesellschaft fur Natur- und Volkerkunde Ostasiens, XXXV A).
Hand catalog. o.p.
Hucker, 446; JAS, 2/62

0472 Fu, Lo-shu, tr. A Documentary Chronicle of Sino-Western Rela-
C tions 1644-1820. Tucson: University of Arizona Press, 1966.
2 v. (Association for Asian Studies, Monographs and Papers,
XXII). 66-18529.
Choice, 6/67; JAS, 8/67; Pacific Affairs, Fall-Winter/67-68

0473 Goodrich, Luther Carrington. The Literary Inquisition of
B Ch'ien-lung. 2d ed. with addenda and corrigenda. N.Y.:
Paragon, 1966 (orig. pub. by Waverly Press, 1935). 275 pp.
66-11100. (R). (M-University).
Sup. 67, 3239; Hucker, 511; JAOS, 12/35

0474 Greenberg, Michael. British Trade and the Opening of China,
A 1800-42. Cambridge: University, 1951. 238 pp. A52-9218.
o.p.
AUFS, 743; Hucker, 561; FEQ, 11/51; Am. Econ. R., 9/52;
Pacific Affairs, 12/52

0475 Grimm, Tilemann. Erziehung und Politik im Konfuzianischen China
C der Ming-Zeit, 1368-1644. Hamburg: Gesellschaft fur Natur-
und Volkerkunde Ostasiens, 1960. 176 pp. (Mitteilungen
der Gesellschaft fur Natur- und Volkerkunde Ostasiens,
XXXV B). Hand catalog.
Hucker, 445; JAS, 11/60

0476 Ho, Ping-ti. The Ladder of Success in Imperial China; Aspects
A of Social Mobility, 1368-1911. N.Y.: Columbia University
Press, 1962. 385 pp. 62-10451.
JAS, 11/64; AHR, 10/63; Am. Soc. R., 8/63; Ann. Am. Acad.,
7/63; TLS, 11/14/63

0477 Hou, Chi-ming. Foreign Investment and Economic Development
A in China, 1840-1937. Cambridge, Mass.: Harvard Univer-
sity Press, 1965. 306 pp. (Harvard East Asian Series, 21).
65-22069.
Choice, 9/66; JAS, 2/67; AHR, 10/66; J. Pol. Econ., 8/66;
Library Journal, 12/15/66

0478 Hsiao, Kung-ch'uan. Rural China; Imperial Control in the
A Nineteenth Century. Seattle: University of Washington
Press, 1960. 783 pp. 60-15803.
Hucker, 1821; JAS, 8/61; Am. Anthropologist, 10/61; Am.
Soc. R., 8/61; Ann. Am. Acad., 11/61; JAOS, 1-3/62

0479 Hsieh, Pao Chao. The Government of China (1644-1911). N.Y.:
C Octagon, 1966 (orig. pub. by Johns Hopkins, 1925). 414 pp.
66-18027. (R). (M-University).
Hucker, 510

0480 Hsu, Immanuel Chung-yueh. China's Entrance into the Family of
A Nations: The Diplomatic Phase, 1858-1880 by Immanuel C. Y.
Hsu. fore. by William Langer. Cambridge, Mass.: Harvard
University Press, 1960. 255 pp. (Harvard East Asian Series,
5). 60-5738 rev.
Sup. 61, 2798; Hucker, 661; JAS, 11/60; AHR, 10/60;
Library Journal, 3/15/60; TLS, 12/30/60

0481 Hsu, Immanuel Chung-yueh. The Ili Crisis; A Study of Sino-
B Russian Diplomacy, 1871-1881. Oxford: Clarendon, 1965.
230 pp. 66-1409.
Choice, 9/66; JAS, 8/66; Library Journal, 1/1/68; TLS,
2/10/66

0482 Huc, Evariste Regis. The Chinese Empire: Being a Sequel to
C the Work Entitled "Recollections of a Journey through Tar-
tary and Thibet." London: Longman, Brown, Green and
Longmans, 1855. 2 v. 4-29888. o.p.

0483 Huc, Evariste Regis. Travels in Tartary, Thibet and China,
C 1844-1846. tr. by William Hazlitt. N.Y.: Harper, 1928.
2 v. 29-8715. o.p. (M-University).
AUFS, 1185

0484 Hucker, Charles O. The Censorial System of Ming China.
C Stanford, Calif.: Stanford University Press, 1966.
406 pp. (Stanford Studies in the Civilizations of Eastern
Asia). 66-10916.
Sup. 67, 3242; Choice, 2/67; JAS, 2/68; AHR, 1/67;
Ann. Am. Acad., 5/67; Library Journal, 7/68

0485 Hucker, Charles O. The Traditional Chinese State in Ming
A Times (1368-1644). Tucson: University of Arizona Press,
1961. 85 pp. 61-15391.

Sup. 63, 2917; Hucker 444; JAS, 8/62; JAOS, 1-3/62

0486 Hudson, Geoffrey Francis. Europe and China; A Survey of Their
A   Relations from the Earliest Times to 1800. Boston:
     Beacon, 1961 (orig. pub. by Arnold, 1931). 336 pp.
     A63-5056. (R).
     Hucker, 134; AHR, 10/32

0487 Hughes, Ernest Richard. The Invasion of China by the Western
C   World. ed. by R. S. Dawson. 2d ed. N.Y.: Barnes & Noble,
     1968 (orig. pub. by Macmillan, 1938). 317 pp. 73-213. (R).
     Hucker, 728; Choice, 5/69; Am. J. Soc., 9/38; Am. Pol. Sci.
     R., 8/38; Am. Soc. R., 12/38; Ann. Am. Acad., 7/38

0488 Hunter, William C. The 'Fan Kwae' at Canton before Treaty
B   Days, 1825-1844, by an Old Resident. N.Y.: Paragon, 1965
     (orig. pub. in London, 1822). 97 pp. 42-50527. (R).
     Hucker, 683

0489 Hussey, Harry. Venerable Ancestor; The Life and Times of
B   Tz'u Hsi, 1835-1908, Empress of China. Garden City, N.Y.:
     Doubleday, 1949. 354 pp. 49-11056. o.p.
     Hucker, 611

0490 Kammerer, Albert. La Decouverte de la Chine par les Portugais
C   au XVIeme Siecle et la Cartographie des Portulans. Leiden:
     Brill, 1944. 260 pp. AF47-6702.
     Hucker, 582

0491 K'ang, Yu-wei. Ta T'ung Shu. The One-World Philosophy of K'ang
B   Yu-wei. tr. from Chinese by Laurence G. Thompson. N.Y.:
     Hillary House, 1958. 300 pp. A58-4956 rev.
     AUFS, 747; Hucker, 649

0492 Ku, Chieh-Kang. The Autobiography of a Chinese Historian,
B   Being the Preface to a Symposium on Ancient Chinese
     History (Ku shih pien). tr. and annotated by Arthur W.
     Hummel. Taipei: Ch'eng-wen Publishing Co., dist. by Chinese
     Materials and Research Aids Service Center, 1966 (orig. pub.
     by Brill, 1931). 199 pp. Hand catalog. (R).
     Hucker, 1628

0493 Kuei, Wan-jung. T'ang-yin-pi-shih. Parallel Cases from
C   Under the Pear-tree, a 13th Century Manual of Jurisprudence
     and Detection. tr. from Chinese with notes and intro. by
     R. H. van Gulik. Leiden: Brill, 1956. 198 pp. 57-970.
     Hucker, 1874

0494 Lamb, Alastair. Britain and Chinese Central Asia; The Road to
A   Lhasa, 1767 to 1905. N.Y.: Humanities, 1960. 387 pp.
     61-1070.
     Hucker, 678; JAS, 2/63

0495 Lamb, Alastair. British Missions to Cochin China: 1778-
C   1822. Kuala Lumpur: Printcraft, 1961. 248 pp. (Royal
     Asiatic Society. Journal of the Malayan Branch, Singapore,
     Vol. 34, Parts 3 and 4). Hand catalog.
     Sup. 63, 2921; JAS, 11/62

0496 Latourette, Kenneth Scott. A History of Christian Missions in
B   China. N.Y.: Russell & Russell, 1967 (orig. pub. by Mac-
     millan, 1929). 930 pp. 66-24721. (R). (M-University).
     AUFS, 749; Hucker, 548; AHR, 7/29; J. Religion, 10/29;
     Pol. Sci. Q., 12/29

0497 Laufer, Berthold. Chinese Clay Figures. Chicago: Field Museum
C   of Natural History, 1914- (Publication 177). 15-8603.
     o.p.
     Hucker, 1910

0498 Lensen, George Alexander. The Russo-Chinese War. Tallahassee,
B   Fla.: Diplomatic Press, 1967. 315 pp. 67-26314.
     Choice, 3/68; JAS, 5/68; Pacific Affairs, Spring/68

0499 Levenson, Joseph Richmond. Liang Ch'i-ch'ao and the Mind of
A   Modern China. Cambridge, Mass.: Harvard University Press,
     1959. 256 pp. 53-5069.
     AUFS, 750; Hucker, 749; FEQ, 11/54

0500 Li, Chien-nung. The Political History of China, 1840-1928.
B   tr. and ed. by Ssu-yu Teng and Jeremy Ingalls. Stanford,
     Calif.: Stanford University Press, 1968 (orig. pub. by
     Van Nostrand, 1956). 545 pp. 67-26648. (R).
     Hucker, 604; AHR, 4/57; Am. Pol. Sci. R., 9/57; Library
     Journal, 9/15/56; Pacific Affairs, 6/57; TLS, 6/14/57

0501 Liang, Fang-chung. The Single-wip Method (I-t'iao-pien fa) of
B   Taxation in China. tr. by Wang Yu-ch'uan. Cambridge,

Mass.: Harvard University Press, 1956. 71 pp. 56-4991.
o.p.
Hucker, 448

0502 MacNair, Harley Farnsworth, ed. Modern Chinese History; Selected
B   Readings. N.Y.: Paragon, 1967 (orig. pub. by Commercial
     Press, 1923). 910 pp. 67-29257. (R).
     Hucker, 658

0503 Malone, Carroll Brown. History of the Peking Summer Palaces
C   under the Ch'ing Dynasty. N.Y.: Paragon, 1966 (orig. pub.
     by University of Illinois, 1934). 247 pp. 66-30338. (R).
     Hucker, 527; AHR, 4/35

0504 Mayers, William Frederick. The Chinese Government. A Manual of
C   Chinese Titles, Categorically Arranged and Explained, with
     an Index. 3d ed. rev. by G. M. H. Playfair. Taipai:
     Ch'eng-wen Publishing Co., dist. by Chinese Materials and
     Research Aids Service Center, 1966 (orig. pub. by Kelly &
     Walsh, 1897). 196 pp. Hand catalog. (R).
     Hucker, 542

0505 Meadows, Thomas Taylor. The Chinese and Their Rebellions,
A   Viewed in Connection with Their National Philosophy,
     Ethics, Legislation, and Administration. To Which is Added
     an Essay on Civilization and Its Present State in the East
     and West. Stanford, Calif.: Academic Reprints, 1953.
     656 pp. 54-2175. o.p.
     Hucker, 625

0506 Michael, Franz H. The Origin of Manchu Rule in China; Frontier
A   and Bureaucracy as Interacting Forces in the Chinese
     Empire. N.Y.: Octagon, 1965 (orig. pub. by Johns Hopkins
     Press, 1942). 127 pp. 65-25880. (R).
     AUFS, 754; Hucker, 509; FEQ, 5/43; Am. Pol. Sci. R., 6/42;
     Ann. Am. Acad., 7/42; Pacific Affairs, 9/42

0507 Morse, Hosea Ballou. The Chronicles of the East India Company,
B   Trading to China, 1635-1834. Taipei: Chinese Materials
     and Research Aids Service Center (orig. pub. by Clarendon,
     1926-29). 5 v. 26-9732. (R).
     Hucker, 560; Am. Econ. R., 12/26; AHR, 10/26

0508 Morse, Hosea Ballou. The International Relations of the Chinese
B   Empire. Taipei: Chinese Materials and Research Aids Ser-
     vice Center, 1966 (orig. pub. by Longmans, Green, 1910-
     18). 3 v. 11-2033. (R).
     AUFS, 755; Hucker, 662

0509 Morse, Hosea Ballou. The Trade and Administration of Chinese
C   Empire, 1966. Taipei: Ch'eng-wen Publishing Co., dist. by
     Chinese Materials and Research Aids Service Center, 1966
     (orig. pub. by Longmans, Green, 1920). 451 pp. NUC 67-43061.
     (R).
     Hucker, 667

0510 Parsons, James B. A Preliminary Analysis of the Ming
C   Dynasty Bureaucracy. Kyoto: Kansai Asiatic Society, 1959.
     16 pp. (Occasional Papers of the Kansai Asiatic Society,
     VII). Hand catalog.
     Hucker, 1848

0511 Pelcovits, Nathan Albert. Old China Hands and the Foreign
A   Office. N.Y.: Octagon, 1967 (orig. pub. by American Insti-
     tute of Pacific Relations, 1948). 349 pp. 78-76003. (R).
     AUFS, 756; Hucker, 677; AHR, 10/48; Am. Pol. Sci. R., 4/48;
     Ann. Am. Acad., 5/48; FEQ, 8/48; Pacific Affairs, 9/48

0512 Powell, Ralph L. The Rise of Chinese Military Power, 1895-
A   1912. Princeton, N.J.: Princeton University Press, 1955.
     383 pp. 55-6247. o.p.
     Hucker, 647; AHR, 1/56; Ann. Am. Acad., 3/56; Library
     Journal, 8/55

0513 Rawlinson, John L. China's Struggle for Naval Development,
B   1839-1895. Cambridge, Mass.: Harvard University Press,
     1967. 318 pp. (Harvard East Asian Series, 25). 66-10127.
     Choice, 7-8/67; JAS, 11/67; AHR, 12/67; JAOS, 10-12/67

0514 Reichwein, Adolf. China and Europe: Intellectual and Artistic
A   Contacts in the Eighteenth Century. tr. by J. C. Powell.
     N.Y.: Barnes & Noble, 1968 (orig. pub. by Knopf, 1925).
     174 pp. 25-9577. (R).
     Hucker, 574

0515 Ricci, Matteo. China in the Sixteenth Century: the Journals of
B   Matthew Ricci, 1583-1610. tr. from Latin by Louis J.
     Gallagher. N.Y.: Random House, 1953. 616 pp. 53-9708.

o.p.
Hucker, 546

0516 Rosso, Antonio Sisto. Apostolic Legations to China of the
C   Eighteenth Century. South Pasadena, Calif.: P. D. and Ione
     Perkins, 1948. 502 pp. 49-25178. o.p.
     Hucker, 552; FEQ, 2/52

0517 Rowbotham, Arnold Horrex. Missionary and Mandarin, the
A   Jesuits at the Court of China. N.Y.: Russell & Russell,
     1966 (orig. pub. by University of California Press, 1942).
     374 pp. 66-13253. (R).
     AUFS, 759; Hucker, 1307; FEQ, 5/43

0518 Serruys, Henry. Sino-Jurced Relations During the Yung-lo
C   Period 1403-1424. Wiesbaden: Otto Harrassowitz, 1955.
     118 pp. 56-38257. o.p.
     Hucker, 498

0519 Shih, Vincent Yu-chung. The Taiping Ideology; Its Sources,
B   Interpretations, and Influences. Seattle: University
     of Washington Press, 1967. 553 pp. (Far Eastern and
     Russian Institute Publications on Asia, 15). 66-19571.
     Choice, 6/68; JAS, 8/68; Library Journal, 4/15/68; TLS,
     8/22/68

0520 Spector, Stanley. Li Hung-chang and the Huai Army; A Study
A   in Nineteenth-Century Chinese Regionalism. intro. by
     Franz Michael. Seattle: University of Washington Press,
     1964. 359 pp. (Washington University Publications on
     Asia). 64-11052.
     Sup. 65, 3106; JAS, 2/66; AHR, 7/65; Library Journal,
     9/15/64

0521 Spence, Jonathan D. Ts'ao Yin and the K'ang-hsi Emperor;
A   Bondservant and Master. New Haven, Conn.: Yale Univer-
     sity Press, 1966. 329 pp. (Yale Historical Publications
     Miscellany, 85). 66-21537.
     Choice, 7-8/67; JAS, 8/68; AHR, 7/67; Library Journal,
     11/15/66; TLS, 3/16/67

0522 Stanley, Charles Johnson. Late Ch'ing Finance: Hu Kuang-yung
B   as an Innovator. Cambridge, Mass.: Harvard University
     Press, 1961. 117 pp. 62-1254. o.p.
     JAS, 8/62

0523 Sun, I-tu (Jen). Chinese Railways and British Interests, 1898-
C   1911, by E-tu Zen Sun. N.Y.: King's Crown, 1954. 230 pp.
     54-12129 rev. o.p.
     Hucker, 676; FEQ, 8/55; AHR, 4/55; Ann. Am. Acad., 5/55

0524 Sun Tzu. The Art of War; The Oldest Military Treatise in the
C   World. Taipei: Literature House, dist. by Chinese Materials
     and Research Aids Service Center, 1964 (orig. pub. by Luzac,
     1910). 204 pp. Hand catalog. (R).
     Hucker, 1899

0525 T'an, Ch'un-lin. The Boxer Catastrophe, by Chester C. Tan.
A   N.Y.: Octagon, 1967 (orig. pub. by Columbia University
     Press, 1955). 276 pp. 66-18057. (R). (M-University).
     Hucker, 653; JAS, 2/57; AHR, 4/56; Ann. Am. Acad., 3/56;
     Library Journal, 3/6/56; Pacific Affairs, 9/56

0526 Teng, Ssu-yu. Chang Hsi and the Treaty of Nanking, 1842. Chi-
B   cago: University of Chicago Press, 1944. 119 pp. A45-937.
     o.p.
     Hucker, 671; FEQ, 2/52; AHR, 10/45

0527 Teng, Ssu-yu. China's Response to the West; A Documentary
A   Survey, 1839-1923. Cambridge, Mass.: Harvard University
     Press in cooperation with Institute of Pacific Relations,
     1954. 296 pp. 53-5061 rev.
     Hucker, 607; FEQ, 8/55; Library Journal, 3/15/54

0528 Teng, Ssu-yu. New Light on the History of the Taiping Rebel-
B   lion. N.Y.: Russell & Russell, 1966 (orig. pub. by
     Harvard University Press, 1950). 132 pp. 66-13241. (R).
     Hucker, 618; FEQ, 8/51; AHR, 10/50; Am. Pol. Sci. R., 9/50;
     Pacific Affairs, 6/50

0529 Teng, Ssu-yu. The Nien Army and their Guerilla Warfare, 1851-
A   1868. N.Y.: Humanities, 1961. 254 pp. Hand catalog.
     JAS, 5/62; JAOS, 10-12/62

0530 Wakeman, Frederic E. Strangers at the Gate; Social Disorder
A   in South China, 1839-1861. Berkeley: University of California
     Press, 1966. 276 pp. (Center for Chinese Studies).
     66-25349.

Choice, 7-8/67; JAS, 8/67; AHR, 10/67; Library Journal,
1/1/67

0531 Waley, Arthur. The Opium War through Chinese Eyes. Stanford,
B   Calif.: Stanford University Press, 1968 (orig. pub. by
     Allen & Unwin, 1958). 257 pp. 68-12334. (R).
     Hucker, 669; JAS, 11/59; AHR, 1/60; Ann. Am. Acad., 11/59;
     Library Journal, 5/1/59; TLS, 3/20/59

0532 Walker, Richard Louis, ed. China and the West: Cultural Col-
C   lision; Selected Documents. New Haven, Conn.: Far Eastern
     Publications, Yale University, 1956. 254 pp. 56-58515.
     o.p.
     Hucker, 657

0533 Williams, Samuel Wells. The Middle Kingdom; A Survey of the
B   Geography, Government, Literature, Social Life, Arts, and
     History of the Chinese Empire and Its Inhabitants.
     N.Y.: Paragon, 1966 (orig. pub. by Scribner's, 1883).
     2 v. 66-16895. (R). (M-University).
     Hucker, 10

0534 Wright, Mary Clabaugh. The Last Stand of Chinese Conserva-
A   tism; The T'ung-chih Restoration, 1862-1874. Stanford,
     Calif.: Stanford University Press, 1957. 426 pp. 57-5946.
     AUFS, 767; Hucker, 617; JAS, 5/58; AHR, 1/58; Am. Pol. Sci.
     R., 3/58; JAOS, 7-9/58; Library Journal, 3/1/57; Pacific
     Affairs, 3/58; TLS, 4/25/58

0535 Wright, Stanley Fowler. Hart and the Chinese Customs. Belfast:
B   Mullan, 1950. 949 pp. 51-2518.
     Hucker, 673; FEQ, 8/52

0536 Wu, Ai-ch'en. China and the Soviet Union; A Study of Sino-
B   Soviet Relations. Port Washington, N.Y.: Kennikat, 1968
     (orig. pub. by John Day, 1950). 434 pp. 67-29610. (R).
     Hucker, 703; AHR, 7/51; Pacific Affairs, 3/51; TLS,
     12/22/50

0537 Yen, Sophia Su-fei. Taiwan in China's Foreign Relations,
B   1836-1874. Hamden, Conn.: Shoe String Press, 1965. 404 pp.
     65-7577.
     Choice, 11/65; JAS, 5/66

0538 Yule, Sir Henry, ed. and tr. Cathay and the Way Thither; Being
C   a Collection of Medieval Notices of China. new ed., rev. by
     Henri Cordier. Taipei: Ch'eng-wen Publishing Co., dist. by
     Chinese Materials and Research Aids Service Center, 1966
     (orig. pub. by Hakluyt Society, 1913-16). 4 v. in 2.
     5-40435. (R).
     Hucker, 135

0539 Yung, Wing. My Life in China and America. N.Y.: Holt, 1909.
B   286 pp. 9-31843. o.p.
     Hucker, 696; Ann. Am. Acad., 5/10

HISTORY
REVOLUTION AND REPUBLIC

0540 Abend, Hallett Edward. My Life in China, 1926-1941. N.Y.:
C   Harcourt, Brace, 1943. 396 pp. 43-15741. o.p. (M-Uni-
     versity).
     Hucker, 628; FEQ, 5/44; Am. Pol. Sci. R., 8/43; Library
     Journal, 7/1/43; TLS, 8/28/43

0541 Anders, Leslie. The Ledo Road; General Joseph W. Stilwell's
C   Highway to China. Norman: University of Oklahoma Press,
     1965. 255 pp. 65-11232.
     Choice, 10/65; JAS, 5/66; Library Journal, 4/15/65

0542 Band, Claire. Two Years with the Chinese Communists. New
B   Haven, Conn.: Yale University Press, 1948. 347 pp.
     48-5830 rev. o.p.
     Hucker, 893; Ann. Am. Acad., 7/48; Pacific Affairs, 9/48

0543 Barnett, A. Doak. China on the Eve of Communist Takeover.
A   N.Y.: Praeger, 1963. 371 pp. (Praeger Publications in
     Russian History and World Communism, No. 130). 63-10824.
     Ann. Am. Acad., 1/64; Library Journal, 7/63

0544 Bergere, Marie Claire, ed. Une Crise Financiere a Shanghai
B   a le Fin de l'Ancien Regime. Paris: Mouton, 1964. 84 pp.
     (Maison des Sciences de l'Homme, Materiaux pour l'Etude
     de la Chine Modern et Contemporaine, Textes, 3).
     NUC 66-74341.
     JAS, 2/66

0545 Berkov, Robert. Strong Man of China; The Story of Chiang
B   Kai-shek. Boston: Houghton Mifflin, 1938. 288 pp.
      38-3985. o.p.
      Am. Pol. Sci. R., 8/38

0546 Bertram, James M. First Act in China; The Story of the Sian
B   Mutiny. N.Y.: Viking, 1938. 284 pp. 38-20738. o.p.
      Hucker, 777; Ann. Am. Acad., 7/38; Pacific Affairs, 3/38

0547 Borg, Dorothy. American Policy and the Chinese Revolution,
A   1925-1928. N.Y.: Octagon, 1967 (orig. pub. by Macmillan,
      1947). 440 pp. 67-18753. (R).
      AUFS, 778; Hucker, 812; FEQ, 11/47; AHR, 10/47; Am. Pol.
      Sci. R., 12/47;

0548 Brandt, Conrad. Stalin's Failure in China 1924-1927. N.Y.:
A   Norton, 1966 (orig. pub. by Harvard University Press,
      1958). 226 pp. (Norton Library, N352). NUC 67-85293.
      (R).
      AUFS, 903; Hucker, 872; JAS, 5/59; AHR, 4/59; Am. Pol.
      Sci. R., 6/59; TLS, 5/8/59

0549 Buck, John Lossing. Chinese Farm Economy; A Study of 2866 Farms
B   in Seventeen Localities and Seven Provinces of China. Chi-
      cago: University of Chicago Press for University of Nanking,
      1930. 476 pp. 31-6710. o.p.
      Hucker, 2200; Am. J. Soc., 9/31; Geog. R., 4/31

0550 Buck, John Lossing. Land Utilization in China; A Study of
B   16,786 Farms in 168 Localities, and 38,256 Farm Families
      in Twenty-two Provinces in China, 1929-1933. N.Y.: Para-
      gon, 1964 (orig. pub. by University of Chicago Press, 1937).
      494 pp. 64-18448. (R).
      Hucker, 2199; JAS, 8/65; Ann. Am. Acad., 11/38; Pacific
      Affairs, 12/38

0551 Buck, Mrs. Pearl Sydenstricker. The Good Earth. N.Y.: John
B   Day, 1931. 375 pp. 31-26625.
      TLS, 4/30/31

0552 Buck, Mrs. Pearl Sydenstricker. My Several Worlds, a Personal
B   Record. N.Y.: John Day, 1954. 407 pp. 54-10460.

0553 Carlson, Evans Fordyce. The Chinese Army; Its Organization
B   and Military Efficiency. N.Y.: Institute of Pacific Rela-
      tions, 1940. 139 pp. 40-14507. o.p.
      Hucker, 1937; Am. Pol. Sci. R., 12/40

0554 Carlson, Evans Fordyce. Twin Stars of China, a Behind-the-
B   Scenes Story of China's Valiant Struggle for Existence,
      by a U.S. Marine Who Lived & Moved with the People.
      N.Y.: Dodd, Mead, 1940. 331 pp. 40-27687. o.p.
      Hucker, 804

0555 Chang, Chia-ao. The Inflationary Spiral; The Experience in
B   China, 1939-1950. Cambridge: Technology Press of M.I.T.,
      1958. 394 pp. 58-6083. o.p.
      Hucker, 2280; JAS, 5/59; Am. Econ. R., 12/59; Ann. Am.
      Acad., 1/59; Pacific Affairs, 9/59

0556 Chang, Chia-sen. The Third Force in China. N.Y.: Bookman,
B   1952. 345 pp. 53-5815.
      Hucker, 801; Library Journal, 2/1/53; Pacific Affairs,
      9/53; Pol. Sci. Q., 6/53

0557 Chao, Pu-wei (Yang). Autobiography of a Chinese Woman, Bu wei
B   Yang Chao. tr. from Chinese by Yuenren Chao. N.Y.:
      John Day, 1947. 327 pp. 47-1800. o.p.
      Hucker, 737; FEQ, 8/47; Library Journal, 3/1/47

0558 Chassin, Lionel Max. The Communist Conquest of China; A
B   History of the Civil War, 1945-1949. tr. by T. Osato and
      L. Gelas. Cambridge, Mass.: Harvard University Press,
      1965. 264 pp. 65-22043.
      Choice, 2/66; JAS, 5/66; AHR, 7/66; Ann. Am. Acad., 2/66;
      Library Journal, 8/65; TLS, 3/3/66

0559 Ch'en, Han-sheng. Landlord and Peasant in China; A Study of
B   the Agrarian Crisis in South China. N.Y.: International
      Publishers, 1936. 144 pp. A38-206. o.p. (M-University).
      Hucker, 2210; Am. Econ. R., 3/37; Am. Soc. R., 8/37;
      Ann. Am. Acad., 3/37; J. Pol. Econ., 12/37; Pacific Affairs,
      9/37

0560 Ch'en, Jerome. Yuan Shih-K'ai, 1859-1916; Brutus Assumes the
B   Purple. Stanford, Calif.: Stanford University Press,
      1961. 290 pp. 61-14066.
      Sup. 63, 2905; JAS, 11/62

0561 Ch'en, Kung-po. The Communist Movement in China; An Essay
C   Written in 1924. ed. with an intro. by C. Martin Wilbur.
      N.Y.: Octagon, 1966 (orig. pub. by Columbia University
      Press, 1960). 138 pp. 65-28873. (R).
      Choice, 12/66; JAS, 11/67; Library Journal, 9/1/66

0562 Chen, Stephen. Sun Yat-sen, a Portrait. N.Y.: John Day, 1946.
B   242 pp. 46-25215. o.p.
      Hucker, 760; FEQ, 2/47; Library Journal, 6/15/46

0563 Cheng, Yu-k'uei. Foreign Trade and Industrial Development
B   of China, an Historical and Integrated Analysis through
      1948. Washington: University Press of Washington, D.C.,
      1956. 278 pp. 56-12632. o.p.
      AUFS, 786; Hucker, 2220; JAS, 2/58; Am. Econ. R., 6/57;
      AHR, 7/57

0564 Chennault, Claire Lee. Way of a Fighter; The Memoirs of Claire
B   Lee Chennault. ed. by Robert Hotz. N.Y.: Putnam, 1949.
      375 pp. 49-845. o.p.
      Hucker, 818

0565 Chiang, Kai-shek. China's Destiny & Chinese Economic Theory.
B   N.Y.: Roy, 1947. 347 pp. 47-30072. o.p.
      Hucker, 771; FEQ, 11/50; Pol. Sci. Q., 12/47

0566 Chiang, Kai-shek. The Collected Wartime Messages of Generalis-
C   simo Chiang Kai-shek, 1937-1945. N.Y.: Kraus, 1969 (orig.
      pub. by John Day, 1946). 2 v. 46-7008. (R).
      Hucker, 772; FEQ, 2/47

0567 Chiang, Kai-shek. Resistance and Reconstruction, Messages
C   during China's Six Years of War, 1937-1943. N.Y.:
      Harper, 1943. 322 pp. 43-10514. o.p. (M-University).
      FEQ, 2/44; Library Journal, 7/43

0568 Chiang, Kai-shek. Soviet Russia in China, a Summing-up at
B   Seventy. rev. abr. ed. tr. under the direction of Madame
      Chiang Kai-shek. N.Y.: Farrar, Straus, Cudahy, 1965. 218 pp.
      65-9173.
      Hucker, 768; JAS, 2/58

0569 Chiang, Monlin. Tides from the West, a Chinese Autobiography.
B   New Haven, Conn.: Yale University Press, 1947. 282 pp.
      47-4798. o.p.
      Hucker, 739; FEQ, 11/47; Ann. Am. Acad., 9/47; Library
      Journal, 4/15/47

0570 Chiang, Wen-han. The Chinese Student Movement. N.Y.: King's
B   Crown, 1948. 176 pp. 48-7286. o.p.

0571 Ch'ien, Tuan-sheng. The Government and Politics of China.
A   Cambridge, Mass.: Harvard University Press for the
      International Secretariat, Institute of Pacific Relations,
      1950. 526 pp. 50-8563.
      Sup. 61, 2792; Hucker, 729; FEQ, 5/51

0572 Chin, Wen-ssu. China and the League of Nations; The Sino-
C   Japanese Controversy, by Wunsz King. Jamaica, N.Y.:
      St. John's University Press, 1965. 104 pp. (Asia in
      the Modern World, 5). 65-17177.
      Choice, 5/66; JAS, 2/66

0573 Chin, Wen-ssu. China at the Paris Peace Conference in 1919, by
B   Wunsz King. Jamaica, N.Y.: St. John's University Press,
      1961. 39 pp. 61-59840.
      JAS, 5/66

0574 Chin, Wen-ssu. China at the Washington Conference, 1921-1922,
B   by Wunsz King. Jamaica, N.Y.: St. John's University Press,
      1963. 71 pp. (Asia in the Modern World, No. 3). 63-14976.
      JAS, 5/66

0575 Ching, Hsuan-tung. The Last Manchu: the Autobiography of Henry
C   Pu Yi, Last Emperor of China. ed. with an intro. by Paul
      Kramer. tr. by Kuo Ying Paul Tsai. N.Y.: Putnam, 1967.
      318 pp. 67-10588.

0576 Chou, Shun-hsin. The Chinese Inflation, 1937-1949. N.Y.:
A   Columbia University Press, 1963. 319 pp. (Studies of
      the East Asian Institute). 62-18260.
      Am. Econ. R., 6/64; Library Journal, 7/63

0577 Chow, Chung-cheng. The Lotus Pool. tr. by Joyce Emerson.
C   N.Y.: Appleton-Century-Crofts, 1961. 272 pp. 61-14881.
      o.p.
      Sup. 63, 2906; JAS, 8/62; Library Journal, 12/15/61

0578 Chu, Ch'ang-ling. Reformer in Modern China, Chang Chien, 1853-
B   1926. N.Y.: Columbia University Press, 1965. 256 pp.
        65-10541.
        Choice, 2/66; JAS, 5/66; AHR, 4/66; Library Journal, 3/1/65

0579 Clifford, Nicholas Rowland. Retreat from China; British Pol-
A   icy in the Far East, 1937-1941. Seattle: University of Wash-
        ington Press, 1967. 222 pp. 67-12395.
        Choice, 9/67; JAS, 11/67; AHR, 4/68

0580 Clubb, Oliver Edmund. 20th Century China. N.Y.: Columbia Uni-
B   versity Press, 1964. 470 pp. 64-11041.
        Sup. 65, 3089; Choice, 6/64; JAS, 8/64; AHR, 10/64;
        Library Journal, 1/15/64; TLS, 4/16/64

0581 Clyde, Paul Hibbert. International Rivalries in Manchuria,
B   1689-1922. 2d ed., rev. N.Y.: Octagon, 1965 (orig.
        pub. by Ohio State University Press, 1928). 323 pp.
        66-17493. (R). (M-University).
        Hucker, 699; Silberman, 421

0582 Coox, Alvin D. Year of the Tiger. Tokyo: Orient/West,
A   1964. 162 pp.
        JAS, 8/65; Japan Q., 4-6/65

0583 De Francis, John Francis. Nationalism and Language Reform in
A   China. Princeton, N.J.: Princeton University Press, 1950.
        306 pp. 51-119 rev. o.p. (M-University).
        AUFS, 1027; Hucker, 65; FEQ, 11/51; AHR, 7/51; Am. Pol. Sci.
        R., 9/51; JAOS, 10-12/51; Pacific Affairs, 6/51

0584 Dulles, Foster Rhea. China and America; The Story of Their
B   Relations since 1784. Port Washington, N.Y.: Kennikat,
        1968 (orig. pub. by Princeton University Press, 1946).
        277 pp. 67-29611. (R).
        Hucker, 686; FEQ, 2/47; Am. Pol. Sci. R., 12/46; Ann. Am.
        Acad., 11/46; Pol. Sci. Q., 12/46

0585 Epstein, Israel. The Unfinished Revolution in China. Boston:
C   Little, Brown, 1947. 442 pp. 47-4043. o.p.
        Hucker, 805; FEQ, 5/48; Library Journal, 6/15/47

0586 Feis, Herbert. The China Tangle; The American Effort in China
A   from Pearl Harbor to the Marshall Mission. Princeton, N.J.:
        Princeton University Press, 1953. 445 pp. 53-10142.
        Hucker, 819; FEQ, 5/54; Library Journal, 10/1/53

0587 Finch, Percy. Shanghai and Beyond. N.Y.: Scribner's, 1953.
C   357 pp. 53-7276. o.p.
        AUFS, 924; FEQ, 5/54; Library Journal, 2/1/53

0588 Finney, Charles Grandison. The Old China Hands. Garden City,
C   N.Y.: Doubleday, 1961. 258 pp. 61-9506. o.p.
        Library Journal, 1/1/62

0589 Fishel, Wesley R. The End of Extraterritoriality in China.
B   Berkeley: University of California Press, 1952. 318 pp.
        52-6592. o.p.
        Hucker, 825; FEQ, 2/53

0590 Fleming, Peter. One's Company - A Journey to China. London:
C   Cape, 1934. 319 pp. 34-30523. o.p.

0591 Folsom, Kenneth E. Friends, Guests, and Colleagues; The
C   Mu-Fu System in the Late Ch'ing Period. Berkeley: Uni-
        versity of California Press, 1968. 234 pp. 67-26479.
        Choice, 9/68; JAS, 8/68

0592 Forman, Harrison. Report from Red China. N.Y.: Holt, 1945.
C   250 pp. 45-2284. o.p.
        Hucker, 894

0593 Franke, Wolfgang. Chinas Kulturelle Revolution; Die Bewegung
C   vom 4 Mai 1919. Munich: R. Oldenbourg, 1957. 89 pp.
        Hand catalog.
        Hucker, 757; JAS, 2/60

0594 Friedman, Irving S. British Relations with China: 1931-1939.
C   N.Y.: International Secretariat, Institute of Pacific Rela-
        tions, 1940. 255 pp. 40-11697. o.p.
        Hucker, 843; Silberman, 486; FEQ, 8/42; Am. Pol. Sci. R.,
        12/40; Ann. Am. Acad., 1/41

0595 Frillmann, Paul. China; The Remembered Life, by Paul Frillmann
A   and Graham Peck. intro. by John K. Fairbank. Boston:
        Houghton Mifflin, 1968. 291 pp. 67-15527.
        Choice, 1/69; Library Journal, 3/15/68

0596 Gale, Esson McDowell. Salt for the Dragon; A Personal History
B   of China, 1908-1945. East Lansing: Michigan State College
        Press, 1953. 225 pp. 53-9494.
        Hucker, 735; FEQ, 2/54; AHR, 10/53

0597 Gillin, Donald G. Warlord: Yen Hsi-shan in Shansi Province,
A   1911-1950. Princeton, N.J.: Princeton University Press,
        1967. 334 pp. 66-14308.
        Choice, 9/67; JAS, 2/68; Ann. Am. Acad., 9/67

0598 Gould, Randall. China in the Sun. Garden City, N.Y.: Double-
B   day, 1946. 403 pp. 46-317. o.p.
        Hucker, 740; FEQ, 8/46; Am. Pol. Sci. R., 8/46

0599 Hahn, Emily. Chiang Kai-shek, an Unauthorized Biography.
C   Garden City, N.Y.: Doubleday, 1955. 382 pp. 55-5582.
        o.p. (M-University).
        Hucker, 767; Library Journal, 3/1/55

0600 Hahn, Emily. The Soong Sisters. Garden City, N.Y.: Double-
C   day, 1943. 349 pp. 43-3571 rev. o.p.
        Hucker, 781

0601 Han, Suyin, pseud. Birdless Summer; China: Autobiography,
C   History. N.Y.: Putnam, 1968. 347 pp. 68-25435.

0602 Han, Suyin, pseud. The Crippled Tree: China, Biography, History,
C   Autobiography. N.Y.: Putnam, 1965. 461 pp. 65-20715. o.p.
        Library Journal, 11/15/65; TLS, 11/11/65

0603 Han, Suyin, pseud. A Mortal Flower; China: Autobiography, His-
C   tory. N.Y.: Putnam, 1966. 412 pp. 66-20297. o.p.
        Library Journal, 11/1/66

0604 Hauser, Ernest O. Shanghai; City for Sale. N.Y.: Harcourt,
C   Brace, 1940. 323 pp. 40-6570 rev. o.p.
        Am. Pol. Sci. R., 10/40; Pacific Affairs, 9/40

0605 Ho, Kan-chih. A History of the Modern Chinese Revolution.
C   Peking: Foreign Languages Press, 1959. 627 pp. 60-3095.
        Hucker, 902

0606 Holcombe, Arthur Norman. The Chinese Revolution; A Phase in
B   the Regeneration of a World Power. Cambridge, Mass.: Har-
        vard University Press, 1930. 401 pp. 30-5261. o.p.
        AHR, 10/30; Am. Pol. Sci. R., 5/30; Ann. Am. Acad., 11/30

0607 Holden, Reuben Andrus. Yale in China; The Mainland, 1901-1951.
B   New Haven, Conn.: Yale in China Association, dist. by Human
        Relations Area Files, 1964. 327 pp. 64-25916.

0608 Hou, Fu-wu. Central Government of China 1912-1928, an Insti-
B   tutional Study by Franklin W. Houn. Madison: University of
        Wisconsin Press, 1957. 246 pp. 57-9807.
        Hucker, 744; JAS, 2/58; AHR, 10/57

0609 Hsia, T. A. Enigma of the Five Martyrs; A Study of the Leftist
B   Literary Movement in Modern China. Berkeley: Institute
        of International Studies, University of California, 1962.
        150 pp. 63-6008. o.p.
        JAS, 8/65

0610 Hsiao, Tso-liang. Power Relations within the Communist
A   Movement, 1930-1934; A Study of Documents. Seattle:
        University of Washington Press, 1961. 404 pp. 61-11573.
        AHR, 10/63; China Q., 10-12/62; Pol. Sci. Q., 12/62

0611 Hsiao, Yu. Mao Tse-tung and I Were Beggars. Syracuse, N.Y.:
B   Syracuse University Press, 1959. 266 pp. 59-15411.
        Hucker, 866; Ann. Am. Acad., 9/60

0612 Hsu, Francis L. K. Americans and Chinese. London: Cresset,
A   1955. 457 pp. 62-6654. o.p.
        Hucker, 1062; AHR, 10/53; Am. Soc. R., 12/53; Ann. Am.
        Acad., 11/53; Library Journal, 5/15/53

0613 Hsueh, Chun-tu. Huang Hsing and the Chinese Revolution. Stan-
B   ford, Calif.: Stanford University Press, 1968 (orig. pub.
        in 1961). 260 pp. (Stanford University Series: History,
        Economics and Political Science, 20). 61-6531. (R).
        Sup. 63, 2915; JAS, 5/62

0614 Hu, Shih. The Chinese Renaissance. 2d ed. N.Y.: Paragon,
C   1964 (orig. pub. by University of Chicago Press, 1934).
        110 pp. (Haskell Lectures, 1933). 63-21052. (R). (M-Uni-
        versity).
        Sup. 65, 3095; Hucker, 755; JAS, 11/64; JAOS, 6/35;
        J. Philosophy, 6/21/34; J. Religion, 10/34

0615 Israel, John. Student Nationalism in China, 1927-1937. Stan-
A   ford, Calif.: Stanford University Press, 1966. 253 pp.
     (Hoover Institution). 66-15300.
     Sup. 67, 3243; Choice, 4/67; JAS, 5/67; AHR, 4/67; Am. Pol.
     Sci. R., 12/67; Ann. Am. Acad., 5/67; Library Journal,
     8/66; Pol. Sci. Q., 12/67

0616 Jansen, Marius B. The Japanese and Sun Yat-sen. Cambridge,
A   Mass.: Harvard University Press, 1954. 274 pp. 53-8021.
     AUFS, 827; Hucker, 758; Silberman, 419; FEQ, 5/55; AHR,
     10/55; Am. Pol. Sci. R., 3/55; Ann. Am. Acad., 7/55; Library
     Journal, 11/15/54

0617 Johnson, Chalmers A. Peasant Nationalism and Communist Power,
B   the Emergence of Revolutionary China, 1937-1945. Stanford,
     Calif.: Stanford University Press, 1968 (orig. pub. in 1962).
     256 pp. 62-16949. (R).
     Sup. 63, 2920; JAS, 8/63; AHR, 10/63; Am. Pol. Sci. R.,
     9/63; China Q., 7-9/63; Library Journal, 11/15/62; Pacific
     Affairs, Fall/63; TLS, 10/18/63

0618 Johnston, Sir Reginald Fleming. Twilight in the Forbidden City.
C   London: Gollancz, 1934. 486 pp. 34-27253. o.p.
     Hucker, 753

0619 Jones, Francis Clifford. Manchuria since 1931. London:
C   Royal Institute of International Affairs, 1949. 256 pp.
     A50-9046. o.p.
     Hucker, 796; Silberman, 497; FEQ, 8/50; Library Journal,
     9/15/49

0620 Jones, Francis Clifford. Shanghai and Teintsin, with Special
C   Reference to Foreign Interests. N.Y.: Institute of
     Pacific Relations, 1940. 182 pp. 43-7168. o.p.
     Hucker, 2090

0621 Kates, George Norbert. The Years That Were Fat; The Last of
C   Old China. intro. by John K. Fairbank. Cambridge, Mass.:
     M.I.T. Press, 1967 (orig. pub. in 1952). 268 pp. NUC
     68-60386. (R).
     JAS, 2/68; FEQ, 11/52; Library Journal, 3/1/52

0622 Koo, Hui-lan (Oei). Hui-lan Koo (Madame Wellington Koo)
C   an Autobiography As Told to Mary Van Rensselaer Thayer.
     N.Y.: Dial, 1943. 421 pp. 43-16023. o.p.

0623 Kotenev, Anatol M. New Lamps for Old; An Interpretation of
C   Events in Modern China and Whither They Lead. Shanghai:
     North-China Daily News and Herald, 1931. 371 pp. 31-30817.
     o.p.
     AUFS, 833

0624 La Fargue, Thomas Edward. China and the World War. Stanford,
C   Calif.: Stanford University Press, 1937. 278 pp.
     37-39237. o.p.
     AHR, 7/38; Am. Pol. Sci. R., 6/38; JAOS, 9/38

0625 Lampard, David. A Present from Peking. Garden City, N.Y.:
B   Doubleday, 1965. 353 pp. 65-13097. o.p.

0626 Latourette, Kenneth Scott. The History of Early Relations
C   between the United States and China, 1784-1844. N.Y.: Kraus,
     1964 (orig. pub. by Yale University Press, 1917). 209 pp.
     (Transactions of the Connecticut Academy of Arts and
     Sciences, August, 1917). 65-1071. (R).

0627 Latourette, Kenneth Scott. A History of Modern China. Balti-
C   more: Penguin, 1954. 233 pp. 55-1351. o.p.
     Hucker, 722

0628 Lattimore, Owen. The Making of Modern China, a Short History.
C   London: Allen & Unwin, 1945. 212 pp. 45-4334. o.p.
     FEQ, 11/44

0629 Lattimore, Owen. Manchuria; Cradle of Conflict. rev. ed.
B   N.Y.: Macmillan, 1935. 343 pp. 35-6659. o.p.
     AUFS, 4986; Am. Pol. Sci. R., 8/35

0630 League of Nations. Commission of Enquiry into the Sino-
B   Japanese Dispute. Report. 1932. 291 pp. 50-53932.
     AUFS, 838

0631 Levenson, Joseph Richmond. Confucian China and Its Modern
A   Fate. Berkeley: University of California Press, 1958-1965.
     3 v. 58-2791 rev. 2.
     AUFS, 942; Hucker, 648; Choice, 5/66, 9/64; JAS, 5/59,
     5/66; AHR, 1/59, 4/65; Library Journal, 9/15/64, 3/15/65;
     TLS, 8/29/58, 8/26/65

0632 Levi, Werner. Modern China's Foreign Policy. Minneapolis:
B   University of Minnesota Press, 1953. 399 pp. 53-10470.
     AUFS, 839; Hucker, 824; FEQ, 11/54; AHR, 10/54; Pacific
     Affairs, 9/54

0633 Linebarger, Paul Myron Anthony. The China of Chiang K'ai-shek;
B   A Political Study. Boston: World Peace Foundation, 1941.
     449 pp. 41-11374. o.p. (M-University).
     AUFS, 844; Hucker, 783; FEQ, 11/41; Am. Pol. Sci. R., 12/41;
     Pacific Affairs, 12/41

0634 Linebarger, Paul Myron Anthony. Government in Republican China.
C   N.Y.: McGraw-Hill, 1938. 203 pp. 38-25848. o.p. (M-Uni-
     versity).
     Hucker, 1934; FEQ, 11/41; Am. Pol. Sci. R., 12/38

0635 Linebarger, Paul Myron Anthony. The Political Doctrines of Sun
C   Yat-sen; An Exposition of the San min chu i. Baltimore:
     Johns Hopkins Press, 1937. 278 pp. 37-12528.
     Hucker, 1929; AHR, 10/37; Am. Pol. Sci. R., 6/37; Ann.
     Am. Acad., 5/37; TLS, 5/8/37

0636 Linebarger, Paul Myron Anthony. Sun Yat Sen and the Chinese
C   Republic. N.Y.: Century, 1925. 371 pp. 25-4930. o.p.
     Hucker, 762

0637 Liu, Chih-pu. A Military History of Modern China, 1924-1949.
A   Princeton, N.J.: Princeton University Press, 1956. 312 pp.
     56-8386. o.p.
     AUFS, 846; JAS, 2/57; Library Journal, 8/56

0638 Liu, Kwang-ching, ed. American Missionaries in China; Papers
B   from Harvard Seminars. Cambridge, Mass.: Harvard Univer-
     sity Press, 1966. 310 pp. (Harvard East Asian Monographs,
     21). 66-31266.
     Choice, 4/67; JAS, 5/67

0639 Liu, Kwang-ching. Anglo-American Steamship Rivalry in China,
B   1862-1874. Cambridge, Mass.: Harvard University Press,
     1962. 218 pp. (Harvard East Asian Series, 8). 62-9426.
     Sup. 63, 2923; JAS, 11/62; AHR, 10/62; Pacific Affairs,
     Fall/62

0640 Liu, Ta-Chung. The Economy of the Chinese Mainland: National
A   Income and Economic Development, 1933-1959. Princeton,
     N.J.: Princeton University Press, 1965. 771 pp. 64-12223.
     Choice, 7-8/65; JAS, 5/66; Am. Econ. R., 6/65; Ann. Am.
     Acad., 7/65; J. Pol. Econ., 8/65; TLS, 6/24/65

0641 Loh, Pichon Pei Yung, ed. The Kuomintang Debacle of 1949; Col-
B   lapse or Conquest? Boston: Heath, 1965. 114 pp. (Problems
     in Asian Civilizations). 64-8154.
     Choice, 11/65

0642 MacNair, Harley Farnsworth. China in Revolution; An Analysis
B   of Politics and Militarism under the Republic. N.Y.: Fertig,
     1968 (orig. pub. by University of Chicago Press, 1931).
     244 pp. 31-28310. (R).
     AUFS, 847; Hucker, 743; Am. Pol. Sci. R., 2/32

0643 MacNair, Harley Farnsworth. The Real Conflict between China
B   and Japan; An Analysis of Opposing Ideologies. Chicago:
     University of Chicago Press, 1938. 215 pp. 38-27812. o.p.
     Hucker, 794

0644 Mao's China; Party Reform Documents, 1942-44. tr. by Boyd
A   Compton. Seattle: University of Washington Press, 1952.
     278 pp. 51-12273.
     AUFS, 953; Hucker, 876; FEQ, 11/52; Pacific Affairs, 12/52

0645 Maugham, William Somerset. On a Chinese Screen. London:
B   Heinemann, 1953. 237 pp. 22-19940.

0646 McCormick, Thomas J. China Market: America's Quest for
B   Informal Empire 1893-1901. Chicago: Quadrangle, 1967.
     241 pp. 67-21637.
     Choice, 4/68; JAS, 5/68; J. Am. Hist., 3/68

0647 McLane, Charles B. Soviet Policy and the Chinese Communists,
A   1931-1946. N.Y.: Columbia University Press, 1958. 310 pp.
     58-11903. o.p.
     Hucker, 874; AHR, 7/59; Ann. Am. Acad., 5/59; Library
     Journal, 10/1/58

0648 Meng, S. M. The Tsungli Yamen: Its Organization and Functions.
B   Cambridge, Mass.: Harvard University Press, 1962. 146 pp.
     (Harvard East Asian Monographs). 62-53393.
     Sup. 63, 2925

0649 Michael, Franz H. The Taiping Rebellion; History and Documents.
A   Vol. I: History. Seattle: University of Washington Press,
     1966. 244 pp. (University of Washington Publications on
     Asia). 66-13538.
     Sup. 67, 3246; Choice, 9/66; JAS, 5/67; AHR, 4/67;
     Library Journal, 6/15/66; Pacific Affairs, Spring-Summer/66;
     Pol. Sci. Q., 9/67

0650 Miles, Milton E. A Different Kind of War: the Little-known
C   Story of the Combined Guerilla Forces Created in China
     by the U.S. Navy and the Chinese During World War II,
     as prepared by Hawthorne Daniel from the original manu-
     script. fore. by Arleigh Burke. Garden City, N.Y.:
     Doubleday, 1967. 629 pp. 67-10399.
     Choice, 9/68; JAS, 2/69; Library Journal, 10/15/67

0651 Misselwitz, Henry Francis. The Dragon Stirs; An Intimate
C   Sketch-Book of China's Kuomintang Revolution, 1927-29.
     N.Y.: Harbinger, 1941. 293 pp. 41-11787. o.p.
     Hucker, 784

0652 Murphey, Rhoads. Shanghai, Key to Modern China. Cambridge,
B   Mass.: Harvard University Press, 1953. 232 pp. 53-5073.
     o.p.
     AUFS, 852; FEQ, 11/54

0653 Ning, Lao T'ai-t'ai. A Daughter of Han; The Autobiography of
B   a Chinese Working Woman, by Ida Pruitt. Stanford, Calif.:
     Stanford University Press, 1967 (orig. pub. by Yale Uni-
     versity Press, 1945). 254 pp. 68-10633. (R).
     Hucker, 2055; Choice, 12/68; FEQ, 5/46; Library Journal,
     11/1/45

0654 North, Robert Carver. Chinese Communism. N.Y.: McGraw-Hill,
B   1966. 256 pp. (World University Library). 64-66180.
     Choice, 11/66

0655 North, Robert Carver. Kuomintang and Chinese Communist Elites.
B   Stanford, Calif.: Stanford University Press, 1952.
     130 pp. 52-3689. o.p.
     Hucker, 775; FEQ, 5/53; AHR, 4/53; Am. Soc. R., 8/53;
     Pacific Affairs, 6/53

0656 North, Robert Carver. M. N. Roy's Mission to China; The Com-
B   munist-Kuomintang Split of 1927. tr. by Helen I. Powers.
     Berkeley: University of California Press, 1963. 399 pp.
     63-21387.
     China Q., 7-9/68; Pacific Affairs, Spring/64; Pol. Sci. Q.,
     6/64

0657 North, Robert Carver. Moscow and Chinese Communists. 2d ed.
A   Stanford, Calif.: Stanford University Press, 1963. 310 pp.
     62-18742.
     AUFS, 957; Hucker, 869; FEQ, 5/54; Am. Pol. Sci. R., 6/63;
     Library Journal, 4/1/63; Pol. Sci. Q., 3/64

0658 Peck, Graham. Two Kinds of Time; Illustrated by the Author.
A   Boston: Houghton Mifflin, 1950. 725 pp. 50-10600. o.p.
     AUFS, 855; Hucker, 802; FEQ, 8/51

0659 Powell, John Benjamin. My Twenty-five Years in China. N.Y.:
C   Macmillan, 1945. 436 pp. 45-9203. o.p.
     Hucker, 734; FEQ, 5/46

0660 Price, Ernest Batson. The Russo-Japanese Treaties of 1907-
B   1916 concerning Manchuria and Mongolia. Baltimore: Johns
     Hopkins Press, 1933. 164 pp. 33-20423. o.p. (M-Uni-
     versity).
     AUFS, 1230; Am. Pol. Sci. R., 10/33; Pol. Sci. Q., 12/33

0661 Rankin, Karl Lott. China Assignment. Seattle: University
B   of Washington Press, 1964. 343 pp. 64-20488.
     Choice, 12/64; JAS, 5/65; J. Am. Hist., 6/65; Library
     Journal, 12/15/64

0662 Reinsch, Paul Samuel. An American Diplomat in China. N.Y.:
B   Paragon, 1967 (orig. pub. by Doubleday, 1922). 396 pp.
     NUC 68-1766. (R).
     Am. Pol. Sci. R., 8/22; Ann. Am. Acad., 5/22

0663 Remer, Charles Frederick. The Foreign Trade of China. Taipei:
C   Ch'eng-wen Publishing Co., dist. by Chinese Materials
     and Research Aids Service Center, 1967 (orig. pub. by
     Commercial, 1926). 269 pp. Hand catalog. (R). (M-Uni-
     versity).

0664 Remer, Charles Frederick. Readings in Economics for China,
C   Selected Materials with Explanatory Introductions. Shang-
     hai: Commercial, 1926. 685 pp. Agr 23-917. o.p.

0665 Richardson, Hugh Edward. A Short History of Tibet. N.Y.:
A   Dutton, 1962. 308 pp. 61-6023.
     JAS, 2/63; Library Journal, 8/62; TLS, 12/21/62

0666 Rigg, Robert B. Red China's Fighting Hordes, a Realistic Account
C   of the Chinese Communist Army by a U.S. Army Officer. Har-
     risburg, Pa.: Military Service Publishing Co., 1951. 378 pp.
     51-14765 rev. o.p.
     Hucker, 1960; Pacific Affairs, 12/52

0667 Romanus, Charles F. Stilwell's Command Problems. Washington:
A   Office of Chief of Military History, Dept. of the Army,
     1956. 518 pp. 55-60004. o.p.
     JAS, 2/58

0668 Romanus, Charles F. Stilwell's Mission to China. Washington:
A   Office of Chief of Military History, Dept. of the Army,
     1953. 441 pp. 53-60349. o.p.
     Hucker, 817; FEQ, 11/53

0669 Romanus, Charles F. Time Runs Out in CBI. Washington: Office
A   of Chief of Military History, Dept. of the Army, 1959.
     428 pp. 59-60003. o.p.
     JAS, 8/60

0670 Rosinger, Lawrence Kaelter. China's Wartime Politics, 1937-1944.
B   Princeton, N.J.: Princeton University Press, 1945. 133 pp.
     45-10186. o.p.
     Hucker, 807; FEQ, 2/45; Am. Pol. Sci. R., 2/45; Ann. Am.
     Acad., 3/45; Pol. Sci. Q., 3/45

0671 Rowe, David Nelson. China among the Powers. N.Y.: Harcourt,
B   Brace, 1945. 205 pp. 45-1826. o.p.
     Hucker, 806; FEQ, 8/45; Ann. Am. Acad., 7/45; Pol. Sci. Q.,
     6/45

0672 Rowe, David Nelson. Modern China, a Brief History. Prince-
C   ton, N.J.: Van Nostrand, 1959. 192 pp. 59-15095.
     Hucker, 724; China Q., 7-9/60

0673 Rue, John E. Mao Tse-tung in Opposition, 1927-1935. Stanford,
A   Calif.: Stanford University Press, 1966. 387 pp. 66-15302.
     Sup. 67, 3248; Choice, 5/67; JAS, 8/67; AHR, 7/67; Library
     Journal, 12/1/66; Pol. Sci. Q., 12/67

0674 Russell, Edward Frederick Langley Russell. Knights of the Bush-
B   ido, the Shocking History of Japanese War Atrocities. N.Y.:
     Dutton, 1958. 334 pp. 58-9587.
     TLS, 9/12/58

0675 Scalapino, Robert A. The Chinese Anarchist Movement. Berke-
A   ley: Center for Chinese Studies, Institute of International
     Studies, University of California, 1961. 81 pp. A63-86 rev.
     o.p. (M-University).
     JAS, 11/61

0676 Schiffrin, Harold Z. Sun Yat-sen and the Origins of the Chinese
A   Revolution. Berkeley: University of California Press, 1968.
     412 pp. 68-26530.

0677 Schurmann, Herbert Franz, comp. The China Reader: Republican
B   China. N.Y.: Random House, 1967. 394 pp. 66-21489.
     Choice, 1/68; JAS, 2/68

0678 Scott, Robert Lee. Flying Tiger: Chennault of China. Gar-
C   den City, N.Y.: Doubleday, 1959. 285 pp. 59-7000.
     AUFS, 869; Library Journal, 2/1/59

0679 Selle, Earl Albert. Donald of China. N.Y.: Harper, 1948.
B   374 pp. 48-5343. o.p. (M-University).
     Hucker, 780; Pacific Affairs, 9/48

0680 Sharman, Lyon. Sun Yat-Sen, His Life and Its Meaning; A
A   Critical Biography. Stanford, Calif.: Stanford Univer-
     sity Press, 1968 (orig. pub. by John Day, 1934). 418 pp.
     68-17141. (R).
     AUFS, 871; Hucker, 759

0681 Sheridan, James E. Chinese Warlord; The Career of Feng
A   Yu-hsiang. Stanford, Calif.: Stanford University Press,
     1966. 386 pp. 65-18978.
     Choice, 12/66; AHR, 7/67; Library Journal, 4/1/66; TLS,
     4/13/67

0682 Smedley, Agnes. Battle Hymn of China. N.Y.: Knopf, 1943.
C   528 pp. 43-12192. o.p.
     Hucker, 899; FEQ, 5/44; Library Journal, 8/43

0683 Smedley, Agnes. China Fights Back; An American Woman with
C   the Eighth Route Army. N.Y.: Vanguard, 1938. 282 pp.
      38-27564. o.p.

0684 Smedley, Agnes. The Great Road; The Life and Times of Chu
A   Teh. N.Y.: Monthly Review Press, 1956. 461 pp. 56-11272.
      AUFS, 973; Hucker, 864; JAS, 8/57; Pacific Affairs, 6/57

0685 Snow, Edgar. Far Eastern Front. N.Y.: Smith & Haas, 1933.
B   336 pp. 33-27375. o.p.

0686 Snow, Edgar. Random Notes on Red China (1936-1945). Cam-
B   bridge, Mass.: Harvard University Press, 1957. 148 pp.
      58-146. o.p.
      JAS, 11/58

0687 Snow, Edgar. Red Star over China. 1st rev. and enl. ed. N.Y.:
A   Grove, 1968. 543 pp. 68-17724.
      AUFS, 975; Choice, 11/68; Hucker, 778; Library Journal, 7/68

0688 Snow, Helen (Foster). Inside Red China. N.Y.: Doubleday,
B   Doran, 1939. 356 pp. 39-27102 rev. o.p.

0689 Snow, Helen (Foster). Women in Modern China. The Hague: Mouton,
B   1967. 264 pp. 67-18165.
      China Q., 1-3/68

0690 Stein, Guenther. The Challenge of Red China. N.Y.: McGraw-
C   Hill, 1945. 490 pp. 45-8957. o.p.
      Hucker, 895; Library Journal, 10/15/45

0691 Stilwell, Joseph Warren. The Stilwell Papers. ed. by Theo-
A   dore H. White. N.Y.: Sloane Associates, 1948. 357 pp.
      48-6966. o.p.
      AUFS, 875; Hucker, 816; Library Journal, 4/15/48

0692 Stuart, John Leighton. Fifty Years in China; The Memoirs of
B   John Leighton Stuart, Missionary and Ambassador. N.Y.:
      Random House, 1954. 346 pp. 54-7808. o.p.
      Hucker, 733; Library Journal, 10/15/54

0693 Sues, Ilona Ralf. Shark's Fins and Millet. Boston: Little,
C   Brown, 1944. 331 pp. 44-187. o.p.
      Hucker, 736; Am. J. Soc., 9/44; Pacific Affairs, 12/44

0694 Sun, Yat-sen. San Min Chu I, the Three Principles of the
B   People. tr. by Frank W. Price. Nanking: Ministry of
      Information, 1947. 317 pp. A49-5367. o.p.
      AUFS, 882; Hucker, 764

0695 Swarup, Shanti. A Study of the Chinese Communist Movement.
B   N.Y.: Oxford, 1966. 289 pp. 66-71987.
      Choice, 12/66; JAS, 11/67; Pol. Sci. Q., 12/67; TLS, 4/11/66

0696 T'ang, Leang-li. The Inner History of the Chinese Revolution.
B   London: Routledge, 1930. 391 pp. 30-27099. o.p.
      Ann. Am. Acad., 11/30

0697 Tang, Peter S. H. Russian and Soviet Policy in Manchuria
B   and Outer Mongolia, 1911-1931. Durham, N.C.: Duke Uni-
      versity Press, 1959. 494 pp. 59-7084.
      Hucker, 841

0698 Tawney, Richard Henry. Land and Labour in China. N.Y.: Octagon,
C   1964 (orig. pub. by Allen & Unwin, 1932). 207 pp. 64-16384.
      (R).
      AUFS, 886; Hucker, 2126; Geog. R., 7/33; J. Pol. Econ., 10/33

0699 Taylor, George E. The Struggle for North China. N.Y.: Inter-
A   national Secretariat, Institute of Pacific Relations, 1940.
      250 pp. 41-51528. o.p.
      AUFS, 887; Hucker, 792; FEQ, 5/42; Am. Pol. Sci. R., 6/41;
      Ann. Am. Acad., 5/41; Pacific Affairs, 6/41

0700 Toland, John. The Flying Tigers. N.Y.: Random House, 1963.
C   170 pp. (Landmarks Books, 105). 63-18286.
      Library Journal, 1/15/64

0701 Tong, Hollington Kong. Chiang Kai-Shek, Soldier and Statesman,
B   Authorized Biography. Shanghai: China Publishing, 1937.
      2 v. 38-32771. o.p.

0702 Tong, Te-kong. United States Diplomacy in China, 1844-60.
B   Seattle: University of Washington Press, 1964. 332 pp.
      64-11051.
      Choice, 2/65; JAS, 2/65; AHR, 4/65; Library Journal, 9/15/64

0703 Trotskii, Lev. Problems of the Chinese Revolution. tr. by
C   Max Schachtman. 2d ed. N.Y.: Paragon, 1962 (orig. pub. by
      Pioneer, 1932). 432 pp. A63-5007. (R).
      JAS, 11/66

0704 Tsou, Tang. America's Failure in China: 1941-50. Chicago: Uni-
A   versity of Chicago Press, 1963. 614 pp. 63-13072.
      Sup. 65, 3108; JAS, 2/64; AHR, 1/64; Am. Pol. Sci. R., 3/64;
      China Q., 4-6/64; Pol. Sci. Q., 12/64

0705 U.S. Department of State. The China White Paper, August, 1949.
B   Stanford, Calif.: Stanford University Press, 1967 (orig.
      pub. by U. S. Dept. of State, 1949 under title United States
      Relations with China, with Special Reference to the Period,
      1944-1949). 1079 pp. 67-26650. (R).
      AUFS, 993; Hucker, 820; Choice, 4/68; FEQ, 11/50

0706 Utley, Freda. The China Story. Chicago: Regnery, 1951.
C   274 pp. 51-3311.
      Hucker, 822; FEQ, 5/52; Ann. Am. Acad., 11/51; Library
      Journal, 5/15/51; Pacific Affairs, 9/51

0707 Van Slyke, Lyman P. Enemies and Friends; The United Front
A   in Chinese Communist History. Stanford, Calif.: Stan-
      ford University Press, 1967. 330 pp. 67-26531.
      Choice, 6/68; JAS, 8/68; AHR, 6/68

0708 Varg, Paul. The Making of a Myth: the United States and
A   China, 1897-1912. East Lansing: Michigan State Univer-
      sity Press, 1968. 184 pp. 68-20411.
      Choice, 11/68; JAS, 2/69; Library Journal, 10/1/68

0709 Wang, Yi Chu. Chinese Intellectuals and the West, 1872-
A   1949. Chapel Hill: University of North Carolina Press,
      1966. 557 pp. 66-10207.
      Choice, 1/67; JAS, 11/66; AHR, 10/66; Ann. Am. Acad., 11/66;
      J. Am. Hist., 12/66; Library Journal, 3/1/66; Pacific
      Affairs, Spring-Summer/67; Pol. Sci. Q., 6/67; TLS, 12/1/66

0710 Wehrle, Edmund S. Britain, China, and the Antimissionary
C   Riots, 1891-1900. Minneapolis: University of Minnesota
      Press, 1966. 223 pp. 66-15064.
      Choice, 11/66; JAS, 11/66; AHR, 10/66; Ann. Am. Acad., 9/66;
      Library Journal, 11/15/65

0711 Wei, Wen-ch'i. China and Soviet Russia. Princeton, N.J.: Van
B   Nostrand, 1956. 379 pp. 56-9014. o.p.
      Hucker, 838; JAS, 11/57; AHR, 4/57; Am. Pol. Sci. R., 9/57;
      Ann. Am. Acad., 3/57; Library Journal, 5/1/56; TLS, 4/5/57

0712 White, Theodore Harold. The Mountain Road. N.Y.: Sloane Assoc-
B   iates, 1958. 347 pp. 58-6394. o.p.
      Library Journal, 5/15/58

0713 White, Theodore Harold. Thunder Out of China. N.Y.: Apollo
A   (orig. pub. by Sloane Associates, 1946). 331 pp. 46-11919.
      (R).
      AUFS, 891; Hucker, 799

0714 Whiting, Allen Suess. Sinkiang: Pawn or Pivot? East Lansing:
B   Michigan State University Press, 1958. 314 pp. 58-11509.
      Hucker, 840; JAS, 8/59; AHR, 1/60; Am. Pol. Sci. R., 6/59;
      Ann. Am. Acad., 5/59; Pacific Affairs, 12/59; TLS, 8/7/59

0715 Whiting, Allen Suess. Soviet Policies in China, 1917-1924.
A   Stanford, Calif.: Stanford University Press, 1968 (orig.
      pub. by Columbia University Press, 1954). 350 pp.
      68-12355. (R).
      AUFS, 892; Hucker, 880; FEQ, 8/55; AHR, 7/55; Ann. Am. Acad.,
      9/55; Pacific Affairs, 9/55

0716 Wieger, Leon, ed. and tr. Chine Modern...par le p. Leon Wieger.
B   Hien-hien: Imprimiere Editions, 1920-32. 10 v. 32-17022.
      o.p.

0717 Wilbur, Clarence Martin, ed. Documents on Communism, Nationalism,
B   and Soviet Advisers on China, 1918-1927; Papers Seized in
      the Peking Raid. N.Y.: Columbia University Press, 1956.
      617 pp. 56-6813. o.p.
      AUFS, 996; Hucker, 875; JAS, 11/57

0718 Winfield, Gerald Freeman. China, the Land and the People.
C   N.Y.: Sloane Associates in cooperation with American Insti-
      tute of Pacific Relations, 1948. 437 pp. 48-9514. o.p.
      Hucker, 8; FEQ, 5/49; Library Journal, 12/15/48

0719 Wint, Guy. Dragon and Sickle; How the Communist Revolution Hap-
C   pened in China. N.Y.: Praeger, 1959. 107 pp. 59-7728. o.p.
      JAS, 8/60

0720 Wu, Lien-te. Plague Fighter; The Autobiography of a Modern
B   Chinese Physician. Cambridge: Heffer, 1959. 667 pp.
  59-1837.
  JAS, 11/59

0721 Yakhontoff, Victor A. The Chinese Soviets. N.Y.: Coward-
C   McCann, 1934. 296 pp. 34-25723. o.p. (M-University).
  Hucker, 890

0722 Young, Arthur Nichols. China and the Helping Hand, 1937-1945.
A   Cambridge, Mass.: Harvard University Press, 1963. 502 pp.
  (Harvard East Asian Series, 12). 63-20774.
  Choice, 3/64; JAS, 8/64; Ann. Am. Acad., 11/64; Library
  Journal, 12/1/63

0723 Young, Arthur Nichols. China's Wartime Finance and Inflation,
A   1937-1945. Cambridge, Mass.: Harvard University Press,
  1965. 421 pp. (Harvard East Asian Series, 20). 65-22049.
  Choice, 11/66; JAS, 8/66; Am. Econ. R., 12/66; AHR, 7/66;
  J. Pol. Econ., 6/66; Library Journal, 11/1/65

0724 Yu, George T. Party Politics in Republican China; The Kuo-
A   mintang, 1912-1924. Berkeley: University of California
  Press, 1966. 203 pp. 66-13089.
  Choice, 11/66; JAS, 8/67; AHR, 4/67; Am. Pol. Sci. R., 12/66;
  Ann. Am. Acad., 1/67; Library Journal, 5/15/66; Pacific
  Affairs, Spring-Summer/66; Pol. Sci. Q., 6/67

0725 Zolotow, Maurice. Maurice William and Sun Yat-sen. London:
B   Hale, 1948. 128 pp. 49-24346. o.p.

HISTORY
COMMUNIST

0726 Barnett, A. Doak. Communist China and Asia; Challenge to
A   American Policy. N.Y.: Harper, 1960. 575 pp. 60-5956.
  Sup. 61, 2788; Hucker, 846; JAS, 11/60

0727 Barnett, A. Doak. Communist China: the Early Years, 1949-55.
A   N.Y.: Praeger, 1964. 336 pp. 64-22487.
  Sup. 65, 3084; Choice, 2/65; JAS, 8/65; Ann. Am. Acad.,
  9/65

0728 Belden, Jack. China Shakes the World. N.Y.: Harper, 1949.
A   524 pp. 49-11358. o.p. (M-University).
  AUFS, 900; Hucker, 800

0729 Bertram, James M. Return to China. London: Heinemann, 1957.
B   251 pp. 58-18363. o.p.

0730 Blum, Robert. The United States and China in World Affairs.
B   ed. by A. Doak Barnett. N.Y.: McGraw-Hill, 1966. 287 pp.
  (United States and China in World Affairs Series/Council
  on Foreign Relations). 66-26490.
  Sup. 67, 3234; Choice, 7-8/67; JAS, 8/67; Library Journal,
  11/1/66

0731 Bodde, Derk. Peking Diary: 1948-1949, a Year of Revolution.
A   Greenwich, Conn.: Fawcett, 1967 (orig. pub. by Abelard-
  Schuman, 1950). 288 pp. NUC 68-76595. (R).
  AUFS, 901; Hucker, 977; FEQ, 8/51; AHR, 4/51; Am. J. Soc.,
  3/51; Library Journal, 10/1/50; Pacific Affairs, 6/51;
  TLS, 10/5/51

0732 Boorman, Howard L. Moscow-Peking Axis: Strengths and Strains.
B   N.Y.: Harper for Council on Foreign Relations, 1957.
  227 pp. 56-7909. o.p.
  AUFS, 902; Hucker, 1012; JAS, 2/58; Am. Pol. Sci. R.,
  9/57; Ann. Am. Acad., 9/57; Library Journal, 4/1/57;
  Pol. Sci. Q., 9/57

0733 Boyd, R. C. Communist China's Foreign Policy. N.Y.: Praeger,
B   1962. 147 pp. (Praeger Publications in Russian History
  and World Communism, No. 107). 62-13750. o.p.
  JAS, 2/63; Ann. Am. Acad., 11/62; China Q., 7-9/64; Library
  Journal, 5/1/62; TLS, 8/10/62

0734 Brandt, Conrad. A Documentary History of Chinese Communism.
A   N.Y.: Atheneum, 1966 (orig. pub. by Harvard University
  Press, 1952). 552 pp. 66-60102/CD. (R).
  AUFS, 904; Hucker, 871; FEQ, 5/53; AHR, 4/53; Ann. Am.
  Acad., 3/53; Library Journal, 2/15/53; Pacific Affairs,
  6/53; TLS, 1/30/53

0735 Cartier-Bresson, Henri. From One China to the Other. text
B   by Han Suyin (pseud.). N.Y.: Universe, 1956. 56-11623.
  o.p.

JAS, 8/57; TLS, 10/5/56

0736 Chakravarti, Prithwis Chandra. India's China Policy. Bloom-
B   ington: Indiana University Press, 1962. 180 pp. 62-8970.
  o.p.
  Library Journal, 3/15/62

0737 Chao, Kuo-chun. Thirty Years of the Communist Movement in
B   China: a Chronology of Major Developments, 1920-1950.
  Cambridge, Mass.: Russian Research Center, Harvard Uni-
  versity, 1950. o.p.

0738 Ch'en, Hsi-en. Thought Reform of the Chinese Intellectuals.
B   Hong Kong: Hong Kong University Press, 1960. 247 pp.
  60-4137 rev.
  Hucker, 940; JAS, 8/61; China Q., 7-9/62

0739 Ch'en, Jerome. Mao and the Chinese Revolution. With Thirty-
A   Seven Poems by Mao Tse-tung. tr. by Michael Bullock and
  Jerome Ch'en. N.Y.: Oxford, 1965. 419 pp. 65-2375.
  Sup. 65, 3087; Choice, 6/65; JAS, 11/65; Ann. Am. Acad.,
  11/65; Library Journal, 6/1/65; TLS, 3/25/65

0740 Chicago China Conference, 1966. Contemporary China; Papers.
B   ed. by Ruth Adams. N.Y.: Pantheon, 1966. 336 pp. 66-23986.
  Choice, 6/67

0741 Chou, Ching-wen. Ten Years of Storm; The True Story of the
C   Communist Regime in China, by Chow, Ching-wen. ed. and
  tr. by Lai Ming. N.Y.: Holt, Rinehart and Winston, 1960.
  323 pp. 60-12858. o.p.
  Library Journal, 9/15/60

0742 Chou, Ts'e-tsung. The May Fourth Movement: Intellectual Revo-
A   lution in Modern China. Stanford, Calif.: Stanford Uni-
  versity Press, 1968 (orig. pub. by Harvard University Press,
  1960). 486 pp. (Harvard East Asian Series, 6). 67-26647.
  (R).
  Sup. 61, 2793; Hucker, 754; AHR, 1/61; Ann. Am. Acad., 11/60;
  China Q., 4-6/61; JAOS, 8-9/61; Pacific Affairs, Summer/61;
  Pol. Sci. Q., 12/60; TLS, 4/7/61

0743 Clark, Gerald. Impatient Giant: Red China Today. N.Y.: McKay,
C   1959. 212 pp. 59-12259.
  Hucker, 967; Library Journal, 9/15/59; TLS, 4/22/60

0744 Clubb, Oliver Edmund. The United States and the Sino-Soviet
C   Bloc in Southeast Asia. Washington: Brookings Institution,
  1962. 173 pp. 62-21276.
  Sup. 63, 2908; AHR, 4/63; Ann. Am. Acad., 5/63; China Q.,
  4-6/63

0745 Communist China 1955-1959; Policy Documents with Analysis.
B   fore. by Robert R. Bowie and John K. Fairbank. Cambridge,
  Mass.: Harvard University Press for Center for Inter-
  national Affairs and the East Asian Research Center,
  1962. 611 pp. 62-11394.
  Sup. 63, 2909; JAS, 2/63, 8/64

0746 Conlon Associates, Ltd. United States Foreign Policy: Asia.
C   Washington: Government Printing Office, 1959. 157 pp.
  (Studies Prepared at the Request of the Commitee on Foreign
  Relations, United States Senate, No. 5). 60-60164 rev. o.p.
  Hucker, 1016

0747 Cooley, John K. East Wind Over Africa; Red China's African
C   Offensive. N.Y.: Walker, 1965. 246 pp. 65-22132.
  Choice, 2/66; Library Journal, 10/15/65

0748 Doolin, Dennis J. Territorial Claims in the Sino-Soviet Con-
B   flict; Documents & Analysis. Stanford, Calif.: Hoover
  Institution on War, Revolution, and Peace, 1965. 77 pp.
  (Hoover Institution Studies, 7). 65-19766.
  Choice, 3/66

0749 Dutt, Vidya Prakash. China and the World; An Analysis of
C   Communist China's Foreign Policy. rev. ed. N.Y.: Praeger,
  1966. 356 pp. (Praeger Publications in Russian History
  and World Communism, 177). 66-15447.
  Choice, 10/66

0750 Elegant, Robert S. China's Red Masters; Political Biographies
C   of the Chinese Communist Leaders. N.Y.: Twayne, 1951.
  264 pp. 51-10445. o.p.
  AUFS, 922; FEQ, 2/52

0751 Fairbank, John King. China: the People's Middle Kingdom and
A   the U.S.A. Cambridge, Mass.: Harvard University Press,

1967. 145 pp. 67-17307.
Choice, 1/68; JAS, 2/68; J. Am. Hist., 9/67; TLS, 12/14/67

0752 Fairbank, John King. Communist China and Taiwan in United
B   States Foreign Policy. Storrs: University of Connecticut,
1960. 61 pp. (4th annual Brien McMahon Lecture). 61-63940.
o.p.
Hucker, 1017

0753 Feuerwerker, Albert. Chinese Communist Studies of Modern Chinese
B   History. Cambridge, Mass.: Harvard University Press, 1961.
287 pp. (Harvard University Chinese Economic and Political
Studies: Special Series). 61-19595.
Sup. 63, 2911; JAS, 5/62; China Q., 10-12/62

0754 Fisher, Margaret Welpley. Himalayan Battleground; Sino-Indian
C   Rivalry in Ladakh. N.Y.: Praeger, 1963. 205 pp. 63-11121.
Am. Pol. Sci. R., 3/64; Ann. Am. Acad., 5/64; Library
Journal, 8/63; Pacific Affairs, Spring/64; TLS, 6/2/64

0755 Fisher, Margaret Welpley. Indian Views of Sino-Indian Rela-
C   tions. Berkeley: Institute of International Studies,
University of California, 1956. 163 pp. (Indian Press
Digests-Monograph Series, No. 1). A56-9495. o.p.
Hucker, 1002

0756 Fitzgerald, Charles Patrick. The Birth of Communist China.
C   N.Y.: Praeger, 1966. 288 pp. (Pelican Original, A694).
65-27021.
Choice, 7-8/65; Library Journal, 4/1/66

0757 Fitzgerald, Charles Patrick. The Chinese View of their
B   Place in the World. N.Y.: Oxford, 1964. 72 pp.
(Chatham House Essay, 1). 64-1590.
Choice, 12/64; JAS, 2/65

0758 Fitzgerald, Charles Patrick. Flood Tide in China. London:
B   Cresset, 1958. 285 pp. 59-723.
Hucker, 962

0759 Fitzgerald, Charles Patrick. Revolution in China. N.Y.:
C   Praeger, 1952. 289 pp. 52-8621. o.p.
AUFS, 925; Hucker, 933; FEQ, 5/53; Library Journal, 9/1/52;
TLS, 9/12/52

0760 Friends, Society of. American Friends Service Committee. A New
C   China Policy; Some Quaker Proposals. New Haven, Conn.:
Yale University Press, 1965. 68 pp. 65-15048.
Sup. 65, 3103; Choice, 10/65

0761 Garthoff, Raymond L., ed. Sino-Soviet Military Relations.
C   N.Y.: Praeger, 1966. 285 pp. 66-18900.
Sup. 67, 3237; Choice, 6/67; Library Journal, 10/1/66

0762 Ginsburgs, George. Communist China and Tibet; The First Dozen
A   Years. The Hague: M. Nijhoff, 1964. 218 pp. 65-84502.
JAS, 11/65

0763 Gluckstein, Ygael. Mao's China; Economic and Political Survey.
B   Chester Springs, Pa.: Dufour, 1957. 438 pp. 57-3556.
AUFS, 928; Hucker, 1948; TLS, 10/11/57

0764 Great Cultural Revolution in China. comp. and ed. by the
C   Asia Research Centre. Rutland, Vt.: Tuttle, 1968.
507 pp. 67-8722.
Choice, 9/68

0765 Greene, Felix. Awakened China; The Country Americans Don't
C   Know. Garden City, N.Y.: Doubleday, 1961. 425 pp. 61-9512.
JAS, 8/62; Library Journal, 11/15/61

0766 Greene, Felix. A Curtain of Ignorance; How the American
C   Public has been Misinformed about China. Garden City,
N.Y.: Doubleday, 1964. 340 pp. 64-11717.
Choice, 12/64; Library Journal, 9/1/64

0767 Griffith, Samuel B. Peking and People's Wars; An Analysis
B   of Statements by Official Spokesmen of the Chinese
Communist Party on the Subject of Revolutionary Strategy.
N.Y.: Praeger, 1966. 142 pp. 66-18902.
Choice, 4/67; Library Journal, 10/15/66

0768 Griffith, William E. The Sino-Soviet Rift, Analyzed and
B   Documented. Cambridge, Mass.: M.I.T. Press, 1964. 508 pp.
(Center for International Studies, Studies in Interna-
tional Communism). 63-22708.
Sup. 65, 5796; Choice, 7-8/65; Library Journal, 1/15/65;
TLS, 12/31/64

0769 Guillain, Robert. 600 Million Chinese. tr. by Mervyn Savill.
B   N.Y.: Criterion, 1957. 310 pp. 57-8260.
AUFS, 929; Hucker, 963; Library Journal, 9/15/57

0770 Halperin, Morton H. China and the Bomb. N.Y.: Praeger for
B   the Center for International Affairs and East Asian
Research Center, Harvard University, 1965. 166 pp.
65-15646.
Sup. 65, 3094; Choice, 6/65; Am. Pol. Sci. R., 12/65;
Ann. Am. Acad., 3/66; Library Journal, 3/15/65

0771 Halperin, Morton H. Communist China and Arms Control. N.Y.:
B   Praeger, 1965. 191 pp. (Praeger Special Studies in Inter-
national Politics and Public Affairs). 65-26757.
Choice, 5/66; JAS, 11/66; Ann. Am. Acad., 5/66

0772 Halpern, Abraham Meyer, ed. Policies Toward China; Views from
A   Six Continents. N.Y.: McGraw-Hill, 1965. 528 pp. (United
States and China in World Affairs). 65-24892.
Choice, 10/66; JAS, 2/67; AHR, 10/66; Library Journal,
1/15/66

0773 Hinton, Harold C. China's Relations with Burma and Vietnam;
B   A Brief Survey. N.Y.: International Secretariat, Institute
of Pacific Relations, 1958. 64 pp. 58-2644. o.p.
Hucker, 990; JAS, 5/59

0774 Hinton, Harold C. Communist China in World Politics. Boston:
B   Houghton Mifflin, 1966. 527 pp. 66-400.
Sup. 67, 3241; Choice, 6/66; JAS, 2/67; Library Journal,
5/15/66

0775 Hsieh, Alice Langley. Communist China's Strategy in the
B   Nuclear Era. Englewood Cliffs, N.J.: Prentice-Hall,
1962. 204 pp. 62-12563. o.p.
Am. Pol. Sci. R., 9/62; Ann. Am. Acad., 11/62; Library
Journal, 6/15/62

0776 Hsu, Kai-yu. Chou En-lai: China's Grey Eminence. Garden
A   City, N.Y.: Doubleday, 1968. 294 pp. 68-10566.
Choice, 7-8/68; China Q., 7-9/68

0777 Hudson, Geoffrey Francis. The Sino-Soviet Dispute. N.Y.:
C   Praeger, 1961. 227 pp. 61-15894. o.p.
Am. Pol. Sci. R., 9/62; Ann. Am. Acad., 3/62; Pol. Sci. Q.,
9/62

0778 Isaacs, Harold Robert. Images of Asia, American Views of China
A   and India. N.Y.: Putnam, 1962 (orig. pub. by John Day,
1958 under the title Scratches on Our Minds). 416 pp.
58-5692. (R).
AUFS, 936; JAS, 5/62; Ann. Am. Acad., 9/58; Library Journal,
2/15/58

0779 Isaacs, Harold Robert. The Tragedy of the Chinese Revolution.
A   rev. ed. Stanford, Calif.: Stanford University Press,
1951. 382 pp. 51-12683. o.p.
AUFS, 937; Hucker, 878; FEQ, 5/53; Ann. Am. Acad., 1/52;
China Q., 7-9/52; Pol. Sci. Q., 9/52; TLS, 7/18/52

0780 Jackson, William Arthur Douglas. The Russo-Chinese Border-
C   lands; Zone of Peaceful Contact or Potential Conflict?
Princeton, N.J.: Van Nostrand, 1962. 126 pp. (Searchlight
Book, No. 2). 62-4176.
Sup. 63, 2918; JAS, 8/64

0781 Karol, K. S. China: the Other Communism. tr. from French by
C   Tom Bailstow. N.Y.: Hill & Wang, 1967. 474 pp. 66-27608.
Sup. 67, 3244; Choice, 11/67; Library Journal, 3/15/67

0782 Klochko, Mikhail Antonovich. Soviet Scientist in Red China.
B   tr. by Andrew MacAndrew. N.Y.: Praeger, 1964. 213 pp.
64-16681.
Sup. 65, 3096; Choice, 1/65; JAS, 5/66; China Q., 1-3/65;
Library Journal, 1/1/65; TLS, 2/25/65

0783 Koningsberger, Hans. Love and Hate in China. N.Y.: McGraw-
B   Hill, 1966. 150 pp. 66-19286.
Choice, 12/66

0784 Kuo, Pin-chia. China: New Age and New Outlook. N.Y.: Knopf,
C   1956. 231 pp. 56-5605.
Hucker, 935; JAS, 11/56; Library Journal, 2/1/56; Pacific
Affairs, 9/56; TLS, 7/20/56

0785 Lall, Arthur. How Communist China Negotiates. N.Y.:
B   Columbia University Press, 1968. 291 pp. 67-29051.

Choice, 10/68; China Q., 1-3/69; Library Journal, 3/15/68

0786 Landman, Lynn. Profile of Red China. N.Y.: Simon & Schuster,
C   1951. 245 pp. 51-5047. o.p. (M-University).
      Library Journal, 8/51

0787 Latourette, Kenneth Scott. China. Englewood Cliffs, N.J.:
C   Prentice-Hall, 1964. 152 pp. (The Modern Nations in
      Historical Perspective). 64-23560.
      Choice, 2/65; JAS, 5/65; AHR, 10/65; Library Journal, 3/15/65

0788 Li, Ch'i. Preliminary Study of Selected Terms. Berkeley:
B   East Asia Studies, Institute of International Studies, Uni-
      versity of California, 1956. 23 pp. 62-58111. o.p.

0789 Lifton, Robert Jay. Thought Reform and the Psychology of Total-
A   ism; A Study of "Brainwashing" in China. N.Y.: Norton, 1961.
      510 pp. 61-5934.
      Hucker, 942; JAS, 8/61; Ann. Am. Acad., 5/61; Library
      Journal, 2/15/61; TLS, 8/11/61

0790 Lindsay, Michael. China and the Cold War; A Study in Interna-
B   tional Politics. Carlton: Melbourne, 1955. 286 pp.
      55-1680.
      AUFS, 945; Hucker, 984; FEQ, 8/56

0791 Liu, Shao-t'ang. Out of Red China. tr. from Chinese by
C   Jack Chia and Henry Walter. N.Y.: Duell, Sloan & Pearce,
      1953. 269 pp. 52-12620. o.p.
      Library Journal, 2/1/53

0792 MacFarquhar, Roderick, ed. The Hundred Flowers Campaign and
A   the Chinese Intellectuals. epilogue by G. F. Hudson.
      N.Y.: Praeger, 1960. 324 pp. 60-10877. o.p.
      Sup. 61, 2803; Hucker, 941; JAS, 2/61; Ann. Am. Acad., 5/61;
      Library Journal, 9/1/60; Pacific Affairs, Spring/61; TLS,
      12/30/60

0793 Mao, Tse-tung. Selected Works. N.Y.: International Publishers,
A   1954- 54-9751.
      Hucker, 868; JAS, 5/63; China Q., 7-9/62

0794 Mehnert, Klaus. Peking and Moscow. tr. from the German by
B   Leila Vennewitz. N.Y.: Putnam, 1963. 522 pp. 63-16176.
      Sup. 65, 5802; JAS, 5/63; China Q., 10-12/64; Library
      Journal, 11/15/63; TLS, 5/21/64

0795 Meisner, Maurice J. Li Ta-chao and the Origins of Chinese
A   Marxism. Cambridge, Mass.: Harvard University Press,
      1967. 326 pp. (Harvard East Asian Series, 27). 67-10904.
      Choice, 1/68; JAS, 2/68; AHR, 12/67; Library Journal, 3/1/67;
      Pacific Affairs, Spring/68; TLS, 1/18/68

0796 Mende, Tibor. China and Her Shadow. London: Thames & Hud-
B   son, 1961. 360 pp. 62-1393. o.p.

0797 Moraes, Francis Robert. Report on Mao's China. N.Y.: Mac-
B   millan, 1953. 212 pp. 53-9391. o.p.
      AUFS, 954; Hucker, 965; Am. Pol. Sci. R., 9/53; Ann. Am.
      Acad., 11/53; Library Journal, 6/15/53; Pacific Affairs,
      9/53

0798 Moraes, Francis Robert. The Revolt in Tibet. N.Y.: Mac-
C   millan, 1960. 223 pp. 60-6644.
      JAS, 11/60; Am. Pol. Sci. R., 12/60; Ann. Am. Acad.,
      9/60; Library Journal, 1/1/60; TLS, 3/25/60

0799 Panikkar, Kavalam Madhava. In Two Chinas, Memoirs of a Diplo-
C   mat. London: Allen & Unwin, 1955. 183 pp. 55-4527. o.p.
      Hucker, 970

0800 Payne, Pierre Stephen Robert. Mao Tse-tung, Ruler of Red
B   China. N.Y.: Schuman, 1950. 303 pp. 50-10288. o.p.
      Hucker, 863; Library Journal, 9/15/60

0801 Portisch, Hugo. Red China Today. tr. from German by H. von
C   Koschembahr. Chicago: Quadrangle, 1966. 383 pp. 66-11872.
      Choice, 11/66; Ann. Am. Acad., 11/66; Library Journal,
      5/15/66

0802 Princeton University Conference. The United States and Communist
B   China. Papers Delivered at the Sixty-ninth Meeting of
      the Princeton University Conference Feb. 25-26, 1965.
      ed. by William W. Lockwood. Princeton, N.J.: 1965. 71 pp.
      65-5991. o.p.
      JAS, 8/66

0803 Rasmussen, Albert Henry. China Trader. N.Y.: Crowell, 1954.
C   274 pp. 54-5530. o.p. (M-University).
      TLS, 8/13/54

0804 Rickett, Allyn. Prisoners of Liberation. N.Y.: Cameron, 1957.
B   288 pp. 57-13896. o.p.
      AUFS, 963; Hucker, 968; JAS, 2/58

0805 Rostow, Walt Whitman. The Prospects for Communist China. Cam-
C   bridge, Mass.: Technology Press of M.I.T., 1954. 379 pp.
      54-13288.
      AUFS, 964; Hucker, 931; FEQ, 5/55; Am. Econ. R., 6/55; Am.
      Soc. R., 6/55; Ann. Am. Acad., 5/55; Pacific Affairs, 6/55;
      TLS, 4/29/55

0806 Roy, Manabendra Nath. Revolution and Counter-Revolution in
C   China. Calcutta: National Book Agency (orig. pub. by Renais-
      sance, 1946). 689 pp. 50-1167. (R).
      Hucker, 888

0807 Schram, Stuart. Mao Tse-tung. N.Y.: Simon & Schuster,
A   1967. 351 pp. 67-12918.
      Choice, 10/67; China Q., 7-9/68; Library Journal, 5/1/67;
      TLS, 10/12/67

0808 Schurmann, Herbert Franz, comp. The China Reader: Communist
B   China. N.Y.: Random House, 1967. 667 pp. 66-21489.
      Choice, 1/68; JAS, 2/68

0809 Schwartz, Benjamin Isadore. Chinese Communism and the Rise of
A   Mao. Cambridge, Mass.: Harvard University Press, 1951.
      258 pp. 51-12067.
      AUFS, 968; Hucker, 870; FEQ, 8/52; Am. Soc. R., 12/51; Ann.
      Am. Acad., 3/52; J. Pol. Econ., 3/52; Library Journal, 8/51

0810 Shao, Leng Chuan. Japan and Communist China. Kyoto: 1959.
B   130 pp. Hand catalog.

0811 Sherwani, Latif Ahmed. India, China, and Pakistan. Karachi:
C   Council for Pakistan Studies, 1967. 140 pp. SA68-657.

0812 Snow, Edgar. The Other Side of the River, Red China Today.
A   N.Y.: Random House, 1962. 810 pp. 61-6243.
      JAS, 8/63; Ann. Am. Acad., 9/63; China Q., 4-6/63; Library
      Journal, 5/15/63; Pacific Affairs, Summer/63; Pol. Sci. Q.,
      12/63; TLS, 5/17/63

0813 Snow, Helen (Foster). The Chinese Labor Movement by Nym
B   Wales, pseud. N.Y.: John Day, 1945. 235 pp. 45-146. o.p.
      Hucker, 2066; FEQ, 11/45

0814 Snow, Helen (Foster). Red Dust; Autobiographies of the Chi-
A   nese Communists, As Told to Nym Wales, pseud. Stanford,
      Calif.: Stanford University Press, 1952. 238 pp.
      52-5970. o.p.
      Hucker, 867; FEQ, 11/52; Ann. Am. Acad., 7/52

0815 Soviet and Chinese Communism; Similarities and Differences.
C   ed. by Donald W. Treadgold. Seattle: University of Washing-
      ton Press, 1967. 452 pp. 66-19575.
      Choice, 9/67; AHR, 12/67

0816 Steele, Archibald Trojan. The American People and China. N.Y.:
B   McGraw-Hill, 1966. 325 pp. (The United States and China
      in World Affairs). 65-28736.
      Choice, 6/66; JAS, 5/67; AHR, 10/66; Ann. Am. Acad., 11/66;
      Library Journal, 11/15/66

0817 Steiner, H. Arthur, ed. Chinese Communism in Action. Los
C   Angeles: Political Science 159, University of California,
      1953. 3 v. 54-185. o.p.

0818 Steiner, H. Arthur. The International Position of Communist
C   China, Political and Ideological Directions of Foreign Policy.
      Thirteenth Conference, Institute of Pacific Relations, Lahore,
      Pakistan, February, 1958. N.Y.: Institute of Pacific Rela-
      tions, 1958. 42 pp. 58-3925. o.p.
      Hucker, 979

0819 Suigo, Carlo. In the Land of Mao Tse-tung. tr. from Ital-
C   ian by Muriel Currey. ed. by Clifford Witting. London:
      Allen & Unwin, 1953. 311 pp. A55-2811. o.p.

0820 Swearingen, Arthur Rodger. Soviet and Chinese Communist Power
C   in the World Today. N.Y.: Basic Books, 1966. 127 pp.
      66-29266.
      Choice, 5/67; Library Journal, 12/1/66

CHINA - HISTORY

0821 Tang, Peter S. H. Communist China Today. 2d ed. rev. and enl.
C   Washington: Research Institute on the Sino-Soviet Bloc,
     1961. 61-18067. o.p.
     Hucker, 934; JAS, 11/58, 8/62; China Q., 4-6/63

0822 Thomas, S. B. Communist China and Her Neighbors. Toronto:
C   Canadian Institute of International Affairs, 1955. 16 pp.
     55-3250. o.p. (M-University).
     Hucker, 985

0823 U.S. Congress. Senate Committee on Foreign Relations. China,
C   Vietnam, and the United States; Highlights of the Hear-
     ings of the Senate Foreign Relations Committee. Washing-
     ton: Public Affairs Press, 1966. 218 pp. 66-25442. o.p.
     Sup. 67, 3253; Choice, 4/67; Library Journal, 10/15/66

0824 Van der Sprenkel, Otto P. N. B., ed. New China; Three Views, by
B   Otto B. Van der Sprenkel, Robert Guillain and Michael Lindsay.
     London: Turnstile, 1950. 241 pp. 51-2194. o.p.
     AUFS, 994; Hucker, 978; FEQ, 11/51; Library Journal,
     3/1/51; TLS, 12/15/50

0825 Walker, Richard Louis. China under Communism, the First
C   Five Years. New Haven, Conn.: Yale University Press, dist.
     by Lawrence Verry, 1955. 403 pp. 55-6422.
     AUFS, 995; Hucker, 927; FEQ, 2/56; Library JOurnal, 6/15/55

0826 Whiting, Allen Suess. China Crosses the Yalu; The Decision
B   to Enter the Korean War. Stanford, Calif.: Stanford Uni-
     versity Press, 1969 (orig. pub. by Macmillan, 1960). 219 pp.
     (Rand Series). 68-13744. (R).
     Hucker, 949; JAS, 5/61; AHR, 7/61; Am. Pol. Sci. R., 3/61;
     Ann. Am. Acad., 5/61; China Q., 1-3/62; Library Journal,
     10/15/60; Pacific Affairs, Fall/61; TLS, 6/23/61

0827 Wint, Guy. Common Sense About China. N.Y.: Macmillan, 1960.
A   176 pp. 60-15049.
     Sup. 61, 2807; Hucker, 922; JAS, 5/61; China Q., 7-9/60;
     Library Journal, 10/15/60; Pacific Affairs, Winter/61;
     TLS, 2/2/60

0828 Young, Kenneth Todd. Negotiating with the Chinese Communists:
C   the United States Experience, 1953-1967. N.Y.: McGraw-
     Hill for Council on Foreign Relations, 1968. 461 pp.
     (United States and China in World Affairs/Council on For-
     eign Relations). 67-28088.
     Choice, 10/68; JAS, 2/69; Library Journal, 1/1/68

0829 Zagoria, Donald S. The Sino-Soviet Conflict, 1956-1961.
A   Princeton, N.J.: Princeton University Press, 1962. 484 pp.
     62-10890.
     Sup. 63, 2930; JAS, 11/62; AHR, 10/62; Am. Pol. Sci. R.,
     9/62; Ann. Am. Acad., 1/63; China Q., 7-9/63; Library
     Journal, 3/1/62; Pacific Affairs, Spring/63; Pol. Sci. Q.,
     9/62; TLS, 8/24/62

GOVERNMENT AND POLITICS

0830 Barnett, A. Doak. Cadres, Bureaucracy and Political Power in
C   Communist China. with contrib. by Ezra Vogel. N.Y.: Co-
     lumbia University Press, 1967. 563 pp. (Studies of the East
     Asian Institute of Columbia University). 67-15895.
     Choice, 4/68; Ann. Am. Acad., 3/68; Library Journal, 6/1/67

0831 Barnett, A. Doak. China After Mao, with Selected Documents.
A   Princeton, N.J.: Princeton University Press, 1967. 287 pp.
     (Walter E. Edge Lectures). 67-14406.
     Choice, 7-8/67; Ann. Am. Acad., 3/68

0832 Ch'en, Hsi-en, comp. The Chinese Communist Regime; Documents
C   and Commentary. N.Y.: Praeger, 1967. 344 pp. (Praeger
     Publications in Russian History and World Communism, 191).
     67-18969.
     Choice, 4/68; JAS, 5/68; Library Journal, 8/67

0833 Cohen, Arthur A. The Communism of Mao Tse-tung. Chicago:
B   University of Chicago Press, 1964. 210 pp. 64-23420.
     Sup. 65, 3090; Choice, 11/64; JAS, 2/66

0834 Cohen, Jerome Alan. The Criminal Process in the People's
A   Republic of China, 1949-1963; An Introduction. Cambridge,
     Mass.: Harvard University Press, 1968. 706 pp.
     (Harvard Studies in East Asian Law, 2). 68-14252.
     Choice, 10/68; JAS, 11/68; China Q., 1-3/68

0835 Doolin, Dennis J. The Chinese People's Republic. by Dennis J.
C   Doolin and Robert C. North. Stanford, Calif.: Hoover Insti-
     tution on War, Revolution, and Peace, 1966. 68 pp. (Hoover
     Institution Studies, 14). 65-19769.

CHINA - GOVERNMENT AND POLITICS

Choice, 3/67; China Q., 7-9/68

0836 Doolin, Dennis J., ed. and tr. Communist China; The Politics of
A   Student Opposition. Stanford, Calif.: Hoover Institution on
     War, Revolution, and Peace, 1964. 70 pp. 64-16879.
     JAS, 2/65; China Q., 4-6/65

0837 George, Alexander L. The Chinese Communist Army in Action;
B   The Korean War and Its Aftermath. N.Y.: Columbia
     University Press, 1967. 255 pp. 67-12659.
     Choice, 1/68; AHR, 2/68; Ann. Am. Acad., 11/67; Pacific
     Affairs, Fall-Winter/67-68; TLS, 10/12/67

0838 Gittings, John. The Role of the Chinese Army. N.Y.: Oxford for
B   Royal Institute of International Affairs, 1967. 331 pp.
     67-80303.
     Sup. 67, 3238; Choice, 3/68; AHR, 2/68; Library Journal,
     8/67; TLS, 1/18/68

0839 Griffith, Samuel B. The Chinese People's Liberation Army.
B   N.Y.: McGraw-Hill, 1967. 398 pp. (Council on Foreign
     Relations/United States and China in World Affairs).
     67-16302.
     Choice, 11/67; Ann. Am. Acad., 11/67; Library Journal,
     6/15/67; Pacific Affairs, Fall-Winter/67-68; TLS, 8/25/68

0840 Hsia, T. A. The Commune in Retreat As Evidenced in Terminol-
B   ogy and Semantics. Berkeley: Center for Chinese Studies,
     Institute of International Studies, University of Cali-
     fornia, 1964. 91 pp. (Studies in Chinese Communist
     Terminology No. 11). 65-63417. o.p.
     JAS, 2/66

0841 Hsia, T. A. Metaphor, Myth, Ritual, and the People's Commune.
B   Berkeley: Center for Chinese Studies, Institute of Inter-
     national Studies, University of California, 1961. 60 pp.
     (Studies in Chinese Communist Terminology No. 7). 61-64267.
     o.p.
     JAS, 2/66

0842 Hsia, T. A. A Terminological Study of the Hsia-Fang Movement.
C   Berkeley: Center for Chinese Studies, Institute of Inter-
     national Studies, University of California, 1963. 68 pp.
     (Studies in Chinese Communist Terminology No. 10). NUC
     64-18351. o.p.
     JAS, 2/66

0843 Joffe, Ellis. Party and Army: Professionalism and Political
A   Control in the Chinese Officer Corps, 1949-1964. Cambridge,
     Mass.: Harvard University Press for the East Asian Research
     Center, 1965. 198 pp. (Harvard East Asian Monographs, 19).
     65-29001.
     Choice, 4/66; JAS, 5/66

0844 Leng, Shao-chuan. Justice in Communist China: a Survey
B   of the Judicial System of the Chinese People's Republic.
     Dobbs Ferry, N.Y.: Oceana, 1967. 196 pp. 67-14398.
     Choice, 11/68; Library Journal, 2/15/68

0845 Leng, Shao Chuan. Sun Yat-sen and Communism. by Shao Chuan
A   Leng and Norman D. Palmer. N.Y.: Praeger, 1961. 234 pp.
     60-16426. o.p.

0846 Lewis, John Wilson. Chinese Communist Party Leadership and
B   the Succession of Mao Tse-tung; An Appraisal of Tensions.
     Washington: External Research Staff, U.S. Dept. of State,
     1964. 35 pp. NUC 64-47659. o.p.

0847 Lewis, John Wilson. Leadership in Communist China. Ithaca, N.Y.:
A   Cornell University Press, 1963. 305 pp. 63-12090.
     JAS, 11/65; Am. J. Soc., 3/64; Am. Pol. Sci. R., 12/63;
     Am. Soc. R., 2/65; China Q., 11-12/63; Pacific Affairs,
     Fall/64; Pol. Sci. Q., 6/65

0848 Lewis, John Wilson, ed. Major Doctrines of Communist China.
B   N.Y.: Norton, 1964. 343 pp. 64-10892.
     Sup. 65, 3100; Choice, 9/64; JAS, 2/65

0849 Liu, Shao-ch'i. How to Be a Good Communist. 2d rev. ed.
C   Peking: Foreign Languages Press, 1952. 118 pp. 55-20000.
     o.p.
     Hucker, 1351

0850 Mao, Tse-tung. Basic Tactics. tr. with an intro. by Stuart R.
B   Schram. N.Y.: Praeger, 1966. 149 pp. 66-18912.
     Choice, 7-8/67; Am. Pol. Sci. R., 12/67; Library Journal,
     12/1/66

0851 Mao, Tse-tung. China's "New Democracy". N.Y.: New Century, 1945.
C   47 pp. 46-20896. o.p.
     Hucker, 891; FEQ, 11/50

0852 Mao, Tse-tung. The Political Thought of Mao Tse-tung, Anthology
A   by Stuart R. Schram. N.Y.: Praeger, 1963. 319 pp. (Praeger
     Publications in Russian History and World Communism, No. 134).
     63-18539.
     Choice, 3/64; JAS, 8/64; China Q., 1-3/65; Library Journal,
     12/1/63; TLS, 6/25/64

0853 Mao, Tse-tung. Quotations from Chairman Mao Tse-tung.
C   ed. and with an intro., essay and notes by Stuart R.
     Schram. N.Y.: Praeger, 1968. 182 pp. 68-20400.
     Choice, 10/68; Library Journal, 8/68; TLS, 8/15/68

0854 Moseley, George, ed. and tr. The Party and the National Ques-
B   tion in China. Cambridge, Mass.: M.I.T. Press, 1966. 186 pp.
     66-27573.
     Choice, 7-8/67

0855 Mu, Fu-sheng, pseud. The Wilting of the Hundred Flowers; The
C   Chinese Intelligensia Under Mao. N.Y.: Praeger, 1963.
     324 pp. (Praeger Publications in Russian History and World
     Communism, No. 122). 63-9812.
     JAS, 8/63; Am. Pol. Sci. R., 9/63; Ann. Am. Acad., 11/63;
     China Q., 4-6/63; Library Journal, 3/15/63; TLS, 5/17/63

0856 National Council of the Churches of Christ in the U.S.A.
C   Division of Foreign Missions. Far Eastern Office. Docu-
     ments of the Three-Self Movement; Source Materials for
     the Study of the Protestant Church in Communist China.
     Francis Jones, consultant and ed. N.Y.: National Council,
     1963. 209 pp. o.p.
     JAS, 8/64; China Q., 10-12/64

0857 The Politics of the Chinese Red Army; A Translation of the Bulle-
B   tin of Activities of the People's Liberation Army. ed. by
     J. C. Cheng, with the collaboration of C. Han and others.
     Stanford, Calif.: Hoover Institution on War, Revolution, and
     Peace, 1966. 776 pp. 65-28426.
     JAS, 2/67; Library Journal, 6/1/66

0858 Powell, Ralph L. Politico-Military Relationships in Communist
B   China. Washington: External Research Staff, U.S. Dept. of
     State, 1963. 21 pp. 64-60730. o.p.

0859 Pye, Lucian W. The Spirit of Chinese Politics; A Psycho-
B   cultural Study of the Authority Crisis in Political
     Development. Cambridge, Mass.: M.I.T. Press, 1968.
     255 pp. 68-14451.
     Choice, 12/68; China Q., 1-3/69; Library Journal, 8/68

0860 Schurmann, Herbert Franz. Ideology and Organization in Communist
A   China. Berkeley: University of California Press, 1966.
     540 pp. 66-15324.
     Sup. 67, 3249; Choice, 2/67; JAS, 2/67; Am. Pol. Sci. R.,
     3/67; Library Journal, 5/15/66; Pol. Sci. Q., 12/67

0861 Serruys, Paul Leo Mary. Survey of the Chinese Language Reform
B   and the Anti-Illiteracy Movement in Communist China. Berke-
     ley: Center for Chinese Studies, Institute of International
     Studies, University of California, 1962. 208 pp. (Studies
     in Chinese Communist Terminology, No. 8). 62-63221. o.p.
     (M-University).
     China Q., 4-6/63

0862 Thomas, S. B. Government and Administration in Communist
C   China. rev. 2d ed. N.Y.: International Secretariat, Insti-
     tute of Pacific Relations, 1955. 196 pp. A55-8710. o.p.
     AUFS, 988; Hucker, 1944; FEQ, 8/55

0863 Tiewes, Frederick C. Provincial Party Personnel in Mainland
A   China, 1950-1966. N.Y.: East Asian Institute, Columbia
     University, 1967. 114 pp. 66-30799.
     Choice, 1/68; JAS, 11/67

0864 Townsend, James Roger. Political Participation in Communist
A   China. Berkeley: University of California Press, 1967.
     233 pp. 67-11422.
     Choice, 10/67; JAS, 2/68; Library Journal, 3/1/67

0865 Wu, Chun-hsi. Dollars Dependents and Dogma; Overseas Chinese
B   Remittances to Communist China. intro. by C. F. Remer.
     Stanford, Calif.: Hoover Institution on War, Revolution,
     and Peace, 1967. 231 pp. 67-24368.
     JAS, 8/68; China Q., 7-9/68

ECONOMICS

0866 Aird, John Shields. The Size, Composition, and Growth of the
A   Population of Mainland China. Washington: Bureau of the
     Census, U.S. Dept. of Commerce, 1961. 100 pp. (Interna-
     tional Population Statistics Reports. Series P-90, No. 15).
     A61-9631.
     JAS, 2/62

0867 Buck, John Lossing. Food and Agriculture in Communist China.
B   N.Y.: Praeger, 1966. 171 pp. 65-28286.
     Choice, 11/66; JAS, 2/67; Pacific Affairs, Fall-Winter/66-67;
     TLS, 5/18/67

0868 Chandrasekhar, Sripati. China's Population; Census and Vital
B   Statistics. Hong Kong: Hong Kong University Press, 1959.
     69 pp. NUC 59-4756.
     Hucker, 2190; JAS, 5/60

0869 Chao, Kang. The Construction Industry in Communist China.
C   Chicago: Aldine, 1968. 237 pp. 66-23161.
     Choice, 10/68

0870 Chao, Kang. The Rate and Pattern of Industrial Growth in
C   Communist China. Ann Arbor: University of Michigan
     Press, 1965. 188 pp. 65-11514.
     Choice, 11/66; JAS, 5/66; Am. Econ. R., 6/66; J. Pol. Econ.,
     4/66; Library Journal, 6/15/65

0871 Chen, Nai-ruenn. Chinese Economic Statistics; A Handbook
A   for Mainland China. Chicago: Aldine, 1967. 539 pp.
     66-15200.
     Choice, 3/68; Ann. Am. Acad., 11/67; TLS, 12/26/67

0872 Ch'en, Ta. Population in Modern China. Chicago: University
B   of Chicago Press, 1946. 126 pp. A46-3756. o.p. (M-
     University).
     Hucker, 2191; FEQ, 5/47; Am. Pol. Sci. R., 4/47; Am. Soc. R.,
     4/47; Ann. Am. Acad., 7/47

0873 Cheng, Chu-yuan. The China Mainland Market under Communist
C   Control. Kowloon: Union Research Institute, 1956. 96 pp.
     57-35238.
     Hucker, 2254

0874 Cheng, Chu-yuan. Communist China's Economy, 1949-62: Struc-
A   tural Changes and Crisis. South Orange, N.J.: Seton Hall
     University Press, 1963. 217 pp. 63-11865. o.p.
     JAS, 2/64; China Q., 7-9/63

0875 Cheng, Chu-yuan. Economic Relations Between Peking and
B   Moscow, 1949-63. N.Y.: Praeger, 1964. 119 pp. (Praeger
     Special Studies in International Economics). 64-23512. o.p.
     Choice, 7-8/65; JAS, 11/65; China Q., 4-6/65

0876 Cheng, Chu-yuan. Income and Standard of Living in Mainland
B   China. Kowloon: Union Research Institute, 1957. 2 v.
     60-35360.
     Hucker, 2175

0877 Cheng, Chu-yuan. Monetary Affairs of Communist China. Kowloon:
C   Union Research Institute, 1954. 160 pp. 55-40585.
     Hucker, 2282

0878 Cheng, Chu-yuan. Scientific and Engineering Manpower in
A   Communist China, 1949-1963. Washington: National Science
     Foundation, dist. by Government Printing Office, 1965.
     588 pp. 66-60439.
     JAS, 11/66

0879 China (People's Republic of China, 1949-). First Five-year
B   Plan for Development of the National Economy of the People's
     Republic of China in 1953-1957. Peking: Foreign Languages
     Press, 1956. 231 pp. 57-47651. o.p.

0880 Clubb, Oliver Edmund. Chinese Communist Development Programs
C   in Manchuria, with a Supplement on Inner Mongolia. N.Y.:
     International Secretariat, Institute of Pacific Relations,
     1954. 46 pp. 55-14203. o.p.
     Hucker, 2176

0881 Donnithorne, Audrey. China's Economic System. N.Y.: Praeger,
B   1967. 592 pp. 67-23967.
     Choice, 9/68; Library Journal, 7/67; TLS, 12/28/67

0882 Ecklund, George N. Financing the Chinese Government Budget,
B   Mainland China, 1950-1959. Chicago: Aldine, 1966.

CHINA - ECONOMICS

133 pp. 66-15201.
Choice, 10/67; Ann. Am. Acad., 7/67; Library Journal, 3/15/67

0883　Eckstein, Alexander. Communist China's Economic Growth
A　　and Foreign Trade, Implications for U.S. Policy. N.Y.:
　　　McGraw-Hill, 1966. 366 pp. 65-28588.
　　　JAS, 2/67; Am. Econ. R., 12/66; Ann. Am. Acad., 1/67;
　　　J. Pol. Econ., 8/67; Library Journal, 1/15/66; Pacific
　　　Affairs, Fall-Winter/66-67; Pol. Sci. Q., 6/67

0884　Eckstein, Alexander et. al. The National Income of Communist
C　　China. N.Y.: Free Press of Glencoe, 1962. 215 pp.
　　　61-9164.
　　　Sup. 63, 2910; JAS, 11/62; Am. Econ. R., 12/62; Ann. Am.
　　　Acad., 9/62; China Q., 10-12/62; Library Journal, 5/15/62

0885　An Economic Profile of Mainland China; Studies Prepared for the
A　　Joint Economic Committee, Congress of the United States.
　　　Washington: Government Printing Office, 1967. 2 v.
　　　67-60884.

0886　Economic Trends in Communist China. ed. by Alexander Eckstein,
A　　Walter Galenson, and Ta-chang Liu. Chicago: Aldine, 1968.
　　　757 pp. (Social Science Research Council). 68-19887.
　　　Choice, 4/69

0887　Ho, Ping-ti. Studies on the Population of China, 1368-1953.
A　　Cambridge, Mass.: Harvard University Press, 1959. 341 pp.
　　　(Harvard East Asian Series, 4). 59-12970.
　　　Sup. 63, 2913; Hucker, 2186; JAS, 5/62; AHR, 4/60; Ann. Am.
　　　Acad., 9/60; Library Journal, 1/1/60; Pol. Sci. Q., 12/60;
　　　TLS, 3/25/60

0888　Hughes, Trevor Jones. The Economic Development of Communist
C　　China, 1949-1958. N.Y.: Oxford for the Royal Institute of
　　　International Affairs, 1959. 223 pp. 60-650.
　　　Sup. 61, 2800; Hucker, 2161; JAS, 11/60

0889　Kirby, E. Stuart. Introduction to the Economic History of
C　　China. London: Allen & Unwin, 1954. 202 pp. 54-1075.
　　　o.p. (M-University).
　　　Hucker, 2127; Am. Econ. R., 12/54; Ann. Am. Acad., 7/54;
　　　TLS, 4/16/54

0890　Li, Choh-min. Economic Development of Communist China; An
A　　Appraisal of the First Five Years of Industrialization.
　　　Berkeley: University of California Press, 1959. 284 pp.
　　　58-13330.
　　　AUFS, 943; Hucker, 2160; JAS, 2/60; Am. Econ. R., 9/59; Am.
　　　Pol. Sci. R., 9/59; Ann. Am. Acad., 9/59; Pacific Affairs,
　　　12/59

0891　Liu, Ta-chun. China's Economic Stabilization and Reconstruc-
B　　tion, by D. K. Lieu. New Brunswick, N.J.: Rutgers Uni-
　　　versity Press, 1948. o.p.
　　　Hucker, 2155; Am. Econ. R., 12/48; Pacific Affairs, 9/48

0892　Shen, Tsung-han. Agricultural Resources of China. Ithaca,
A　　N.Y.: Cornell University Press, 1951. 407 pp. 51-7098.
　　　Hucker, 2198; FEQ, 5/52

0893　Sladkovskii, M. I. History of Economic Relations Between
C　　Russia and China. tr. by M. Roublev. Sinological editor:
　　　G. Grause. N.Y.: Daniel Davey, 1967. 299 pp. (Israel
　　　Program for Scientific Translations). 67-7663.
　　　Choice, 4/68; Am. Econ. R., 3/68

0894　Walker, Kenneth Richard. Planning in Chinese Agriculture;
C　　Socialisation and the Private Sector, 1956-1962. Chicago:
　　　Aldine, 1965. 109 pp. 65-16721.
　　　Choice, 4/66; JAS, 8/66; Am. Econ. R., 6/66; Ann. Am.
　　　Acad., 5/66; J. Pol. Econ., 6/66

0895　Wu, Yuan-li. An Economic Survey of Communist China. N.Y.:
B　　Bookman, 1956. 566 pp. 56-13636.
　　　Hucker, 2164; JAS, 11/56; Am. Econ. R., 12/56; Ann. Am.
　　　Acad., 9/56; Geog. R., 10/56; Library Journal, 3/15/56;
　　　Pol. Sci. Q., 12/56; TLS, 7/27/56

0896　Wu, Yuan-Li. The Economy of Communist China; An Introduction.
B　　N.Y.: Praeger, 1965. 225 pp. 65-18082.
　　　Choice, 2/66; JAS, 8/66; Am. Econ. R., 6/66; Ann. Am. Acad.,
　　　5/66; TLS, 7/28/66

CHINA - SOCIOLOGY,
ANTHROPOLOGY AND LINGUISTICS

SOCIOLOGY, ANTHROPOLOGY AND LINGUISTICS

0897　Burgess, John Stewart. The Guilds of Peking. Taipei: Ch'eng-wen
C　　Publishing Co., dist. by Chinese Materials and Research
　　　Aids Service Center, 1966 (orig. pub. by Columbia University
　　　Press, 1928). 270 pp. NUC 68-74755. (R). (M-University).
　　　Hucker, 2064; Am. Econ. R., 6/29; J. Pol. Econ., 6/29

0898　Ch'en, Ta. Emigrant Communities in South China; A Study of
C　　Overseas Migration and Its Influence on Standards of Living
　　　and Social Change. N.Y.: Secretariat, Institute of Pacific
　　　Relations, 1940. 287 pp. 40-12776. o.p.
　　　Hucker, 2076

0899　Chiang, I. A Chinese Childhood. N.Y.: John Day, 1952. 303 pp.
C　　52-11035. o.p.
　　　Hucker, 1991

0900　Ch'u, T'ung-tsu. Law and Society in Traditional China. The
A　　Hague: Mouton, 1961. 304 pp. 62-19813.
　　　Sup. 63, 2907; JAS, 5/62

0901　Eberhard, Wolfram. Guilt and Sin in Traditional China.
B　　Berkeley: University of California Press, 1967. 141 pp.
　　　67-12297.
　　　Choice, 3/68; JAS, 5/68; Library Journal, 5/1/67

0902　Fei, Hsiao-t'ung. Peasant Life in China; A Field Study of
A　　Country Life in the Yangtze Valley. London: Routledge,
　　　1939. 300 pp. 39-15658.
　　　Hucker, 2071

0903　Freedman, Maurice. Lineage Organization in Southeastern China.
A　　London: Athlone, 1958. 151 pp. (London School of Eco-
　　　nomics Monographs on Social Anthropology, 18). 58-3785.
　　　Hucker, 2047; JAS, 5/60

0904　Fried, Morton Herbert. Fabric of Chinese Society; A Study
A　　of the Social Life of a Chinese County Seat. N.Y.: Octagon,
　　　1969 (orig. pub. by Praeger, 1953). 243 pp. 52-11994. (R).
　　　(M-University).
　　　AUFS, 812; Hucker, 2075; FEQ, 2/54; Ann. Am. Acad., 7/53;
　　　Library Journal, 3/15/53; Pacific Affairs, 9/53

0905　Gamble, Sidney David. Ting Hsien, a North China Rural Commu-
B　　nity. Stanford, Calif.: Stanford University Press, 1968
　　　(orig. pub. by Institute of Pacific Relations, 1954).
　　　472 pp. 68-13743. (R).
　　　Hucker, 2074; Choice, 3/69; FEQ, 11/54; Am. Anthropologist,
　　　4/55; Am. J. Soc., 3/55; Am. Pol. Sci. R., 3/55; Am. Soc. R.,
　　　10/54; Ann. Am. Acad., 9/54

0906　Geddes, William Robert. Peasant Life in Communist China.
B　　Ithaca, N.Y.: Society for Applied Anthropology, Cornell
　　　University, 1963. 66 pp. (Monograph No. 6). 63-5144.
　　　o.p.

0907　Hinton, William. Fanshen; A Documentary of Revolution in a
C　　Chinese Village. N.Y.: Monthly Review Press, 1967. 637 pp.
　　　66-23525.
　　　Choice, 7-8/67; JAS, 2/68; Library Journal, 3/1/67

0908　Hu, Hsien-chin. The Common Descent Group in China and its
C　　Functions. ed. by Ralph Linton. N.Y.: Johnson, 1964 (orig.
　　　pub. by Viking Fund, 1948). 204 pp. (Viking Fund Publica-
　　　tions in Anthropology, 10). NUC 67-40970. (R). (M-Uni-
　　　versity).
　　　Hucker, 2040; FEQ, 5/51

0909　Levy, Marion Joseph. The Family Revolution in Modern China.
A　　N.Y.: Octagon, 1963 (orig. pub. by Harvard University
　　　Press, 1949). 390 pp. 63-20892. (R).
　　　AUFS, 840; Hucker, 2034; FEQ, 2/52; Am. Anthropologist,
　　　1/50; Pacific Affairs, 12/49

0910　Liu, William Thomas, ed. Chinese Society Under Communism; A
B　　Reader. N.Y.: Wiley, 1967. 496 pp. 66-29625.
　　　Choice, 1/68; JAS, 11/67; Am. Soc. R., 10/67

0911　Michigan. University. Center for Chinese Studies. Occasional
C　　Papers. The Cultural Revolution: 1967 in Review. by Carl
　　　Riskin, Michael Oksenberg, Robert Scalapino, and Ezra Vogel.
　　　Ann Arbor: Center for Chinese Studies, University of Mich-
　　　igan, 1968- (Papers in Chinese Studies, No. 2, July, 1968).

CHINA - SOCIOLOGY, ANTHROPOLOGY AND LINGUISTICS

0912   Yang, Ch'ing-k'un. The Chinese Family in the Communist Revo-
B   lution. fore. by Talcott Parsons. Cambridge, Mass.: M.I.T.
       Press (orig. pub. by Harvard University Press, 1959).
       246 pp. 59-14897. (R).
       Sup. 61, 2809; Hucker, 2033; Am. Soc. R., 12/60; Library
       Journal, 1/1/60; Pacific Affairs, 9/60

LANGUAGE AND LITERATURE
LITERATURE
EARLY PERIOD
PROSE

0913   Acton, Harold Mario Mitchell and I-hsieh Li, trs. Four Cau-
C   tionary Tales. pref. by Arthur Waley. N.Y.: A. A. Wyn,
       1948. 159 pp. 47-29848. o.p.

0914   Bauer, Wolfgang. The Golden Casket; Chinese Novellas of Two
A   Millenia. tr. by Christopher Levenson. N.Y.: Harcourt,
       Brace & World, 1964. 391 pp. 64-18278.
       Library Journal, 11/15/64

0915   Chai, Ch'u, ed. and tr. A Treasury of Chinese Literature; A New
A   Prose Anthology, Including Fiction and Drama. N.Y.: Appleton-
       Century, 1965. 484 pp. 65-11681.
       Choice, 6/66; JAS, 5/66; JAOS, 7-9/66; Library Journal,
       3/1/65

0916   Chang, Tsu. The Dwelling of Playful Goddesses; China's First
C   Novelette, by Chang Wen-ch'eng. annotated tr. by Howard
       S. Levy. Tokyo: Dai Nippon Insatsu, dist. by Paragon, 1965.
       2 v. 65-15788.
       JAS, 8/66

0917   Chin p'ing mei. The Golden Lotus; A Translation from the Chinese
A   Original by Clement Egerton. N.Y.: Dover, 1954. 4 v.
       54-4573.
       Hucker, 1700

0918   The Dragon King's Daughter; Ten Tang Dynasty Stories. Pe-
C   king: Foreign Languages Press, 1954. 100 pp. 56-47384.
       o.p.

0919   Eberhard, Wolfram, ed. and tr. Chinese Fairy Tales and Folk
C   Tales. London: Paul, Trench, Trubner, 1937. 304 pp.
       38-6187. o.p.
       Hucker, 1712

0920   Eberhard, Wolfram. Folktales of China. rev. ed. Chicago:
A   University of Chicago Press, 1965. 267 pp. 65-25440.
       Choice, 6/66; Library Journal, 8/1/66

0921   Edwards, Evangeline Dora. Chinese Prose Literature of the T'ang
B   Period, A.D. 618-906. London: A. Probsthain, 1937-38. 2 v.
       38-10507 rev. o.p.
       AUFS, 1054; Hucker, 1611

0922   Edwards, Evangeline Dora, ed. The Dragon Book, comp. and ed.
C   by E. D. Edwards. London: William Hodge, 1938. 367 pp.
       39-14127. o.p.
       Hucker, 1655

0923   Feng, Meng-lung. Stories from a Ming Collection. Translations
B   of Chinese Short Stories Published in the Seventeenth Century,
       by Cyril Birch. N.Y.: Grove, 1968 (orig. pub. by Indiana
       University Press, 1959). 205 pp. (UNESCO Collection of
       Representative Works, Chinese Series). 59-9848. (R).
       Hucker, 1659; JAS, 8/59

0924   Giles, Herbert Allen, ed. and tr. Gems of Chinese Literature,
B   in Two Volumes Bound as One. 2d rev. and enl. ed. N.Y.:
       Paragon, 1965 (orig. pub. by Kelly & Walsh, 1923). 430 pp.
       64-18450. (R).
       Hucker, 1575; Choice, 4/67

0925   Hsi yu chi. Monkey, by Wu Ch'eng-en. tr. from Chinese by
A   Arthur Waley. London: Allen & Unwin, 1942. 305 pp.
       A43-273.
       AUFS, 1059; Hucker, 1697; FEQ, 5/45

0926   Kao, K'o-i, ed. Chinese Wit and Humor. N.Y.: Coward-McCann,
B   1946. 347 pp. 46-6653. o.p.
       Hucker, 1654; Library Journal, 8/46

0927   Ko Lien Hua Ying. Flower Shadows Behind the Curtain; A Sequel
B   to Chin P'ing Mei. tr. by V. Kean from F. Kuhn's German
       version of the original Chinese. intro. by F. Kuhn. London:
       The Bodley Head, 1959. 432 pp. Hand catalog. o.p.

CHINA - LANGUAGE AND LITERATURE

Hucker, 1701

0928   Li, Ju-chen. Flowers in the Mirror. tr. by Lin Tai-yi. Lon-
A   don: Peter Owen, 1965. 310 pp. NUC 66-71903.

0929   Li, Yu. Jou Pu Tuan; The Prayer Mat of Flesh. tr. by Richard
B   Martin from the German version by Franz Kuhn. N.Y.: Grove,
       1963. 376 pp. 63-9803. o.p.
       JAS, 2/64

0930   Lin, Yutang. Famous Chinese Short Stories Retold by Lin Yutang.
B   N.Y.: Washington Square, 1961 (orig. pub. by John Day, 1952).
       299 pp. NUC 63-26649. (R).
       Hucker, 1650; FEQ, 5/54

0931   Lin, Yutang, comp. and tr. The Importance of Understanding;
C   Translations from the Chinese. Cleveland: World, 1960.
       494 pp. 60-6690. o.p.
       Hucker, 1609; Library Journal, 3/15/60

0932   Lin, Yutang, tr. Widow, Nun and Courtesan; Three Novelettes
C   from the Chinese. N.Y.: John Day, 1951. 266 pp.
       51-10944 rev. 2. o.p.
       Hucker, 1710; Am. Soc. R., 11/51; Library Journal, 6/1/51

0933   Liu, E. The Travels of Lao Ts'an. tr. from Chinese by Harold
A   Shadick. Ithaca, N.Y.: Cornell University Press, 1966
       (orig. pub. in 1952). 277 pp. NUC 68-1914. (R).
       AUFS, 1067; Hucker, 1704; Choice, 12/67

0934   Lo, Kuan-chung. Romance of the Three Kingdoms. San Kuo Chih
A   Yen-i. tr. by C. H. Brewitt-Taylor. Rutland, Vt.: Tuttle,
       1959. 2 v. 59-10407 rev. o.p.
       Hucker, 1694

0935   Lung t'u Kung an. The Strange Cases of Magistrate Pao; Chinese
C   Tales of Crime and Detection. tr. from Chinese and retold
       by Leon Comber. Rutland, Vt.: Tuttle, 1964. 137 pp.
       64-19359.

0936   P'u, Sung-ling. Strange Stories from a Chinese Studio. tr. and
B   annotated by Herbert A. Giles. 3d ed. rev. Shanghai:
       Kelly & Walsh, 1916. 488 pp. 24-18340 rev. o.p.
       AUFS, 1073; Hucker, 1651

0937   Shen, Fu. Chapters from a Floating Life; The Autobiography of
C   a Chinese Artist. tr. from Chinese by Shirley M. Black.
       London: Oxford, 1960. 108 pp. 60-4904. o.p.
       Hucker, 1711

0938   Shui Hu Ch'uan. All Men are Brothers. tr. from Chinese
A   by Pearl S. Buck. N.Y.: John Day, 1968 (orig. pub. by
       Grove, 1957). 2 v. 57-8648. (R).
       AUFS, 1076; Hucker, 1695

0939   Shui Hu Ch'uan. Water Margin, written by Shih Nai-an. tr.
C   by J. H. Jackson. N.Y.: Paragon, 1968 (orig. pub. in
       Shanghai, 1937). 2 v. 67-31568. (R).
       Hucker, 1696

0940   Smith, Arthur Henderson. Proverbs and Common Sayings from the
C   Chinese, Together with Much Related and Unrelated Matter,
       Interspersed with Observations on Chinese Things in General.
       N.Y.: Dover, 1965 (orig. pub. by American Presbyterian
       Mission Press, 1914). 374 pp. 64-18446. (R).
       Choice, 6/66; JAS, 8/66

0941   Ts'ao, Chan. Dream of the Red Chamber. by Tsao Hsueh-chin.
A   with a continuation by Kao Ou. tr. from Chinese by
       Chi-chen Wang. N.Y.: Twayne, 1958. 574 pp. 58-1761.
       AUFS, 1084; Hucker, 1702; JAS, 5/59; Library Journal, 5/15/58

0942   Ts'ao, Chan. Dream of the Red Chamber. Hung Lou Meng. A
A   Chinese Novel of the Early Ching Period. tr. from Chinese
       by Franz Kuhn. tr. from German by Florence and Isabel
       McHugh. N.Y.: Pantheon, 1958. 582 pp. 58-6097. o.p.
       Hucker, 1703; JAS, 5/59

0943   Wang, Chi-chen, tr. Traditional Chinese Tales. N.Y.: Colum-
B   bia University Press, 1944. 225 pp. A44-727 rev. o.p.
       (M-University).
       AUFS, 1095; Hucker, 1649; FEQ, 8/44; Library Journal, 11/15/43

0944   Werner, Edward Theodore Chalmers. Myths and Legends of China.
C   N.Y.: Brentano, 1922. 453 pp. 23-5292. o.p.
       Hucker, 1085

0945 Wu, Ching-tzu. The Scholars. tr. by Yang Hsien-yi and
A   Gladys Yang. Peking: Foreign Languages Press, 1957.
    721 pp. A58-4116. o.p.
    Hucker, 1698

0946 Wu tse tien ssu ta chian. Dee Goong An. Three Murder Cases
C   Solved by Judge Dee, an Old Chinese Detective Novel Trans-
    lated from the Original Chinese with Introduction and Notes,
    by R. H. van Gulik. Tokyo: Toppan Printing Co., 1949.
    237 pp. 57-17542.

0947 Yang, Hsien-i, tr. The Courtesan's Jewel Box; Chinese Stories
A   of the Xth-XVIIth Centuries. Peking: Foreign Languages
    Press, 1957. 553 pp. 57-41973. o.p.
    AUFS, 1100; JAS, 5/59

0948 Yang, Hsien-i, tr. The Man Who Sold a Ghost; Chinese Tales of
C   the 3rd-6th Centuries. Peking: Foreign Languages Press,
    1958. 162 pp. Hand catalog. o.p.

0949 Yang, Hsien-i. Stories About Not Being Afraid of Ghosts. Pe-
C   king: Foreign Languages Press, 1961. 89 pp. Hand cata-
    log. o.p.

0950 Yen, Hui-ch'ing, comp. and tr. Stories of Old China. tr. by
C   W. W. Yeng. Shanghai: New Art and Literature Publishing
    House, 1958. 178 pp. NUC 63-39119.

LANGUAGE AND LITERATURE
LITERATURE
EARLY PERIOD
POETRY

0951 Ayscough, Florence (Wheelock), tr. Fir-Flower Tablets; Poems
C   Translated from the Chinese. English versions by Amy Lowell.
    Boston: Houghton Mifflin, 1921. 227 pp. 22-3648. o.p.
    Hucker, 1566

0952 Ch'en, Jerome. Poems of Solitude, tr. from Chinese by Jerome
B   Ch'en and Michael Bullock. London: Abelard-Schuman, 1960.
    118 pp. 60-14523.
    TLS, 2/3/61

0953 Ch'u, Ta-kao. Chinese Lyrics. tr. by Ch'u Ta-kao. pref. by
B   Sir Arthur Quiller-Couch. Cambridge: University, 1937.
    55 pp. 38-2934. o.p.
    Hucker, 1562; TLS, 8/7/37

0954 Ch'u Tz'u. Ch'u Tz'u: the Songs of the South, an Ancient Chinese
A   Anthology, by David Hawkes. Oxford: Clarendon, 1959.
    229 pp. 59-1155. o.p.
    AUFS, 1052; Hucker, 1583; JAS, 11/59; JAOS, 4-6/59

0955 Ch'u, Yuan. Li Sao and Other Poems. tr. by Yang Hsien-yi and
C   Gladys Yang. Peking: Foreign Languages Press, 1953. 84 pp.
    55-32706. o.p.

0956 Davis, Albert Richard, ed. The Penguin Book of Chinese Verse.
C   tr. by Robert Kotewall and Norman L. Smith. Baltimore:
    Penguin, 1962. 84 pp. 62-6274.

0957 Demieville, Paul, ed. Anthologie de la Poesie Chinoise
B   Classique. Paris: Gallimard, 1962. 571 pp. NUC 64-37030.

0958 Frodsham, J. D., comp. An Anthology of Chinese Verse: Han, Wei,
A   Chin and the Northern and Southern Dynasties. Oxford: Clar-
    endon, 1967. 198 pp. (Oxford Library of East Asian Lit-
    eratures). 67-95155.
    Choice, 9/68; JAS, 11/68; TLS, 9/28/67

0959 Graham, Angus Charles, ed. and tr. Poems of the Late T'ang.
A   Baltimore: Penguin, 1965. 173 pp. (UNESCO Collection
    of Representative Works: Chinese Series). 66-804.
    Choice, 10/66; JAOS, 7-9/66

0960 Gulik, Robert Hans van. Hsi K'ang and his Poetical Essay on
C   the Lute. Tokyo: Sophia University, 1941. 90 pp. 42-4465.
    Hucker, 1590; JAOS, 12/41

0961 Han-shan. Cold Mountain; 100 Poems by the T'ang Poet Han-shan.
B   tr. and with intro. by Burton Watson. N.Y.: Grove, 1962.
    122 pp. 62-15847. o.p.
    JAS, 8/63; JAOS, 10-12/62

0962 Han, Ying. Han Shih Wai Chuan: Han Ying's Illustrations of
C   the Didactic Application of the Classic of Songs. tr.
    by James Robert Hightower. Cambridge, Mass.: Harvard
    University Press, 1952. 368 pp. 52-9389.
    Hucker, 1657

0963 Hart, Henry Hersch, comp. and tr. A Chinese Market; Lyrics
C   from the Chinese in English Verse, by Henry H. Hart. fore.
    by E. T. Werner. Peking: French Bookstore, 1931. 101 pp.
    32-34108. o.p.

0964 Huang, Wen. Poems From China. tr. by Wong Man. Hong Kong:
C   Creation Books, 1950. 241 pp. 52-22125.

0965 Li, Po. The Works of Li Po, the Chinese Poet. Done into English
A   Verse by Shigeyoshi Obata. N.Y.: Paragon, 1964 (orig. pub.
    by Dutton, 1922). 236 pp. 65-26103. (R).
    Hucker, 1598

0966 Lin, Pu. Lin Ho-ching. tr. and annotated by Max Perleberg.
C   Hong Kong: K. Weiss, 1952. 150 pp. 55-36458.

0967 Lu, Yu. The Rapier of Lu, Patriot Poet of China. tr. and
C   biography by Clara M. Candlin. London: Murray, 1946. 68 pp.
    48-10659.
    Hucker, 1606

0968 Mackintosh, Duncan Robert, comp. A Collection of Chinese Lyrics;
B   Rendered into Verse by Alan Ayling from Translations of
    the Chinese. London: Routledge & Paul, 1965. 254 pp.
    66-2532.
    JAS, 5/67

0969 Payne, Pierre Stephen Robert. The White Pony; An Anthology
B   of Chinese Poetry from the Earliest Times to the Present
    Day. newly tr. N.Y.: New American Library, 1960 (orig.
    pub. by John Day, 1947). 320 pp. 47-6700. (R).
    Hucker, 1560; Library Journal, 12/1/47

0970 Rexroth, Kenneth. One Hundred Poems from the Chinese. N.Y.:
C   New Directions, 1956. 159 pp. 56-13351.
    Hucker, 1577; JAS, 8/58

0971 Shih Ching. The Book of Odes. Chinese text, transcription and
C   tr. by Bernhard Karlgren. Stockholm: Museum of Far Eastern
    Antiquities, 1950. 270 pp. 52-65061.
    AUFS, 1074; Hucker, 1537

0972 Shih Ching. The Book of Songs. tr. from Chinese by Arthur
A   Waley. N.Y.: Grove, 1960. 358 pp. 60-6341. o.p.
    AUFS, 1075; Hucker, 1536

0973 Shih Ching. The Confucian Odes, the Classic Anthology Defined
C   by Confucius. tr. by Ezra Pound. N.Y.: J. Laughlin, 1959
    (orig. pub. by Harvard University Press, 1954). 223 pp.
    (New Directions Paperback, 81). 59-13170. (R).
    Hucker, 1538; FEQ, 2/55

0974 Su, Shih. Selections from the Works of Su Tung-p'o (A.D. 1036-
C   1101). tr. by Cyril Drummond Le Gros Clark. London:
    Cape, 1931. 180 pp. 32-23257. o.p.
    Hucker, 1604

0975 Su, Shih. Su Tung-P'o, Selections from a Sung Dynasty Poet.
A   tr. with intro. by Burton Watson. N.Y.: Columbia University
    Press, 1965. 139 pp. (UNESCO Collection of Representative
    Works: Chinese Series). 65-13619.
    Sup. 65, 3107; Choice, 11/65; JAS, 11/66; JAOS, 4-6/66;
    Library Journal, 2/1/65; TLS, 5/19/66

0976 Su Tung-p'o. The Prose-Poetry of Su Tung-p'o; Being Transla-
B   tions into English...with Introductory Essays, Notes and
    Commentaries by Cyril Drummond Le Gros Clark. N.Y.:
    Paragon, 1964 (orig. pub. by Kegan Paul, 1935). 280 pp.
    NUC 65-61237. (R).
    Hucker, 1605; JAOS, 3/36

0977 T'ang-shih san-pai shou. The Jade Mountain; A Chinese Anthology,
A   Being Three Hundred Poems of the T'ang Dynasty, 618-906.
    tr. by Witter Bynner from the texts of Kiang Kang-hu.
    Garden City, N.Y.: Doubleday, 1964 (orig. pub. by Knopf,
    1929). 238 pp. 64-4615. (R).
    AUFS, 1080; Hucker, 1554; Choice, 12/64

0978 T'ao, Ch'ien. Poems. tr. by Lily Pao-hu Chang and Mar-
B   jorie Sinclair. Honolulu: University of Hawaii Press,
    1953. 133 pp. 53-8575. o.p.
    Hucker, 1592

0979 T'ao, Ch'ien. T'ao the Hermit; Sixty Poems. tr. by William
B   Acker. N.Y.: Thames & Hudson, 1952. 157 pp. 53-3610.
    o.p.
    AUFS, 1083; Hucker, 1591; TLS, 7/25/52

0980 Ting, Walasse, comp. Chinese Moonlight: 63 Poems by 33 Poets.
C   tr. and recomposed by Walasse Ting. Copenhagen: Permild
    and Rosengreen, dist. by Wittenborn, 1967. 71 pp. 67-21795.

0981 Trevelyan, Robert Calverley, ed. From the Chinese. Oxford:
C   Clarendon, 1945. 92 pp. A46-622. o.p.

0982 Tu, Fu. Selected Poems. comp. by Feng Chih. tr. by Rewi Alley.
C   Peking: Foreign Languages Press, 1962. 178 pp. NUC 63-
    63022. o.p.

0983 Tu, Fu. Tu Fu, the Autobiography of a Chinese Poet, A.D.
C   712-770. tr. by Florence Ayscough. Boston: Houghton
    Mifflin, 1929-34. 2 v. 29-29750 rev. o.p.

0984 Tun-huang Manuscripts. English. Ballads and Stories from Tun-
A   huang; An Anthology, by Arthur Waley. London: Allen &
    Unwin, 1960. 273 pp. 61-4417.
    JAS, 5/62

0985 Waley, Arthur, tr. Chinese Poems, Selected from 170 Chinese
A   Poems, More Translations from the Chinese, The Temple
    and The Book of Songs. London: Allen & Unwin, 1946.
    213 pp. 47-5287.
    AUFS, 1087

0986 Waley, Arthur, tr. More Translations from the Chinese.
B   N.Y.: Knopf, 1937. 144 pp. 19-17614. o.p.

0987 Waley, Arthur. The Real Tripitaka, and Other Pieces. London:
C   Allen & Unwin, 1952. 291 pp. 55-18728.
    Hucker, 1658

0988 Waley, Arthur, tr. The Temple, and Other Poems. N.Y.:
B   Knopf, 1923. 150 pp. 23-17912. o.p.
    AUFS, 1092; Hucker, 1551

0989 Waley, Arthur, tr. Translations from the Chinese. N.Y.:
B   Knopf, 1941. 325 pp. 41-4061.
    Hucker, 1561

0990 Wang, Wei. Poems. tr. by Chang Yin-nan and Lewis C. Walmsley.
B   Rutland, Vt.: Tuttle, 1958. 159 pp. 58-7723. o.p.
    Hucker, 1596; JAS, 5/59

LANGUAGE AND LITERATURE
LITERATURE
EARLY PERIOD
DRAMA

0991 Arlington, Lewis Charles. The Chinese Drama from the Earliest
C   Times Until Today. N.Y.: Blom, 1966 (orig. pub. in 1930).
    177 pp. 65-19614. (R).

0992 Arlington, Lewis Charles, ed. and tr. Famous Chinese Plays.
B   N.Y.: Russell & Russell, 1963 (orig. pub. by Vetch, 1937).
    443 pp. 63-15147. (R).
    Hucker, 1676

0993 Chu, Su-ch'en. Fifteen Strings of Cash; A Kunchu Opera. tr.
C   by Yang Hsien-yi and Gladys Yang. Peking: Foreign Lang-
    uages Press, 1957. 84 pp. 59-34753. o.p.

0994 The Forsaken Wife (A Pingchu Opera). tr. by Yang Hsien-yi and
C   Gladys Yang. Peking: Foreign Languages Press, 1958. 70 pp.
    Hand catalog.

0995 Hsi hsiang chi. The Romance of the Western Chamber (Hsi hsiang
A   chi), a Chinese Play Written in the Thirteenth Century. tr.
    by S. I. Hsiung. N.Y.: Columbia University Press, 1968
    (orig. pub. by Methuen, 1935). 281 pp. 68-22412. (R).
    AUFS, 1130; Hucker, 1675

0996 Hsi hsiang chi. The West Chamber, a Medieval Drama. tr. from
A   original Chinese with notes by Henry Hart. fore. by Edward
    Thomas Williams. Stanford, Calif.: Stanford University
    Press, 1936. 192 pp. 36-22471. o.p.
    Hucker, 1677; JAOS, 6/37

0997 Hung, Sheng. The Palace of Eternal Youth. tr. by Yang Hsien-
A   yi and Gladys Yang. Peking: Foreign Languages Press, 1955.
    322 pp. 57-35395. o.p.

0998 Kuan, Han-ch'ing. Selected Plays. tr. by Yang Hsien-yi and
A   Gladys Yang. Shanghai: New Art & Literature, 1958. 237 pp.
    61-39292. o.p.
    AUFS, 1131

0999 Kuang-tung yueh chu tuan. The Runaway Maid; A Cantonese Opera.
C   rev. by the Cantonese Opera Company of Kwangtung. tr. by
    Gladys Yang. Peking: Foreign Languages Press, 1958. 64 pp.
    59-25096.

1000 Li, Hsing-tao. The Circle of Chalk; A Play in Five Acts, Adapted
C   from Chinese by Klabund (pseud.). English version by James
    Laver. London: Heinemann, 1929. 107 pp. o.p.

1001 Li, Hsing-tao. The Story of the Circle of Chalk; A Drama
C   from the Old Chinese. tr. by Frances Hume from French
    of Stanislas Julien. London: Rodale, 1954. 124 pp.
    A55-8680. o.p.

1002 Lin Yin Chi. Love Under the Willows; A Szechuan Opera. Liang
C   Shanpo and Chu Ying-tai. tr. by Yang Hsien-yi and Gladys
    Yang. Peking: Foreign Languages Press, 1956. 85 pp.
    57-41511.

1003 Scott, Adolphe Clarence, ed. Traditional Chinese Plays: Ssu Lang
A   Visits His Mother; Ssu lang t'an mu. The Butterfly Dream; Hu
    tieh meng. Madison: University of Wisconsin Press, 1967.
    165 pp. 66-22854.
    Library Journal, 4/1/67; TLS, 9/28/67

1004 Wang Pao-ch'uan. Lady Precious Stream; An Old Chinese Play Done
A   into English According to Its Traditional Style by S. I.
    Hsiung. London: Methuen, 1934. 168 pp.
    35-11934.
    Hucker, 1678

1005 Yang, Hsien-i. The Fisherman's Revenge; A Peking Opera. tr.
C   by Yang Hsien-yi and Gladys Yang. Peking: Foreign Languages
    Press, 1956. 53 pp. Hand catalog.

LANGUAGE AND LITERATURE
LITERATURE
EARLY PERIOD
HISTORY AND CRITICISM

1006 Birch, Cyril, comp. and ed. associate ed., Donald Keene. An-
A   thology of Chinese Literature. N.Y.: Grove, 1965- (UNESCO
    Collection of Representative Works, Chinese Series).
    65-14202.
    Sup. 67, 3233; Choice, 6/66; JAS, 11/66; JAOS, 4-6/66;
    Library Journal, 1/1/66

1007 Bishop, John Lyman. The Colloquial Short Story in China; A
B   Study of the San-yen Collections. Cambridge, Mass.:
    Harvard University Press, 1956. 144 pp. 56-7211.
    AUFS, 1047; JAS, 11/56

1008 Bishop, John Lyman, ed. Studies in Chinese Literature. Cam-
B   bridge, Mass.: Harvard University Press, 1965. 245 pp.
    65-13836.

1009 Ch'en, Shou-yi. Chinese Literature; A Historical Introduction.
C   N.Y.: Ronald, 1961. 665 pp. 61-9426.
    Hucker, 1519; JAS, 5/62; JAOS, 4-6/62

1010 Chou, Shu-jen. A Brief History of Chinese Fiction, by Lu Hsun
B   (pseud.). Peking: Foreign Languages Press, 1959. 462 pp.
    60-3865.
    Hucker, 1647

1011 Dieny, Jean-Pierre. Aux Origines de la Poesie Classique en
C   Chine. Etude sur la Poesie Lyrique a l'Epoque des Han.
    Leiden: Brill, 1968. 176 pp. (T'oung Pao, Monographie IV).
    68-93582.

1012 Feng, Shu-lan. A Short History of Classical Chinese Litera-
C   ture by Feng Yuan-chun. tr. by Yang Hsien-yi and Gladys
    Yang. Peking: Foreign Languages Press, 1958. 132 pp.
    60-1450. o.p.
    Hucker, 1526; FEQ, 8/50

1013 Frodsham, J. D. The Murmuring Stream: the Life and Works of
A   the Chinese Nature Poet Hsieh Ling-yun (385-433), Duke of
    K'ang-lo. Kuala Lumpur: University of Malaya Press, dist.
    by Oxford, 1967. 2 v. 68-143150.
    JAS, 5/69

1014 Giles, Herbert Allen. A History of Chinese Literature. N.Y.:
B   Ungar, 1966. 498 pp. 66-26507. (M-University).
    AUFS, 1055

1015 Halson, Elizabeth. Peking Opera; A Short Guide. N.Y.: Oxford,
B   1966. 92 pp. 66-31690/MN.
      JAS, 8/67

1016 Hawkes, David. A Little Primer of Tu Fu. Oxford: Clarendon,
B   1967. 243 pp. 67-105047.
      JAS, 11/68; TLS, 9/28/67

1017 Hervouet, Y. Un Poete de Cour Sous les Han: Sseu-ma Siang-
C   jou. Paris: Presses Universitaires, 1964. 478 pp.
      67-39197.

1018 Ho, Shih-chun. Jou Lin Wai Che, le Roman des Lettres; Etudes
C   sur un Roman Satirique Chinois. Paris: L. Rodstein, 1933.
      207 pp.
      Hucker, 1691

1019 Holzman, Donald. La Vie et la Pensee de Hi K'ang (223-262).
B   Leiden: Brill, 1957. 186 pp. A59-4991.
      Hucker, 250; JAS, 5/64

1020 Hsia, Chih-tsing. The Classic Chinese Novel; A Critical Intro-
A   duction. N.Y.: Columbia University Press, 1968. 413 pp.
      68-18997.
      Choice, 1/68; JAS, 2/69; Library Journal, 5/1/68

1021 Hu, P'in-ch'ing. Li Ch'ing-chao. N.Y.: Twayne, 1966. 128 pp.
C   (TWAS, 5). 66-16122.
      Choice, 10/67

1022 Hung, William. Tu Fu, China's Greatest Poet. Cambridge, Mass.:
A   Harvard University Press, 1952. 300 pp. 52-5034. o.p.
      Hucker, 1599; FEQ, 2/53

1023 Irwin, Richard Gregg. The Evolution of a Chinese Novel: Shui-
B   hu-chuan. Cambridge, Mass.: Harvard University Press,
      1953. 231 pp. 53-10476. o.p.
      AUFS, 1063; Hucker, 1686; FEQ, 11/54; JAOS, 4-6/54

1024 Lai, Ming. A History of Chinese Literature. N.Y.: Putnam,
C   1966 (orig. pub. by John Day, 1964). 439 pp. 64-20468 rev.
      (R).
      Choice, 11/65; JAS, 5/65; JAOS, 7-9/65; Library Journal,
      10/1/64; TLS, 8/6/64

1025 Lin, Yutang. The Gay Genius; The Life and Times of Su Tung po.
C   N.Y.: John Day, 1947. 427 pp. 47-11617 rev. o.p.
      Hucker, 1603; FEQ, 5/48

1026 Liu, Hsieh. The Literary Mind and the Carving of Dragons; A
B   Study of Thought and Pattern in Chinese Literature. tr. by
      Vincent Yu-chung Shih. N.Y.: Columbia University Press, 1959.
      298 pp. 58-13768.
      Hucker, 1610; JAS, 5/60; JAOS, 7-9/60; Library Journal,
      4/15/59; Pacific Affairs, 9/59; TLS, 12/4/59

1027 Liu, Jo-yu. The Art of Chinese Poetry, by James J. Y. Liu.
A   Chicago: University of Chicago Press, 1962. 165 pp.
      62-53199.
      JAS, 2/64

1028 Liu, Jo-yu. The Chinese Knight-Errant, by James J. Y. Liu.
B   Chicago: University of Chicago Press, 1967. 242 pp.
      66-14112.
      Choice, 7-8/68; JAS, 5/68

1029 Liu, Jo-yu. Elizabethan and Yuan; A Brief Comparison of Some
C   Conventions in Poetic Drama, by James Liu. London: The
      China Society, 1955. 12 pp. (China Society Occasional
      Papers, 8).
      Hucker, 1666

1030 Liu, Ts'un-jen. The Authorship of the Feng Shen Yen i. Wies-
B   baden: Otto Harrassowitz, 1962. 326 pp. (Buddhist and
      Taoist Influences on Chinese Novels, Vol. I). NUC
      63-26810.

1031 Liu, Ts'un-jen. Wu Ch'eng-en, His Life and Career. Leiden:
C   Brill, 1967. 102 pp. (T'oung Pao offprint). 68-86791.

1032 Liu, Wu-chi. An Introduction to Chinese Literature. Bloom-
A   ington: Indiana University Press, 1966. 321 pp. 66-12729.
      Sup. 67, 3245; Choice, 5/67; JAS, 5/67; Library Journal,
      7/66; TLS, 4/20/66

1033 Lu, Chi. The Art of Letters; Lu Chi's "Wen-fu" A.D. 302. tr.
B   by E. R. Hughes. Princeton, N.J.: Princeton University
      Press, 1951. 261 pp. (Bollingen Series, Vol. 29). 51-13302.
      Hucker, 1588

1034 March, Benjamin. Chinese Shadow-figure Plays and their Making.
C   Detroit: Puppetry Imprints, 1938. 57 pp. 38-19584. o.p.
      Hucker, 1674

1035 Margoulies, Georges. Evolution de la Prose Artistique Chi-
C   noise. Munchen: Encyclopadie-Verlag, 1929. 334 pp. 31-5098.

1036 Margoulies, Georges. Le "Fou" dans le Wen-siuan, Etude et
C   Textes. Paris: Geuthner, 1926. 138 pp. 33-34621.

1037 Margoulies, Georges. Histoire de La Litterature Chinoise:
C   Poesie. Paris: Payot, 1951. 417 pp. 52-27648.
      Hucker, 1559

1038 Margoulies, Georges. Histoire de la Litterature Chinoise:
C   Prose. Paris: Payot, 1949. 336 pp.

1039 Mote, Frederick W. The Poet Kao Ch'i, 1336-1374. Princeton,
A   N.J.: Princeton University Press, 1962. 261 pp. 62-7411.
      JAOS, 10-12/62

1040 Scott, Adolphe Clarence. The Classical Theatre of China. N.Y.:
A   Macmillan, 1957. 250 pp. o.p.
      AUFS, 1134; Hucker, 1661; JAS, 2/58; TLS, 5/10/57

1041 Scott, Adolphe Clarence. An Introduction to the Chinese Thea-
C   tre. Singapore: Donald Moore, 1958. 92 pp. NUC 64-44435.

1042 Teele, Roy Earl. Through a Glass Darkly; A Study of English
C   Translations of Chinese Poetry. Ann Arbor: 1949. 173 pp.
      A50-323. o.p.
      Hucker, 1558

1043 Thiele, Margaret Rossiter. None But the Nightingale, an Intro-
C   duction to Chinese Literature. Rutland, Vt.: Tuttle, 1967.
      159 pp. 67-20950.
      Choice, 7-8/68; Pacific Affairs, Spring/68

1044 Waley, Arthur. The Life and Times of Po Chu-i, 772-846 A.D.
A   N.Y.: Hillary House, 1951 (orig. pub. by Allen & Unwin,
      1949). 238 pp. 52-55888. (R).
      AUFS, 1088; Hucker, 1601; FEQ, 8/51; TLS, 1/20/50

1045 Waley, Arthur. The Poetry and Career of Li Po, 701-162 A.D.
A   N.Y.: Hillary House, 1958 (orig. pub. in 1950). 123 pp.
      51-13161. (R).
      AUFS, 1090; Hucker, 1597

1046 Waley, Arthur. Yuan Mei, Eighteenth Century Chinese Poet.
A   N.Y.: Macmillan, 1957. 227 pp. 57-13771.
      AUFS, 1094; Hucker, 1607; JAS, 2/60; JAOS, 7-9/57; TLS,
      2/22/57

1047 Watson, Burton. Early Chinese Literature. N.Y.: Columbia
A   University Press, 1962. 304 pp. 62-17552.
      JAS, 8/63

1048 Wen-lin; Studies in the Chinese Humanities. ed. by Chow Tse-
C   tsung. Madison: University of Wisconsin Press, 1968.
      325 pp. 67-20756.
      JAS, 5/69

1049 Wimsatt, Genevieve Blanche. Chinese Shadow Shows. Cambridge,
C   Mass.: Harvard University Press, 1936. 68 pp. 37-4449.
      o.p.
      Hucker, 1673

1050 Wimsatt, Genevieve Blanche. Selling Wilted Peonies; Biography
C   and Songs of Yu Hsuan-chi, T'ang Poetess. N.Y.: Columbia
      University Press, 1936. 119 pp. 37-1811 rev. o.p.
      JAOS, 6/37

1051 Wu, Shih-ch'ang. On the Red Chamber Dream; A Critical Study
C   of Two Annotated Manuscripts of the XVIIIth Century.
      Oxford: Clarendon, 1961. 391 pp. 61-1936.
      JAS, 11/61; JAOS, 1-3/62

1052 Wylie, Alexander. Notes on Chinese Literature: With Introduc-
C   tory Remarks on the Progressive Advancement of the Art;
      And a List of Translations from the Chinese into Various
      European Languages. 2d ed. N.Y.: Paragon, 1964 (orig.
      pub. by Presbyterian Mission, 1922). 307 pp. 64-18442.
      (R).
      JAS, 2/65

1053 Yoshikawa, Kojiro. An Introduction to Sung Poetry. tr. by
A   Burton Watson. Cambridge, Mass.: Harvard University

Press, 1967. 191 pp. 67-14347.
Choice, 2/68; JAS, 5/68; TLS, 1/4/68

1054 Zucker, Adolf Eduard. The Chinese Theater. Boston: Little,
C   Brown, 1925. 234 pp. 25-23016. o.p.
        AUFS, 1137; Hucker, 1664

LANGUAGE AND LITERATURE
LITERATURE
MODERN PERIOD
PROSE

1055 Chang, Eileen. Naked Earth. Hong Kong: Union Press, 1956.
C   365 pp. Hand catalog.

1056 Chang, Eileen. The Rice-sprout Song. N.Y.: Scribners, 1955.
C   182 pp. 55-7192. o.p.
        Library Journal, 5/1/55

1057 Chang, T'ien-i. Big Lin and Little Lin. tr. by Gladys Yang.
C   Peking: Foreign Languages Press, 1958. 157 pp. Hand
        catalog.

1058 Chang, T'ien-i. Stories of Chinese Young Pioneers by Chang
C   Tien-yi. Peking: Foreign Languages Press, 1954. 49 pp.
        57-45357. o.p.

1059 Chao, Shu-li. Changes in Li Village. tr. by Gladys Yang.
B   Peking: Foreign Languages Press, 1953. 224 pp. 55-37564.
        o.p.
        AUFS, 1105

1060 Chao, Shu-li. Rhymes of Li Yu-tsai and Other Stories. 2d ed.
A   Peking: Foreign Languages Press, 1954. 155 pp. 58-19521.

1061 Chao, Shu-li. Sanliwan Village. tr. by Gladys Yang. Peking:
B   Foreign Languages Press, 1957. 275 pp. 58-31671. o.p.

1062 Ch'en, Ch'i-t'ung. The Long March. Peking: Foreign Languages
C   Press, 1956. 168 pp. 57-58106. o.p.

1063 Chen, Chi-ying. Fool in the Reeds. 4th ed. tr. by Eileen
C   Chang. Hong Kong: Rainbow Press, 1961. 295 pp. NUC
        64-61530.

1064 Chen, Teng-ko. Living Hell. tr. by Sidney Shapiro. Peking:
C   Foreign Languages Press, 1955. 147 pp.

1065 Chiang, Ping-chih. The Sun Shines over the Sangkan River
A   by Ting Ling (pseud.). tr. by Yang Hsien-yi and Gladys
        Yang. Peking: Foreign Languages Press, 1954. 348 pp.
        54-31827. o.p.
        AUFS, 1106

1066 Chiang, Ping-chih. When I Was in Sha Chuan and Other Stories.
C   tr. by Pusheng Kung. Bombay: Kutub Publishers, preface
        date, 1945. 118 pp. o.p

1067 Chou, Erh-fu. Morning in Shanghai. tr. by A. C. Barnes. Pe-
C   king: Foreign Languages Press, 1962- 664 pp. NUC 63-3225.

1068 Chou, Li-po. Great Changes in a Mountain Village, a Novel.
A   tr. by Derek Bryan. Peking: Foreign Languages Press,
        1961- 353 pp. Hand catalog.

1069 Chou, Li-po. The Hurricane. tr. from Chinese by Hsu Meng-
C   hsiung. Peking: Foreign Languages Press, 1955. 409 pp.
        A56-5663.
        AUFS, 1107

1070 Chou, Li-po. Sowing the Clouds, a Collection of Chinese Short
C   Stories, by Chou Li-po, Li Chun and others. Peking: Foreign
        Languages Press, 1961. 146 pp. NUC 63-3228. o.p.

1071 Chou, Shu-jen. Ah Q and Others, Selected Stories of Lusin
A   (pseud.). tr. by Chi-chen Wang. N.Y.: Columbia University
        Press, 1941. 219 pp. 41-10678. o.p. (M-University).
        AUFS, 1108; Hucker, 1751; FEQ, 5/42

1072 Chou, Shu-jen. Chosen Pages from Lu Hsun (pseud.), the Literary
C   Mentor of the Chinese Revolution. N.Y.: Cameron Associates,
        1959. 315 pp. Hand catalog. o.p.

1073 Chou, Shu-jen. Selected Stories of Lu Hsun (pseud.). Peking:
C   Foreign Languages Press, 1954. 251 pp. 56-37158. o.p.

1074 Chou, Shu-jen. Selected Works of Lu Hsun (pseud.). Peking:
A   Foreign Languages Press, 1956- 57-35404. o.p.

Hucker, 1753

1075 Chu, Po. Tracks in the Snowy Forest. tr. by Sidney Shapiro.
C   Peking: Foreign Languages Press, 1962. 548 pp. NUC 63-3367.

1076 Feng, Hsueh-feng. Fables. tr. by Gladys Yang. Peking:
C   Foreign Languages Press, 1953. 70 pp. 57-20220. o.p.

1077 Homeward Journey and Other Stories, by Contemporary Chinese
C   Writers. tr. by Gladys Yang. Peking: Foreign Languages
        Press, 1957. 234 pp. 58-15367. o.p.

1078 Hsiao, Chun. Village in August, by T'ien Chun, pseud. N.Y.:
B   Smith & Durrell, 1942. 313 pp. 42-11707. o.p.
        AUFS, 1113; Pacific Affairs, 9/42

1079 Hsu, Kuang-yao. The Plains are Ablaze. tr. by Sidney Shapiro.
C   Peking: Foreign Languages Press, 1955. 277 pp. A56-5729.
        o.p.

1080 Hu, K'o. Steeled in Battles. tr. by Tang Sheng. Peking:
C   Foreign Languages Press, 1955. 130 pp. 58-17706.

1081 Hu, Wan-ch'un. Man of a Special Cut. Peking: Foreign Languages
C   Press, 1963. 183 pp. NUC 65-2189.

1082 I Knew All Along and Other Stories by Contemporary Chinese
C   Writers. Peking: Foreign Languages Press, 1960. 172 pp.
        Hand catalog.

1083 K'ang, Cho. When the Sun Comes Up. Peking: Foreign Languages
C   Press, 1961. 175 pp. Hand catalog.

1084 Kao, Yu-pao. My Childhood. Peking: Foreign Languages Press,
C   1960. 379 pp. Hand catalog.

1085 Kao, Yun-lan. Annals of a Provincial Town. tr. by Sidney
C   Shapiro. Peking: Foreign Languages Press, 1959. 306 pp.
        62-19805.

1086 Kuo, Kuo-fu. Among the Ominans. tr. by Huai-yuan Shang.
C   Peking: Foreign Languages Press, 1961. 348 pp. 62-46451.

1087 Li, Fei-kan. Living Amongst Heroes. by Pa Chin (pseud.).
C   Peking: Foreign Languages Press, 1954. 132 pp. 57-35603.
        o.p.

1088 Li, Liu-ju. Sixty Stirring Years, a Novel in Three Volumes.
C   Peking: Foreign Languages Press, 1961- NUC 63-50932. o.p.

1089 Liang, Pin. Keep the Red Flag Flying. tr. by Gladys
C   Yang. Peking: Foreign Languages Press, 1961. 528 pp.
        63-6530.

1090 Liu, Ching. Wall of Bronze. tr. by Sidney Shapiro. Peking:
C   Foreign Languages Press, 1954. 283 pp. 55-38605.

1091 Liu, Pai-yu. Flames Ahead. Peking: Foreign Languages Press,
C   1954. 166 pp. 57-34675.

1092 Liu, Pai-yu. Six A.M. and Other Stories. Peking: Foreign
C   Languages Press, 1953. 149 pp. 57-35388.

1093 Lu, Chu-kuo. The Battle of Samgkumryung. tr. by A. M.
C   Condron. Peking: Foreign Languages Press, 1961. 162 pp.
        Hand catalog.

1094 Ma, Chia. Unfading Flowers. Peking: Foreign Languages
C   Press, 1961. 106 pp. NUC 63-42012.

1095 Ma, Feng. The Sun Has Risen. Peking: Foreign Languages
C   Press, 1961. 174 pp. NUC 63-42013.

1096 Mirages and Sea-Markets, a Collection of Modern Chinese Essays.
C   Peking: Foreign Languages Press, 1962. 122 pp. NUC 63-28310.

1097 A New Home and Other Stories, by Contemporary Chinese Writers.
C   Peking: Foreign Languages Press, 1955. 166 pp. Hand
        catalog. o.p.

1098 Pai, Wei. The Chus Reach Heaven. tr. by Yang Hsien-yi and
C   Gladys Yang. Peking: Foreign Languages Press, 1954.
        108 pp. 55-3971.

1099 Registration and Other Stories, by Contemporary Chinese Writers.
C   Peking: Foreign Languages Press, 1956. 210 pp. Hand cata-
        log. o.p.

1100 Shen, Ts'ung-wen. The Chinese Earth; Stories. tr. by Ching
C   Ti and Robert Payne. London: Allen & Unwin, 1947. 289 pp.
      56-43546. o.p.

1101 Shen, Yen-ping. Midnight by Mao Tun (pseud.). tr. by Hsu
A   Meng-hsiung. Peking: Foreign Languages Press, 1957.
      524 pp. 58-22593. o.p.
      AUFS, 1117

1102 Shen, Yen-ping. Spring Silkworms and Other Stories, by Mao
C   Tun (pseud.). tr. by Sidney Shapiro. Peking: Foreign Lan-
      guages Press, 1956. 278 pp. 57-34699. o.p.

1103 Shu, Ch'ing-ch'un. City of Cats. by Lao sheh. tr. by James
C   E. Dew. Ann Arbor: Center for Chinese Studies, University
      of Michigan, 1964. 64 pp. (Occasional Papers No. 3).
      64-63813. o.p.

1104 Shu, Ch'ing-ch'un. Divorce. tr. by Evan King. St. Peters-
B   burg, Fla.: King Publications, 1948. 444 pp. 48-18747 rev.

1105 Shu, Ch'ing-ch'un. Dragon Beard Ditch; A Play in Three Acts, by
C   Lao Sheh (pseud.). tr. by Liao Hung-ying. Peking: Foreign
      Languages Press, 1956. 97 pp. 61-46449.

1106 Shu, Ch'ing-ch'un. The Drum Singers. tr. from Chinese by
A   Helena Kuo. N.Y.: Harcourt, Brace, 1952. 283 pp. 52-6438.
      o.p.
      FEQ, 11/52; Library Journal, 3/1/52

1107 Shu, Ch'ing-ch'un (Lau Shaw, pseud.). Heavensent. London:
B   Dent, 1951. 284 pp. o.p.

1108 Shu, Ch'ing-ch'un. The Quest for Love of Lao Lee. tr. by
B   Helen Kuo. N.Y.: Reynal & Hitchcock, 1948. 306 pp.
      48-9236. o.p.

1109 Shu, Ch'ing-ch'un. Rickshaw Boy, by Lau Shaw (pseud.). tr.
A   from Chinese by Evan King, pseud. Garden City, N.Y.: Sun
      Dial, 1946. 315 pp. 47-2841 rev. o.p.
      AUFS, 1120; Hucker, 1754; FEQ, 5/46; Library Journal, 7/45

1110 Shu, Ch'ing-ch'un. The Yellow Storm by Lau Shaw (pseud.).
B   tr. from Chinese by Ida Pruitt. N.Y.: Harcourt, Brace,
      1951. 533 pp. 51-9088. o.p.
      AUFS, 1121; Hucker, 1755; Library Journal, 2/1/51; TLS,
      10/26/51

1111 Snow, Edgar, ed. Living China, Modern Chinese Short Stories.
B   N.Y.: Reynal & Hitchcock, 1937. 360 pp. 37-27319. o.p.
      AUFS, 1122; Hucker, 1749; Pacific Affairs, 3/37; TLS, 11/21/36

1112 Stories of the Chinese People's Volunteers. tr. by the Teachers
C   of the English Faculty of the Foreign Languages Depart-
      ment of Futan University. Peking: Foreign Languages Press,
      1960. 258 pp. Hand catalog.

1113 Tu, P'eng-ch'eng. Defend Yenan! tr. by Sidney Shapiro.
C   Peking: Foreign Languages Press, 1958. 404 pp. Hand
      catalog. o.p.

1114 Tu, P'eng-ch'eng. In Days of Peace. Peking: Foreign Lan-
C   guages Press, 1962. 219 pp. NUC 63-76507.

1115 Wang, Chi-chen, tr. Contemporary Chinese Stories. N.Y.:
A   Columbia University Press, 1944. 242 pp. A44-726 rev.
      o.p.
      AUFS, 1124; Hucker, 1745; FEQ, 8/44; Library Journal,
      11/15/43

1116 Wang, Chi-chen, ed. Stories of China at War. N.Y.: Columbia
B   University Press, 1947. 158 pp. A47-1034. o.p.
      Hucker, 1746; Library Journal, 12/15/46

1117 Wang, Huo. Chieh Chen-Kuo, Guerilla Hero and Coal Miner.
C   Peking: Foreign Languages Press, 1961. 122 pp.

1118 Wang, Wen-shih. The Night of the Snowstorm. Peking: Foreign
C   Languages Press, 1961. 222 pp. Hand catalog. o.p.

1119 Wang, Yuan-chien. An Ordinary Labourer. Peking: Foreign
C   Languages Press, 1961. 183 pp. 64-33730.

1120 Wu, Hung-tsao. New Chinese Writing. Taipei: Heritage Press,
C   1962. 170 pp.

1121 Yang, I. The Bright Future. tr. by Tang Sheng. Peking:
C   Foreign Languages Press, 1958. 105 pp. Hand catalog.

1122 Yang, I. Uncle Kao, by Ouyang Shan (pseud.). tr. by Kuo Mei-
C   hua. Peking: Foreign Languages Press, 1957. 296 pp.
      57-48991.

1123 Yang, Shuo. A Thousand Miles of Lovely Land. tr. by Yuan
C   Ko-chia. Peking: Foreign Languages Press, 1957. 236 pp.
      57-40848. o.p.

1124 Yeh, Chun-chan, tr. Three Seasons and Other Stories. Lon-
C   don: Staples Press, 1947. 136 pp. Hand catalog. o.p.

1125 Yeh, Shao-chun. Schoolmaster Ni Huan-chih; Novel. tr. by A. C.
B   Barnes. Peking: Foreign Languages Press, 1958. 383 pp.
      59-31782. o.p.

1126 The Young Coal-Miner and Other Stories, by Contemporary Chinese
C   Writers. Peking: Foreign Languages Press, 1958. 176 pp.
      59-24097. o.p.

1127 Yu, Ho-lin. Harvest, by Yeh Tzu (pseud.). tr. by Tang Sheng
C   and Ma Ching-chun. Peking: Foreign Languages Press, 1960.
      183 pp. 61-28139.

1128 Yuan, Chia-hua, ed. and tr. Contemporary Chinese Short Stories.
B   N.Y.: Carrington, 1946. 169 pp. A48-5659. o.p.

LANGUAGE AND LITERATURE
LITERATURE
MODERN PERIOD
POETRY

1129 Acton, Harold Mario Mitchell. Modern Chinese Poetry. London:
C   Duckworth, 1936. 176 pp. 36-23555. o.p.

1130 Alley, Rewi, ed. and tr. Poems of Revolt; Some Chinese Voices
C   Over the Last Century. Peking: New World Press, 1962.
      228 pp. 64-30877. o.p.

1131 Cheng, Ch'i-yu. New China in Verse. Berkeley, Calif.: Gil-
C   lick Press, 1944. 120 pp. 44-30097. o.p.

1132 Hsu, Kai-yu, ed. and tr. Twentieth Century Chinese Poetry,
A   an Anthology. Garden City, N.Y.: Doubleday, 1963. 434 pp.
      63-7725.
      JAOS, 1-3/64; Library Journal, 4/15/63; Pacific Affairs,
      Fall/63

1133 New Chinese Poetry. tr. by Yu Kwang-chung. Taipei: Heritage
C   Press, 1960. 94 pp. Hand catalog.
      JAS, 11/61

1134 Payne, Pierre Stephen Robert, ed. Contemporary Chinese Poetry,
C   an Anthology. London: Routledge, 1947. 168 pp.
      A48-4463. o.p. (M-University).
      Hucker, 1747

1135 Wang, Chao-ming. Poems of Wang Ching-wei. tr. by Seyuan
C   Shu. London: Allen & Unwin, 1938. 96 pp. 39-757. o.p.

LANGUAGE AND LITERATURE
LITERATURE
MODERN PERIOD
DRAMA

1136 Ho, Ching-chih. The White-Haired Girl; An Opera in Five Acts.
B   tr. by Yang Hsien-yi and Gladys Yang. Peking: Foreign Lan-
      guages Press, 1954. 97 pp. 55-29783. o.p.
      AUFS, 1129; Hucker, 1758

1137 Hu, K'o. Locust Tree Village; A Play in Five Acts. Peking:
C   Foreign Languages Press, 1961. 126 pp. NUC 63-23461.

1138 Kuo, Mo-jo. Chu Yuan, a Play in Five Acts. tr. by Yang
C   Hsien-yi and Gladys Yang. Peking: Foreign Languages
      Press, 1953. 126 pp. 55-32878.
      AUFS, 1132

1139 Shen, Tuan-hsien. The Test, a Play in Five Acts. tr. by Ying
C   Yu. Peking: Foreign Languages Press, 1956. 107 pp. Hand
      catalog.

1140 Tien, Han. Kuan Han-ching: a Play. Peking: Foreign Languages
C   Press, 1961. 134 pp. Hand catalog.

1141 Tien, Han, ed. The White Snake, a Peking Opera. tr. by
C   Yang Hsien-yi and Gladys Yang. Peking: Foreign Languages
      Press, 1957. 79 pp. Hand catalog. o.p.

1142 Tsogtnarin. Golden Eagle. Translation of Chin Ying, a Play.
C   Peking: Foreign Languages Press, 1961. 100 pp. NUC 64-46554.

1143 Tuan, Cheng-pin. Taming the Dragon and the Tiger; A Play in
C   Six Scenes. by Tuan Cheng-pin and Tu Shih-tsun. tr. by
     A. C. Barnes. Peking: Foreign Languages Press, 1961.
     106 pp. Hand catalog.

1144 Wan, Chia-pao. Bright Skies, by Tsao Yu, pseud. tr. by Cheng
B   Pei-chi. Peking: Foreign Languages Press, 1960. 127 pp.
     Hand catalog.

1145 Wan, Chia-pao. Sunrise; A Play in Four Acts. tr. by A. C.
B   Barnes. Peking: Foreign Languages Press, 1960. 189 pp.
     Hand catalog. o.p.

1146 Wan, Chia-pao. Thunderstorm; A Play by Tsao Yu. tr. by Wang
B   Tso-liang and A. C. Barnes. 2d ed. Peking: Foreign Lan-
     guages Press, 1964. 164 pp. NUC 66-91168. o.p.

LANGUAGE AND LITERATURE
LITERATURE
MODERN PERIOD
HISTORY AND CRITICISM

1147 Birch, Cyril, ed. Chinese Communist Literature. N.Y.:
A   Praeger, 1963. 254 pp. 63-18538.
     Library Journal, 8/63

1148 Boven, Henri Van. Histoire de la Litterature Chinoise
B   Moderne. Peiping: Catholic University, 1946. 187 pp.
     49-15732. o.p.

1149 Chao, Chung. The Communist Program for Literature and Art
C   in China. Kowloon: Union Research Institute, 1955.
     157 pp. 56-349.
     Hucker, 1415; FEQ, 8/56

1150 Chou, En-lai, et al. The People's New Literature: Four
C   Reports at the First All-China Conference of Writers
     and Artists. Peking: Cultural Press, 1950. 136 pp. o.p.

1151 Chou, Yang. China's New Literature and Art; Essays and
C   Addresses. Peking: Foreign Languages Press, 1954. 156 pp.
     57-35757. o.p.

1152 Chou, Yang. A Great Debate on the Literary Front. Appendix:
C   Clear the Road and Advance Boldly! by Shao Chuan-lin.
     tr. by Yang Hsien-yi and Gladys Yang. Peking: Foreign
     Languages Press, 1958. 72 pp. 59-22364.

1153 Fokkema, D. W. Literary Doctrine in China and Soviet Influ-
A   ence, 1956-1960. The Hague: Mouton, 1965. 296 pp. 65-23876.
     JAS, 8/66

1154 Goldman, Merle. Literary Dissent in Communist China.
A   Cambridge, Mass.: Harvard University Press, 1967.
     343 pp. (Harvard East Asian Series, 29). 67-17311.
     Choice, 5/68; JAS, 5/68

1155 Hsia, Chih-tsing. A History of Modern Chinese Fiction, 1917-
A   1957. with appendix on Taiwan by Tsi-an Hsia. New Haven,
     Conn.: Yale University Press, 1961. 662 pp. 60-13273.
     Hucker, 1713; JAS, 11/61; Library Journal, 12/15/60

1156 Hsia, Tsi-an. The Gate of Darkness, Studies on the Leftist
B   Literary Movement in China. Seattle: University of
     Washington Press, 1968. 266 pp. 68-8510.

1157 Hsiao, Ch'ien. Etching of a Tormented Age; A Glimpse of Con-
C   temporary Chinese Literature. London: Allen & Unwin,
     1942. 48 pp. A42-3665 rev. o.p.

1158 Huang, Sung-k'ang. Lu Hsun and the New Culture Movement
C   of Modern China. Amsterdam: Djambatan, 1957. 158 pp.
     58-33802.
     JAS, 2/59

1159 Krebsova, Berta. Lu Sun, Sa Vie et Son Oeuvre. Prague: Acad-
C   emie Tchecoslavaque des Sciences, 1953. 111 pp. 56-17185.

1160 Lang, Olga. Pa Chin and His Writings; Chinese Youth Between
A   the Two Revolutions. Cambridge, Mass.: Harvard
     University Press, 1967. 402 pp. (Harvard East Asian
     Series, 28). 67-17314.
     Choice, 11/68; JAS, 5/68; AHR, 4/68; TLS, 2/29/68

1161 Monsterleet, Jean. Sommets de la Litterature Chinoise Con-
C   temporaine. Paris: Domat, 1953. 167 pp. 53-33054.

1162 Prusek, Jaroslav. Die Literatur Des Befreiten China und
C   Ihre Volkstraditionen. tr. by Pavel Eisner und Ubers von
     Wilhelm Gampert. Prague: Artia, 1955. 736 pp. 56-3856.

1163 Prusek, Jaroslav, ed. Studies in Modern Chinese Literature
C   Berlin: Akadamie-Verlag, 1964. 179 pp. NUC 66-2065.
     JAS, 5/66

1164 Schyns, Joseph. 1500 Chinese Novels and Plays. Kentfield,
C   Calif.: Gregg International, 1965 (orig. pub. in Peking,
     1948). 546 pp. NUC 66-92546. (R).
     Hucker, 1722

1165 Scott, Adolphe Clarence. Literature and the Arts in Twentieth
A   Century China. Gloucester, Mass.: Peter Smith, 1968 (orig.
     pub. by Doubleday, 1963). 212 pp. 68-3339. (R).

1166 Scott, Adolphe Clarence. Mei Lan-fang, Leader of the Pear Gar-
B   den. N.Y.: Oxford, 1959. 139 pp. 60-16031.
     Hucker, 1721; JAS, 5/61

1167 Tagore, Amitendranath. Literary Debates in Modern China,
B   1918-1937. Tokyo: Centre for East Asian Cultural Studies
     1967. 280 pp. (East Asian Cultural Studies Series,
     No. 11). NUC 68-69915.
     JAS, 5/68

1168 Ting, I. A Short History of Modern Chinese Literature by Ting
C   Yi. Peking: Foreign Languages Press, 1959. 310 pp.
     60-31434. o.p.
     Hucker, 1741

1169 Yang, I-fan. The Case of Hu Feng. Hong Kong: Union Research
C   Institute, 1956. 169 pp. 57-35727.
     Hucker, 1740

PHILOSOPHY AND RELIGION
GENERAL

1170 Briere, O. Fifty Years of Chinese Philosophy, 1898-1948. ed.,
A   with intro., by Dennis J. Doolin. tr. from French by Laur-
     ence G. Thompson. N.Y.: Praeger, 1965 (orig. pub. by Allen
     & Unwin, 1956). 159 pp. 65-21106. (R).
     Hucker, 1328; Choice, 9/66; JAS, 8/57; JAOS, 1-3/57

1171 Chan, Wing-tsit. Religious Trends in Modern China. N.Y.:
A   Columbia University Press, 1953. 327 pp. (American Council
     of Learned Societies; Lectures on the History of Religions,
     n.s. 3). 53-7012. (M-University).
     AUFS, 582; Hucker, 1331; FEQ, 11/53

1172 Chou, I-ch'ing. La Philosophie Chinoise, par Chow Yih-ching.
C   Paris: Presses Universitaires, 1956. 126 pp. Hand catalog.

1173 Creel, Herrlee Glessner. Chinese Thought, from Confucius to
B   Mao Tse-tung. N.Y.: New American Library, 1960 (orig. pub.
     by University of Chicago, 1953). 240 pp. 53-10054. (R).
     AUFS, 585; Hucker, 1044; FEQ, 8/55; Am. Anthropologist,
     4/54; Pacific Affairs, 12/53; TLS, 11/5/54

1174 East-West Philosophers' Conference. The Chinese Mind; Essen-
B   tials of Chinese Philosophy and Culture. ed. by Charles
     A. Moore, with the assistance of Aldyth V. Morris. Hono-
     lulu: East-West Center Press, 1967. 402 pp. 66-24011.
     JAS, 8/68; Library Journal, 1/1/68

1175 Feng, Yu-lan. A History of Chinese Philosophy, by Fung Yu-lan.
A   tr. by Derk Bodde. Princeton, N.J.: Princeton University
     Press, 1952-53. 2 v. A52-9807 rev. o.p.
     AUFS, 587; Hucker, 1046; FEQ, 8/53, 5/54

1176 Granet, Marcel. La Pensee Chinoise. Paris: La Renaissance
B   du Livre, 1934. 614 pp. 34-13974.

1177 Groot, Jan Jakob Maria de. The Religious System of China; Its
C   Ancient Forms, Evolution, History and Present Aspect, Manners,
     Customs and Social Institutions Connected Therewith. N.Y.:
     Paragon, 1964 (orig. pub. by Brill, 1892-1910). 6 v.
     NUC 65-90096. (R).
     Hucker, 1059

1178 Groot, Jan Jakob Maria de. Sectarianism and Religious Perse-
C   cution in China. N.Y.: Paragon, 1963 (orig. pub. by Johan-
     nes Muller, 1903-04). 2 v. NUC 65-51769. (R).
     Hucker, 1071

1179 Hughes, Ernest Richard, ed. and tr. Chinese Philosophy in
A   Classical Times. N.Y.: Dutton, 1954. 336 pp. 54-3630.
       AUFS, 596; Hucker, 1051

1180 Kuan, Chung. Kuan-tzu; A Repository of Early Chinese Thought.
C   A Translation and Study of Twelve Chapters, by W. Allyn
       Rickett. fore. by Derke Bodde. Hong Kong: Hong Kong Uni-
       versity Press, 1965- 66-4314.
       Choice, 1/67; TLS, 12/1/66

1181 Kwok, Danny Wynn Ye. Scientism in Chinese Thought, 1900-1950.
C   New Haven, Conn.: Yale University Press, 1965. 231 pp.
       (Yale Historical Publications, Miscellany, 82). 65-22330.
       Choice, 7-8/66; JAS, 11/66; Library Journal, 12/1/65; TLS,
       4/21/66

1182 Mo, Ti. The Ethical and Political Works of Motse. tr. from
C   original Chinese by Yi-Pao Mei. London: A. Probsthain, 1929.
       275 pp. 30-4133. o.p.
       AUFS, 600; Hucker, 1221

1183 Nivison, David S. The Life and Thought of Chang Hsueh-ch'eng
B   (1738-1801). Stanford, Calif.: Stanford University
       Press, 1966. 336 pp. (Studies in Civilization of Eastern
       Asia). 65-13112.
       Choice, 9/66; JAS, 11/67; JAOS, 10-12/67; Library Journal,
       11/15/65; TLS, 9/22/66

1184 Soothill, William Edward. The Three Religions of China; Lectures
B   Delivered at Oxford. 3d ed. N.Y.: Oxford, 1930. 271 pp.
       24-13494. o.p.
       AUFS, 604; Hucker, 1052

1185 Waley, Arthur. Three Ways of Thought in Ancient China. Gar-
B   den City, N.Y.: Doubleday, 1956. 216 pp. 56-5973.
       AUFS, 607; Hucker, 1132; JAOS, 3/41

1186 Weber, Max. The Religion of China: Confucianism and Taoism.
A   tr. and ed. by Hans H. Gerth. with an intro. by C. K. Yang.
       N.Y.: Macmillan, 1964. 308 pp. 64-9025.
       AUFS, 609; Hucker, 1106; JAS, 5/65; FEQ, 5/52

1187 Wright, Arthur F., ed. Studies in Chinese Thought. Chicago:
B   University of Chicago Press, 1953. 317 pp. 53-13533.
       AUFS, 612; Hucker, 1064; FEQ, 5/55; AHR, 7/54; Ann. Am.
       Acad., 7/54

1188 Yang, Ch'ing-k'un. Religion in Chinese Society; A Study of Con-
A   temporary Social Functions of Religion and Some of Their
       Historical Factors. Berkeley: University of California
       Press, 1961. 473 pp. 61-7520
       JAS, 8/62

PHILOSOPHY AND RELIGION
CONFUCIANISM

1189 Bruce, Joseph Percy. Chu Hsi and His Masters; An Introduction
C   to Chu Hsi and the Sung School of Chinese Philosophy. Lon-
       don: A. Probsthain, 1923. 336 pp. 23-11243. o.p. (M-
       University).
       AUFS, 614

1190 Chang, Chia-sen. The Development of Neo-Confucian Thought,
C   by Carsun Chang. N.Y.: Bookman, 1957- 58-177.
       Hucker, 1139; JAS, 11/58, 11/63

1191 Chang, Chia-sen. Wang Yang-ming: the Idealist Philosopher of
C   Sixteenth-Century China by Carsun Chang. Jamaica, N.Y.:
       St. John's University Press, 1962. 102 pp. 62-12341.
       JAOS, 7-9/62

1192 Chou, I-ch'ing. La Philosophie Morale dans le Neo-Confu-
C   cianisme (Tcheou Touen-yi) par Chow Yi-ching. Paris:
       Presses Universitaires, 1954. 230 pp. A54-3489 rev.
       Hucker, 1153; FEQ, 11/54

1193 Chu, Hsi. The Philosophy of Human Nature, by Chu Hsi. tr. from
B   Chinese with notes by J. Percy Bruce. London: A. Probsthain,
       1922. 44 pp. 23-7674 rev. 2. o.p.
       Hucker, 1148

1194 Chu, Hsi, comp. Reflections of Things at Hand; The Neo-
B   Confucian Anthology. N.Y.: Columbia University Press,
       1967. 441 pp. 65-22548.

1195 Chung-yung. The Conduct of Life; or, The Universal Order of
C   Confucius; A Translation of One of the Four Confucian Books
       Hitherto Known as The Doctrine of the Mean by Ku Hung Ming.
       London: Murray, dist. by Paragon, 1908. 60 pp. (Wisdom

of the East Series). W9-170. o.p. (M-University).

1196 Confucius. The Analects of Confucius. tr. and annotated by
A   Arthur Waley. N.Y.: Hillary House, 1964 (orig. pub. in
       1936). 268 pp. 39-5047. (R).
       AUFS, 620; Hucker, 1120; J. Philosophy, 9/28/39

1197 Confucius. The Analects of Confucius; or, The Conversations of
B   Confucius with His Disciples and Certain Others. tr. into
       English by William Edward Soothill. ed. by Lady Hosie.
       London: Oxford, 1962 (orig. pub. in 1937). 254 pp. NUC
       68-38770. (R).
       Hucker, 1122

1198 Confucius. K'ung Tzu Chia Yu. The School Sayings of Confucius.
C   intro., tr. of sections 1-10 with critical notes by R. P.
       Kramers. Leiden: Brill, 1950. 406 pp. (Sinica Leidensia,
       7).
       Hucker, 1126

1199 Creel, Herrlee Glessner. Confucius and the Chinese Way.
B   N.Y.: Harper, 1960 (orig. pub. by John Day, 1949 under
       the title Confucius, the Man and the Myth). 363 pp.
       60-5492. (R).
       AUFS, 625; Hucker, 170; FEQ, 2/50; AHR, 10/49; JAOS, 7-9/50

1200 Dubs, Homer Hasenpflug. Hsuntze, the Moulder of Ancient Con-
C   fucianism. Taipei: Ch'eng-wen Publishing Co., dist. by
       Chinese Materials and Research Aids Service Center, 1966
       (orig. pub. by A. Probsthain, 1927). 308 pp. NUC 66-76897.
       (R).
       AUFS, 626; Hucker, 1136; JAOS, 3/29

1201 Graham, Angus Charles. Two Chinese Philosophers: Ch'eng Ming-tao
B   and Ch'eng Yi-ch'uan. London: Lund Humphries, 1958. 195 pp.
       59-33740. o.p.
       Hucker, 1149; JAS, 11/59; JAOS, 4-6/59

1202 Hsun-tze. The Works of Hsuntze. tr. from Chinese with notes by
C   Homer H. Dubs. Taipei: Ch'eng-wen Publishing Co., dist. by
       Chinese Materials and Research Aids Service Center, 1966
       (orig. pub. by A. Probsthain, 1928). 336 pp. NUC 68-42525.
       (R).
       AUFS, 631, Hucker, 1137

1203 Huang, Hsiu-chi. Lu Hsiang-shan...a Twelfth Century Chinese
C   Idealist Philosopher. New Haven, Conn.: American Orien-
       tal Society, 1944. 116 pp. 45-5004. o.p.
       Hucker, 1155; FEQ, 11/45

1204 I Ching. The I Ching; or, Book of Changes. The Richard Wil-
C   helm translation rendered into English by Cary F. Baynes.
       3d ed. Princeton, N.J.: Princeton University Press,
       1967. 740 pp. (Bollingen Series, Vol. 19). 67-24740.
       AUFS, 597; Choice, 10/68; Hucker, 1533; JAOS, 10-12/50

1205 I Ching. The Yi King. tr. by James Legge. ed. with new intro.
C   by Ch'u Chai and Winberg Chai. New Hyde Park, N.Y.: Uni-
       versity Books, 1964 (orig. pub. by Clarendon, 1882). 448 pp.
       (Sacred Books of the East, Vol. 16). 64-25866. (R).
       Choice, 5/65

1206 Kaizuka, Shigeki. Confucius. tr. from Japanese by Geoffrey
C   Bownas. N.Y.: Hillary House, 1956. 191 pp. A57-3058.
       Hucker, 171

1207 Legge, James, ed. and tr. The Chinese Classics. tr. into Eng-
B   lish, with preliminary essays and explanatory notes. Hong
       Kong: Hong Kong University Press, 1960 (orig. pub. by
       Trubner, 1875-1909). 5 v. 61-4012. (R). (M-University).
       Hucker, 1530; JAS, 2/63

1208 Li, Chi. The Li Ki. tr. by James Legge. Delhi: Motilal Banar-
C   sidass, 1966 (orig. pub. by Clarendon, 1885). 2 v. (Sacred
       Books of the East, Vols. 27-28). 32-15906. (R).

1209 Mencius: Mencius. A New Translation Arranged and Annotated for
B   the General Reader by W. A. C. H. Dobson. Toronto: Uni-
       versity of Toronto Press, 1963. 215 pp. 63-23889.
       JAS, 5/64; JAOS, 9-12/63

1210 Nivison, David S., ed. Confucianism in Action. contrib. by
B   William Theodore De Bary and others. Stanford, Calif.:
       Stanford University Press, 1969 (orig. pub. in 1959).
       390 pp. (Studies in the Civilizations of Eastern Asia).
       59-7433. (R).
       Sup. 61, 2804; Hucker, 1098; JAS, 8/60; AHR, 4/60; Ann. Am.
       Acad., 1/60; Library Journal, 6/15/59; Pacific Affairs, 3/60

1211 Richards, Ivor Armstrong. Mencius on the Mind; Experiments in
B   Multiple Definition. London: Paul, Trench, Trubner, 1932.
     131 pp. 32-21317.
     Hucker, 1128; JAOS, 9/33

1212 Sargent, Galen Eugene. Tchou Hi contre le Bouddhisme. Paris:
C   Imprimerie Nationale, 1955. 158 pp.
     Hucker, 1152

1213 Schwartz, Benjamin Isadore. In Search of Wealth and Power:
B   Yen Fu and the West. Cambridge, Mass.: Harvard Univer-
     sity Press, 1964. 298 pp. (Harvard East Asian Series,
     16). 64-16069.
     Sup. 65, 3105; Choice, 7-8/64; JAS, 11/64; Am. Pol. Sci. R.,
     3/65; JAOS, 7-9/65; Library Journal, 7/64; Pacific Affairs,
     Spring/65; Pol. Sci. Q., 12/65; TLS, 11/26/64

1214 Shryock, John Knight. The Origin and Development of the State
C   Cult of Confucius; An Introductory Study. N.Y.: Paragon,
     1966 (orig. pub. by Century, 1932). 298 pp. 66-21765. (R).
     Hucker, 1168; Am. Pol. Sci. R., 8/32; J. Philosophy, 11/10/32

1215 Ssu shu. The Four Books: Confucian Analects, The Great Learning,
A   The Doctrine of the Mean, and The Works of Mencius. tr.
     by James Legge. N.Y.: Paragon, 1966 (orig. dist. by P. D.
     and Ione Perkins, 1930). 1014 pp. 66-16894. (R).

1216 Ta hsueh. The Great Learning & the Mean-in-Action. tr. from
B   Chinese by E. R. Hughes. N.Y.: Dutton, 1943. 176 pp.
     43-1988. o.p.
     AUFS, 641

1217 Wang, Ch'ang-chih. La Philosophie Morale de Wang Yang-ming...
C   par Wang Tch'ang-tche. Paris: Geuthner, 1936. 217 pp.
     (Varietes Sinologiques, 63). 42-43210.
     Hucker, 1162

1218 Wang, Shou-jen. Instructions for Practical Living and Other
A   Neo-Confucian Writings, by Wang Yang-ming. tr. by Wing-
     tsit Chan. N.Y.: Columbia University Press, 1963. 358 pp.
     62-16688.
     JAS, 11/64

1219 Wilhelm, Hellmut. Change; Eight Lectures on the I Ching. tr.
C   from German by Cary F. Baynes. Princeton, N.J.: Princeton
     University Press, 1960. 111 pp. (Bollingen Series, Vol.
     62). 60-11791.
     Hucker, 1532; JAS, 8/61; JAOS, 1-3/61

1220 Wright, Arthur F., ed. The Confucian Persuasion. contrib. by
B   James Cahill and others. Stanford, Calif.: Stanford Uni-
     versity Press, 1969 (orig. pub. in 1960). 390 pp. (Studies
     in the Civilizations of Eastern Asia). 60-8561. (R).
     Sup. 61, 2808; Hucker, 1097; JAS, 5/61; JAOS, 4-6/62

PHILOSOPHY AND RELIGION
TAOISM

1221 Chuang-tsu. Basic Writings. tr. by Burton Watson. N.Y.:
A   Columbia University Press, 1964. 148 pp. 64-21079.
     Choice, 12/65

1222 Chuang-tzu. A New Selected Translation with an Exposition of
A   the Philosophy of Kuo Hsiang, by Yu-lan Fung. 2d ed.
     N.Y.: Paragon, 1964 (orig. pub. by Commercial Press, 1933).
     164 pp. 64-18451. (R).
     AUFS, 643; Hucker, 1199

1223 Ho-Shang-Kung, pseud. Commentary on Lao-tse. tr. and annotated
C   by Eduard Erkes. Ascona: Artibus Asiae, 1958. 135 pp.
     Hand catalog.
     Hucker, 1192

1224 Lao-tzu. Tao Teh Ching. tr. by John C. H. Wu. ed. by Paul
B   K. T. Sih. Jamaica, N.Y.: St. John's University Press,
     1961. 115 pp. 60-16884.

1225 Lao-tzu. Tao Te Ching, the Book of the Way and Its Virtue.
C   tr. from Chinese by J. J. L. Duyvendak. London: Murray,
     1954. 172 pp. 54-4621. o.p.
     AUFS, 646; Hucker, 1186

1226 Lao-tzu. Tao Te Ching, a New Translation by Ch'u Ta-Kao.
B   5th ed. London: Allen & Unwin, 1959. 95 pp. A60-1769.
     o.p.
     Hucker, 1187

1227 Lao-tzu. The Way and Its Power; A Study of the Tao Te Ching
B   and Its Place in Chinese Thought, by Arthur Waley. N.Y.:
     Macmillan, 1956 (orig. pub. by Allen & Unwin, 1934). 262 pp.
     58-5092. (R).
     AUFS, 647; Hucker, 1185

1228 Lao-tzu. The Way of Lao Tzu. (Tao-te ching). tr. by Wing-tsit
A   Chan. N.Y.: Bobbs-Merrill, 1963. 285 pp. 62-21266.

1229 Lieh-tzu. The Book of Lieh-tzu. A New Translation by A. C.
C   Graham. London: Murray, dist. by Paragon, 1961. 183 pp.
     (Wisdom of the East Series). 62-51659.
     Hucker, 1203; JAS, 11/61

1230 Lieh-tzu. Taoist Teachings from the Book of Lieh Tzu. tr.
C   from Chinese with intro. and notes by Lionel Giles. 2d ed.
     London: Murray, dist. by Paragon, 1947. 121 pp. (Wisdom
     of the East Series). CA14-275p.
     Hucker, 1204

1231 Liu, Hsiang. Le Lie-sien Tchouan, Biographie Legendaires des
C   Immortels Taoistes de l'Antiquite. tr. and annotated by
     Max Kaltenmark. Peking: Centre d'Etudes Sinologiques de
     Pekin, 1953. 204 pp. o.p.
     Hucker, 1214

1232 The Texts of Taoism. tr. by James Legge. N.Y.: Julian Press,
C   1959. 790 pp. 58-14214. o.p.
     Hucker, 1184

1233 Welch, Holmes. The Parting of the Way; Lao Tzu and the Taoist
C   Movement. Boston: Beacon, 1957. 204 pp. 57-7729.
     AUFS, 652; Hucker, 1176; JAS, 11/58; Am. Soc. R., 8/57

PHILOSOPHY AND RELIGION
BUDDHISM

1234 Asvaghosa. The Awakening of Faith, Attributed to Asvaghosha.
B   tr. with commentary by Yoshita S. Hakeda. N.Y.: Columbia
     University Press, 1967. 128 pp. 67-13778.
     Choice, 5/68

1235 Beal, Samuel. A Catena of Buddhist Scriptures from the Chinese.
C   London: Trubner, 1871. 436 pp. 32-13515. o.p.
     AUFS, 654

1236 Beal, Samuel, tr. The Life of Hiuen-Tsiang by the Shaman Hwui Li.
C   new ed. N.Y.: Dutton, 1916. o.p.
     Hucker, 1273

1237 Burtt, Edwin Arthur, ed. The Teachings of the Compassionate
B   Buddha. N.Y.: New American Library, 1955. 247 pp. 55-5474.
     AUFS, 1552; Hucker, 1238; Silberman, 625

1238 Chao Lun. The Book of Chao, a Translation from the Original
C   Chinese. tr. by Walter Liebenthal. Peiping: Catholic Uni-
     versity, 1948. 195 pp. o.p.
     Hucker, 1295

1239 Ch'en, Kenneth Kuan Sheng. Buddhism in China, a Historical
A   Survey. Princeton, N.J.: Princeton University Press,
     1964. 560 pp. (Princeton Studies in the History of
     Religion, Council of the Humanities, The Virginia and
     Richard Stewart Memorial Lectures, 1). 63-23402.
     Sup. 65, 3088; Choice, 3/65; JAS, 8/65; JAOS, 7-9/65

1240 Chou, Hsiang-kuang. T'ai Hsu, His Life and Teachings. Alla-
C   habad: Indo-Chinese Literature Publications, 1957. 74 pp.
     58-43903. o.p.
     JAS, 8/58

1241 Demieville, Paul. La Concile de Lhasa; Une Controverse Sur
C   le Quitisme entre Bouddhistes de l'Inde et de la Chine
     au VIII Siecle de l'Ere Chretienne. Paris: Imprimerie
     Nationale, 1952- A55-689.

1242 Hui'neng. The Platform Sutra of the Sixth Patriach. tr. by
B   P. Yampolsky. N.Y.: Columbia University Press, 1967.
     272 pp. Hand catalog.
     JAS, 5/68

1243 Lankavatara-sutra. The Lankavatara Sutra; A Mahayana Text, Trans-
C   lated for the First Time from the Original Sanskrit by Dai-
     setz Teitaro Suzuki. N.Y.: Humanities, 1966 (orig. pub.
     by Routledge and Kegan Paul, 1956). 300 pp. 57-37460. (R).
     AUFS, 1575; Hucker, 1293; JAOS, 3/33

1244 Reichelt, Karl Ludvig. Truth and Tradition in Chinese Buddhism;
B   A Study of Chinese Mahayana Buddhism. tr. from Norwegian by

Kathrina Van Wagenen Bugge. Shanghai: Commercial Press, 1927. 330 pp. 28-8949. o.p.
Hucker, 1258

1245 Robinson, Richard H., tr. Chinese Buddhist Verse. N.Y.: Para-
C gon, 1966 (orig. pub. by Grove, 1954). 85 pp. 55-25496.
(R).
AUFS, 665; Hucker, 1297

1246 Robinson, Richard H. Early Madhyamika in India and China.
C Madison: University of Wisconsin Press, 1967. 347 pp.
66-22853.

1247 Saddharmapundarika. The Lotus of the Wonderful Law; or, The
B Lotus Gospel, by W. E. Soothill. Oxford: Clarendon, 1930.
275 pp. o.p. 30-31901. o.p. (M-University).
Hucker, 1292; JAOS, 6/31; TLS, 7/17/30

1248 Surangamasutra. The Surangama Sutra (leng Yen Ching); Chinese
C Rendering by Master Paramiti of Central North India at
Chih Chih Monastery, Canton, China, A.D. 705. tr. by
Upasaka Lu K'uan Yu (Charles Luk). N.Y.: Hillary House,
1966. 262 pp. 66-70040.
Choice, 4/67; JAS, 5/67

1249 Vasu-bandhau. Vijnaptimatratasiddhi, la Siddhi de Hiuan-Tsang.
C tr. and annotated by Louis de La Vallee Poussin. Paris:
Geuthner, 1928-1929. 2 v. 32-34323.

1250 Vasu-bandhu. Un Systeme de Philosophie Bouddhique. Materiaux
C pour L'Etude du Systeme Vijnaptimatra by Sylvain Levi. Paris:
Champion, 1932. 206 pp.

1251 Vasu-bandhu. Wei Shih Er shih Lun or the Treatise in Twenty
C Stanzas on Representation-Only, by Vasubandhu. tr. from
the Chinese version of Hsuan Tsang, Tripitaka Master of
the T'ang Dynasty, by Clarence H. Hamilton. N.Y.: Kraus,
1966 (orig. pub. by American Oriental Society, 1938).
82 pp. 39-16886. (R). (M-University).

1252 Wright, Arthur F. Buddhism in Chinese History. Stanford,
B Calif.: Stanford University Press, 1959. 144 pp. 59-7432.
AUFS, 671; Hucker, 1249; JAS, 11/59; JAOS, 10-12/59

**PHILOSOPHY AND RELIGION
OTHER RELIGIONS**

1253 Basic Writings of Mo Tzu, Hsun Tzu, and Han Fei Tzu. tr. by
B Burton Watson. N.Y.: Columbia University Press, 1967.
140 pp. 67-16170.
Choice, 11/67

1254 Ch'u, Yuan. The Nine Songs, a Study of Shamanism in Ancient
B China by Arthur Waley. London: Allen & Unwin, 1955. 64 pp.
55-28909.
AUFS, 584; Hucker, 1584; JAS, 11/56

1255 Dore, Henri. Researches into Chinese Superstitions. tr. from
C the French with notes, historical and explanatory, by M.
Kennelly. Taipei: Chinese Materials and Research Aids
Service Center (orig. pub. by T'usewei Press, 1914-).
11 v. in 5. 26-18204. (R).
Hucker, 1092

1256 Han, Fei. The Complete Works of Han Fei Tzu...A Classic of
B Chinese Legalism. tr. from Chinese with intro. and notes
by W. K. Liao. London: A. Probsthain, 1939- 41-11756.
o.p.
Hucker, 1228; JAS, 11/60

1257 Hodous, Lewis. Folkways in China. London: A. Probsthain,
C 1929. 248 pp. 29-12220. o.p.
Hucker, 1084; JAOS, 6/30

1258 Hu, Shih. The Development of the Logical Method in Ancient
B China. 2d ed. with intro. by Hyman Kublin. N.Y.: Para-
gon, 1963 (orig. pub. by Oriental, 1922). 187 pp. 63-21053.
(R). (M-University).
AUFS, 594; JAS, 11/64

1259 Mei, Yi-pao. Motse, the Neglected Rival of Confucius. London:
C A. Probsthain, 1934. 222 pp. 35-10340. o.p.
Hucker, 1220

1260 Tun, Li-ch'en. Annual Customs and Festivals in Peking As Recorded
C in the Yen-ching Sui-shih-chi. tr. and annotated by Derk
Bodde. 2d ed. rev. Hong Kong: Hong Kong University Press,
dist. by Oxford, 1965 (orig. pub. by Vetch, 1936). 147 pp.

65-8424. (R). (M-University).
Hucker, 1076

1261 Wang, Ch'ung. Lun-heng. tr. from Chinese and annotated by
C Alfred Forke. 2d ed. N.Y.: Paragon, 1962 (orig. pub. by
Luzac, 1907). 2 v. 63-411. (R).
Hucker, 1235

1262 White, William Charles. Chinese Jews; A Compilation of Matters
C Relating to the Jews of K'ai-feng Fu. 2d ed. N.Y.: Paragon,
1966 (orig. pub. by University of Toronto Press, 1942).
625 pp. 66-31664. (R).
Sup. 67, 3255; Hucker, 1301; JAOS, 10-12/67

**FINE ARTS AND ARCHITECTURE
GENERAL**

1263 Davidson, J. Leroy. The Lotus Sutra in Chinese Art; A Study in
C Buddhist Art to the Year 1000. New Haven, Conn.: Yale Uni-
versity Press, 1954. 105 pp. 54-5604. o.p.
Hucker, 1409; FEQ, 5/55; Library Journal, 9/1/54

1264 Grousset, Rene. Chinese Art and Culture. tr. by Haakon Che-
B valier. N.Y.: Orion, 1959. 331 pp. 59-13323. o.p.
Hucker, 1402; Library Journal, 1/15/60; Pacific Affairs,
9/60; TLS, 3/4/60

1265 Lee, Sherman E. and Wai-kam Ho. Chinese Art under the Mongols:
C the Yuan Dynasty (1279-1368). Cleveland: Cleveland
Museum of Art, 1968. 403 pp. 68-9276.

1266 Salmony, Alfred. Antler and Tongue; An Essay on Ancient Chi-
C nese Symbolism and Its Implications. Ascona: Artibus Asiae,
1954. 57 pp. (Artibus Asiae Supplementum XIII). 55-1320.
Hucker, 1510

1267 Sickman, Laurence C. The Art and Architecture of China. by
A Laurence Sickman and Alexander Soper. Baltimore: Penguin,
1956. 334 pp. 56-1125.
AUFS, 1018; Hucker, 1394; JAS, 11/56; Library Journal,
4/1/56

1268 Soper, Alexander Coburn. Literary Evidence for Early Buddhist
C Art in China. Ascona: Artibus Asiae, 1959. 296 pp. (Sup-
plementum XIX). A59-4696.
Hucker, 1408

1269 Speiser, Werner. The Art of China: Spirit and Society. tr. by
B George Lawrence. N.Y.: Crown, 1961. 256 pp. 61-10700.

1270 Sullivan, Michael. Chinese Art in the Twentieth Century.
B Berkeley: University of California Press, 1959. 110 pp.
59-16314. o.p.
Hucker, 1414; JAS, 5/60

1271 Sullivan, Michael. An Introduction to Chinese Art. Berkeley:
B University of California Press, 1961. 223 pp. 61-3831.
o.p.
Hucker, 1398; JAS, 2/62; JAOS, 1-3/62

1272 Sullivan, Michael. A Short History of Chinese Art. Berkeley:
A University of California Press, 1967. 279 pp. 67-21260.
Choice, 4/68; JAS, 5/68

1273 Vincent, Irene (Vongehr). The Sacred Oasis; Caves of the
B Thousand Buddhas, Tun Huang. Chicago: University of
Chicago Press, 1953. 114 pp. A53-5284. o.p.
Hucker, 1483; TLS, 2/26/54

1274 Watson, William. China Before the Han Dynasty. N.Y.: Praeger,
C 1962. 264 pp. 61-14105.
TLS, 9/21/62

1275 Willetts, William. Foundations of Chinese Art from Neolithic
A Pottery to Modern Architecture. N.Y.: McGraw-Hill, 1965.
456 pp. 64-66127.
Library Journal, 10/15/65

**FINE ARTS AND ARCHITECTURE
FINE ARTS**

1276 Bachhofer, Ludwig. A Short History of Chinese Art. N.Y.:
B Pantheon, 1946. 139 pp. 47-952. o.p.
AUFS, 1001; Hucker, 1400; FEQ, 5/48

1277 Barnard, Noel. Bronze Casting and Bronze Alloys in Ancient
C China. Canberra: Australian National University, 1961.
336 pp. 62-6942.

JAS, 5/62

1278 Bulling, A. The Meaning of China's Most Ancient Art; An Inter-
C   pretation of Pottery Patterns from Kansu (Ma Ch'ang and Pan-
      shan) and Their Development in the Shang, Chou and Han Peri-
      ods. Leiden: Brill, 1952. 150 pp. 53-29440.
      Hucker, 1513

1279 Chen, Chih-Mai. Chinese Calligraphers and their Art.
C   N.Y.: Cambridge, 1967. 286 pp. 65-22861.
      Choice, 10/67; JAS, 11/67; Library Journal, 12/1/67;
      TLS, 11/30/67

1280 Chiang, I. Chinese Calligraphy; An Introduction to Its Aesthetic
A   and Technique. fore. by Sir Herbert Read. 2d ed. London:
      Methuen, 1954. 230 pp. A55-2398.
      Hucker, 1486

1281 Feddersen, Martin. Chinese Decorative Art; A Handbook for
B   Collectors and Connoisseurs. 2d ed., rev. and enl. tr.
      by Arthur Lane. London: Faber & Faber, 1961. 286 pp.
      Hand catalog.

1282 Freer Gallery of Art, Washington D.C. The Freer Chinese
C   Bronzes, by John Alexander Pope and others. Washington:
      Smithsonian Institution, 1967- (Freer Gallery of Art,
      Oriental Studies, No. 7). 68-61307.

1283 Honey, William Bowyer. The Ceramic Art of China, and Other
A   Countries of the Far East. London: Faber & Faber, 1945.
      238 pp. 45-10141. o.p.
      AUFS, 1011; Hucker, 1431; Silberman, 848

1284 Jenyns, Soame. Later Chinese Porcelain; The Ch'ing Dynasty,
C   1644-1912. 2d ed. London: Faber & Faber, 1959. 111 pp.
      60-735.
      Hucker, 1434

1285 Jenyns, Soame. Ming Pottery and Porcelain. London: Faber
C   & Faber, 1953. 160 pp. 53-4516. o.p.
      Hucker, 1433

1286 Loehr, Max. Ritual Vessels of Bronze Age China. N.Y.: Asia
B   Society, dist. by New York Graphic, 1968. 183 pp.
      68-30798.

1287 Rudolph, Richard C. Han Tomb Art of West China: a Collection of
C   First- and Second-Century Reliefs by Richard C. Rudolph in
      collaboration with Wen Yu. Berkeley: University of Cali-
      fornia Press, 1951. 67 pp. 51-11148. o.p.
      Hucker, 1447; FEQ, 2/52

1288 Watson, William. Ancient Chinese Bronzes. London: Faber
B   & Faber, 1962. 117 pp. Hand catalog.
      JAS, 11/63

FINE ARTS AND ARCHITECTURE
FINE ARTS
PAINTING

1289 Acker, William Reynolds Beal. Some T'ang and Pre-T'ang Texts
C   on Chinese Painting. Leiden: Brill, 1954. 414 pp. 55-3283.
      Hucker, 1488

1290 Cahill, James. Chinese Painting. Geneva: Skira, 1960. 211 pp.
A   (Treasures of Asia). 60-15594.
      Sup. 61, 2790; Hucker, 1465; JAS, 5/61; JAOS, 1-3/62;
      Library Journal, 1/15/61; TLS, 3/10/61

1291 Cahill, James Francis. Fantastics and Eccentrics in Chinese
B   Painting. N.Y.: Asia Society, dist. by Abrams, 1967.
      122 pp. 67-16859.
      Choice, 9/67

1292 Chiang, I. The Chinese Eye, an Interpretation of Chinese Paint-
A   ing. 4th ed. London: Methuen, 1960 (orig. pub. in 1936).
      239 pp. Hand catalog. (R).
      Hucker, 1477; TLS, 11/23/35, 1/21/55

1293 Driscoll, Lucy. Chinese Calligraphy, by Lucy Driscoll and
B   Kenji Toda. 2d ed. N.Y.: Paragon, 1964 (orig. pub. by
      University of Chicago Press, 1935). 70 pp. 64-24329.
      (R).
      AUFS, 1005; Hucker, 1487; JAOS, 12/35

1294 Goepper, Roger. The Essence of Chinese Painting. tr. by Michael
A   Bullock. London: Lund Humphries, 1963. 244 pp. 65-829.
      o.p.

1295 Gray, Basil. Buddhist Cave Paintings at Tun-huang. Chicago:
C   University of Chicago Press, 1959. 86 pp. 59-5771. o.p.
      Hucker, 1482

1296 Gulik, Robert Hans van. Chinese Pictorial Art as Viewed by the
C   Connoisseur, Notes on the Means and Methods of Traditional
      Chinese Connoisseurship of Pictorial Art, Based upon a
      Study of the Art of Mounting Scrolls in China and Japan.
      Roma: Isituto Italiano per il Medio ed Estremo Oriente,
      1958. 537 pp. 59-31931.
      Hucker, 1473

1297 Kuo, Hsi. An Essay on Landscape Painting by Kuo Hsi. tr. by
B   Shio Sakanishi. London: Murray, dist. by Paragon, 1935.
      64 pp. (Wisdom of the East Series). 36-7175.
      Hucker, 1491

1298 Kuo, Jo-hsu. Experiences in Painting (T'u-hua chien-wen chih).
C   An Eleventh Century History of Chinese Painting, Together
      with the Chinese Text in Facsimile. tr. and annotated by
      Alexander Coburn Soper. Washington: American Council of
      Learned Societies, 1951. 216 pp. 52-190.
      Hucker, 1489

1299 Lee, Sherman E. Chinese Landscape Painting. 2d ed. rev. Cleve-
B   land: Cleveland Museum of Art, dist. by Abrams, 1962. 169 pp.
      62-11141.

1300 Lee, Sherman E. Streams and Mountains Without End; A Northern
C   Sung Handscroll and Its Significance in the History of Early
      Chinese Painting, by Sherman E. Lee and Wen Fong. Ascona:
      Artibus Asiae, 1955. 57 pp. (Supplementum XIV). A56-6593.
      Hucker, 1474; FEQ, 2/56

1301 Li, Chu-tsing. The Autumn Colors on the Ch'iao and Hua
C   Mountains; A Landscape by Chao Meng-fu. Ascona: Artibus
      Asiae, 1965. 109 pp. (Supplementum XXI). 66-4539.
      JAOS, 7-9/65

1302 Lin, Yutang. The Chinese Theory of Art, Translations From the
B   Masters of Chinese Art. N.Y.: Putnam, 1967. 244 pp.
      67-21121.
      JAS, 2/68; Library Journal, 2/1/68; TLS, 11/16/67

1303 Loehr, Max. Chinese Landscape Woodcuts; From an Imperial
C   Commentary to the Tenth-century Printed Edition of the
      Buddhist Canon. Cambridge, Mass.: Harvard University
      Press, 1968. 114 pp. 67-22868.
      Choice, 11/68; Library Journal, 6/15/68

1304 Rowley, George. Principles of Chinese Painting. 2d ed. Prince-
A   ton, N.J.: Princeton University Press, 1959. 85 pp. 60-325.
      Hucker, 1472; FEQ, 2/48

1305 Sakanishi, Shio, tr. The Spirit of the Brush, Being the Out-
C   look of Chinese Painters on Nature, from Eastern China
      to Five Dynasties, A.D. 317-960. N.Y.: Grove, 1939.
      108 pp. 39-8538 rev. o.p.
      Hucker, 1490

1306 Siren, Osvald. The Chinese on the Art of Painting: Translations
C   and Comments. N.Y.: Schocken, 1963 (orig. pub. by Vetch,
      1936). 261 pp. 63-20262. (R).
      Hucker, 1492; JAOS, 12/36

1307 Siren, Osvald. Chinese Painting: Leading Masters and Principles.
B   N.Y.: Ronald, 1956- A57-1105.
      AUFS, 1020; Hucker, 1466

1308 Sullivan, Michael. The Birth of Landscape Painting in China.
C   Berkeley: University of California Press, 1962. 213 pp.
      60-16863.
      JAS, 8/63; JAOS, 4-6/62; Library Journal, 5/1/62; TLS,
      6/29/62

1309 Swann, Peter C. Chinese Painting. N.Y.: Universe Books, 1958.
B   153 pp. 58-11096. o.p.
      Hucker, 1470; JAS, 5/60; Library Journal, 12/1/58; TLS,
      3/13/59

1310 Sze, Mai-Mai. The Tao of Painting, a Study of the Ritual Dis-
B   position of Chinese Painting. 2d ed. Princeton, N.J.:
      Princeton University Press, 1963. 587 pp. (Bollingen

Series, Vol. 49). 64-2864.
Hucker, 1471; Library Journal, 5/1/57

1311 Waley, Arthur. An Introduction to the Study of Chinese Paint-
B   ing. N.Y.: Grove, 1958. 261 pp. 58-6228. o.p.
      AUFS, 1022; Hucker, 1469

FINE ARTS AND ARCHITECTURE
FINE ARTS
SCULPTURE

1312 Siren, Osvald. Chinese Sculpture from the Fifth to the Four-
B   teenth Century; Over 900 Specimens in Stone, Bronze, Lacquer
      and Wood, Principally from Northern China. London: Benn,
      1925. 4 v. 25-17954. o.p.
      Hucker, 1456

FINE ARTS AND ARCHITECTURE
ARCHITECTURE

1313 Boyd, Andrew Charles Hugh. Chinese Architecture and Town Plan-
B   ning, 1500 B.C.-A.D. 1911. Chicago: University of Chicago
      Press, 1962. 166 pp. 63-9735.
      JAS, 8/63; Arch. Forum, 4/63; TLS, 11/30/62

1314 Prip-Moller, Johannes. Chinese Buddhist Monasteries; Their
C   Plan and Its Function as a Setting for Buddhist Monastic
      Life. 2d ed. N.Y.: Oxford, 1967. 396 pp. 68-2487.
      JAS, 11/68

1315 Siren, Osvald. Gardens of China. N.Y.: Ronald, 1949. 141 pp.
B   Agr 49-79.
      Hucker, 1501; FEQ, 8/50; JAOS, 10-12/51; Library Journal,
      9/15/49

PERFORMING ARTS

1316 Alley, Rewi. Peking Opera; An Introduction Through Pictures
C   by Eva Siao. Peking: New World Press, 1957. 99 pp.
      58-16732. o.p.

1317 Chao, Mei-po. The Yellow Bell; A Brief Sketch of the History of
B   Chinese Music. Baldwin, Md.: Barberry Hill, 1934. 61 pp.
      34-40479. o.p.
      Hucker, 1777

1318 Grey, Beryl. Through the Bamboo Curtain. N.Y.: Reynal, dist.
C   by Morrow, 1966. 127 pp. 66-5581.
      Choice, 3/67

1319 Gulik, Robert Hans van. The Lore of the Chinese Lute; An Essay
C   in Ch'in Ideology. Tokyo: Sophia University, 1940. 224 pp.
      41-12381.
      Hucker, 1778; JAOS, 12/41

1320 Reinhard, Kurt. Chinesische Musik. Eisenach und Kassel:
C   Erich Roth, 1956. 246 pp. 57-17248.
      Hucker, 1774

1321 Soulie, Charles George. Theatre et Musique Modernes en Chine,
B   Avec une Etude Technique de la Musique Chinoise et Trans-
      cription pour Piano par Andre Gailhard. Paris: Geuthner,
      1926. 195 pp. 28-24553.
      Hucker, 1779

EDUCATION AND MASS COMMUNICATION

1322 Biggerstaff, Knight. The Earliest Modern Government Schools
A   in China. Ithaca, N.Y.: Cornell University Press, 1961.
      276 pp. 61-14951.
      Sup. 63, 2903; JAS, 8/62

1323 Buck, Mrs. Pearl Sydenstricker. Tell the People, Talks with
C   James Yen About the Mass Education Movement. N.Y.: John
      Day, 1945. 84 pp. 45-2762. o.p.

1324 Chao, Chung. Students in Mainland China, by Chao Chung and Yang
C   I-fan. 3d ed. Kowloon: Union Research Institute, 1958.
      139 pp. Hand catalog.
      Hucker, 1966

1325 Ch'en, Li-fu. Chinese Education During the War (1937-1942) by
C   Chen Li-fu. Chungking: Ministry of Education, 1943. 41 pp.
      43-18642. o.p.
      Hucker, 1941

1326 Chi, Tung-wei. Education for the Proletariat in Communist
B   China. Kowloon: Union Research Institute, 1954. 73 pp.
      55-39760.
      Hucker, 1968

1327 Chung, Shih. Higher Education in Communist China. Kowloon:
C   Union Research Institute, 1953. 97 pp. 55-41537.
      Hucker, 1967

1328 Franke, Wolfgang. The Reform and Abolition of the Traditional
A   Chinese Examination System. Cambridge, Mass.: Harvard Uni-
      versity Press, 1960. 100 pp. 61-1281.

1329 Fraser, Stewart, ed. Chinese Communist Education; Records of
A   the First Decade. Nashville, Tenn.: Vanderbilt University
      Press, 1965. 542 pp. 64-18962.
      Sup. 67, 3236; Choice, 10/65; JAS, 5/66; Am. Pol. Sci. R.,
      12/65; Library Journal, 7/65

1330 Galt, Howard Spilman. The Development of Chinese Educational
B   Theory; The Historical Development of the Theory of Educa-
      tion in China to the Close of the Han Dynasty, A.D. 220.
      Shanghai: Commercial Press, 1929. 180 pp. A32-2590. o.p.

1331 Galt, Howard Spilman. A History of Chinese Educational Insti-
B   tutions. London: A. Probsthain, 1952- 52-4827.
      Hucker, 1528; FEQ, 11/52

1332 Gregg, Alice Henrietta. China and Educational Autonomy; The
B   Changing Role of the Protestant Educational Missionary in
      China, 1807-1937. Syracuse, N.Y.: Syracuse University
      Press, 1946. 285 pp. A47-3119. o.p. (M-University).

1333 Hevi, Emmanuel John. An African Student in China. N.Y.:
B   Praeger, 1963. 220 pp. 63-18529.
      JAS, 2/65; China Q., 1-3/65

1334 Hu, Ch'ang-tu. Chinese Education Under Communism. N.Y.:
A   Bureau of Publications, Teachers College, Columbia
      University, 1962. 157 pp. 62-20698. o.p.

1335 Kuo, Ping-wen. The Chinese System of Public Education. N.Y.:
B   Teachers College, Columbia University, 1915. 209 pp.
      15-17201. o.p.
      Hucker, 1914

1336 Lewis, Ida Belle. The Education of Girls in China. N.Y.:
B   Teachers College, Columbia University, 1919. 92 pp.
      20-7788. o.p.
      Hucker, 2056

1337 Lin, Yu-t'ang. A History of the Press and Public Opinion in
B   China. Chicago: University of Chicago Press, 1936. 179 pp.
      37-27194. o.p.
      Hucker, 114; Am. J. Soc., 11/37; Am. Pol. Sci. R., 6/37;
      TLS, 8/7/37

1338 Lindsay, Michael. Notes on Educational Problems in Communist
A   China, 1941-47. N.Y.: International Secretariat, Insti-
      tute of Pacific Relations, 1950. 194 pp. 50-7573. o.p.

1339 Nunn, Godfrey Raymond. Publishing in Mainland China. Cam-
A   bridge, Mass.: M.I.T. Press, 1966. 83 pp. (Report No. 4).
      66-17756.
      JAS, 2/67

1340 Orleans, Leo A. Professional Manpower and Education in Com-
A   munist China. Washington: Government Printing Office,
      1961. 260 pp. 61-61233. o.p.
      Hucker, 2229; JAS, 2/62; China Q., 10-12/61

1341 Peake, Cyrus. Nationalism and Education in Modern China. N.Y.:
A   Columbia University Press, 1932. 240 pp. 32-26886. o.p.

1342 Purcell, Victor William Williams Saunders. Problems of Chinese
B   Education. London: Kegan Paul, Trench, Trubner, 1936.
      261 pp. 37-3092. o.p.
      Hucker, 1939

1343 Tsang, Chiu-sam. Society, Schools and Progress in China. N.Y.:
A   Pergamon, 1968. 333 pp. 68-21109.

1344 Tung, Chi-ping and Humphrey Evans. The Thought Revolution.
C   N.Y.: Coward-McCann, 1966. 254 pp. 66-13121.
      JAS, 2/68

CHINA - EDUCATION AND
MASS COMMUNICATION

1345　U.S. Office of Education. Basic Principles Underlying the
A　　Chinese Communist Approach to Education, by Chester Cheng.
　　　Washington: U.S. Office of Education, 1961. 24 pp. (Infor-
　　　mation on Education Around the World Series, No. 51).

1346　Wilson, John Tuzo. One Chinese Moon. N.Y.: Hill & Wang, 1959.
B　　274 pp. 59-14657. o.p.

1347　Yen, Maria, pseud. The Umbrella Garden; A Picture of Student
C　　Life in Red China. adapted from Chinese by Maria Yen
　　　with Richard M. McCarthy. N.Y.: Macmillan, 1954. 268 pp.
　　　54-12389. o.p.
　　　AUFS, 1000; Hucker, 964; FEQ, 5/55

1348　Yu, Te-chi. Mass Persuasion in Communist China, by Frederick
A　　T. C. Yu. N.Y.: Praeger, 1964. 186 pp. (Praeger Publica-
　　　tions in Russian History and World Communism, 145). 64-13389.
　　　Choice, 7-8/64; Ann. Am. Acad., 1/65; Library Journal,
　　　5/1/64; Pol. Sci. Q., 9/65

1349　Zi, Etienne. Pratique des Examens Litteraires en Chine.
C　　Shanghai: Mission Catholique, 1894. (Varietes Sino-
　　　logiques, 5). 50-42950. o.p.
　　　Hucker, 1840

SCIENCE AND TECHNOLOGY

1350　American Association for the Advancement of Science. Sciences
A　　in Communist China; A Symposium Presented at the New
　　　York Meeting of the American Association for the Advance-
　　　ment of Science, December 26-27, 1960. ed. by Sidney H.
　　　Gould. Washington: 1961. 872 pp. (Publication No. 68).
　　　61-14965 rev. o.p.

1351　Bennett, Adrian Arthur. John Fryer: the Introduction of Western
B　　Science and Technology into Nineteenth-Century China. Cam-
　　　bridge, Mass.: Harvard University Press, 1967. 157 pp.
　　　(East Asian Monographs, 24). 68-4092.

1352　Croizier, Ralph C. Traditional Medicine in Modern China:
B　　Science, Nationalism, and the Tensions of Cultural Change.
　　　Cambridge, Mass.: Harvard University Press, 1968.
　　　325 pp. (Harvard East Asian Series, 34). 68-17624.
　　　Choice, 11/68; China Q., 1-3/69; Library Journal, 7/68;
　　　TLS, 12/5/68

1353　Elia, Pasquale M. d'. Galileo in China; Relations through the
B　　Roman College between Galileo and the Jesuit Scientist-
　　　Missionaries (1610-1640). tr. by Rufus Sutter and Matthew
　　　Sciasia. Cambridge, Mass.: Harvard University Press,
　　　1960. 115 pp. 61-5252. o.p.
　　　Hucker, 1379; JAOS, 1-3/62

1354　Huang-ti Nei Ching Su Wen. Huang-Tu nei chung su wen. The
C　　Yellow Emporer's Classic of Internal Medicine. new ed.
　　　Chapters 1-34 tr. with an intro. by Ilza Veith. Berkeley:
　　　University of California Press, 1966. 260 pp. 66-21112.
　　　Hucker, 1374; Choice, 7-8/67; FEQ, 5/51; Science, 5/7/67

1355　Huard, Pierre Alphonse. La Medecine Chinoise au Cours des
C　　Siecles. Paris: R. Dacosta, 1959. 190 pp. 59-51354.
　　　Hucker, 1375

1356　Hume, Edward Hicks. The Chinese Way in Medicine. Baltimore:
C　　Johns Hopkins Press, 1940. 189 pp. 40-32412. o.p.
　　　Hucker, 1373; FEQ, 5/42

1357　Ko, Hung. Alchemy, Medicine, Religion in the China of A.D. 320:
C　　the Nei P'ien of Ko Hung (Pao-p'u tzu). tr. by James R.
　　　Ware. Cambridge, Mass.: M.I.T. Press, 1967. 388 pp.
　　　66-23548.
　　　Choice, 10/67; JAS, 11/67

1358　Needham, Joseph. Chinese Astronomy and the Jesuit Mission:
A　　an Encounter of Cultures. London: China Society, 1958.
　　　20 pp. 60-2893.
　　　Hucker, 1380

1359　Needham, Joseph. The Development of Iron and Steel Technology
A　　in China. London: The Newcomen Society for the Study of
　　　History of Engineering and Technology, the Science Museum,
　　　1958. 76 pp. 59-1313.
　　　Hucker, 1361

1360　Needham, Joseph. Science and Civilisation in China. Cam-
A　　bridge: University, 1954- 54-4723.
　　　AUFS, 693; Hucker, 136; Choice, 4/66; JAS, 11/59; FEQ, 8/55;

CHINA - SCIENCE AND TECHNOLOGY

AHR, 4/60, 1/63; Library Journal, 9/1/54, 5/1/66; Pacific
Affairs, Fall/63; TLS, 10/15/54, 2/10/66

1361　Snapper, Isidore. Chinese Lessons to Western Medicine; A Con-
C　　tribution to Geographical Medicine from the Clinics of
　　　Peiping Union Medical College. 2d ed. N.Y.: Grune &
　　　Stratton, 1965 (orig. pub. by Interscience Publications,
　　　1941). 416 pp. 64-7771. (R).
　　　Hucker, 1376

1362　Wang, Chi-min. History of Chinese Medicine; Being a Chronicle
C　　of Medical Happenings in China from Ancient Times to the
　　　Present Period, by K. Chimin Wong and Wu Lien-teh. 2d ed.
　　　Shanghai: National Quarantine Service, 1936. 906 pp.
　　　37-34871. o.p.
　　　Hucker, 1372

BIBLIOGRAPHIES

1363 A Bibliography on Japanese Buddhism. ed. by Bando Shojun and
B   others. Tokyo: CIIB Press, 1958. 180 pp. A59-8335.
     Silberman, 622

1364 Borton, Hugh. A Selected List of Books and Articles on Japan
B   in English, French, and German. rev. and enl. Cambridge,
     Mass.: Harvard University Press for Harvard-Yenching Insti-
     tute, 1954. 272 pp. 53-5055.
     AUFS, 158; Silberman, 9; FEQ, 2/42

1365 Kato, Genchi. A Bibliography of Shinto in Western Languages,
B   from the Oldest Times till 1952. Tokyo: Meiji Jingu Shamu-
     sho, 1953. 58 pp. 58-15934 rev.
     Silberman, 600

1366 Nachod, Oskar. Bibliographie von Japan, 1906-1926 (-1938-1943).
C   Leipzig: K. W. Hiersmann, 1928- 29-4184 rev. 2.
     Silberman, 21, 22

1367 Nachod, Oskar. Bibliography of the Japanese Empire, 1906-1926.
C   Leipzig: K. W. Hiersemann, 1928. 2 v. 29-4185. o.p.
     Silberman, 23

1368 Nihon PEN Kurabu. Japanese Literature in European Languages,
A   a Bibliography. Tokyo: Kasai, 1957. 69 pp. 61-32222.
     Silberman, 865

REFERENCE BOOKS

1369 Chaplin, Hamako Ito. A Manual of Japanese Writing. New Haven,
A   Conn.: Yale University Press, 1967. 3 v. 66-21510.
     JAS, 8/68

1370 Economic Statistics of Japan. Tokyo: Bank of Japan. annual.
B

1371 Foreign Trade of Japan. Japan External Trade Organization.
A   Tokyo. annual.

1372 Fukuda, Naomi, ed. Union Catalog of Books on Japan in West-
A   ern Languages. Tokyo: International House Library, 1968.
     543 pp. Hand catalog.

1373 Hall, John Whitney. Japanese History; A Guide to Japanese
C   Reference and Research Materials. Ann Arbor: University
     of Michigan Press, 1954. 165 pp. (Center for Japanese
     Studies. Bibliography Series). 54-62413. o.p.
     Sup. 61, 2762; Silberman, 163

1374 Hall, John Whitney. Japanese History; New Dimensions of
B   Approach and Understanding. Washington: Service Center
     for Teachers of History, 1961. 63 pp. (Publication No. 34).
     61-9919. o.p.
     Sup. 61, 2763; Silberman, 144

1375 Henderson, Harold Gould. Handbook of Japanese Grammar.
B   rev. ed. Boston: Houghton Mifflin, 1948. 360 pp. 48-4731.
     Silberman, 135

1376 Japan Biographical Encyclopedia and Who's Who. 1958-
A   58-1808 rev.

1377 Japan Economic Yearbook. Tokyo: Oriental Economist, 1954-
B   Biennial, Irregular.

1378 Japan Statistical Yearbook. Tokyo: Japanese Government,
A   Office of Prime Minister, Bureau of Statistics. annual.

1379 Kenkyusha's New English-Japanese Dictionary on Bilingual
C   Principles. new ed. N.Y.: Japan Publications Trading
     Co., 1956. 2213 pp. Hand catalog.
     AUFS, 410; Silberman, 110

1380 Kenkyusha's New Japanese-English Dictionary. new ed., ed. by
B   Senkichiro Katsumata. N.Y.: Japan Publications Trading
     Co., 1954. 2136 pp. Hand catalog.
     AUFS, 411; Silberman, 111

1381 Lehmann, Winfred Phillip. A Grammar of Formal Written Japan-
C   ese, by W. P. Lehmann and Lloyd Faust. Cambridge, Mass.:
     Harvard University Press, 1951. 153 pp. (Harvard-Yenching
     Institute Studies, V). 51-587 rev. o.p.
     Silberman, 128; FEQ, 11/51

1382 List of Japanese Economic and Business Periodicals in English.
B   Tokyo: Japan Economic Research Center, 1967.

1383 Miller, Roy Andrew. The Japanese Language. Chicago:
A   University of Chicago Press, 1967. 428 pp. 67-16777.
     JAS, 11/68

1384 Morris, Ivan I. Dictionary of Selected Forms in Classical
C   Japanese Literature. N.Y.: Columbia University Press,
     1966. 155 pp. 66-13020.
     Choice, 10/67; JAS, 11/66

1385 Nelson, Andrew Nathaniel. The Modern Reader's Japanese-
B   English Character Dictionary. 2d rev. ed. Rutland,
     Vt.: Tuttle, 1966. 1108 pp. Hand catalog.
     JAS, 2/63; Japan Q., 4-6/62; JAOS, 4-6/62

1386 Papinot, Edmond. Historical and Geographical Dictionary
B   of Japan. N.Y.: Ungar, 1964 (orig. pub. by Sansaisha,
     1910). 2 v. 64-25236. (R).
     Choice, 4/65

1387 Rose-Innes, Arthur. Beginners' Dictionary of Chinese-Japa-
C   nese Characters, with Common Abbreviations, Variants and
     Numerous Compounds. 4th ed. rev. Tokyo: Meisei Sha, 1959.
     507 pp. Hand catalog.
     AUFS, 413; Silberman, 108

1388 Sansom, George Bailey. An Historical Grammar of Japanese.
B   Oxford: Clarendon, 1928. 347 pp. 28-23697.
     Silberman, 127

1389 Webb, Herschel. Research in Japanese Sources, a Guide. N.Y.:
C   Columbia University Press for East Asian Institute, 1965.
     170 pp. 64-21202.
     Sup. 65, 3074; Choice, 7-8/65; JAS, 8/65; Library Journal,
     1/1/65

JOURNALS

1390 Asiatic Society of Japan Transactions. Tokyo, 1872 ff.
B   irregular. In three series: 1st, 1872-1922, 2nd, 1924-
     1940, 3rd, 1948ff. 5-22827. (R-Kraus).
     Sup. 61, 2784; Silberman, 29

1391 Contemporary Japan. Tokyo: Foreign Affairs Association of
C   Japan, 1932-
     Silberman, 41

1392 Contemporary Religions in Japan. v.1- 1960-
C

1393 Economic Survey of Japan. Japanese Government Economic Plan-
A   ning Agency. Tokyo: Japan Times.

1394 Japan Illustrated. v.1- 1963-
B

1395 Japan Quarterly. Tokyo: Asahi Shimbun, v.1- Oct./Dec.,
B   1954-
     Silberman, 42

1396 Japan Times Weekly. v.1- 1938-
C

1397 Journal of Social and Political Ideas in Japan. v.1- 1963-
C   Tokyo: Center for Japanese Social and Political Studies.
     JAS, 11/63

1398 Monumenta Nipponica. Tokyo: Sophia University, 1938-1943,
B   1951-
     Silberman, 34

1399 Oriental Economist. Tokyo: Oriental Economist, 1934-
C   Silberman, 43

GENERAL BOOKS

1400 Boxer, Charles Ralph. Jan Compagnie in Japan, 1600-1850; an
B   Essay on the Cultural, Artistic and Scientific Influence
     Exercised by the Hollanders in Japan from the Seventeenth
     to the Nineteenth Centuries. 2d rev. ed. The Hague: Ni-
     jhoff, 1950. 198 pp. 51-1183.
     AUFS, 184; Silberman, 289; FEQ, 5/51

1401 Embree, John Fee. The Japanese. Washington: Smithsonian
C   Institution, 1943. 42 pp. 43-51696. o.p.
     AUFS, 160; FEQ, 8/43

1402 Griffis, William Elliot. The Mikado's Empire. l2th ed.
B   N.Y.: Harper, 1913. 2 v. 13-3305. o.p.

1403 Hall, John Whitney. Twelve Doors to Japan. N.Y.: McGraw-
A   Hill, 1965. 649 pp. 64-66015.
      Choice, 2/66; JAS, 11/66; Am. Anthropologist, 6/66;
      Am. Pol. Sci. R., 12/66; Library Journal, 3/1/66;
      Pacific Affairs, Spring-Summer/66

1404 Harvard University. East Asian Research Center. Papers on
C   Japan. Cambridge, Mass., 1961- 59-2493 rev. 2.

1405 Hearn, Lafcadio. Glimpses of Unfamiliar Japan. N.Y.: AMS,
B   1968 (orig. pub. by Houghton Mifflin, 1894). 2 v.
      4-16699. (R).

1406 Hearn, Lafcadio. Japan, an Attempt at Interpretation. Rut-
B   land, Vt.: Tuttle, 1955. 498 pp. 56-249 rev.
      AUFS, 194

1407 Japan. Mombusho. Nihon Yunesuko Kokunai Iinkai. Japan;
C   Its Land, People, and Culture. rev. ed. comp. by Japanese
      National Commission for UNESCO. Tokyo: Printing Bureau, Min-
      istry of Finance, dist. by Japan Publications Trading Co.,
      1964. 885 pp. 65-71358.
      Silberman, 1

1408 Michigan. University. Center for Japanese Studies. Occa-
C   sional Papers. Ann Arbor, Mich.: Center for Japanese
      Studies, 1951- 54-33454.
      Silberman, 28

1409 Olson, Lawrence Alexander. Dimensions of Japan; A Collection
B   of Reports Written for the American Universities Field Staff.
      N.Y.: American Universities Field Staff, 1963. 403 pp.
      63-14762.
      Sup. 63, 2893; JAS, 8/65; Am. Anthropologist, 2/64;
      Am. Pol. Sci. R., 3/64; Am. Soc. R., 6/64; Japan Q.,
      7-9/64; Library Journal, 8/63

1410 Orient/West. The Japanese Image. ed. by Maurice Schneps and
C   Alvin D. Coox. Philadelphia: Orient/West, 1965. 381 pp.
      65-6136. o.p.
      JAS, 8/66

1411 Schwantes, Robert S. Japanese and Americans, a Century
B   of Cultural Relations. N.Y.: Harper for Council on Foreign
      Relations, 1955. 380 pp. 55-7220. o.p.
      AUFS, 281; Silberman, 430; FEQ, 5/56; Japan Q., 1-3/57;
      Library Journal, 8/55

1412 Tsunoda, Ryusaku, ed. Sources of the Japanese Tradition.
A   N.Y.: Columbia University Press, 1958. 928 pp. 58-7167.
      AUFS, 175; Silberman, 152; JAS, 2/59; Ann. Am. Acad., 1/59;
      Japan Q., 1-3/59; JAOS, 10-12/59; Library Journal, 7/58;
      Pacific Affairs, 3/59

1413 Ueda, Makoto. Literary and Art Theories in Japan. Cleve-
B   land, Ohio: Case Western Reserve University Press, 1967.
      274 pp. 67-14521.
      Choice, 7-8/68; JAS, 8/68; Library Journal, 3/1/68

1414 Varley, H. Paul. A Syllabus of Japanese Civilization. N.Y.:
A   Columbia University Press, 1968. 98 pp. (Companion to
      Asian Studies/Committee on Oriental Studies). 68-55815.

1415 Webb, Herschel. An Introduction to Japan. 2d ed. N.Y.: Colum-
B   bia University Press, 1957. 130 pp. 54-12312.
      AUFS, 176; Silberman, 2; JAS, 2/58; Library Journal, 2/15/55;
      Pacific Affairs, 12/55

GEOGRAPHY

1416 Isida, Ryujiro. Geography of Japan. Tokyo: Kokusai Bunka Shin-
B   kokai, 1961. 124 pp. (Series on Japanese Life and Cul-
      ture, 2). NUC 65-2427.
      Choice, 6/66; JAS, 2/65

1417 Society of Japanese Regional Geography. Regional Geography
C   of Japan. Tokyo: Society of Japanese Regional Geography,
      1957. 6 v.
      Silberman, 76

1418 Trewartha, Glenn Thomas. Japan, a Physical, Cultural and Regional
A   Geography. Madison: University of Wisconsin Press, 1965.
      652 pp. 65-11200.
      Silberman, 75; Choice, 11/65; FEQ, 8/45

HISTORY
GENERAL

1419 Honjo, Eijiro. The Social and Economic History of Japan.
B   N.Y.: Russell & Russell, 1965 (orig. pub. by Kyoto
      Institute for Research in Economic History of Japan,
      1935). 410 pp. 65-18809. (R).
      AUFS, 165; Silberman, 230

1420 Murdoch, James. A History of Japan. N.Y.: Ungar, 1964 (orig.
B   pub. by Routledge, 1903-26). 3 v. in 6. 64-15695. (R).
      AUFS, 167; Silberman, 155; Choice, 4/65

1421 Reischauer, Edwin Oldfather. Japan, Past and Present.
A   3d ed. rev. N.Y.: Knopf, 1964. 323 pp. 64-12896.
      AUFS, 169; Silberman, 149; Choice, 5/64; FEQ, 8/53

1422 Sansom, Sir George Bailey. A History of Japan. Stanford,
A   Calif.: Stanford University Press, 1958-63. (Studies
      in the Civilization of Eastern Asia). 3 v. 58-11694.
      Sup. 61, 2777; Sup. 65, 3071; AUFS, 204; Hucker, 306;
      Silberman, 147, 148; JAS, 8/59, 8/64; AHR, 7/59, 1/62, 7/64;
      Ann. Am. Acad., 5/64; Japan Q., 10-12/59, 1-3/62, 10-12/64;
      JAOS, 1-3/59, 9-12/61; Library Journal, 10/15/63; TLS,
      4/24/59, 10/13/61, 8/6/64

1423 Sansom, Sir George Bailey. Japan, a Short Cultural History.
A   rev. ed. N.Y.: Appleton-Century, 1943. 554 pp. 43-18417.
      AUFS, 170; Hucker, 132; Silberman, 146; Pacific Affairs, 6/44

1424 Sansom, Sir George Bailey. Japan in World History. N.Y.:
C   International Secretariat, Institute of Pacific Relations,
      1951. 94 pp. 51-13888. o.p.
      Silberman, 153; AHR, 7/52; Pacific Affairs, 6/52; TLS,
      12/21/51

1425 Sansom, Sir George Bailey. The Western World and Japan, a Study
A   in the Interaction of European and Asiatic Cultures. N.Y.:
      Knopf, 1950. 504 pp. 50-5199.
      AUFS, 172; Hucker, 559; Silberman, 278; FEQ, 5/51; AHR,
      7/50; Am. Pol. Sci. R., 8/50; Ann. Am. Acad., 9/50; JAOS,
      7-9/50; Library Journal, 2/1/50; TLS, 10/27/50

1426 Takekoshi, Yosaburo. The Economic Aspects of the History
A   of the Civilization of Japan. London: Dawsons, dist. by
      Paragon, 1967 (orig. pub. by Macmillan, 1930). 3 v.
      68-96138. (R).
      Silberman, 277; AHR, 4/31

1427 Takizawa, Matsuyo. The Penetration of Money Economy in Japan
C   and Its Effects upon Social and Political Institutions.
      N.Y.: AMS, 1968 (orig. pub. by Columbia University Press,
      1927). 159 pp. 68-54302. (R).
      Silberman, 274

1428 Tsunoda, Ryusaku, tr. Japan in the Chinese Dynastic Histories:
C   Later Han through Ming Dynasties. ed. by L. Carrington Good-
      rich. South Pasadena, Calif.: P. D. and Ione Perkins,
      1951. 187 pp. 53-67. o.p.
      Hucker, 133; Silberman, 196

1429 Yamagiwa, Joseph Koshimi, ed. Readings in Japanese History.
C   Ann Arbor: University of Michigan Press, 1966. 2 v.
      66-31440.
      JAS, 5/67

1430 Yanaga, Chitoshi. Japan since Perry. Hamden, Conn.: Archon,
B   1966 (orig. pub. by McGraw-Hill, 1949). 723 pp.
      66-16779. (R).
      AUFS, 300; Silberman, 316; FEQ, 11/50; AHR, 4/50; Ann. Am.
      Acad., 1/50; JAOS, 7-9/50; Pacific Affairs, 12/49

1431 Yoshida, Shigeru. Japan's Decisive Century, 1867-1967.
B   N.Y.: Praeger, 1967. 110 pp. 67-22296.
      Choice, 7-8/68; Library Journal, 7/67; TLS, 8/1/68

HISTORY
EARLY HISTORY

1432 Groot, Gerard. The Prehistory of Japan. ed. by Bertram S.
C   Kraus. N.Y.: Columbia University Press, 1951. 128 pp.
      51-11028. o.p.
      Silberman, 173; FEQ, 2/52; JAOS, 10-12/52

1433 Haguenauer, Charles. Origines de la Civilisation Japonais;
B   Introduction a l'Etude de la Prehistoire du Japon.
      Paris: Imprimerie Nationale, 1956- 58-15251.

Silberman, 175; JAS, 2/60

1434 Kidder, Jonathan Edward. Japan Before Buddhism. rev. ed.
A   N.Y.: Praeger, 1966. 284 pp. (Ancient Peoples and Places
      Series, Vol. 10). 66-12521.
      Silberman, 172; Choice, 10/67; JAS, 5/60; Japan Q., 7-9/60

1435 Nihongi; Chronicles of Japan from the Earliest Times to
B   A.D. 697. tr. from original Chinese and Japanese by
      W. G. Aston. London: Allen & Unwin, 1956. 443 pp.
      A56-5065.
      Silberman, 192; Japan Q., 1-3/57

1436 Reischauer, Robert Karl. Early Japanese History, c.40 B.C.-
B   A.D. 1167. Gloucester, Mass.: Peter Smith, 1967 (orig.
      pub. by Princeton University Press, 1937). 2 v. 67-8701.
      (R).
      Silberman, 187; JAOS, 3/39; TLS, 1/1/38

1437 Yasumaro. Translation of "Ko-ji-ki"....or "Records of Ancient
B   Matters", by Basil Hall Chamberlain. 2d ed. with annota-
      tions by W. G. Aston. New Hyde Park, N.Y.: University
      Books, 1966 (orig. pub. by J. L. Thompson, 1932). 495 pp.
      33-20689. (R).
      Silberman, 193

HISTORY
PRE-MODERN

1438 Alcock, Sir Rutherford. The Capital of the Tycoon: a Narra-
B   tive of Three Years' Residence in Japan. St. Clair Shores,
      Mich.: Scholarly Press (orig. pub. by Harper 1863). 2 v.
      16-5665. (R).
      Silberman, 355

1439 Asakawa, Kan'ichi, ed. and tr. The Documents of Iriki. new ed.
C   Tokyo: Japan Society for Promotion of Science, 1955. 442 pp.
      59-24424.
      Silberman, 219; Japan Q., 10-12/57

1440 Asakawa, Kan'ichi. The Early Institutional Life of Japan; A
B   Study in the Reform of 645 A.D. 2d ed. N.Y.: Paragon,
      1963 (orig. pub. by Tokyo Shueisha, 1903). 355 pp.
      63-21051. (R).
      AUFS, 178; Silberman, 208; JAS, 5/65

1441 Beasley, William G. Great Britain and the Opening of Japan,
B   1834-1858. London: Luzac, 1951. 227 pp. 52-39372.
      AUFS, 180; Silberman, 292; FEQ, 2/53

1442 Beasley, William G., ed. and tr. Select Documents on Japanese
B   Foreign Policy, 1853-1868. N.Y.: Oxford, 1955. 359 pp.
      55-4067.
      AUFS, 181; Silberman, 293; FEQ, 8/56

1443 Bohner, Hermann. Shotoku Taishi. Tokyo: Deutsche Gesellschaft
C   fur Natur- und Volkerkunde Ostasiens, 1940. 1033 pp.
      (Deutsche Gesellschaft fur Natur- und Volkerkunde Ostasiens,
      Mitteilungen, Supplement Bd. XV).
      Silberman, 203

1444 Borton, Hugh. Peasant Uprisings in Japan of the Tokugawa
C   Period. New Hyde Park, N.Y.: University Books, 1966 (orig.
      pub. by Asiatic Society of Japan, 1938). 210 pp. AC38-2555
      rev. (R).
      AUFS, 182; Silberman, 268

1445 Boxer, Charles Ralph. The Christian Century in Japan, 1549-
A   1650. rev. ed. Berkeley: University of California Press,
      1967. 535 pp. NUC 68-28062.
      AUFS, 183; Silberman, 241; FEQ, 11/52; Ann. Am. Acad.,
      11/51; JAOS, 10-12/52; TLS, 9/14/51

1446 Brown, Delmer Myers. Money Economy in Medieval Japan; A Study
C   in the Use of Coins. New Haven, Conn.: Institute of Far
      Eastern Languages, Yale University, 1951. 128 pp.
      (Association for Asian Studies, Monographs and Papers,
      I). A52-10471 rev.
      Silberman, 1505; FEQ, 11/52; JAOS, 4-6/53

1447 Cocks, Richard. Diary of Richard Cocks, Cape-Merchant in
C   the English Factory in Japan, 1615-22. ed. by Edward M.
      Thompson. London: printed for Hakluyt Society, 1883. 2 v.
      5-40455. o.p.
      Silberman, 298

1448 Cooper, Michael, ed. They Came to Japan, an Anthology of
C   European Reports on Japan, 1543-1640. Berkeley: University

      of California Press, 1965. 439 pp. 65-19250.
      Sup. 67, 3212; Choice, 4/66; Library Journal, 11/1/65

1449 Dening, Walter. The Life of Toyotomi Hideyoshi. 4th ed. Tokyo:
B   Hokuseido, 1955. 558 pp. 56-1288.
      Silberman, 236; Japan Q., 10-12/56

1450 Golovnin, Vasilii Mikhailovich. Narrative of My Captivity
C   in Japan, during the Years 1811, 1812 and 1813. London:
      Printed for H. Colburn, 1818. 2 v. 4-28643. o.p.

1451 Griffis, William Elliot. Townsend Harris, First American
B   Envoy in Japan. Boston: Houghton Mifflin, 1895. 351 pp.
      4-17023. o.p. (M-University).

1452 Hall, John Whitney. Government and Local Power in Japan,
A   500 to 1700, a Study Based on Bizen Province. Princeton,
      N.J.: Princeton University Press, 1966. 446 pp. 65-14307.
      Choice, 9/66; JAS, 11/66; AHR, 10/66; Am. Pol. Sci. R.,
      12/66; Ann. Am. Acad., 11/66; Japan Q., 10-12/66; Library
      Journal, 2/15/66; Pacific Affairs, Fall-Winter/66-67

1453 Hall, John Whitney, comp. Studies in the Institutional History
C   of Early Modern Japan. Princeton, N.J.: Princeton Uni-
      versity Press, 1968. 396 pp. 68-15766.

1454 Hall, John Whitney. Tanuma Okitsugu, 1719-1788, Forerunner
B   of Modern Japan. Cambridge, Mass.: Harvard University
      Press, 1955. 208 pp. 52-5396.
      AUFS, 192; Silberman, 247; FEQ, 5/56; AHR, 4/56; JAOS,
      1-3/56; Pacific Affairs, 9/56

1455 Harris, Townsend. The Complete Journal of Townsend Harris,
A   First American Consul and Minister to Japan. intro. and
      notes by Mario Emilio Cosenza. 2d rev. ed. Rutland, Vt.:
      Tuttle, 1959. 616 pp. 59-9397.
      Silberman, 312

1456 Hayashi, Tadasu. The Secret Memoirs of Count Tadasu Hayashi
C   (1850-1913). ed. by A. M. Pooley. N.Y.: Putnam, 1915.
      331 pp. 15-16413. o.p.
      Silberman, 410

1457 Honjo, Eijiro. Economic Theory and History of Japan in the
C   Tokugawa Period. N.Y.: Russell & Russell, 1965 (orig.
      pub. by Maruzen, 1943). 350 pp. 65-18808. (R).
      Silberman, 272

1458 Jouon des Longrais, Frederic. Age de Kamakura: Sources (1150-
B   1333). Tokyo: Maison Franco-Japonais, 1950- 50-29222.
      Silberman, 221

1459 Kaempfer, Engelbert. The History of Japan, Together with a
A   Description of the Kingdom of Siam, 1690-92. tr. from
      Dutch by J. G. Scheuchzer. N.Y.: Macmillan, 1906. 3 v.
      6-32382. o.p.
      AUFS, 196

1460 Keene, Donald. The Japanese Discovery of Europe; Honda
B   Toshiaki and Other Discoverers, 1720-1798. rev. ed. Stan-
      ford, Calif.: Stanford University Press, 1969 (orig. pub.
      in 1952). 255 pp. 69-13180. (R).
      AUFS, 197; Silberman, 279; FEQ, 2/55; Library Journal,
      9/15/54; Pacific Affairs, 9/55

1461 Laures, John. Nobunaga und das Christentum. Tokyo: Sophia-
C   Universitat, 1950. 54 pp. (Monumenta Nipponica Monographs,
      No. 10). 51-28771.
      Silberman, 242

1462 Lensen, George Alexander. The Russian Push Toward Japan;
B   Russo-Japanese Relations, 1697-1875. Princeton, N.J.:
      Princeton University Press, 1959. 533 pp. 59-9608.
      o.p. (M-University).
      Silberman, 302; JAS, 2/60; AHR, 3/60; Am. Pol. Sci. R.,
      12/59; Ann. Am. Acad., 1/60; Japan Q., 10-12/59; Pacific
      Affairs, 12/59

1463 Lensen, George Alexander. Russia's Japan Expedition of 1852
C   to 1855. Gainesville: University of Florida Press, 1955.
      208 pp. 55-8081. o.p.
      Silberman, 304; FEQ, 2/56

1464 Macauley, Edward Yorke. With Perry in Japan; The Diary of
C   Edward Yorke McCauley. Princeton, N.J.: Princeton
      University Press, 1942. 124 pp. 43-1901. o.p. (M-Uni-
      versity).
      AHR, 7/43

1465 Morris, Ivan I. The World of the Shining Prince; Court Life in
A   Ancient Japan. N.Y.: Knopf, 1964. 336 pp. 64-12310.
        Sup. 65, 3067; Choice, 11/64; Japan Q., 1-3/65; Library
        Journal, 9/1/64

1466 Nachod, Oskar. Die Beziehungen der Niederlandischen Ostin-
B   dischen Kompagnie zu Japan im Siebzehenten Jahrhundert.
        Leipzig: R. Friese, 1897. 444 pp. 38-11905. o.p.
        Silberman, 291

1467 Perry, Matthew Calbraith. Narrative of the Expedition of an
A   American Squadron to the China Seas and Japan, Performed in
        the Years 1852, 1853, and 1854, Under the Command of
        Commodore M. C. Perry, U.S. Navy, by Order of the Government
        of the United States. ed. by Francis L. Hawks. N.Y.: AMS,
        1967 (orig. pub. by Nicholson, 1856). 3 v. 1-4228. (R).
        Silberman, 307

1468 Rogers, Philip George. The First Englishman in Japan; The Story
C   of Will Adams. London: Harvill, 1956. 143 pp. 56-58999.
        o.p.
        Silberman, 296; JAS, 2/58; Japan Q., 1-3/57

1469 Sadler, Arthur Lindsay. The Maker of Modern Japan; The Life
B   of Tokugawa Ieyasu. London: Allen & Unwin, 1937. 429 pp.
        37-7531.
        Silberman, 235; FEQ, 8/42

1470 Sheldon, Charles David. The Rise of the Merchant Class in
B   Tokugawa Japan, 1600-1868; An Introductory Survey. Locust
        Valley, N.Y.: Augustin, 1958. 205 pp. (Association for
        Asian Studies, Monographs and Papers, V). A59-8765.
        AUFS, 205; Silberman, 261; JAS, 8/59

1471 Shinoda, Minoru. The Founding of the Kamakura Shogunate,
B   1180-1185, With Selected Translations from the Azuma Kagami.
        N.Y.: Columbia University Press, 1960. 385 pp. (Columbia
        University Records of Civilization: Sources and Studies,
        No. 57). 59-10433.
        Sup. 61, 2779; Silberman, 218; JAS, 11/60; AHR, 7/60;
        Ann. Am. Acad., 9/60; Library Journal, 2/1/60; Pacific
        Affairs, Summer/61; TLS, 1/27/61

1472 Smith, Thomas Carlyle. The Agrarian Origins of Modern Japan.
A   Stanford, Calif.: Stanford University Press, 1959. 250 pp.
        59-7429.
        Silberman, 259; JAS, 11/59; Am. Anthropologist, 12/59; Am.
        Econ. R., 3/60; AHR, 7/60; Ann. Am. Acad., 11/59; Geog. R.,
        7/60; Japan Q., 7-9/60; Library Journal, 5/15/59; Pacific
        Affairs, 3/60; Pol. Sci. Q., 12/60

1473 Statler, Oliver. Japanese Inn. N.Y.: Random House, 1961.
C   365 pp. 61-6236.
        Sup. 61, 2781; Japan Q., 7-9/61; Library Journal, 3/1/61;
        Pacific Affairs, Summer/62; TLS, 2/9/62

1474 Straelen, Henricus van. Yoshida Shoin, Forerunner of the
C   Meiji Restoration; A Biographical Study. Leiden: Brill,
        1952. 149 pp. (T'oung Pao Monograph, No. 2). 52-12675.
        Silberman, 285

1475 Totman, Conrad D. Politics in the Tokugawa Bakufu,
C   1600-1843. Cambridge, Mass.: Harvard University
        Press, 1967. 346 pp. (Harvard East Asian Series,
        30). 67-22873.
        Choice, 10/68; JAS, 11/68

1476 Tsuchiya, Takao. An Economic History of Japan. tr. by Michi-
C   taro Shidehara. rev. by Neil Skene Smith. Tokyo: Asiatic
        Society of Japan, 1937. 269 pp. AC38-2554.
        AUFS, 208; Silberman, 229

1477 Tsukahira, Toshio George. Feudal Control in Tokugawa Japan;
C   The Sankin Kotai System. Cambridge, Mass.: Harvard
        University Press, 1966. 228 pp. 67-3532.
        Sup. 67, 3228; JAS, 5/67

1478 Varley, H. Paul. The Onin War; History of Its Origins and
B   Background with a Selective Translation of The Chronicle
        of Onin. N.Y.: Columbia University Press, 1967. 238 pp.
        (Studies in Oriental Culture, 1). 66-14595.
        Sup. 67, 3229; Choice, 11/67; JAS, 8/68; AHR, 10/67; Ann.
        Am. Acad., 11/67; Library Journal, 1/1/67

1479 Webb, Herschel. The Japanese Imperial Institution in the
B   Tokugawa Period. N.Y.: Columbia University Press, 1968.
        296 pp. (East Asian Institute, Columbia University).

68-11912.
Choice, 12/68

HISTORY
MODERN TO 1945

1480 Akita, George. Foundations of Constitutional Govern-
C   ment in Modern Japan, 1868-1900. Cambridge, Mass.:
        Harvard University Press, 1967. 292 pp. 65-13835.
        Choice, 9/67; JAS, 2/68; AHR, 10/67; Ann. Am. Acad., 9/67

1481 Anethan, Albert d', Baron. The d'Anethan Dispatches from Japan,
C   1894-1910; The Observations of Baron Albert d'Anethan,
        Belgian Minister Plenipotentiary and Dean of the Diplo-
        matic Corps. sel., tr., and ed. with an historical intro.
        by George Alexander Lensen. Tallahassee, Fla.: Diplomatic
        Press in cooperation with Sophia University, 1967. 272 pp.
        67-26670.
        Choice, 4/68

1482 Baelz, Erwin O. E. Von. Awakening Japan: the Diary of a Ger-
C   man Doctor. tr. from German by Eden and Cedar Paul.
        N.Y.: Viking, 1932. 406 pp. 32-13595. o.p.
        Pol. Sci. Q., 12/32

1483 Bailey, Thomas Andrew. Theodore Roosevelt and the Japanese-
C   American Crises; An Account of the International Compli-
        cations Arising from the Race Problem on the Pacific
        Coast. Gloucester, Mass.: Peter Smith, 1964 (orig. pub.
        by Stanford University Press, 1934). 353 pp. 64-56762.
        (R).
        Silberman, 434; Am. Pol. Sci. R., 6/35; Ann. Am. Acad.,
        5/35; Pacific Affairs, 9/35; Pol. Sci. Q., 12/35

1484 Beckmann, George M. The Japanese Communist Party, 1922-1945.
C   by George M. Beckmann and Okubo Genji. Stanford, Calif.:
        Stanford University Press, 1969. 453 pp. 68-26776.

1485 Beckmann, George M. The Making of the Meiji Constitution; The
B   Oligarchs and the Constitutional Development of Japan,
        1868-1891. Lawrence: University of Kansas Press, 1957.
        158 pp. 57-10705. o.p. (M-University).
        AUFS, 218; Silberman, 368; JAS, 5/58

1486 Blacker, Carmen. The Japanese Enlightenment: a Study of
B   the Writings of Fukuzawa Yukichi. N.Y.: Cambridge, 1964.
        185 pp. (Cambridge University Oriental Publication
        No. 10). 64-1805.
        Sup. 65, 3055; JAS, 5/65; Japan Q., 10-12/64; JAOS, 4-6/64

1487 Borton, Hugh. Japan's Modern Century. N.Y.: Ronald, 1955.
A   524 pp. 55-10667.
        AUFS, 221; Silberman, 317; AHR, 4/56; Am. Pol. Sci. R.,
        3/56; Ann. Am. Acad., 7/56; Pacific Affairs, 6/56; Pol. Sci.
        Q., 6/56

1488 Brown, Delmer Myers. Nationalism in Japan; An Introductory
B   Historical Analysis. Berkeley: University of California
        Press, 1955. 336 pp. 54-6469. o.p.
        AUFS, 222; Silberman, 321; FEQ, 8/55; AHR, 7/55; Ann. Am.
        Acad., 5/55; Japan Q., 7-9/56; Library Journal, 3/1/55

1489 Butow, Robert Joseph Charles. Japan's Decision to Surrender.
A   Stanford, Calif.: Stanford University Press, 1954.
        259 pp. 54-8145.
        Silberman, 538; FEQ, 2/55; AHR, 4/55; Am. Pol. Sci. R.,
        12/54; Ann. Am. Acad., 1/55; Japan Q., 1-3/56; Library
        Journal, 10/1/54; Pacific Affairs, 12/55; TLS, 5/6/55

1490 Butow, Robert Joseph Charles. Tojo and the Coming of the War.
B   Princeton, N.J.: Princeton University Press, 1961. 584 pp.
        61-6287.
        Sup. 61, 2756; JAS, 2/62; AHR, 10/61; Am. Pol. Sci. R.,
        12/61; Japan Q., 10-12/61; JAOS, 1-3/62; Pol. Sci. Q.,
        3/62; TLS, 12/15/61

1491 Byas, Hugh. Government by Assassination. N.Y.: Knopf, 1942.
B   369 pp. 42-25289. o.p.
        Silberman, 452; FEQ, 5/43; Pacific Affairs, 3/43

1492 Cary, Otis. A History of Christianity in Japan. N.Y.: Revell,
B   1909. 2 v. 9-22916. o.p.
        Silberman, 656

1493 Conroy, Francis Hilary. The Japanese Frontier in Hawaii,
C   1868-1898. Berkeley: University of California Press, 1953.
        175 pp. (University of California Publications in History,
        Vol. 46). A53-9799. o.p.

Silberman, 433; FEQ, 5/54

1494 Conroy, Francis Hilary. The Japanese Seizure of Korea: 1868-
A 1910, a Study of Realism and Idealism in International
Relations. Philadelphia: University of Pennsylvania
Press, 1960. 544 pp. 60-6936.
Silberman, 424a; JAS, 2/63; Ann. Am. Acad., 9/61; Library
Journal, 3/1/61; Pacific Affairs, Winter/61

1495 Craig, Albert M. Choshu in the Meiji Restoration. Cambridge,
A Mass.: Harvard University Press, 1961. 385 pp. (Harvard
Historical Monographs, 47). 61-8839.
Sup. 61, 2759; Silberman, 341

1496 Crowley, James B. Japan's Quest for Autonomy; National Security
A and Foreign Policy, 1930-1938. Princeton, N.J.: Princeton
University Press, 1966. 428 pp. 66-10552.
Sup. 67, 3213; Choice, 7-8/67; JAS, 8/67; Ann. Am. Acad.,
7/67; Pacific Affairs, Spring-Summer/67; TLS, 7/6/67

1497 Dennett, Tyler. Roosevelt and the Russo-Japanese War, a Crit-
B ical Study of American Policy in East Asia in 1902-5.
Gloucester, Mass.: Peter Smith, 1959 (orig. pub. by Double-
day, Page, 1925). 357 pp. 60-2036. (R).
Silberman, 436; AHR, 10/25; Am. Pol. Sci. R., 8/25

1498 Dennis, Alfred Lewis Pinneo. The Anglo-Japanese Alliance. N.Y.:
B Johnson, 1967 (orig. pub. by University of California Press,
1923). 111 pp. A23-1030. (R).
Silberman, 408

1499 Dulles, Foster Rhea. Yankees and Samurai; America's Role in
B the Emergence of Modern Japan: 1791-1900. N.Y.: Harper
& Row, 1965. 275 pp. 65-20427.
Choice, 11/65; AHR, 7/66; Ann. Am. Acad., 1/66; Library
Journal, 10/1/65

1500 Duus, Peter. Party Rivalry and Political Change in Taisho
B Japan. Cambridge, Mass.: Harvard University Press, 1968.
317 pp. (Harvard East Asian Series, 35). 68-21972.
Choice, 2/69

1501 Elsbree, Willard H. Japan's Role in Southeast Asian Na-
C tionalist Movements, 1940 to 1945. Cambridge, Mass.: Har-
vard University Press, 1953. 182 pp. 53-13171. o.p.
AUFS, 1268; Silberman, 548; FEQ, 11/54; AHR, 7/54; Am. Pol.
Sci. R., 6/54; Ann. Am. Acad., 7/54; Pacific Affairs,
3/54; TLS, 8/6/54

1502 Esthus, Raymond A. Theodore Roosevelt and Japan. Seattle:
C University of Washington Press, 1967. 329 pp. 66-19567.
Sup. 67, 3215; Choice, 5/67; JAS, 11/67; AHR, 10/67;
Japan Q., 7-9/67; J. Am. Hist., 6/67; Pacific Affairs,
Spring-Summer/67; TLS, 9/28/67

1503 Falk, Edwin Albert. Togo and the Rise of Japanese Sea Power.
C N.Y.: Longmans, Green, 1936. 508 pp. 36-5811. o.p.
Silberman, 396; AHR, 1/37; Am. Pol. Sci. R., 8/36;
TLS, 6/27/36

1504 Feis, Herbert. The Atomic Bomb and the End of the War in the
A Pacific. rev. ed. Princeton, N.J.: Princeton University
Press, 1966 (orig. pub. in 1961 under the title Japan
Subdued). 199 pp. 66-13312.
Silberman, 525; JAS, 11/61; AHR, 10/61; Am. Pol. Sci. R.,
9/61; Ann. Am. Acad., 11/61; Japan Q., 7-9/61; Library
Journal, 6/1/61; Pol. Sci. Q., 12/67; TLS, 12/15/61

1505 Feis, Herbert. Contest Over Japan. N.Y.: Norton, 1967.
C 187 pp. 67-16603.
Choice, 9/68; AHR, 4/68; J. Am. Hist., 3/68; Library
Journal, 9/15/67

1506 Feis, Herbert. The Road to Pearl Harbor; The Coming of the
C War Between the United States and Japan. Princeton,
N.J.: Princeton University Press, 1950. 356 pp.
50-9585.
Silberman, 513; FEQ, 11/51

1507 Fujii, Jintaro, ed. Outline of Japanese History in the Meiji Era.
C tr. by Hattie K. and Kenneth E. Colton. Tokyo: Obunsha,
1958. 544 pp. (Japanese Culture in the Meiji Era, Vol. VII).
59-52559.
Silberman, 335

1508 Fukuzawa, Yukichi. Autobiography. rev. ed. tr. by C. Blacker.
A N.Y.: Columbia University Press, 1966. 407 pp. 66-15468.
Choice, 10/66; Library Journal, 8/66

1509 Grew, Joseph Clark. Ten Years in Japan, a Contemporary Record
B Drawn from Diaries and Private and Official Papers. Joseph
C. Grew, United States Ambassador to Japan, 1932-1942.
N.Y.: Simon & Schuster, 1944. 554 pp. 44-40123. o.p.
AUFS, 235; Silberman, 519; FEQ, 11/44; Am. Pol. Sci. R.,
10/44; Library Journal, 5/1/44; TLS, 9/23/44

1510 Grew, Joseph Clark. Turbulent Era; A Diplomatic Record
B of Forty Years, 1904-1945. Boston: Houghton Mifflin,
1952. 2 v. 52-5262. o.p.
AUFS, 306; Silberman, 518; AHR, 7/53; Ann. Am. Acad.,
3/53; TLS, 4/17/53

1511 Griffis, William Elliot. The Mikado: Institution and Person,
C a Study of the International Political Forces of Japan.
Princeton, N.J.: Princeton University Press, 1915.
346 pp. 15-24757. o.p.

1512 Gubbins, John Harington. The Making of Modern Japan, an
C Account of the Progress of Japan from Pre-feudal Days to
Constitutional Government and the Position of a Great
Power, with Chapters on Religion, the Complex Family
System, Education, etc. New Hyde Park, N.Y.: University
Books, 1966 (orig. pub. by Seeley, Service, 1922).
316 pp. 23-5147. (R).

1513 Idditti, Smimasa. The Life of Marquis Shigenobu Okuma, a
B Maker of New Japan. Tokyo: Hokuseido, 1940. 423 pp.
41-2559.
Silberman, 357

1514 Iglehart, Charles W. A Century of Protestant Christianity in
A Japan. Rutland, Vt.: Tuttle in cooperation with the Japanese
Committee, Division of Foreign Missions, National Council of
the Churches of Christ in the U.S.A., 1959. 384 pp.
59-11758.
Sup. 61, 2765; Silberman, 663; JAS, 8/60; Japan Q., 4-6/60

1515 Ike, Nobutaka. The Beginnings of Political Democracy in
B Japan. Baltimore: Johns Hopkins Press, 1950. 246 pp.
50-14240. o.p. (M-University).
AUFS, 246; Silberman, 365; FEQ, 8/51; Am. Anthropologist,
7/51; AHR, 8/51

1516 Ike, Nobutaka, ed. and tr. Japan's Decision for War; Rec-
A ords of the 1941 Policy Conferences. Stanford, Calif.:
Stanford University Press, 1967. 306 pp. 67-13659.
Choice, 9/67; JAS, 5/68; Ann. Am. Acad., 11/67; Library
Journal, 2/15/67; Pacific Affairs, Spring-Summer/67

1517 Ikle, Frank William. German-Japanese Relations, 1936-1940.
C N.Y.: Bookman, 1956. 243 pp. 57-13764. o.p.
Silberman, 488; JAS, 2/58

1518 Ishii, Kikujiro. Diplomatic Commentaries. tr. and ed. by
C William R. Langdon. Baltimore: Johns Hopkins Press, 1936.
351 pp. 36-7778. o.p.
Silberman, 524; Am. Pol. Sci. R., 10/36; Ann. Am. Acad.,
7/36; TLS, 5/9/36

1519 Ito, Hirobumi. Commentaries on the Constitution of the
B Empire of Japan. tr. by Miyoji Ito. Tokyo: Igirisu-
horitsu Gakko, 22nd Year of Meiji, 1889. 259 pp. 1-1269.
Silberman, 1246

1520 Iwata, Masakazu. Okubo Toshimichi, the Bismarck of Japan.
C Berkeley: University of California Press, 1964. 376 pp.
(University of California Center for Japanese and Korean
Studies Publication). 64-25533.
Sup. 65, 3060; Choice, 6/65; JAS, 11/65; Library Journal,
2/1/65; Pacific Affairs, Spring/65

1521 Jansen, Marius B., ed. Changing Japanese Attitudes toward
A Modernization. Princeton, N.J.: Princeton University
Press for the Conference on Modern Japan of the Associa-
tion for Asian Studies, 1965. 546 pp. (Conference on
Modern Japan of the Association for Asian Studies). 63-23406.
Sup. 65, 3061; Choice, 10/65; JAS, 2/66; Japan Q., 7-9/65;
JAOS, 1-3/66

1522 Jansen, Marius B. Sakamoto Ryoma and the Meiji Restoration.
A Princeton, N.J.: Princeton University Press, 1961.
423 pp. 61-6909.
Sup. 61, 2766; Silberman, 340; Japan Q., 10-12/61; JAOS,
4-6/62

1523 Johnson, Chalmers A. An Instance of Treason; Ozaki Hotsumi
B   and the Sorge Spy Ring. Stanford, Calif.: Stanford Uni-
     versity Press, 1964. 278 pp. 64-14556.
     Sup. 65, 3062; Choice, 10/64; JAS, 5/65; AHR, 1/65;
     Am. Pol. Sci. R., 3/65; TLS, 8/12/65

1524 Jones, Francis Clifford. Extraterritoriality in Japan and
B   the Diplomatic Relations Resulting in Its Abolition,
     1853-1899. New Haven, Conn.: Yale University Press, 1931.
     237 pp. 31-30406. o.p.
     Silberman, 400

1525 Karig, Walter. Battle Report(s)...Prepared from Official
C   Sources. N.Y.: Farrar & Rinehart for Council on Books
     in Wartime, 1944- 44-4769 rev. 2. o.p.
     Silberman, 527; FEQ, 2/48, 2/53; Library Journal, 12/1/44,
     4/15/52

1526 Kato, Masuo. The Lost War, a Japanese Reporter's Inside
B   Story. N.Y.: Knopf, 1946. 264 pp. 46-6474. o.p.
     FEQ, 5/47

1527 Kublin, Hyman. Asian Revolutionary, the Life of Sen Kata-
B   yama. Princeton, N.J.: Princeton University Press, 1964.
     370 pp. 63-7156.
     Sup. 65, 3064; Choice, 6/64; JAS, 11/64; Japan Q., 7-9/64;
     Library Journal, 4/15/64; TLS, 8/13/64

1528 Kuno, Yoshi Saburo. Japanese Expansion on the Asiatic
C   Continent; A Study in the History of Japan with Special
     Reference to Her International Relations with China,
     Korea, and Russia. Port Washington, N.Y.: Kennikat, 1968
     (orig. pub. by University of California Press, 1937-40).
     2 v. 67-27615. (R).
     Hucker, 492; Silberman, 237; FEQ, 11/41; TLS, 11/20/37

1529 Lu, David J. From the Marco Polo Bridge to Pearl Harbor,
B   Japan's Entry into World War II. fore. by Herbert Feis.
     Washington: Public Affairs Press, 1961. 274 pp. 61-15692.
     o.p.
     Sup. 63, 2887; JAS, 8/62

1530 Maki, John McGilvrey. Japanese Militarism, Its Cause and
B   Cure. N.Y.: Knopf, 1945. 258 pp. 45-3717. o.p.
     Silberman, 1362; FEQ, 11/45; Pacific Affairs, 12/45;
     Pol. Sci. Q., 12/45

1531 Marshall, Byron K. Capitalism and Nationalism in Prewar
B   Japan; The Ideology of the Business Elite, 1868-1941.
     Stanford, Calif.: Stanford University Press, 1967.
     163 pp. 67-26528.
     Choice, 9/68; JAS, 8/68; Library Journal, 12/1/67

1532 Maxon, Yale Candee. Control of Japanese Foreign Policy,
C   a Study of Civil-Military Rivalry, 1930-1945. Berkeley:
     University of California Press, 1957. 286 pp. A57-9540.
     o.p.
     AUFS, 257; Silberman, 441; JAS, 2/58; AHR, 1/58; Ann. Am.
     Acad., 7/58; Pacific Affairs, 6/58

1533 McLaren, Walter Wallace. A Political History of Japan during
B   the Meiji Era, 1867-1912. N.Y.: Russell & Russell, 1966
     (orig. pub. by Scribner's, 1916). 379 pp. 65-17910. (R).
     (M-University).
     AUFS, 258; Silberman, 353; TLS, 8/3/16

1534 Mears, Helen. Mirror for Americans: Japan. Boston: Hough-
C   ton Mifflin, 1948. 329 pp. 48-8353. o.p.
     Library Journal, 8/48; TLS, 12/25/48

1535 Moore, Frederick. With Japan's Leaders; An Intimate Record
C   of Fourteen Years as Counsellor to the Japanese Govern-
     ment, ending December 7, 1941. N.Y.: Scribner's, 1942.
     365 pp. 42-17502. o.p.
     FEQ, 5/43

1536 Morley, James William. The Japanese Thrust Into Siberia, 1918.
B   N.Y.: Columbia University Press, 1957. 395 pp. (Studies
     of the Russian Institute). 57-5805. o.p.
     AUFS, 4839; Silberman, 493; JAS, 5/58; AHR, 4/58; Am. Pol.
     Sci. R., 4/58

1537 Najita, Tetsuo. Hara Kei in the Politics of Compromise,
C   1905-1915. Cambridge, Mass.: Harvard University
     Press, 1967. 314 pp. (Harvard East Asian Series,
     31). 67-27090.
     Choice, 5/68; JAS, 5/68

1538 Nish, Ian Hill. The Anglo-Japanese Alliance; The Diplomacy
B   of Two Island Empires, 1894-1907. London: Athlone, 1966.
     420 pp. (University of London Historical Studies, 18).
     66-73701.
     Sup. 67, 3221; Choice, 1/67; JAS, 11/67; AHR, 1/67;
     Japan Q., 1-3/67; Pacific Affairs, Spring-Summer/66

1539 Norman, E. Herbert. Japan's Emergence as a Modern State;
A   Political and Economic Problems of the Meji Period.
     N.Y.: International Secretariat, Institute of Pacific
     Relations, 1940. 254 pp. 40-8128. o.p.
     AUFS, 264; Silberman, 336; FEQ, 8/43; Am. Econ. R., 9/40;
     Am. Pol. Sci. R., 8/40; Ann. Am. Acad., 10/40

1540 Norman, E. Herbert. Soldier and Peasant in Japan: the Origins
C   of Conscription. Vancouver: University of British Columbia
     Press, 1965 (orig. pub. by Institute of Pacific Relations,
     1943). 76 pp. NUC 67-46889. (R).
     Silberman, 393

1541 Okuma, Shigenobu, comp. Fifty Years of New Japan. 2d ed.
B   London: Smith Elder & Co., 1909. 2 v. 20-7617. o.p.
     AUFS, 268; Silberman, 362; AHR, 7/10

1542 Omura, Bunji. The Last Genro, Prince Saionji, the Man Who
C   Westernized Japan. Philadelphia: Lippincott, 1938.
     442 pp. 38-7536. o.p.
     AHR, 1/39; Am. J. Soc., 9/38; Am. Pol. Sci. R., 12/38;
     Pacific Affairs, 12/38

1543 Oya, Soichi, ed. Japan's Longest Day. comp. by Pacific War
C   Research Society. Palo Alto, Calif.: Kodansha, 1968.
     339 pp. 68-17573.
     Choice, 11/68

1544 Paske-Smith, Montague. Western Barbarians in Japan and
B   Formasa in Tokugawa Days, 1603-1868. N.Y.: Paragon,
     1968 (orig. pub. by Thompson, 1930). 431 pp. 68-30741.
     (R).
     Silberman, 297

1545 Pittau, Joseph. Political Thought in Early Meiji Japan,
C   1868-1889. Cambridge, Mass.: Harvard University Press,
     1967. 250 pp. (Harvard East Asian Series, 24).
     65-22065.
     Sup. 67, 3225; Choice, 10/67; JAS, 11/67; Japan Q., 10-12/67;
     JAOS, 10-12/67; Library Journal, 12/15/66

1546 Reischauer, Robert Karl. Japan, Government-Politics.
C   N.Y.: Nelson, 1939. 221 pp. 39-3379. o.p.
     AUFS, 274; Silberman, 1189; Am. Pol. Sci. R., 12/39;
     Pol. Sci. Q., 6/39

1547 Satow, Sir Ernest Mason. A Diplomat in Japan; The Inner
B   History of the Critical Years in the Evolution of Japan
     When the Ports were Opened and the Monarchy Restored...
     London: Seeley, Service, 1921. 427 pp. 21-8608. o.p.
     Silberman, 411

1548 Scalapino, Robert A. Democracy and the Party Movement in
A   Prewar Japan, the Failure of the First Attempt. Berkeley:
     University of California Press, 1953. 471 pp. 53-10608.
     AUFS, 279; Silberman, 320; AHR, 4/54; Ann. Am. Acad., 1/54;
     Pacific Affairs, 12/53; Pol. Sci. Q., 6/54

1549 Schroeder, Paul W. The Axis Alliance and Japanese-American
B   Relations, 1941. Ithaca, N.Y.: Cornell University Press
     for American Historical Association, 1958. 246 pp.
     58-2112.
     Silberman, 515; AHR, 10/58; Am. Pol. Sci. R., 12/59;
     Ann. Am. Acad., 7/58

1550 Shibusawa, Keizo, ed. Japanese Life and Culture in the Meiji
C   Era. tr. by Charles Terry. Tokyo: Obunsha, 1958. 397 pp.
     (Japanese Culture in the Meiji Era, Vol. V). 59-52562.
     Silberman, 1367

1551 Shigemitsu, Mamoru. Japan and Her Destiny; My Struggle
A   for Peace. tr. by Oswald White. N.Y.: Dutton, 1958.
     392 pp. 57-5005. o.p.
     Silberman, 478; JAS, 2/61; Library Journal, 7/58;
     Pol. Sci. Q., 12/58; TLS, 6/6/58

1552 Smith, Thomas Carlyle. Political Change and Industrial Develop-
B   ment in Japan: Government Enterprise, 1868-1880. Stanford,
     Calif.: Stanford University Press, 1955. 126 pp.
     55-6687.
     AUFS, 283; Silberman, 386; FEQ, 5/56; AHR, 4/56; Library
     Journal, 6/15/56; Pacific Affairs, 3/56

1553 Storry, Richard. The Double Patriots, a Study of Japanese
B   Nationalism. Boston: Houghton Mifflin, 1957. 335 pp.
      57-9520. o.p.
      AUFS, 284; Silberman, 374; Japan Q., 1-3/58

1554 Storry, Richard. A History of Modern Japan. N.Y.: Barnes &
C   Noble, 1962. 287 pp. 60-4354.
      Sup. 61, 2782; Silberman, 318; JAS, 5/61; Japan Q., 1-3/61;
      Library Journal, 2/15/58; Pacific Affairs, 9/58; TLS,
      10/11/57

1555 Sugimoto, Etsu Inagaki. A Daughter of the Samurai; How a
C   Daughter of Feudal Japan, Living Hundreds of Years in One
      Generation, Became a Modern American. Rutland, Vt.:
      Tuttle, 1966 (orig. pub. by Doubleday, 1926). 314 pp.
      66-15849. (R).
      AUFS, 285; Choice, 4/67

1556 Takeuchi, Tatsuji. War and Diplomacy in the Japanese
B   Empire. N.Y.: Russell & Russell, 1966 (orig. pub. by
      Doubleday, Doran, 1935). 505 pp. 66-27158. (R).
      AUFS, 288; Silberman, 399; Am. Pol. Sci. R., 8/36; TLS,
      4/25/36

1557 Tanaka, Giichi. Japan's Dream of World Empire; The Tanaka
C   Memorial. N.Y.: Harper, 1942. 118 pp. 42-3102. o.p.

1558 Tasaki, Hanama. Long the Imperial Way. Boston: Houghton
B   Mifflin, 1949. 372 pp. 50-3997. o.p.
      Library Journal, 6/15/50

1559 Togo, Shigenori. The Cause of Japan. tr. and ed. by Togo
B   Fumihiko and Ben Bruce Blakeney. N.Y.: Simon & Schuster,
      1956. 372 pp. 56-9916. o.p.
      AUFS, 319; Silberman, 479; JAS, 8/57; Japan Q., 4-6/57;
      Library Journal, 9/15/56

1560 Tolischus, Otto David. Tokyo Record. N.Y.: Reynal & Hitchcock,
C   1943. 462 pp. 43-3080. o.p.
      FEQ, 8/43; Pacific Affairs, 9/43; TLS, 7/24/43

1561 Totten, George Oakley, ed. Democracy in Prewar Japan; Ground-
B   work or Facade? Boston: Heath, 1965. 107 pp. (Problems in
      Asian Civilization). 65-19459.
      Choice, 11/66

1562 Utley, Freda. Japan's Feet of Clay. N.Y.: Norton, 1937.
C   393 pp. 37-27234. o.p.
      Am. Econ. R., 9/37; Pacific Affairs, 3/37; TLS, 11/28/36

1563 Ward, Robert Spencer. Asia for the Asiatics? The Techniques of
C   Japanese Occupation. Chicago: University of Chicago
      Press, 1945. 204 pp. A45-3653. o.p.
      Silberman, 549; FEQ, 5/46; Am. Pol. Sci. R., 10/45; Ann. Am.
      Acad., 11/45; Pacific Affairs, 12/45

1564 White, John Albert. The Diplomacy of the Russo-Japanese War.
C   Princeton, N.J.: Princeton University Press, 1964. 410 pp.
      63-23417.
      Sup. 65, 3075; Choice, 1/65; JAS, 11/65; AHR, 7/65

1565 Wilson, Robert Arden. Genesis of the Meiji Government in Japan,
B   1868-1871. Berkeley: University of California Press, 1957.
      149 pp. (University of California Publications in History,
      Vol. 56). A58-9047. o.p.
      Silberman, 367; JAS, 11/59

1566 Wohlstetter, Roberta. Pearl Harbor; Warning and Decision.
B   Stanford, Calif.: Stanford University Press, 1962.
      426 pp. 62-15966.
      AHR, 1/63; Library Journal, 9/1/62; Pacific Affairs,
      Winter/62-63; TLS, 2/15/63

1567 Yanagida, Kunio, ed. Japanese Manners & Customs in the Meiji
C   Era. tr. by Charles S. Terry. Tokyo: Obunsha, 1957.
      335 pp. (Japanese Culture in the Meiji Era, Vol. IV).
      A59-8764.
      Silberman, 1368

1568 Yoshihashi, Takehiko. Conspiracy at Mukden; The Rise of the
C   Japanese Military. New Haven, Conn.: Yale University Press,
      1963. 274 pp. 63-17025.
      Sup. 65, 3076; JAS, 8/64; AHR, 7/64; Am. Pol. Sci. R., 9/64;
      Japan Q., 10-12/64; Library Journal, 3/15/64; TLS, 6/18/64

1569 Young, Arthur Morgan. Imperial Japan, 1926-1938. N.Y.: Morrow,
B   1938. 328 pp. 38-27898. o.p.

AUFS, 301; Silberman, 438

1570 Young, Arthur Morgan. Japan in Recent Times, 1912-1926. N.Y.:
C   Morrow, 1929. 347 pp. 29-26885. o.p. (M-University).
      AUFS, 302; Silberman, 437

HISTORY
POST-WAR

1571 American Assembly. The United States and Japan. ed. by Her-
B   bert Passin. Englewood Cliffs, N.J.: Prentice-Hall, 1966.
      174 pp. 66-14703.
      Sup. 67, 3224; Am. Pol. Sci. R., 6/67; Ann. Am. Acad., 2/67;
      Japan Q., 7-9/66; Library Journal, 3/15/66

1572 Baerwald, Hans H. The Purge of Japanese Leaders Under the
B   Occupation. Berkeley: University of California Press,
      1959. 111 pp. (University of California Publications in
      Political Science, Vol. 8). 59-63933. o.p.
      Sup. 61, 2755; Silberman, 567; JAS, 5/60; Japan Q., 7-9/60

1573 Kawai, Kazuo. Japan's American Interlude. Chicago: Univer-
A   sity of Chicago Press, 1960. 257 pp. 59-14111.
      Sup. 61, 2768; Silberman, 551; JAS, 11/60; AHR, 7/60;
      Am. Pol. Sci. R., 12/60; Ann. Am. Acad., 9/60; Library
      Journal, 3/15/60; Pacific Affairs, 9/60

1574 Kurzman, Dan. Kishi and Japan; The Search for the Sun. fore.
A   by James A. Michener. N.Y.: Obolensky, 1960. 394 pp.
      60-9041.
      Sup. 63, 2886; Silberman, 586; JAS, 2/63; Library Journal,
      11/15/60; Pacific Affairs, Fall/61

1575 Martin, Edwin M. The Allied Occupation of Japan. Stanford,
C   Calif.: Stanford University Press, 1948. 155 pp.
      48-9639. o.p.
      Silberman, 556; FEQ, 8/49; Am. Econ. R., 12/49; Ann. Am.
      Acad., 3/49; Pacific Affairs, 6/49

1576 Mendel, Douglas Heusted. The Japanese People and Foreign
C   Policy; A Study of Public Opinion in Post-Treaty Japan.
      fore. by Edwin O. Reischauer. Berkeley: University of Cali-
      fornia Press, 1961. 269 pp. 61-14553. o.p.
      Sup. 63, 2890; JAS, 8/62; Japan Q., 7-9/62

1577 Packard, George R. Protest in Tokyo; The Security Treaty Crisis
B   of 1960. Princeton, N.J.: Princeton University Press, 1966.
      423 pp. 65-17156.
      Sup. 67, 3222; Choice, 10/67; JAS, 11/66; Am. Pol. Sci. R.,
      6/67; Ann. Am. Acad., 12/66; Library Journal, 9/66;
      Pol. Sci. Q., 6/67

1578 Reischauer, Edwin Oldfather. The United States and Japan.
A   3d ed. Cambridge, Mass.: Harvard University Press,
      1965. 396 pp. (American Foreign Policy Library). 64-8057.
      AUFS, 369; Silberman, 3; Choice, 9/65; Japan Q., 4-6/58;
      Library Journal, 3/15/65

1579 Sebald, William Joseph. With MacArthur in Japan; A Personal
C   History of the Occupation. N.Y.: Norton, 1965. 318 pp.
      64-23883.
      Choice, 9/65; Library Journal, 6/1/65

1580 U.S. Department of State. Treaty of Peace with Japan.
C   Signed at San Francisco, September 8, 1951, Proclaimed by
      President of the U.S., April 28, 1952. Washington:
      Dept. of State, 1952. (Department of State Publication
      4613. Treaties and Other International Acts Series, 2490).
      o.p.
      Silberman, 580

1581 Wildes, Harry Emerson. Typhoon in Tokyo; The Occupation and Its
B   Aftermath. N.Y.: Macmillan, 1954. 356 pp. 54-10175. o.p.
      Silberman, 555; FEQ, 11/54; Ann. Am. Acad., 11/54

1582 Willoughby, Charles Andrew. MacArthur, 1941-1951. N.Y.:
C   McGraw-Hill, 1954. 441 pp. 54-11277. o.p.
      Silberman, 535

GOVERNMENT AND POLITICS

1583 Burks, Ardath W. The Government of Japan. 2d ed. N.Y.:
A   Crowell, 1964. 283 pp. 64-14572.
      JAS, 8/62

1584 Colbert, Evelyn (Speyer). The Left Wing in Japanese Politics.
C   N.Y.: International Secretariat, Institute of Pacific Rela-
      tions, 1952. 353 pp. 52-9711. o.p.

Silberman, 1344; FEQ, 2/53; Library Journal, 6/15/52

1585 Cole, Allan Burnett. Japanese Society and Politics: the Im-
C pact of Social Stratification and Mobility on Politics.
Boston: Graduate School, 1956. 158 pp. (Studies in Politi-
cal Science, No. 1). 57-59505. o.p. (M-University).
AUFS, 340; Silberman, 1329; JAS, 5/57

1586 Cole, Allan Burnett. Political Tendencies of Japanese in
C Small Enterprises; With Special Reference to the Social
Democratic Party. N.Y.: Institute of Pacific Relations,
1959. 155 pp. 59-1191. o.p. (M-University).
Silberman, 1336; JAS, 2/60

1587 Cole, Allan Burnett. Socialist Parties in Postwar Japan.
B contr. chapter by Ronald P. Dore. New Haven, Conn.:
Yale University Press, 1966. 490 pp. (Studies on
Japan's Social Democratic Parties, Vol. II). 66-21511.
Choice, 10/67; JAS, 8/67; Ann. Am. Acad., 7/67; Japan Q.,
7-9/67

1588 Conference on Nineteenth Century Japanese Elites, University
C of Arizona, 1963. Modern Japanese Leadership; Transition
and Change. ed. by Bernard S. Silberman and H. D. Haroo-
tunian with ten collaborating authors. Tucson: University
of Arizona Press, 1966. 433 pp. 66-18532.
Choice, 6/67; JAS, 5/67; AHR, 4/67

1589 Conference on Political Modernization in Japan and Turkey,
C Gould House, 1962. Political Modernization in Japan and
Turkey. ed. by Robert E. Ward and Dankwart A. Rustow.
Princeton, N.J.: Princeton University Press, 1964.
502 pp. 63-16238.
Sup. 65, 3056; JAS, 11/64; Pacific Affairs, Spring/65;
Pol. Sci. Q., 12/65

1590 Fujii, Shinichi. The Essentials of Japanese Constitutional
C Law. Tokyo: Yuhikaku, 1940. 463 pp. 40-14329.
Silberman, 1245

1591 Henderson, Dan Fenno. Conciliation and Japanese Law, Tokugawa
C and Modern. Seattle: University of Washington Press, 1965.
2 v. (Association for Asian Studies, Monographs and Papers,
XIII). 64-18425.
JAS, 5/66; JAOS, 10-12/65

1592 Japan. Constitution. The Constitution of Japan and Criminal
C Laws. Tokyo: Japan Trade Guide Publishing Co., 1951.
198 pp. 51-33946.
Silberman, 1300

1593 Japan. Constitution. The Constitution of Japan, Effective
B May 3, 1947. Washington: Government Printing Office, 1947.
13 pp. (Department of State Publication 2836, Far Eastern
Series, 22). 47-31999. o.p.
Silberman, 1301

1594 Japan. Laws, Statutes, etc. The Civil Code of Japan. Tokyo:
C Civil Affairs Bureau, General Secretariat, Supreme Court,
1950. 221 pp. 51-208.
Silberman, 1308

1595 Japan. Laws, Statutes, etc. The Criminal Code of Japan, as
C Amended in 1947, and the Minor Offenses Law of Japan. tr. by
Thomas L. Blakemore. Rutland, Vt.: Tuttle, 1950. 186 pp.
50-14942.
Silberman, 1309

1596 Japan. Saiko Saibansho. Court and Constitution in Japan;
C Selected Supreme Court Decisions, 1948-1960, by John M.
Maki. Seattle: University of Washington Press, 1964.
445 pp. (University of Washington Publication on Asia).
63-9940.
Sup. 65, 3065; Choice, 4/64; JAS, 8/64; Japan Q., 1-3/65

1597 Langdon, Frank. Politics in Japan. Boston: Little, Brown,
B 1967. 290 pp. 66-28736.

1598 Langer, Paul Fritz. The Japanese Communists and Their Struggle
C for Power. Santa Monica, Calif.: Rand Corporation, 1962.
39 pp. 62-39667. o.p.

1599 Maki, John McGilvrey. Government and Politics in Japan; The
C Road to Democracy. N.Y.: Praeger, 1962. 275 pp. 62-13735.
Sup. 63, 2888; JAS, 11/62; Am. Pol. Sci. R., 3/63; Japan Q.,
10-12/62; Library Journal, 7/62; Pacific Affairs, Winter/62-
63; Pol. Sci. Q., 9/63

1600 Maruyama, Masao. Thought and Behaviour in Modern Japanese
B Politics. ed. by Ivan Morris. N.Y.: Oxford, 1963.
344 pp. 63-5967.
Sup. 65, 3066; JAS, 11/64; AHR, 7/64; Ann. Am. Acad.,
7/64; TLS, 9/13/63

1601 McNelly, Theodore. Contemporary Government of Japan. Boston:
C Houghton Mifflin, 1963. 228 pp. 63-3353.
Sup. 63, 2889; JAS, 2/64

1602 Miller, Frank O. Minobe Tatsukichi, Interpreter of Constitu-
C tionalism in Japan. Berkeley: University of California
Press, 1965. 392 pp. (Publications for the Center for
Japanese and Korean Studies). 64-18644.
Choice, 11/65; JAS, 2/66; AHR, 1/66; Am. Pol. Sci. R.,
3/66; Ann. Am. Acad., 11/65; TLS, 1/20/66

1603 Morris, Ivan I. Nationalism and the Right Wing in Japan; A
C Study of Post-war Trends. N.Y.: Oxford for the Royal Insti-
tute of International Affairs, 1960. 476 pp. 60-2705.
Sup. 61, 2773; Silberman, 1357; JAS, 11/60; AHR, 1/61;
Am. Pol. Sci. R., 12/60; Ann. Am. Acad., 1/61; Japan Q.,
10-12/60; Pacific Affairs, 9/60; Pol. Sci. Q., 9/61;
TLS, 8/5/60

1604 Political Handbook of Japan. Tokyo: Tokyo News Service, 1949-
C 50-2733.
Silberman, 1194a

1605 Quigley, Harold Scott. Japanese Government and Politics; An
C Introductory Study. N.Y.: Century, 1932. 442 pp.
32-30112. o.p.
Silberman, 585; Am. Pol. Sci. R., 2/33; Ann. Am. Acad.,
3/33

1606 Quigley, Harold Scott. The New Japan, Government and Politics.
C Minneapolis: University of Minnesota Press, 1956. 456 pp.
55-11708.
Silberman, 564; FEQ, 8/56; AHR, 7/56; Am. Pol. Sci. R., 9/56;
Ann. Am. Acad., 9/56; Japan Q., 7-9/56; Library Journal,
1/15/56

1607 Scalapino, Robert A. The Japanese Communist Movement,
B 1920-1966. Berkeley: University of California Press,
1967. 412 pp. 67-14443.
Sup. 67, 3226; Choice, 10/67; JAS, 2/68; Library Journal,
3/15/67

1608 Scalapino, Robert A. Parties and Politics in Contemporary Japan.
A Berkeley: University of California Press, 1962. 190 pp.
61-14279.
Sup. 63, 2896; JAS, 11/62; Am. Pol. Sci. R., 9/62; Japan
Q., 10-12/62; Library Journal, 1/1/62

1609 Steiner, Kurt. Local Government in Japan. Stanford, Calif.:
B Stanford University Press, 1965. 564 pp. 64-17005.
Choice, 12/65; JAS, 8/66; AHR, 7/66; Am. Pol. Sci. R.,
12/65; Japan Q., 1-3/66; Library Journal, 5/1/65; Pol.
Sci. Q., 6/66

1610 Supreme Commander for the Allied Powers. Government Section.
B Political Reorientation of Japan, September 1945 to
September 1948; Report. St. Clair Shores, Mich.: Scholarly
Press (orig. pub. by Government Printing Office, 1949).
2 v. 50-60501. (R).
AUFS, 374; Silberman, 562

1611 Swearingen, Rodger. Red Flag in Japan; International Commu-
C nism in Action, 1919-1951. Cambridge, Mass.: Harvard Uni-
versity Press, 1952. 276 pp. 52-6434. o.p.
Silberman, 443; FEQ, 5/53; Am. Pol. Sci. R., 12/52; Ann.
Am. Acad., 11/52; Library Journal, 7/52; Pacific Affairs,
9/53; Pol. Sci. Q., 12/53; TLS, 1/30/53

1612 Totten, George Oakley. The Social Democratic Movement in
C Pre-war Japan. New Haven, Conn.: Yale University Press,
1966. 455 pp. (Studies on Japan's Social Democratic
Parties, Vol. I). 66-12515 rev.
Sup. 67, 3227; Choice, 10/67; JAS, 2/68; AHR, 4/67; Library
Journal, 10/1/66

1613 Tsukahira, Toshio George. The Postwar Evolution of Communist
C Strategy in Japan. Cambridge, Mass.: Center for International
Studies, M.I.T., 1954. 89 pp. 55-32093. o.p.

1614 Tsuneishi, Warren Michio. Japanese Political Style; An Intro-
B duction to the Government and Politics of Modern Japan.
N.Y.: Harper & Row, 1966. 226 pp. (Harper's Comparative
Government Series). 66-11467 rev.

49

JAPAN - GOVERNMENT AND POLITICS

Choice, 10/67

1615 Uyehara, Cecil H. and others. Comparative Platforms of Japanese
C   Major Parties: Social Democratic Party of Japan Reunified
on October 13, 1955; Japan Liberal Democratic Party, Re-
sulting from a Merger on November 15, 1955. Boston:
Fletcher School of Law and Diplomacy, 1955. 65 pp. o.p.
Silberman, 1352; FEQ, 8/56

1616 Von Mehren, Arthur Taylor, ed. Law in Japan; The Legal Order in
C   a Changing Society. Cambridge, Mass.: Harvard University
Press, 1963. 706 pp. 62-19220.
Sup. 65, 3073; JAS, 8/64; Am. Pol. Sci. R., 6/64; Japan
Q., 7-9/64; Library Journal, 11/15/63

1617 Ward, Robert Edward. Five Studies in Japanese Politics. Ann
B   Arbor: University of Michigan Press, 1957. 121 pp. 57-63486.
o.p.
JAS, 5/58

1618 Ward, Robert Edward. Japan's Political System. Englewood Cliffs,
A   N.J.: Prentice-Hall, 1967. 126 pp. (Comparative Asian
Governments). 67-20230.
Choice, 2/68; JAS, 2/68

1619 Ward, Robert Edward. Political Development in Modern Japan.
C   Princeton, N.J.: Princeton University Press, 1968.
637 pp. 66-14309.
JAS, 2/69

ECONOMICS

1620 Allen, George Cyril. Japan's Economic Expansion. N.Y.:
B   Oxford, 1965. 296 pp. 65-6197.
Sup. 67, 3211; Choice, 3/66; JAS, 5/66; Japan Q., 4-6/66;
TLS, 12/2/65

1621 Allen, George Cyril. A Short Economic History of Modern Japan,
A   1867-1937. rev. ed. N.Y.: Praeger, 1963. 237 pp. 63-9172.
AUFS, 214; Silberman, 323; JAS, 11/63; Japan Q., 7-9/63

1622 Ayusawa, Iwao Frederick. A History of Labor in Modern Japan.
A   Honolulu: East-West Center Press, 1966. 406 pp. 66-30068.
Choice, 10/67; JAS, 11/67; Library Journal, 5/15/67

1623 Bisson, Thomas Arthur. Zaibatsu Dissolution in Japan. Berke-
C   ley: University of California Press, 1954. 314 pp. 54-6468.
o.p.
Silberman, 575; FEQ, 11/54; AHR, 10/54; Ann. Am. Acad., 7/54

1624 Broadbridge, Seymour A. Industrial Dualism in Japan: a
B   Problem of Economic Growth and Structural Change.
Chicago: Aldine, 1967. 105 pp. 66-23159.
Choice, 1/68; JAS, 11/67; Ann. Am. Acad., 11/67; Library
Journal, 5/15/67

1625 Cohen, Jerome Bernard. Japan's Economy in War and Recon-
B   struction. Minneapolis: University of Minnesota Press for
Institute of Pacific Relations, 1949. 545 pp. 49-9272 rev.
o.p.
AUFS, 229; Silberman, 577; FEQ, 5/50; Am. Econ. R., 12/49;
Am. Soc. R., 12/49; Ann. Am. Acad., 11/49

1626 Cohen, Jerome Bernard. Japan's Postwar Economy. Bloomington:
C   Indiana University Press, 1958. 262 pp. 57-10725. o.p.
AUFS, 338; Silberman, 576; JAS, 5/59; Am. Econ. R., 6/59;
Ann. Am. Acad., 3/59; Geog. R., 10/59; J. Pol. Econ., 6/59;
Pol. Sci. Q., 6/59

1627 Dore, Ronald Philip. Land Reform in Japan. N.Y.: Oxford, 1959.
B   510 pp. 59-1526. o.p.
AUFS, 346; Silberman, 1565; JAS, 2/60; Am. J. Soc., 11/59;
Ann. Am. Acad., 1/60; Japan Q., 10-12/59; J. Pol. Econ.,
10/60; Pacific Affairs, 6/60; Pol. Sci. Q., 9/59; TLS,
2/24/59

1628 Emi, Koichi. Government Fiscal Activity and Economic
C   Growth in Japan, 1868-1960. Tokyo: Kinokuniya, 1963.
186 pp. 64-32272.

1629 Fuji Ginko. Banking in Modern Japan. 2d ed. Tokyo: Research
C   Division, Fuji Bank, 1967. 299 pp. Hand catalog.

1630 Hadley, Eleanor M. Antitrust in Japan. Princeton, N.J.:
B   Princeton University Press, 1969. 985 pp. 68-56312.

1631 Hewes, Laurence Ilsley. Japan: Land and Men, an Account
C   of the Japanese Land Reform Program, 1945-51. Ames:

JAPAN - ECONOMICS

Iowa State College Press, 1955. 154 pp. 55-9962 rev.
o.p.
Silberman, 572; FEQ, 8/56

1632 Hirschmeier, Johannes. The Origins of Entrepreneurship in
B   Meiji Japan. Cambridge, Mass.: Harvard University
Press, 1964. 354 pp. (Harvard University East Asian
Research Center. Harvard East Asian Studies, 17). 64-20973.
Sup. 65, 3058; Choice, 2/65; JAS, 11/65; Am. Econ. R.,
9/65; AHR, 4/65; Library Journal, 9/15/64

1633 Hollerman, Leon. Japan's Dependence on the World Economy;
B   The Approach Toward Economic Liberalization. Princeton,
N.J.: Princeton University Press, 1967. 291 pp. 66-26586.
Choice, 4/68; JAS, 5/68; Pacific Affairs, Spring/68

1634 Huh, Kyung-Mo. Japan's Trade in Asia: Developments Since
C   1926, Prospects for 1970. N.Y.: Praeger, 1966. 283 pp.
(Praeger Special Studies in International Economics and
Development). 66-15449.
Choice, 9/67

1635 Hunsberger, Warren S. Japan and the United States in World
B   Trade. N.Y.: Harper & Row for Council on Foreign Relations,
1964. 492 pp. 64-24790. o.p.
Choice, 2/65; AHR, 5/65; Ann. Am. Acad., 7/65; Japan Q.,
4-6/65

1636 Japan. Mombusho. Nihon Yunesuko Kokunai Iinkai. The Role
C   of Education in the Social and Economic Development of
Japan. Tokyo: Ministry of Education, 1966. 429 pp.
NUC 67-35296.

1637 Kokusai Shokuryo. Nogyo Kyokai. Agriculture in Japan. Tokyo:
C   Japan FAO Association, 1953. 62 pp. 54-29294 rev.

1638 Levine, Solomon Bernard. Industrial Relations in Postwar
B   Japan. Urbana: University of Illinois Press, 1958.
200 pp. 58-6997.
AUFS, 360; Silberman, 1589; JAS, 5/59; Am. Econ. R., 3/59;
Am. Soc. R., 2/59; Ann. Am. Acad., 3/59; Japan Q., 10-12/58;
J. Pol. Econ., 10/59; Library Journal, 8/58; Pacific Affairs,
12/58

1639 Lockwood, William Wirt. The Economic Development of Japan:
A   Growth and Structural Change, 1868-1938. Princeton,
N.J.: Princeton University Press, 1954. 603 pp. 54-6077.
AUFS, 252; Silberman, 322; FEQ, 8/55; Am. Econ. R., 6/55;
Ann. Am. Acad., 5/55; Japan Q., 1-3/56; J. Pol. Econ.,
8/55; Pacific Affairs, 6/55; Pol. Sci. Q., 12/55; TLS,
4/29/55

1640 Lockwood, William Wirt, ed. The State and Economic Enterprise
A   in Japan; Essays in the Political Economy of Growth.
Princeton, N.J.: Princeton University Press, 1965. 753 pp.
(Studies in the Modernization of Japan, 2). 65-15386.
Choice, 2/66; JAS, 5/66; Ann. Am. Acad., 5/66; Library
Journal, 11/15/65

1641 Nakamura, James I. Agricultural Production and the Economic
C   Development of Japan, 1873-1922. Princeton, N.J.: Prince-
ton University Press, 1966. 257 pp. (Studies of the East
Asian Institute, Columbia University). 66-11975.
Choice, 5/67; Am. Econ. R., 9/67; Pacific Affairs, Spring-
Summer/67

1642 Nihon Ginko. Tokeikyoku. Hundred-Year Statistics of the Japa-
A   nese Economy (with two supplements). Tokyo: Statistics
Dept., Bank of Japan, 1966. 616 pp. NUC 68-60340.

1643 Ogura, Takekazu, ed. Agricultural Development in Modern Japan.
A   Tokyo: Japan FAO Association, 1963. 688 pp. 65-77317.

1644 Ohara, Keiji, ed. Japanese Trade & Industry in the Meiji-Taisho
B   Era. tr. and adapted by Okata Tamotsu. Tokyo: Obunsha,
1957. 566 pp. A59-8760 rev.
Silberman, 383

1645 Okawa, Kazushi. The Growth Rate of the Japanese Economy Since
B   1878. Tokyo: Kinokuniya, 1957. 250 pp. (Hitotsubashi
University, Institute of Economic Research, Series 1).
A59-3538.
Silberman, 1490

1646 Patrick, Hugh T. Monetary Policy and Central Banking in
B   Contemporary Japan. Bombay: University of Bombay Press,
1962. 219 pp. (Series in Monetary and International Economics, No. 5). SA64-1456.

JAPAN - ECONOMICS

JAS, 11/64

1647 Rosovsky, Henry. Capital Formation in Japan, 1868-1940.
A   N.Y.: Free Press of Glencoe, 1961. 358 pp. 61-12874.
      Sup. 63, 2895; JAS, 11/62

1648 Schumpeter, Elizabeth Boody, ed. The Industrialization of Japan
C   and Manchoukuo, 1930-1940: Population, Raw Materials and
      Industry. N.Y.: Macmillan, 1940. 944 pp. 40-35446. o.p.
      Am. Econ. R., 3/41; Ann. Am. Acad., 5/41; Pacific Affairs,
      6/41

1649 Seki, Keizo. The Cotton Industry of Japan. Tokyo: Japan
C   Society for the Promotion of Science, 1956. 417 pp.
      57-27081.

1650 Shinohara, Miyohei. Growth and Cycles in the Japanese Eco-
B   nomy. Tokyo: Kinokuniya, 1962. 349 pp. 63-58420.

1651 Sumiya, Mikio. Social Impact of Industrialization in Japan.
C   Tokyo: Japan National Commission for UNESCO, 1963.
      278 pp. NUC 66-62270.

1652 Taeuber, Irene Barnes. The Population of Japan. Princeton,
C   N.J.: Princeton University Press, 1958. 461 pp. 58-7122.
      Silberman, 266; JAS, 5/59; Am. Anthropologist, 4/59; Am.
      J. Soc., 11/59; Am. Soc. R., 6/59; Ann. Am. Acad., 6/59;
      Geog. R., 4/59; Japan Q., 1-3/59; Library Journal, 8/58

1653 Tohata, Seiichi, comp. The Modernization of Japan. Tokyo:
B   Institute of Asian Economic Affairs, 1966- 68-1427.
      JAS, 11/66

1654 Tokyo Keizai Kenkyu Senta. Postwar Economic Growth in Japan;
A   Selected Papers of the First Conference of the Tokyo
      Economic Research Center. ed. by Ryutaro Komiya. Berke-
      ley: University of California Press, 1966. 260 pp. 66-22705.
      JAS, 6/67

1655 U.S. Department of State. Mission on Japanese Combines. Report
B   of Mission on Japanese Combines. Part I, Analytical and Tech-
      nical Data, Report to Department of State and War Dept., Mar.
      1946. (Dept. of State Publication 2628/Far Eastern Ser-
      ies 14). o.p.
      Silberman, 463

1656 U.S. Strategic Bombing Survey. The Effects of Strategic
C   Bombing on Japan's War Economy. Washington: Over-All Eco-
      nomics Effect Division, 1946. 244 pp. 47-32980. o.p.

1657 Yamamura, Kozo. Economic Policy in Postwar Japan; Growth vs
C   Economic Democracy. Berkeley: University of California
      Press, 1967. 226 pp. (Center for Japanese and Korean
      Studies). 67-29726.
      Choice, 12/68; JAS, 11/68; Am. Econ. R., 9/68; Library
      Journal, 12/1/67; Pacific Affairs, Fall/68

1658 Yamanaka, Tokutaro, comp. Small Business in Japan. Tokyo:
B   Japan Times, 1960. 368 pp. 61-4047.

SOCIOLOGY, ANTHROPOLOGY AND LINGUISTICS

1659 Abegglen, James C. The Japanese Factory; Aspects of Its
A   Social Organization. Glencoe, Ill.: Free Press, 1958.
      142 pp. 58-7482. o.p.
      AUFS, 324; Silberman, 1591; JAS, 11/58; Am. Anthropologist,
      12/56; Am. Soc. R., 10/58; Ann. Am. Acad., 9/58; Pacific
      Affairs, 12/58

1660 Aspects of Social Change in Modern Japan. ed. by R. P. Dore.
A   Princeton, N.J.: Princeton University Press, 1967. 474 pp.
      66-11973.
      JAS, 8/68

1661 Basabe, Fernando M. Japanese Youth Confronts Religion; A So-
B   ciological Survey, by Fernando M. Basabe, in collaboration
      with Anzai Shin and Alphonso M. Nebreda. Tokyo: Sophia
      University in cooperation with Tuttle, 1967. 183 pp.
      67-28418.
      Choice, 10/68

1662 Beardsley, Richard King. Village Japan. Chicago: University of
A   Chicago Press, 1959. 498 pp. 58-13802.
      AUFS, 329; Silberman, 1410; JAS, 2/60; Am. Anthropologist,
      8/60; Am. Pol. Sci. R., 3/60; Am. Soc. R., 4/60; Ann. Am.
      Acad., 3/60; Geog. R., 7/60; Japan Q., 10-12/59; JAOS,
      10-12/59; Library Journal, 3/17/59

JAPAN - SOCIOLOGY, ANTHROPOLOGY AND LINGUISTICS

1663 Benedict, Ruth Fulton. The Chrysanthemum and the Sword; Pat-
A   terns of Japanese Culture. Boston: Houghton Mifflin, 1946.
      324 pp. 46-11843.
      AUFS, 219; Silberman, 1380; FEQ, 8/47; Library Journal,
      10/15/46

1664 Bennett, John William. Paternalism in the Japanese Economy:
B   Anthropological Studies of Oyabun-Kobun Patterns. by John
      W. Bennett and Iwao Ishino. Minneapolis: University of
      Minnesota Press, 1963. 307 pp. 63-16068.
      Choice, 1/64; JAS, 8/64

1665 Bennett, John William. In Search of Identity; The Japanese
B   Overseas Scholar in America and Japan. Minneapolis: Uni-
      versity of Minnesota Press, 1958. 369 pp. 58-10879.
      AUFS, 330; Silberman, 1460; JAS, 8/59; Am. Anthropologist,
      8/59; Am. J. Soc., 3/60; Ann. Am. Acad., 9/59; Library
      Journal, 10/15/58

1666 Blood, Robert O. Love Match and Arranged Marriage; A Tokyo-
B   Detroit Comparison. N.Y.: Free Press of Glencoe, 1967.
      264 pp. 67-12511.
      Choice, 3/68; Am. Soc. R., 8/68

1667 Chambliss, William Jones. Chiarijima Village: Land Tenure,
B   Taxation, and Local Trade, 1818-1884. Tucson: University
      of Arizona Press, 1965. 159 pp. (Association for Asian
      Studies, Monographs and Papers, XIX). 64-8756.
      Choice, 7-8/66; JAS, 11/66

1668 Cook, Alice Hanson. An Introduction to Japanese Trade Unionism.
B   Ithaca: New York State School of Industrial and Labor Rela-
      tions, Cornell University, 1966. 216 pp. 66-63380.

1669 Cornell, John Bilheimer. Two Japanese Villages: Matsunagi, a
B   Japanese Mountain Community by John B. Cornell; Kurusu,
      a Japanese Agricultural Community by Robert J. Smith.
      Ann Arbor: University of Michigan Press, 1956. 232 pp.
      56-1904. o.p.
      JAS, 5/57; JAOS, 4-6/57

1670 De Vos, George. Japan's Invisible Race; Caste in Culture and
B   Personality. Berkeley: University of California Press, 1966.
      415 pp. 66-16422.
      Sup. 67, 3214; Choice, 1/68; JAS, 5/67; Am. Soc. R., 10/67;
      Ann. Am. Acad., 11/67

1671 Dore, Ronald Philip. City Life in Japan; A Study of the Tokyo
A   Ward. Berkeley: University of California Press, 1958.
      472 pp. 59-16060.
      AUFS, 345; Silberman, 1408; JAS, 8/59; Japan Q., 7-9/59

1672 Embree, John Fee. The Japanese Nation, a Social Survey.
B   N.Y.: Farrar & Rinehart, 1945. 308 pp. 45-6450. o.p.
      AUFS, 230; Silberman, 595; FEQ, 11/46; Am. Pol. Sci. R.,
      12/45; Ann. Am. Acad., 11/45; Pacific Affairs, 12/45

1673 Embree, John Fee. Suye Mura, a Japanese Village. Chicago:
B   University of Chicago Press, 1939. 354 pp. 40-1477.
      AUFS, 231; Silberman, 1409; Am. Anthropologist, 10/40;
      Am. J. Soc., 9/40; Am. Soc. R., 4/40; JAOS, 9/40;
      Pacific Affairs, 12/40

1674 Fukutake, Tadashi. Japanese Rural Society. N.Y.: Oxford,
B   1967. 230 pp. 67-8869.
      Japan Q., 10-12/67

1675 Gibney, Frank. Five Gentlemen of Japan; The Portrait of a
B   Nation's Character. N.Y.: Farrar, Straus & Young, 1953.
      373 pp. 53-7052. o.p.
      AUFS, 234; Silberman, 1383; Library Journal, 2/1/53; Pacific
      Affairs, 9/53; TLS, 9/11/53

1676 Grad, Andrew Jonah. Land and Peasant in Japan; An Introductory
C   Survey. N.Y.: International Secretariat, Institute of
      Pacific Relations, 1952. 262 pp. 52-12003 rev. o.p.
      (M-University).
      Silberman, 1566; FEQ, 5/53

1677 Hasegawa, Nyozekan. The Japanese Character; A Cultural
C   Profile. tr. by J. Bester. Palo Alto, Calif.: Kodansha,
      1966. 157 pp. (Japanese National Commission for UNESCO
      Publication). 66-19819.
      Choice, 2/67; Japan Q., 10-12/66

1678 Lifton, Robert Jay. Death in Life; Survivors of Hiroshima.
C   N.Y.: Random House, 1968. 594 pp. 67-22658.

JAPAN - SOCIOLOGY, ANTHROPOLOGY AND LINGUISTICS

Choice, 11/68; Library Journal, 1/15/68

1679 Mishima, Sumio (Seo). The Broader Way; A Woman's Life in the
C   New Japan. N.Y.: John Day, 1953. 247 pp. 53-6588. o.p.
     Silberman, 1407; Library Journal, 5/15/53

1680 Mitchell, Richard H. The Korean Minority in Japan. Berkeley:
B   University of California Press, 1967. 186 pp. 67-18074.
     Choice, 6/68; Ann. Am. Acad., 7/68; Pacific Affairs,
     Summer/68

1681 Nakane, Chie. Kinship and Economic Organization in Rural
B   Japan. N.Y.: Humanities, 1967. 203 pp. 66-10915.

1682 Nishikiori, Hideo. Togo-mura, a Village in Northern Japan.
C   tr. by Toshio Sano, annotated by John Embree. N.Y.: Inter-
     national Secretariat, Institute of Pacific Relations, 1945.
     114 pp. A47-934. o.p.

1683 Norbeck, Edward. Changing Japan. N.Y.: Holt, Rinehart &
B   Winston, 1965. 82 pp. 65-23200.
     JAS, 8/66

1684 Norbeck, Edward. Takashima, a Japanese Fishing Community.
B   Salt Lake City: University of Utah Press, 1954. 231 pp.
     54-3502. o.p.
     Silberman, 1411; FEQ, 11/54

1685 Plath, David William. The After Hours; Modern Japan and the
A   Search for Enjoyment. Berkeley: University of California
     Press, 1964. 222 pp. 64-16133.
     Sup. 65, 3070; Choice, 9/64; JAS, 5/65; Ann. Am. Acad.,
     11/64; Japan Q., 10-12/64; Library Journal, 8/64

1686 Riesman, David. Conversations in Japan; Modernization, Politics,
A   and Culture. by David Riesman and Evelyn Thompson Riesman.
     N.Y.: Basic Books, 1967. 371 pp. 67-17861.
     Choice, 1/68; Library Journal, 6/15/67

1687 Shiso no Kagaku Kenkyukai. Japanese Popular Culture; Studies
B   in Mass Communications and Cultural Change Made at the
     Institute of the Science of Thought, Japan. Rutland, Vt.:
     Tuttle, 1959. 223 pp. 58-5088.
     Silberman, 1405

1688 Silberman, Bernard S., ed. Japanese Character and Culture;
A   A Book of Selected Readings. Tucson: University of
     Arizona Press, 1962. 421 pp. 61-63840.
     JAS, 2/63; Am. Anthropologist, 4/63; Am. Pol. Sci. R.,
     3/63; Japan Q., 7-9/63; Pacific Affairs, Fall/63

1689 Vogel, Ezra F. Japan's New Middle Class; The Salary Man and
A   His Family in a Tokyo Suburb. Berkeley: University
     of California Press, 1963. 299 pp. 63-21263.
     JAS, 11/64; Am. Anthropologist, 8/64; Ann. Am. Acad.,
     11/64; Library Journal, 10/1/63

1690 Whitehill, Arthur Murray. The Other Worker; A Comparative Study
B   of Industrial Relations in the United States and Japan. by
     Arthur M. Whitehill and Shin-Ichi Takezawa. Honolulu:
     East-West Center Press, 1968. 481 pp. 67-21409.
     Choice, 4/69

1691 Wilkinson, Thomas Oberson. The Urbanization of Japanese
B   Labor 1868-1955. Amherst: University of Massachusetts
     Press, 1965. 243 pp. 65-26242.
     JAS, 8/66

LANGUAGE AND LITERATURE
LITERATURE

1692 Keene, Donald, ed. Anthology of Japanese Literature, from the
A   Earliest Era to the Mid-Nineteenth Century. N.Y.: Grove,
     1955. 442 pp. 55-5110.
     AUFS, 417; Silberman, 878; FEQ, 8/56; Japan Q., 10-12/56;
     Library Journal, 11/1/55

1693 Keene, Donald. Japanese Literature; An Introduction for
A   Western Readers. N.Y.: Grove, 1955. 114 pp. 55-6276.
     AUFS, 418; Silberman, 866

1694 Kokusai Bunka Shinkokai, Tokyo. Introduction to Contemporary
B   Japanese Literature, ed. by the Kokusai Bunka Shinkokai.
     Tokyo: 1939-1959. 2 v. 39-12994 rev.
     AUFS, 471; Silberman, 875, 937

JAPAN - LANGUAGE AND LITERATURE

1695 Miyamori, Asataro, ed. and tr. Masterpieces of Japanese Poetry,
C   Ancient and Modern. 2d ed. Tokyo: Taiseido Shobo, 1956.
     2 v. in 1. 37-29969 rev.
     AUFS, 420; Silberman, 1037

LANGUAGE AND LITERATURE
LITERATURE
EARLY PERIOD
PROSE

1696 Blyth, Reginald Horace. Japanese Humour. Tokyo: Japan
C   Travel Bureau, 1957. 184 pp. 57-14606.

1697 Fujiwara Michitsuna no haha. The Gossamer Years, the Diary of
A   a Noblewoman of Heian, Japan. tr. by Edward Seidensticker.
     Rutland, Vt.: Tuttle, 1964. 201 pp. (UNESCO Collection of
     Representative Works. Japanese Series). 64-22750.
     Sup. 65, 3063; JAS, 2/66; JAOS, 10-12/65

1698 Gikeiki. Yoshitsune; A Fifteenth-Century Japanese Chronicle.
B   tr. with intro. by Helen Craig McCullough. Stanford, Calif.:
     Stanford University Press, 1966. 367 pp. (UNESCO Collec-
     tion of Representative Works: Japanese Series). 65-19810.
     Sup. 67, 3219; Choice, 11/66; JAS, 11/67; Library Journal,
     8/66

1699 Ihara, Saikaku. Five Women Who Loved Love. tr. by Wm. Theodore
A   de Bary. Rutland, Vt.: Tuttle, 1956. 264 pp. 55-10619.
     AUFS, 431; Silberman, 922

1700 Ihara, Saikaku. The Japanese Family Storehouse, or, the
B   Millionaire's Gospel Modernized. tr. by G. W. Sargent.
     Cambridge: University, 1959. 281 pp. 59-1893.
     Silberman, 921; JAS, 8/60; Japan Q., 1-3/60

1701 Ihara, Saikaku. This Scheming World. tr. by Masanori Takatsuka
B   and David C. Stubbs. Rutland, Vt.: Tuttle, 1965. 128 pp.
     (Library of Japanese Literature). 65-17850.
     Choice, 3/67; JAS, 8/66

1702 Ise Monogatari. English. Tales of Ise; Lyrical Episodes
A   from Tenth-Century Japan. tr. by Helen Craig McCullough.
     Stanford, Calif.: Stanford University Press, 1968. 277 pp.
     68-17135.

1703 Jippensha, Ikku. Shank's Mare, Being a Translation of the Tokaido
B   Volumes of Hizakurige, Japan's Great Comic Novel of Travel
     and Ribaldry. Rutland, Vt.: Tuttle, 1960 (orig. pub. in
     1920). 414 pp. 60-14370. (R).
     AUFS, 433; Silberman, 927; JAS, 8/61

1704 Kamo, Chomei. The Ten Foot Square Hut and Tales of the Heike,
C   Being Two Thirteenth Century Japanese Classics. tr. by
     A. L. Sadler. Sydney: Angus & Robertson, 1928. 271 pp.
     AUFS, 434; Silberman, 907

1705 Ki no Tsurayuki. The Tosa Diary. tr. from Japanese by Wil-
B   liam N. Porter. London: Frowde, 1912. 148 pp. S41-52.
     o.p.
     Silberman, 889

1706 Murasaki Shikibu. The Tale of Genji: a Novel in Six Parts.
A   tr. from Japanese by Arthur Waley. Boston: Houghton Mif-
     flin, 1935. 2 v. 36-27029. o.p.
     AUFS, 439; Silberman, 895

1707 Omori, Annie Shepley, tr. Diaries of Court Ladies of Old Japan.
C   Boston: Houghton Mifflin, 1920. 200 pp. 21-128. o.p.
     AUFS, 441; Silberman, 890

1708 Reischauer, Edwin Oldfather, ed. and tr. Translations from
B   Early Japanese Literature. Cambridge, Mass.: Harvard Uni-
     versity Press for Harvard-Yenching Institute, 1951. 467 pp.
     51-10360.
     AUFS, 443; Silberman, 904; FEQ, 8/52

1709 Sei Shonagon. The Pillowbook of Sei Shonagon. tr. by Ivan
A   Morris. N.Y.: Columbia University Press, 1967. 2 v.
     (UNESCO Collection of Representative Works). 67-24962.
     Choice, 4/69; JAS, 11/68; Library Journal, 1/1/68

1710 Taiheike. The Taiheki: a Chronicle of Medieval Japan. tr.
B   with intro. and notes by Helen Craig McCulloch. N.Y.:
     Columbia University Press, 1959. 401 pp. (Columbia Uni-
     versity Records of Civilization: Sources and Studies, No.
     59). 59-6662.
     Silberman, 909; JAS, 5/60; JAOS, 4-6/59; Library Journal,
     4/15/59; Pacific Affairs, 12/59; TLS, 3/15/60

1711 Yoshida, Kenko. Essays in Idleness; The Tsurezuregusa of
A   Kenko. tr. by Donald Keene. N.Y.: Columbia University
       Press, 1967. 213 pp. (Columbia College Program of
       Translations from the Oriental Classics/Records of
       Civilization: Sources and Studies, LXXVIII). 67-23566.
       Choice, 7-8/68; JAS, 5/69

1712 Zolbrod, Leon M. Takizawa Bakin. N.Y.: Twayne, 1967. 162 pp.
C   (Twayne World Authors Series). 67-12269.
       JAS, 8/68; Library Journal, 1/1/68; Pacific Affairs, Summer/68

LANGUAGE AND LITERATURE
LITERATURE
EARLY PERIOD
POETRY

1713 Blyth, Reginald Horace. Haiku. rev. ed. Tokyo: Hokuseido,
B   dist. by Japan Publications Trading Co., 1963-1964. 4 v.
       53-20278.
       AUFS, 426; Silberman, 1064

1714 Blyth, Reginald Horace. Senryu; Japanese Satirical Verses.
B   Tokyo: Hokuseido, 1949. 230 pp. 52-20528.
       AUFS, 428; Silberman, 1067

1715 Bownas, Geoffrey, ed. and tr. The Penguin Book of Japanese
A   Verse. tr., ed., and intro. by Geoffrey Bownas and Anthony
       Thwaite. Baltimore: Penguin, 1964. 242 pp. (Penguin
       Poets, D77). 64-6583.
       Sup. 65, 3069; Choice, 11/64; Japan Q., 10-12/64

1716 Brower, Robert Hopkins. Japanese Court Poetry. Stanford,
A   Calif.: Stanford University Press, 1961. 527 pp. (Studies
       in the Civilizations of Eastern Asia). 61-10925.
       Sup. 63, 2881; JAS, 8/62; Japan Q., 4-6/62; JAOS, 7-9/62

1717 Fujiwara, Sadaie. Fujiwara Teika's Superior Poems of Our
B   Time; A Thirteenth-Century Poetic Treatise and Sequence.
       Stanford, Calif.: Stanford University Press, 1967. 148 pp.
       (UNESCO Collection of Representative Works). 67-17300.
       JAS, 5/68; Library Journal, 8/67

1718 Henderson, Harold Gould, ed. and tr. An Introduction to Haiku;
A   An Anthology of Poems and Poets from Basho to Shiki. Garden
       City, N.Y.: Doubleday, 1958. 179 pp. 58-11314.
       AUFS, 430; Silberman, 1060; JAS, 8/59; Library Journal,
       1/15/59

1719 Ichikawa, Sanki, ed. Haikai and Haiku. Tokyo: Nippon Gakujutsu
B   Shinkokai, 1958. 191 pp. Hand catalog.
       Silberman, 1063

1720 Kobayashi, Issa. The Autumn Wind; A Selection from the Poems
B   of Issa. tr. by Lewis Mackenzie. London: Murray, dist.
       by Paragon, 1957. 115 pp. (Wisdom of the East Series).
       59-2658.
       Silberman, 1075; Japan Q., 4-6/58

1721 Kobayashi, Issa. The Year of My Life. tr. by Nobuyuki Yuasa.
B   Berkeley: University of California Press, 1960. 140 pp.
       60-9651 rev. o.p.
       Silberman, 1073

1722 Man'yoshu. The Manyoshu; The Nippon Gakujutsu Shinkokai Trans-
A   lation of One Thousand Poems with the Texts in Romaji, with
       a New Foreword by Donald Keene. N.Y.: Columbia University
       Press, 1965 (orig. pub. by University of Chicago Press,
       1941). 502 pp. (Records of Civilization: Sources &
       Studies, LXX). 65-15376. (R).
       Choice, 11/65; Library Journal, 6/1/65

1723 Matsuo, Basho. The Narrow Road to the Deep North, and Other
A   Travel Sketches. tr. by Nobuyuki Yuasa. Baltimore: Penguin,
       1966. 167 pp. (Penguin Classics). 67-71320.
       Choice, 7-8/67; Japan Q., 4-6/67

1724 Miner, Earl Roy. An Introduction to Japanese Court Poetry.
A   Stanford, Calif.: Stanford University Press, 1968. 173 pp.
       68-17138.

1725 Okuma, Kotomichi. A Grass Path, Selected Poems from Sokeishu.
C   tr. by Yukuo Uyehara and Marjorie Sinclair. Honolulu:
       University of Hawaii Press, 1955. 72 pp. 55-10495.
       Silberman, 1077; Japan Q., 7-9/56

1726 Rexroth, Kenneth. One Hundred Poems from the Japanese.
C   N.Y.: New Directions, 1955. 143 pp. 56-2557.
       FEQ, 5/56; Japan Q., 10-12/56

1727 Waley, Arthur, tr. Japanese Poetry; The 'Uta'. London: Lund,
B   Humphries, 1956. 110 pp. Hand catalog.
       AUFS, 447; Silberman, 1043

1728 Yasuda, Kenneth. The Japanese Haiku, Its Essential Nature,
C   History, and Possibilities in English with Selected Examples.
       Rutland, Vt.: Tuttle, 1958. 232 pp. 57-8795.
       Silberman, 1061; JAS, 8/58; Japan Q., 4-6/58

LANGUAGE AND LITERATURE
LITERATURE
EARLY PERIOD
DRAMA

1729 Anderson, George Lincoln, ed. The Genius of the Oriental
C   Theater. N.Y.: New American Library, 1966. 416 pp.
       66-22974.
       Choice, 3/67

1730 Araki, James T. The Ballad-Drama of Medieval Japan. Berkeley:
B   University of California Press, 1964. 289 pp. 64-24887.
       Choice, 11/65; JAS, 2/66; JAOS, 7-9/65; Pacific Affairs,
       Fall-Winter/65-66

1731 Bowers, Faubion. Japanese Theatre. N.Y.: Hermitage, 1952.
B   294 pp. 52-12701.
       AUFS, 495; Silberman, 1093; FEQ, 8/53; Library Journal,
       10/15/52

1732 Chikamatsu, Monzaemon. The Battles of Coxinga, Chikamatsu's
B   Puppet Play, Its Background and Importance. by Donald
       Keene. N.Y.: Cambridge, 1951. 205 pp. 54-34551.
       AUFS, 496; Hucker, 524; Silberman, 1147; FEQ, 2/55

1733 Chikamatsu, Monzaemon. The Love Suicide at Amijima (Shinju
C   Ten no Amijima). A Study of a Japanese Domestic Tragedy.
       study by Donald H. Shively. Cambridge, Mass.: Harvard
       University Press, 1953. 173 pp. 52-10757 rev. o.p.
       AUFS, 497; Silberman, 1148; FEQ, 5/54

1734 Chikamatsu, Monzaemon. Major Plays. tr. by Donald Keene.
A   N.Y.: Columbia University Press, 1961. 485 pp. (UNESCO
       Collection of Representative Works). 61-15106.
       JAOS, 1-3/62

1735 Ernst, Earle, ed. Three Japanese Plays from the Traditional
B   Theatre. London: Oxford, 1959. 200 pp. 59-1489 rev.
       o.p.
       Silberman, 1096; JAS, 8/60; Japan Q., 7-9/60; Library
       Journal, 5/1/59; TLS, 4/24/59

1736 Kawatake, Mokuami. The Love of Izayoi & Seishin; A Kabuki
B   Play. tr. by Frank T. Motofuji. Rutland, Vt.: Tuttle,
       1966. 172 pp. (Library of Japanese Literature).
       66-16266.
       Choice, 2/68

1737 Namiki, Gohei. Kanjincho; A Japanese Kabuki Play. by A. C.
C   Scott. N.Y.: Samuel French, 1968 (orig. pub. in Tokyo, 1953).
       50 pp. 55-57023. (R).

1738 Nippon Gakujutsu Shinkokai. Dai 17 Sho (Nihon Koten Hon'yaku)
A   Iinkai. Japanese Noh Drama; Ten Plays Selected and Trans-
       lated from the Japanese. Tokyo: Nippon Gakujutsu Shin-
       kokai, 1955-1960. 3 v. 60-21422.
       Silberman, 1122

1739 O'Neill, P. G. Early No Drama: Its Background, Character, and
C   Development, 1300-1450. London: Lund Humphries, 1959.
       223 pp. 59-31584.
       Silberman, 1112; JAS, 5/60; Japan Q., 7-9/59

1740 O'Neill, P. G. A Guide to No. 2d ed. Tokyo: Hinoki Shoten,
C   1960. 229 pp. NUC 63-52409.
       Silberman, 1113

1741 Sakanishi, Shio, tr. Japanese Folk-plays: the Ink-Smeared Lady
A   and Other Kyooen. Rutland, Vt.: Tuttle, 1960. 150 pp.
       (UNESCO Collection of Representative Works: Japanese Series).
       60-1954.
       JAS, 11/60; Japan Q., 7-9/60

1742 Sakanishi, Shio, tr. Kyogen; Comic Interludes of Japan.
B   Boston: Marshall Jones, 1938. 150 pp. 38-16902. o.p.
       AUFS, 517; Silberman, 1128; JAOS, 3/39

1743 Segawa, Joko. Genyadana; A Japanese Kabuki Play. by A. C.
B   Scott. Tokyo: Hokuseido, 1953. 52 pp. 53-11699.

1744   Waley, Arthur. The No Plays of Japan. N.Y.: Grove, 1957
A   (orig. pub. by Knopf, 1922). 319 pp. 57-7376. (R).
       AUFS, 520; Silberman, 1121

LANGUAGE AND LITERATURE
LITERATURE
EARLY PERIOD
HISTORY AND CRITICISM

1745   Aston, William George. A History of Japanese Literature. N.Y.:
C   Johnson, 1965 (orig. pub. by Heinemann, 1899). 420 pp.
       99-768. (R).
       AUFS, 424; Silberman, 876

1746   Hibbett, Howard. The Floating World in Japanese Fiction. N.Y.:
A   Oxford, 1959. 232 pp. 59-3936. o.p.
       Silberman, 910; JAS, 5/60; Japan Q., 1-3/60

1747   Kokusai Bunka Shinkokai, Tokyo. Introduction to Classic Japa-
B   nese Literature. Tokyo: 1948. 443 pp. 50-31232 rev.
       AUFS, 419; Silberman, 873

1748   Okazaki, Yoshie, comp. Japanese Literature in the Meiji Era.
C   tr. by V. H. Viglielmo. Tokyo: Obunsha, 1955. 673 pp.
       (Japanese Culture in the Meiji Era, Vol. I). 56-22381.
       Silberman, 935

LANGUAGE AND LITERATURE
LITERATURE
MODERN PERIOD
PROSE

1749   Akutagawa, Ryunosuke. Hell Screen ("Jigoku Hen") and Other
C   Stories. tr. from Japanese by W. H. H. Norman. Tokyo:
       Hokuseido, 1948. 177 pp. 52-21547.
       AUFS, 449

1750   Akutagawa, Ryunosuke. Kappa. tr. from Japanese by Seichi
C   Shiojiri. new ed. Tokyo: Hokuseido, 1949. 136 pp.
       52-21548.
       Silberman, 1001

1751   Akutagawa, Ryunosuke. Rashomon, and Other Stories. tr. by
C   Takashi Kojima. enl. ed. N.Y.: Liveright, 1968. 119 pp.
       67-97739.

1752   Akutagawa, Ryunosuke. Tales Grotesque and Curious. tr. from
B   Japanese by Glenn W. Shaw. rev. ed. Tokyo: Hokuseido, dist.
       by Japan Publications Trading Co., 1963. 144 pp. 52-46785.
       AUFS, 452

1753   Akutagawa, Ryunosuke. The Three Treasures. tr. by Sasaki
C   Takamasa. 2d ed. rev. and enl. Tokyo: Hokuseido, 1951.
       142 pp. 60-20214.

1754   Akutagawa, Ryunosuke. TuTze-Chun. tr. by Dorothy Britton.
B   Tokyo: Kodansha, dist. by Japan Publications Trading Co.,
       1965. 59 pp. 65-12283.
       Choice, 1/66

1755   Arishima, Takeo. The Agony of Coming into the World. tr.
C   by Seiji Fujita. Tokyo: Hokuseido, 1955. 103 pp. 57-27401.

1756   Dazai, Osamu, pseud. No Longer Human. tr. by Donald Keene.
B   Norfolk, Conn: New Directions, 1958. 177 pp. 58-9509.
       Silberman, 1003; TLS, 6/30/58

1757   Dazai, Osamu, pseud. The Setting Sun. tr. by Donald Keene.
B   Norfolk, Conn.: J. Laughlin, 1956. 189 pp. 56-13350 rev.
       AUFS, 456; Silberman, 1004; JAS, 2/57; Library Journal,
       9/15/56

1758   Hasegawa, Tatsunosuke. An Adopted Husband (Sono Omokage). tr.
C   from the original Japanese of Futabei, by Buchachiro Mitzui
       and Gregg M. Sinclair. N.Y.: Knopf, 1919. 275 pp. 19-10549
       rev. o.p. (M-University).

1759   Hasegawa, Tatsunosuke. Mediocrity. tr. from Japanese by
C   Glenn W. Shaw. Tokyo: Hokuseido, 1927. 195 pp. Hand
       catalog.

1760   Hayashi, Fumiko. Floating Cloud (Ukigumo). tr. by Y. Koita-
C   bashi. Tokyo: Information, 1957. 110 pp. A58-5446.
       Silberman, 1007

1761   Japan Writers' Society. Young Forever and Five Other Novel-
C   ettes, by Contemporary Japanese Authors. Tokyo: Hokuseido,
       1941. 142 pp. A42-566 rev. 2.

1762   Kawabata, Yasunari. Snow Country. tr., with an intro. by Ed-
B   ward G. Seidensticker. N.Y.: Knopf, 1956. 175 pp.
       56-8910.
       AUFS, 467; Silberman, 1010; Library Journal, 12/15/56;
       TLS, 7/5/57

1763   Kawabata, Yasunari. Thousand Cranes. tr. by Edward Seiden-
B   sticker. N.Y.: Knopf, 1959. 147 pp. 59-6220.
       Library Journal, 1/1/59; TLS, 6/5/59

1764   Keene, Donald, ed. and tr. The Old Woman, The Wife, and The
B   Archer; Three Modern Japanese Short Novels. N.Y.: Viking,
       1961. 172 pp. 61-16603. o.p.
       Sup. 63, 2885; JAS, 8/62; Library Journal, 9/1/61;
       TLS, 5/18/62

1765   McKinnon, Richard N., ed. The Heart is Alone; A Selection
C   of 20th Century Japanese Short Stories. Tokyo: Hokuseido,
       1957. 171 pp. 57-14222.
       AUFS, 473; Silberman, 958; JAS, 8/58

1766   Mishima, Yukio, pseud. Confessions of a Mask. tr. by Mere-
B   dith Weatherby. Norfolk, Conn.: New Directions, 1958.
       255 pp. 58-12637.
       AUFS, 474; Silberman, 1014; JAS, 2/59

1767   Mishima, Yukio, pseud. Death in Midsummer, and Other Stories.
B   N.Y.: New Directions, 1966. 181 pp. 66-17819.
       Choice, 1/67; Library Journal, 4/1/66; TLS, 4/20/67

1768   Mishima, Yukio, pseud. The Sound of Waves. tr. by Meredith
B   Weatherby. N.Y.: Knopf, 1956. 182 pp. 56-8911.
       Silberman, 1013; Library Journal, 8/56

1769   Mishima, Yukio, pseud. The Temple of the Golden Pavilion.
B   tr. by Ivan Morris. N.Y.: Knopf, 1959. 262 pp. 59-7222.
       AUFS, 476; Silberman, 1015; Library Journal, 5/15/59

1770   Mori, Ogai. The Wild Geese. tr. by Kingo Ochiai and Sanford
B   Goldstein. Rutland, Vt.: Tuttle, 1959. 119 pp. 59-14087.
       Sup. 61, 2775; JAS, 8/60; JAOS, 4-6/60

1771   Mori, Rintaro. Sansho-Dayu, by Ogai Mori (pseud.). tr. by
C   Tsutomi Fukuda. Tokyo: Hokuseido, 1952. 72 pp.
       FEQ, 11/54

1772   Morris, Ivan I., ed. Modern Japanese Stories: an Anthology.
A   London: Eyre & Spottiswoode, dist. by Lawrence Verry, 1965
       (orig. pub. in 1961). 528 pp. (UNESCO Collection of Rep-
       resentative Works: Japanese Series). 61-11971. (R).
       Sup. 63, 2891; Choice, 5/66; JAS, 8/62; JAOS, 4-6/62

1773   Natsume, Soseki. Botchan (Master Darling). tr. by Yasotaro
C   Morri. Rutland, Vt.: Tuttle, 1968 (orig. pub. in 1922).
       188 pp. 68-11974. (R).
       Choice, 1/69; Silberman, 1025

1774   Natsume, Soseki. Kokoro, a Novel. tr. by Edwin McClellan.
A   Chicago: Regnery, 1957. 248 pp. 57-10097.
       AUFS, 479; Silberman, 1024; JAS, 8/58

1775   Natsume, Soseki. Kusamakura and Buncho. tr. by Umeji Sasaki.
C   Tokyo: Iwanami-shoten, 1927. 276 pp.

1776   Natsume, Soseki. Ten Nights' Dreams and Our Cat's Grave. tr.
C   by Sankichi Hata and Dofu Shirai. Tokyo: Tokyo News
       Service, 1949. 112 pp. 57-19173.

1777   Natsume, Soseki. Within My Glass Doors. tr. by Iwao Matsuhara
C   and E. T. Iglehart. Tokyo: Shinseido, 1928. 154 pp.
       52-50336.

1778   Noma, Hiroshi. Zone of Emptiness. tr. from French by Bernard
C   Frechtman. Cleveland: World, 1956. 317 pp. 56-9260. o.p.
       AUFS, 483; Library Journal, 9/1/56

1779   Oe, Kenzaburo. A Personal Matter. N.Y.: Grove, 1968. 214 pp.
B   68-22007.
       Library Journal, 7/68

1780   Ooka, Shohei. Fires on the Plain. tr. from Japanese by
B   Ivan Morris. N.Y.: Knopf, 1957. 246 pp. 57-5651. o.p.
       AUFS, 484; Silberman, 1030; Library Journal, 7/57; TLS,
       4/12/57

1781   Osaragi, Jiro, pseud. Homecoming. tr. from Japanese by Brewster
B   Horwitz. N.Y.: Knopf, 1955. 303 pp. 54-12040.
       AUFS, 482; Silberman, 1028; Japan Q., 10-12/55; Library
       Journal, 12/1/54; TLS, 9/9/55

1782 Ryan, Marleigh Grayer. Japan's First Modern Novel: Ukigumo
A   of Futabatei Shimei. N.Y.: Columbia University Press,
    1967. 381 pp. (UNESCO Collection of Representative Works).
    67-15896.
    Choice, 3/68; JAS, 5/68

1783 Seidensticker, Edward G. Kafu the Scribbler; The Life and
A   Writings of Nagai Kafu, 1879-1959. Stanford, Calif.:
    Stanford University Press, 1965. 360 pp. 65-21492.
    Choice, 9/66; JAS, 11/66; Japan Q., 4-6/66; Library Journal,
    12/1/65

1784 Takeyama, Michio. Harp of Burma. tr. by Howard Hibbett.
B   Rutland, Vt.: Tuttle, 1966. 132 pp. (UNESCO Collection
    of Contemporary Works/Library of Japanese Literature).
    66-20570.
    Choice, 5/67

1785 Tanizaki, Jun'ichiro. Ashikari and the Story of Shunkin;
B   Modern Japanese Novels. tr. from Japanese by Roy Humpher-
    son and Hajime Okita. Tokyo: Hokuseido, 1936. 172 pp.
    38-2496 rev.
    AUFS, 487

1786 Tanizaki, Jun'ichiro. Diary of a Mad Old Man. tr. from Jap-
B   anese by Howard Hibbett. N.Y.: Knopf, 1965. 177 pp.
    65-11115.
    Choice, 11/65; Library Journal, 8/65

1787 Tanizaki, Jun'ichiro. The Makioka Sisters. tr. from Japanese
A   by Edward G. Seidensticker. N.Y.: Knopf, 1957. 530 pp.
    57-10311.
    AUFS, 488; Silberman, 1031; JAS, 8/58; Library Journal,
    9/15/57

1788 Tanizaki, Jun'ichiro. Seven Japanese Tales. tr. from Japanese
A   by Howard Hibbett. N.Y.: Knopf, 1963. 298 pp. 62-15574.
    Library Journal, 7/63; TLS, 5/5/64

1789 Tanizaki, Jun'ichiro. Some Prefer Nettles. tr. from Japanese
B   by Edward G. Seidensticker. N.Y.: Knopf, 1955. 202 pp.
    55-5616.
    AUFS, 489; Silberman, 1032; Japan Q., 10-12/55; Library
    Journal, 4/1/55

1790 Tokutomi, Kenjiro. Nami-ko, a Realistic Novel. tr. from
C   Japanese by Sakae Shioya and E. F. Edgett. Boston:
    Turner, 1904. 314 pp. 4-7710. o.p. (M-University).

1791 Yoshikawa, Eiji. The Heike Story. tr. from Japanese by
C   Fuki Wooyenaka Uramatsu. N.Y.: Knopf, 1956. 626 pp.
    56-5778. o.p.
    Silberman, 1035; Japan Q., 4-6/57; Library Journal, 11/1/56

LANGUAGE AND LITERATURE
LITERATURE
MODERN PERIOD
POETRY

1792 Green Hill Poems, by Kiyoshi Sato (and others). Tokyo: Hoku-
C   seido, 1953. 182 pp. 55-42250.
    Silberman, 1084

1793 Ishikawa, Hajime. A Handful of Sand. tr. by Shio Sakanishi.
B   Boston: Marshall Jones, 1934. 77 pp. 34-35669. o.p.
    AUFS, 464

1794 Ishikawa, Takuboku. Poems to Eat. tr. by Carl Sesar. Palo
B   Alto, Calif.: Kodansha, 1966. 168 pp. 66-19820.
    Choice, 10/66

1795 Ito, Kojiro. Songs of a Cowherd. tr. from works of Sachio
B   Ito by Shio Sakanishi. Boston: Marshall Jones, 1936.
    74 pp. (Modern Japanese Poets Series, 3). 37-475.
    o.p. (M-University).

1796 Kono, Ichiro, ed. An Anthology of Modern Japanese Poetry.
B   Tokyo: Kenkyusha, 1957. 173 pp. A59-7331.
    AUFS, 472; Silberman, 1081

1797 Ninomiya, Takamichi, ed. The Poetry of Living Japan; An
A   Anthology. N.Y.: Grove, 1957. 104 pp. 58-12186. o.p.
    AUFS, 480; Silberman, 1080

1798 Yosano, Akiko. Tangled Hair; Translated from the Works of the
B   Poet Akiko Yosano, by Shio Sakanishi. Boston: Marshall
    Jones, 1935. 71 pp. 36-137. o.p. (M-University).

AUFS, 493

LANGUAGE AND LITERATURE
LITERATURE
MODERN PERIOD
DRAMA

1799 Mishima, Yukio, pseud. Five Modern No Plays. tr. from
A   Japanese by Donald Keene. N.Y.: Knopf, 1957. 198 pp.
    57-8684 rev.
    AUFS, 510; Silberman, 1152; JAS, 5/58

1800 Mishima, Yukio, pseud. Madame de Sade. tr. by Donald Keene.
B   N.Y.: Grove, 1967. 108 pp. 67-19616.
    Choice, 4/68; Library Journal, 8/67

1801 Mishima, Yukio, pseud. Twilight Sunflower; A Play in Four Acts.
C   tr. by Shigeho Shinozaki and A. Warren Virgil. Tokyo:
    Hokuseido, 1958. 143 pp. Hand catalog.
    Silberman, 1154

1802 Mushakoji, Saneatsu. The Passion, by S. Mushakoji and Three
C   Other Japanese Plays. Honolulu: Oriental Literature
    Society, University of Hawaii, 1933. 178 pp. 36-543. o.p.
    Silberman, 1158

1803 Yamamoto, Yuzo. Three Plays. tr. from Japanese by Glenn
C   W. Shaw. Tokyo: Hokuseido, 1935. 358 pp. 36-4894.
    Silberman, 1155

LANGUAGE AND LITERATURE
LITERATURE
MODERN PERIOD
HISTORY AND CRITICISM

1804 Keene, Donald. Modern Japanese Literature, an Anthology.
A   N.Y.: Grove, 1956. 440 pp. 56-8439.
    AUFS, 468; Silberman, 956; JAS, 5/57

1805 Ueda, Makoto. Zeami, Basho, Yeats, Pound: a Study in Japanese
C   and English Poetics. The Hague: Mouton, 1965. 165 pp.
    (Studies in General and Comparative Literature, I). 65-28168.

PHILOSOPHY AND RELIGION
GENERAL

1806 Anesaki, Masaharu. History of Japanese Religion, with Special
A   Reference to the Social and Moral Life of the Nation.
    Rutland, Vt.: Tuttle, 1963. 423 pp. 63-19395/CD.
    AUFS, 125; Silberman, 591; JAS, 5/64

1807 Anesaki, Masaharu. Religious Life of the Japanese People.
A   rev. by Hideo Kishimoto. Honolulu: East-West Center Press,
    1965. 105 pp. (Series on Japanese Life and Culture, 4).
    64-584. o.p. (M-University).
    AUFS, 126; Choice, 12/65; JAS, 2/65

1808 Bellah, Robert Neelly. Tokugawa Religion, the Values of Pre-
A   Industrial Japan. Glencoe, Ill.: Free Press, 1957. 249 pp.
    57-6748.
    AUFS, 127; Silberman, 594; JAS, 5/63; Am. Soc. R., 10/57;
    Ann. Am. Acad., 11/57; J. Religion, 10/57; Pacific Affairs,
    9/57

1809 Benl, Oscar, ed. Japanische Geisteswelt; Vom Mythus zur Gegen-
C   wart. Baden-Baden: Holle Verlag, 1956. 419 pp. Hand
    catalog.
    Silberman, 589

1810 Bunce, William K., ed. Religions in Japan: Buddhism, Shinto, and
B   Christianity. Rutland, Vt.: Tuttle, 1962. 194 pp. Hand
    catalog.
    AUFS, 130; Silberman, 590

1811 East-West Philosophers' Conference. The Japanese Mind; Essen-
B   tials of Japanese Philosophy and Culture. ed. by Charles
    A. Moore with the assistance of Aldyth V. Morris. Hono-
    lulu: East-West Center Press, 1964. 357 pp. (East-West
    Philosophers' Conference, 1964). 67-16704.
    Choice, 6/68; JAS, 11/68

1812 Griffis, William Elliot. The Religions of Japan, from the
C   Dawn of History to the Era of the Meiji. N.Y.: Scribner's,
    1895. 457 pp. 4-4213. o.p. (M-University).

1813 Gundert, Wilhelm. Japanische Religionsgeschichte, die Reli-
C   gionen der Japaner und Koreaner in Geschichtlichen Abriss
    Dargestellt. Tokyo: Japanisch-Deutches Kulturinstitut,

1935. 267 pp. 36-6168.
Silberman, 592

1814 Hori, Ichiro. Folk Religion in Japan: Continuity and Change.
B   ed. by Joseph M. Kitagawa and Alan L. Miller. Chicago: Uni-
       versity of Chicago Press, 1968. 278 pp. 67-30128.
       JAS, 2/69; Library Journal, 8/68

1815 Kishimoto, Hideo. Japanese Religion in the Meiji Era. tr.
B   by John F. Howes. Tokyo: Obunsha, 1956. 377 pp. (Japanese
       Culture in the Meiji Era, Vol. II). 57-2109.
       Silberman, 593; JAS, 8/57

1816 Kitagawa, Joseph Mitsuo. Religion in Japanese History. N.Y.:
A   Columbia University Press, 1966. 475 pp. (Lectures on
       the History of Religions, Sponsored by the American Council
       of Learned Societies, New Series, 7). 65-23669.
       Choice, 6/67; JAS, 8/67; AHR, 10/67; Library Journal, 1/15/66

1817 Kosaka, Masaaki, ed. Japanese Thought in the Meiji Era. tr.
B   by David Abosch. Tokyo: Pan-Pacific Press, 1958. 512 pp.
       (Japanese Culture in the Meiji Era, Vol. IX). 59-65049.
       Silberman, 335

1818 Okakura, Kakuzo. The Book of Tea. intro. and notes by E. F.
B   Bleiler. N.Y.: Dover, 1965 (orig. pub. in 1906). 76 pp.
       56-13134. (R).
       Silberman, 862

PHILOSOPHY AND RELIGION
SHINTO

1819 Dumoulin, Heinrich. Kamo Mabuchi (1697-1769); Ein Beitrag Zur
C   Japanischen Religions- und Geistesgeschichte. Tokyo: Sophia
       University Press, 1943- (Monumenta Nipponica Monograph, 8).
       50-41347.
       Silberman, 691

1820 Herbert, Jean. Shinto; At the Fountain-head of Japan. pref.
C   by Yukitada Sasaki. N.Y.: Stein and Day, 1967. 622 pp.
       66-24531.
       Choice, 11/67; Library Journal, 6/15/67

1821 Holtom, Daniel Clarence. Modern Japan and Shinto Nationalism;
B   A Study of Present-day Trends in Japanese Religions.
       rev. ed. N.Y.: Paragon, 1963 (orig. pub. by University
       of Chicago Press, 1947). 226 pp. 66-22615. (R).
       Sup. 65, 3059; JAS, 11/64; FEQ, 8/43

1822 Holtom, Daniel Clarence. The National Faith of Japan; A
B   Study in Modern Shinto. N.Y.: Paragon, 1965 (orig.
       pub. by Dutton, 1938). 329 pp. 65-26102. (R).
       AUFS, 134; Silberman, 607; JAOS, 12/40; J. Religion, 7/38

1823 Kato, Genchi. A Study of Shinto, the Religion of the Japanese
C   Nation. Tokyo: Zaidan-hojin-Meiji-seitoku-kinen-gakkai,
       1926. 255 pp. 28-16775.
       AUFS, 136; Silberman, 610

1824 Muraoka, Tsunetsuga. Studies in Shinto Thought. tr. by Delmer
B   Brown and James Araki. Tokyo: Japanese Ministry of Educa-
       tion, 1964. 264 pp. NUC 65-10734.

1825 Ono, Motonori. Shinto: the Kami Way. Tokyo: Bridgway, dist.
B   by Tuttle, 1962. 116 pp. 61-14033.
       Sup. 63, 2894; JAS, 5/62

1826 Posonby-Fane, Richard Arthur Brabazon. Visiting Famous Shinto
C   Shrines in Japan. Kyoto: The Ponsonby Memorial Society, 1964.
       439 pp. 66-32263.
       JAS, 5/66

PHILOSOPHY AND RELIGION
BUDDHISM

1827 Anesaki, Masaharu. Nichiren, the Buddhist Prophet. Gloucester,
C   Mass.: Peter Smith, 1966 (orig. pub. by Harvard University
       Press, 1916). 160 pp. 67-2824. (R). (M-University).
       Silberman, 638; Choice, 2/68

1828 Bloom, Alfred. Shinran's Gospel of Pure Grace. Tucson:
C   University of Arizona Press, 1965. 97 pp. (Association
       for Asian Studies, Monographs and Papers, XX). 64-8757.
       Choice, 2/67

1829 Blyth, Reginald Horace. Zen and Zen Classics. Tokyo: Hokuseido,
C   dist. by Japan Publications Trading Co., 1963-66. 5 v.
       62-51117 rev.

JAOS, 7-9/62

1830 Dumoulin, Heinrich. Ostliche Meditation und Christliche
B   Mystik. Munchen: Alber, 1966. 339 pp. 67-82534.

1831 Dumoulin, Heinrich. Zen; Geschichte und Gestalt. Berne:
C   Francke Verlag, 1959. 332 pp. (Sammlung Dalps, 87).
       Hand catalog.
       Silberman, 639

1832 Eliot, Sir Charles Norton Edgecumbe. Japanese Buddhism.
A   London: Routledge & Kegan Paul, 1935. 449 pp. 35-6584.
       AUFS, 141; Silberman, 624; JAS, 8/60; J. Philosophy, 6/20/35

1833 Kamstra, J. H. Encounter or Syncretism, the Initial Growth
B   of Japanese Buddhism. Leiden: Brill, 1967. 508 pp.
       68-81683.

1834 Kidder, Jonathan Edward. Japanese Temples; Sculpture, Paint-
A   ings, Gardens, and Architecture. Tokyo: Bijutsu Shuppan-
       sha, 1964. 554 pp. NUC 66-35074.

1835 Lassalle, Hugo. Zen Buddhismus. von Hugo M. Enomiya. Koln:
B   Bachem, 1966. 449 pp. 66-66205.

1836 Saunders, Ernest Dale. Buddhism in Japan, With an Outline
C   of Its Origins in India. Philadelphia: University of
       Pennsylvania Press, 1964. 328 pp. 64-10900.
       Sup. 65, 3072; Choice, 4/65; JAS, 5/65

1837 Shunjo. Honen, the Buddhist Saint; His Life and Teaching. tr.
C   by Harper Havelock Coates and Ryugaku Ishizuka. Kyoto: Soci-
       ety for Publication of Sacred Books of the World, 1949. 5 v.
       49-29237.
       AUFS, 145; Silberman, 636

1838 Suzuki, Daisetz Teitaro. Essays in Zen Buddhism, First
C   Series. N.Y.: Grove, 1961 (orig. pub. by Harper, 1949).
       383 pp. 50-13886. (R).
       AUFS, 147; Silberman, 646

1839 Suzuki, Daisetz Teitaro. Essays in Zen Buddhism, Second
C   Series. London: Rider, 1958. 326 pp. Hand catalog. o.p.
       AUFS, 147; Silberman, 647; JAOS, 6/34

1840 Suzuki, Daisetz Teitaro. Essays in Zen Buddhism, Third
C   Series. London: Luzac, 1934. 350 pp. 35-2983. o.p.
       AUFS, 147; Silberman, 648

1841 Suzuki, Daisetz Teitaro. The Training of the Zen Buddhist
C   Monk. New Hyde Park, N.Y.: University Books, 1965 (orig.
       pub. by Eastern Buddhist Society, 1934). 161 pp.
       65-23523. (R).
       Choice, 5/66; JAOS, 12/37

1842 Suzuki, Daisetz Teitaro. Zen and Japanese Culture. rev. and
C   and enl. 2d ed. Princeton, N.J.: Princeton University Press,
       1959. 478 pp. (Bollingen Series, Vol. 64). 58-12174.
       Silberman, 643; J. Religion, 4/60; TLS, 3/15/60

1843 Takakusu, Junjiro. The Essentials of Buddhist Philosophy. ed.
B   by W. T. Chan and Charles A. Moore. 2d ed. Honolulu: Uni-
       versity of Hawaii Press, 1949. 221 pp. A51-1982. o.p.
       (M-University).
       Hucker, 1240; JAOS, 1-3/50

1844 Visser, Marinus Willem de. Ancient Buddhism in Japan; Sutras
C   and Ceremonies in Use in the Seventh and Eighth Centuries
       A.D. and their History in Later Times. Leiden: Brill,
       1935. 2 v. 39-3106.
       Silberman, 632

PHILOSOPHY AND RELIGION
CHINESE THOUGHT IN

1845 Ishigoro, Tadaatsu, ed. Ninomiya, Sontoku; His Life and Evening
C   Talks. Tokyo: Kenkyusha, 1955.
       Silberman, 689

1846 Ogyu, Sorai. The Political Writings of Ogyu Sorai. by J. R.
C   McEwan. London: Cambridge, 1962. 153 pp. (Cambridge
       University Oriental Publication, No. 7). 62-52873.
       Sup. 63, 2892; JAS, 5/63

1847 Smith, Warren W. Confucianism in Modern Japan; A Study of
C   Conservatism in Japanese Intellectual History. Tokyo:
       Hokuseido, 1959. 285 pp. 60-137.
       Sup. 61, 2780; Silberman, 678; JAS, 11/60

JAPAN - PHILOSOPHY AND RELIGION

1848 Spae, Joseph John. Ito Jinsai, a Philosopher, Educator
C   and Sinologist of the Tokugawa Period. N.Y.: Paragon,
       1965 (orig. pub. by Catholic University, Peking, 1948).
       278 pp. A48-5462. (R).
       AUFS, 155; Silberman, 684

PHILOSOPHY AND RELIGION
OTHER RELIGIONS

1849 Laures, John. The Catholic Church in Japan; A Short History.
C   Rutland, Vt.: Tuttle, 1954. 252 pp. A55-7332.
       Silberman, 661; JAOS, 4-6/55; J. Religion, 7/55

1850 Laures, John. Kirishitan Bunko; A Manual of Books and Docu-
B   ments on the Early Christian Missions in Japan, (With
       First Supplement). Tokyo: Sophia University Press, 1940.
       344 pp. 50-47693.
       Silberman, 654; FEQ, 2/42, 2/49; Japan Q., 4-6/58

1851 Miura, Isshu. Zen Dust; The History of the Koan and Koan Study
C   in Rinzai (Lin-Chi) Zen. by Isshu Miura and Ruth Fuller
       Sasaki. with background notes, descriptive bibliography,
       genealogical charts, maps and reproductions of drawings
       by Haskuin. N.Y.: Harcourt, Brace & World, 1967. 574 pp.
       66-10044.
       JAS, 11/67

FINE ARTS AND ARCHITECTURE
GENERAL

1852 Anesaki, Masaharu. Art, Life, and Nature in Japan. Boston:
C   Marshall Jones, 1932. 178 pp. 33-1620. o.p.
       Silberman, 731

1853 Floral Art of Japan, prepared by Issotei Nishikawa. N.Y.:
B   Japan Publications Trading Co., 1964. (Tourist Library,
       N.S. 1). 61-11568.
       Silberman, 837

1854 Harada, Jiro. Japanese Gardens. Boston: T. Branford, 1956.
A   160 pp. 56-12490.
       Silberman, 830; JAS, 2/58

1855 Horiguchi, Sutemi. Tradition of Japanese Garden. 2d ed. Hono-
C   lulu: East-West Center Press, 1963. 185 pp. 64-2824.
       Library Journal, 5/15/64

1856 Iwamiya, Takeji. Design and Craftsmanship of Japan: Stone,
B   Metal, Fibers and Fabrics, Bamboo. introductory essay by
       Donald Richie. N.Y.: Abrams, 1965. 182 pp. 64-22626.
       Choice, 12/65

1857 Japanese Handicrafts, prepared by Y. Okada. Tokyo: Japan Travel
B   Bureau, 1956- (Tourist Library, N.S. 21). 62-10306.
       Silberman, 832

1858 Joly, Henri L. Legend in Japanese Art, a Description of
A   Historical Episodes, Legendary Characters, Folk-Lore
       Myths, Religious Symbolism Illustrated in the Arts of
       Old Japan. Rutland, Vt.: Tuttle, 1967 (orig. pub.
       by Bodley Head, 1908). 623 pp. 67-16411. (R).
       Choice, 10/67; Library Journal, 8/67; TLS, 11/6/67

1859 Kaemmerer, Eric A. Trades and Crafts of Old Japan; Leaves
B   from a Contemporary Album. Rutland, Vt.: Tuttle, 1961.
       112 pp. 61-14030.
       Sup. 63, 2884

1860 Kidder, Jonathan Edward. Early Japanese Art; The Great Tombs
C   and Treasures. Princeton, N.J.: Van Nostrand, 1964. 354 pp.
       64-57443. o.p.
       Choice, 10/65; TLS, 3/25/65

1861 Kobayashi, Norio. Bonsai - Miniature Potted Trees. 7th ed.
B   Tokyo: Japan Travel Bureau, 1957. 177 pp. (Tourist Library,
       N.S. 13). 57-8540.
       Silberman, 836

1862 Kojiro, Yuichiro. Forms in Japan. tr. by Kenneth Yasuda.
B   Honolulu: East-West Center Press, 1965. 184 pp. 64-7591.
       Choice, 10/65; JAS, 2/66; Library Journal, 8/65; TLS,
       12/23/65

1863 Lancaster, Clay. The Japanese Influence in America. N.Y.:
B   Walton H. Rawls, dist. by Twayne, 1963. 292 pp. 63-18860.
       Choice, 3/64; JAS, 5/65; Library Journal, 2/15/64

JAPAN - FINE ARTS AND
ARCHITECTURE

1864 Maeda, Yasuji. Japanese Decorative Design. Tokyo: Japan
B   Travel Bureau, 1960. 157 pp. (Tourist Library, N.S. 23).
       59-15732.
       Silberman, 857

1865 Munsterberg, Hugo. The Folk Arts of Japan. Rutland, Vt.:
C   Tuttle, 1958. 168 pp. 58-7496.
       AUFS, 393; Silberman, 831; Japan Q., 7-9/58; JAOS, 10-12/58;
       Library Journal, 7/58

1866 Newsom, Samuel. A Thousand Years of Japanese Gardens. 4th ed.
B   Tokyo: Tokyo News Service, 1959. 318 pp.
       Silberman, 829

1867 Noma, Seiroku. Masks. English adaptation by Merideth Weatherby.
C   Rutland, Vt.: Tuttle, 1957. unpaged. 57-8793.
       Silberman, 854

1868 Oka, Hideyuki. How to Wrap Five Eggs; Japanese Design in
A   Traditional Packaging. fore. by George Nelson. tr. and
       adapted for Western Readers by Atsuko Nii and Ralph Fried-
       rich. N.Y.: Harper & Row, 1967. 203 pp. 67-19619.
       Choice, 7-8/68

1869 Okakura, Kakuzo. The Ideals of the East, with Special Refer-
C   ence to the Art of Japan. London: Murray, 1903. 244 pp.
       3-11515. o.p.

1870 Paine, Robert Treat. The Art and Architecture of Japan. Balti-
A   more: Penguin, 1955. 316 pp. 55-12839.
       AUFS, 399; Silberman, 721; FEQ, 5/56; Library Journal,
       1/1/56; TLS, 1/27/56

1871 Robinson, Basil William. A Primer of Japanese Sword Blades.
C   N.Y.: Paragon, 1965 (orig. pub. by Dyer, 1955). 95 pp.
       59-21053. (R).
       Silberman, 851

1872 Sadler, Arthur Lindsay. Cha-no-yu, the Japanese Tea Ceremony.
C   Rutland, Vt.: Tuttle, 1963 (orig. pub. by Kegan, Paul,
       Trench and Trubner, 1934). 245 pp. 62-19787. (R).
       Silberman, 864; Japan Q., 10-12/63

1873 Sato, Shozo. The Art of Arranging Flowers; A Complete Guide
B   to Japanese Ikebana. N.Y.: Abrams, 1966. 366 pp.
       65-20323.
       Choice, 7-8/67; Library Journal, 1/15/67

1874 Tatsui, Matsunosuke. Japanese Gardens. N.Y.: Japan Publica-
B   tions Trading Co., 19- (Tourist Library, N.S. 5).
       62-13698.
       Silberman, 828

1875 Tea Cult of Japan, prepared by Y. Fukukita. Tokyo: Japan Travel
A   Bureau, 1934- (Tourist Library, N.S. 4). 59-13187 rev.
       Silberman, 863

1876 Tokyo. National Museum. Pageant of Japanese Art. Tokyo:
A   Toto Bunka, 1952-54. 6 v. 57-29427.
       AUFS, 403; Silberman, 733

1877 Tsuda, Noritake. Handbook of Japanese Art. Tokyo: Sanseido,
B   1935. 525 pp. 36-20290.
       Silberman, 732

1878 Ueno, Naoteur, ed. Japanese Arts and Crafts in the Meiji Era.
C   English adaptation by Richard Lane. Tokyo: Pan-Pacific
       Press, 1958. 224 pp. (Japanese Culture in the Meiji Era,
       Vol. VIII). 59-52560.
       Silberman, 725

1879 Warner, Langdon. The Enduring Art of Japan. Cambridge,
C   Mass.: Harvard University Press, 1952. 113 pp. 52-8220.
       AUFS, 406; Silberman, 724; FEQ, 11/53

1880 Yamada, Chisaburoh, ed. Decorative Arts of Japan. Tokyo: Ko-
A   dansha, dist. by Japan Publications Trading Co., 1964.
       262 pp. 63-22011.
       Choice, 11/65; Library Journal, 9/15/64; TLS, 12/23/65

1881 Yamada, Tokubei. Japanese Dolls. 2d ed. Tokyo: Japan Travel
B   Bureau, 1959. 190 pp. (Tourist Library, N.S. 17).
       59-13186.
       Silberman, 856

1882 Yanagisawa, Soen. Tray Landscapes (Bonkei and Bonseki). rev. ed.
B   N.Y.: Japan Publications Trading Co., 1964. 193 pp.

(Tourist Library, N.S. 19). 56-1256.
Silberman, 835; JAS, 2/58

FINE ARTS AND ARCHITECTURE
FINE ARTS

1883 Anesaki, Masaharu. Buddhist Art in its Relation to Buddhist
C   Ideals, with Special Reference to Buddhism in Japan.
      Boston: Houghton Mifflin, 1915. 73 pp. 16-100. o.p.
      Silberman, 727

1884 Arai, Hakuseki. The Sword Book in Honcho Gunkiko and the Book
C   of Same, Ko Hi Sei Gi of Inaba Tsurio. tr. by Henri L.
      Joly and Inada Hogitaro. Rutland, Vt.: Tuttle, 1963.
      176 pp. 63-6519.

1885 Art Treasures from Japan. Exhibition, Los Angeles County Mu-
C   seum of Art, September 29, 1965-November 7, 1965, and Other
      Institutions. Palo Alto, Calif.: Kodansha, 1965. 196 pp.
      65-23948.

1886 Boyer, Martha Hagensen. Japanese Export Lacquers from the
C   Seventeenth Century in the National Museum of Denmark.
      Copenhagen: The National Museum, 1959. 149 pp. 60-4349.

1887 Buhot, Jean. Histoire des Arts du Japon. Paris: Vanoest,
C   1949- A51-3611.
      Silberman, 720

1888 Feddersen, Martin. Japanese Decorative Art; A Handbook for
B   Collectors and Connoisseurs. Boston: Boston Book and Art
      Shop, 1962. 286 pp. 61-9623.

1889 Harada, Jiro. A Glimpse of Japanese Ideals; Lectures on
B   Japanese Art and Culture. Tokyo: Japan Kokusai Bunka Shin-
      kokai, 1937. 239 pp. 38-15940.
      AUFS, 389

1890 Herberts, Kurt. Oriental Lacquer; Art and Technique.
C   London: Thames & Hudson, 1962. 513 pp. Hand catalog.

1891 Jenyns, Roger Soame. Japanese Porcelain. N.Y.: Praeger, 1965.
C   351 pp. 65-13447.
      Choice, 6/66; Library Journal, 12/15/65

1892 Kidder, Jonathan Edward. Prehistoric Japanese Arts; The Jomon
C   Pottery of Japan. contrib. by Teruya Esaka. Palo Alto,
      Calif.: Kodansha, 1968. 308 pp. 68-17458.
      JAS, 2/59; Japan Q., 1-3/58

1893 Kumagaya, Nobuo and Miroru Ooka. History of Buddhist Art in
C   Japan. South Pasadena, Calif.: P. D. and Ione Perkins,
      1940. o.p.
      Silberman, 728

1894 Lee, Sherman E. Japanese Decorative Style. Cleveland:
A   Cleveland Museum of Art, dist. by Abrams, 1961. 161 pp.
      61-9910.

1895 Miller, Roy Andrew. Japanese Ceramics. N.Y.: Crown, 1962.
A   19 pp. 62-1506.
      Silberman, 843; Japan Q., 10-12/60; JAOS, 4-6/61; Library
      Journal, 8/60

1896 Minamoto, Hoshu. An Illustrated History of Japanese Art.
C   Kyoto: K. Hoshino, 1935. 264 pp. 36-9490

1897 Minnich, Helen Benton. Japanese Costume and the Makers of Its
C   Elegant Tradition. Rutland, Vt.: Tuttle, 1963. 374 pp.
      62-15063.
      JAS, 5/64; Japan Q., 1-3/64; JAOS, 10-12/66

1898 Mitsuoka, Tadanari. Ceramic Art of Japan. Tokyo: Japan
B   Travel Bureau, 1949. 190 pp. (Tourist Library, 8).
      A51-3512.
      Silberman, 845

1899 Munsterberg, Hugo. The Arts of Japan; An Illustrated History.
B   Rutland, Vt.: Tuttle, 1957. 201 pp. 56-13414.
      Silberman, 723; JAS, 2/58; Japan Q., 4-6/63; Library
      Journal, 7/57

1900 Noma, Seiroku. The Arts of Japan, Ancient and Medieval. tr.
A   and adapt. by John Rosenfield. Palo Alto, Calif.: Kodansha,
      1965. 236 pp. 65-19186.
      Choice, 6/66; JAS, 11/66; Library Journal, 12/1/65

1901 Okada, Yuzuru. Netsuke, a Miniature Art of Japan. Tokyo:
B   Japan Travel Bureau, 1951. 212 pp. (Tourist Library,
      N.S. 14). A52-9342.
      Silberman, 850

1902 Rague, Beatrix Von. Geschichte Der Japanischen Lackkunst.
C   Berlin: De Gruyter, 1967. 380 pp. NUC 67-55214.

1903 Sagara, Tokuzo. Japanese Fine Arts. 4th ed. Tokyo: Japan
B   Travel Bureau, 1958. 249 pp. (Tourist Library, N.S. 9).
      58-12786.
      Silberman, 726

1904 Sanders, Herbert H. The World of Japanese Ceramics. Palo Alto,
C   Calif.: Kodansha, 1967. 267 pp. 67-16771.

1905 Swann, Peter C. An Introduction to the Arts of Japan. N.Y.:
B   Praeger, 1958. 220 pp. 58-12088. o.p.
      Silberman, 722; JAS, 8/60; JAOS, 5-6/67; Library Journal,
      12/15/58; TLS, 9/5/58

1906 Yashiro, Yukio, ed. Art Treasures of Japan. Tokyo: Koku-
C   sai Bunka Shinkokai, 1960. 2 v. 63-2165.
      Japan Q., 1-3/61

1907 Yashiro, Yukio. 2000 Years of Japanese Art. ed. by Peter
B   C. Swann. N.Y.: Abrams, 1958. 268 pp. 58-13478.
      AUFS, 407; Silberman, 735; Japan Q., 7-9/59; TLS, 4/17/59

FINE ARTS AND ARCHITECTURE
FINE ARTS
PAINTING

1908 Akiyama, Terukazu. Japanese Painting. Geneva: Skira, dist. by
A   World, 1961. 216 pp. 61-15270.
      Silberman, 756

1909 Binyon, Laurence. Japanese Colour Prints. Boston: Boston
A   Book and Art Shop, 1960 (orig. pub. by Frederick Publishers,
      1955). 230 pp. 59-14161. (R).
      Silberman, 785

1910 Bowie, Henry P. On the Laws of Japanese Painting; An Intro-
C   duction to the Study of the Art of Japan. N.Y.: Dover,
      1951 (orig. pub. in 1911). 117 pp. 52-9794. (R).
      Silberman, 758

1911 Fujikake, Shizuya. Japanese Wood-block Prints. rev. ed.
B   Tokyo: Japan Travel Bureau, 1954. 219 pp. (Tourist Lib-
      rary, N.S. 10). 56-1608.
      Silberman, 783

1912 Hillier, Jack Ronald. Japanese Colour Prints. London: Phai-
B   don, dist. by Praeger, 1966. 87 pp. 67-31916.
      Choice, 5/67

1913 Hillier, Jack Ronald. The Japanese Print: a New Approach.
B   Rutland, Vt.: Tuttle, 1960. 184 pp. 60-51853.
      JAS, 5/62

1914 Holloway, Owen E. Graphic Art of Japan; The Classical School.
C   London: A. Tiranti, 1957. 135 pp. A58-3264.
      Japan Q., 1-3/58

1915 Ishida, Mosaku. Japanese Buddhist Prints. English adaptation
C   by Charles S. Terry. N.Y.: Abrams for Kodansha, 1964.
      195 pp. 64-20004.
      Choice, 11/64; JAS, 11/65; Art Bul., 6/65; Library Journal,
      11/1/64

1916 Katsushika, Hokusai. The Hokusai Sketchbooks; Selections from
B   the Manga. ed. by James A. Michener. Rutland, Vt.: Tuttle,
      1958. 286 pp. 58-9983.
      Silberman, 795; JAS, 5/59; Japan Q., 10-12/58; JAOS, 1-3/59;
      Library Journal, 10/1/58

1917 Kurth, Julius. Die Geschichte des Japanischen Holzschnitts.
C   Leipzig: Hiersemann, 1925-1929. 3 v. 31-32662.
      Silberman, 782

1918 Lane, Richard Douglas. Masters of the Japanese Print, Their
A   World and Their Work. Garden City, N.Y.: Doubleday, 1962.
      319 pp. 62-12098.
      JAS, 8/63; Japan Q., 4-6/63; JAOS, 10-12/62

1919 Ledoux, Louis Vernon. Japanese Prints, Buncho to Utamaro, in
C the Collection of Louis V. Ledoux. N.Y.: Weyhe, 1948.
192 pp. A50-9099. o.p.
FEQ, 11/49; JAOS, 4-6/50

1920 Ledoux, Louis Vernon. Japanese Prints by Harunobu and Shunsho
C in the Collection of Louis V. Ledoux. N.Y.: Wehye, 1945.
152 pp. 45-7008. o.p.
FEQ, 8/48; JAOS, 7-9/47

1921 Ledoux, Louis Vernon. Japanese Prints, Hokusai and Hiroshige,
C in the Collection of Louis V. Ledoux. Princeton, N.J.:
Princeton University Press, 1951. 51-12844. o.p.
FEQ, 5/52; JAOS, 4-6/52

1922 Ledoux, Louis Vernon. Japanese Prints of the Primitive Period
C in the Collection of Louis V. Ledoux. N.Y.: Weyhe, 1942.
186 pp. 42-14640. o.p.
JAOS, 7-9/47

1923 Ledoux, Louis Vernon. Japanese Prints, Sharaku to Toyokuni, in
C the Collection of Louis V. Ledoux. Princeton, N.J.:
Princeton University Press, 1950. unpaged. 50-6469. o.p.
Silberman, 780; JAOS, 7-9/51

1924 Miyagawa, Torao. Modern Japanese Painting; An Art in Transi-
C tion. Palo Alto, Calif.: Kodansha, 1967. 131 pp. 67-16770.
Choice, 9/67; Library Journal, 9/15/67

1925 Narazaki, Muneshige. The Japanese Print; Its Evolution and
A Essence. Palo Alto, Calif.: Kodansha, 1966. 274 pp.
66-12551.

1926 Robertson, Ronald G. Contemporary Printmaking in Japan.
B N.Y.: Crown, 1965. 120 pp. 65-24320.
Choice, 9/66; Library Journal, 2/15/66

1927 Rosenfield, John M. Japanese Arts of the Heian Period:
A 794-1185. N.Y.: Asia Society, dist. by New York Graphic,
1967. 135 pp. 67-22187.
Choice, 7-8/68; Library Journal, 4/1/68

1928 Seckel, Dietrich. Emakimono, the Art of the Japanese Painted
A Hand Scroll. N.Y.: Pantheon, 1959. 238 pp. 59-4934.
Silberman, 761; Library Journal, 1/1/60; TLS, 2/19/60

1929 Sharaku, Toshusai. Sharaku, by Juzo Suzuki. tr. by John
B Bestor. Palo Alto, Calif.: Kodansha, 1968. 96 pp.
(Masterworks of Ukiyo-e, Vol. 2). 68-13740.
Choice, 12/68; Library Journal, 7/68

1930 Statler, Oliver. Modern Japanese Prints: an Art Reborn.
A Rutland, Vt.: Tuttle, 1956. 209 pp. 56-6810.
AUFS, 400; Silberman, 786; JAS, 5/57; Japan Q., 4-6/57;
Library Journal, 11/1/56

1931 Stern, Harold P. Masters of the Japanese Print; Ukiyoe Hanga.
A N.Y.: Abrams, 1969. 323 pp. 69-12794.

1932 Toda, Kenji. Japanese Scroll Painting. Chicago: University
C of Chicago Press, 1935. 167 pp. 35-4632. o.p.
Silberman, 763

1933 United Nations. UNESCO. Japan: Ancient Buddhist Paintings.
C intro. by Takaaki Matsushita. Greenwich, Conn.: New York
Graphic, 1959. 21 pp. (UNESCO World Art Series, 11).
60-1597.

1934 Waterhouse, David B. Harunobu and His Age; The Development of
C Colour Printing in Japan. London: The Trustees of the
British Museum, 1964. 326 pp. 65-28917.
JAS, 5/65; JAOS, 7-9/65

1935 Yoshida, Toshi. Japanese Print-Making; A Handbook of Traditional
A & Modern Techniques. Rutland, Vt.: Tuttle, 1966. 176 pp.
66-20674.
Choice, 7-8/67; Library Journal, 1/15/67

FINE ARTS AND ARCHITECTURE
FINE ARTS
SCULPTURE

1936 Kidder, Jonathan Edward. The Birth of Japanese Art. N.Y.:
B Praeger, 1965. 209 pp. 65-16808.
Choice, 10/65; JAS, 2/66; Library Journal, 8/65; TLS,
12/23/65

1937 Miki, Fumio. Haniwa, the Clay Sculpture of Protohistoric
C Japan. Rutland, Vt.: Tuttle, 1960. 160 pp. 60-9286.
Silberman, 745; JAS, 2/61; Japan Q., 1-3/61; JAOS, 1-3/61;
Library Journal, 8/60

1938 Noguchi, Isamu. A Sculptor's World. fore. by R. Buckminster
A Fuller. N.Y.: Harper & Row, 1968. 259 pp. 67-22505.
Choice, 12/68; Library Journal, 6/1/68

1939 Noma, Seiroku. Japanese Sculpture. Tokyo: Board of Tourist
B Industry, Japanese Government Railways, 1939. 99 pp.
(Tourist Library, 29). 40-9656.
Silberman, 740

1940 Warner, Langdon. Japanese Sculpture of the Suiko Period.
C intro. by Lorraine d'O Warner. New Haven, Conn.: Yale
University Press, 1923. 80 pp. 24-2015. o.p.
Silberman, 744

1941 Warner, Langdon. Japanese Sculpture of the Tempyo Period;
C Masterpieces of the Eighth Century. ed. and arr. by James
Marshall Plumer. Cambridge, Mass.: Harvard University
Press, 1964. 217 pp. 64-23111.
Silberman, 742; Choice, 2/65; Art. Bul., 6/65; JAOS, 8-9/61;
Library Journal, 12/15/64; TLS, 6/10/65

1942 Watson, William. Sculpture of Japan, From the Fifth to the
A Fifteenth Century. London: Studio, 1959. 216 pp. 60-41576.
o.p.
Silberman, 738; Library Journal, 4/1/60; TLS, 2/19/60

FINE ARTS AND ARCHITECTURE
ARCHITECTURE

1943 Alcx, William. Japanese Architecture. N.Y.: Braziller,
B 1963. 127 pp. 63-7516.

1944 Asahi Shimbun Sha. Ise, Prototype of Japanese Architecture.
C Cambridge, Mass.: M.I.T. Press, 1965. 212 pp. 64-7970.
Choice, 9/65; JAS, 2/66

1945 Cram, Ralph Adams. Impressions of Japanese Architecture and
A the Allied Arts. N.Y.: Dover, 1966 (orig. pub. by
Marshall Jones, 1930). 242 pp. 66-25705. (R).
Silberman, 808

1946 Futagawa, Yukio. The Roots of Japanese Architecture; A Photo-
A graphic Quest. N.Y.: Harper & Row, 1963. 207 pp. 63-16240.
Library Journal, 10/1/63

1947 Japan. Imperial Treasury (Shosoin). The Shosoin, an Eighth
C Century Treasury House. comp. by Mosaku Ishida and Gunchi
Moda. English resume by Harada Jiro. Tokyo: Mainichi
Newspapers, 1954. 20 pp.
Silberman, 814

1948 Japanese Architecture. prepared by H. Kishida. Tokyo: Japan
A Travel Bureau, 1935- (Tourist Library, N.S. 6).
60-11616 rev.
Silberman, 805

1949 New York. Museum of Modern Art. The Architecture of Japan.
C by Arthur Drexler. N.Y.: 1955. 286 pp. 55-5987. o.p.
Japan Q., 4-6/57; Library Journal, 3/1/56

1950 Sadler, Arthur Lindsay. A Short History of Japanese Archi-
A tecture. Rutland, Vt.: Tuttle, 1962. 160 pp. 62-21539.

1951 Seike, Kiyoshi. Contemporary Japanese Houses. Palo Alto,
A Calif.: Kodansha, 1964. 205 pp. 64-25254.

1952 Soper, Alexander Coburn. The Evolution of Buddhist Architecture
C in Japan. Princeton, N.J.: Princeton University Press,
1942. 330 pp. (Monographs in Art and Archaeology, 22).
42-24943. o.p. (M-University).
Silberman, 810

1953 Taut, Bruno. Houses and People of Japan. 2d ed. Tokyo:
C Sanseido, 1958. 326 pp. Hand catalog.
Silberman, 822

PERFORMING ARTS

1954 Ashihara, Hidesato. The Japanese Dance. 2d ed. Tokyo: Japan
A   Travel Bureau, 1965. 164 pp. NUC 66-33916.

1955 Embree, John Fee, comp. Japanese Peasant Songs. Philadelphia:
B   American Folklore Society, 1944. 96 pp. (Memoirs of the
     American Folklore Society, Vol. 38). 44-2122. o.p.
     Silberman, 1179

1956 Ernst, Earle. The Kabuki Theatre. N.Y.: Oxford, 1956.
A   296 pp. 56-14007.
     AUFS, 502; Silberman, 1133; TLS, 8/10/56

1957 Garfias, Robert. Gagaku, the Music and Dances of the Japanese
A   Imperial Household. N.Y.: Theater Art Books, 1959. 59-3783.
     Silberman, 1170

1958 Harich-Schneider, Eta. The Rhythmical Patterns in Gagaku and
C   Bugaku. Leiden: Brill, 1954. 109 pp. A56-2858.
     Silberman, 1174

1959 Hattori, Ryuttaro, comp. Japanese Folk-Songs with Piano
B   Accompaniment. 4th ed. Tokyo: Japan Times, 1960.
     Silberman, 1180

1960 Keene, Donald. Bunraku; The Art of the Japanese Puppet Theatre.
A   Tokyo: Kodansha, dist. by Japan Publications Trading Co.,
     1965. 287 pp. 65-19187.
     Japan Q., 1-3/66

1961 Komiya, Toyotaka, ed. Japanese Music and Drama in the Meiji Era.
C   tr. and adapted by Edward Seidensticker and Donald Keene.
     Tokyo: Obunsha, 1956. 535 pp. (Japanese Culture in the
     Meiji Era, Vol. IV). A59-8756.
     Silberman, 1169

1962 Malm, William P. Japanese Music and Musical Instruments.
A   Rutland, Vt.: Tuttle, 1959. 299 pp. 59-10411 rev.
     Sup. 61, 2772; Silberman, 1165; JAS, 5/60; Japan Q., 4-6/60;
     JAOS, 4-6/60; Library Journal, 12/1/59; Music Lib. Assn.
     Notes, 6/60

1963 Piggott, Sir Francis Taylor. The Music and Musical Instruments
C   of Japan. 2d ed. Yokohama: Kelly & Walsh, 1909. 196 pp.
     10-20826. o.p.
     Silberman, 1167

1964 Scott, Adolf Clarence. The Kabuki Theatre of Japan. N.Y.:
B   Collier, 1966 (orig. pub. by Macmillan, 1955). 317 pp.
     NUC 67-62445. (R).
     Silberman, 1134; Library Journal, 2/1/56; TLS, 9/23/55

1965 Scott, Adolphe Clarence. The Puppet Theatre of Japan. Rutland,
C   Vt.: Tuttle, 1963. 173 pp. 63-21179.
     Choice, 3/64; JAS, 2/65; JAOS, 7-9/64

1966 Shaver, Ruth M. Kabuki Costume. Rutland, Vt.: Tuttle, 1966.
C   396 pp. 66-15266.
     Choice, 4/67; Library Journal, 12/1/66

1967 Tanabe, Hisao. Japanese Music. 2d ed. Tokyo: Kokusai Bunka
B   Shinkokai, 1959. 74 pp. Hand catalog.

EDUCATION AND MASS COMMUNICATION

1968 Anderson, Ronald Stone. Japan: Three Epochs of Modern Education.
B   Washington: U.S. Dept. of Health, Education, and Welfare,
     Office of Education, 1959. 219 pp. HEW59-38. o.p.
     Silberman, 1464

1969 Bryant, William Cullen. English Language Teaching in Japanese
B   Schools. N.Y.: Japan Society, 1955. o.p.
     Silberman, 1485

1970 Dore, Ronald Philip. Education in Tokugawa Japan. Berkeley:
A   University of California Press, 1965. 346 pp. (University
     of California Center for Japanese and Korean Studies
     Publication). 65-1744.
     Choice, 7-8/65; JAS, 11/65; Am. Soc. R., 10/65; Ann. Am.
     Acad., 11/65; Japan Q., 7-9/65; JAOS, 4-6/65; TLS, 1/20/66

1971 Eells, Walter Crosby. The Literature of Japanese Education, 1945-
B   1954. Hamden, Conn.: Archon, 1966 (orig. pub. by Shoe-
     string Press, 1955). 210 pp. 55-12032. (R).
     Silberman, 1463; Japan Q., 10-12/56

1972 Hall, Robert King. Education for a New Japan. New Haven,
B   Conn.: Yale University Press, 1949. 503 pp. 49-9201. o.p.
     (M-University).
     Silberman, 1472; FEQ, 8/50; Pacific Affairs, 3/50

1973 Hall, Robert King. Shushin: the Ethics of a Defeated Nation.
B   N.Y.: Bureau of Publications, Teachers College, Columbia
     University, 1949. 244 pp. 49-10209. o.p.
     Silberman, 1471; FEQ, 11/50

1974 Japan. Ministry of Education. Kokutai no Hongi Cardinal
B   Principles of the National Entity of Japan. tr. by
     John Owen Gauntlett. ed. by Robert King Hall. Cambridge,
     Mass.: Harvard University Press, 1949. 200 pp. 49-9335
     rev. o.p. (M-University).
     AUFS, 135; Silberman, 1470; FEQ, 5/50; Am. Pol. Sci. R.,
     10/47; Am. Soc. R., 8/49

1975 Kobayashi, Victor Nobuo. John Dewey in Japanese Educational
B   Thought. Ann Arbor: University of Michigan School of Educa-
     tion, 1964. 198 pp. (Comparative Education Dissertation
     Series, No. 2). 65-63281.
     JAS, 11/65

1976 Passin, Herbert. Society and Education in Japan. N.Y.: Bureau
A   of Publications, Teachers College, Columbia University, 1965.
     347 pp. (Studies of the East Asian Institute, Columbia Uni-
     versity). 65-19168.
     Sup. 67, 3223; Choice, 9/65; JAS, 5/66

1977 Richie, Donald. The Films of Akira Kurosawa. Berkeley:
A   University of California Press, 1965. 218 pp. 65-26695.
     Choice, 4/66; Library Journal, 1/15/65; TLS, 2/24/66

1978 Supreme Commander for the Allied Forces. Civil Information
B   and Education Section. Education in the New Japan.
     Tokyo: General Headquarters, Supreme Commander for the
     Allied Powers, Civil Information and Education Section,
     Education Division, 1948. 2 v. 48-4912. o.p.
     Silberman, 1473

1979 Whittemore, Edward P. The Press in Japan Today, a Case Study.
B   Columbia: University of South Carolina Press, 1961.
     91 pp. (Institute of International Studies. Studies
     in International Affairs, No. 1). 61-64390. o.p.
     Sup. 63, 2898; JAS, 8/62; Japan Q., 4-6/62

BIBLIOGRAPHIES

1980 California. University. Institute of East Asiatic Studies.
A   Korean Studies Guide. comp. for the Institute of East
     Asiatic Studies, University of California, by B. H. Hazard,
     Jr. (and others). ed. by Richard Marcus. Berkeley: Uni-
     versity of California Press, 1954. 220 pp. 54-7843. o.p.
     AUFS, 525

1981 Chung, Yong Sun, comp. A Selected Bibliography on Korea,
C   1959-1963. Seoul: Korean Research and Publication, Inc.,
     dist. by Cellar Book Shop, 1966. 117 pp. 65-9439.
     Choice, 6/67

1982 Gompertz, Godfrey St. George Montague. Bibliography of Western
C   Literature on Korea from the Earliest Times until 1950.
     Seoul: Korea Branch, Royal Asiatic Society, 1963. (Trans-
     actions, Vol. XL).

1983 U.S. Library of Congress. Reference Department. Korea: an
B   Annotated Bibliography. Washington: Library of Congress,
     1950. 3 v. 50-62963 rev. o.p.
     Silberman, 1625

REFERENCE BOOKS

1984 Martin, Samuel Elmo. A Korean-English Dictionary. New Haven,
C   Conn.: Yale University Press, 1967. 1902 pp. (Yale
     Language Texts). 67-24503.
     Choice, 6/68; JAS, 8/68; Library Journal, 4/1/68

1985 Yang, Key Paik. Reference Guide to Korean Materials, 1945-1959.
B   Washington: 1960. 131 pp. 60-50260. o.p.

JOURNALS

1986 Asiatic Research Bulletin. Seoul: Research Center, Korea
B   University.

1987 Journal of Asiatic Studies. Seoul: Korea University.
C

1988 Journal of Social Sciences and Humanities. Seoul: Bulletin
C   of the Korean Research Center, 1955-

1989 Korean Affairs. Seoul: The Council on Korean Affairs, 1962-
C

1990 The Korean Studies Series. Seoul: The Korean Research Center,
C   1955-

1991 Koreana Quarterly. Seoul: International Research Center, 1959-
B   Silberman, 1647

1992 Royal Asiatic Society of Great Britain and Ireland. Korea
B   Branch. Transactions. Seoul: The Society, 1900- (R-Kraus,
     M-Microphoto).
     Silberman, 1646

GENERAL BOOKS

1993 Chong, Kyong-jo. Korea Tomorrow, Land of the Morning Calm.
C   N.Y.: Macmillan, 1956. 384 pp. 56-1184. o.p.
     FEQ, 8/56; Am. Pol. Sci. R., 6/56; Ann. Am. Acad., 9/56;
     Library Journal, 3/1/56; TLS, 3/10/56

1994 Chong, Kyong-jo. New Korea; New Land of the Morning Calm.
B   N.Y.: Macmillan, 1962. 274 pp. 62-15611.
     Sup. 63, 2899; JAS, 8/62; AHR, 4/63; Am. Pol. Sci. R.,
     6/63; Ann. Am. Acad., 9/63; Library Journal, 9/15/62;
     Pacific Affairs, Fall/63

1995 Grad, Andrew Jonah. Modern Korea. N.Y.: John Day for Inter-
C   national Secretariat, Institute of Pacific Relations, 1944.
     330 pp. 44-47020. o.p.
     AUFS, 537; Silberman, 1910; FEQ, 11/45; Pacific Affairs,
     3/45

1996 Jung, In-hah, ed. The Feel of Korea; A Symposium of American
C   Comment. Seoul: Hollym Corporation, 1966. 369 pp. 66-9059.

1997 Kang, Younghill. The Grass Roof. Chicago: Follett, 1966
B   (orig. pub. by Scribner's, 1939). 377 pp. 66-27984. (R).
     AUFS, 545

1998 Keith, Elizabeth. Old Korea, the Land of Morning Calm. N.Y.:
C   Hutchinson, 1946. 72 pp. 47-6028. o.p.

AUFS, 546; Silberman, 1624

1999 Korea: Its Land, People, and Culture of All Ages. Seoul:
B   Hakwon-Sa, 1960. 718 pp. 60-2998.
     Silberman, 1619

2000 Korea (Republic) Yunesuk'o Hanguk Wiwonhoe. UNESCO Korean
B   Survey. Seoul: Dong-a, 1960. 936 pp. 60-52083.
     Silberman, 1617a

2001 McCune, Shannon Boyd-Bailey. Korea, Land of Broken Calm. Prince-
A   ton, N.J.: Van Nostrand, 1966. 221 pp. 66-16903.
     Sup. 67, 3231; JAS, 11/66

2002 Osgood, Cornelius. The Koreans and Their Culture. N.Y.:
B   Ronald, 1951. 387 pp. 51-271.
     AUFS, 563; Silberman, 1616; Am. Anthropologist, 7/51;
     AHR, 7/51; Am. Soc. R., 6/51; Ann. Am. Acad., 9/51; JAOS,
     10-12/51; Library Journal, 2/15/51; Pacific Affairs, 9/51

2003 Portway, Donald. Korea; Land of the Morning Calm. London:
C   Harrap, 1953. 187 pp. A54-1865. o.p.
     AUFS, 565

2004 Rutt, Richard. Korean Works and Days: Notes from the Diary
A   of a Country Priest. Rutland, Vt.: Tuttle, 1964. 231 pp.
     63-15271.
     Sup. 65, 3080; Choice, 10/64; Japan Q., 1-3/65

2005 Yi, Miryok. The Yalu Flows, a Korean Childhood. tr. by H. A.
C   Hammelmann. East Lansing: Michigan State University Press,
     1956. 149 pp. 56-12105.
     Silberman, 1902; JAS, 5/57; TLS, 8/6/54

GEOGRAPHY

2006 McCune, Shannon Boyd-Bailey. Korea's Heritage; A Regional and
B   Social Geography. Rutland, Vt.: Tuttle, 1956. 250 pp.
     56-6807.
     AUFS, 558; Silberman, 1671; JAS, 2/57; Ann. Am. Acad.,
     7/57; Pacific Affairs, 12/56

HISTORY
GENERAL

2007 Berger, Carl. The Korea Knot, a Military-Political History.
B   rev. ed. Philadelphia: University of Pennsylvania Press,
     1965. 255 pp. 64-24503.
     Choice, 11/65; JAS, 2/58

2008 Hulbert, Homer Bezaleel. History of Korea. ed. by Clarence
B   Norwood Weems. N.Y.: Hillary House, 1962. 2 v. 62-9992.
     Sup. 63, 2900; JAS, 11/62

2009 Kim, Ch'ang-sun. Fifteen-Year History of North Korea. Washing-
B   ton: U.S. Joint Publications Research Service, 1963. 198 pp.
     (JPRS 18925). NUC 65-27380.

2010 Nelson, Melvin Frederick. Korea and the Old Orders in Eastern
B   Asia. N.Y.: Russell & Russell, 1967 (orig. pub. by Louisiana
     State University Press, 1945). 326 pp. 66-27132. (R).
     AUFS, 561; Silberman, 1806; FEQ, 5/46; AHR, 10/45; Am. Pol.
     Sci. R., 8/45; Ann. Am. Acad., 11/45

HISTORY
PRE-MODERN

2011 Rockhill, William Woodville. China's Intercourse with Korea
C   from the XVth Century to 1895. New Hyde Park, N.Y.: Uni-
     versity Books, 1966 (orig. pub. by Luzac, 1905). 60 pp.
     6-7316. (R). (M-University).
     Silberman, 1742

HISTORY
MODERN TO 1945

2012 Harrington, Fred Harvey. God, Mammon, and the Japanese:
C   Dr. Horace N. Allen and Korean-American Relations,
     1884-1905. Madison: University of Wisconsin Press, 1944.
     362 pp. 44-2219.
     Silberman, 1816; FEQ, 8/44; AHR, 10/44; Am. Pol. Sci. R.,
     12/44; Ann. Am. Acad., 7/44; Pacific Affairs, 7/30/44;
     Pol. Sci. Q., 6/44

2013 Kim, Chong Ik Eugene. Korea and the Politics of Imperialism,
B   1876-1910. by C. I. Eugene Kim and Han-Kyo Kim. Berke-
     ley: University of California Press, 1967. 260 pp.
     (Center for Japanese and Korean Studies). 68-12037.

Choice, 11/68; Pacific Affairs, Fall/68

2014 Korea. (Government-General of Chosen, 1910-1945). A Short
C History of Korea. comp. by Center for East Asian Cultural
Studies. Honolulu: East-West Center Press, 1964. 84 pp.
65-2830. o.p.
Choice, 1/66; JAS, 11/65

2015 McCune, George MacAfee, ed. Korean-American Relations; Documents
B Pertaining to the Far Eastern Diplomacy of the United
States. Berkeley: University of California Press,
1951- 2 v. 51-1111.
Silberman, 1812; JAS, 11/64; FEQ, 2/52; Am. Pol. Sci. R.,
6/51

2016 Suh, Dae-Sook. The Korean Communist Movement, 1918-1948.
A Princeton, N.J.: Princeton Universtity Press, 1967. 406 pp.
66-17711.
Choice, 10/67; JAS, 2/68; AHR, 10/67; Am. Pol. Sci. R.,
12/67; Library Journal, 3/15/67

2017 Weems, Benjamin B. Reform, Rebellion, and the Heavenly Way.
B Tucson: University of Arizona Press, 1964. 122 pp. (Association for Asian Studies, Monographs and Papers, XV).
64-17267.
Sup. 65, 3082; Choice, 4/65; JAS, 5/65

HISTORY
POST-WAR

2018 Cho, Soon Sung. Korea in World Politics, 1940-1950; An
B Evaluation of American Responsibility. Berkeley: University of California Press, 1967. 338 pp. (Center
for Japanese and Korean Studies). 67-14968.
Choice, 12/68; JAS, 5/68; Ann. Am. Acad., 1/68; TLS,
12/21/67

2019 Clark, Mark Wayne. From the Danube to the Yalu. N.Y.:
C Harper, 1954. 369 pp. 54-6010. o.p. (M-University).
Silberman, 1785; Library Journal, 5/15/54; TLS, 9/17/54

2020 Fehrenbach, T. R. This Kind of War; A Study in Unpreparedness.
A N.Y.: Macmillan, 1963. 688 pp. 63-9972.
JAS, 5/64; Ann. Am. Acad., 9/63; Library Journal, 6/15/63

2021 Geer, Andrew Clare. The New Breed; The Story of the U.S.
C Marines in Korea. N.Y.: Harper, 1952. 395 pp. 52-5438.
o.p.

2022 Goodrich, Leland Matthew. Korea; A Study of U.S. Policy in
B the United Nations. N.Y.: Council on Foreign Relations,
1956. 235 pp. 56-9751. o.p. (M-University).
AUFS, 536; Silberman, 1794; JAS, 2/58; Library Journal,
9/15/56

2023 Hahm, Pyong-choon. The Korean Political Tradition and Law.
C Seoul: Hollym Corporation, 1967. 249 pp. (Royal Asiatic
Society, Korea Branch, Monograph Series, No. 1). 68-2912.
JAS, 11/68

2024 Heinl, Robert Debs, Jr. Victory at High Tide; The Inchon-
C Seoul Campaign. Philadelphia: Lippincott, 1968. 315 pp.
(Great Battles of History). 68-11129.
Choice, 11/68; Library Journal, 12/15/67

2025 Joy, Charles Turner. How Communists Negotiate. N.Y.: Macmil-
C lan, 1955. 178 pp. 55-13828. o.p.
Silberman, 1791; Library Journal, 11/15/55

2026 Kahn, Ely Jacques. The Peculiar War; Impressions of a Reporter
B in Korea. N.Y.: Random House, 1952. 211 pp. 52-5554. o.p.
Silberman, 1783

2027 Marshall, Samuel Lyman Atwood. Pork Chop Hill; The American
C Fighting Man in Action, Korea, Spring, 1953. N.Y.:
Apollo, 1965 (orig. pub. by Morrow, 1956). 315 pp.
56-9545. (R).

2028 Marshall, Samuel Lyman Atwood. The River and the Gauntlet;
B Defeat of the Eighth Army by the Chinese Communist Forces,
November, 1950, in the Battle of the Chongchon River,
Korea. N.Y.: Morrow, 1953. 385 pp. 53-5337. o.p.
Silberman, 1789; Library Journal, 5/1/53

2029 McCune, George MacAfee. Korea Today. Cambridge, Mass.: Harvard
A University Press, 1950. 372 pp. 50-8875. o.p.
AUFS, 556; Silberman, 1889; FEQ, 8/51; Am. Pol. Sci. R.,
12/50; Library Journal, 8/50; Pol. Sci. Q., 12/50

2030 Meade, Edward Grant. American Military Government in Korea.
C N.Y.: King's Crown, 1951. 281 pp. 51-9103. o.p.
AUFS, 559; Silberman, 1776; FEQ, 8/51; Am. Soc. R., 6/51;
Ann. Am. Acad., 5/51; Pacific Affairs, 9/51; Pol. Sci. Q.,
12/51

2031 Paige, Glenn D. The Korean People's Democratic Republic.
B Stanford, Calif.: Hoover Institution on War, Revolution,
and Peace, 1966. 60 pp. 65-27783.
JAS, 2/67

2032 Poats, Rutherford M. Decision in Korea. N.Y.: McBride,
C 1954. 340 pp. 54-7378. o.p.
AUFS, 564; Silberman, 1786; Library Journal, 6/1/54

2033 Rees, David. Korea: the Limited War. N.Y.: St. Martin's,
C 1964. 511 pp. 64-14946.
Sup. 65, 3079; Choice, 7-8/64; Library Journal, 5/15/64;
TLS, 4/23/64

2034 Ridgway, Matthew B. The Korean War: How We Met the Challenge,
A How All-out Asian War Was Averted, Why MacArthur Was
Dismissed, Why Today's War Objectives Must be Limited.
Garden City, N.Y.: Doubleday, 1967. 291 pp. 67-11172.
Choice, 4/68; Library Journal, 9/15/67

2035 Riley, John W. The Reds Take a City; The Communist Occupa-
B tion of Seoul, with Eyewitness Accounts. tr. by Hugh
Heung-wu Cynn. New Brunswick, N.J.: Rutgers University
Press, 1951. 210 pp. 51-13868. o.p.
Silberman, 1788

2036 Scalapino, Robert A., ed. North Korea Today. N.Y.: Praeger,
A 1963. 141 pp. 63-20152.
Sup. 65, 3081; JAS, 5/64; Am. Pol. Sci. R., 6/64; Library
Journal, 12/1/63; TLS, 4/6/64

2037 United Nations Command. Military Armistice in Korea and
C Temporary Supplementary Agreement, Signed at Panmunjon,
Korea, July 27, 1958, Entered into Force July 27, 1953.
Washington: Government Printing Office, 1953. 127 pp.
54-61053. o.p.
Silberman, 1795

2038 U.S. Department of State. Office of Public Affairs. Korea,
C 1945 to 1948; A Report on Political Developments and Economic Resources with Selected Documents. Washington: Dept.
of State, 1948. 124 pp. 48-47165. o.p.
Silberman, 1777

2039 Vatcher, William H. Panmunjom; The Story of the Korean
B Military Armistice Negotiations. N.Y.: Praeger, 1958.
322 pp. 58-7887. o.p.
JAS, 11/58; AHR, 1/59; Ann. Am. Acad., 7/58

2040 White, William Lindsay. Back Down the Ridge. N.Y.: Harcourt,
B Brace, 1953. 182 pp. 53-5642. o.p.

2041 Yu, Hon. Study of North Korea. Seoul: Research Institute
C of Internal and External Affairs, 1966. 317 pp. 68-44186.

GOVERNMENT AND POLITICS

2042 Henderson, Gregory. Korea, the Politics of the Vortex.
A Cambridge, Mass.: Harvard University Press, 1968. 479 pp.
68-25611.
Choice, 2/69; JAS, 2/69

2043 Kim, Chong Ik Eugene. A Pattern of Political Development;
B Korea. Kalamazoo, Mich.: Korea Research and Publication,
Inc., 1964. 200 pp. 64-56446. mimeo. o.p.
JAS, 11/65

2044 Koh, Byung Chul, comp. Aspects of Administrative Development
B in South Korea. Seoul: Korea Research and Publications,
dist. by Cellar Book Shop, 1967. 144 pp. (Monograph
Series on Korea, 4). 68-634.
Choice, 7-8/68

2045 Lee, Chong-sik. The Politics of Korean Nationalism. Berkeley:
A University of California Press for the Center for Japanese
Studies, 1963. 342 pp. 63-19029.
Sup. 65, 3077; JAS, 5/64; Ann. Am. Acad., 7/64; Library
Journal, 11/1/63; TLS, 3/2/64

2046 Pak, Chong-hui. Our Nation's Path; Ideology of Social Recon-
C struction. Seoul: Dong-a, 1962. 172 pp. NUC 63-35548.

KOREA - GOVERNMENT AND POLITICS

2047 Reeve, W. D. The Republic of Korea, a Political and Economic
A   Study. N.Y.: Oxford, 1963. 197 pp. 63-25579.
     JAS, 8/64

ECONOMICS

2048 Agriculture in Korea. Seoul: Ministry of Agriculture and
C   Forestry, 1965. 192 pp.

2049 Chung, Joseph Sang-hoon, ed. Patterns of Economic Develop-
B   ment: Korea. Seoul: Korea Research and Publications,
     dist. by Cellar Book Shop, 1966. 241 pp. (Monograph
     Series on Korea, 3). 67-567.
     Choice, 9/67; JAS, 5/67

2050 Kim, Byong Kuk. Central Banking Experiment in a Developing
B   Economy; Case Study of Korea. Seoul: The Korean Research
     Center, 1965. 282 pp. (The Korean Studies Series, Vol. 12).
     K66-510.

2051 Lyons, Gene Martin. Military Policy and Economic Aid; The
C   Korean Case, 1950-1953. Columbus: Ohio State University
     Press, 1961. 298 pp. 61-7301.
     Sup. 63, 2901; JAS, 8/62; AHR, 10/61; Am. Pol. Sci. R.,
     3/62

2052 United Nations. Food and Agricultural Organization. Rehabil-
B   itation and Development of Agriculture, Forestry and Fish-
     eries in South Korea. Report prepared for the United
     Nations Korean Reconstruction Agency by a Mission selected
     by the Food and Agricultural Organization of the United
     Nations. N.Y.: Columbia University Press, 1954. 428 pp.
     54-11917. o.p.
     Silberman, 1926

LANGUAGE AND LITERATURE
LITERATURE
EARLY PERIOD
PROSE

2053 Chong, In-sob, ed. and tr. Folk Tales from Korea. N.Y.:
C   Grove, 1953. 257 pp. 53-12953. o.p.
     AUFS, 526; Silberman, 1880; JAS, 5/57; FEQ, 2/54; TLS,
     10/31/52

2054 Kim, So-un. The Story Bag; A Collection of Korean Folk tales.
C   Rutland, Vt.: Tuttle, 1955. 229 pp. 55-13738.
     Silberman, 1881

2055 Voorhees, Melvin B. Korean Tales. N.Y.: Simon & Schuster,
C   1952. 209 pp. 52-13787. o.p.

LANGUAGE AND LITERATURE
LITERATURE
EARLY PERIOD
POETRY

2056 Lee, Peter H., comp. and tr. Anthology of Korean Poetry From
A   the Earliest Era to the Present. N.Y.: John Day, 1964.
     196 pp. (UNESCO Collection of Representative Works:
     Korean Series). 64-14198. o.p.
     Sup. 65, 3078; Choice, 10/64; JAS, 11/64; Library Journal,
     10/1/64

2057 Pai, Inez (Kong), ed. and tr. The Ever White Mountain; Korean
B   Lyrics in the Classical Sijo Form. Rutland, Vt.: Tuttle,
     1965. 175 pp. 65-26821.
     Choice, 4/66; JAS, 11/66

LANGUAGE AND LITERATURE
LITERATURE
EARLY PERIOD
HISTORY AND CRITICISM

2058 Lee, Peter H. Korean Literature: Topics and Themes. Tucson:
B   University of Arizona Press, 1965. 141 pp. (Associa-
     tion for Asian Studies, Monographs and Papers, XVI).
     64-19167.
     Choice, 10/65; JAS, 11/65

KOREA - LANGUAGE AND LITERATURE

LANGUAGE AND LITERATURE
LITERATURE
MODERN PERIOD
PROSE

2059 Kim, Richard E. The Martyred, a Novel. N.Y.: Braziller, 1964.
A   316 pp. 64-10785.
     Choice, 3/64; Library Journal, 4/1/64; TLS, 10/29/64

PHILOSOPHY AND RELIGION
GENERAL

2060 Moffett, Samuel Hugh. The Christians of Korea. N.Y.: Friend-
C   ship Press, 1962. 174 pp. 62-17527.

2061 Palmer, Spencer John. Korea and Christianity; The Problem
C   of Identification and Tradition. Seoul: Hollym Corpora-
     tion, 1967. 174 pp. NUC 68-60983.

FINE ARTS AND ARCHITECTURE
FINE ARTS

2062 Kim, Chae-won. Treasures of Korean Art; 2000 Years of Cer-
B   amics, Sculpture, and Jeweled Arts. N.Y.: Abrams, 1966.
     283 pp. 66-23402.
     Choice, 4/67; Library Journal, 1/15/67; TLS, 10/6/66

2063 McCune, Evelyn. The Arts of Korea; An Illustrated History.
B   Rutland, Vt.: Tuttle, 1962. 452 pp. 61-11122.
     Sup. 63, 2902; JAS, 8/62; Library Journal, 2/1/62; TLS,
     9/21/62

EDUCATION AND MASS COMMUNICATION

2064 Korea University. Asiatic Research Center. A Brief History
C   of the Asiatic Research Center. Seoul: 1964.

2065 Meinecke, Charlotte Drummond. Education in Korea. Seoul·
C   Ministry of Education, Republic of Korea, 1958. 70 pp.
     59-32817.
     Silberman, 1906

2066 United Nations. UNESCO-UNKRA Educational Planning Mission to
C   Korea. Rebuilding Education in the Republic of Korea;
     Report. Paris: UNESCO, 1954. 221 pp. 54-14822. o.p.
     Silberman, 1909

JOURNALS

2067 Joint Commission on Rural Reconstruction in China. 1950-
B   Hucker, 2178

2068 Tzu Yu Chung-Kuo Chih Kung Yeh. (Industry of Free China).
C   v.1- 1954-
     Hucker, 2180

GEOGRAPHY

2069 Hsieh, Chiao-min. Taiwan-ilha Formosa; A Geography in Per-
A   spective. Washington: Butterworth's, 1964. 372 pp.
     64-22305. o.p.
     JAS, 2/66

HISTORY
GENERAL

2070 Campbell, William. Formosa under the Dutch, Described from
C   Contemporary Records with Explanatory Notes and a Bibli-
     ography of the Island. Taipei: Ch'eng-wen Publishing Co.,
     dist. by Chinese Materials and Research Aids Service
     Center, 1967 (orig. pub. by Kegan Paul, 1903). 629 pp.
     NUC 63-39189. (R).
     Hucker, 585

2071 China Institute of International Affairs. China and the United
C   Nations; Report of a Study Group Set up by the China Insti-
     tute of International Affairs. N.Y.: Manhattan for Carne-
     gie Endowment for International Peace, 1959. 285 pp.
     60-16005. o.p.
     Hucker, 826

2072 Durdin, Tillman. China and the World. The Rebirth of For-
C   mosa by Robert Aura Smith. N.Y.: Foreign Policy Association,
     1953. 63 pp. 53-9998. o.p.

2073 Joint Commission on Rural Reconstruction in China (U.S. and
C   China). Rural Taiwan, Problem and Promise, by Arthur F.
     Raper, project evaluation advisor. Taipei: Joint Commission
     on Rural Reconstruction in China, 1953. 296 pp. 54-36127.

2074 Mancall, Mark, ed. Formosa Today. N.Y.: Praeger, 1964.
A   171 pp. 64-13491.
     Choice, 10/64; Library Journal, 9/15/64; TLS, 1/14/65

2075 Riggs, Fred Warren. Formosa under Chinese Nationalist Rule.
C   N.Y.: Macmillan, 1952. 195 pp. 52-3209. o.p.
     AUFS, 864; Hucker, 850; FEQ, 5/53; Am. Pol. Sci. R., 12/52;
     Ann. Am. Acad., 1/53; Pacific Affairs, 6/53

2076 Sneider, Vern J. A Pail of Oysters. N.Y.: Putnam, 1953.
B   311 pp. 52-13648. o.p.

GOVERNMENT AND POLITICS

2077 Gallin, Bernard. Hsin Hsing, Taiwan; A Chinese Village
A   in Change. Berkeley: University of California Press,
     1966. 324 pp. 66-14734.
     Choice, 12/67; JAS, 8/67

2078 Kerr, George H. Formosa Betrayed. Boston: Houghton Mifflin,
A   1965. 514 pp. 65-20221.
     Choice, 6/66; JAS, 8/66; TLS, 12/8/66

ECONOMICS

2079 Ginsburg, Norton Sydney. The Economic Resources and Development
C   of Formosa. N.Y.: International Secretariat, Institute of
     Pacific Relations, 1953. 58 pp. 54-995. o.p.
     Hucker, 2184

2080 Ho, Yhi-Min. Agricultural Development of Taiwan, 1903-
B   1960. Nashville, Tenn.: Vanderbilt University Press,
     1966. 172 pp. 66-25966.
     Choice, 9/67; JAS, 8/67

2081 Jacoby, Neil Hermon. U.S. Aid to Taiwan; A Study of Foreign
C   Aid, Self-help, and Development. N.Y.: Praeger, 1966.
     364 pp. 66-21784.
     Choice, 3/68; JAS, 8/67; Am. Econ. R., 9/67; Ann. Am.
     Acad., 7/67

2082 Joint Commission on Rural Reconstruction in China (U.S. and
B   China). A Decade of Rural Progress, 1948-1958; Tenth
     Anniversary Review of the Major Accomplishments of the

Joint Commission on Rural Reconstruction. Taipei: 1958.
68 pp. A59-1185.
Hucker, 2181

2083 Shen, Tsung-han. Agricultural Development on Taiwan Since
A   World War II. Ithaca, N.Y.: Cornell University Press,
     1964. 399 pp. 64-18144.
     Choice, 7-8/65; JAS, 2/66

2084 U.S. Mutual Security Mission to China. Economic Progress of
C   Free China, 1951-1958. Taipei: 1958. 83 pp. 58-62448.
     o.p.
     Hucker, 2182

2085 U.S. Mutual Security Mission to China. Urban and Industrial
C   Taiwan, Crowded and Resourceful, by Arthur F. Raper.
     Taipei: 1954. 370 pp. 55-60504.
     Hucker, 2185

SOCIOLOGY, ANTHROPOLOGY AND LINGUISTICS

2086 Barclay, George W. Colonial Development and Population in
B   Taiwan. Princeton, N.J.: Princeton University Press,
     1954. 274 pp. 52-13153.
     AUFS, 774; FEQ, 11/55; Am. Anthropologist, 4/55; Am. Pol.
     Sci. R., 12/54; Ann. Am. Acad., 11/54; Geog. R., 7/55; J.
     Pol. Econ., 8/55

2087 Wolf, Margery. The House of Lim: a Study of a Chinese Farm
A   Family. N.Y.: Appleton-Century-Crofts, 1968. 147 pp.
     68-11211.
     Choice, 3/69; JAS, 11/68

HISTORY
GENERAL

2088 Endacott, G. B. A History of Hong Kong. N.Y.: Oxford, 1958.
B   322 pp. 58-4392.
       Hucker, 679; AHR, 4/59; TLS, 2/6/59

2089 Lo, Hsiang-lin. Hong Kong and Western Cultures. Honolulu:
B   East-West Center Press, 1964. 345 pp. 65-7535.
       Choice, 9/65

2090 Rand, Christopher. Hong Kong, the Island Between. N.Y.:
B   Knopf, 1952. 244 pp. 52-10942. o.p.
       AUFS, 960; Library Journal, 9/15/52

GOVERNMENT AND POLITICS

2091 Endacott, G. B. Government and People in Hong Kong, 1841-
A   1962, a Constitutional History. Hong Kong: Hong Kong Uni-
       versity Press, dist. by Oxford, 1964. 263 pp. 65-2252.
       Choice, 2/66; JAS, 11/65; AHR, 10/65; TLS, 9/16/65

ECONOMICS

2092 Potter, Jack M. Capitalism and the Chinese Peasant: Social
B   and Economic Change in a Hong Kong Village. Berkeley:
       University of California Press, 1968. 215 pp. 68-10688.
       JAS, 11/68

2093 Szczepanik, Edward F. The Economic Growth of Hong Kong. London:
A   Oxford for Royal Institute of International Affairs, 1960
       (orig. pub. in 1958). 186 pp. 61-1573. (R).
       JAS, 5/60

BIBLIOGRAPHIES

2094 Uchida, Naosaku. The Overseas Chinese; A Bibliographical Essay
A   Based on the Resources of the Hoover Institution. Stan-
       ford, Calif.: Hoover Institution on War, Revolution, and
       Peace, 1959. 134 pp. (Bibliographical Series, 7). 60-1670.
       o.p.

GENERAL BOOKS

2095 Fried, Morton Herbert. Colloquium on Overseas Chinese. N.Y.:
B   International Secretariat, Institute of Pacific Relations,
       1958. 80 pp. 58-3235. o.p.

2096 MacNair, Harley Farnsworth. The Chinese Abroad, Their Position
B   and Protection; A Study in International Law and Relations.
       Shanghai: Commercial, 1924. 340 pp. 25-17605. o.p.

2097 Purcell, Victor William Williams Saunders. The Chinese in South-
A   east Asia. 2d ed. N.Y.: Oxford, 1965. 623 pp. 65-4234.
       Hucker, 118; FEQ, 2/52

HISTORY
GENERAL

2098 Chiu, Ping. Chinese Labor in California, 1850-1880, an
B   Economic Study. Madison: State Historical Society of
       Wisconsin for Dept. of History, University of Wisconsin,
       1963. 180 pp. 63-63578.

2099 Elegant, Robert S. The Dragon's Seed; Peking and the Over-
C   seas Chinese. N.Y.: St. Martin's, 1959. 319 pp.
       59-10511. o.p.
       JAS, 2/60; Library Journal, 5/15/59; Pacific Affairs, 12/59

2100 Williams, Lea E. Overseas Chinese Nationalism, the Genesis
B   of the Pan-Chinese Movement in Indonesia, 1900-1916.
       Glencoe, Ill.: Free Press, 1960. 235 pp. 60-9582.
       Hucker, 2103

GOVERNMENT AND POLITICS

2101 Coughlin, Richard J. Double Identity; The Chinese in Modern
B   Thailand. N.Y.: Oxford, 1960. 222 pp. 60-4015.
       JAS, 8/61; Am. Anthropologist, 6/61; Am. Soc. R., 4/61;
       Ann. Am. Acad., 11/61

2102 Pye, Lucian W. Guerilla Communism in Malaya; Its Social and
A   Political Meaning. Princeton, N.J.: Princeton Univer-
       sity Press, 1956. 369 pp. 56-10827.
       AUFS, 1429; Ann. Am. Acad., 5/57

SOCIOLOGY, ANTHROPOLOGY AND LINGUISTICS

2103 Barth, Gunther Paul. Bitter Strength; A History of the Chinese
A   in the United States, 1850-1870. Cambridge, Mass.:
       Harvard University Press, 1964. 305 pp. 64-21785.
       Choice, 7-8/65; JAS, 5/66; AHR, 7/65; Library Journal, 1/1/65

2104 Comber, Leon. The Traditional Mysteries of Chinese Secret
B   Societies in Malaya. Singapore: Donald Moore for Eastern
       Universities Press, 1961. 113 pp. NUC 63-4480.

2105 Dillon, Richard H. The Hatchet Men: the Story of Tong Wars
B   in San Francisco's Chinatown. N.Y.: Coward-McCann, 1962.
       375 pp. 62-14747.
       Library Journal, 9/1/62

2106 Kaye, Barrington. Upper Nankin Street, Singapore; A Socio-
B   logical Study of Chinese Households Living in a Densely
       Populated Area. Singapore: University of Malaya Press,
       1960. 439 pp. 60-51064.
       JAS, 5/61

2107 Lee, Rose Hum. The Chinese in the United States of America.
B   N.Y.: Oxford, 1960. 465 pp. 60-3959. o.p.
       Am. J. Soc., 3/61; Am. Pol. Sci. R., 2/61, 3/61; Ann. Am.
       Acad., 3/61; China Q., 1-3/61; Pacific Affairs, Winter/61

2108 Leigh, Michael B. The Chinese Community of Sarawak; A Study
B   of Communal Relations. Singapore: Malaysia Publishing
       House for Dept. of History, University of Singapore,
       1964. 68 pp. (Singapore Studies on Malaysia, No. 6).
       SA66-7066.

2109 Newell, William Hare. Treacherous River: a Study of Rural
A   Chinese in North Malaya. Kuala Lumpur: University of

Malaya Press, dist. by Oxford, 1962. 233 pp. 63-2972.
JAS, 11/65

2110   Skinner, George William. Chinese Society in Thailand: an Ana-
  C   lytical History. Ithaca, N.Y.: Cornell University Press,
          1957. 459 pp. 57-3051.
          AUFS, 1373; Hucker, 2097; Ann. Am. Acad., 11/57; Library
          Journal, 10/1/57

2111   Skinner, George William. Leadership and Power in the Chinese
  B   Community of Thailand. Ithaca, N.Y.: Cornell University
          Press for Association for Asian Studies, 1958. 363 pp.
          (Association for Asian Studies, Monographs and Papers,
          III). 58-1987.
          AUFS, 1374; Hucker, 2098; JAS, 11/58; AHR, 1/59; Am. J. Soc.,
          7/59; Ann. Am. Acad., 7/58

2112   Stewart, Watt. Chinese Bondage in Peru; A History of the
  A   Chinese Coolie in Peru, 1849-1874. Durham, N.C.: Duke
          University Press, 1951. 247 pp. 51-10928. o.p.
          FEQ, 2/52

2113   Tan, Giok-lan. The Chinese of Sukabumi: a Study in Social
  B   and Cultural Accommodation. Ithaca, N.Y.: Modern Indo-
          nesia Project, Southeast Asia Program, Dept. of Asian
          Studies, Cornell University, 1963. 314 pp. (Modern
          Indonesia Project, Monograph Series). NUC 64-42481.
          JAS, 8/64

2114   Wickberg, Edgar. The Chinese in Philippine Life, 1850-1898.
  A   New Haven, Conn: Yale University Press, 1965. 280 pp.
          65-22475.
          Sup. 67, 3270; Choice, 1/66; JAS, 5/66; AHR, 4/66; Library
          Journal, 8/65

Index

1659 Abegglen, James C. The Japanese Factory; Aspects of Its
A   Social Organization. Glencoe, Ill.: Free Press, 1958.
     142 pp. 58-7482. o.p.
     AUFS, 324; Silberman, 1591; JAS, 11/58; Am. Anthropologist,
     12/56; Am. Soc. R., 10/58; Ann. Am. Acad., 9/58; Pacific
     Affairs, 12/58

0540 Abend, Hallett Edward. My Life in China, 1926-1941. N.Y.:
C   Harcourt, Brace, 1943. 396 pp. 43-15741. o.p. (M-Uni-
     versity).
     Hucker, 628; FEQ, 5/44; Am. Pol. Sci. R., 8/43; Library
     Journal, 7/1/43; TLS, 8/28/43

1289 Acker, William Reynolds Beal. Some T'ang and Pre-T'ang Texts
C   on Chinese Painting. Leiden: Brill, 1954. 414 pp. 55-3283.
     Hucker, 1488

1129 Acton, Harold Mario Mitchell. Modern Chinese Poetry. London:
C   Duckworth, 1936. 176 pp. 36-23555. o.p.

0913 Acton, Harold Mario Mitchell and I-hsieh Li, trs. Four Cau-
C   tionary Tales. pref. by Arthur Waley. N.Y.: A. A. Wyn,
     1948. 159 pp. 47-29848. o.p.

2048 Agriculture in Korea. Seoul: Ministry of Agriculture and
C   Forestry, 1965. 192 pp.

0866 Aird, John Shields. The Size, Composition, and Growth of the
A   Population of Mainland China. Washington: Bureau of the
     Census, U.S. Dept. of Commerce, 1961. 100 pp. (Interna-
     tional Population Statistics Reports. Series P-90, No. 15).
     A61-9631.
     JAS, 2/62

1480 Akita, George. Foundations of Constitutional Govern-
C   ment in Modern Japan, 1868-1900. Cambridge, Mass.:
     Harvard University Press, 1967. 292 pp. 65-13835.
     Choice, 9/67; JAS, 2/68; AHR, 10/67; Ann. Am. Acad., 9/67

1908 Akiyama, Terukazu. Japanese Painting. Geneva: Skira, dist. by
A   World, 1961. 216 pp. 61-15270.
     Silberman, 756

1749 Akutagawa, Ryunosuke. Hell Screen ("Jigoku Hen") and Other
C   Stories. tr. from Japanese by W. H. H. Norman. Tokyo:
     Hokuseido, 1948. 177 pp. 52-21547.
     AUFS, 449

1750 Akutagawa, Ryunosuke. Kappa. tr. from Japanese by Seichi
C   Shiojiri. new ed. Tokyo: Hokuseido, 1949. 136 pp.
     52-21548.
     Silberman, 1001

1751 Akutagawa, Ryunosuke. Rashomon, and Other Stories. tr. by
C   Takashi Kojima. enl. ed. N.Y.: Liveright, 1968. 119 pp.
     67-97739.

1752 Akutagawa, Ryunosuke. Tales Grotesque and Curious. tr. from
B   Japanese by Glenn W. Shaw. rev. ed. Tokyo: Hokuseido, dist.
     by Japan Publications Trading Co., 1963. 144 pp. 52-46785.
     AUFS, 452

1753 Akutagawa, Ryunosuke. The Three Treasures. tr. by Sasaki
C   Takamasa. 2d ed. rev. and enl. Tokyo: Hokuseido, 1951.
     142 pp. 60-20214.

1754 Akutagawa, Ryunosuke. TuTze-Chun. tr. by Dorothy Britton.
B   Tokyo: Kodansha, dist. by Japan Publications Trading Co.,
     1965. 59 pp. 65-12283.
     Choice, 1/66

1438 Alcock, Sir Rutherford. The Capital of the Tycoon: a Narra-
B   tive of Three Years' Residence in Japan. St. Clair Shores,
     Mich.: Scholarly Press (orig. pub. by Harper, 1863). 2 v.
     16-5665. (R).
     Silberman, 355

1943 Alex, William. Japanese Architecture. N.Y.: Braziller,
B   1963. 127 pp. 63-7516.

1620 Allen, George Cyril. Japan's Economic Expansion. N.Y.:
B   Oxford, 1965. 296 pp. 65-6197.
     Sup. 67, 3211; Choice, 3/66; JAS, 5/66; Japan Q., 4-6/66;
     TLS, 12/2/65

1621 Allen, George Cyril. A Short Economic History of Modern Japan,
A   1867-1937. rev. ed. N.Y · Praeger, 1963. 237 pp. 63-9172.

AUFS, 214; Silberman, 323; JAS, 11/63; Japan Q., 7-9/63

0146 Allen, George Cyril. Western Enterprise in Far Eastern Eco-
A   nomic Development, China and Japan. N.Y.: Macmillan, 1954.
     291 pp. 54-2001.
     AUFS, 69; Hucker, 663; Silberman, 1561; Ann. Am. Acad.,
     7/54; Pacific Affairs, 9/54; TLS, 3/26/54

1316 Alley, Rewi. Peking Opera; An Introduction Through Pictures
C   by Eva Siao. Peking: New World Press, 1957. 99 pp.
     58-16732. o.p.

1130 Alley, Rewi, ed. and tr. Poems of Revolt; Some Chinese Voices
C   Over the Last Century. Peking: New World Press, 1962.
     228 pp. 64-30877. o.p.

0020 Amerasia. v.1-11. 1937-1947.
C

0308 American Academy of Political and Social Science. Contemporary
B   China and the Chinese. ed. by Howard L. Boorman. Phila-
     delphia: American Academy of Political and Social Science,
     1959. 220 pp. 59-1059. o.p.

0118 American Assembly. The United States and the Far East. ed. by
B   Willard L. Thorp. 2d ed. Englewood Cliffs, N.J.: Pren-
     tice-Hall, 1962. 188 pp. 62-3632.
     AUFS, 70

1571 American Assembly. The United States and Japan. ed. by Her-
B   bert Passin. Englewood Cliffs, N.J.: Prentice-Hall, 1966.
     174 pp. 66-14703.
     Sup. 67, 3224; Am. Pol. Sci. R., 6/67; Ann. Am. Acad., 2/67;
     Japan Q., 7-9/66; Library Journal, 3/15/66

1350 American Association for the Advancement of Science. Sciences
A   in Communist China; A Symposium Presented at the New
     York Meeting of the American Association for the Advance-
     ment of Science, December 26-27, 1960. ed. by Sidney H.
     Gould. Washington: 1961. 872 pp. (Publication No. 68).
     61-14965 rev. o.p.

0021 American Oriental Society. Journal, v.1- 1843/49-
A   (R-Kraus).
     AUFS, 2; Hucker, 38

0134 American Universities Field Staff. Expectant Peoples, Nation-
B   alism and Development. ed. by K. H. Silvert. pref. by
     Kenneth W. Thompson. N.Y.: Random House for American
     Universities Field Staff, 1963. 489 pp. 63-19716.
     Sup. 65, 3052; Choice, 3/64; Am. Anthropologist, 8/64;
     Am. J. Soc., 11/64; Am. Soc. R., 10/64; Ann. Am. Acad.,
     9/64; Library Journal, 4/15/64

0001 American Universities Field Staff. Select Bibliography: Asia,
A   Africa, Eastern Europe, Latin America. N.Y.: American
     Universities Field Staff, 1960. 534 pp. Supplement,
     1961; Supplement, 1963; Supplement, 1965; Supplement, 1967.
     60-10482.
     Silberman, 13

0541 Anders, Leslie. The Ledo Road; General Joseph W. Stilwell's
C   Highway to China. Norman: University of Oklahoma Press,
     1965. 255 pp. 65-11232.
     Choice, 10/65; JAS, 5/66; Library Journal, 4/15/65

0430 Anderson, Flavia. The Rebel Emperor. London: Gollancz, 1958.
C   356 pp. 58-4562. o.p.
     Hucker, 623

1729 Anderson, George Lincoln, ed. The Genius of the Oriental
C   Theater. N.Y.: New American Library, 1966. 416 pp.
     66-22974.
     Choice, 3/67

1968 Anderson, Ronald Stone. Japan: Three Epochs of Modern Education.
B   Washington: U.S. Dept. of Health, Education, and Welfare,
     Office of Education, 1959. 219 pp. HEW59-38. o.p.
     Silberman, 1464

0352 Andersson, Johan Gunnar. Children of the Yellow Earth; Studies
A   in Prehistoric China. N.Y.: Macmillan, 1934. 345 pp.
     35-2425. o.p.
     Hucker, 142

1852 Anesaki, Masaharu. Art, Life, and Nature in Japan. Boston:
C   Marshall Jones, 1932. 178 pp. 33-1620. o.p.
     Silberman, 731

1883 Anesaki, Masaharu. Buddhist Art in its Relation to Buddhist
C   Ideals, with Special Reference to Buddhism in Japan.
     Boston:sHoughton Mifflin, 1915. 73 pp. 16-100. o.p.
     Silberman, 727

1806 Anesaki, Masaharu. History of Japanese Religion, with Special
A   Reference to the Social and Moral Life of the Nation.
     Rutland, Vt.: Tuttle, 1963. 423 pp. 63-19395/CD.
     AUFS, 125; Silberman, 591; JAS, 5/64

1827 Anesaki, Masaharu. Nichiren, the Buddhist Prophet. Gloucester,
C   Mass.: Peter Smith, 1966 (orig. pub. by Harvard University
     Press, 1916). 160 pp. 67-2824. (R). (M-University).
     Silberman, 638; Choice, 2/68

1807 Anesaki, Masaharu. Religious Life of the Japanese People.
A   rev. by Hideo Kishimoto. Honolulu: East-West Center Press,
     1965. 105 pp. (Series on Japanese Life and Culture, 4).
     64-584. o.p. (M-University).
     AUFS, 126; Choice, 12/65; JAS, 2/65

1481 Anethan, Albert d', Baron. The d'Anethan Dispatches from Japan,
C   1894-1910; The Observations of Baron Albert d'Anethan,
     Belgian Minister Plenipotentiary and Dean of the Diplo-
     matic Corps. sel., ed. and ed. with an historical intro.
     by George Alexander Lensen. Tallahassee, Fla.: Diplomatic
     Press in cooperation with Sophia University, 1967. 272 pp.
     67-26670.
     Choice, 4/68

0119 Angus, Henry Forbes. Canada and the Far East, 1940-1953.
B   Toronto: University of Toronto Press, 1953. 129 pp.
     53-13495.
     AUFS, 73; FEQ, 11/54; AHR, 10/54; Am. Pol. Sci. R., 6/54;
     Ann. Am. Acad., 11/54; Library Journal, 3/15/54

0431 Appleton, William Worthen. A Cycle of Cathay; The Chinese Vogue
B   in England during the Seventeenth and Eighteenth Centuries.
     N.Y.: Columbia University Press, 1951. 182 pp. 51-9335.
     o.p.
     Hucker, 575; FEQ, 2/52

1884 Arai, Hakuseki. The Sword Book in Honcho Gunkiko and the Book
C   of Same, Ko Hi Sei Gi of Inaba Tsurio. tr. by Henri L.
     Joly and Inada Hogitaro. Rutland, Vt.: Tuttle, 1963.
     176 pp. 63-6519.

1730 Araki, James T. The Ballad-Drama of Medieval Japan. Berkeley:
B   University of California Press, 1964. 289 pp. 64-24887.
     Choice, 11/65; JAS, 2/66; JAOS, 7-9/65; Pacific Affairs,
     Fall-Winter/65-66

1755 Arishima, Takeo. The Agony of Coming into the World. tr.
C   by Seiji Fujita. Tokyo: Hokuseido, 1955. 103 pp. 57-27401.

0991 Arlington, Lewis Charles. The Chinese Drama from the Earliest
C   Times Until Today. N.Y.: Blom, 1966 (orig. pub. in 1930).
     177 pp. 65-19614. (R).

0992 Arlington, Lewis Charles, ed. and tr. Famous Chinese Plays.
B   N.Y.: Russell & Russell, 1963 (orig. pub. by Vetch, 1937).
     443 pp. 63-15147. (R).
     Hucker, 1676

0022 Ars Asiatica, v.1-18. 1914-35.
B

0023 Ars Orientalis. v.1- 1954-
B   Sup. 61, 2749

1885 Art Treasures from Japan. Exhibition, Los Angeles County Mu-
C   seum of Art, September 29, 1965-November 7, 1965, and Other
     Institutions. Palo Alto, Calif.: Kodansha, 1965. 196 pp.
     65-23948.

0024 Artibus Asiae, v.1- 1925- (R-Johnson).
A

1944 Asahi Shimbun Sha. Ise, Prototype of Japanese Architecture.
C   Cambridge, Mass.: M.I.T. Press, 1965. 212 pp. 64-7970.
     Choice, 9/65; JAS, 2/66

1439 Asakawa, Kan'ichi, ed. and tr. The Documents of Iriki. new ed.
C   Tokyo: Japan Society for Promotion of Science, 1955. 442 pp.
     59-24424.
     Silberman, 219; Japan Q., 10-12/57

1440 Asakawa, Kan'ichi. The Early Institutional Life of Japan; A
B   Study in the Reform of 645 A.D. 2d ed. N.Y.: Paragon,

1963 (orig. pub. by Tokyo Shueisha, 1903). 355 pp.
63-21051. (R).
AUFS, 178; Silberman, 208; JAS, 5/65

0178 Asanga. La Somme du Grand Vehicule d'Asanga (Mahayanasamgraha)
C   par Etienne Lamotte. Louvain: Bureaux du Museon, 1938-39.
     2 v. 42-46855.

1954 Ashihara, Hidesato. The Japanese Dance. 2d ed. Tokyo: Japan
A   Travel Bureau, 1965. 164 pp. NUC 66-33916.

0025 Asia and the Americas. v.1-46. 1898-1946.
C

0026 Asia Major, v.1-10. 1924-35. n.s.v.1- 1949- (R-Johnson).
B   Hucker, 31; Silberman, 39

0010 Asia Society. American Institutions and Organizations Interested
A   in Asia: a Reference Directory. ed. by Ward Morehouse. 2d
     ed. N.Y.: Taplinger for Asia Society, 1961. 581 pp.
     61-11435.
     Sup. 63, 2873; JAS, 5/62; Library Journal, 9/1/61

0027 Asian Recorder. v.1- 1955-
C   Sup. 61, 2750

0028 Asian Survey, v.1- 1961- (1932-61 as Far Eastern Sur-
A   vey, v.1-30). (R-Kraus).
     AUFS, 86; Hucker, 27

1986 Asiatic Research Bulletin. Seoul: Research Center, Korea
B   University.

1390 Asiatic Society of Japan Transactions. Tokyo, 1872 ff.
B   irregular. In three series: 1st, 1872-1922, 2nd, 1924-
     1940, 3rd, 1948ff. 5-22827. (R-Kraus).
     Sup. 61, 2784; Silberman, 29

0328 Aspects de la Chine: Langue, Histoire, Religions, Philosophie,
B   Litterature, Arts; par E. Balazs et al. Paris: Presses
     Universitaires, 1959. 2 v. Hand catalog.
     Sup. 61, 2787; Hucker, 6; JAS, 2/61

1660 Aspects of Social Change in Modern Japan. ed. by R. P. Dore.
A   Princeton, N.J.: Princeton University Press, 1967. 474 pp.
     66-11973.
     JAS, 8/68

1745 Aston, William George. A History of Japanese Literature. N.Y.:
C   Johnson, 1965 (orig. pub. by Heinemann, 1899). 420 pp.
     99-768. (R).
     AUFS, 424; Silberman, 876

1234 Asvaghosa. The Awakening of Faith, Attributed to Asvaghosha.
B   tr. with commentary by Yoshita S. Hakeda. N.Y.: Columbia
     University Press, 1967. 128 pp. 67-13778.
     Choice, 5/68

0951 Ayscough, Florence (Wheelock), tr. Fir-Flower Tablets; Poems
C   Translated from the Chinese. English versions by Amy Lowell.
     Boston: Houghton Mifflin, 1921. 227 pp. 22-3648. o.p.
     Hucker, 1566

1622 Ayusawa, Iwao Frederick. A History of Labor in Modern Japan.
A   Honolulu: East-West Center Press, 1966. 406 pp. 66-30068.
     Choice, 10/67; JAS, 11/67; Library Journal, 5/15/67

1276 Bachhofer, Ludwig. A Short History of Chinese Art. N.Y.:
B   Pantheon, 1946. 139 pp. 47-952. o.p.
     AUFS, 1001; Hucker, 1400; FEQ, 5/48

0432 Backhouse, Sir Edmund Trelawny. Annals & Memoirs of the Court
B   of Peking (from the 16th to the 20th Century). Boston:
     Houghton Mifflin, 1914. 531 pp. 14-30273. o.p.
     AUFS, 727; Hucker, 477; AHR, 7/14; Am. Pol. Sci. R., 8/14

1482 Baelz, Erwin O. E. Von. Awakening Japan: the Diary of a Ger-
C   man Doctor. tr. from German by Eden and Cedar Paul.
     N.Y.: Viking, 1932. 406 pp. 32-13595. o.p.
     Pol. Sci. Q., 12/32

1572 Baerwald, Hans H. The Purge of Japanese Leaders Under the
B   Occupation. Berkeley: University of California Press,
     1959. 111 pp. (University of California Publications in
     Political Science, Vol. 8). 59-63933. o.p.
     Sup. 61, 2755; Silberman, 567; JAS, 5/60; Japan Q., 7-9/60

0309 Bagchi, Prabodh Chandra. India and China; A Thousand Years
A   of Cultural Relations. 2d ed., rev. N.Y.: Philosophical
     Library, 1951. 234 pp. A52-8492. o.p.

Hucker, 119; FEQ, 11/52

1483   Bailey, Thomas Andrew. Theodore Roosevelt and the Japanese-
C   American Crises; An Account of the International Compli-
       cations Arising from the Race Problem on the Pacific
       Coast. Gloucester, Mass.: Peter Smith, 1964 (orig. pub.
       by Stanford University Press, 1934). 353 pp. 64-56762.
       (R).
       Silberman, 434; Am. Pol. Sci. R., 6/35; Ann. Am. Acad.,
       5/35; Pacific Affairs, 9/35; Pol. Sci. Q., 12/35

0310   Balazs, Etienne. Chinese Civilization and Bureaucracy;
A   Variations on a Theme. tr. by H. Wright. ed. by
       Arthur F. Wright. New Haven, Conn.: Yale University Press
       for East Asian Research Center, Harvard University and
       Council on East Asian Studies, Yale University, 1964.
       309 pp. 64-20909.
       Sup. 65, 3083; Choice, 2/65; JAS, 5/65

0433   Bales, William Leslie. Tso Tsungt'ang, Soldier and Statesman
C   of Old China. Shanghai: Kelly & Walsh, 1937. 436 pp.
       38-5016. o.p. (M-University).
       Hucker, 641

0135   Ball, William Macmahon. Nationalism and Communism in East
B   Asia. 2d ed. rev. Carlton: Melbourne University Press,
       1956. 220 pp. 56-4246. o.p. (M-University).
       AUFS, 74; JAS, 8/57; FEQ, 8/53

0542   Band, Claire. Two Years with the Chinese Communists. New
B   Haven, Conn.: Yale University Press, 1948. 347 pp.
       48-5830 rev. o.p.
       Hucker, 893; Ann. Am. Acad., 7/48; Pacific Affairs, 9/48

0434   Banno, Masataka. China and the West, 1858-1861; The Origins
A   of the Tsungli Yamen. Cambridge, Mass.: Harvard Univer-
       sity Press, 1964. 367 pp. (Harvard East Asian Series,
       15). 64-13419.
       Choice, 9/64; JAS, 11/64; AHR, 1/65; JAOS, 7-9/64; Pacific
       Affairs, Winter/64-65; TLS, 4/8/65

2086   Barclay, George W. Colonial Development and Population in
B   Taiwan. Princeton, N.J.: Princeton University Press,
       1954. 274 pp. 52-13153.
       AUFS, 774; FEQ, 11/55; Am. Anthropologist, 4/55; Am. Pol.
       Sci. R., 12/54; Ann. Am. Acad., 11/54; Geog. R., 7/55; J.
       Pol. Econ., 8/55

1277   Barnard, Noel. Bronze Casting and Bronze Alloys in Ancient
C   China. Canberra: Australian National University, 1961.
       336 pp. 62-6942.
       JAS, 5/62

0830   Barnett, A. Doak. Cadres, Bureaucracy and Political Power in
C   Communist China. with contrib. by Ezra Vogel. N.Y.: Co-
       lumbia University Press, 1967. 563 pp. (Studies of the East
       Asian Institute of Columbia University). 67-15895.
       Choice, 4/68; Ann. Am. Acad., 3/68; Library Journal, 6/1/67

0831   Barnett, A. Doak. China After Mao, with Selected Documents.
A   Princeton, N.J.: Princeton University Press, 1967. 287 pp.
       (Walter E. Edge Lectures). 67-14406.
       Choice, 7-8/67; Ann. Am. Acad., 3/68

0543   Barnett, A. Doak. China on the Eve of Communist Takeover.
A   N.Y.: Praeger, 1963. 371 pp. (Praeger Publications in
       Russian History and World Communism, No. 130). 63-10824.
       Ann. Am. Acad., 1/64; Library Journal, 7/63

0726   Barnett, A. Doak. Communist China and Asia; Challenge to
A   American Policy. N.Y.: Harper, 1960. 575 pp. 60-5956.
       Sup. 61, 2788; Hucker, 846; JAS, 11/60

0727   Barnett, A. Doak. Communist China: the Early Years, 1949-55.
A   N.Y.: Praeger, 1964. 336 pp. 64-22487.
       Sup. 65, 3084; Choice, 2/65; JAS, 8/65; Ann. Am. Acad.,
       9/65

0136   Barnett, A. Doak, ed. Communist Strategies in Asia: a Comparative
A   Analysis of Governments and Parties. N.Y.: Praeger, 1963.
       293 pp. 63-10823.
       Library Journal, 1/15/64

2103   Barth, Gunther Paul. Bitter Strength; A History of the Chinese
A   in the United States, 1850-1870. Cambridge, Mass.:
       Harvard University Press, 1964. 305 pp. 64-21785.
       Choice, 7-8/65; JAS, 5/66; AHR, 7/65; Library Journal, 1/1/65

1661   Basabe, Fernando M. Japanese Youth Confronts Religion; A So-
B   ciological Survey, by Fernando M. Basabe, in collaboration

with Anzai Shin and Alphonso M. Nebreda. Tokyo: Sophia
University in cooperation with Tuttle, 1967. 183 pp.
67-28418.
Choice, 10/68

1253   Basic Writings of Mo Tzu, Hsun Tzu, and Han Fei Tzu. tr. by
B   Burton Watson. N.Y.: Columbia University Press, 1967.
       140 pp. 67-16170.
       Choice, 11/67

0091   Battistini, Lawrence Henry. The Rise of American Influence in
B   Asia and the Pacific. East Lansing: Michigan State Uni-
       versity Press, 1960. 241 pp. 59-15833. o.p.
       Silberman, 432; JAS, 2/61

0914   Bauer, Wolfgang. The Golden Casket; Chinese Novellas of Two
A   Millenia. tr. by Christopher Levenson. N.Y.: Harcourt,
       Brace & World, 1964. 391 pp. 64-18278.
       Library Journal, 11/15/64

1235   Beal, Samuel. A Catena of Buddhist Scriptures from the Chinese.
C   London: Trubner, 1871. 436 pp. 32-13515. o.p.
       AUFS, 654

1236   Beal, Samuel, tr. The Life of Hiuen-Tsiang by the Shaman Hwui Li.
C   new ed. N.Y.: Dutton, 1916. o.p.
       Hucker, 1273

1662   Beardsley, Richard King. Village Japan. Chicago: University of
A   Chicago Press, 1959. 498 pp. 58-13802.
       AUFS, 329; Silberman, 1410; JAS, 2/60; Am. Anthropologist,
       8/60; Am. Pol. Sci. R., 3/60; Am. Soc. R., 4/60; Ann. Am.
       Acad., 3/60; Geog. R., 7/60; Japan Q., 10-12/59; JAOS,
       10-12/59; Library Journal, 3/17/59

1441   Beasley, William G. Great Britain and the Opening of Japan,
B   1834-1858. London: Luzac, 1951. 227 pp. 52-39372.
       AUFS, 180; Silberman, 292; FEQ, 2/53

1442   Beasley, William G., ed. and tr. Select Documents on Japanese
B   Foreign Policy, 1853-1868. N.Y.: Oxford, 1955. 359 pp.
       55-4067.
       AUFS, 181; Silberman, 293; FEQ, 8/56

0011   Beasley, William Gerald and E. G. Pullyblank, eds. Histor-
A   ians of China and Japan. N.Y.: Oxford, 1961. 351 pp.
       (University of London, Historical Writing on the Peoples
       of Asia, Vol. 3). Hand catalog.
       Sup. 63, 2876; Hucker, 1620a; JAS, 5/62; Japan Q., 1-3/62

1484   Beckmann, George M. The Japanese Communist Party, 1922-1945.
C   by George M. Beckmann and Okubo Genji. Stanford, Calif.:
       Stanford University Press, 1969. 453 pp. 68-26776.

1485   Beckmann, George M. The Making of the Meiji Constitution; The
B   Oligarchs and the Constitutional Development of Japan,
       1868-1891. Lawrence: University of Kansas Press, 1957.
       158 pp. 57-10705. o.p. (M-University).
       AUFS, 218; Silberman, 368; JAS, 5/58

0728   Belden, Jack. China Shakes the World. N.Y.: Harper, 1949.
A   524 pp. 49-11358. o.p. (M-University).
       AUFS, 900; Hucker, 800

0147   Bellah, Robert Neely, ed. Religion and Progress in Modern
A   Asia. N.Y.: Free Press of Glencoe, 1965. 246 pp.
       65-16267.
       Sup. 67, 3351; Choice, 1/67; JAS, 5/66; Am. Anthropologist,
       6/66; Am. Soc. R., 10/66; Ann. Am. Acad., 5/66; Library
       Journal, 9/1/65; Pol. Sci. Q., 12/66

1808   Bellah, Robert Neely. Tokugawa Religion, the Values of Pre-
A   Industrial Japan. Glencoe, Ill.: Free Press, 1957. 249 pp.
       57-6748.
       AUFS, 127; Silberman, 594; JAS, 5/63; Am. Soc. R., 10/57;
       Ann. Am. Acad., 11/57; J. Religion, 10/57; Pacific Affairs,
       9/57

0120   Beloff, Max. Soviet Policy in the Far East, 1944-1951. N.Y.:
A   Oxford, 1953. 278 pp. 53-12887. o.p.
       AUFS, 75; Hucker, 835; FEQ, 11/54

0148   Belshaw, Horace. Population Growth and Levels of Consumption,
B   with Special Reference to Countries in Asia. N.Y.: Insti-
       tute of Pacific Relations, 1956. 223 pp. 56-4881. o.p.
       AUFS, 10; Am. Econ. R., 6/57; Am. Pol. Sci. R., 9/57; Ann.
       Am. Acad., 1/57; TLS, 8/3/56

1663   Benedict, Ruth Fulton. The Chrysanthemum and the Sword; Pat-
A   terns of Japanese Culture. Boston: Houghton Mifflin, 1946.

324 pp. 46-11843.
AUFS, 219; Silberman, 1380; FEQ, 8/47; Library Journal, 10/15/46

0149 Benham, Frederic Charles. The Colombo Plan, and Other Essays.
C N.Y.: Royal Institute of International Affairs, 1956. 89 pp. 56-14552.
AUFS, 11; JAS, 8/57

1809 Benl, Oscar, ed. Japanische Geisteswelt; Vom Mythus zur Gegen-
C wart. Baden-Baden: Holle Verlag, 1956. 419 pp. Hand catalog.
Silberman, 589

1351 Bennett, Adrian Arthur. John Fryer: the Introduction of Western
B Science and Technology into Nineteenth-Century China. Cam-
bridge, Mass.: Harvard University Press, 1967. 157 pp. (East Asian Monographs, 24). 68-4092.

1664 Bennett, John William. Paternalism in the Japanese Economy:
B Anthropological Studies of Oyabun-Kobun Patterns. by John
W. Bennett and Iwao Ishino. Minneapolis: University of Minnesota Press, 1963. 307 pp. 63-16068.
Choice, 1/64; JAS, 8/64

1665 Bennett, John William. In Search of Identity; The Japanese
B Overseas Scholar in America and Japan. Minneapolis: Uni-
versity of Minnesota Press, 1958. 369 pp. 58-10879.
AUFS, 330; Silberman, 1460; JAS, 8/59; Am. Anthropologist, 8/59; Am. J. Soc., 3/60; Ann. Am. Acad., 9/59; Library Journal, 10/15/58

2007 Berger, Carl. The Korea Knot, a Military-Political History.
B rev. ed. Philadelphia: University of Pennsylvania Press, 1965. 255 pp. 64-24503.
Choice, 11/65; JAS, 2/58

0544 Bergere, Marie Claire, ed. Une Crise Financiere a Shanghai
B a le Fin de l'Ancien Regime. Paris: Mouton, 1964. 84 pp. (Maison des Sciences de l'Homme, Materiaux pour l'Etude de la Chine Modern et Contemporaine, Textes, 3).
NUC 66-74341.
JAS, 2/66

0545 Berkov, Robert. Strong Man of China; The Story of Chiang
B Kai-shek. Boston: Houghton Mifflin, 1938. 288 pp. 38-3985. o.p.
Am. Pol. Sci. R., 8/38

0435 Bernard, Henri. Matteo Ricci's Scientific Contribution to China.
C tr. by Edward Chalmers Werner. Peiping: Vetch, 1935. 108 pp. 36-17357. o.p.
Hucker, 553; TLS, 9/26/36

0436 Bernard, Henri. Le Pere Matthieu Ricci et la Societe Chinoise de
C son Temps (1552-1610). Tientsin: Hautes Etudes, 1937. 2 v. 38-33085. o.p.

0179 Berry, Thomas Mary. Buddhism. N.Y.: Hawthorne Books, 1967.
A 187 pp. 66-15226.

0231 Berton, Peter Alexander Menquez. Contemporary China; A Research
A Guide. Stanford, Calif.: Hoover Institution on War, Revolu-
tion and Peace, 1967. (Hoover Institution Bibliographical Series, Vol. XXXI). 695 pp. 67-14235.
JAS, 11/68; Library Journal, 7/68

0546 Bertram, James M. First Act in China; The Story of the Sian
B Mutiny. N.Y.: Viking, 1938. 284 pp. 38-20738. o.p.
Hucker, 777; Ann. Am. Acad., 7/38; Pacific Affairs, 3/38

0729 Bertram, James M. Return to China. London: Heinemann, 1957.
B 251 pp. 58-18363. o.p.

0172 The Bible of the World. ed. by Robert O. Ballou. N.Y.: Vik-
C ing, 1939. 1415 pp. 39-27953.
Hucker, 1060

0002 Bibliography of Asian Studies. Ann Arbor: Association for
A Asian Studies, 1956- 43-14717 rev. 2.
Hucker, 16

1363 A Bibliography on Japanese Buddhism. ed. by Bando Shojun and
B others. Tokyo: CIIB Press, 1958. 180 pp. A59-8335.
Silberman, 622

0353 Bielenstein, Hans. The Restoration of the Han Dynasty; With
B Prolegomena on the Historiography of the Hou Han Shu.
Stockholm: 1953- 209 pp. 55-21208.
Hucker, 1624

1322 Biggerstaff, Knight. The Earliest Modern Government Schools
A in China. Ithaca, N.Y.: Cornell University Press, 1961. 276 pp. 61-14951.
Sup. 63, 2903; JAS, 8/62

1909 Binyon, Laurence. Japanese Colour Prints. Boston: Boston
A Book and Art Shop, 1960 (orig. pub. by Frederick Publishers, 1955). 230 pp. 59-14161. (R).
Silberman, 785

0194 Binyon, Laurence. The Spirit of Man in Asian Art. N.Y.:
C Dover, 1965 (orig. pub. by Harvard University Press, 1935). 217 pp. 65-24017. (R).
AUFS, 12; JAOS, 9/35

0232 Biographical Dictionary of Republican China. ed. by Howard L.
A Boorman and Richard C. Howard. N.Y.: Columbia University Press, 1967- 67-12006.
Choice, 6/67, 9/68; AHR, 12/67; Am. Pol. Sci. R., 3/68; Library Journal, 3/1/67, 8/68

1006 Birch, Cyril, comp. and ed. associate ed., Donald Keene. An-
A thology of Chinese Literature. N.Y.: Grove, 1965- (UNESCO Collection of Representative Works, Chinese Series). 65-14202.
Sup. 67, 3233; Choice, 6/66; JAS, 11/66; JAOS, 4-6/66; Library Journal, 1/1/66

1147 Birch, Cyril, ed. Chinese Communist Literature. N.Y.:
A Praeger, 1963. 254 pp. 63-18538.
Library Journal, 8/63

1007 Bishop, John Lyman. The Colloquial Short Story in China; A
B Study of the San-yen Collections. Cambridge, Mass.: Harvard University Press, 1956. 144 pp. 56-7211.
AUFS, 1047; JAS, 11/56

1008 Bishop, John Lyman, ed. Studies in Chinese Literature. Cam-
B bridge, Mass.: Harvard University Press, 1965. 245 pp. 65-13836.

0092 Bisson, Thomas Arthur. America's Far Eastern Policy. N.Y.:
C Institute of Pacific Relations, dist. by Macmillan, 1945. 235 pp. 45-1072. o.p.
Silberman, 507; FEQ, 8/45; Am. Pol. Sci. R., 8/45; Pacific Affairs, 9/45

0093 Bisson, Thomas Arthur. Japan in China. N.Y.: Macmillan, 1938.
B 417 pp. 38-27434. o.p.
AUFS, 777; Hucker, 797; Am. Pol. Sci. R., 10/38; Pacific Affairs, 9/38

1623 Bisson, Thomas Arthur. Zaibatsu Dissolution in Japan. Berke-
C ley: University of California Press, 1954. 314 pp. 54-6468. o.p.
Silberman, 575; FEQ, 11/54; AHR, 10/54; Ann. Am. Acad., 7/54

1486 Blacker, Carmen. The Japanese Enlightenment: a Study of
B the Writings of Fukuzawa Yukichi. N.Y.: Cambridge, 1964. 185 pp. (Cambridge University Oriental Publication No. 10). 64-1805.
Sup. 65, 3055; JAS, 5/65; Japan Q., 10-12/64; JAOS, 4-6/64

0437 Bland, John Otway Percy. China Under the Empress Dowager;
B Being the History of the Life and Times of Tzu Hsi. new
and rev. ed. Taipei: Chinese Materials and Research Aids Service Center (orig. pub. by Houghton Mifflin, 1914). 322 pp. A17-407. (R). (M-University).
AUFS, 730; Hucker, 610; FEQ, 11/41

1666 Blood, Robert O. Love Match and Arranged Marriage; A Tokyo-
B Detroit Comparison. N.Y.: Free Press of Glencoe, 1967. 264 pp. 67-12511.
Choice, 3/68; Am. Soc. R., 8/68

0329 Bloodworth, Dennis. The Chinese Looking Glass. N.Y.: Farrar,
A Straus, & Giroux, 1967. 432 pp. 67-22047.
Choice, 11/67; Library Journal, 6/15/67

1828 Bloom, Alfred. Shinran's Gospel of Pure Grace. Tucson:
C University of Arizona Press, 1965. 97 pp. (Association for Asian Studies, Monographs and Papers, XX). 64-8757.
Choice, 2/67

0730 Blum, Robert. The United States and China in World Affairs.
B ed. by A. Doak Barnett. N.Y.: McGraw-Hill, 1966. 287 pp. (United States and China in World Affairs Series/Council on Foreign Relations). 66-26490.
Sup. 67, 3234; Choice, 7-8/67; JAS, 8/67; Library Journal,

1713   Blyth, Reginald Horace. Haiku. rev. ed. Tokyo: Hokuseido,
B   dist. by Japan Publications Trading Co., 1963-1964. 4 v.
       53-20278.
       AUFS, 426; Silberman, 1064

1696   Blyth, Reginald Horace. Japanese Humour. Tokyo: Japan
C   Travel Bureau, 1957. 184 pp. 57-14606.

1714   Blyth, Reginald Horace. Senryu; Japanese Satirical Verses.
B   Tokyo: Hokuseido, 1949. 230 pp. 52-20528.
       AUFS, 428; Silberman, 1067

1829   Blyth, Reginald Horace. Zen and Zen Classics. Tokyo: Hokuseido,
C   dist. by Japan Publications Trading Co., 1963-66. 5 v.
       62-51117 rev.
       JAOS, 7-9/62

0438   Boardman, Eugene Powers. Christian Influence Upon the Ideology of
A   the Taiping Rebellion, 1851-1864. Madison: University of
       Wisconsin Press, 1952. 188 pp. 52-13339. o.p.
       Hucker, 624; FEQ, 5/53

0311   Bodde, Derk. China's Cultural Tradition, What and Whither?
B   N.Y.: Rinehart, 1957. 90 pp. 57-59558.
       AUFS, 673; Hucker, 9; JAS, 8/58; JAOS, 10-12/57

0354   Bodde, Derk. China's First Unifier; A Study of the Ch'in Dynasty
B   As Seen in the Life of Li Ssu, 280?-208 B.C. London: Oxford,
       1967 (orig. pub. by Brill, 1938). 270 pp. 67-108881. (R).
       AUFS, 698; Hucker, 183; JAOS, 9/38

0731   Bodde, Derk. Peking Diary: 1948-1949, a Year of Revolution.
A   Greenwich, Conn.: Fawcett, 1967 (orig. pub. by Abelard-
       Schuman, 1950). 288 pp. NUC 68-76595. (R).
       AUFS, 901; Hucker, 977; FEQ, 8/51; AHR, 4/51; Am. J. Soc.,
       3/51; Library Journal, 10/1/50; Pacific Affairs, 6/51;
       TLS, 10/5/51

1443   Bohner, Hermann. Shotoku Taishi. Tokyo: Deutsche Gesellschaft
C   fur Natur- und Volkerkunde Ostasiens, 1940. 1033 pp.
       (Deutsche Gesellschaft fur Natur- und Volkerkunde Ostasiens,
       Mitteilungen, Supplement Bd. XV).
       Silberman, 203

0732   Boorman, Howard L. Moscow-Peking Axis: Strengths and Strains.
B   N.Y.: Harper for Council on Foreign Relations, 1957.
       227 pp. 56-7909. o.p.
       AUFS, 902; Hucker, 1012; JAS, 2/58; Am. Pol. Sci. R.,
       9/57; Ann. Am. Acad., 9/57; Library Journal, 4/1/57;
       Pol. Sci. Q., 9/57

0547   Borg, Dorothy. American Policy and the Chinese Revolution,
A   1925-1928. N.Y.: Octagon, 1967 (orig. pub. by Macmillan,
       1947). 440 pp. 67-18753. (R).
       AUFS, 778; Hucker, 812; FEQ, 11/47; AHR, 10/47; Am. Pol.
       Sci. R., 12/47;

0094   Borg, Dorothy. The United States and the Far Eastern Crisis
A   of 1933-1938; From the Manchurian Incident through the
       Initial State of the Undeclared Sino-Japanese War. Cam-
       bridge, Mass.: Harvard University Press, 1964. (Harvard
       East Asian Series, 14). 674 pp. 64-13421.
       Sup. 65, 3085; Choice, 7-8/64; JAS, 11/64; AHR, 1/65;
       Library Journal, 5/15/64; Pacific Affairs, Winter/64-65;
       Pol. Sci. Q., 12/64

1487   Borton, Hugh. Japan's Modern Century. N.Y.: Ronald, 1955.
A   524 pp. 55-10667.
       AUFS, 221; Silberman, 317; AHR, 4/56; Am. Pol. Sci. R.,
       3/56; Ann. Am. Acad., 7/56; Pacific Affairs, 6/56; Pol. Sci.
       Q., 6/56

1444   Borton, Hugh. Peasant Uprisings in Japan of the Tokugawa
C   Period. New Hyde Park, N.Y.: University Books, 1966 (orig.
       pub. by Asiatic Society of Japan, 1938). 210 pp. AC38-2555
       rev. (R).
       AUFS, 182; Silberman, 268

1364   Borton, Hugh. A Selected List of Books and Articles on Japan
B   in English, French, and German. rev. and enl. Cambridge,
       Mass.: Harvard University Press for Harvard-Yenching Insti-
       tute, 1954. 272 pp. 53-5055.
       AUFS, 158; Silberman, 9; FEQ, 2/42

0191   Bossert, Helmuth Theodor, ed. Decorative Art of Asia and
C   Egypt; Four Hundred Decorative Motifs in Color, Forming a
       Survey of the Applied Art of Egypt, China, Japan, Siam,
       Tibet, of the Lapps and Siberian and Islamic Peoples.

N.Y.: Praeger, 1956. 13 pp. 56-9928. o.p.

1148   Boven, Henri Van. Histoire de la Litterature Chinoise
B   Moderne. Peiping: Catholic University, 1946. 187 pp.
       49-15732. o.p.

1731   Bowers, Faubion. Japanese Theatre. N.Y.: Hermitage, 1952.
B   294 pp. 52-12701.
       AUFS, 495; Silberman, 1093; FEQ, 8/53; Library Journal,
       10/15/52

0168   Bowers, Faubion. Theatre in the East; A Survey of Asian Dance
C   and Drama. N.Y.: Grove, 1960 (orig. pub. by Nelson, 1956).
       374 pp. NUC 63-6677. (R). o.p.
       Hucker, 1672; JAS, 11/56; Library Journal, 7/56; TLS,
       8/10/56

1910   Bowie, Henry P. On the Laws of Japanese Painting; An Intro-
C   duction to the Study of the Art of Japan. N.Y.: Dover,
       1951 (orig. pub. in 1911). 117 pp. 52-9794. (R).
       Silberman, 758

1715   Bownas, Geoffrey, ed. and tr. The Penguin Book of Japanese
A   Verse. tr., ed., and intro. by Geoffrey Bownas and Anthony
       Thwaite. Baltimore: Penguin, 1964. 242 pp. (Penguin
       Poets, D77). 64-6583.
       Sup. 65, 3069; Choice, 11/64; Japan Q., 10-12/64

1445   Boxer, Charles Ralph. The Christian Century in Japan, 1549-
A   1650. rev. ed. Berkeley: University of California Press,
       1967. 535 pp. NUC 68-28062.
       AUFS, 183; Silberman, 241; FEQ, 11/52; Ann. Am. Acad.,
       11/51; JAOS, 10-12/52; TLS, 9/14/51

0439   Boxer, Charles Ralph. Fidalgos in the Far East, 1550-1770; Fact
B   and Fancy in the History of Macao. The Hague: Nijhoff, 1948.
       297 pp. 49-21659.
       Hucker, 557; FEQ, 2/52

1400   Boxer, Charles Ralph. Jan Compagnie in Japan, 1600-1850; an
B   Essay on the Cultural, Artistic and Scientific Influence
       Exercised by the Hollanders in Japan from the Seventeenth
       to the Nineteenth Centuries. 2d rev. ed. The Hague: Ni-
       jhoff, 1950. 198 pp. 51-1183.
       AUFS, 184; Silberman, 289; FEQ, 5/51

0440   Boxer, Charles Ralph, ed. South China in the Sixteenth Century,
C   Being the Narratives of Galeote Pereira, Fr. Gaspar da
       Cruz, and Fr. Martin de Rada (1550-1575). tr. by editor.
       Lichtenstein: Kraus, 1967 (orig. pub. by Hakluyt Society,
       1953). 388 pp. (Works issued by the Hakluyt Society, 2d
       ser. No. 106). NUC 68-28970. (R).
       Sup. 61, 2789; Hucker, 573; FEQ, 5/56

1313   Boyd, Andrew Charles Hugh. Chinese Architecture and Town Plan-
B   ning, 1500 B.C.-A.D. 1911. Chicago: University of Chicago
       Press, 1962. 166 pp. 63-9735.
       JAS, 8/63; Arch. Forum, 4/63; TLS, 11/30/62

0733   Boyd, R. C. Communist China's Foreign Policy. N.Y.: Praeger,
B   1962. 147 pp. (Praeger Publications in Russian History
       and World Communism, No. 107). 62-13750. o.p.
       JAS, 2/63; Ann. Am. Acad., 11/62; China Q., 7-9/64; Library
       Journal, 5/1/62; TLS, 8/10/62

1886   Boyer, Martha Hagensen. Japanese Export Lacquers from the
C   Seventeenth Century in the National Museum of Denmark.
       Copenhagen: The National Museum, 1959. 149 pp. 60-4349.

0441   Braga, Jose Maria. China Landfall, 1513. Hong Kong: K. Weiss,
C   1956.
       Hucker, 584

0442   Braga, Jose Maria. The Western Pioneers and Their Discovery
B   of Macao. Macao: Imprensa Nacional, 1949. 248 pp. 51-24246.
       Hucker, 569

0734   Brandt, Conrad. A Documentary History of Chinese Communism.
A   N.Y.: Atheneum, 1966 (orig. pub. by Harvard University
       Press, 1952). 552 pp. 66-60102/CD. (R).
       AUFS, 904; Hucker, 871; FEQ, 5/53; AHR, 4/53; Ann. Am.
       Acad., 3/53; Library Journal, 2/15/53; Pacific Affairs,
       6/53; TLS, 1/30/53

0548   Brandt, Conrad. Stalin's Failure in China 1924-1927. N.Y.:
A   Norton, 1966 (orig. pub. by Harvard University Press,
       1958). 226 pp. (Norton Library, N352). NUC 67-85293.
       (R).
       AUFS, 903; Hucker, 872; JAS, 5/59; AHR, 4/59; Am. Pol.
       Sci. R., 6/59; TLS, 5/8/59

0137 Brecher, Michael. The New States of Asia, a Political Analysis.
B   N.Y.: Oxford, 1963. 226 pp. 64-549.
     Sup. 65, 3043; Choice, 9/64; Ann. Am. Acad., 9/64; JAOS,
     4-6/65; TLS, 7/9/64

1170 Briere, O. Fifty Years of Chinese Philosophy, 1898-1948. ed.,
A   with intro., by Dennis J. Doolin. tr. from French by Laur-
     ence G. Thompson. N.Y.: Praeger, 1965 (orig. pub. by Allen
     & Unwin, 1956). 159 pp. 65-21106. (R).
     Hucker, 1328; Choice, 9/66; JAS, 8/57; JAOS, 1-3/57

0198 British Museum. Dept. of Oriental Printed Books and Manuscripts.
B   Descriptive Catalogue of the Chinese Manuscripts from Tun-
     huang in the British Museum, by Lionel Giles. London:
     Trustees of the British Museum, 1957. 334 pp. 58-31979.
     Hucker, 263; JAS, 8/58; JAOS, 4-6/58

1624 Broadbridge, Seymour A. Industrial Dualism in Japan: a
B   Problem of Economic Growth and Structural Change.
     Chicago: Aldine, 1967. 105 pp. 66-23159.
     Choice, 1/68; JAS, 11/67; Ann. Am. Acad., 11/67; Library
     Journal, 5/15/67

0268 The Broadsheet. v.1- 1964-
C

1716 Brower, Robert Hopkins. Japanese Court Poetry. Stanford,
A   Calif.: Stanford University Press, 1961. 527 pp. (Studies
     in the Civilizations of Eastern Asia). 61-10925.
     Sup. 63, 2881; JAS, 8/62; Japan Q., 4-6/62; JAOS, 7-9/62

1446 Brown, Delmer Myers. Money Economy in Medieval Japan; A Study
C   in the Use of Coins. New Haven, Conn.: Institute of Far
     Eastern Languages, Yale University, 1951. 128 pp.
     (Association for Asian Studies, Monographs and Papers,
     I). A52-10471 rev.
     Silberman, 1505; FEQ, 11/52; JAOS, 4-6/53

1488 Brown, Delmer Myers. Nationalism in Japan; An Introductory
B   Historical Analysis. Berkeley: University of California
     Press, 1955. 336 pp. 54-6469. o.p.
     AUFS, 222; Silberman, 321; FEQ, 8/55; AHR, 7/55; Ann. Am.
     Acad., 5/55; Japan Q., 7-9/56; Library Journal, 3/1/55

1189 Bruce, Joseph Percy. Chu Hsi and His Masters; An Introduction
C   to Chu Hsi and the Sung School of Chinese Philosophy. Lon-
     don: A. Probsthain, 1923. 336 pp. 23-11243. o.p. (M-
     University).
     AUFS, 614

1969 Bryant, William Cullen. English Language Teaching in Japanese
B   Schools. N.Y.: Japan Society, 1955. o.p.
     Silberman, 1485

0549 Buck, John Lossing. Chinese Farm Economy; A Study of 2866 Farms
B   in Seventeen Localities and Seven Provinces of China. Chi-
     cago: University of Chicago Press for University of Nanking,
     1930. 476 pp. 31-6710. o.p.
     Hucker, 2200; Am. J. Soc., 9/31; Geog. R., 4/31

0867 Buck, John Lossing. Food and Agriculture in Communist China.
B   N.Y.: Praeger, 1966. 171 pp. 65-28286.
     Choice, 11/66; JAS, 2/67; Pacific Affairs, Fall-Winter/66-67;
     TLS, 5/18/67

0550 Buck, John Lossing. Land Utilization in China; A Study of
B   16,786 Farms in 168 Localities, and 38,256 Farm Families
     in Twenty-two Provinces in China, 1929-1933. N.Y.: Para-
     gon, 1964 (orig. pub. by University of Chicago Press, 1937).
     494 pp. 64-18448. (R).
     Hucker, 2199; JAS, 8/65; Ann. Am. Acad., 11/38; Pacific
     Affairs, 12/38

0551 Buck, Mrs. Pearl Sydenstricker. The Good Earth. N.Y.: John
B   Day, 1931. 375 pp. 31-26625.
     TLS, 4/30/31

0552 Buck, Mrs. Pearl Sydenstricker. My Several Worlds, a Personal
B   Record. N.Y.: John Day, 1954. 407 pp. 54-10460.

1323 Buck, Mrs. Pearl Sydenstricker. Tell the People, Talks with
C   James Yen About the Mass Education Movement. N.Y.: John
     Day, 1945. 84 pp. 45-2762. o.p.

0184 Buhot, Jean. Chinese and Japanese Art; With Sections on Korea
C   and Vietnam. tr. from French by Remy Inglis Hall. ed. by
     Charles McCurdy. Garden City, N.Y.: Anchor Books, 1967.
     428 pp. 67-10368.
     Choice, 2/68; JAS, 5/68; Library Journal, 12/1/67

1887 Buhot, Jean. Histoire des Arts du Japon. Paris: Vanoest,
C   1949- A51-3611.
     Silberman, 720

0003 Bulletin of Far Eastern Bibliography. Washington: American
A   Council of Learned Societies, 1936-1940. 5 v. 42-6022 rev.

1278 Bulling, A. The Meaning of China's Most Ancient Art; An Inter-
C   pretation of Pottery Patterns from Kansu (Ma Ch'ang and Pan-
     shan) and Their Development in the Shang, Chou and Han Peri-
     ods. Leiden: Brill, 1952. 150 pp. 53-29440.
     Hucker, 1513

1810 Bunce, William K., ed. Religions in Japan: Buddhism, Shinto, and
B   Christianity. Rutland, Vt.: Tuttle, 1962. 194 pp. Hand
     catalog.
     AUFS, 130; Silberman, 590

0443 Bunger, Karl. Quellen zur Rechtgeschichte der T'ang-zeit.
C   Peking: Catholic University, 1946. (Monumenta Serica Mono-
     graph, IX). o.p.
     Hucker, 287

0897 Burgess, John Stewart. The Guilds of Peking. Taipei: Ch'eng-wen
C   Publishing Co., dist. by Chinese Materials and Research
     Aids Service Center, 1966 (orig. pub. by Columbia University
     Press, 1928). 270 pp. NUC 68-74755. (R). (M-University).
     Hucker, 2064; Am. Econ. R., 6/29; J. Pol. Econ., 6/29

1583 Burks, Ardath W. The Government of Japan. 2d ed. N.Y.:
A   Crowell, 1964. 283 pp. 64-14572.
     JAS, 8/62

1237 Burtt, Edwin Arthur, ed. The Teachings of the Compassionate
B   Buddha. N.Y.: New American Library, 1955. 247 pp. 55-5474.
     AUFS, 1552; Hucker, 1238; Silberman, 625

0121 Buss, Claude Albert. The Far East; A History of Recent and
B   Contemporary International Relations in East Asia. N.Y.:
     Macmillan, 1955. 738 pp. 55-2617. o.p.
     AUFS, 77; Silberman, 331; FEQ, 11/55; TLS, 11/18/55

1489 Butow, Robert Joseph Charles. Japan's Decision to Surrender.
A   Stanford, Calif.: Stanford University Press, 1954.
     259 pp. 54-8145.
     Silberman, 538; FEQ, 2/55; AHR, 4/55; Am. Pol. Sci. R.,
     12/54; Ann. Am. Acad., 1/55; Japan Q., 1-3/56; Library
     Journal, 10/1/54; Pacific Affairs, 12/55; TLS, 5/6/55

1490 Butow, Robert Joseph Charles. Tojo and the Coming of the War.
B   Princeton, N.J.: Princeton University Press, 1961. 584 pp.
     61-6287.
     Sup. 61, 2756; JAS, 2/62; AHR, 10/61; Am. Pol. Sci. R.,
     12/61; Japan Q., 10-12/61; JAOS, 1-3/62; Pol. Sci. Q.,
     3/62; TLS, 12/15/61

1491 Byas, Hugh. Government by Assassination. N.Y.: Knopf, 1942.
B   369 pp. 42-25289. o.p.
     Silberman, 452; FEQ, 5/43; Pacific Affairs, 3/43

0444 Cahen, Gaston. History of the Relations of Russia and China
C   under Peter the Great, 1689-1730. tr. and ed. by W.
     Sheldon Ridge. Banger, Me.: University Prints-Reprints,
     1967 (orig. pub. in Shanghai, 1914 under title Some Early
     Russo-Chinese Relations). 128 pp. (Russian Series, 4).
     67-23371. (R).
     AUFS, 733; Choice, 5/68

1290 Cahill, James. Chinese Painting. Geneva: Skira, 1960. 211 pp.
A   (Treasures of Asia). 60-15594.
     Sup. 61, 2790; Hucker, 1465; JAS, 5/61; JAOS, 1-3/62;
     Library Journal, 1/15/61; TLS, 3/10/61

1291 Cahill, James Francis. Fantastics and Eccentrics in Chinese
B   Painting. N.Y.: Asia Society, dist. by Abrams, 1967.
     122 pp. 67-16859.
     Choice, 9/67

1980 California. University. Institute of East Asiatic Studies.
A   Korean Studies Guide. comp. for the Institute of East
     Asiatic Studies, University of California, by B. H. Hazard,
     Jr. (and others). ed. by Richard Marcus. Berkeley: Uni-
     versity of California Press, 1954. 220 pp. 54-7843. o.p.
     AUFS, 525

0122 Cameron, Meribeth Elliot. China, Japan and the Powers. N.Y.:
B   Ronald, 1952. 682 pp. 52-6194.
     AUFS, 78; Silberman, 326; FEQ, 2/53; Library Journal,
     7/52

0445 Cameron, Meribeth Elliot. The Reform Movement in China, 1898-
A   1912. Stanford, Calif.: Stanford University Press, 1931.
     223 pp. 31-32244. o.p.
     Hucker, 646; Am. J. Soc., 9/32; Am. Pol. Sci. S., 2/32;
     Ann. Am. Acad., 5/32

0446 Campbell, Charles Soutter. Special Business Interests and the
B   Open Door Policy. Hamden, Conn.: Shoe String Press, 1968
     (orig. pub. by Yale University Press, 1951). 88 pp.
     (Yale Historical Publications, 53). 68-21689. (R).
     Hucker, 692

2070 Campbell, William. Formosa under the Dutch, Described from
C   Contemporary Records with Explanatory Notes and a Bibli-
     ography of the Island. Taipei: Ch'eng-wen Publishing Co.,
     dist. by Chinese Materials and Research Aids Service
     Center, 1967 (orig. pub. by Kegan Paul, 1903). 629 pp.
     NUC 63-39189. (R).
     Hucker, 585

0553 Carlson, Evans Fordyce. The Chinese Army; Its Organization
B   and Military Efficiency. N.Y.: Institute of Pacific Rela-
     tions, 1940. 139 pp. 40-14507. o.p.
     Hucker, 1937; Am. Pol. Sci. R., 12/40

0554 Carlson, Evans Fordyce. Twin Stars of China, a Behind-the-
B   Scenes Story of China's Valiant Struggle for Existence,
     by a U.S. Marine Who Lived & Moved with the People.
     N.Y.: Dodd, Mead, 1940. 331 pp. 40-27687. o.p.
     Hucker, 804

0095 Carnegie Endowment for International Peace. Division of Inter-
C   national Law. The Sino-Japanese Negotiations of 1915,
     Japanese and Chinese Documents and Chinese Official State-
     ment. Washington: Carnegie Endowment, 1921. 76 pp.
     21-21869. o.p.
     Hucker, 750

0233 Carnegie Endowment for International Peace. Treaties and
B   Agreements with and Concerning China, 1919-29. Wash-
     ington: Carnegie Endowment, 1957. o.p.
     Hucker, 828

0355 Carter, Thomas Francis. The Invention of Printing in China
A   and Its Spread Westward. rev. by L. Carrington Goodrich.
     2d ed. N.Y.: Ronald, 1955. 293 pp. 55-5418.
     AUFS, 699; Hucker, 335; FEQ, 2/56; TLS, 8/27/55

0735 Cartier-Bresson, Henri. From One China to the Other. text
B   by Han Suyin (pseud.). N.Y.: Universe, 1956. 56-11623.
     o.p.
     JAS, 8/57; TLS, 10/5/56

1492 Cary, Otis. A History of Christianity in Japan. N.Y.: Revell,
B   1909. 2 v. 9-22916. o.p.
     Silberman, 656

0166 Ceadel, Eric B., ed. Literatures of the East, an Appreciation.
C   London: Murray, 1953. 194 pp. 54-1444.
     AUFS, 14; Hucker, 1523

0915 Chai, Ch'u, ed. and tr. A Treasury of Chinese Literature; A New
A   Prose Anthology, Including Fiction and Drama. N.Y.: Appleton-
     Century, 1965. 484 pp. 65-11681.
     Choice, 6/66; JAS, 5/66; JAOS, 7-9/66; Library Journal,
     3/1/65

0736 Chakravarti, Prithwis Chandra. India's China Policy. Bloom-
B   ington: Indiana University Press, 1962. 180 pp. 62-8970.
     o.p.
     Library Journal, 3/15/62

1667 Chambliss, William Jones. Chiarijima Village: Land Tenure,
B   Taxation, and Local Trade, 1818-1884. Tucson: University
     of Arizona Press, 1965. 159 pp. (Association for Asian
     Studies, Monographs and Papers, XIX). 64-8756.
     Choice, 7-8/66; JAS, 11/66

0199 Chan, Wing-tsit. Chinese Philosophy, 1949-1963; An Annotated
C   Bibliography of Mainland China Publications. Honolulu:
     East-West Center Press, 1967. 290 pp. 65-20582.
     Choice, 6/67; JAS, 8/68

0200 Chan, Wing-tsit. An Outline and Annotated Bibliography of
A   Chinese Philosophy. New Haven, Conn.: Far Eastern Pub-
     lications, Yale University, 1959. 127 pp. Supplement,
     1961; Supplement, 1965. 60-9.
     Hucker, 1022

1171 Chan, Wing-tsit. Religious Trends in Modern China. N.Y.:
A   Columbia University Press, 1953. 327 pp. (American Council
     of Learned Societies; Lectures on the History of Religions,
     n.s. 3). 53-7012. (M-University).
     AUFS, 582; Hucker, 1331; FEQ, 11/53

0234 Chan, Wing-tsit, comp. and tr. A Source Book of Chinese Phi-
A   losophy. Princeton, N.J.: Princeton University Press,
     1963. 856 pp. 62-7398.
     JAS, 5/64; JAOS, 1-3/64; Library Journal, 10/1/63; TLS,
     4/9/64

0150 Chandrasekhar, Sripati, ed. Asia's Population Problems; With
B   a Discussion of Population and Immigration in Australia.
     N.Y.: Praeger, 1967. 311 pp. 66-21773.
     Choice, 10/67; JAS, 2/68; Library Journal, 5/1/67

0868 Chandrasekhar, Sripati. China's Population; Census and Vital
B   Statistics. Hong Kong: Hong Kong University Press, 1959.
     69 pp. NUC 59-4756.
     Hucker, 2190; JAS, 5/60

0555 Chang, Chia-ao. The Inflationary Spiral; The Experience in
B   China, 1939-1950. Cambridge: Technology Press of M.I.T.,
     1958. 394 pp. 58-6083. o.p.
     Hucker, 2280; JAS, 5/59; Am. Econ. R., 12/59; Ann. Am.
     Acad., 1/59; Pacific Affairs, 9/59

1190 Chang, Chia-sen. The Development of Neo-Confucian Thought,
C   by Carsun Chang. N.Y.: Bookman, 1957- 58-177.
     Hucker, 1139; JAS, 11/58, 11/63

0556 Chang, Chia-sen. The Third Force in China. N.Y.: Bookman,
B   1952. 345 pp. 53-5815.
     Hucker, 801; Library Journal, 2/1/53; Pacific Affairs,
     9/53; Pol. Sci. Q., 6/53

1191 Chang, Chia-sen. Wang Yang-ming: the Idealist Philosopher of
C   Sixteenth-Century China by Carsun Chang. Jamaica, N.Y.:
     St. John's University Press, 1962. 102 pp. 62-12341.
     JAOS, 7-9/62

0447 Chang, Chung-li. The Chinese Gentry; Studies on Their Role in
A   Nineteenth-Century Chinese Society. Seattle: University of
     Washington Press, 1968 (orig. pub. in 1955). 250 pp.
     NUC 69-7002. (R).
     Hucker, 1831; FEQ, 2/56; AHR, 1/56; Am. J. Soc., 5/56; Ann.
     Am. Acad., 1/56; Pacific Affairs, 3/56

1055 Chang, Eileen. Naked Earth. Hong Kong: Union Press, 1956.
C   365 pp. Hand catalog.

1056 Chang, Eileen. The Rice-sprout Song. N.Y.: Scribners, 1955.
C   182 pp. 55-7192. o.p.
     Library Journal, 5/1/55

0448 Chang, Hsin-pao. Commissioner Lin and the Opium War. Cam-
B   bridge, Mass.: Harvard University Press, 1964. 319 pp.
     (Harvard East Asian Series, 18). 64-21786.
     Choice, 2/65; JAS, 5/65; AHR, 7/65; Library Journal, 11/15/64

0356 Chang, Kwang-chih. The Archaeology of Ancient China. rev. ed.
B   New Haven, Conn.: Yale University Press, 1968. 483 pp.
     68-24780.
     Choice, 3/69; JAS, 2/64, 5/69; Am. Anthropologist, 2/64;
     JAOS, 4-6/62, 1-3/66; Library Journal, 5/1/63; TLS, 4/2/64

1057 Chang, T'ien-i. Big Lin and Little Lin. tr. by Gladys Yang.
C   Peking: Foreign Languages Press, 1958. 157 pp. Hand
     catalog.

1058 Chang, T'ien-i. Stories of Chinese Young Pioneers by Chang
C   Tien-yi. Peking: Foreign Languages Press, 1954. 49 pp.
     57-45357. o.p.

0916 Chang, Tsu. The Dwelling of Playful Goddesses; China's First
C   Novelette, by Chang Wen-ch'eng. annotated tr. by Howard
     S. Levy. Tokyo: Dai Nippon Insatsu, dist. by Paragon, 1965.
     2 v. 65-15788.
     JAS, 8/66

1149 Chao, Chung. The Communist Program for Literature and Art
C   in China. Kowloon: Union Research Institute, 1955.
     157 pp. 56-349.
     Hucker, 1415; FEQ, 8/56

1324 Chao, Chung. Students in Mainland China, by Chao Chung and Yang
C   I-fan. 3d ed. Kowloon: Union Research Institute, 1958.
     139 pp. Hand catalog.
     Hucker, 1966

0869   Chao, Kang. The Construction Industry in Communist China.
C   Chicago: Aldine, 1968. 237 pp. 66-23161.
       Choice, 10/68

0870   Chao, Kang. The Rate and Pattern of Industrial Growth in
C   Communist China. Ann Arbor: University of Michigan
       Press, 1965. 188 pp. 65-11514.
       Choice, 11/66; JAS, 5/66; Am. Econ. R., 6/66; J. Pol. Econ.,
       4/66; Library Journal, 6/15/65

0201   Chao, Kuo-chun. Selected Works in English for a Topical Study
B   of Modern China, 1840-1952. Cambridge, Mass.: Regional
       Studies Program on East Asia, Harvard University, 1952.
       38 pp. o.p.

0737   Chao, Kuo-chun. Thirty Years of the Communist Movement in
B   China: a Chronology of Major Developments, 1920-1950.
       Cambridge, Mass.: Russian Research Center, Harvard Uni-
       versity, 1950. o.p.

1238   Chao Lun. The Book of Chao, a Translation from the Original
C   Chinese. tr. by Walter Liebenthal. Peiping: Catholic Uni-
       versity, 1948. 195 pp. o.p.
       Hucker, 1295

1317   Chao, Mei-po. The Yellow Bell; A Brief Sketch of the History of
B   Chinese Music. Baldwin, Md.: Barberry Hill, 1934. 61 pp.
       34-40479. o.p.
       Hucker, 1777

0557   Chao, Pu-wei (Yang). Autobiography of a Chinese Woman, Bu wei
B   Yang Chao. tr. from Chinese by Yuenren Chao. N.Y.:
       John Day, 1947. 327 pp. 47-1800. o.p.
       Hucker, 737; FEQ, 8/47; Library Journal, 3/1/47

1059   Chao, Shu-li. Changes in Li Village. tr. by Gladys Yang.
B   Peking: Foreign Languages Press, 1953. 224 pp. 55-37564.
       o.p.
       AUFS, 1105

1060   Chao, Shu-li. Rhymes of Li Yu-tsai and Other Stories. 2d ed.
A   Peking: Foreign Languages Press, 1954. 155 pp. 58-19521.

1061   Chao, Shu-li. Sanliwan Village. tr. by Gladys Yang. Peking:
B   Foreign Languages Press, 1957. 275 pp. 58-31671. o.p.

1369   Chaplin, Hamako Ito. A Manual of Japanese Writing. New Haven,
A   Conn.: Yale University Press, 1967. 3 v. 66-21510.
       JAS, 8/68

0558   Chassin, Lionel Max. The Communist Conquest of China; A
B   History of the Civil War, 1945-1949. tr. by T. Osato and
       L. Gelas. Cambridge, Mass.: Harvard University Press,
       1965. 264 pp. 65-22043.
       Choice, 2/66; JAS, 5/66; AHR, 7/66; Ann. Am. Acad., 2/66;
       Library Journal, 8/65; TLS, 3/3/66

0357   Chau Ju-kua: His Work on the Chinese and Arab Trade in the Twelfth
C   and Thirteenth Centuries, Entitled Chu-fan-chi. tr. from
       Chinese and annotated by Friedrich Hirth and W. W. Rockhill.
       N.Y.: Paragon, 1966 (orig. pub. by Imperial Academy of Sci-
       ences, 1911). 2 v. 66-30339. (R). (M-University).
       Hucker, 344

0358   Chavannes, Edouard. Documents sur Les Tou-kiue (Turcs) Occi-
C   dentaux. St. Petersbourg: Commissionnaires de l'Acadamie
       Imperiale des Sciences, 1903. 378 pp. 6-24267.
       Hucker, 286

1062   Ch'en, Ch'i-t'ung. The Long March. Peking: Foreign Languages
C   Press, 1956. 168 pp. 57-58106. o.p.

1063   Chen, Chi-ying. Fool in the Reeds. 4th ed. tr. by Eileen
C   Chang. Hong Kong: Rainbow Press, 1961. 295 pp. NUC
       64-61530.

1279   Chen, Chih-Mai. Chinese Calligraphers and their Art.
C   N.Y.: Cambridge, 1967. 286 pp. 65-22861.
       Choice, 10/67; JAS, 11/67; Library Journal, 12/1/67;
       TLS, 11/30/67

0559   Ch'en, Han-sheng. Landlord and Peasant in China; A Study of
B   the Agrarian Crisis in South China. N.Y.: International
       Publishers, 1936. 144 pp. A38-206. o.p. (M-University).
       Hucker, 2210; Am. Econ. R., 3/37; Am. Soc. R., 8/37;
       Ann. Am. Acad., 3/37; J. Pol. Econ., 12/37; Pacific Affairs,
       9/37

0832   Ch'en, Hsi-en, comp. The Chinese Communist Regime; Documents
C   and Commentary. N.Y.: Praeger, 1967. 344 pp. (Praeger
       Publications in Russian History and World Communism, 191).

67-18969.
       Choice, 4/68; JAS, 5/68; Library Journal, 8/67

0738   Ch'en, Hsi-en. Thought Reform of the Chinese Intellectuals.
B   Hong Kong: Hong Kong University Press, 1960. 247 pp.
       60-4137 rev.
       Hucker, 940; JAS, 8/61; China Q., 7-9/62

0739   Ch'en, Jerome. Mao and the Chinese Revolution. With Thirty-
A   Seven Poems by Mao Tse-tung. tr. by Michael Bullock and
       Jerome Ch'en. N.Y.: Oxford, 1965. 419 pp. 65-2375.
       Sup. 65, 3087; Choice, 6/65; JAS, 11/65; Ann. Am. Acad.,
       11/65; Library Journal, 6/1/65; TLS, 3/25/65

0952   Ch'en, Jerome. Poems of Solitude, tr. from Chinese by Jerome
B   Ch'en and Michael Bullock. London: Abelard-Schuman, 1960.
       118 pp. 60-14523.
       TLS, 2/3/61

0560   Ch'en, Jerome. Yuan Shih-K'ai, 1859-1916; Brutus Assumes the
B   Purple. Stanford, Calif.: Stanford University Press,
       1961. 290 pp. 61-14066.
       Sup. 63, 2905; JAS, 11/62

1239   Ch'en, Kenneth Kuan Sheng. Buddhism in China, a Historical
A   Survey. Princeton, N.J.: Princeton University Press,
       1964. 560 pp. (Princeton Studies in the History of
       Religion, Council of the Humanities, The Virginia and
       Richard Stewart Memorial Lectures, 1). 63-23402.
       Sup. 65, 3088; Choice, 3/65; JAS, 8/65; JAOS, 7-9/65

0561   Ch'en, Kung-po. The Communist Movement in China; An Essay
C   Written in 1924. ed. with an intro. by C. Martin Wilbur.
       N.Y.: Octagon, 1966 (orig. pub. by Columbia University
       Press, 1960). 138 pp. 65-28873. (R).
       Choice, 12/66; JAS, 11/67; Library Journal, 9/1/66

1325   Ch'en, Li-fu. Chinese Education During the War (1937-1942) by
C   Chen Li-fu. Chungking: Ministry of Education, 1943. 41 pp.
       43-18642. o.p.
       Hucker, 1941

0871   Chen, Nai-ruenn. Chinese Economic Statistics; A Handbook
A   for Mainland China. Chicago: Aldine, 1967. 539 pp.
       66-15200.
       Choice, 3/68; Ann. Am. Acad., 11/67; TLS, 12/26/67

0235   Ch'en, Shou-j'ung. A Concise English-Chinese Dictionary, with
B   Romanized Standard Pronunciation. 2d ed. Stanford, Calif.:
       Stanford University Press, 1955. 416 pp. 55-9693.
       Hucker, 85

1009   Ch'en, Shou-yi. Chinese Literature; A Historical Introduction.
C   N.Y.: Ronald, 1961. 665 pp. 61-9426.
       Hucker, 1519; JAS, 5/62; JAOS, 4-6/62

0562   Chen, Stephen. Sun Yat-sen, a Portrait. N.Y.: John Day, 1946.
B   242 pp. 46-25215. o.p.
       Hucker, 760; FEQ, 2/47; Library Journal, 6/15/46

0898   Ch'en, Ta. Emigrant Communities in South China; A Study of
C   Overseas Migration and Its Influence on Standards of Living
       and Social Change. N.Y.: Secretariat, Institute of Pacific
       Relations, 1940. 287 pp. 40-12776. o.p.
       Hucker, 2076

0872   Ch'en, Ta. Population in Modern China. Chicago: University
B   of Chicago Press, 1946. 126 pp. A46-3756. o.p. (M-
       University).
       Hucker, 2191; FEQ, 5/47; Am. Pol. Sci. R., 4/47; Am. Soc. R.,
       4/47; Ann. Am. Acad., 7/47

1064   Chen, Teng-ko. Living Hell. tr. by Sidney Shapiro. Peking:
C   Foreign Languages Press, 1955. 147 pp.

1131   Cheng, Ch'i-yu. New China in Verse. Berkeley, Calif.: Gil-
C   lick Press, 1944. 120 pp. 44-30097. o.p.

0873   Cheng, Chu-yuan. The China Mainland Market under Communist
C   Control. Kowloon: Union Research Institute, 1956. 96 pp.
       57-35238.
       Hucker, 2254

0874   Cheng, Chu-yuan. Communist China's Economy, 1949-62: Struc-
A   tural Changes and Crisis. South Orange, N.J.: Seton Hall
       University Press, 1963. 217 pp. 63-11865. o.p.
       JAS, 2/64; China Q., 7-9/63

0875   Cheng, Chu-yuan. Economic Relations Between Peking and
B   Moscow, 1949-63. N.Y.: Praeger, 1964. 119 pp. (Praeger

Special Studies in International Economics). 64-23512. o.p.
Choice, 7-8/65; JAS, 11/65; China Q., 4-6/65

0876   Cheng, Chu-yuan. Income and Standard of Living in Mainland
B   China. Kowloon: Union Research Institute, 1957. 2 v.
       60-35360.
       Hucker, 2175

0877   Cheng, Chu-yuan. Monetary Affairs of Communist China. Kowloon:
C   Union Research Institute, 1954. 160 pp. 55-40585.
       Hucker, 2282

0878   Cheng, Chu-yuan. Scientific and Engineering Manpower in
A   Communist China, 1949-1963. Washington: National Science
       Foundation, dist. by Government Printing Office, 1965.
       588 pp. 66-60439.
       JAS, 11/66

0359   Cheng, Te-k'un. Archaeology in China. Cambridge: Heffer,
B   1959- 59-1455.
       Hucker, 137, 152; Choice, 5/67; JAOS, 9-12/63

0449   Ch'eng, T'ien-fang. A History of Sino-Russian Relations.
C   Washington: Public Affairs Press, 1957. 389 pp. 57-6908.
       o.p.
       Hucker, 839; Library Journal, 8/57

0563   Cheng, Yu-k'uei. Foreign Trade and Industrial Development
B   of China, an Historical and Integrated Analysis through
       1948. Washington: University Press of Washington, D.C.,
       1956. 278 pp. 56-12632. o.p.
       AUFS, 786; Hucker, 2220; JAS, 2/58; Am. Econ. R., 6/57;
       AHR, 7/57

0564   Chennault, Claire Lee. Way of a Fighter; The Memoirs of Claire
B   Lee Chennault. ed. by Robert Hotz. N.Y.: Putnam, 1949.
       375 pp. 49-845. o.p.
       Hucker, 818

0330   Chi, Ch'ao-ting. Key Economic Areas in Chinese History as
A   Revealed in the Development of Public Works for Water-
       Control. 2d ed. N.Y.: Paragon, 1963 (orig. pub. by Allen &
       Unwin, 1936). 168 pp. 63-24179. (R).
       Hucker, 111; JAS, 5/64; AHR, 7/37; Pacific Affairs, 9/36;
       TLS, 2/22/36

1326   Chi, Tung-wei. Education for the Proletariat in Communist
B   China. Kowloon: Union Research Institute, 1954. 73 pp.
       55-39760.
       Hucker, 1968

1280   Chiang, I. Chinese Calligraphy; An Introduction to Its Aesthetic
A   and Technique. fore. by Sir Herbert Read. 2d ed. London:
       Methuen, 1954. 230 pp. A55-2398.
       Hucker, 1486

0899   Chiang, I. A Chinese Childhood. N.Y.: John Day, 1952. 303 pp.
C   52-11035. o.p.
       Hucker, 1991

1292   Chiang, I. The Chinese Eye, an Interpretation of Chinese Paint-
A   ing. 4th ed. London: Methuen, 1960 (orig. pub. in 1936).
       239 pp. Hand catalog. (R).
       Hucker, 1477; TLS, 11/23/35, 1/21/55

0565   Chiang, Kai-shek. China's Destiny & Chinese Economic Theory.
B   N.Y.: Roy, 1947. 347 pp. 47-30072. o.p.
       Hucker, 771; FEQ, 11/50; Pol. Sci. Q., 12/47

0566   Chiang, Kai-shek. The Collected Wartime Messages of Generalis-
C   simo Chiang Kai-shek, 1937-1945. N.Y.: Kraus, 1969 (orig.
       pub. by John Day, 1946). 2 v. 46-7008. (R).
       Hucker, 772; FEQ, 2/47

0567   Chiang, Kai-shek. Resistance and Reconstruction, Messages
C   during China's Six Years of War, 1937-1943. N.Y.:
       Harper, 1943. 322 pp. 43-10514. o.p. (M-University).
       FEQ, 2/44; Library Journal, 7/43

0568   Chiang, Kai-shek. Soviet Russia in China, a Summing-up at
B   Seventy. rev. abr. ed. tr. under the direction of Madame
       Chiang Kai-shek. N.Y.: Farrar, Straus, Cudahy, 1965. 218 pp.
       65-9173.
       Hucker, 768; JAS, 2/58

0569   Chiang, Monlin. Tides from the West, a Chinese Autobiography.
B   New Haven, Conn.: Yale University Press, 1947. 282 pp.
       47-4798. o.p.
       Hucker, 739; FEQ, 11/47; Ann. Am. Acad., 9/47; Library
       Journal, 4/15/47

1065   Chiang, Ping-chih. The Sun Shines over the Sangkan River
A   by Ting Ling (pseud.). tr. by Yang Hsien-yi and Gladys
       Yang. Peking: Foreign Languages Press, 1954. 348 pp.
       54-31827. o.p.
       AUFS, 1106

1066   Chiang, Ping-chih. When I Was in Sha Chuan and Other Stories.
C   tr. by Pusheng Kung. Bombay: Kutub Publishers, preface
       date, 1945. 118 pp. o.p.

0450   Chiang, Siang-tseh. The Nien Rebellion. Seattle: University of
A   Washington Press, 1968 (orig. pub. in 1954). 159 pp.
       54-3971. (R).
       Hucker, 640; FEQ, 5/55; JAOS, 4-6/56

0570   Chiang, Wen-han. The Chinese Student Movement. N.Y.: King's
B   Crown, 1948. 176 pp. 48-7286. o.p.

0740   Chicago China Conference, 1966. Contemporary China; Papers.
B   ed. by Ruth Adams. N.Y.: Pantheon, 1966. 336 pp. 66-23986.
       Choice, 6/67

0051   Chicago. University. Committee for the Comparative Study of
B   New Nations. Old Societies and New States, the Quest for
       Modernity in Asia and Africa. ed. by Clifford Geertz.
       N.Y.: Free Press of Glencoe, 1963. 310 pp. 63-8416.
       Sup. 65, 3046; JAS, 2/64; Am. Anthropologist, 8/64; Am. J.
       Soc., 3/64; Am. Pol. Sci. R., 3/64

0571   Ch'ien, Tuan-sheng. The Government and Politics of China.
A   Cambridge, Mass.: Harvard University Press for the
       International Secretariat, Institute of Pacific Relations,
       1950. 526 pp. 526 pp. 50-8563.
       Sup. 61, 2792; Hucker, 729; FEQ, 5/51

1732   Chikamatsu, Monzaemon. The Battles of Coxinga, Chikamatsu's
B   Puppet Play, Its Background and Importance. by Donald
       Keene. N.Y.: Cambridge, 1951. 205 pp. 54-34551.
       AUFS, 496; Hucker, 524; Silberman, 1147; FEQ, 2/55

1733   Chikamatsu, Monzaemon. The Love Suicide at Amijima (Shinju
C   Ten no Amijima). A Study of a Japanese Domestic Tragedy.
       study by Donald H. Shively. Cambridge, Mass.: Harvard
       University Press, 1953. 173 pp. 52-10757 rev. o.p.
       AUFS, 497; Silberman, 1148; FEQ, 5/54

1734   Chikamatsu, Monzaemon. Major Plays. tr. by Donald Keene.
A   N.Y.: Columbia University Press, 1961. 485 pp. (UNESCO
       Collection of Representative Works). 61-15106.
       JAOS, 1-3/62

0917   Chin p'ing mei. The Golden Lotus; A Translation from the Chinese
A   Original by Clement Egerton. N.Y.: Dover, 1954. 4 v.
       54-4573.
       Hucker, 1700

0360   Chin shu. English. Selections. Account of the T'u-yu-hun in
C   the History of the Chin Dynasty. tr. and annotated by Thomas
       D. Carroll. Berkeley: University of California Press, 1953.
       47 pp. (Chinese Dynastic Histories Translations, No. 4).
       A54-5210. o.p.
       Hucker, 267; FEQ, 11/54; JAOS, 7-9/55

0572   Chin, Wen-ssu. China and the League of Nations; The Sino-
C   Japanese Controversy, by Wunsz King. Jamaica, N.Y.:
       St. John's University Press, 1965. 104 pp. (Asia in
       the Modern World, 5). 65-17177.
       Choice, 5/66; JAS, 2/66

0573   Chin, Wen-ssu. China at the Paris Peace Conference in 1919, by
B   Wunsz King. Jamaica, N.Y.: St. John's University Press,
       1961. 39 pp. 61-59840.
       JAS, 5/66

0574   Chin, Wen-ssu. China at the Washington Conference, 1921-1922,
B   by Wunsz King. Jamaica, N.Y.: St. John's University Press,
       1963. 71 pp. (Asia in the Modern World, No. 3). 63-14976.
       JAS, 5/66

0096   China. Assessor to the Commission of Enquiry into Sino-Japa-
C   nese Dispute. Memoranda Presented to the Lytton Commission,
       by V. K. Wellington Koo, assessor. N.Y.: The Chinese Cul-
       tural Society, 1932-33. 3 v. 33-7709 rev. 2. o.p.
       Hucker, 789

0236   China Handbook. 1937/43- comp. by Chinese Ministry of Infor-
C   mation. Taipei: China Publishing Co., 1937- 43-14605.
       Am. Pol. Sci. R., 4/44; Pacific Affairs, 6/44

2071 China Institute of International Affairs. China and the United
C Nations; Report of a Study Group Set up by the China Institute of International Affairs. N.Y.: Manhattan for Carnegie Endowment for International Peace, 1959. 285 pp.
60-16005. o.p.
Hucker, 826

0451 China. Laws, Statutes, etc. Manuel du Code Chinois, par le P.
C Guy Boulais. Taipai: Ch'eng-wen Publishing Co., dist. by
Chinese Materials and Research Aids Service Center, 1966
(orig. pub. by Mission Catholique, 1923-24). 2 v. (Varietes
Sinologiques, 55). Hand catalog. (R).
Hucker, 1886

0269 China Monthly Review. v.1-124. 1917-1953. (1917-21 as
B Millard's Review; 1921-23 as Weekly Review of the Far
East; 1923-50 as China Weekly Review). (M-Microphoto).

0879 China (People's Republic of China, 1949-). First Five-year
B Plan for Development of the National Economy of the People's
Republic of China in 1953-1957. Peking: Foreign Languages
Press, 1956. 231 pp. 57-47651. o.p.

0270 China Pictorial. v.1- 1951- (M-IDC).
C

0271 The China Post. Taiwan. 1952-
C

0272 The China Quarterly, v.1- 1960- (M-IDC).
A Hucker, 25

0273 China Reconstructs. v.1- 1952- (M-IDC).
C Hucker, 2159

0274 China Report. v.1- 1964-
C

0275 China Review. v.1-25. 1872-1901. (M-Research Publications).
C

0237 The China Year Book. 1912-39. ed. by H. G. W. Woodhead.
C Shanghai: North China Daily News and Herald. 20 v.
12-20762 rev. (R-Kraus).
Hucker, 718

0238 China Yearbook, 1937/43- Taipei: China Publishing Co.
C 43-14605.
Hucker, 849

0276 Chinese Art Society of America, Inc. Archives, 1- 1945-
C (M-IDC).
JAS, 2/58; FEQ, 2/52, 8/56

0277 Chinese Communist Affairs. v.1- 1964-
C

0278 Chinese Culture, v.1- 1957-
C Hucker, 39

0331 Chinese Dynastic Histories Translations. Berkeley: University
C of California Press, 1952-
Hucker, 1641

0279 Chinese Economic Bulletin. v.1-27. 1921-1935.
C

0280 Chinese Economic Journal and Bulletin. v.1-20. 1927-1937.
C

0281 Chinese Economic Studies. v.1- 1967-
C

0282 Chinese Education. v.1- 1968-
C

0283 Chinese Law and Government. v.1- 1968-
C

0284 Chinese Literature. v.1- 1951-
C Hucker, 1757

0285 Chinese Repository. v.1-20. 1832-51. (R-Kraus, M-Microphoto,
C M-Research Publications).
Hucker, 616

0286 Chinese Social and Political Science Review. v.1-24. 1916-41.
B (M-Research Publications).
Hucker, 40

0287 Chinese Studies in History and Philosophy. v.1- 1967-
C

0288 Chinese Studies in Sociology and Anthropology. v.1- 1966-
A

0239 Ch'ing Administrative Terms; A Translation of the Terminology
C of the Six Boards with Explanatory Notes. tr. and ed. by
E-tu Zen Sun. Cambridge, Mass.: Harvard University Press,
1961. 421 pp. 61-15279.
Sup. 63, 2927; JAS, 5/62

0575 Ching, Hsuan-tung. The Last Manchu: the Autobiography of Henry
C Pu Yi, Last Emperor of China. ed. with an intro. by Paul
Kramer. tr. by Kuo Ying Paul Tsai. N.Y.: Putnam, 1967.
318 pp. 67-10588.

0289 Ch'ing Hua Hsueh Pao. v.1-15. 1924-1948. n.s.v.1- 1956-
C Hucker, 35

2098 Chiu, Ping. Chinese Labor in California, 1850-1880, an
B Economic Study. Madison: State Historical Society of
Wisconsin for Dept. of History, University of Wisconsin,
1963. 180 pp. 63-63578.

0361 Chiu T'ang shu. Biography of An Lu-shan. tr. and annotated
C by Howard S. Levy. Berkeley: University of California Press,
1960. 122 pp. (Chinese Dynastic Histories Translations,
No. 8). 61-63071. o.p.
Hucker, 319; JAS, 2/62

2018 Cho, Soon Sung. Korea in World Politics, 1940-1950; An
B Evaluation of American Responsibility. Berkeley: University of California Press, 1967. 338 pp. (Center
for Japanese and Korean Studies). 67-14968.
Choice, 12/68; JAS, 5/68; Ann. Am. Acad., 1/68; TLS,
12/21/67

0452 Ch'oe, Pu. Diary: a Record of Drifting Across the Sea. tr.
C with intro. and notes by John Meskill. Tucson: University
of Arizona Press, 1965. 177 pp. (Association for Asian
Studies, Monographs and Papers, XVII). 64-19165.
Choice, 10/66; JAS, 11/65; JAOS, 10-12/65; Library Journal,
6/15/65

2053 Chong, In-sob, ed. and tr. Folk Tales from Korea. N.Y.:
C Grove, 1953. 257 pp. 53-12953. o.p.
AUFS, 526; Silberman, 1880; JAS, 5/57; FEQ, 2/54; TLS,
10/31/52

1993 Chong, Kyong-jo. Korea Tomorrow, Land of the Morning Calm.
C N.Y.: Macmillan, 1956. 384 pp. 56-1184. o.p.
FEQ, 8/56; Am. Pol. Sci. R., 6/56; Ann. Am. Acad., 9/56;
Library Journal, 3/1/56; TLS, 3/10/56

1994 Chong, Kyong-jo. New Korea; New Land of the Morning Calm.
B N.Y.: Macmillan, 1962. 274 pp. 62-15611.
Sup. 63, 2899; JAS, 8/62; AHR, 4/63; Am. Pol. Sci. R.,
6/63; Ann. Am. Acad., 9/63; Library Journal, 9/15/62;
Pacific Affairs, Fall/63

0741 Chou, Ching-wen. Ten Years of Storm; The True Story of the
C Communist Regime in China, by Chow, Ching-wen. ed. and
tr. by Lai Ming. N.Y.: Holt, Rinehart and Winston, 1960.
323 pp. 60-12858. o.p.
Library Journal, 9/15/60

1150 Chou, En-lai, et al. The People's New Literature: Four
C Reports at the First All-China Conference of Writers
and Artists. Peking: Cultural Press, 1950. 136 pp. o.p.

1067 Chou, Erh-fu. Morning in Shanghai. tr. by A. C. Barnes. Pe-
C king: Foreign Languages Press, 1962- 664 pp. NUC 63-3225.

1240 Chou, Hsiang-kuang. T'ai Hsu, His Life and Teachings. Alla-
C habad: Indo-Chinese Literature Publications, 1957. 74 pp.
58-43903. o.p.
JAS, 8/58

1172 Chou, I-ch'ing. La Philosophie Chinoise, par Chow Yih-ching.
C Paris: Presses Universitaires, 1956. 126 pp. Hand catalog.

1192 Chou, I-ch'ing. La Philosophie Morale dans le Neo-Confu-
C cianisme (Tcheou Touen-yi) par Chow Yi-ching. Paris:
Presses Universitaires, 1954. 230 pp. A54-3489 rev.
Hucker, 1153; FEQ, 11/54

1068 Chou, Li-po. Great Changes in a Mountain Village, a Novel.
A tr. by Derek Bryan. Peking: Foreign Languages Press,
1961- 353 pp. Hand catalog.

1069 Chou, Li-po. The Hurricane. tr. from Chinese by Hsu Meng-
C   hsiung. Peking: Foreign Languages Press, 1955. 409 pp.
     A56-5663.
     AUFS, 1107

1070 Chou, Li-po. Sowing the Clouds, a Collection of Chinese Short
C   Stories, by Chou Li-po, Li Chun and others. Peking: Foreign
     Languages Press, 1961. 146 pp. NUC 63-3228. o.p.

0453 Ch'ou pan i wu shih mo. China's Management of the American Bar-
B   barians; A Study of Sino-American Relations, 1841-1861, with
     Documents. by Earl Swisher. New Haven, Conn.: Yale Univer-
     sity Press for the Far Eastern Association, 1953. 844 pp.
     (Association for Asian Studies, Monographs and Papers, VI).
     54-2170.
     Hucker, 685; FEQ, 11/54

1071 Chou, Shu-jen. Ah Q and Others, Selected Stories of Lusin
A   (pseud.). tr. by Chi-chen Wang. N.Y.: Columbia University
     Press, 1941. 219 pp. 41-10678. o.p. (M-University).
     AUFS, 1108; Hucker, 1751; FEQ, 5/42

1010 Chou, Shu-jen. A Brief History of Chinese Fiction, by Lu Hsun
B   (pseud.). Peking: Foreign Languages Press, 1959. 462 pp.
     60-3865.
     Hucker, 1647

1072 Chou, Shu-jen. Chosen Pages from Lu Hsun (pseud.), the Literary
C   Mentor of the Chinese Revolution. N.Y.: Cameron Associates,
     1959. 315 pp. Hand catalog. o.p.

1073 Chou, Shu-jen. Selected Stories of Lu Hsun (pseud.). Peking:
C   Foreign Languages Press, 1954. 251 pp. 56-37158. o.p.

1074 Chou, Shu-jen. Selected Works of Lu Hsun (pseud.). Peking:
A   Foreign Languages Press, 1956- 57-35404. o.p.
     Hucker, 1753

0576 Chou, Shun-hsin. The Chinese Inflation, 1937-1949. N.Y.:
A   Columbia University Press, 1963. 319 pp. (Studies of
     the East Asian Institute). 62-18260.
     Am. Econ. R., 6/64; Library Journal, 7/63

0742 Chou, Ts'e-tsung. The May Fourth Movement: Intellectual Revo-
A   lution in Modern China. Stanford, Calif.: Stanford Uni-
     versity Press, 1968 (orig. pub. by Harvard University Press,
     1960). 486 pp. (Harvard East Asian Series, 6). 67-26647.
     (R).
     Sup. 61, 2793; Hucker, 754; AHR, 1/61; Ann. Am. Acad., 11/60;
     China Q., 4-6/61; JAOS, 8-9/61; Pacific Affairs, Summer/61;
     Pol. Sci. Q., 12/60; TLS, 4/7/61

0240 Chou, Ts'e-tsung. Research Guide to the May Fourth Movement:
B   Intellectual Revolution in Modern China, 1915-1924.
     Cambridge, Mass.: Harvard University Press, 1963. 297 pp.
     (Harvard East Asian Series, 13). 63-22745.
     JAS, 8/64

1151 Chou, Yang. China's New Literature and Art; Essays and
C   Addresses. Peking: Foreign Languages Press, 1954. 156 pp.
     57-35757. o.p.

1152 Chou, Yang. A Great Debate on the Literary Front. Appendix:
C   Clear the Road and Advance Boldly! by Shao Chuan-lin.
     tr. by Yang Hsien-yi and Gladys Yang. Peking: Foreign
     Languages Press, 1958. 72 pp. 59-22364.

0577 Chow, Chung-cheng. The Lotus Pool. tr. by Joyce Emerson.
C   N.Y.: Appleton-Century-Crofts, 1961. 272 pp. 61-14881.
     o.p.
     Sup. 63, 2906; JAS, 8/62; Library Journal, 12/15/61

0578 Chu, Ch'ang-ling. Reformer in Modern China, Chang Chien, 1853-
B   1926. N.Y.: Columbia University Press, 1965. 256 pp.
     65-10541.
     Choice, 2/66; JAS, 5/66; AHR, 4/66; Library Journal, 3/1/65

1193 Chu, Hsi. The Philosophy of Human Nature, by Chu Hsi. tr. from
B   Chinese with notes by J. Percy Bruce. London: A. Probsthain,
     1922. 44 pp. 23-7674 rev. 2. o.p.
     Hucker, 1148

1194 Chu, Hsi, comp. Reflections of Things at Hand; The Neo-
B   Confucian Anthology. N.Y.: Columbia University Press,
     1967. 441 pp. 65-22548.

1075 Chu, Po. Tracks in the Snowy Forest. tr. by Sidney Shapiro.
C   Peking: Foreign Languages Press, 1962. 548 pp. NUC 63-3367.

0993 Chu, Su-ch'en. Fifteen Strings of Cash; A Kunchu Opera. tr.
C   by Yang Hsien-yi and Gladys Yang. Peking: Foreign Lang-

uages Press, 1957. 84 pp. 59-34753. o.p.

0953 Ch'u, Ta-kao. Chinese Lyrics. tr. by Ch'u Ta-kao. pref. by
B   Sir Arthur Quiller-Couch. Cambridge: University, 1937.
     55 pp. 38-2934. o.p.
     Hucker, 1562; TLS, 8/7/37

0900 Ch'u, T'ung-tsu. Law and Society in Traditional China. The
A   Hague: Mouton, 1961. 304 pp. 62-19813.
     Sup. 63, 2907; JAS, 5/62

0454 Ch'u, T'ung-tsu. Local Government in China under the Ching.
A   Stanford, Calif.: Stanford University Press, 1966 (orig.
     pub. by Harvard University Press, 1962). 360 pp.
     (Harvard East Asian Series, 9). 62-11396. (R).
     JAS, 11/63; AHR, 1/63; Ann. Am. Acad., 1/63; Library Journal,
     6/15/62; Pol. Sci. Q., 6/63

0954 Ch'u Tz'u. Ch'u Tz'u: the Songs of the South, an Ancient Chinese
A   Anthology, by David Hawkes. Oxford: Clarendon, 1959.
     229 pp. 59-1155. o.p.
     AUFS, 1052; Hucker, 1583; JAS, 11/59; JAOS, 4-6/59

0955 Ch'u, Yuan. Li Sao and Other Poems. tr. by Yang Hsien-yi and
C   Gladys Yang. Peking: Foreign Languages Press, 1953. 84 pp.
     55-32706. o.p.

1254 Ch'u, Yuan. The Nine Songs, a Study of Shamanism in Ancient
B   China by Arthur Waley. London: Allen & Unwin, 1955. 64 pp.
     55-28909.
     AUFS, 584; Hucker, 1584; JAS, 11/56

1221 Chuang-tsu. Basic Writings. tr. by Burton Watson. N.Y.:
A   Columbia University Press, 1964. 148 pp. 64-21079.
     Choice, 12/65

1222 Chuang-tzu. A New Selected Translation with an Exposition of
A   the Philosophy of Kuo Hsiang, by Yu-lan Fung. 2d ed.
     N.Y.: Paragon, 1964 (orig. pub. by Commercial Press, 1933).
     164 pp. 64-18451. (R).
     AUFS, 643; Hucker, 1199

2049 Chung, Joseph Sang-hoon, ed. Patterns of Economic Develop-
B   ment: Korea. Seoul: Korea Research and Publications,
     dist. by Cellar Book Shop, 1966. 241 pp. (Monograph
     Series on Korea, 3). 67-567.
     Choice, 9/67; JAS, 5/67

1327 Chung, Shih. Higher Education in Communist China. Kowloon:
C   Union Research Institute, 1953. 97 pp. 55-41537.
     Hucker, 1967

1981 Chung, Yong Sun, comp. A Selected Bibliography on Korea,
C   1959-1963. Seoul: Korean Research and Publication, Inc.,
     dist. by Cellar Book Shop, 1966. 117 pp. 65-9439.
     Choice, 6/67

1195 Chung-yung. The Conduct of Life; or, The Universal Order of
C   Confucius; A Translation of One of the Four Confucian Books
     Hitherto Known as The Doctrine of the Mean by Ku Hung Ming.
     London: Murray, dist. by Paragon, 1908. 60 pp. (Wisdom
     of the East Series). W9-170. o.p. (M-University).

0743 Clark, Gerald. Impatient Giant: Red China Today. N.Y.: McKay,
C   1959. 212 pp. 59-12259.
     Hucker, 967; Library Journal, 9/15/59; TLS, 4/22/60

2019 Clark, Mark Wayne. From the Danube to the Yalu. N.Y.:
C   Harper, 1954. 369 pp. 54-6010. o.p. (M-University).
     Silberman, 1785; Library Journal, 5/15/54; TLS, 9/17/54

0579 Clifford, Nicholas Rowland. Retreat from China; British Pol-
A   icy in the Far East, 1937-1941. Seattle: University of Wash-
     ington Press, 1967. 222 pp. 67-12395.
     Choice, 9/67; JAS, 11/67; AHR, 4/68

0880 Clubb, Oliver Edmund. Chinese Communist Development Programs
C   in Manchuria, with a Supplement on Inner Mongolia. N.Y.:
     International Secretariat, Institute of Pacific Relations,
     1954. 46 pp. 55-14203. o.p.
     Hucker, 2176

0580 Clubb, Oliver Edmund. 20th Century China. N.Y.: Columbia Uni-
B   versity Press, 1964. 470 pp. 64-11041.
     Sup. 65, 3089; Choice, 6/64; JAS, 8/64; AHR, 10/64;
     Library Journal, 1/15/64; TLS, 4/16/64

0744 Clubb, Oliver Edmund. The United States and the Sino-Soviet
C   Bloc in Southeast Asia. Washington: Brookings Institution,
     1962. 173 pp. 62-21276.

Sup. 63, 2908; AHR, 4/63; Ann. Am. Acad., 5/63; China Q., 4-6/63

0123   Clune, Frank. Ashes of Hiroshima; A Post-war Trip to Japan
C   and China. Sydney: Angus & Robertson, 1950. 299 pp.
       51-10012.

0097   Clyde, Paul Hibbert. The Far East, a History of the Western
A   Impact and the Eastern Response, 1830-1965. 4th ed.
       Englewood Cliffs, N.J.: Prentice-Hall, 1966. 511 pp.
       66-10814.
       Sup. 67, 3208; Choice, 5/66; JAS, 2/67

0581   Clyde, Paul Hibbert. International Rivalries in Manchuria,
B   1689-1922. 2d ed., rev. N.Y.: Octagon, 1965 (orig.
       pub. by Ohio State University Press, 1928). 323 pp.
       66-17493. (R). (M-University).
       Hucker, 699; Silberman, 421

0455   Clyde, Paul Hibbert, ed. United States Policy Toward China;
B   Diplomatic and Public Documents, 1839-1939. N.Y.:
       Russell & Russell, 1964 (orig. pub. by Duke University
       Press, 1940). 321 pp. 64-15018. (R). (M-University).
       Choice, 4/65; Hucker, 690; FEQ, 2/42; Am. Pol. Sci. R.,
       10/40; Ann. Am. Acad., 1/41; Pacific Affairs, 12/40

1447   Cocks, Richard. Diary of Richard Cocks, Cape-Merchant in
C   the English Factory in Japan, 1615-22. ed. by Edward M.
       Thompson. London: printed for Hakluyt Society, 1883. 2 v.
       5-40455. o.p.
       Silberman, 298

0833   Cohen, Arthur A. The Communism of Mao Tse-tung. Chicago:
B   University of Chicago Press, 1964. 210 pp. 64-23420.
       Sup. 65, 3090; Choice, 11/64; JAS, 2/66

0834   Cohen, Jerome Alan. The Criminal Process in the People's
A   Republic of China, 1949-1963; An Introduction. Cambridge,
       Mass.: Harvard University Press, 1968. 706 pp.
       (Harvard Studies in East Asian Law, 2). 68-14252.
       Choice, 10/68; JAS, 11/68; China Q., 1-3/68

1625   Cohen, Jerome Bernard. Japan's Economy in War and Recon-
B   struction. Minneapolis: University of Minnesota Press for
       Institute of Pacific Relations, 1949. 545 pp. 49-9272 rev.
       o.p.
       AUFS, 229; Silberman, 577; FEQ, 5/50; Am. Econ. R., 12/49;
       Am. Soc. R., 12/49; Ann. Am. Acad., 11/49

1626   Cohen, Jerome Bernard. Japan's Postwar Economy. Bloomington:
C   Indiana University Press, 1958. 262 pp. 57-10725. o.p.
       AUFS, 338; Silberman, 576; JAS, 5/59; Am. Econ. R., 6/59;
       Ann. Am. Acad., 3/59; Geog. R., 10/59; J. Pol. Econ., 6/59;
       Pol. Sci. Q., 6/59

0456   Cohen, Paul A. China and Christianity; The Missionary Movement
A   and the Growth of Chinese Anti-foreignism, 1860-1870.
       Cambridge, Mass.: Harvard University Press, 1963. 392 pp.
       (Harvard East Asian Series, 11). 63-19135.
       JAS, 8/64; AHR, 10/64; Ann. Am. Acad., 3/64; Library Journal,
       1/1/64

1584   Colbert, Evelyn (Speyer). The Left Wing in Japanese Politics.
C   N.Y.: International Secretariat, Institute of Pacific Rela-
       tions, 1952. 353 pp. 52-9711. o.p.
       Silberman, 1344; FEQ, 2/53; Library Journal, 6/15/52

1585   Cole, Allan Burnett. Japanese Society and Politics: the Im-
C   pact of Social Stratification and Mobility on Politics.
       Boston: Graduate School, 1956. 158 pp. (Studies in Politi-
       cal Science, No. 1). 57-59505. o.p. (M-University).
       AUFS, 340; Silberman, 1329; JAS, 5/57

1586   Cole, Allan Burnett. Political Tendencies of Japanese in
C   Small Enterprises; With Special Reference to the Social
       Democratic Party. N.Y.: Institute of Pacific Relations,
       1959. 155 pp. 59-1191. o.p. (M-University).
       Silberman, 1336; JAS, 2/60

1587   Cole, Allan Burnett. Socialist Parties in Postwar Japan.
B   contr. chapter by Ronald P. Dore. New Haven, Conn.:
       Yale University Press, 1966. 490 pp. (Studies on
       Japan's Social Democratic Parties, Vol. II). 66-21511.
       Choice, 10/67; JAS, 8/67; Ann. Am. Acad., 7/67; Japan Q.,
       7-9/67

0457   Collis, Maurice. Foreign Mud, Being an Account of the Opium Im-
B   broglio at Canton in the 1830's and the Anglo-Chinese War that
       Followed. N.Y.: Norton, 1968 (orig. pub. by Knopf, 1947).
       300 pp. 47-31165. (R). (M-University).

AUFS, 739; Hucker, 672; FEQ, 8/48

0089   Collis, Maurice. The Grand Peregrination, Being the Life and
C   Adventures of Fernao Mendes Pinto. N.Y.: Macmillan, 1949.
       313 pp. 50-233. o.p.
       Hucker, 592

0312   Collis, Maurice. The Great Within. London: Faber & Faber,
C   1941. 349 pp. 42-2761
       Hucker, 482

0362   Collis, Maurice. Marco Polo. N.Y.: New Directions, 1960.
B   190 pp. 60-14665. o.p.
       Hucker, 403

0012   Columbia University. Columbia College. A Guide to the Oriental
A   Classics, Prepared by the Staff of the Oriental Studies
       Program, Columbia College, and Edited by Wm. Theodore De Bary.
       N.Y.: Columbia University Press, 1964. 199 pp. 63-20463.
       Sup. 65, 3045; Choice, 9/64

2104   Comber, Leon. The Traditional Mysteries of Chinese Secret
B   Societies in Malaya. Singapore: Donald Moore for Eastern
       Universities Press, 1961. 113 pp. NUC 63-4480.

0241   Commercial Press. A Comprehensive English-Chinese Dictionary.
B   2d rev. ed. Shanghai: Commercial Press, 1948. 1502 pp.
       46-44900. o.p.

0745   Communist China 1955-1959; Policy Documents with Analysis.
B   fore. by Robert R. Bowie and John K. Fairbank. Cambridge,
       Mass.: Harvard University Press for Center for Inter-
       national Affairs and the East Asian Research Center,
       1962. 611 pp. 62-11394.
       Sup. 63, 2909; JAS, 2/63, 8/64

1588   Conference on Nineteenth Century Japanese Elites, University
C   of Arizona, 1963. Modern Japanese Leadership; Transition
       and Change. ed. by Bernard S. Silberman and H. D. Haroo-
       tunian with ten collaborating authors. Tucson: University
       of Arizona Press, 1966. 433 pp. 66-18532.
       Choice, 6/67; JAS, 5/67; AHR, 4/67

0169   Conference on Oriental Classics in General Education, Columbia
A   University, 1958. Approaches to the Oriental Classics; Asian
       Literature and Thought in General Education. ed. by Wm.
       Theodore De Bary. N.Y.: Columbia University Press, 1959.
       262 pp. 59-9905.
       JAS, 5/60; Library Journal, 5/15/59; Pacific Affairs, 12/59

1589   Conference on Political Modernization in Japan and Turkey,
C   Gould House, 1962. Political Modernization in Japan and
       Turkey. ed. by Robert E. Ward and Dankwart A. Rustow.
       Princeton, N.J.: Princeton University Press, 1964.
       502 pp. 63-16238.
       Sup. 65, 3056; JAS, 11/64; Pacific Affairs, Spring/65;
       Pol. Sci. Q., 12/65

1196   Confucius. The Analects of Confucius. tr. and annotated by
A   Arthur Waley. N.Y.: Hillary House, 1964 (orig. pub. in
       1936). 268 pp. 39-5047. (R).
       AUFS, 620; Hucker, 1120; J. Philosophy, 9/28/39

1197   Confucius. The Analects of Confucius; or, The Conversations of
B   Confucius with His Disciples and Certain Others. tr. into
       English by William Edward Soothill. ed. by Lady Hosie.
       London: Oxford, 1962 (orig. pub. in 1937). 254 pp. NUC
       68-38770. (R).
       Hucker, 1122

1198   Confucius. K'ung Tzu Chia Yu. The School Sayings of Confucius.
C   intro., tr. of sections 1-10 with critical notes by R. P.
       Kramers. Leiden: Brill, 1950. 406 pp. (Sinica Leidensia,
       7).
       Hucker, 1126

0746   Conlon Associates, Ltd. United States Foreign Policy: Asia.
C   Washington: Government Printing Office, 1959. 157 pp.
       (Studies Prepared at the Request of the Commitee on Foreign
       Relations, United States Senate, No. 5). 60-60164 rev. o.p.
       Hucker, 1016

1493   Conroy, Francis Hilary. The Japanese Frontier in Hawaii,
C   1868-1898. Berkeley: University of California Press, 1953.
       175 pp. (University of California Publications in History,
       Vol. 46). A53-9799. o.p.
       Silberman, 433; FEQ, 5/54

1494   Conroy, Francis Hilary. The Japanese Seizure of Korea: 1868-
A   1910, a Study of Realism and Idealism in International

Relations. Philadelphia: University of Pennsylvania
Press, 1960. 544 pp. 60-6936.
Silberman, 424a; JAS, 2/63; Ann. Am. Acad., 9/61; Library
Journal, 3/1/61; Pacific Affairs, Winter/61

0458 Constant, Charles Samuel de. Les Memoires de Charles de Constant
C sur le Commerce a la Chine par Louis Dermigny. Paris:
S.E.V.P.E.N., 1964. 491 pp. (Ecole Pratique des Hautes
Etudes-VI Section-Centre de Recherches Historiques). NUC
66-5605.
JAS, 5/66

0290 Contemporary China, v.1- 1955-
B Hucker, 909

0242 Contemporary China; Economic and Social Studies, Documents,
B Bibliography, Chronology, 1955-. ed. by E. Stuart Kirby.
Hong Kong: Hong Kong University Press, 1955- 57-22028.
Hucker, 1974; JAS, 11/57, 8/59, 8/64; China Q., 4-6/62

1391 Contemporary Japan. Tokyo: Foreign Affairs Association of
C Japan, 1932-
Silberman, 41

1392 Contemporary Religions in Japan. v.1- 1960-
C

1668 Cook, Alice Hanson. An Introduction to Japanese Trade Unionism.
B Ithaca: New York State School of Industrial and Labor Relations, Cornell University, 1966. 216 pp. 66-63380.

0747 Cooley, John K. East Wind Over Africa; Red China's African
C Offensive. N.Y.: Walker, 1965. 246 pp. 65-22132.
Choice, 2/66; Library Journal, 10/15/65

1448 Cooper, Michael, ed. They Came to Japan, an Anthology of
C European Reports on Japan, 1543-1640. Berkeley: University
of California Press, 1965. 439 pp. 65-19250.
Sup. 67, 3212; Choice, 4/66; Library Journal, 11/1/65

0582 Coox, Alvin D. Year of the Tiger. Tokyo: Orient/West,
A 1964. 162 pp.
JAS, 8/65; Japan Q., 4-6/65

0202 Cordier, Henri. Bibliotheca Sinica. Dictionnaire Bibliogra-
A phiques des Ouvrages Relatifs a l'Empire Chonois. Taipei:
Ch'eng-wen Publishing Co., dist. by Chinese Materials and
Research Aids Service Center, 1966 (orig. pub. by Guil-
moto, 1904-24). 5 v. (R). (M-IDC).
Hucker, 19

1669 Cornell, John Bilheimer. Two Japanese Villages: Matsunagi, a
B Japanese Mountain Community by John B. Cornell; Kurusu,
a Japanese Agricultural Community by Robert J. Smith.
Ann Arbor: University of Michigan Press, 1956. 232 pp.
56-1904. o.p.
JAS, 5/57; JAOS, 4-6/57

2101 Coughlin, Richard J. Double Identity; The Chinese in Modern
B Thailand. N.Y.: Oxford, 1960. 222 pp. 60-4015.
JAS, 8/61; Am. Anthropologist, 6/61; Am. Soc. R., 4/61;
Ann. Am. Acad., 11/61

0151 Cowan, Charles Donald, ed. The Economic Development of China
B and Japan; Studies in Economic History and Political
Economy. N.Y.: Humanities, 1964. 255 pp. (Praeger
Studies on Modern Asia and Africa, 4). 64-14125.
Choice, 7-8/64; Ann. Am. Acad., 3/65; Pacific Affairs,
Spring/65; TLS, 3/26/64

1495 Craig, Albert M. Choshu in the Meiji Restoration. Cambridge,
A Mass.: Harvard University Press, 1961. 385 pp. (Harvard
Historical Monographs, 47). 61-8839.
Sup. 61, 2759; Silberman, 341

1945 Cram, Ralph Adams. Impressions of Japanese Architecture and
A the Allied Arts. N.Y.: Dover, 1966 (orig. pub. by
Marshall Jones, 1930). 242 pp. 66-25705. (R).
Silberman, 808

0363 Creel, Herrlee Glessner. The Birth of China; A Study of the
A Formative Period of Chinese Civilization. N.Y.: Ungar,
1954. 402 pp. 54-5633.
AUFS, 700; Hucker, 153; JAOS, 9/37

1173 Creel, Herrlee Glessner. Chinese Thought, from Confucius to
B Mao Tse-tung. N.Y.: New American Library, 1960 (orig. pub.
by University of Chicago, 1953). 240 pp. 53-10054. (R).
AUFS, 585; Hucker, 1044; FEQ, 8/55; Am. Anthropologist,
4/54; Pacific Affairs, 12/53; TLS, 11/5/54

0243 Creel, Herrlee Glessner. Chinese Writing. Washington: Amer-
A ican Council on Education, 1943. 16 pp. 43-10984.
Hucker, 72

1199 Creel, Herrlee Glessner. Confucius and the Chinese Way.
B N.Y.: Harper, 1960 (orig. pub. by John Day, 1949 under
the title Confucius, the Man and the Myth). 363 pp.
60-5492. (R).
AUFS, 625; Hucker, 170; FEQ, 2/50; AHR, 10/49; JAOS, 7-9/50

0074 Cressey, George Babcock. Asia's Lands and Peoples, a Geog-
A raphy of One-third of the Earth and Two-thirds of Its
People. 3d ed. N.Y.: McGraw-Hill, 1963. 663 pp. 62-22087.
AUFS, 19; Sup. 65, 3044; Hucker, 50; Silberman, 81; FEQ,
5/45; Am. Anthropologist, 6/64; Library Journal, 3/15/64

0322 Cressey, George Babcock. China's Geographic Foundations,
B a Survey of the Land and Its People. N.Y.: McGraw-Hill,
1934. 436 pp. 34-1104. o.p.
Hucker, 48; Am. J. Soc., 11/34; Am. Pol. Sci. R., 6/34;
Ann. Am. Acad., 5/34; J. Pol. Econ., 12/34; Pol. Sci. Q.,
9/34

0323 Cressey, George Babcock. Land of the 500 Million; A Geography
B of China. N.Y.: McGraw-Hill, 1955. 387 pp. 55-8895.
Hucker, 46; FEQ, 8/56; Geog. R., 10/56; Library Journal,
1/1/56; Pacific Affairs, 6/56

0244 Cressy, Earl Herbert. Understanding China; A Handbook of
C Background Information on Changing China. N.Y.: Nelson,
1957. 278 pp. 57-11898. o.p.
JAS, 8/58

1352 Croizier, Ralph C. Traditional Medicine in Modern China:
B Science, Nationalism, and the Tensions of Cultural Change.
Cambridge, Mass.: Harvard University Press, 1968.
325 pp. (Harvard East Asian Series, 34). 68-17624.
Choice, 11/68; China Q., 1-3/69; Library Journal, 7/68;
TLS, 12/5/68

1496 Crowley, James B. Japan's Quest for Autonomy; National Security
A and Foreign Policy, 1930-1938. Princeton, N.J.: Princeton
University Press, 1966. 428 pp. 66-10552.
Sup. 67, 3213; Choice, 7-8/67; JAS, 8/67; Ann. Am. Acad.,
7/67; Pacific Affairs, Spring-Summer/67; TLS, 7/6/67

0364 Crump, James Irving. Intrigues; Studies of the Chan-kuo ts'e.
B Ann Arbor: University of Michigan Press, 1964. 212 pp.
64-17440.
JAS, 2/66; JAOS, 1-3/66

0291 Current Scene; Developments in Mainland China. v.1- 1961-
C

0098 Curry, Roy Watson. Woodrow Wilson and Far Eastern Policy,
B 1913-1921. N.Y.: Octagon, 1968 (orig. pub. by Bookman,
1957). 411 pp. 68-22300. (R).
Hucker, 814; Silberman, 517

0099 Dallin, David J. The Rise of Russia in Asia. New Haven,
B Conn.: Yale University Press, 1949. 293 pp. 49-9059. o.p.
AUFS, 20; Hucker, 702; Silberman, 417; FEQ, 5/50; Library
Journal, 4/15/49; Pol. Sci. Q., 9/49

0100 Dallin, David J. Soviet Russia and the Far East. New Haven,
B Conn.: Yale University Press, 1948. 398 pp. 48-9035 rev.
o.p.
AUFS, 80; Hucker, 834; Silberman, 491; FEQ, 5/49; AHR, 4/49;
Am. Pol. Sci. R., 6/49; Ann. Am. Acad., 5/49; Library
Journal, 10/15/48; Pacific Affairs, 6/49

1263 Davidson, J. Leroy. The Lotus Sutra in Chinese Art; A Study in
C Buddhist Art to the Year 1000. New Haven, Conn.: Yale Uni-
versity Press, 1954. 105 pp. 54-5604. o.p.
Hucker, 1409; FEQ, 5/55; Library Journal, 9/1/54

0203 Davidson, Martha. A List of Published Translations from Chinese
C into English, French, and German. tentative ed. Ann Arbor,
Mich.: J. W. Edwards for American Council of Learned Soci-
eties, 1952-57. 2 pts. 52-4721 rev. o.p.
AUFS, 1039; Hucker, 1520; JAS, 8/59; FEQ, 5/54; JAOS,
10-12/58

0956 Davis, Albert Richard, ed. The Penguin Book of Chinese Verse.
C tr. by Robert Kotewall and Norman L. Smith. Baltimore:
Penguin, 1962. 84 pp. 62-6274.

0459 Dawson, Raymond Stanley. The Chinese Chamelion: an Analysis of
B European Conceptions of Chinese Civilization. N.Y.: Oxford,

1967. 235 pp. 67-81516.
Choice, ll/67; JAS, ll/67; Library Journal, 8/67; TLS, 5/18/67

0313 Dawson, Raymond Stanley, ed. The Legacy of China. N.Y.:
C   Oxford, 1964. 392 pp. 64-6757.
     Sup. 65, 309l; Choice, 12/64; JAS, 5/65

1756 Dazai, Osamu, pseud. No Longer Human. tr. by Donald Keene.
B   Norfolk, Conn: New Directions, 1958. 177 pp. 58-9509.
     Silberman, l003; TLS, 6/30/58

1757 Dazai, Osamu, pseud. The Setting Sun. tr. by Donald Keene.
B   Norfolk, Conn.: J. Laughlin, 1956. 189 pp. 56-13350 rev.
     AUFS, 456; Silberman, l004; JAS, 2/57; Library Journal,
     9/15/56

0013 De Bary, William Theodore, ed. Approaches to Asian Civiliza-
A   tions. N.Y.: Columbia University Press, 1964. 293 pp.
     63-20226.
     JAS, 2/65

0314 De Bary, William Theodore, ed. Sources of Chinese Tradition.
A   contrib. by Yi-pao Mei and others. N.Y.: Columbia Uni-
     versity Press, 1960. 976 pp. (Records of Civilization:
     Sources and Studies, 55, Introduction to Oriental Civiliza-
     tions, 3). 60-99ll.
     Sup. 6l, 2794; Hucker, l045; JAS, 5/61; Ann. Am. Acad.,
     1/61; Library Journal, 5/1/60; Pacific Affairs, Summer/61

0365 Debnicki, Aleksy. The Chu-shu-chi-nien as a Source to the Social
C   History of Ancient China. Warszawa: Panstwowe Wydawnictwo
     Naukowe, 1956. Hand catalog.
     Hucker, 174

0583 De Francis, John Francis. Nationalism and Language Reform in
A   China. Princeton, N.J.: Princeton University Press, 1950.
     306 pp. 51-119 rev. o.p. (M-University).
     AUFS, l027; Hucker, 65; FEQ, 11/51; AHR, 7/51; Am. Pol. Sci.
     R., 9/51; JAOS, 10-12/51; Pacific Affairs, 6/51

0957 Demieville, Paul, ed. Anthologie de la Poesie Chinoise
B   Classique. Paris: Gallimard, 1962. 571 pp. NUC 64-37030.

1241 Demieville, Paul. La Concile de Lhasa; Une Controverse Sur
C   le Quitisme entre Bouddhistes de l'Inde et de la Chine
     au VIII Siecle de l'Ere Chretienne. Paris: Imprimerie
     Nationale, 1952- A55-689.

1449 Dening, Walter. The Life of Toyotomi Hideyoshi. 4th ed. Tokyo:
B   Hokuseido, 1955. 558 pp. 56-1288.
     Silberman, 236; Japan Q., 10-12/56

0101 Dennett, Tyler. Americans in Eastern Asia; A Critical Study of
A   the United States' Policy in the Far East in the 19th Century.
     N.Y.: Barnes & Noble, 1963 (orig. pub. in 1922). 725 pp.
     NUC 64-38454. (R).
     AUFS, 81; Hucker, 689; Silberman, 314; JAS, 2/64; FEQ, 5/42;
     AHR, 4/23

1497 Dennett, Tyler. Roosevelt and the Russo-Japanese War, a Crit-
B   ical Study of American Policy in East Asia in 1902-5.
     Gloucester, Mass.: Peter Smith, 1959 (orig. pub. by Double-
     day, Page, 1925). 357 pp. 60-2036. (R).
     Silberman, 436; AHR, 10/25; Am. Pol. Sci. R., 8/25

1498 Dennis, Alfred Lewis Pinneo. The Anglo-Japanese Alliance. N.Y.:
B   Johnson, 1967 (orig. pub. by University of California Press,
     1923). 111 pp. A23-1030. (R).
     Silberman, 408

0460 Der Ling, Princess. Son of Heaven. N.Y.: Appleton-Century,
C   1935. 248 pp. 35-5894. o.p.
     Hucker, 612

0461 Der Ling, Princess. "Mrs. Thaddeus G. White". Two Years in the
B   Forbidden City. N.Y.: Moffat, Yard and Co., 1911. 383 pp.
     11-29741. o.p.

0052 The Developing World; AUFS Readings - Vol. I- N.Y.: American
C   Universities Field Staff, 1966- 66-29570.
     Sup. 67, 3204

1670 De Vos, George. Japan's Invisible Race; Caste in Culture and
B   Personality. Berkeley: University of California Press, 1966.
     415 pp. 66-16422.
     Sup. 67, 3214; Choice, 1/68; JAS, 5/67; Am. Soc. R., 10/67;
     Ann. Am. Acad., 11/67

1011 Dieny, Jean-Pierre. Aux Origines de la Poesie Classique en
C   Chine. Etude sur la Poesie Lyrique a l'Epoque des Han.
     Leiden: Brill, 1968. 176 pp. (T'oung Pao, Monographie IV).
     68-93582.

2105 Dillon, Richard H. The Hatchet Men: the Story of Tong Wars
B   in San Francisco's Chinatown. N.Y.: Coward-McCann, 1962.
     375 pp. 62-14747.
     Library Journal, 9/1/62

0881 Donnithorne, Audrey. China's Economic System. N.Y.: Praeger,
B   1967. 592 pp. 67-23967.
     Choice, 9/68; Library Journal, 7/67; TLS, 12/28/67

0835 Doolin, Dennis J. The Chinese People's Republic. by Dennis J.
C   Doolin and Robert C. North. Stanford, Calif.: Hoover Insti-
     tution on War, Revolution, and Peace, 1966. 68 pp. (Hoover
     Institution Studies, 14). 65-19769.
     Choice, 3/67; China Q., 7-9/68

0836 Doolin, Dennis J., ed. and tr. Communist China; The Politics of
A   Student Opposition. Stanford, Calif.: Hoover Institution on
     War, Revolution, and Peace, 1964. 70 pp. 64-16879.
     JAS, 2/65; China Q., 4-6/65

0748 Doolin, Dennis J. Territorial Claims in the Sino-Soviet Con-
B   flict; Documents & Analysis. Stanford, Calif.: Hoover
     Institution on War, Revolution, and Peace, 1965. 77 pp.
     (Hoover Institution Studies, 7). 65-19766.
     Choice, 3/66

1255 Dore, Henri. Researches into Chinese Superstitions. tr. from
C   the French with notes, historical and explanatory, by M.
     Kennelly. Taipei: Chinese Materials and Research Aids
     Service Center (orig. pub. by T'usewei Press, 1914-).
     11 v. in 5. 26-18204. (R).
     Hucker, 1092

1671 Dore, Ronald Philip. City Life in Japan; A Study of the Tokyo
A   Ward. Berkeley: University of California Press, 1958.
     472 pp. 59-16060.
     AUFS, 345; Silberman, 1408; JAS, 8/59; Japan Q., 7-9/59

1970 Dore, Ronald Philip. Education in Tokugawa Japan. Berkeley:
A   University of California Press, 1965. 346 pp. (University
     of California Center for Japanese and Korean Studies
     Publication). 65-1744.
     Choice, 7-8/65; JAS, ll/65; Am. Soc. R., 10/65; Ann. Am.
     Acad., 11/65; Japan Q., 7-9/65; JAOS, 4-6/65; TLS, 1/20/66

1627 Dore, Ronald Philip. Land Reform in Japan. N.Y.: Oxford, 1959.
B   510 pp. 59-1526. o.p.
     AUFS, 346; Silberman, 1565; JAS, 2/60; Am. J. Soc., 11/59;
     Ann. Am. Acad., 1/60; Japan Q., 10-12/59; J. Pol. Econ.,
     10/60; Pacific Affairs, 6/60; Pol. Sci. Q., 9/59; TLS,
     2/24/59

0918 The Dragon King's Daughter; Ten Tang Dynasty Stories. Pe-
C   king: Foreign Languages Press, 1954. 100 pp. 56-47384.
     o.p.

1293 Driscoll, Lucy. Chinese Calligraphy, by Lucy Driscoll and
B   Kenji Toda. 2d ed. N.Y.: Paragon, 1964 (orig. pub. by
     University of Chicago Press, 1935). 70 pp. 64-24329.
     (R).
     AUFS, l005; Hucker, l487; JAOS, 12/35

1200 Dubs, Homer Hasenpflug. Hsuntze, the Moulder of Ancient Con-
C   fucianism. Taipei: Ch'eng-wen Publishing Co., dist. by
     Chinese Materials and Research Aids Service Center, 1966
     (orig. pub. by A. Probsthain, 1927). 308 pp. NUC 66-76897.
     (R).
     AUFS, 626; Hucker, ll36; JAOS, 3/29

0584 Dulles, Foster Rhea. China and America; The Story of Their
B   Relations since 1784. Port Washington, N.Y.: Kennikat,
     1968 (orig. pub. by Princeton University Press, 1946).
     277 pp. 67-29611. (R).
     Hucker, 686; FEQ, 2/47; Am. Pol. Sci. R., 12/46; Ann. Am.
     Acad., 11/46; Pol. Sci. Q., 12/46

1499 Dulles, Foster Rhea. Yankees and Samurai; America's Role in
B   the Emergence of Modern Japan: 1791-1900. N.Y.: Harper
     & Row, 1965. 275 pp. 65-20427.
     Choice, ll/65; AHR, 7/65; Ann. Am. Acad., 1/66; Library
     Journal, 10/1/65

0180 Dumoulin, Heinrich. A History of Zen Buddhism. N.Y.: Pantheon,
A   1963. 335 pp. 62-17386. o.p.
     Japan Q., 10-12/63; JAOS, 7-9/65

1819 Dumoulin, Heinrich. Kamo Mabuchi (1697-1769); Ein Beitrag Zur
C   Japanischen Religions- und Geistesgeschichte. Tokyo: Sophia
       University Press, 1943- (Monumenta Nipponica Monograph, 8).
       50-41347.
       Silberman, 691

1830 Dumoulin, Heinrich. Ostliche Meditation und Christliche
B   Mystik. Munchen: Alber, 1966. 339 pp. 67-82534.

1831 Dumoulin, Heinrich. Zen; Geschichte und Gestalt. Berne:
C   Francke Verlag, 1959. 332 pp. (Sammlung Dalps, 87).
       Hand catalog.
       Silberman, 639

2072 Durdin, Tillman. China and the World. The Rebirth of For-
C   mosa by Robert Aura Smith. N.Y.: Foreign Policy Association,
       1953. 63 pp. 53-9998. o.p.

0749 Dutt, Vidya Prakash. China and the World; An Analysis of
C   Communist China's Foreign Policy. rev. ed. N.Y.: Praeger,
       1966. 356 pp. (Praeger Publications in Russian History
       and World Communism, 177). 66-15447.
       Choice, 10/66

1500 Duus, Peter. Party Rivalry and Political Change in Taisho
B   Japan. Cambridge, Mass.: Harvard University Press, 1968.
       317 pp. (Harvard East Asian Series, 35). 68-21972.
       Choice, 2/69

0075 East, William Gordon, ed. The Changing Map of Asia, a Political
A   Geography. rev. ed. London: Methuen, dist. by Barnes &
       Noble, 1966 (orig. pub. in 1950). 434 pp. 59-1411. (R).
       Silberman, 85

1174 East-West Philosophers' Conference. The Chinese Mind; Essen-
B   tials of Chinese Philosophy and Culture. ed. by Charles
       A. Moore, with the assistance of Aldyth V. Morris. Hono-
       lulu: East-West Center Press, 1967. 402 pp. 66-24011.
       JAS, 8/68; Library Journal, 1/1/68

1811 East-West Philosophers' Conference. The Japanese Mind; Essen-
B   tials of Japanese Philosophy and Culture. ed. by Charles
       A. Moore with the assistance of Aldyth V. Morris. Hono-
       lulu: East-West Center Press, 1964. 357 pp. (East-West
       Philosophers' Conference, 1964). 67-16704.
       Choice, 6/68; JAS, 11/68

0053 Eastern and Western World; Selected Readings. ed. by S. Hofstra.
B   The Hague: W. van Hoeve for Netherlands Universities Founda-
       tion for International Co-operation, 1953. 181 pp. 53-40444.

0462 Eastman, Lloyd E. Throne and Mandarins: China's Search for a
A   Policy during the Sino-French Controversy, 1880-1885.
       Cambridge, Mass.: Harvard University Press, 1967. 254 pp.
       (Harvard Historical Studies, Vol. XXIX). 67-12098.
       Choice, 11/67; JAS, 11/67; AHR, 2/68

0919 Eberhard, Wolfram, ed. and tr. Chinese Fairy Tales and Folk
C   Tales. London: Paul, Trench, Trubner, 1937. 304 pp.
       38-6187. o.p.
       Hucker, 1712

0366 Eberhard, Wolfram. Conquerors and Rulers; Social Forces in
B   Medieval China. 2d ed. N.Y.: Heinman, 1956. 129 pp.
       52-11731.
       AUFS, 703; Hucker, 328

0920 Eberhard, Wolfram. Folktales of China. rev. ed. Chicago:
A   University of Chicago Press, 1965. 267 pp. 65-25440.
       Choice, 6/66; Library Journal, 8/1/66

0901 Eberhard, Wolfram. Guilt and Sin in Traditional China.
B   Berkeley: University of California Press, 1967. 141 pp.
       67-12297.
       Choice, 3/68; JAS, 5/68; Library Journal, 5/1/67

0332 Eberhard, Wolfram. A History of China. tr. by E. W. Dickes.
B   2d ed., rev. Berkeley: University of California Press, 1960.
       358 pp. A62-8636.
       Hucker, 103; FEQ, 8/51

0882 Ecklund, George N. Financing the Chinese Government Budget,
B   Mainland China, 1950-1959. Chicago: Aldine, 1966.
       133 pp. 66-15201.
       Choice, 10/67; Ann. Am. Acad., 7/67; Library Journal, 3/15/67

0883 Eckstein, Alexander. Communist China's Economic Growth
A   and Foreign Trade, Implications for U.S. Policy. N.Y.:
       McGraw-Hill, 1966. 366 pp. 65-28588.
       JAS, 2/67; Am. Econ. R., 12/66; Ann. Am. Acad., 1/67;
       J. Pol. Econ., 8/67; Library Journal, 1/15/66; Pacific

Affairs, Fall-Winter/66-67; Pol. Sci. Q., 6/67

0884 Eckstein, Alexander et. al. The National Income of Communist
C   China. N.Y.: Free Press of Glencoe, 1962. 215 pp.
       61-9164.
       Sup. 63, 2910; JAS, 11/62; Am. Econ. R., 12/62; Ann. Am.
       Acad., 9/62; China Q., 10-12/62; Library Journal, 5/15/62

0885 An Economic Profile of Mainland China; Studies Prepared for the
A   Joint Economic Committee, Congress of the United States.
       Washington: Government Printing Office, 1967. 2 v.
       67-60884.

1370 Economic Statistics of Japan. Tokyo: Bank of Japan. annual.
B

1393 Economic Survey of Japan. Japanese Government Economic Plan-
A   ning Agency. Tokyo: Japan Times.

0886 Economic Trends in Communist China. ed. by Alexander Eckstein,
A   Walter Galenson, and Ta-chang Liu. Chicago: Aldine, 1968.
       757 pp. (Social Science Research Council). 68-19887.
       Choice, 4/69

0921 Edwards, Evangeline Dora. Chinese Prose Literature of the T'ang
B   Period, A.D. 618-906. London: A. Probsthain, 1937-38. 2 v.
       38-10507 rev. o.p.
       AUFS, 1054; Hucker, 1611

0922 Edwards, Evangeline Dora, ed. The Dragon Book, comp. and ed.
C   by E. D. Edwards. London: William Hodge, 1938. 367 pp.
       39-14127. o.p.
       Hucker, 1655

1971 Eells, Walter Crosby. The Literature of Japanese Education, 1945-
B   1954. Hamden, Conn.: Archon, 1966 (orig. pub. by Shoe-
       string Press, 1955). 210 pp. 55-12032. (R).
       Silberman, 1463; Japan Q., 10-12/56

0750 Elegant, Robert S. China's Red Masters; Political Biographies
C   of the Chinese Communist Leaders. N.Y.: Twayne, 1951.
       264 pp. 51-10445. o.p.
       AUFS, 922; FEQ, 2/52

2099 Elegant, Robert S. The Dragon's Seed; Peking and the Over-
C   seas Chinese. N.Y.: St. Martin's, 1959. 319 pp.
       59-10511. o.p.
       JAS, 2/60; Library Journal, 5/15/59; Pacific Affairs, 12/59

1353 Elia, Pasquale M. d'. Galileo in China; Relations through the
B   Roman College between Galileo and the Jesuit Scientist-
       Missionaries (1610-1640). tr. by Rufus Sutter and Matthew
       Sciasia. Cambridge, Mass.: Harvard University Press,
       1960. 115 pp. 61-5252. o.p.
       Hucker, 1379; JAOS, 1-3/62

1832 Eliot, Sir Charles Norton Edgecumbe. Japanese Buddhism.
A   London: Routledge & Kegan Paul, 1935. 449 pp. 35-6584.
       AUFS, 141; Silberman, 624; JAS, 8/60; J. Philosophy, 6/20/35

1501 Elsbree, Willard H. Japan's Role in Southeast Asian Na-
C   tionalist Movements, 1940 to 1945. Cambridge, Mass.: Har-
       vard University Press, 1953. 182 pp. 53-13171. o.p.
       AUFS, 1268; Silberman, 548; FEQ, 11/54; AHR, 7/54; Am. Pol.
       Sci. R., 6/54; Ann. Am. Acad., 7/54; Pacific Affairs,
       3/54; TLS, 8/6/54

1401 Embree, John Fee. The Japanese. Washington: Smithsonian
C   Institution, 1943. 42 pp. 43-51696. o.p.
       AUFS, 160; FEQ, 8/43

1672 Embree, John Fee. The Japanese Nation, a Social Survey.
B   N.Y.: Farrar & Rinehart, 1945. 308 pp. 45-6450. o.p.
       AUFS, 230; Silberman, 595; FEQ, 11/46; Am. Pol. Sci. R.,
       12/45; Ann. Am. Acad., 11/45; Pacific Affairs, 12/45

1955 Embree, John Fee, comp. Japanese Peasant Songs. Philadelphia:
B   American Folklore Society, 1944. 96 pp. (Memoirs of the
       American Folklore Society, Vol. 38). 44-2122. o.p.
       Silberman, 1179

1673 Embree, John Fee. Suye Mura, a Japanese Village. Chicago:
B   University of Chicago Press, 1939. 354 pp. 40-1477.
       AUFS, 231; Silberman, 1409; Am. Anthropologist, 10/40;
       Am. J. Soc., 9/40; Am. Soc. R., 4/40; JAOS, 9/40;
       Pacific Affairs, 12/40

1628 Emi, Koichi. Government Fiscal Activity and Economic
C   Growth in Japan, 1868-1960. Tokyo: Kinokuniya, 1963.
       186 pp. 64-32272.

2091 Endacott, G. B. Government and People in Hong Kong, 1841-
A   1962, a Constitutional History. Hong Kong: Hong Kong Uni-
     versisy Press, dist. by Oxford, 1964. 263 pp. 65-2252.
     Choice, 2/66; JAS, 11/65; AHR, 10/65; TLS, 9/16/65

2088 Endacott, G. B. A History of Hong Kong. N.Y.: Oxford, 1958.
B   322 pp. 58-4392.
     Hucker, 679; AHR, 4/59; TLS, 2/6/59

0367 Ennin. Diary; The Record of a Pilgrimage to China in Search
A   of the Law. tr. from Chinese by Edwin O. Reischauer. N.Y.:
     Ronald, 1955. 454 pp. 55-5553.
     Hucker, 281; Silberman, 634; FEQ, 11/55; Ann. Am. Acad.,
     11/55; Library Journal, 6/15/55; Pacific Affairs, 12/55

0585 Epstein, Israel. The Unfinished Revolution in China. Boston:
C   Little, Brown, 1947. 442 pp. 47-4043. o.p.
     Hucker, 805; FEQ, 5/48; Library Journal, 6/15/47

1956 Ernst, Earle. The Kabuki Theatre. N.Y.: Oxford, 1956.
A   296 pp. 56-14007.
     AUFS, 502; Silberman, 1133; TLS, 8/10/56

1735 Ernst, Earle, ed. Three Japanese Plays from the Traditional
B   Theatre. London: Oxford, 1959. 200 pp. 59-1489 rev.
     o.p.
     Silberman, 1096; JAS, 8/60; Japan Q., 7-9/60; Library
     Journal, 5/1/59; TLS, 4/24/59

1502 Esthus, Raymond A. Theodore Roosevelt and Japan. Seattle:
C   University of Washington Press, 1967. 329 pp. 66-19567.
     Sup. 67, 3215; Choice, 5/67; JAS, 11/67; AHR, 10/67;
     Japan Q., 7-9/67; J. Am. Hist., 6/67; Pacific Affairs,
     Spring-Summer/67; TLS, 9/28/67

0102 Eudin, Xenia Joukoff. Soviet Russia and the East, 1920-1927,
B   a Documentary Survey. Stanford, Calif.: Stanford Uni-
     versity Press, 1957. 478 pp. 56-8690.
     Hucker, 883; JAS, 2/58; AHR, 4/58; Pacific Affairs, 9/58;
     Pol. Sci. Q., 3/58; TLS, 1/3/58

0185 Eumorfopoulos, George. The George Eumorfopoulos Collection;
C   Catalogue of the Chinese and Corean Bronzes, Sculpture,
     Jades, Jewellery and Miscellaneous Objects. by W. Per-
     ceval Yetts. London: Benn, 1929- 30-16020. o.p.
     Hucker, 1426

0192 Eumorfopoulos, George. The George Eumorfopoulos Collection;
C   Catalogue of the Chinese, Corean and Persian Pottery and
     Porcelain. London: Benn, 1925-28. 6 v. 26-5494. o.p.
     Hucker, 1443

0751 Fairbank, John King. China: the People's Middle Kingdom and
A   the U.S.A. Cambridge, Mass.: Harvard University Press,
     1967. 145 pp. 67-17307.
     Choice, 1/68; JAS, 2/68; J. Am. Hist., 9/67; TLS, 12/14/67

0315 Fairbank, John King, ed. Chinese Thought and Institutions.
A   Chicago: University of Chicago Press, 1957. 438 pp. 57-5272.
     AUFS, 676; Hucker, 1063; JAS, 5/60; AHR, 4/58; Am. J. Soc.,
     1/59; Am. Pol. Sci. R., 9/58; Am. Soc. R., 6/58; Ann. Am.
     Acad., 9/58; JAOS, 10-12/58; TLS, 4/25/58

0463 Fairbank, John King. Ch'ing Administration; Three Studies.
C   Cambridge, Mass.: Harvard University Press, 1960. 218 pp.
     (Harvard-Yenching Institute Studies, XIX). 60-7991.
     Hucker, 513

0464 Fairbank, John King, comp. Ch'ing Documents; An Introductory
C   Syllabus. 2d ed. rev. Cambridge, Mass.: Harvard University
     Press, 1959. 2 v. 60-3385.
     Hucker, 520; FEQ, 5/53; JAOS, 1-3/53

0752 Fairbank, John King. Communist China and Taiwan in United
B   States Foreign Policy. Storrs: University of Connecticut,
     1960. 61 pp. (4th annual Brien McMahon Lecture). 61-63940.
     o.p.
     Hucker, 1017

0204 Fairbank, John King. Japanese Studies of Modern China; A Biblio-
C   graphical Guide to Historical and Social-Science Research
     on the 19th and 20th Centuries. Rutland, Vt.: Tuttle for
     Harvard-Yenching Institute, 1955. 331 pp. A55-7749.
     FEQ, 2/56

0205 Fairbank, John King. Modern China; A Bibliographical Guide to
B   Chinese Works, 1898-1937. Cambridge, Mass.: Harvard Uni-
     versity Press, 1950. 608 pp. (Harvard-Yenching Institute
     Studies, I). 50-5236.

Hucker, 717; FEQ, 8/51; AHR, 7/50; Pacific Affairs, 6/50

0465 Fairbank, John King. Trade and Diplomacy on the China Coast; The
A   Opening of the Treaty Ports, 1842-1854. Stanford, Calif.:
     Stanford University Press, 1968 (orig. pub. by Harvard
     University Press, 1953). 2 v. 65-100264. (R).
     AUFS, 741; Hucker 660; AHR, 10/54; Am. Pol. Sci. R., 6/54;
     Ann. Am. Acad., 4/54

0333 Fairbank, John King. The United States and China. new ed.
A   rev. and enl. Cambridge, Mass.: Harvard University
     Press, 1958. 365 pp. 58-11552.
     AUFS, 806; Hucker, 2; JAS, 5/60; FEQ, 5/49; Library Journal,
     9/1/58

1503 Falk, Edwin Albert. Togo and the Rise of Japanese Sea Power.
C   N.Y.: Longmans, Green, 1936. 508 pp. 36-5811. o.p.
     Silberman, 396; AHR, 1/37; Am. Pol. Sci. R., 8/36;
     TLS, 6/27/36

0029 Far East Digest. nos. 1-135. 1947-1958.
C

0030 Far Eastern Ceramic Bulletin. v.1-12. 1948-60.
C

0031 Far Eastern Economic Review, v.1- 1946- (M-Microphoto).
B   Hucker, 2158

1281 Feddersen, Martin. Chinese Decorative Art; A Handbook for
B   Collectors and Connoisseurs. 2d ed., rev. and enl. tr.
     by Arthur Lane. London: Faber & Faber, 1961. 286 pp.
     Hand catalog.

1888 Feddersen, Martin. Japanese Decorative Art; A Handbook for
B   Collectors and Connoisseurs. Boston: Boston Book and Art
     Shop, 1962. 286 pp. 61-9623.

2020 Fehrenbach, T. R. This Kind of War; A Study in Unpreparedness.
A   N.Y.: Macmillan, 1963. 688 pp. 63-9972.
     JAS, 5/64; Ann. Am. Acad., 9/63; Library Journal, 6/15/63

0902 Fei, Hsiao-t'ung. Peasant Life in China; A Field Study of
A   Country Life in the Yangtze Valley. London: Routledge,
     1939. 300 pp. 39-15658.
     Hucker, 2071

1504 Feis, Herbert. The Atomic Bomb and the End of the War in the
A   Pacific. rev. ed. Princeton, N.J.: Princeton University
     Press, 1966 (orig. pub. in 1961 under the title Japan
     Subdued). 199 pp. 66-13312.
     Silberman, 525; JAS, 11/61; AHR, 10/61; Am. Pol. Sci. R.,
     9/61; Ann. Am. Acad., 11/61; Japan Q., 7-9/61; Library
     Journal, 6/1/61; Pol. Sci. Q., 12/67; TLS, 12/15/61

0586 Feis, Herbert. The China Tangle; The American Effort in China
A   from Pearl Harbor to the Marshall Mission. Princeton, N.J.:
     Princeton University Press, 1953. 445 pp. 53-10142.
     Hucker, 819; FEQ, 5/54; Library Journal, 10/1/53

1505 Feis, Herbert. Contest Over Japan. N.Y.: Norton, 1967.
C   187 pp. 67-16603.
     Choice, 9/68; AHR, 4/68; J. Am. Hist., 3/68; Library
     Journal, 9/15/67

1506 Feis, Herbert. The Road to Pearl Harbor; The Coming of the
C   War Between the United States and Japan. Princeton,
     N.J.: Princeton University Press, 1950. 356 pp.
     50-9585.
     Silberman, 513; FEQ, 11/51

1076 Feng, Hsueh-feng. Fables. tr. by Gladys Yang. Peking:
C   Foreign Languages Press, 1953. 70 pp. 57-20220. o.p.

0923 Feng, Meng-lung. Stories from a Ming Collection. Translations
B   of Chinese Short Stories Published in the Seventeenth Century,
     by Cyril Birch. N.Y.: Grove, 1968 (orig. pub. by Indiana
     University Press, 1959). 205 pp. (UNESCO Collection of
     Representative Works, Chinese Series). 59-9848. (R).
     Hucker, 1659; JAS, 8/59

1012 Feng, Shu-lan. A Short History of Classical Chinese Litera-
C   ture by Feng Yuan-chun. tr. by Yang Hsien-yi and Gladys
     Yang. Peking: Foreign Languages Press, 1958. 132 pp.
     60-1450. o.p.
     Hucker, 1526; FEQ, 8/50

1175 Feng, Yu-lan. A History of Chinese Philosophy, by Fung Yu-lan.
A   tr. by Derk Bodde. Princeton, N.J.: Princeton University
     Press, 1952-53. 2 v. A52-9807 rev. o.p.

AUFS, 587; Hucker, l046; FEQ, 8/53, 5/54

0245 Fenn, Courtenay Hughes. Chinese-English Pocket Dictionary.
B   rev. Amer. ed. Cambridge, Mass.: Harvard University Press,
       1944. 694 pp. 50-4925l.
       Hucker, 86

0193 Fenollosa, Ernest Francisco. Epochs of Chinese and Japanese
A   Art, an Outline History of East Asiatic Design. new and
       rev. ed. N.Y.: Dover, 1963 (orig. pub. in 1913). 2 v.
       63-5655. (R).
       Hucker, 1411; Silberman, 716; JAS, 5/65

0334 Feuerwerker, Albert. Approaches to Modern Chinese History.
A   Berkeley: University of California Press, 1967. 356 pp.
       67-15640.
       Choice, 2/68

0466 Feuerwerker, Albert. China's Early Industrialization; Sheng
A   Hsuan-huai (1844-1916) and Mandarin Enterprise. Cambridge,
       Mass.: Harvard University Press, 1958. 311 pp. 58-12967.
       AUFS, 742; Hucker, 2219; JAS, 8/59

0753 Feuerwerker, Albert. Chinese Communist Studies of Modern Chinese
B   History. Cambridge, Mass.: Harvard University Press, 1961.
       287 pp. (Harvard University Chinese Economic and Political
       Studies: Special Series). 61-19595.
       Sup. 63, 29ll; JAS, 5/62; China Q., 10-12/62

0152 Field, Frederick Vanderbilt, ed. An Economic Survey of the
C   Pacific Area. N.Y.: International Secretariat, Institute
       of Pacific Relations, 1941- 42-8899. o.p.
       Silberman, 1497

0587 Finch, Percy. Shanghai and Beyond. N.Y.: Scribner's, 1953.
C   357 pp. 53-7276. o.p.
       AUFS, 924; FEQ, 5/54; Library Journal, 2/1/53

0588 Finney, Charles Grandison. The Old China Hands. Garden City,
C   N.Y.: Doubleday, 1961. 258 pp. 61-9506. o.p.
       Library Journal, 1/1/62

0589 Fishel, Wesley R. The End of Extraterritoriality in China.
B   Berkeley: University of California Press, 1952. 318 pp.
       52-6592. o.p.
       Hucker, 825; FEQ, 2/53

0754 Fisher, Margaret Welpley. Himalayan Battleground; Sino-Indian
C   Rivalry in Ladakh. N.Y.: Praeger, 1963. 205 pp. 63-11121.
       Am. Pol. Sci. R., 3/64; Ann. Am. Acad., 5/64; Library
       Journal, 8/63; Pacific Affairs, Spring/64; TLS, 6/2/64

0755 Fisher, Margaret Welpley. Indian Views of Sino-Indian Rela-
C   tions. Berkeley: Institute of International Studies,
       University of California, 1956. 163 pp. (Indian Press
       Digests-Monograph Series, No. 1). A56-9495. o.p.
       Hucker, 1002

0756 Fitzgerald, Charles Patrick. The Birth of Communist China.
C   N.Y.: Praeger, 1966. 288 pp. (Pelican Original, A694).
       65-27021.
       Choice, 7-8/65; Library Journal, 4/1/66

0467 Fitzgerald, Charles Patrick. China: a Short Cultural History.
B   4th rev. ed. N.Y.: Praeger, 1954. 621 pp. 54-6804.
       AUFS, 678; Hucker, 102

0757 Fitzgerald, Charles Patrick. The Chinese View of their
B   Place in the World. N.Y.: Oxford, 1964. 72 pp.
       (Chatham House Essay, 1). 64-1590.
       Choice, 12/64; JAS, 2/65

0368 Fitzgerald, Charles Patrick. The Empress Wu. Melbourne: Cheshire
B   for Australian National University, 1955. 252 pp. 58-27599.
       Hucker, 316; JAS, 8/58

0758 Fitzgerald, Charles Patrick. Flood Tide in China. London:
B   Cresset, 1958. 285 pp. 59-723.
       Hucker, 962

0759 Fitzgerald, Charles Patrick. Revolution in China. N.Y.:
C   Praeger, 1952. 289 pp. 52-862l. o,p.
       AUFS, 925; Hucker, 933; FEQ, 5/53; Library Journal, 9/1/52;
       TLS, 9/12/52

0369 Fitzgerald, Charles Patrick. Son of Heaven, a Biography of Li
B   Shih-Min, Founder of the T'ang Dynasty. Cambridge: Uni-
       versity, 1933. 232 pp. 35-40l6. o.p.
       Hucker, 3l4

0468 Fleming, Peter. Bayonets to Lhasa; The First Full Account of the
C   British Invasion of Tibet in 1904. N.Y.: Harper, 1961.
       319 pp. 61-6431. o.p.
       Hucker, 680; Library Journal, 4/1/61; TLS, 2/3/61

0590 Fleming, Peter. One's Company - A Journey to China. London:
C   Cape, 1934. 319 pp. 34-30523. o.p.

0469 Fleming, Peter. The Siege at Peking. N.Y.: Harper, 1959.
B   273 pp. 59-10580.
       Hucker, 654; JAS, 8/60; AHR, 10/60; Library Journal, 9/15/59;
       TLS, 6/26/59

1853 Floral Art of Japan, prepared by Issotei Nishikawa. N.Y.:
B   Japan Publications Trading Co., 1964. (Tourist Library,
       N.S. 1). 61-11568.
       Silberman, 837

1153 Fokkema, D. W. Literary Doctrine in China and Soviet Influ-
A   ence, 1956-1960. The Hague: Mouton, 1965. 296 pp. 65-23876.
       JAS, 8/66

0591 Folsom, Kenneth E. Friends, Guests, and Colleagues; The
C   Mu-Fu System in the Late Ch'ing Period. Berkeley: Uni-
       versity of California Press, 1968. 234 pp. 67-26479.
       Choice, 9/68; JAS, 8/68

1371 Foreign Trade of Japan. Japan External Trade Organization.
A   Tokyo. annual.

0592 Forman, Harrison. Report from Red China. N.Y.: Holt, 1945.
C   250 pp. 45-2284. o.p.
       Hucker, 894

0246 Forrest, Robert Andrew Dermod. The Chinese Language. London:
C   Faber & Faber, 1948. 352 pp. 48-21629.
       AUFS, 1029; Hucker, 66; FEQ, 8/50

0994 The Forsaken Wife (A Pingchu Opera). tr. by Yang Hsien-yi and
C   Gladys Yang. Peking: Foreign Languages Press, 1958. 70 pp.
       Hand catalog.

0206 Franke, Herbert. Sinologie. Bern: A. Francke, 1953.
B   216 pp. A55-7033.
       Hucker, 21

0335 Franke, Otto. Geschichte des Chinesischen Reiches; Eine
B   Darstellung Seiner Entstehung, Seines Wesens und Seiner
       Entwicklung bis zur Neuesten Zeit. Berlin: De Gruyter,
       1930- 31-2382.
       Hucker, 104; FEQ, 8/52, 8/53; JAOS, 10-12/62

0593 Franke, Wolfgang. Chinas Kulturelle Revolution; Die Bewegung
C   vom 4 Mai 1919. Munich: R. Oldenbourg, 1957. 89 pp.
       Hand catalog.
       Hucker, 757; JAS, 2/60

0470 Franke, Wolfgang. Preliminary Notes on the Important Chinese
C   Literary Sources for the History of the Ming Dynasty (1368-
       1644). Chengtu: Chinese Cultural Studies Research Institute,
       West China Union University, 1948. 118 pp. (Studia Serica
       Monographs, Series A, No. 2). o.p.
       Hucker, 442

1328 Franke, Wolfgang. The Reform and Abolition of the Traditional
A   Chinese Examination System. Cambridge, Mass.: Harvard Uni-
       versity Press, 1960. 100 pp. 61-1281.

0370 Frankel, Hans Hermann, ed. and tr. Biographies of Meng Hao-jan.
C   Berkeley: University of California Press, 1952. 25 pp.
       (Chinese Dynastic Histories Translations, No. 1). A52-9556.
       Hucker, 327; FEQ, 5/53

0336 Frankel, Hans Hermann, comp. Catalogue of Translations from the
C   Chinese Dynastic Histories for the Period 220-960. Berkeley:
       University of California Press, 1957. 295 pp. (Chinese
       Dynastic Histories Translations, Supplement No. 1). A58-9014.
       Hucker, 247; JAS, 11/58

1329 Fraser, Stewart, ed. Chinese Communist Education; Records of
A   the First Decade. Nashville, Tenn.: Vanderbilt University
       Press, 1965. 542 pp. 64-18962.
       Sup. 67, 3236; Choice, 10/65; JAS, 5/66; Am. Pol. Sci. R.,
       12/65; Library Journal, 7/65

0903 Freedman, Maurice. Lineage Organization in Southeastern China.
A   London: Athlone, 1958. 151 pp. (London School of Eco-
       nomics Monographs on Social Anthropology, 18). 58-3785.
       Hucker, 2047; JAS, 5/60

83

1282 Freer Gallery of Art, Washington D.C. The Freer Chinese
C   Bronzes, by John Alexander Pope and others. Washington:
     Smithsonian Institution, 1967- (Freer Gallery of Art,
     Oriental Studies, No. 7). 68-61307.

2095 Fried, Morton Herbert. Colloquium on Overseas Chinese. N.Y.:
B   International Secretariat, Institute of Pacific Relations,
     1958. 80 pp. 58-3235. o.p.

0904 Fried, Morton Herbert. Fabric of Chinese Society; A Study
A   of the Social Life of a Chinese County Seat. N.Y.: Octagon,
     1969 (orig. pub. by Praeger, 1953). 243 pp. 52-11994. (R).
     (M-University).
     AUFS, 812; Hucker, 2075; FEQ, 2/54; Ann. Am. Acad., 7/53;
     Library Journal, 3/15/53; Pacific Affairs, 9/53

0594 Friedman, Irving S. British Relations with China: 1931-1939.
C   N.Y.: International Secretariat, Institute of Pacific Rela-
     tions, 1940. 255 pp. 40-11697. o.p.
     Hucker, 843; Silberman, 486; FEQ, 8/42; Am. Pol. Sci. R.,
     12/40; Ann. Am. Acad., 1/41

0760 Friends, Society of. American Friends Service Committee. A New
C   China Policy; Some Quaker Proposals. New Haven, Conn.:
     Yale University Press, 1965. 68 pp. 65-15048.
     Sup. 65, 3103; Choice, 10/65

0471 Friese, Heinz. Das Dienstleistungs-Systen der Ming-zeit. Weis-
C   baden: Otto Harrassowitz, 1959. 163 pp. (Mitteilungen der
     Gesellschaft fur Natur- und Volkerkunde Ostasiens, XXXV A).
     Hand catalog. o.p.
     Hucker, 446; JAS, 2/62

0595 Frillmann, Paul. China; The Remembered Life, by Paul Frillmann
A   and Graham Peck. intro. by John K. Fairbank. Boston:
     Houghton Mifflin, 1968. 291 pp. 67-15527.
     Choice, 1/69; Library Journal, 3/15/68

0958 Frodsham, J. D., comp. An Anthology of Chinese Verse: Han, Wei,
A   Chin and the Northern and Southern Dynasties. Oxford: Clar-
     endon, 1967. 198 pp. (Oxford Library of East Asian Lit-
     eratures). 67-95155.
     Choice, 9/68; JAS, 11/68; TLS, 9/28/67

1013 Frodsham, J. D. The Murmuring Stream: the Life and Works of
A   the Chinese Nature Poet Hsieh Ling-yun (385-433), Duke of
     K'ang-lo. Kuala Lumpur: University of Malaya Press, dist.
     by Oxford, 1967. 2 v. 68-143150.
     JAS, 5/69

0153 Froelich, Walter, ed. Land Tenure, Industrialization and
C   Social Stability: Experience and Prospects in Asia.
     Milwaukee, Wis.: Marquette University Press, 1961.
     301 pp. (Marquette Asian Studies, 2). 61-10914.
     Sup. 63, 2871

0472 Fu, Lo-shu, tr. A Documentary Chronicle of Sino-Western Rela-
C   tions 1644-1820. Tucson: University of Arizona Press, 1966.
     2 v. (Association for Asian Studies, Monographs and Papers,
     XXII). 66-18529.
     Choice, 6/67; JAS, 8/67; Pacific Affairs, Fall-Winter/67-68

1629 Fuji Ginko. Banking in Modern Japan. 2d ed. Tokyo: Research
C   Division, Fuji Bank, 1967. 299 pp. Hand catalog.

1507 Fujii, Jintaro, ed. Outline of Japanese History in the Meiji Era.
C   tr. by Hattie K. and Kenneth E. Colton. Tokyo: Obunsha,
     1958. 544 pp. (Japanese Culture in the Meiji Era, Vol. VII).
     59-52559.
     Silberman, 335

1590 Fujii, Shinichi. The Essentials of Japanese Constitutional
C   Law. Tokyo: Yuhikaku, 1940. 463 pp. 40-14329.
     Silberman, 1245

1911 Fujikake, Shizuya. Japanese Wood-block Prints. rev. ed.
B   Tokyo: Japan Travel Bureau, 1954. 219 pp. (Tourist Lib-
     rary, N.S. 10). 56-1608.
     Silberman, 783

1697 Fujiwara Michitsuma no haha. The Gossamer Years, the Diary of
A   a Noblewoman of Heian, Japan. tr. by Edward Seidensticker.
     Rutland, Vt.: Tuttle, 1964. 201 pp. (UNESCO Collection of
     Representative Works. Japanese Series). 64-22750.
     Sup. 65, 3063; JAS, 2/66; JAOS, 10-12/65

1717 Fujiwara, Sadaie. Fujiwara Teika's Superior Poems of Our
B   Time; A Thirteenth-Century Poetic Treatise and Sequence.
     Stanford, Calif.: Stanford University Press, 1967. 148 pp.
     (UNESCO Collection of Representative Works). 67-17300.
     JAS, 5/68; Library Journal, 8/67

1372 Fukuda, Naomi, ed. Union Catalog of Books on Japan in West-
A   ern Languages. Tokyo: International House Library, 1968.
     543 pp. Hand catalog.

1674 Fukutake, Tadashi. Japanese Rural Society. N.Y.: Oxford,
B   1967. 230 pp. 67-8869.
     Japan Q., 10-12/67

1508 Fukuzawa, Yukichi. Autobiography. rev. ed. tr. by C. Blacker.
A   N.Y.: Columbia University Press, 1966. 407 pp. 66-15468.
     Choice, 10/66; Library Journal, 8/66

1946 Futagawa, Yukio. The Roots of Japanese Architecture; A Photo-
A   graphic Quest. N.Y.: Harper & Row, 1963. 207 pp. 63-16240.
     Library Journal, 10/1/63

0596 Gale, Esson McDowell. Salt for the Dragon; A Personal History
B   of China, 1908-1945. East Lansing: Michigan State College
     Press, 1953. 225 pp. 53-9494.
     Hucker, 735; FEQ, 2/54; AHR, 10/53

2077 Gallin, Bernard. Hsin Hsing, Taiwan; A Chinese Village
A   in Change. Berkeley: University of California Press,
     1966. 324 pp. 66-14734.
     Choice, 12/67; JAS, 8/67

1330 Galt, Howard Spilman. The Development of Chinese Educational
B   Theory; The Historical Development of the Theory of Educa-
     tion in China to the Close of the Han Dynasty, A.D. 220.
     Shanghai: Commercial Press, 1929. 180 pp. A32-2590. o.p.

1331 Galt, Howard Spilman. A History of Chinese Educational Insti-
B   tutions. London: A. Probsthain, 1952- 52-4827.
     Hucker, 1528; FEQ, 11/52

0905 Gamble, Sidney David. Ting Hsien, a North China Rural Commu-
B   nity. Stanford, Calif.: Stanford University Press, 1968
     (orig. pub. by Institute of Pacific Relations, 1954).
     472 pp. 68-13743. (R).
     Hucker, 2074; Choice, 3/69; FEQ, 11/54; Am. Anthropologist,
     4/55; Am. J. Soc., 3/55; Am. Pol. Sci. R., 3/55; Am. Soc. R.,
     10/54; Ann. Am. Acad., 9/54

0337 Gardner, Charles Sidney. Chinese Traditional Historiography.
A   Cambridge, Mass.: Harvard University Press, 1961. 124 pp.
     (Harvard Historical Monographs, No. 11). Hand catalog.
     Sup. 63, 2912; Hucker, 1622; JAS, 5/62

0207 Gardner, Charles Sidney, ed. A Union List of Selected Western
B   Books on China in American Libraries. 2d ed. N.Y.:
     Burt Franklin, 1967 (orig. pub. by American Council of
     Learned Societies, 1932). 111 pp. 32-5871. (R).
     JAOS, 6/32

1957 Garfias, Robert. Gagaku, the Music and Dances of the Japanese
A   Imperial Household. N.Y.: Theater Art Books, 1959. 59-3783.
     Silberman, 1170

0761 Garthoff, Raymond L., ed. Sino-Soviet Military Relations.
C   N.Y.: Praeger, 1966. 285 pp. 66-18900.
     Sup. 67, 3237; Choice, 6/67; Library Journal, 10/1/66

0906 Geddes, William Robert. Peasant Life in Communist China.
B   Ithaca, N.Y.: Society for Applied Anthropology, Cornell
     University, 1963. 66 pp. (Monograph No. 6). 63-5144.
     o.p.

2021 Geer, Andrew Clare. The New Breed; The Story of the U.S.
C   Marines in Korea. N.Y.: Harper, 1952. 395 pp. 52-5438.
     o.p.

0247 Gentzler, J. Mason. A Syllabus of Chinese Civilization. N.Y.:
B   Columbia University Press, 1968. 107 pp. (Companion to
     Asian Studies/Committee on Oriental Studies). 68-55814.
     Choice, 4/69

0292 Geological Society of China. Bulletin. v.1- 1922-
B   Hucker, 53

0837 George, Alexander L. The Chinese Communist Army in Action;
B   The Korean War and Its Aftermath. N.Y.: Columbia
     University Press, 1967. 255 pp. 67-12659.
     Choice, 1/68; AHR, 2/68; Ann. Am. Acad., 11/67; Pacific
     Affairs, Fall-Winter/67-68; TLS, 10/12/67

0371 Gernet, Jacques. Daily Life in China on the Eve of the Mongol
B   Invasion, 1250-1276. tr. by H. M. Wright. N.Y.: Macmillan,
     1962. 254 pp. 62-4325.
     Hucker, 339

0186 Getty, Alice. The Gods of Northern Buddhism; Their History,
B   Iconography, and Progressive Evolution through the
        Northern Buddhist Countries. Rutland, Vt.: Tuttle, 1962
        (orig. pub. by Oxford, 1914). 220 pp. 62-13617. (R).
        JAS, 8/63

0248 Gibert, Lucien. Dictionnaire Historique et Geographique
C   de la Mandchourie. Hong Kong: La Societe des Missions-
        Etrangeres, 1934. 1040 pp. AC35-2634.
        Hucker, 127

1675 Gibney, Frank. Five Gentlemen of Japan; The Portrait of a
B   Nation's Character. N.Y.: Farrar, Straus & Young, 1953.
        373 pp. 53-7052. o.p.
        AUFS, 234; Silberman, 1383; Library Journal, 2/1/53; Pacific
        Affairs, 9/53; TLS, 9/11/53

1698 Gikeiki. Yoshitsune; A Fifteenth-Century Japanese Chronicle.
B   tr. with intro. by Helen Craig McCullough. Stanford, Calif.:
        Stanford University Press, 1966. 367 pp. (UNESCO Collec-
        tion of Representative Works: Japanese Series). 65-19810.
        Sup. 67, 3219; Choice, 11/66; JAS, 11/67; Library Journal,
        8/66

0249 Giles, Herbert Allen. A Chinese Biographical Dictionary. N.Y.:
C   Burt Franklin, 1966 (orig. pub. by Kelly & Walsh, 1898).
        Hand catalog. (R).
        Hucker, 91

0250 Giles, Herbert Allen. A Chinese-English Dictionary. 2d ed.
C   rev. and enl. N.Y.: Paragon, 1964 (orig. pub. by Kelly &
        Walsh, 1912). 2 v. 64-8885. (R).
        Hucker, 87

0924 Giles, Herbert Allen, ed. and tr. Gems of Chinese Literature,
B   in Two Volumes Bound as One. 2d rev. and enl. ed. N.Y.:
        Paragon, 1965 (orig. pub. by Kelly & Walsh, 1923). 430 pp.
        64-18450. (R).
        Hucker, 1575; Choice, 4/67

1014 Giles, Herbert Allen. A History of Chinese Literature. N.Y.:
B   Ungar, 1966. 498 pp. 66-26507. (M-University).
        AUFS, 1055

0597 Gillin, Donald G. Warlord: Yen Hsi-shan in Shansi Province,
A   1911-1950. Princeton, N.J.: Princeton University Press,
        1967. 334 pp. 66-14308.
        Choice, 9/67; JAS, 2/68; Ann. Am. Acad., 9/67

2079 Ginsburg, Norton Sydney. The Economic Resources and Development
C   of Formosa. N.Y.: International Secretariat, Institute of
        Pacific Relations, 1953. 58 pp. 54-995. o.p.
        Hucker, 2184

0076 Ginsburg, Norton Sydney. Pattern of Asia. Englewood Cliffs,
A   N.J.: Prentice-Hall, 1958. 929 pp. 58-8513.
        AUFS, 23; Hucker, 49; JAS, 11/58

0762 Ginsburgs, George. Communist China and Tibet; The First Dozen
A   Years. The Hague: M. Nijhoff, 1964. 218 pp. 65-84502.
        JAS, 11/65

0838 Gittings, John. The Role of the Chinese Army. N.Y.: Oxford for
B   Royal Institute of International Affairs, 1967. 331 pp.
        67-80303.
        Sup. 67, 3238; Choice, 3/68; AHR, 2/68; Library Journal,
        8/67; TLS, 1/18/68

0763 Gluckstein, Ygael. Mao's China; Economic and Political Survey.
B   Chester Springs, Pa.: Dufour, 1957. 438 pp. 57-3556.
        AUFS, 928; Hucker, 1948; TLS, 10/11/57

1294 Goepper, Roger. The Essence of Chinese Painting. tr. by Michael
A   Bullock. London: Lund Humphries, 1963. 244 pp. 65-829.
        o.p.

1154 Goldman, Merle. Literary Dissent in Communist China.
A   Cambridge, Mass.: Harvard University Press, 1967.
        343 pp. (Harvard East Asian Series, 29). 67-17311.
        Choice, 5/68; JAS, 5/68

1450 Golovnin, Vasilii Mikhailovich. Narrative of My Captivity
C   in Japan, during the Years 1811, 1812 and 1813. London:
        Printed for H. Colburn, 1818. 2 v. 4-28643. o.p.

1982 Gompertz, Godfrey St. George Montague. Bibliography of Western
C   Literature on Korea from the Earliest Times until 1950.
        Seoul: Korea Branch, Royal Asiatic Society, 1963. (Trans-
        actions, Vol. XL).

2022 Goodrich, Leland Matthew. Korea; A Study of U.S. Policy in
B   the United Nations. N.Y.: Council on Foreign Relations,
        1956. 235 pp. 56-9751. o.p. (M-University).
        AUFS, 536; Silberman, 1794; sJAS, 2/58; Library Journal,
        9/15/56

0473 Goodrich, Luther Carrington. The Literary Inquisition of
B   Ch'ien-lung. 2d ed. with addenda and corrigenda. N.Y.:
        Paragon, 1966 (orig. pub. by Waverly Press, 1935). 275 pp.
        66-11100. (R). (M-University).
        Sup. 67, 3239; Hucker, 511; JAOS, 12/35

0338 Goodrich, Luther Carrington. A Short History of the Chinese
C   People. 3d ed. N.Y.: Harper, 1959. 295 pp. 59-7025.
        AUFS, 681; Hucker, 99; FEQ, 5/44

0339 Goodrich, Luther Carrington. A Syllabus of the History of Chinese
B   Civilization and Culture. 6th ed. N.Y.: China Society of
        America, 1958. 59 pp. A60-3148. o.p.
        Sup. 61, 2796; Hucker, 13; FEQ, 2/42

0598 Gould, Randall. China in the Sun. Garden City, N.Y.: Double-
B   day, 1946. 403 pp. 46-317. o.p.
        Hucker, 740; FEQ, 8/46; Am. Pol. Sci. R., 8/46

1676 Grad, Andrew Jonah. Land and Peasant in Japan; An Introductory
C   Survey. N.Y.: International Secretariat, Institute of
        Pacific Relations, 1952. 262 pp. 52-12003 rev. o.p.
        (M-University).
        Silberman, 1566; FEQ, 5/53

1995 Grad, Andrew Jonah. Modern Korea. N.Y.: John Day for Inter-
C   national Secretariat, Institute of Pacific Relations, 1944.
        330 pp. 44-47020. o.p.
        AUFS, 537; Silberman, 1910; FEQ, 11/45; Pacific Affairs,
        3/45

0959 Graham, Angus Charles, ed. and tr. Poems of the Late T'ang.
A   Baltimore: Penguin, 1965. 173 pp. (UNESCO Collection
        of Representative Works: Chinese Series). 66-804.
        Choice, 10/66; JAOS, 7-9/66

1201 Graham, Angus Charles. Two Chinese Philosophers: Ch'eng Ming-tao
B   and Ch'eng Yi-ch'uan. London: Lund Humphries, 1958. 195 pp.
        59-33740. o.p.
        Hucker, 1149; JAS, 11/59; JAOS, 4-6/59

0372 Granet, Marcel. Chinese Civilization. tr. by Kathleen E.
A   Innes and Mabel R. Brailsford. N.Y.: Meridian, 1958.
        444 pp. 58-8529. o.p.
        Hucker, 181; JAOS, 6/31

0373 Granet, Marcel. Festivals and Songs of Ancient China. N.Y.:
A   Dutton, 1932. 281 pp. 33-4631. o.p.
        Hucker, 2004; JAOS, 3/34; TLS, 4/28/32

1176 Granet, Marcel. La Pensee Chinoise. Paris: La Renaissance
B   du Livre, 1934. 614 pp. 34-13974.

1295 Gray, Basil. Buddhist Cave Paintings at Tun-huang. Chicago:
C   University of Chicago Press, 1959. 86 pp. 59-5771. o.p.
        Hucker, 1482

0764 Great Cultural Revolution in China. comp. and ed. by the
C   Asia Research Centre. Rutland, Vt.: Tuttle, 1968.
        507 pp. 67-8722.
        Choice, 9/68

1792 Green Hill Poems, by Kiyoshi Sato (and others). Tokyo: Hoku-
C   seido, 1953. 182 pp. 55-42250.
        Silberman, 1084

0474 Greenberg, Michael. British Trade and the Opening of China,
A   1800-42. Cambridge: University, 1951. 238 pp. A52-9218.
        o.p.
        AUFS, 743; Hucker, 561; FEQ, 11/51; Am. Econ. R., 9/52;
        Pacific Affairs, 12/52

0765 Greene, Felix. Awakened China; The Country Americans Don't
C   Know. Garden City, N.Y.: Doubleday, 1961. 425 pp. 61-9512.
        JAS, 8/62; Library Journal, 11/15/61

0766 Greene, Felix. A Curtain of Ignorance; How the American
C   Public has been Misinformed about China. Garden City,
        N.Y.: Doubleday, 1964. 340 pp. 64-11717.
        Choice, 12/64; Library Journal, 9/1/64

0054 Greene, Fred. U.S. Policy and the Security of Asia. N.Y.:
C   McGraw-Hill for Council on Foreign Relations, 1968. 429 pp.

(Council on Foreign Relations/United States and China in World Affairs). 68-11606.
Choice, 7-8/68.

1332 Gregg, Alice Henrietta. China and Educational Autonomy; The
B Changing Role of the Protestant Educational Missionary in China, 1807-1937. Syracuse, N.Y.: Syracuse University Press, 1946. 285 pp. A47-3119. o.p. (M-University).

1509 Grew, Joseph Clark. Ten Years in Japan, a Contemporary Record
B Drawn from Diaries and Private and Official Papers. Joseph C. Grew, United States Ambassador to Japan, 1932-1942. N.Y.: Simon & Schuster, 1944. 554 pp. 44-40123. o.p. AUFS, 235; Silberman, 519; FEQ, 11/44; Am. Pol. Sci. R., 10/44; Library Journal, 5/1/44; TLS, 9/23/44

1510 Grew, Joseph Clark. Turbulent Era; A Diplomatic Record
B of Forty Years, 1904-1945. Boston: Houghton Mifflin, 1952. 2 v. 52-5262. o.p. AUFS, 306; Silberman, 518; AHR, 7/53; Ann. Am. Acad., 3/53; TLS, 4/17/53

1318 Grey, Beryl. Through the Bamboo Curtain. N.Y.: Reynal, dist.
C by Morrow, 1966. 127 pp. 66-5581. Choice, 3/67

1402 Griffis, William Elliot. The Mikado's Empire. 12th ed.
B N.Y.: Harper, 1913. 2 v. 13-3305. o.p.

1511 Griffis, William Elliot. The Mikado: Institution and Person,
C a Study of the International Political Forces of Japan. Princeton, N.J.: Princeton University Press, 1915. 346 pp. 15-24757. o.p.

1812 Griffis, William Elliot. The Religions of Japan, from the
C Dawn of History to the Era of the Meiji. N.Y.: Scribner's, 1895. 457 pp. 4-4213. o.p. (M-University).

1451 Griffis, William Elliot. Townsend Harris, First American
B Envoy in Japan. Boston: Houghton Mifflin, 1895. 351 pp. 4-17023. o.p. (M-University).

0839 Griffith, Samuel B. The Chinese People's Liberation Army.
B N.Y.: McGraw-Hill, 1967. 398 pp. (Council on Foreign Relations/United States and China in World Affairs). 67-16302. Choice, 11/67; Ann. Am. Acad., 11/67; Library Journal, 6/15/67; Pacific Affairs, Fall-Winter/67-68; TLS, 8/25/68

0767 Griffith, Samuel B. Peking and People's Wars; An Analysis
B of Statements by Official Spokesmen of the Chinese Communist Party on the Subject of Revolutionary Strategy. N.Y.: Praeger, 1966. 142 pp. 66-18902. Choice, 4/67; Library Journal, 10/15/66

0768 Griffith, William E. The Sino-Soviet Rift, Analyzed and
B Documented. Cambridge, Mass.: M.I.T. Press, 1964. 508 pp. (Center for International Studies, Studies in International Communism). 63-22708. Sup. 65, 5796; Choice, 7-8/65; Library Journal, 1/15/65; TLS, 12/31/64

0475 Grimm, Tilemann. Erziehung und Politik im Konfuzianischen China
C der Ming-Zeit, 1368-1644. Hamburg: Gesellschaft fur Natur- und Volkerkunde Ostasiens, 1960. 176 pp. (Mitteilungen der Gesellschaft fur Natur- und Volkerkunde Ostasiens, XXXV B). Hand catalog. Hucker, 445; JAS, 11/60

0079 Griswold, Alfred Whitney. The Far Eastern Policy of the United
B States. New Haven, Conn.: Yale University Press, 1964 (orig. pub. by Harcourt, Brace, 1938). 530 pp. 62-809. (R). AUFS, 88; Hucker, 808; Silberman, 431; Choice, 2/65

1432 Groot, Gerard. The Prehistory of Japan. ed. by Bertram S.
C Kraus. N.Y.: Columbia University Press, 1951. 128 pp. 51-11028. o.p. Silberman, 173; FEQ, 2/52; JAOS, 10-12/52

1177 Groot, Jan Jakob Maria de. The Religious System of China; Its
C Ancient Forms, Evolution, History and Present Aspect, Manners, Customs and Social Institutions Connected Therewith. N.Y.: Paragon, 1964 (orig. pub. by Brill, 1892-1910). 6 v. NUC 65-90096. (R). Hucker, 1059

1178 Groot, Jan Jakob Maria de. Sectarianism and Religious Perse-
C cution in China. N.Y.: Paragon, 1963 (orig. pub. by Johannes Muller, 1903-04). 2 v. NUC 65-51769. (R).

Hucker, 1071

1264 Grousset, Rene. Chinese Art and Culture. tr. by Haakon Che-
B valier. N.Y.: Orion, 1959. 331 pp. 59-13323. o.p. Hucker, 1402; Library Journal, 1/15/60; Pacific Affairs, 9/60; TLS, 3/4/60

0055 Grousset, Rene. The Civilizations of the East. tr. from French
A by Catherine Alison Phillips. N.Y.: Cooper Square, 1967 (orig. pub. by Knopf, 1931-34). 4 v. 66-30807. (R). (M-University). AUFS, 24; Choice, 3/69; FEQ, 8/42; TLS, 11/1/34

0374 Grousset, Rene. L'Empire des Steppes: Attila, Gengis-Khan, Tam-
C erlan. 4th ed. Paris: Payot, 1960. Hand catalog. o.p. Hucker, 123

0056 Grousset, Rene. Histoire de l'Extreme-Orient. Paris:
B Geuthner, 1929. 2 v. 30-9378. AUFS, 89

0173 Grousset, Rene. Histoire de La Philosophie Orientale. Paris:
C Nouvelle Librairie Nationale, 1923. 376 pp.

0340 Grousset, Rene. The Rise and Splendour of the Chinese Empire.
A tr. from French by Anthony Watson-Gandy and Terence Gordon. Berkeley: University of California Press, 1953. 312 pp. A53-9939. Hucker, 101; FEQ, 11/53; AHR, 10/53; Library Journal, 5/15/53; Pacific Affairs, 6/53; TLS, 5/9/52

1512 Gubbins, John Harington. The Making of Modern Japan, an
C Account of the Progress of Japan from Pre-feudal Days to Constitutional Government and the Position of a Great Power, with Chapters on Religion, the Complex Family System, Education, etc. New Hyde Park, N.Y.: University Books, 1966 (orig. pub. by Seeley, Service, 1922). 316 pp. 23-5147. (R).

0769 Guillain, Robert. 600 Million Chinese. tr. by Mervyn Savill.
B N.Y.: Criterion, 1957. 310 pp. 57-8260. AUFS, 929; Hucker, 963; Library Journal, 9/15/57

1296 Gulik, Robert Hans van. Chinese Pictorial Art as Viewed by the
C Connoisseur, Notes on the Means and Methods of Traditional Chinese Connoisseurship of Pictorial Art, Based upon a Study of the Art of Mounting Scrolls in China and Japan. Roma: Isituto Italiano per il Medio ed Estremo Oriente, 1958. 537 pp. 59-31931. Hucker, 1473

0960 Gulik, Robert Hans van. Hsi K'ang and his Poetical Essay on
C the Lute. Tokyo: Sophia University, 1941. 90 pp. 42-4465. Hucker, 1590; JAOS, 12/41

1319 Gulik, Robert Hans van. The Lore of the Chinese Lute; An Essay
C in Ch'in Ideology. Tokyo: Sophia University, 1940. 224 pp. 41-12381. Hucker, 1778; JAOS, 12/41

1813 Gundert, Wilhelm. Japanische Religionsgeschichte, die Reli-
C gionen der Japaner und Koreaner in Geschichtlichen Abriss Dargestellt. Tokyo: Japanisch-Deutches Kulturinstitut, 1935. 267 pp. 36-6168. Silberman, 592

1630 Hadley, Eleanor M. Antitrust in Japan. Princeton, N.J.:
B Princeton University Press, 1969. 985 pp. 68-56312.

1433 Haguenauer, Charles. Origines de la Civilisation Japonais;
B Introduction a l'Etude de la Prehistoire du Japon. Paris: Imprimerie Nationale, 1956- 58-15251. Silberman, 175; JAS, 2/60

2023 Hahm, Pyong-choon. The Korean Political Tradition and Law.
C Seoul: Hollym Corporation, 1967. 249 pp. (Royal Asiatic Society, Korea Branch, Monograph Series, No. 1). 68-2912. JAS, 11/68

0599 Hahn, Emily. Chiang Kai-shek, an Unauthorized Biography.
C Garden City, N.Y.: Doubleday, 1955. 382 pp. 55-5582. o.p. (M-University). Hucker, 767; Library Journal, 3/1/55

0600 Hahn, Emily. The Soong Sisters. Garden City, N.Y.: Double-
C day, 1943. 349 pp. 43-3571 rev. o.p. Hucker, 781

0080 Hall, Daniel George Edward. A History of South-East Asia.
B 3d ed. N.Y.: St. Martin's, 1968. 807 pp. 68-15302.

AUFS, 1279; Hucker, 117; FEQ, 5/56; Ann. Am. Acad., 5/56; Library Journal, 12/1/55; Pol. Sci. Q., 6/56; TLS, 11/18/55

1452 Hall, John Whitney. Government and Local Power in Japan,
A   500 to 1700, a Study Based on Bizen Province. Princeton,
      N.J.: Princeton University Press, 1966. 446 pp. 65-14307.
      Choice, 9/66; JAS, 11/66; AHR, 10/66; Am. Pol. Sci.
      R., 12/66; Ann. Am. Acad., 11/66; Japan Q., 10-12/66; Library
      Journal, 2/15/66; Pacific Affairs, Fall-Winter/66-67

1373 Hall, John Whitney. Japanese History; A Guide to Japanese
C   Reference and Research Materials. Ann Arbor: University
      of Michigan Press, 1954. 165 pp. (Center for Japanese
      Studies. Bibliography Series). 54-62413. o.p.
      Sup. 61, 2762; Silberman, 163

1374 Hall, John Whitney. Japanese History; New Dimensions of
B   Approach and Understanding. Washington: Service Center
      for Teachers of History, 1961. 63 pp. (Publication No. 34).
      61-9919. o.p.
      Sup. 61, 2763; Silberman, 144

1453 Hall, John Whitney, comp. Studies in the Institutional History
C   of Early Modern Japan. Princeton, N.J.: Princeton Uni-
      versity Press, 1968. 396 pp. 68-15766.

1454 Hall, John Whitney. Tanuma Okitsugu, 1719-1788, Forerunner
B   of Modern Japan. Cambridge, Mass.: Harvard University
      Press, 1955. 208 pp. 52-5396.
      AUFS, 192; Silberman, 247; FEQ, 5/56; AHR, 4/56; JAOS,
      1-3/56; Pacific Affairs, 9/56

1403 Hall, John Whitney. Twelve Doors to Japan. N.Y.: McGraw-
A   Hill, 1965. 649 pp. 64-66015.
      Choice, 2/66; JAS, 11/66; Am. Anthropologist, 6/66;
      Am. Pol. Sci. R., 12/66; Library Journal, 3/1/66;
      Pacific Affairs, Spring-Summer/66

1972 Hall, Robert King. Education for a New Japan. New Haven,
B   Conn.: Yale University Press, 1949. 503 pp. 49-9201. o.p.
      (M-University).
      Silberman, 1472; FEQ, 8/50; Pacific Affairs, 3/50

1973 Hall, Robert King. Shushin: the Ethics of a Defeated Nation.
B   N.Y.: Bureau of Publications, Teachers College, Columbia
      University, 1949. 244 pp. 49-10209. o.p.
      Silberman, 1471; FEQ, 11/50

0770 Halperin, Morton H. China and the Bomb. N.Y.: Praeger for
B   the Center for International Affairs and East Asian
      Research Center, Harvard University, 1965. 166 pp.
      65-15646.
      Sup. 65, 3094; Choice, 6/65; Am. Pol. Sci. R., 12/65;
      Ann. Am. Acad., 3/66; Library Journal, 3/15/65

0771 Halperin, Morton H. Communist China and Arms Control. N.Y.:
B   Praeger, 1965. 191 pp. (Praeger Special Studies in Inter-
      national Politics and Public Affairs). 65-26757.
      Choice, 5/66; JAS, 11/66; Ann. Am. Acad., 5/66

0772 Halpern, Abraham Meyer, ed. Policies Toward China; Views from
A   Six Continents. N.Y.: McGraw-Hill, 1965. 528 pp. (United
      States and China in World Affairs). 65-24892.
      Choice, 10/66; JAS, 2/67; AHR, 10/66; Library Journal,
      1/15/66

1015 Halson, Elizabeth. Peking Opera; A Short Guide. N.Y.: Oxford,
B   1966. 92 pp. 66-31690/MN.
      JAS, 8/67

1256 Han, Fei. The Complete Works of Han Fei Tzu...A Classic of
B   Chinese Legalism. tr. from Chinese with intro. and notes
      by W. K. Liao. London: A. Probsthain, 1939- 41-11756.
      o.p.
      Hucker, 1228; JAS, 11/60

0961 Han-shan. Cold Mountain; 100 Poems by the T'ang Poet Han-shan.
B   tr. and with intro. by Burton Watson. N.Y.: Grove, 1962.
      122 pp. 62-15847. o.p.
      JAS, 8/63; JAOS, 10-12/62

0601 Han, Suyin, pseud. Birdless Summer; China: Autobiography,
C   History. N.Y.: Putnam, 1968. 347 pp. 68-25435.

0602 Han, Suyin, pseud. The Crippled Tree: China, Biography, History,
C   Autobiography. N.Y.: Putnam, 1965. 461 pp. 65-20715. o.p.
      Library Journal, 11/15/65; TLS, 11/11/65

0603 Han, Suyin, pseud. A Mortal Flower; China: Autobiography, His-
C   tory. N.Y.: Putnam, 1966. 412 pp. 66-20297. o.p.

Library Journal, 11/1/66

0962 Han, Ying. Han Shih Wai Chuan: Han Ying's Illustrations of
C   the Didactic Application of the Classic of Songs. tr.
      by James Robert Hightower. Cambridge, Mass.: Harvard
      University Press, 1952. 368 pp. 52-9389.
      Hucker, 1657

0375 Han, Yu. The Veritable Record of the T'ang Emperor Shun-tsung,
B   February 28, 805 - August 31, 805: Han Yu's Shun-tsung shih-
      lu. tr. with intro. and notes by Bernard S. Soloman. Cam-
      bridge, Mass.: Harvard University Press, 1955. 82 pp.
      55-9441.
      Hucker, 307; FEQ, 2/56; JAOS, 1-3/56

1889 Harada, Jiro. A Glimpse of Japanese Ideals; Lectures on
B   Japanese Art and Culture. Tokyo: Japan Kokusai Bunka Shin-
      kokai, 1937. 239 pp. 38-15940.
      AUFS, 389

1854 Harada, Jiro. Japanese Gardens. Boston: T. Branford, 1956.
A   160 pp. 56-12490.
      Silberman, 830; JAS, 2/58

1958 Harich-Schneider, Eta. The Rhythmical Patterns in Gagaku and
C   Bugaku. Leiden: Brill, 1954. 109 pp. A56-2858.
      Silberman, 1174

2012 Harrington, Fred Harvey. God, Mammon, and the Japanese:
C   Dr. Horace N. Allen and Korean-American Relations,
      1884-1905. Madison: University of Wisconsin Press, 1944.
      362 pp. 44-2219.
      Silberman, 1816; FEQ, 8/44; AHR, 10/44; Am. Pol. Sci. R.,
      12/44; Ann. Am. Acad., 7/44; Pacific Affairs, 7/30/44;
      Pol. Sci. Q., 6/44

1455 Harris, Townsend. The Complete Journal of Townsend Harris,
A   First American Consul and Minister to Japan. intro. and
      notes by Mario Emilio Cosenza. 2d rev. ed. Rutland, Vt.:
      Tuttle, 1959. 616 pp. 59-9397.
      Silberman, 312

0963 Hart, Henry Hersch, comp. and tr. A Chinese Market; Lyrics
C   from the Chinese in English Verse, by Henry H. Hart. fore.
      by E. T. Werner. Peking: French Bookstore, 1931. 101 pp.
      32-34108. o.p.

0032 Harvard Journal of Asiatic Studies, v.1- 1936- (R-Micro-
A   photo, M-IDC).
      AUFS, 25; Hucker, 28; Silberman, 31

0316 Harvard University. East Asian Research Center. Papers on
A   China. Cambridge, Mass.: Harvard University Committee on
      Regional Studies (since 1957, Center for East Asian Studies),
      n.d. 56-2493 rev. 2.
      Hucker, 614

1404 Harvard University. East Asian Research Center. Papers on
C   Japan. Cambridge, Mass., 1961- 59-2493 rev. 2.

1677 Hasegawa, Nyozekan. The Japanese Character; A Cultural
C   Profile. tr. by J. Bester. Palo Alto, Calif.: Kodansha,
      1966. 157 pp. (Japanese National Commission for UNESCO
      Publication). 66-19819.
      Choice, 2/67; Japan Q., 10-12/66

1758 Hasegawa, Tatsunosuke. An Adopted Husband (Sono Omokage). tr.
C   from the original Japanese of Futabei, by Buchachiro Mitzui
      and Gregg M. Sinclair. N.Y.: Knopf, 1919. 275 pp. 19-10549
      rev. o.p. (M-University).

1759 Hasegawa, Tatsunosuke. Mediocrity. tr. from Japanese by
C   Glenn W. Shaw. Tokyo: Hokuseido, 1927. 195 pp. Hand
      catalog.

1959 Hattori, Ryuttaro, comp. Japanese Folk-Songs with Piano
B   Accompaniment. 4th ed. Tokyo: Japan Times, 1960.
      Silberman, 1180

0604 Hauser, Ernest O. Shanghai; City for Sale. N.Y.: Harcourt,
C   Brace, 1940. 323 pp. 40-6570 rev. o.p.
      Am. Pol. Sci. R., 10/40; Pacific Affairs, 9/40

1016 Hawkes, David. A Little Primer of Tu Fu. Oxford: Clarendon,
B   1967. 243 pp. 67-105047.
      JAS, 11/68; TLS, 9/28/67

1760 Hayashi, Fumiko. Floating Cloud (Ukigumo). tr. by Y. Koita-
C   bashi. Tokyo: Information, 1957. 110 pp. A58-5446.
      Silberman, 1007

87

1456 Hayashi, Tadasu. The Secret Memoirs of Count Tadasu Hayashi
C   (1850-1913). ed. by A. M. Pooley. N.Y.: Putnam, 1915.
     331 pp. 15-s6413. o.p.
     Silberman, 410

1405 Hearn, Lafcadio. Glimpses of Unfamiliar Japan. N.Y.: AMS,
B   1968 (orig. pub. by Houghton Mifflin, 1894). 2 v.
     4-16699. (R).

1406 Hearn, Lafcadio. Japan, an Attempt at Interpretation. Rut-
B   land, Vt.: Tuttle, 1955. 498 pp. 56-249 rev.
     AUFS, 194

2024 Heinl, Robert Debs, Jr. Victory at High Tide; The Inchon-
C   Seoul Campaign. Philadelphia: Lippincott, 1968. 315 pp.
     (Great Battles of History). 68-11129.
     Choice, 11/68; Library Journal, 12/15/67

1591 Henderson, Dan Fenno. Conciliation and Japanese Law, Tokugawa
C   and Modern. Seattle: University of Washington Press, 1965.
     2 v. (Association for Asian Studies, Monographs and Papers,
     XIII). 64-18425.
     JAS, 5/66; JAOS, 10-12/65

2042 Henderson, Gregory. Korea, the Politics of the Vortex.
A   Cambridge, Mass.: Harvard University Press, 1968. 479 pp.
     68-25611.
     Choice, 2/69; JAS, 2/69

1375 Henderson, Harold Gould. Handbook of Japanese Grammar.
B   rev. ed. Boston: Houghton Mifflin, 1948. 360 pp. 48-4731.
     Silberman, 135

1718 Henderson, Harold Gould, ed. and tr. An Introduction to Haiku;
A   An Anthology of Poems and Poets from Basho to Shiki. Garden
     City, N.Y.: Doubleday, 1958. 179 pp. 58-11314.
     AUFS, 430; Silberman, 1060; JAS, 8/59; Library Journal,
     1/15/59

1820 Herbert, Jean. Shinto; At the Fountain-head of Japan. pref.
C   by Yukitada Sasaki. N.Y.: Stein and Day, 1967. 622 pp.
     66-24531.
     Choice, 11/67; Library Journal, 6/15/67

1890 Herberts, Kurt. Oriental Lacquer; Art and Technique.
C   London: Thames & Hudson, 1962. 513 pp. Hand catalog.

0251 Herrmann, Albert. An Historical Atlas of China. new ed.
A   Chicago: Aldine, 1966 (orig. pub. by Harvard, 1935 as
     Historical and Commercial Atlas of China). 88 pp. Map
     65-13. (R).
     Hucker, 95; Choice, 12/67; JAS, 8/67; AHR, 1/37; JAOS, 6/37;
     TLS, 8/29/36

1017 Hervouet, Y. Un Poete de Cour Sous les Han: Sseu-ma Siang-
C   jou. Paris: Presses Universitaires, 1964. 478 pp.
     67-39197.

1333 Hevi, Emmanuel John. An African Student in China. N.Y.:
B   Praeger, 1963. 220 pp. 63-18529.
     JAS, 2/65; China Q., 1-3/65

1631 Hewes, Laurence Ilsley. Japan: Land and Men, an Account
C   of the Japanese Land Reform Program, 1945-51. Ames:
     Iowa State College Press, 1955. 154 pp. 55-9962 rev.
     o.p.
     Silberman, 572; FEQ, 8/56

1746 Hibbett, Howard. The Floating World in Japanese Fiction. N.Y.:
A   Oxford, 1959. 232 pp. 59-3936. o.p.
     Silberman, 910; JAS, 5/60; Japan Q., 1-3/60

0208 Hightower, James Robert. Topics in Chinese Literature; Out-
A   lines and Bibliographies. rev. ed. Cambridge, Mass.:
     Harvard University Press, 1953. 141 pp. 53-5058.
     AUFS, 1041; Hucker, 1518; FEQ, 2/51; JAOS, 1-3/51

1912 Hillier, Jack Ronald. Japanese Colour Prints. London: Phai-
B   don, dist. by Praeger, 1966. 87 pp. 67-31916.
     Choice, 5/67

1913 Hillier, Jack Ronald. The Japanese Print: a New Approach.
B   Rutland, Vt.: Tuttle, 1960. 184 pp. 60-51853.
     JAS, 5/62

0773 Hinton, Harold C. China's Relations with Burma and Vietnam;
B   A Brief Survey. N.Y.: International Secretariat, Institute
     of Pacific Relations, 1958. 64 pp. 58-2644. o.p.
     Hucker, 990; JAS, 5/59

0774 Hinton, Harold C. Communist China in World Politics. Boston:
B   Houghton Mifflin, 1966. 527 pp. 66-400.
     Sup. 67, 3241; Choice, 6/66; JAS, 2/67; Library Journal,
     5/15/66

0014 Hinton, Harold C., ed. Major Topics on China and Japan; A Hand-
B   book for Teachers. ed. by Harold C. Hinton and Marius B.
     Jansen. N.Y.: Institute of Pacific Relations, 1957. 326 pp.
     57-4216. o.p. (M-University).
     AUFS, 91; Hucker, 5; JAS, 8/58

0907 Hinton, William. Fanshen; A Documentary of Revolution in a
C   Chinese Village. N.Y.: Monthly Review Press, 1967. 637 pp.
     66-23525.
     Choice, 7-8/67; JAS, 2/68; Library Journal, 3/1/67

1632 Hirschmeier, Johannes. The Origins of Entrepreneurship in
B   Meiji Japan. Cambridge, Mass.: Harvard University
     Press, 1964. 354 pp. (Harvard University East Asian
     Research Center. Harvard East Asian Studies, 17). 64-20973.
     Sup. 65, 3058; Choice, 2/65; JAS, 11/65; Am. Econ. R.,
     9/65; AHR, 4/65; Library Journal, 9/15/64

0154 Ho, Alfred Kuo-liang. The Far East in World Trade; Develop-
C   ments and Growth since 1945. N.Y.: Praeger, 1967. 388 pp.
     (Praeger Special Studies in International Economics and
     Development). 68-14159.
     Choice, 7-8/68; Pacific Affairs, Fall/68

1136 Ho, Ching-chih. The White-Haired Girl; An Opera in Five Acts.
B   tr. by Yang Hsien-yi and Gladys Yang. Peking: Foreign Lan-
     guages Press, 1954. 97 pp. 55-29783. o.p.
     AUFS, 1129; Hucker, 1758

0605 Ho, Kan-chih. A History of the Modern Chinese Revolution.
C   Peking: Foreign Languages Press, 1959. 627 pp. 60-3095.
     Hucker, 902

0476 Ho, Ping-ti. The Ladder of Success in Imperial China; Aspects
A   of Social Mobility, 1368-1911. N.Y.: Columbia University
     Press, 1962. 385 pp. 62-10451.
     JAS, 11/64; AHR, 10/63; Am. Soc. R., 8/63; Ann. Am. Acad.,
     7/63; TLS, 11/14/63

0887 Ho, Ping-ti. Studies on the Population of China, 1368-1953.
A   Cambridge, Mass.: Harvard University Press, 1959. 341 pp.
     (Harvard East Asian Series, 4). 59-12970.
     Sup. 63, 2913; Hucker, 2186; JAS, 5/62; AHR, 4/60; Ann. Am.
     Acad., 9/60; Library Journal, 1/1/60; Pol. Sci. Q., 12/60;
     TLS, 3/25/60

1223 Ho-Shang-Kung, pseud. Commentary on Lao-tse. tr. and annotated
C   by Eduard Erkes. Ascona: Artibus Asiae, 1958. 135 pp.
     Hand catalog.
     Hucker, 1192

1018 Ho, Shih-chun. Jou Lin Wai Che, le Roman des Lettres; Etudes
C   sur un Roman Satirique Chinois. Paris: L. Rodstein, 1933.
     207 pp.
     Hucker, 1691

2080 Ho, Yhi-Min. Agricultural Development of Taiwan, 1903-
B   1960. Nashville, Tenn.: Vanderbilt University Press,
     1966. 172 pp. 66-25966.
     Choice, 9/67; JAS, 8/67

1257 Hodous, Lewis. Folkways in China. London: A. Probsthain,
C   1929. 248 pp. 29-12220. o.p.
     Hucker, 1084; JAOS, 6/30

0606 Holcombe, Arthur Norman. The Chinese Revolution; A Phase in
B   the Regeneration of a World Power. Cambridge, Mass.: Har-
     vard University Press, 1930. 401 pp. 30-5261. o.p.
     AHR, 10/30; Am. Pol. Sci. R., 5/30; Ann. Am. Acad., 11/30

0103 Holcombe, Arthur Norman. The Spirit of the Chinese Revolution;
C   Lowell Institute Lectures, 1930. N.Y.: Knopf, 1930. 185 pp.
     30-25102. o.p.
     Hucker, 731; Am. Pol. Sci. R., 2/31

0607 Holden, Reuben Andrus. Yale in China; The Mainland, 1901-1951.
B   New Haven, Conn.: Yale in China Association, dist. by Human
     Relations Area Files, 1964. 327 pp. 64-25916.

1633 Hollerman, Leon. Japan's Dependence on the World Economy;
B   The Approach Toward Economic Liberalization. Princeton,
     N.J.: Princeton University Press, 1967. 291 pp. 66-26586.
     Choice, 4/68; JAS, 5/68; Pacific Affairs, Spring/68

1914 Holloway, Owen E. Graphic Art of Japan; The Classical School.
C   London: A. Tiranti, 1957. 135 pp. A58-3264.
     Japan Q., 1-3/58

1821 Holtom, Daniel Clarence. Modern Japan and Shinto Nationalism;
B   A Study of Present-day Trends in Japanese Religions.
     rev. ed. N.Y.: Paragon, 1963 (orig. pub. by University
     of Chicago Press, 1947). 226 pp. 66-22615. (R).
     Sup. 65, 3059; JAS, 11/64; FEQ, 8/43

1822 Holtom, Daniel Clarence. The National Faith of Japan; A
B   Study in Modern Shinto. N.Y.: Paragon, 1965 (orig.
     pub. by Dutton, 1938). 329 pp. 65-26102. (R).
     AUFS, 134; Silberman, 607; JAOS, 12/40; J. Religion, 7/38

1019 Holzman, Donald. La Vie et la Pensee de Hi K'ang (223-262).
B   Leiden: Brill, 1957. 186 pp. A59-4991.
     Hucker, 250; JAS, 5/64

1077 Homeward Journey and Other Stories, by Contemporary Chinese
C   Writers. tr. by Gladys Yang. Peking: Foreign Languages
     Press, 1957. 234 pp. 58-15367. o.p.

1283 Honey, William Bowyer. The Ceramic Art of China, and Other
A   Countries of the Far East. London: Faber & Faber, 1945.
     238 pp. 45-10141. o.p.
     AUFS, 1011; Hucker, 1431; Silberman, 848

1457 Honjo, Eijiro. Economic Theory and History of Japan in the
C   Tokugawa Period. N.Y.: Russell & Russell, 1965 (orig.
     pub. by Maruzen, 1943). 350 pp. 65-18808. (R).
     Silberman, 272

1419 Honjo, Eijiro. The Social and Economic History of Japan.
B   N.Y.: Russell & Russell, 1965 (orig. pub. by Kyoto
     Institute for Research in Economic History of Japan,
     1935). 410 pp. 65-18809. (R).
     AUFS, 165; Silberman, 230

1814 Hori, Ichiro. Folk Religion in Japan: Continuity and Change.
B   ed. by Joseph M. Kitagawa and Alan L. Miller. Chicago: Uni-
     versity of Chicago Press, 1968. 278 pp. 67-30128.
     JAS, 2/69; Library Journal, 8/68

1855 Horiguchi, Sutemi. Tradition of Japanese Garden. 2d ed. Hono-
C   lulu: East-West Center Press, 1963. 185 pp. 64-2824.
     Library Journal, 5/15/64

0477 Hou, Chi-ming. Foreign Investment and Economic Development
A   in China, 1840-1937. Cambridge, Mass.: Harvard Univer-
     sity Press, 1965. 306 pp. (Harvard East Asian Series, 21).
     65-22069.
     Choice, 9/66; JAS, 2/67; AHR, 10/66; J. Pol. Econ., 8/66;
     Library Journal, 12/15/66

0608 Hou, Fu-wu. Central Government of China 1912-1928, an Insti-
B   tutional Study by Franklin W. Houn. Madison: University of
     Wisconsin Press, 1957. 246 pp. 57-9807.
     Hucker, 744; JAS, 2/58; AHR, 10/57

0995 Hsi hsiang chi. The Romance of the Western Chamber (Hsi hsiang
A   chi), a Chinese Play Written in the Thirteenth Century. tr.
     by S. I. Hsiung. N.Y.: Columbia University Press, 1968
     (orig. pub. by Methuen, 1935). 281 pp. 68-22412. (R).
     AUFS, 1130; Hucker, 1675

0996 Hsi hsiang chi. The West Chamber, a Medieval Drama. tr. from
A   original Chinese with notes by Henry Hart. fore. by Edward
     Thomas Williams. Stanford, Calif.: Stanford University
     Press, 1936. 192 pp. 36-22471. o.p.
     Hucker, 1677; JAOS, 6/37

0925 Hsi yu chi. Monkey, by Wu Ch'eng-en. tr. from Chinese by
A   Arthur Waley. London: Allen & Unwin, 1942. 305 pp.
     A43-273.
     AUFS, 1059; Hucker, 1697; FEQ, 5/45

1020 Hsia, Chih-tsing. The Classic Chinese Novel; A Critical Intro-
A   duction. N.Y.: Columbia University Press, 1968. 413 pp.
     68-18997.
     Choice, 1/68; JAS, 2/69; Library Journal, 5/1/68

1155 Hsia, Chih-tsing. A History of Modern Chinese Fiction, 1917-
A   1957. with appendix on Taiwan by Tsi-an Hsia. New Haven,
     Conn.: Yale University Press, 1961. 662 pp. 60-13273.
     Hucker, 1713; JAS, 11/61; Library Journal, 12/15/60

0840 Hsia, T. A. The Commune in Retreat As Evidenced in Terminol-
B   ogy and Semantics. Berkeley: Center for Chinese Studies,
     Institute of International Studies, University of Cali-
     fornia, 1964. 91 pp. (Studies in Chinese Communist

     Terminology No. 11). 65-63417. o.p.
     JAS, 2/66

0609 Hsia, T. A. Enigma of the Five Martyrs; A Study of the Leftist
B   Literary Movement in Modern China. Berkeley: Institute
     of International Studies, University of California, 1962.
     150 pp. 63-6008. o.p.
     JAS, 8/65

0841 Hsia, T. A. Metaphor, Myth, Ritual, and the People's Commune.
B   Berkeley: Center for Chinese Studies, Institute of Inter-
     national Studies, University of California, 1961. 60 pp.
     (Studies in Chinese Communist Terminology No. 7). 61-64267.
     o.p.
     JAS, 2/66

0842 Hsia, T. A. A Terminological Study of the Hsia-Fang Movement.
C   Berkeley: Center for Chinese Studies, Institute of Inter-
     national Studies, University of California, 1963. 68 pp.
     (Studies in Chinese Communist Terminology No. 10). NUC
     64-18351. o.p.
     JAS, 2/66

0252 Hsia, Tao-t'ai. China's Language Reforms. New Haven, Conn.:
A   Institute of Far Eastern Languages, Yale University, 1956.
     200 pp. 57-871.
     Hucker, 77; JAS, 5/57

1156 Hsia, Tsi-an. The Gate of Darkness, Studies on the Leftist
B   Literary Movement in China. Seattle: University of
     Washington Press, 1968. 266 pp. 68-8510.

1157 Hsiao, Ch'ien. Etching of a Tormented Age; A Glimpse of Con-
C   temporary Chinese Literature. London: Allen & Unwin,
     1942. 48 pp. A42-3665 rev. o.p.

1078 Hsiao, Chun. Village in August, by T'ien Chun, pseud. N.Y.:
B   Smith & Durrell, 1942. 313 pp. 42-11707. o.p.
     AUFS, 1113; Pacific Affairs, 9/42

0478 Hsiao, Kung-ch'uan. Rural China; Imperial Control in the
A   Nineteenth Century. Seattle: University of Washington
     Press, 1960. 783 pp. 60-15803.
     Hucker, 1821; JAS, 8/61; Am. Anthropologist, 10/61; Am.
     Soc. R., 8/61; Ann. Am. Acad., 11/61; JAOS, 1-3/62

0610 Hsiao, Tso-liang. Power Relations within the Communist
A   Movement, 1930-1934; A Study of Documents. Seattle:
     University of Washington Press, 1961. 404 pp. 61-11573.
     AHR, 10/63; China Q., 10-12/62; Pol. Sci. Q., 12/62

0611 Hsiao, Yu. Mao Tse-tung and I Were Beggars. Syracuse, N.Y.:
B   Syracuse University Press, 1959. 266 pp. 59-15411.
     Hucker, 866; Ann. Am. Acad., 9/60

0775 Hsieh, Alice Langley. Communist China's Strategy in the
B   Nuclear Era. Englewood Cliffs, N.J.: Prentice-Hall,
     1962. 204 pp. 62-12563. o.p.
     Am. Pol. Sci. R., 9/62; Ann. Am. Acad., 11/62; Library
     Journal, 6/15/62

2069 Hsieh, Chiao-min. Taiwan-ilha Formosa; A Geography in Per-
A   spective. Washington: Butterworth's, 1964. 372 pp.
     64-22305. o.p.
     JAS, 2/66

0479 Hsieh, Pao Chao. The Government of China (1644-1911). N.Y.:
C   Octagon, 1966 (orig. pub. by Johns Hopkins, 1925). 414 pp.
     66-18027. (R). (M-University).
     Hucker, 510

0376 Hsu, Cho-yun. Ancient China in Transition; An Analysis of
A   Social Mobility, 722-222 B.C. Stanford, Calif.: Stanford
     University Press, 1969 (orig. pub. in 1965). 238 pp.
     (Studies in the Civilizations of Eastern Asia). 65-13110.
     (R).
     Choice, 12/65; JAS, 5/66; AHR, 4/66; Am. Soc. R., 6/66;
     JAOS, 7-9/66; Library Journal, 5/15/66

0612 Hsu, Francis L. K. Americans and Chinese. London: Cresset,
A   1955. 457 pp. 62-6654. o.p.
     Hucker, 1062; AHR, 10/53; Am. Soc. R., 12/53; Ann. Am.
     Acad., 11/53; Library Journal, 5/15/53

0341 Hsu, Francis L. K. Religion, Science, and Human Crises; A Study
B   of China in Transition and Its Implications for the West.
     London: Routledge & Kegan Paul, 1952. 142 pp. 52-2962.
     Hucker, 1079

0480 Hsu, Immanuel Chung-yueh. China's Entrance into the Family of
A   Nations: The Diplomatic Phase, 1858-1880 by Immanuel C. Y.
      Hsu. fore. by William Langer. Cambridge, Mass.: Harvard
      University Press, 1960. 255 pp. (Harvard East Asian Series,
      5). 60-5738 rev.
      Sup. 61, 2798; Hucker, 661; JAS, 11/60; AHR, 10/60;
      Library Journal, 3/15/60; TLS, 12/30/60

0481 Hsu, Immanuel Chung-yueh. The Ili Crisis; A Study of Sino-
B   Russian Diplomacy, 1871-1881. Oxford: Clarendon, 1965.
      230 pp. 66-1409.
      Choice, 9/66; JAS, 8/66; Library Journal, 1/1/68; TLS,
      2/10/66

0776 Hsu, Kai-yu. Chou En-lai: China's Grey Eminence. Garden
A   City, N.Y.: Doubleday, 1968. 294 pp. 68-10566.
      Choice, 7-8/68; China Q., 7-9/68

1132 Hsu, Kai-yu, ed. and tr. Twentieth Century Chinese Poetry,
A   an Anthology. Garden City, N.Y.: Doubleday, 1963. 434 pp.
      63-7725.
      JAOS, 1-3/64; Library Journal, 4/15/63; Pacific Affairs,
      Fall/63

1079 Hsu, Kuang-yao. The Plains are Ablaze. tr. by Sidney Shapiro.
C   Peking: Foreign Languages Press, 1955. 277 pp. A56-5729.
      o.p.

0209 Hsueh, Chun-tu. The Chinese Communist Movement, 1921-1937;
C   An Annotated Bibliography of Selected Materials in the
      Chinese Collection of the Hoover Institution on War,
      Revolution, and Peace. Stanford, Calif.: Stanford Uni-
      versity Press, 1960. 131 pp. 61-625 rev.
      JAS, 11/68

0210 Hsueh, Chun-tu. The Chinese Communist Movement, 1937-1949;
C   An Annotated Bibliography of Selected Materials in the
      Chinese Collection of the Hoover Institution on War,
      Revolution, and Peace. Stanford, Calif.: Stanford Uni-
      versity Press, 1962. 312 pp. 61-625 rev.
      JAS, 11/68

0613 Hsueh, Chun-tu. Huang Hsing and the Chinese Revolution. Stan-
B   ford, Calif.: Stanford University Press, 1968 (orig. pub.
      in 1961). 260 pp. (Stanford University Series: History,
      Economics and Political Science, 20). 61-6531. (R).
      Sup. 63, 2915; JAS, 5/62

1202 Hsun-tze. The Works of Hsuntze. tr. from Chinese with notes by
C   Homer H. Dubs. Taipei: Ch'eng-wen Publishing Co., dist. by
      Chinese Materials and Research Aids Service Center, 1966
      (orig. pub. by A. Probsthain, 1928). 336 pp. NUC 68-42525.
      (R).
      AUFS, 631; Hucker, 1137

0317 Hu, Ch'ang-tu. China: Its People, Its Society, Its Culture.
B   ed. by Hsiao Hsia. New Haven, Conn.: Human Relations Area
      Files, 1960. 610 pp. 60-7382.
      Hucker, 3; Am. Anthropologist, 10/60; Am. J. Soc., 1/61;
      Am. Pol. Sci. R., 9/60; Am. Soc. R., 7/60; Ann. Am. Acad.,
      11/60; Library Journal, 3/1/60; Pol. Sci. Q., 3/61

1334 Hu, Ch'ang-tu. Chinese Education Under Communism. N.Y.:
A   Bureau of Publications, Teachers College, Columbia
      University, 1962. 157 pp. 62-20698. o.p.

0908 Hu, Hsien-chin. The Common Descent Group in China and its
C   Functions. ed. by Ralph Linton. N.Y.: Johnson, 1964 (orig.
      pub. by Viking Fund, 1948). 204 pp. (Viking Fund Publica-
      tions in Anthropology, 10). NUC 67-40970. (R). (M-Uni-
      versity).
      Hucker, 2040; FEQ, 5/51

1137 Hu, K'o. Locust Tree Village; A Play in Five Acts. Peking:
C   Foreign Languages Press, 1961. 126 pp. NUC 63-23461.

1080 Hu, K'o. Steeled in Battles. tr. by Tang Sheng. Peking:
C   Foreign Languages Press, 1955. 130 pp. 58-17706.

1021 Hu, P'in-ch'ing. Li Ch'ing-chao. N.Y.: Twayne, 1966. 128 pp.
C   (TWAS, 5). 66-16122.
      Choice, 10/67

0614 Hu, Shih. The Chinese Renaissance. 2d ed. N.Y.: Paragon,
C   1964 (orig. pub. by University of Chicago Press, 1934).
      110 pp. (Haskell Lectures, 1933). 63-21052. (R). (M-Uni-
      versity).
      Sup. 65, 3095; Hucker, 755; JAS, 11/64; JAOS, 6/35;
      J. Philosophy, 6/21/34; J. Religion, 10/34

1258 Hu, Shih. The Development of the Logical Method in Ancient
B   China. 2d ed. with intro. by Hyman Kublin. N.Y.: Para-
      gon, 1963 (orig. pub. by Oriental, 1922). 187 pp. 63-21053.
      (R). (M-University).
      AUFS, 594; JAS, 11/64

1081 Hu, Wan-ch'un. Man of a Special Cut. Peking: Foreign Languages
C   Press, 1963. 183 pp. NUC 65-2189.

0377 Huan K'uan. Discourses on Salt and Iron; A Debate on State
B   Control of Commerce and Industry in Ancient China. chap-
      ters I-XIX, tr. by Esson M. Gale. Leiden: Brill, 1931.
      165 pp. 33-4201.
      Hucker, 204

1203 Huang, Hsiu-chi. Lu Hsiang-shan...a Twelfth Century Chinese
C   Idealist Philosopher. New Haven, Conn.: American Orien-
      tal Society, 1944. 116 pp. 45-5004. o.p.
      Hucker, 1155; FEQ, 11/45

1158 Huang, Sung-k'ang. Lu Hsun and the New Culture Movement
C   of Modern China. Amsterdam: Djambatan, 1957. 158 pp.
      58-33802.
      JAS, 2/59

1354 Huang-ti Nei Ching Su Wen. Huang-Tu nei chung su wen. The
C   Yellow Emporer's Classic of Internal Medicine. new ed.
      Chapters 1-34 tr. with an intro. by Ilza Veith. Berkeley:
      University of California Press, 1966. 260 pp. 66-21112.
      Hucker, 1374; Choice, 7-8/67; FEQ, 5/51; Science, 5/7/67

0964 Huang, Wen. Poems From China. tr. by Wong Man. Hong Kong:
C   Creation Books, 1950. 241 pp. 52-22125.

1355 Huard, Pierre Alphonse. La Medecine Chinoise au Cours des
C   Siecles. Paris: R. Dacosta, 1959. 190 pp. 59-51354.
      Hucker, 1375

0482 Huc, Evariste Regis. The Chinese Empire: Being a Sequel to
C   the Work Entitled "Recollections of a Journey through Tar-
      tary and Thibet." London: Longman, Brown, Green and
      Longmans, 1855. 2 v. 4-29888. o.p.

0483 Huc, Evariste Regis. Travels in Tartary, Thibet and China,
C   1844-1846. tr. by William Hazlitt. N.Y.: Harper, 1928.
      2 v. 29-8715. o.p. (M-University).
      AUFS, 1185

0484 Hucker, Charles O. The Censorial System of Ming China.
C   Stanford, Calif.: Stanford University Press, 1966.
      406 pp. (Stanford Studies in the Civilizations of Eastern
      Asia). 66-10916.
      Sup. 67, 3242; Choice, 2/67; JAS, 2/68; AHR, 1/67;
      Ann. Am. Acad., 5/67; Library Journal, 7/68

0211 Hucker, Charles O. China; A Critical Bibliography. Tucson:
A   University of Arizona Press, 1962. 125 pp. 62-10624.
      Sup. 63, 2916; JAS, 5/63

0212 Hucker, Charles O. Chinese History; A Bibliographic Review.
A   Washington: Service Center for Teachers of History,
      1958. 42 pp. 58-59931. o.p.
      AUFS, 685; Hucker, 14

0485 Hucker, Charles O. The Traditional Chinese State in Ming
A   Times (1368-1644). Tucson: University of Arizona Press,
      1961. 85 pp. 61-15391.
      Sup. 63, 2917; Hucker 444; JAS, 8/62; JAOS, 1-3/62

0486 Hudson, Geoffrey Francis. Europe and China; A Survey of Their
A   Relations from the Earliest Times to 1800. Boston:
      Beacon, 1961 (orig. pub. by Arnold, 1931). 336 pp.
      A63-5056. (R).
      Hucker, 134; AHR, 10/32

0777 Hudson, Geoffrey Francis. The Sino-Soviet Dispute. N.Y.:
C   Praeger, 1961. 227 pp. 61-15894. o.p.
      Am. Pol. Sci. R., 9/62; Ann. Am. Acad., 3/62; Pol. Sci. Q.,
      9/62

1179 Hughes, Ernest Richard, ed. and tr. Chinese Philosophy in
A   Classical Times. N.Y.: Dutton, 1954. 336 pp. 54-3630.
      AUFS, 596; Hucker, 1051

0487 Hughes, Ernest Richard. The Invasion of China by the Western
C   World. ed. by R. S. Dawson. 2d ed. N.Y.: Barnes & Noble,
      1968 (orig. pub. by Macmillan, 1938). 317 pp. 73-213. (R).
      Hucker, 728; Choice, 5/69; Am. J. Soc., 9/38; Am. Pol. Sci.
      R., 8/38; Am. Soc. R., 12/38; Ann. Am. Acad., 7/38

0378 Hughes, Ernest Richard. Two Chinese Poets; Vignettes of Han Life
B and Thought. Princeton, N.J.: Princeton University Press,
1960. 266 pp. 59-11078.
Hucker, 211; JAS, 2/61; JAOS, 4-6/62

0888 Hughes, Trevor Jones. The Economic Development of Communist
C China, 1949-1958. N.Y.: Oxford for the Royal Institute of
International Affairs, 1959. 223 pp. 60-650.
Sup. 61, 2800; Hucker, 2161; JAS, 11/60

1634 Huh, Kyung-Mo. Japan's Trade in Asia: Developments Since
C 1926, Prospects for 1970. N.Y.: Praeger, 1966. 283 pp.
(Praeger Special Studies in International Economics and
Development). 66-15449.
Choice, 9/67

1242 Hui'neng. The Platform Sutra of the Sixth Patriach. tr. by
B P. Yampolsky. N.Y.: Columbia University Press, 1967.
272 pp. Hand catalog.
JAS, 5/68

2008 Hulbert, Homer Bezaleel. History of Korea. ed. by Clarence
B Norwood Weems. N.Y.: Hillary House, 1962. 2 v. 62-9992.
Sup. 63, 2900; JAS, 11/62

0104 Hull, Cordell. The Memoirs of Cordell Hull. N.Y.: Macmillan,
B 1948. 2 v. 48-6761. o.p.
Hucker, 815; Am. Pol. Sci. R., 10/48; Ann. Am. Acad.,
7/48; Library Journal, 7/15/48

1356 Hume, Edward Hicks. The Chinese Way in Medicine. Baltimore:
C Johns Hopkins Press, 1940. 189 pp. 40-32412. o.p.
Hucker, 1373; FEQ, 5/42

0997 Hung, Sheng. The Palace of Eternal Youth. tr. by Yang Hsien-
A yi and Gladys Yang. Peking: Foreign Languages Press, 1955.
322 pp. 57-35395. o.p.

1022 Hung, William. Tu Fu, China's Greatest Poet. Cambridge, Mass.:
A Harvard University Press, 1952. 300 pp. 52-5034. o.p.
Hucker, 1599; FEQ, 2/53

1635 Hunsberger, Warren S. Japan and the United States in World
B Trade. N.Y.: Harper & Row for Council on Foreign Relations,
1964. 492 pp. 64-24790. o.p.
Choice, 2/65; AHR, 5/65; Ann. Am. Acad., 7/65; Japan Q.,
4-6/65

0488 Hunter, William C. The 'Fan Kwae' at Canton before Treaty
B Days, 1825-1844, by an Old Resident. N.Y.: Paragon, 1965
(orig. pub. in London, 1822). 97 pp. 42-50527. (R).
Hucker, 683

0489 Hussey, Harry. Venerable Ancestor; The Life and Times of
B Tz'u Hsi, 1835-1908, Empress of China. Garden City, N.Y.:
Doubleday, 1949. 354 pp. 49-11056. o.p.
Hucker, 611

1204 I Ching. The I Ching; or, Book of Changes. The Richard Wil-
C helm translation rendered into English by Cary F. Baynes.
3d ed. Princeton, N.J.: Princeton University Press,
1967. 740 pp. (Bollingen Series, Vol. 19). 67-24740.
AUFS, 597; Choice, 10/68; Hucker, 1533; JAOS, 10-12/50

1205 I Ching. The Yi King. tr. by James Legge. ed. with new intro.
C by Ch'u Chai and Winberg Chai. New Hyde Park, N.Y.: Uni-
versity Books, 1964 (orig. pub. by Clarendon, 1882). 448 pp.
(Sacred Books of the East, Vol. 16). 64-25866. (R).
Choice, 5/65

1082 I Knew All Along and Other Stories by Contemporary Chinese
C Writers. Peking: Foreign Languages Press, 1960. 172 pp.
Hand catalog.

1719 Ichikawa, Sanki, ed. Haikai and Haiku. Tokyo: Nippon Gakujutsu
B Shinkokai, 1958. 191 pp. Hand catalog.
Silberman, 1063

1513 Idditti, Smimasa. The Life of Marquis Shigenobu Okuma, a
B Maker of New Japan. Tokyo: Hokuseido, 1940. 423 pp.
41-2559.
Silberman, 357

1514 Iglehart, Charles W. A Century of Protestant Christianity in
A Japan. Rutland, Vt.: Tuttle in cooperation with the Japanese
Committee, Division of Foreign Missions, National Council of
the Churches of Christ in the U.S.A., 1959. 384 pp.
59-11758.
Sup. 61, 2765; Silberman, 663; JAS, 8/60; Japan Q., 4-6/60

1699 Ihara, Saikaku. Five Women Who Loved Love. tr. by Wm. Theodore
A de Bary. Rutland, Vt.: Tuttle, 1956. 264 pp. 55-10619.
AUFS, 431; Silberman, 922

1700 Ihara, Saikaku. The Japanese Family Storehouse, or, the
B Millionaire's Gospel Modernized. tr. by G. W. Sargent.
Cambridge: University, 1959. 281 pp. 59-1893.
Silberman, 921; JAS, 8/60; Japan Q., 1-3/60

1701 Ihara, Saikaku. This Scheming World. tr. by Masanori Takatsuka
B and David C. Stubbs. Rutland, Vt.: Tuttle, 1965. 128 pp.
(Library of Japanese Literature). 65-17850.
Choice, 3/67; JAS, 8/66

1515 Ike, Nobutaka. The Beginnings of Political Democracy in
B Japan. Baltimore: Johns Hopkins Press, 1950. 246 pp.
50-14240. o.p. (M-University).
AUFS, 246; Silberman, 365; FEQ, 8/51; Am. Anthropologist,
7/51; AHR, 8/51

1516 Ike, Nobutaka, ed. and tr. Japan's Decision for War; Rec-
A ords of the 1941 Policy Conferences. Stanford, Calif.:
Stanford University Press, 1967. 306 pp. 67-13659.
Choice, 9/67; JAS, 5/68; Ann. Am. Acad., 11/67; Library
Journal, 2/15/67; Pacific Affairs, Spring-Summer/67

1517 Ikle, Frank William. German-Japanese Relations, 1936-1940.
C N.Y.: Bookman, 1956. 243 pp. 57-13764. o.p.
Silberman, 488; JAS, 2/58

0155 International Labor Office. The Economic Background of Social
C Policy Including Problems of Industrialization. New Delhi:
International Labor Office, 1947. 221 pp. 48-104.

0253 Irick, Robert L. American-Chinese Relations, 1784-1941; A Survey
B of Chinese-language Materials at Harvard. Cambridge, Mass.:
Harvard University Press, 1960. 296 pp. (Dept. of History,
American Far Eastern Policy Studies: Research Aids, No. 3).
60-4930. o.p.
JAS, 5/62

0081 Iriye, Akira. Across the Pacific; An Inner History of
B American-East Asian Relations. intro. by John K. Fairbank.
N.Y.: Harcourt, Brace & World, 1967. 361 pp. 67-19202.
Choice, 10/68; JAS, 11/68; Library Journal, 10/15/67

0105 Iriye, Akira. After Imperialism, the Search for a New Order
A in the Far East, 1921-1931. Cambridge, Mass.: Harvard
University Press, 1965. 375 pp. (Harvard East Asian
Series, 22). 65-22052.
Sup. 67, 3209; Choice, 6/66; JAS, 8/66; AHR, 7/66

1023 Irwin, Richard Gregg. The Evolution of a Chinese Novel: Shui-
B hu-chuan. Cambridge, Mass.: Harvard University Press,
1953. 231 pp. 53-10476. o.p.
AUFS, 1063; Hucker, 1686; FEQ, 11/54; JAOS, 4-6/54

0778 Isaacs, Harold Robert. Images of Asia, American Views of China
A and India. N.Y.: Putnam, 1962 (orig. pub. by John Day,
1958 under the title Scratches on Our Minds). 416 pp.
58-5692. (R).
AUFS, 936; JAS, 5/62; Ann. Am. Acad., 9/58; Library Journal,
2/15/58

0124 Isaacs, Harold Robert, ed. New Cycle in Asia; Selected
B Documents on Major International Developments in the
Far East, 1943-1947. N.Y.: Macmillan for Institute of
Pacific Relations, 1947. 212 pp. 47-12404. o.p.
AUFS, 94; FEQ, 11/48; Ann. Am. Acad., 5/48; Library Journal,
11/1/47; Pacific Affairs, 9/48

0057 Isaacs, Harold Robert. No Peace for Asia. Cambridge, Mass.:
C M.I.T. Press, 1967 (orig. pub. by Macmillan, 1947). 295 pp.
67-15237. (R).
Choice, 1/68

0779 Isaacs, Harold Robert. The Tragedy of the Chinese Revolution.
A rev. ed. Stanford, Calif.: Stanford University Press,
1951. 382 pp. 51-12683. o.p.
AUFS, 937; Hucker, 878; FEQ, 5/53; Ann. Am. Acad., 1/52;
China Q., 7-9/52; Pol. Sci., 9/52; TLS, 7/18/52

1702 Ise Monogatari. English. Tales of Ise; Lyrical Episodes
A from Tenth-Century Japan. tr. by Helen Craig McCullough.
Stanford, Calif.: Stanford University Press, 1968. 277 pp.
68-17135.

1915 Ishida, Mosaku. Japanese Buddhist Prints. English adaptation
C by Charles S. Terry. N.Y.: Abrams for Kodansha, 1964.
195 pp. 64-20004.
Choice, 11/64; JAS, 11/65; Art Bul., 6/65; Library Journal,

1845 Ishigoro, Tadaatsu, ed. Ninomiya, Sontoku; His Life and Evening
C Talks. Tokyo: Kenkyusha, 1955.
   Silberman, 689

1518 Ishii, Kikujiro. Diplomatic Commentaries. tr. and ed. by
C William R. Langdon. Baltimore: Johns Hopkins Press, 1936.
   351 pp. 36-7778. o.p.
   Silberman, 524; Am. Pol. Sci. R., 10/36; Ann. Am. Acad.,
   7/36; TLS, 5/9/36

1793 Ishikawa, Hajime. A Handful of Sand. tr. by Shio Sakanishi.
B Boston: Marshall Jones, 1934. 77 pp. 34-35669. o.p.
   AUFS, 464

1794 Ishikawa, Takuboku. Poems to Eat. tr. by Carl Sesar. Palo
B Alto, Calif.: Kodansha, 1966. 168 pp. 66-19820.
   Choice, 10/66

1416 Isida, Ryujiro. Geography of Japan. Tokyo: Kokusai Bunka Shin-
B kokai, 1961. 124 pp. (Series on Japanese Life and Cul-
   ture, 2). NUC 65-2427.
   Choice, 6/66; JAS, 2/65

0615 Israel, John. Student Nationalism in China, 1927-1937. Stan-
A ford, Calif.: Stanford University Press, 1966. 253 pp.
   (Hoover Institution). 66-15300.
   Sup. 67, 3243; Choice, 4/67; JAS, 5/67; AHR, 4/67; Am. Pol.
   Sci. R., 12/67; Ann. Am. Acad., 5/67; Library Journal,
   8/66; Pol. Sci. Q., 12/67

1519 Ito, Hirobumi. Commentaries on the Constitution of the
B Empire of Japan. tr. by Miyoji Ito. Tokyo: Igirisu-
   horitsu Gakko, 22nd Year of Meiji, 1889. 259 pp. 1-1269.
   Silberman, 1246

1795 Ito, Kojiro. Songs of a Cowherd. tr. from works of Sachio
B Ito by Shio Sakanishi. Boston: Marshall Jones, 1936.
   74 pp. (Modern Japanese Poets Series, 3). 37-475.
   o.p. (M-University).

1856 Iwamiya, Takeji. Design and Craftsmanship of Japan: Stone,
B Metal, Fibers and Fabrics, Bamboo. introductory essay by
   Donald Richie. N.Y.: Abrams, 1965. 182 pp. 64-22626.
   Choice, 12/65

1520 Iwata, Masakazu. Okubo Toshimichi, the Bismarck of Japan.
C Berkeley: University of California Press, 1964. 376 pp.
   (University of California Center for Japanese and Korean
   Studies Publication). 64-25533.
   Sup. 65, 3060; Choice, 6/65; JAS, 11/65; Library Journal,
   2/1/65; Pacific Affairs, Spring/65

0058 Jackson, Barbara (Ward). The Interplay of East and West,
B Points of Conflict and Co-Operation. N.Y.: Norton, 1957.
   152 pp. 57-8337.
   AUFS, 29; JAS, 2/58; TLS, 6/21/57

0780 Jackson, William Arthur Douglas. The Russo-Chinese Border-
C lands; Zone of Peaceful Contact or Potential Conflict?
   Princeton, N.J.: Van Nostrand, 1962. 126 pp. (Searchlight
   Book, No. 2). 62-4176.
   Sup. 63, 2918; JAS, 8/64

0156 Jacobs, Norman. The Origin of Modern Capitalism and Eastern
B Asia. Hong Kong: Hong Kong University Press, 1958. 243 pp.
   58-59961.
   Hucker, 2028; Silberman, 1506; JAS, 2/60

2081 Jacoby, Neil Hermon. U.S. Aid to Taiwan; A Study of Foreign
C Aid, Self-help, and Development. N.Y.: Praeger, 1966.
   364 pp. 66-21784.
   Choice, 3/68; JAS, 8/67; Am. Econ. R., 9/67; Ann. Am.
   Acad., 7/67

1521 Jansen, Marius B., ed. Changing Japanese Attitudes toward
A Modernization. Princeton, N.J.: Princeton University
   Press for the Conference on Modern Japan of the Associa-
   tion for Asian Studies, 1965. 546 pp. (Conference on
   Modern Japan of the Association for Asian Studies). 63-23406.
   Sup. 65, 3061; Choice, 10/65; JAS, 2/66; Japan Q., 7-9/65;
   JAOS, 1-3/66

0616 Jansen, Marius B. The Japanese and Sun Yat-sen. Cambridge,
A Mass.: Harvard University Press, 1954. 274 pp. 53-8021.
   AUFS, 827; Hucker, 758; Silberman, 419; FEQ, 5/55; AHR,
   10/55; Am. Pol. Sci. R., 3/55; Ann. Am. Acad., 7/55; Library
   Journal, 11/15/54

1522 Jansen, Marius B. Sakamoto Ryoma and the Meiji Restoration.
A Princeton, N.J.: Princeton University Press, 1961.
   423 pp. 61-6909.
   Sup. 61, 2766; Silberman, 340; Japan Q., 10-12/61; JAOS,
   4-6/62

1592 Japan. Constitution. The Constitution of Japan and Criminal
C Laws. Tokyo: Japan Trade Guide Publishing Co., 1951.
   198 pp. 51-33946.
   Silberman, 1300

1593 Japan. Constitution. The Constitution of Japan, Effective
B May 3, 1947. Washington: Government Printing Office, 1947.
   13 pp. (Department of State Publication 2836, Far Eastern
   Series, 22). 47-31999. o.p.
   Silberman, 1301

1947 Japan. Imperial Treasury (Shosoin). The Shosoin, an Eighth
C Century Treasury House. comp. by Mosaku Ishida and Gunchi
   Moda. English resume by Harada Jiro. Tokyo: Mainichi
   Newspapers, 1954. 20 pp.
   Silberman, 814

1594 Japan. Laws, Statutes, etc. The Civil Code of Japan. Tokyo:
C Civil Affairs Bureau, General Secretariat, Supreme Court,
   1950. 221 pp. 51-208.
   Silberman, 1308

1595 Japan. Laws, Statutes, etc. The Criminal Code of Japan, as
C Amended in 1947, and the Minor Offenses Law of Japan. tr. by
   Thomas L. Blakemore. Rutland, Vt.: Tuttle, 1950. 186 pp.
   50-14942.
   Silberman, 1309

1974 Japan. Ministry of Education. Kokutai no Hongi Cardinal
B Principles of the National Entity of Japan. tr. by
   John Owen Gauntlett. ed. by Robert King Hall. Cambridge,
   Mass.: Harvard University Press, 1949. 200 pp. 49-9335
   rev. o.p. (M-University).
   AUFS, 135; Silberman, 1470; FEQ, 5/50; Am. Pol. Sci. R.,
   10/47; Am. Soc. R., 8/49

1407 Japan. Mombusho. Nihon Yunesuko Kokunai Iinkai. Japan;
C Its Land, People, and Culture. rev. ed. comp. by Japanese
   National Commission for UNESCO. Tokyo: Printing Bureau, Min-
   istry of Finance, dist. by Japan Publications Trading Co.,
   1964. 885 pp. 65-71358.
   Silberman, 1

1636 Japan. Mombusho. Nihon Yunesuko Kokunai Iinkai. The Role
C of Education in the Social and Economic Development of
   Japan. Tokyo: Ministry of Education, 1966. 429 pp.
   NUC 67-35296.

1596 Japan. Saiko Saibansho. Court and Constitution in Japan;
C Selected Supreme Court Decisions, 1948-1960, by John M.
   Maki. Seattle: University of Washington Press, 1964.
   445 pp. (University of Washington Publication on Asia).
   63-9940.
   Sup. 65, 3065; Choice, 4/64; JAS, 8/64; Japan Q., 1-3/65

1376 Japan Biographical Encyclopedia and Who's Who. 1958-
A 58-1808 rev.

1377 Japan Economic Yearbook. Tokyo: Oriental Economist, 1954-
B Biennial, Irregular.

1394 Japan Illustrated. v.1- 1963-
B

1395 Japan Quarterly. Tokyo: Asahi Shimbun, v.1- Oct./Dec.,
B 1954-
   Silberman, 42

1378 Japan Statistical Yearbook. Tokyo: Japanese Government,
A Office of Prime Minister, Bureau of Statistics. annual.

1396 Japan Times Weekly. v.1- 1938-
C

1761 Japan Writers' Society. Young Forever and Five Other Novel-
C ettes, by Contemporary Japanese Authors. Tokyo: Hokuseido,
   1941. 142 pp. A42-566 rev. 2.

1948 Japanese Architecture. prepared by H. Kishida. Tokyo: Japan
A Travel Bureau, 1935- (Tourist Library, N.S. 6).
   60-11616 rev.
   Silberman, 805

1857 Japanese Handicrafts, prepared by Y. Okada. Tokyo: Japan Travel
B Bureau, 1956- (Tourist Library, N.S. 21). 62-10306.

Silberman, 832

1891   Jenyns, Roger Soame. Japanese Porcelain. N.Y.: Praeger, 1965.
C   351 pp. 65-13447.
       Choice, 6/66; Library Journal, 12/15/65

1284   Jenyns, Soame. Later Chinese Porcelain; The Ch'ing Dynasty,
C   1644-1912. 2d ed. London: Faber & Faber, 1959. 111 pp.
       60-735.
       Hucker, 1434

1285   Jenyns, Soame. Ming Pottery and Porcelain. London: Faber
C   & Faber, 1953. 160 pp. 53-4516. o.p.
       Hucker, 1433

1703   Jippensha, Ikku. Shank's Mare, Being a Translation of the Tokaido
B   Volumes of Hizakurige, Japan's Great Comic Novel of Travel
       and Ribaldry. Rutland, Vt.: Tuttle, 1960 (orig. pub. in
       1920). 414 pp. 60-14370. (R).
       AUFS, 433; Silberman, 927; JAS, 8/61

0843   Joffe, Ellis. Party and Army: Professionalism and Political
A   Control in the Chinese Officer Corps, 1949-1964. Cambridge,
       Mass.: Harvard University Press for the East Asian Research
       Center, 1965. 198 pp. (Harvard East Asian Monographs, 19).
       65-29001.
       Choice, 4/66; JAS, 5/66

0004   Johns, Francis A. A Bibliography of Arthur Waley. New
B   Brunswick, N.J.: Rutgers University Press, 1968.
       187 pp. 67-20388.
       Choice, 9/68; Library Journal, 5/1/68; TLS, 5/2/68

1523   Johnson, Chalmers A. An Instance of Treason; Ozaki Hotsumi
B   and the Sorge Spy Ring. Stanford, Calif.: Stanford Uni-
       versity Press, 1964. 278 pp. 64-14556.
       Sup. 65, 3062; Choice, 10/64; JAS, 5/65; AHR, 1/65;
       Am. Pol. Sci. R., 3/65; TLS, 8/12/65

0617   Johnson, Chalmers A. Peasant Nationalism and Communist Power,
B   the Emergence of Revolutionary China, 1937-1945. Stanford,
       Calif.: Stanford University Press, 1968 (orig. pub. in 1962).
       256 pp. 62-16949. (R).
       Sup. 63, 2920; JAS, 8/63; AHR, 10/63; Am. Pol. Sci. R.,
       9/63; China Q., 7-9/63; Library Journal, 11/15/62; Pacific
       Affairs, Fall/63; TLS, 10/18/63

0618   Johnston, Sir Reginald Fleming. Twilight in the Forbidden City.
C   London: Gollancz, 1934. 486 pp. 34-27253. o.p.
       Hucker, 753

2067   Joint Commission on Rural Reconstruction in China. 1950-
B   Hucker, 2178

2082   Joint Commission on Rural Reconstruction in China (U.S. and
B   China). A Decade of Rural Progress, 1948-1958; Tenth
       Anniversary Review of the Major Accomplishments of the
       Joint Commission on Rural Reconstruction. Taipei: 1958.
       68 pp. A59-1185.
       Hucker, 2181

2073   Joint Commission on Rural Reconstruction in China (U.S. and
C   China). Rural Taiwan, Problem and Promise, by Arthur F.
       Raper, project evaluation advisor. Taipei: Joint Commission
       on Rural Reconstruction in China, 1953. 296 pp. 54-36127.

1858   Joly, Henri L. Legend in Japanese Art, a Description of
A   Historical Episodes, Legendary Characters, Folk-Lore
       Myths, Religious Symbolism Illustrated in the Arts of
       Old Japan. Rutland, Vt.: Tuttle, 1967 (orig. pub.
       by Bodley Head, 1908). 623 pp. 67-16411. (R).
       Choice, 10/67; Library Journal, 8/67; TLS, 11/6/67

1524   Jones, Francis Clifford. Extraterritoriality in Japan and
B   the Diplomatic Relations Resulting in Its Abolition,
       1853-1899. New Haven, Conn.: Yale University Press, 1931.
       237 pp. 31-30406. o.p.
       Silberman, 400

0619   Jones, Francis Clifford. Manchuria since 1931. London:
C   Royal Institute of International Affairs, 1949. 256 pp.
       A50-9046. o.p.
       Hucker, 796; Silberman, 497; FEQ, 8/50; Library Journal,
       9/15/49

0620   Jones, Francis Clifford. Shanghai and Teintsin, with Special
C   Reference to Foreign Interests. N.Y.: Institute of
       Pacific Relations, 1940. 182 pp. 43-7168. o.p.
       Hucker, 2090

1458   Jouon des Longrais, Frederic. Age de Kamakura: Sources (1150-
B   1333). Tokyo: Maison Franco-Japonais, 1950- 50-29222.
       Silberman, 221

0033   Journal of Asian Studies, v.1- 1941- (1941-56 as Far
A   Eastern Quarterly). (R-AMS).
       AUFS, 30; Hucker, 24; Silberman, 30

1987   Journal of Asiatic Studies. Seoul: Korea University.
C

0034   Journal of Oriental Studies, v.1- 1954- (M-IDC).
B   Hucker, 32

1397   Journal of Social and Political Ideas in Japan. v.1- 1963-
C   Tokyo: Center for Japanese Social and Political Studies.
       JAS, 11/63

1988   Journal of Social Sciences and Humanities. Seoul: Bulletin
C   of the Korean Research Center, 1955-

2025   Joy, Charles Turner. How Communists Negotiate. N.Y.: Macmil-
C   lan, 1955. 178 pp. 55-13828. o.p.
       Silberman, 1791; Library Journal, 11/15/55

1996   Jung, In-hah, ed. The Feel of Korea; A Symposium of American
C   Comment. Seoul: Hollym Corporation, 1966. 369 pp. 66-9059.

1859   Kaemmerer, Eric A. Trades and Crafts of Old Japan; Leaves
B   from a Contemporary Album. Rutland, Vt.: Tuttle, 1961.
       112 pp. 61-14030.
       Sup. 63, 2884

1459   Kaempfer, Engelbert. The History of Japan, Together with a
A   Description of the Kingdom of Siam, 1690-92. tr. from
       Dutch by J. G. Scheuchzer. N.Y.: Macmillan, 1906. 3 v.
       6-32382. o.p.
       AUFS, 196

0138   Kahin, George McTurnan, ed. Major Governments of Asia. 2d ed.
B   Ithaca, N.Y.: Cornell University Press, 1963. 719 pp.
       63-15940.
       AUFS, 31; JAS, 5/59, 5/64

2026   Kahn, Ely Jacques. The Peculiar War; Impressions of a Reporter
B   in Korea. N.Y.: Random House, 1952. 211 pp. 52-5554. o.p.
       Silberman, 1783

1206   Kaizuka, Shigeki. Confucius. tr. from Japanese by Geoffrey
C   Bownas. N.Y.: Hillary House, 1956. 191 pp. A57-3058.
       Hucker, 171

0490   Kammerer, Albert. La Decouverte de la Chine par les Portugais
C   au XVIeme Siecle et la Cartographie des Portulans. Leiden:
       Brill, 1944. 260 pp. AF47-6702.
       Hucker, 582

1704   Kamo, Chomei. The Ten Foot Square Hut and Tales of the Heike,
C   Being Two Thirteenth Century Japanese Classics. tr. by
       A. L. Sadler. Sydney: Angus & Robertson, 1928. 271 pp.
       AUFS, 434; Silberman, 907

1833   Kamstra, J. H. Encounter or Syncretism, the Initial Growth
B   of Japanese Buddhism. Leiden: Brill, 1967. 508 pp.
       68-81683.

1083   K'ang, Cho. When the Sun Comes Up. Peking: Foreign Languages
C   Press, 1961. 175 pp. Hand catalog.

1997   Kang, Younghill. The Grass Roof. Chicago: Follett, 1966
B   (orig. pub. by Scribner's, 1939). 377 pp. 66-27984. (R).
       AUFS, 545

0491   K'ang, Yu-wei. Ta T'ung Shu. The One-World Philosophy of K'ang
B   Yu-wei. tr. from Chinese by Laurence G. Thompson. N.Y.:
       Hillary House, 1958. 300 pp. A58-4956 rev.
       AUFS, 747; Hucker, 649

0926   Kao, K'o-i, ed. Chinese Wit and Humor. N.Y.: Coward-McCann,
B   1946. 347 pp. 46-6653. o.p.
       Hucker, 1654; Library Journal, 8/46

1084   Kao, Yu-pao. My Childhood. Peking: Foreign Languages Press,
C   1960. 379 pp. Hand catalog.

1085   Kao, Yun-lan. Annals of a Provincial Town. tr. by Sidney
C   Shapiro. Peking: Foreign Languages Press, 1959. 306 pp.
       62-19805.

1525   Karig, Walter. Battle Report(s)...Prepared from Official
C   Sources. N.Y.: Farrar & Rinehart for Council on Books

in Wartime, 1944- 44-4769 rev. 2. o.p.
Silberman, 527; FEQ, 2/48, 2/53; Library Journal, 12/1/44, 4/15/52

0254 Karlgren, Bernhard. The Chinese Language, an Essay on Its
A Nature and History. N.Y.: Ronald, 1949. 122 pp. 49-11524.
Hucker, 64; FEQ, 2/51; JAOS, 4-6/50; Pacific Affairs, 3/50

0255 Karlgren, Bernhard. Sound and Symbol in Chinese. London:
B Oxford, 1923. 112 pp. 23-11701.
AUFS, 1032

0781 Karol, K. S. China: the Other Communism. tr. from French by
C Tom Bailstow. N.Y.: Hill & Wang, 1967. 474 pp. 66-27608.
Sup. 67, 3244; Choice, 11/67; Library Journal, 3/15/67

0621 Kates, George Norbert. The Years That Were Fat; The Last of
C Old China. intro. by John K. Fairbank. Cambridge, Mass.:
M.I.T. Press, 1967 (orig. pub. in 1952). 268 pp. NUC
68-60386. (R).
JAS, 2/68; FEQ, 11/52; Library Journal, 3/1/52

1365 Kato, Genchi. A Bibliography of Shinto in Western Languages,
B from the Oldest Times till 1952. Tokyo: Meiji Jingu Shamu-
sho, 1953. 58 pp. 58-15934 rev.
Silberman, 600

1823 Kato, Genchi. A Study of Shinto, the Religion of the Japanese
C Nation. Tokyo: Zaidan-hojin-Meiji-seitoku-kinen-gakkai,
1926. 255 pp. 28-16775.
AUFS, 136; Silberman, 610

1526 Kato, Masuo. The Lost War, a Japanese Reporter's Inside
B Story. N.Y.: Knopf, 1946. 264 pp. 46-6474. o.p.
FEQ, 5/47

1916 Katsushika, Hokusai. The Hokusai Sketchbooks; Selections from
B the Manga. ed. by James A. Michener. Rutland, Vt.: Tuttle,
1958. 286 pp. 58-9983.
Silberman, 795; JAS, 5/59; Japan Q., 10-12/58; JAOS, 1-3/59;
Library Journal, 10/1/58

1762 Kawabata, Yasunari. Snow Country. tr., with an intro. by Ed-
B ward G. Seidensticker. N.Y.: Knopf, 1956. 175 pp.
56-8910.
AUFS, 467; Silberman, 1010; Library Journal, 12/15/56;
TLS, 7/5/57

1763 Kawabata, Yasunari. Thousand Cranes. tr. by Edward Seiden-
B sticker. N.Y.: Knopf, 1959. 147 pp. 59-6220.
Library Journal, 1/1/59; TLS, 6/5/59

1573 Kawai, Kazuo. Japan's American Interlude. Chicago: Univer-
A sity of Chicago Press, 1960. 257 pp. 59-14111.
Sup. 61, 2768; Silberman, 551; JAS, 11/60; AHR, 7/60;
Am. Pol. Sci. R., 12/60; Ann. Am. Acad., 9/60; Library
Journal, 3/15/60; Pacific Affairs, 9/60

0106 Kawakami, Kiyoshi Karl. Manchoukuo, Child of Conflict. N.Y.:
C Macmillan, 1933. 311 pp. 33-8957. o.p.
Hucker, 790; Am. Pol. Sci. R., 6/33; Ann. Am. Acad.,
9/33; J. Religion, 10/33

1736 Kawatake, Mokuami. The Love of Izayoi & Seishin; A Kabuki
B Play. tr. by Frank T. Motofuji. Rutland, Vt.: Tuttle,
1966. 172 pp. (Library of Japanese Literature).
66-16266.
Choice, 2/68

2106 Kaye, Barrington. Upper Nankin Street, Singapore; A Socio-
B logical Study of Chinese Households Living in a Densely
Populated Area. Singapore: University of Malaya Press,
1960. 439 pp. 60-51064.
JAS, 5/61

0139 Kebschull, Harvey G., comp. Politics in Transitional Societies;
C The Challenge of Change in Asia, Africa, and Latin
America. N.Y.: Appleton-Century-Crofts, 1968. 435 pp.
68-13149.
Choice, 11/68

1692 Keene, Donald, ed. Anthology of Japanese Literature, from the
A Earliest Era to the Mid-Nineteenth Century. N.Y.: Grove,
1955. 442 pp. 55-5110.
AUFS, 417; Silberman, 878; FEQ, 8/56; Japan Q., 10-12/56;
Library Journal, 11/1/55

1960 Keene, Donald. Bunraku; The Art of the Japanese Puppet Theatre.
A Tokyo: Kodansha, dist. by Japan Publications Trading Co.,
1965. 287 pp. 65-19187.

Japan Q., 1-3/66

1460 Keene, Donald. The Japanese Discovery of Europe; Honda
B Toshiaki and Other Discoverers, 1720-1798. rev. ed. Stanford, Calif.: Stanford University Press, 1969 (orig. pub.
in 1952). 255 pp. 69-13180. (R).
AUFS, 197; Silberman, 279; FEQ, 2/55; Library Journal,
9/15/54; Pacific Affairs, 9/55

1693 Keene, Donald. Japanese Literature; An Introduction for
A Western Readers. N.Y.: Grove, 1955. 114 pp. 55-6276.
AUFS, 418; Silberman, 866

1804 Keene, Donald. Modern Japanese Literature, an Anthology.
A N.Y.: Grove, 1956. 440 pp. 56-8439.
AUFS, 468; Silberman, 956; JAS, 5/57

1764 Keene, Donald, ed. and tr. The Old Woman, The Wife, and The
B Archer; Three Modern Japanese Short Novels. N.Y.: Viking,
1961. 172 pp. 61-16603. o.p.
Sup. 63, 2885; JAS, 8/62; Library Journal, 9/1/61;
TLS, 5/18/62

1998 Keith, Elizabeth. Old Korea, the Land of Morning Calm. N.Y.:
C Hutchinson, 1946. 72 pp. 47-6028. o.p.
AUFS, 546; Silberman, 1624

1379 Kenkyusha's New English-Japanese Dictionary on Bilingual
C Principles. new ed. N.Y.: Japan Publications Trading
Co., 1956. 2213 pp. Hand catalog.
AUFS, 410; Silberman, 111

1380 Kenkyusha's New Japanese-English Dictionary. new ed., ed. by
B Senkichiro Katsumata. N.Y.: Japan Publications Trading
Co., 1954. 2136 pp. Hand catalog.
AUFS, 411; Silberman, 111

0256 Kennedy, George Alexander. ZH Guide, an Introduction to Sinology.
B New Haven, Conn.: Sinological Seminar, Yale University, 1953.
171 pp. 53-1408.
FEQ, 11/53

0125 Kennedy, Malcolm Duncan. A History of Communism in East
C Asia. N.Y.: Praeger, 1957. 556 pp. 56-5139. o.p.
AUFS, 32; JAS, 2/58; Library Journal, 6/15/57; Pol. Sci.
Q., 12/57; TLS, 8/2/57

0005 Kerner, Robert Joseph. Northeastern Asia, a Select Bibliog-
C raphy. Berkeley: University of California Press, 1939.
2 v. 39-33136.
AUFS, 4599; Silberman, 10; AHR, 7/40; JAOS, 9/40; Pacific
Affairs, 3/40

2078 Kerr, George H. Formosa Betrayed. Boston: Houghton Mifflin,
A 1965. 514 pp. 65-20221.
Choice, 6/66; JAS, 8/66; TLS, 12/8/66

0181 Khantipalo, Phra. What is Buddhism; An Introduction to the
C Teaching of Lord Buddha, with Reference to the Belief In
and Practice of Those Teachings and Their Realization.
Bangkok: Social Science Association Press of Thailand, 1965.
150 pp. NUC 66-16102.
JAS, 5/66

1705 Ki no Tsurayuki. The Tosa Diary. tr. from Japanese by Wil-
B liam N. Porter. London: Frowde, 1912. 148 pp. S41-52.
o.p.
Silberman, 889

1936 Kidder, Jonathan Edward. The Birth of Japanese Art. N.Y.:
B Praeger, 1965. 209 pp. 65-16808.
Choice, 10/65; JAS, 2/66; Library Journal, 8/65; TLS,
12/23/65

1860 Kidder, Jonathan Edward. Early Japanese Art; The Great Tombs
C and Treasures. Princeton, N.J.: Van Nostrand, 1964. 354 pp.
64-57443. o.p.
Choice, 10/65; TLS, 3/25/65

1434 Kidder, Jonathan Edward. Japan Before Buddhism. rev. ed.
A N.Y.: Praeger, 1966. 284 pp. (Ancient Peoples and Places
Series, Vol. 10). 66-12521.
Silberman, 172; Choice, 10/67; JAS, 5/60; Japan Q., 7-9/60

1834 Kidder, Jonathan Edward. Japanese Temples; Sculpture, Paint-
A ings, Gardens, and Architecture. Tokyo: Bijutsu Shuppan-
sha, 1964. 554 pp. NUC 66-35074.

1892 Kidder, Jonathan Edward. Prehistoric Japanese Arts; The Jomon
C Pottery of Japan. contrib. by Teruya Esaka. Palo Alto,

Calif.:, Kodansha, 1968. 308 pp. 68-17458.
JAS, 2/59; Japan Q., 1-3/58

2050 Kim, Byong Kuk. Central Banking Experiment in a Developing
B   Economy; Case Study of Korea. Seoul: The Korean Research
     Center, 1965. 282 pp. (The Korean Studies Series, Vol. 12).
     K66-510.

2062 Kim, Chae-won. Treasures of Korean Art; 2000 Years of Cer-
B   amics, Sculpture, and Jeweled Arts. N.Y.: Abrams, 1966.
     283 pp. 66-23402.
     Choice, 4/67; Library Journal, 1/15/67; TLS, 10/6/66

2009 Kim, Ch'ang-sun. Fifteen-Year History of North Korea. Washing-
B   ton: U.S. Joint Publications Research Service, 1963. 198 pp.
     (JPRS 18925). NUC 65-27380.

2013 Kim, Chong Ik Eugene. Korea and the Politics of Imperialism,
B   1876-1910. by C. I. Eugene Kim and Han-Kyo Kim. Berke-
     ley: University of California Press, 1967. 260 pp.
     (Center for Japanese and Korean Studies). 68-12037.
     Choice, 11/68; Pacific Affairs, Fall/68

2043 Kim, Chong Ik Eugene. A Pattern of Political Development;
B   Korea. Kalamazoo, Mich.: Korea Research and Publication,
     Inc., 1964. 200 pp. 64-56446. mimeo. o.p.
     JAS, 11/65

2059 Kim, Richard E. The Martyred, a Novel. N.Y.: Braziller, 1964.
A   316 pp. 64-10785.
     Choice, 3/64; Library Journal, 4/1/64; TLS, 10/29/64

2054 Kim, So-un. The Story Bag; A Collection of Korean Folk tales.
C   Rutland, Vt.: Tuttle, 1955. 229 pp. 55-13738.
     Silberman, 1881

0107 Kim, Young Hum. East Asia's Turbulent Century, with American
B   Diplomatic Documents. N.Y.: Appleton-Century-Crofts, 1966.
     386 pp. 66-10328.
     Choice, 9/66; Ann. Am. Acad., 9/66

0257 King, Frank H. H. A Research Guide to China Coast Newspapers,
B   1822-1911. Cambridge, Mass.: East Asian Research Center,
     Harvard University, 1965. 235 pp. (Harvard East Asian
     Monograph, 18). 65-5287.

0157 Kirby, E. Stuart. Economic Development in East Asia. N.Y.:
B   Praeger, 1967. 253 pp. 67-26565.
     JAS, 8/68; Library Journal, 12/15/67; TLS, 6/6/68

0889 Kirby, E. Stuart. Introduction to the Economic History of
C   China. London: Allen & Unwin, 1954. 202 pp. 54-1075.
     o.p. (M-University).
     Hucker, 2127; Am. Econ. R., 12/54; Ann. Am. Acad., 7/54;
     TLS, 4/16/54

1815 Kishimoto, Hideo. Japanese Religion in the Meiji Era. tr.
B   by John F. Howes. Tokyo: Obunsha, 1956. 377 pp. (Japanese
     Culture in the Meiji Era, Vol. II). 57-2109.
     Silberman, 593; JAS, 8/57

1816 Kitagawa, Joseph Mitsuo. Religion in Japanese History. N.Y.:
A   Columbia University Press, 1966. 475 pp. (Lectures on
     the History of Religions, Sponsored by the American Council
     of Learned Societies, New Series, 7). 65-23669.
     Choice, 6/67; JAS, 8/67; AHR, 10/67; Library Journal, 1/15/66

0174 Kitagawa, Joseph Mitsuo. Religions of the East. rev. and enl.
B   ed. Philadelphia: Westminster Press, 1968. 351 pp.
     68-7174.

0158 Klein, Sidney. The Pattern of Land Tenure Reform in East Asia
B   after World War II. N.Y.: Bookman, 1958. 260 pp. 58-2808.
     Hucker, 2183

0782 Klochko, Mikhail Antonovich. Soviet Scientist in Red China.
B   tr. by Andrew MacAndrew. N.Y.: Praeger, 1964. 213 pp.
     64-16681.
     Sup. 65, 3096; Choice, 1/65; JAS, 5/66; China Q., 1-3/65;
     Library Journal, 1/1/65; TLS, 2/25/65

1357 Ko, Hung. Alchemy, Medicine, Religion in the China of A.D. 320:
C   the Nei P'ien of Ko Hung (Pao-p'u tzu). tr. by James R.
     Ware. Cambridge, Mass.: M.I.T. Press, 1967. 388 pp.
     66-23548.
     Choice, 10/67; JAS, 11/67

0927 Ko Lien Hua Ying. Flower Shadows Behind the Curtain; A Sequel
B   to Chin P'ing Mei. tr. by V. Kean from F. Kuhn's German
     version of the original Chinese. intro. by F. Kuhn. London:

The Bodley Head, 1959. 432 pp. Hand catalog. o.p.
Hucker, 1701

1720 Kobayashi, Issa. The Autumn Wind; A Selection from the Poems
B   of Issa. tr. by Lewis Mackenzie. London: Murray, dist.
     by Paragon, 1957. 115 pp. (Wisdom of the East Series).
     59-2658.
     Silberman, 1075; Japan Q., 4-6/58

1721 Kobayashi, Issa. The Year of My Life. tr. by Nobuyuki Yuasa.
B   Berkeley: University of California Press, 1960. 140 pp.
     60-9651 rev. o.p.
     Silberman, 1073

1861 Kobayashi, Norio. Bonsai - Miniature Potted Trees. 7th ed.
B   Tokyo: Japan Travel Bureau, 1957. 177 pp. (Tourist Library,
     N.S. 13). 57-8540.
     Silberman, 836

1975 Kobayashi, Victor Nobuo. John Dewey in Japanese Educational
B   Thought. Ann Arbor: University of Michigan School of Educa-
     tion, 1964. 198 pp. (Comparative Education Dissertation
     Series, No. 2). 65-63281.
     JAS, 11/65

2044 Koh, Byung Chul, comp. Aspects of Administrative Development
B   in South Korea. Seoul: Korea Research and Publications,
     dist. by Cellar Book Shop, 1967. 144 pp. (Monograph
     Series on Korea, 4). 68-634.
     Choice, 7-8/68

1862 Kojiro, Yuichiro. Forms in Japan. tr. by Kenneth Yasuda.
B   Honolulu: East-West Center Press, 1965. 184 pp. 64-7591.
     Choice, 10/65; JAS, 2/66; Library Journal, 8/65; TLS,
     12/23/65

1747 Kokusai Bunka Shinkokai, Tokyo. Introduction to Classic Japa-
B   nese Literature. Tokyo: 1948. 443 pp. 50-31232 rev.
     AUFS, 419; Silberman, 873

1694 Kokusai Bunka Shinkokai, Tokyo. Introduction to Contemporary
B   Japanese Literature, ed. by the Kokusai Bunka Shinkokai.
     Tokyo: 1939-1959. 2 v. 39-12994 rev.
     AUFS, 471; Silberman, 875, 937

1637 Kokusai Shokuryo. Nogyo Kyokai. Agriculture in Japan. Tokyo:
C   Japan FAO Association, 1953. 62 pp. 54-29294 rev.

1961 Komiya, Toyotaka, ed. Japanese Music and Drama in the Meiji Era.
C   tr. and adapted by Edward Seidensticker and Donald Keene.
     Tokyo: Obunsha, 1956. 535 pp. (Japanese Culture in the
     Meiji Era, Vol. IV). A59-8756.
     Silberman, 1169

0379 Komroff, Manuel, ed. Contemporaries of Marco Polo. N.Y.: Boni &
B   Liveright, 1928. 358 pp. 28-14790.
     Hucker, 393

0783 Koningsberger, Hans. Love and Hate in China. N.Y.: McGraw-
B   Hill, 1966. 150 pp. 66-19286.
     Choice, 12/66

1796 Kono, Ichiro, ed. An Anthology of Modern Japanese Poetry.
B   Tokyo: Kenkyusha, 1957. 173 pp. A59-7331.
     AUFS, 472; Silberman, 1081

0622 Koo, Hui-lan (Oei). Hui-lan Koo (Madame Wellington Koo)
C   an Autobiography As Told to Mary Van Rensselaer Thayer.
     N.Y.: Dial, 1943. 421 pp. 43-16023. o.p.

2014 Korea. (Government-General of Chosen, 1910-1945). A Short
C   History of Korea. comp. by Center for East Asian Cultural
     Studies. Honolulu: East-West Center Press, 1964. 84 pp.
     65-2830. o.p.
     Choice, 1/66; JAS, 11/65

1999 Korea: Its Land, People, and Culture of All Ages. Seoul:
B   Hakwon-Sa, 1960. 718 pp. 60-2998.
     Silberman, 1619

2000 Korea (Republic) Yunesuk'o Hanguk Wiwonhoe. UNESCO Korean
B   Survey. Seoul: Dong-a, 1960. 936 pp. 60-52083.
     Silberman, 1617a

2064 Korea University. Asiatic Research Center. A Brief History
C   of the Asiatic Research Center. Seoul: 1964.

1989 Korean Affairs. Seoul: The Council on Korean Affairs, 1962-
C

1990 The Korean Studies Series. Seoul: The Korean Research Center,
C 1955-

1991 Koreana Quarterly. Seoul: International Research Center, 1959-
B Silberman, 1647

1817 Kosaka, Masaaki, ed. Japanese Thought in the Meiji Era. tr.
B by David Abosch. Tokyo: Pan-Pacific Press, 1958. 512 pp.
(Japanese Culture in the Meiji Era, Vol. IX). 59-65049.
Silberman, 335

0623 Kotenev, Anatol M. New Lamps for Old; An Interpretation of
C Events in Modern China and Whither They Lead. Shanghai:
North-China Daily News and Herald, 1931. 371 pp. 31-30817.
o.p.
AUFS, 833

0380 Kracke, Edward A. Civil Service in Early Sung China, 960-1067;
B With Particular Emphasis on the Development of Controlled
Sponsorship, to Foster Administrative Responsibility.
Cambridge, Mass.: Harvard University Press, 1953. 262 pp.
52-5399.
AUFS, 706; Hucker, 333; FEQ, 2/54; JAOS, 10-12/53

1159 Krebsova, Berta. Lu Sun, Sa Vie et Son Oeuvre. Prague: Acad-
C emie Tchecoslavaque des Sciences, 1953. 111 pp. 56-17185.

0492 Ku, Chieh-Kang. The Autobiography of a Chinese Historian,
B Being the Preface to a Symposium on Ancient Chinese
History (Ku shih pien). tr. and annotated by Arthur W.
Hummel. Taipei: Ch'eng-wen Publishing Co., dist. by Chinese
Materials and Research Aids Service Center, 1966 (orig. pub.
by Brill, 1931). 199 pp. Hand catalog. (R).
Hucker, 1628

1180 Kuan, Chung. Kuan-tzu; A Repository of Early Chinese Thought.
C A Translation and Study of Twelve Chapters, by W. Allyn
Rickett. fore. by Derke Bodde. Hong Kong: Hong Kong Uni-
versity Press, 1965- 66-4314.
Choice, 1/67; TLS, 12/1/66

0998 Kuan, Han-ch'ing. Selected Plays. tr. by Yang Hsien-yi and
A Gladys Yang. Shanghai: New Art & Literature, 1958. 237 pp.
61-39292. o.p.
AUFS, 1131

0258 Kuang, Ju-ssu. Chinese Written Characters; Their Wit and Wisdom.
C N.Y.: Cobble Hill, dist. by Hill & Wang, 1968 (orig. pub.
by Pantheon, 1944 under title Chinese Wit, Wisdom, and
Written Characters). 72 pp. 45-2993. (R).
Hucker, 73

0999 Kuang-tung yueh chu tuan. The Runaway Maid; A Cantonese Opera.
C rev. by the Cantonese Opera Company of Kwangtung. tr. by
Gladys Yang. Peking: Foreign Languages Press, 1958. 64 pp.
59-25096.

1527 Kublin, Hyman. Asian Revolutionary, the Life of Sen Kata-
B yama. Princeton, N.J.: Princeton University Press, 1964.
370 pp. 63-7156.
Sup. 65, 3064; Choice, 6/64; JAS, 11/64; Japan Q., 7-9/64;
Library Journal, 4/15/64; TLS, 8/13/64

0493 Kuei, Wan-jung. T'ang-yin-pi-shih. Parallel Cases from
C Under the Pear-tree, a 13th Century Manual of Jurisprudence
and Detection. tr. from Chinese with notes and intro. by
R. H. van Gulik. Leiden: Brill, 1956. 198 pp. 57-970.
Hucker, 1874

1893 Kumagaya, Nobuo and Miroru Ooka. History of Buddhist Art in
C Japan. South Pasadena, Calif.: P. D. and Ione Perkins,
1940. o.p.
Silberman, 728

1528 Kuno, Yoshi Saburo. Japanese Expansion on the Asiatic
C Continent; A Study in the History of Japan with Special
Reference to Her International Relations with China,
Korea, and Russia. Port Washington, N.Y.: Kennikat, 1968
(orig. pub. by University of California Press, 1937-40).
2 v. 67-27615. (R).
Hucker, 492; Silberman, 237; FEQ, 11/41; TLS, 11/20/37

1297 Kuo, Hsi. An Essay on Landscape Painting by Kuo Hsi. tr. by
B Shio Sakanishi. London: Murray, dist. by Paragon, 1935.
64 pp. (Wisdom of the East Series). 36-7175.
Hucker, 1491

1298 Kuo, Jo-hsu. Experiences in Painting (T'u-hua chien-wen chih).
C An Eleventh Century History of Chinese Painting, Together
with the Chinese Text in Facsimile. tr. and annotated by
Alexander Coburn Soper. Washington: American Council of

Learned Societies, 1951. 216 pp. 52-190.
Hucker, 1489

1086 Kuo, Kuo-fu. Among the Ominans. tr. by Huai-yuan Shang.
C Peking: Foreign Languages Press, 1961. 348 pp. 62-46451.

1138 Kuo, Mo-jo. Chu Yuan, a Play in Five Acts. tr. by Yang
C Hsien-yi and Gladys Yang. Peking: Foreign Languages
Press, 1953. 126 pp. 55-32878.
AUFS, 1132

0784 Kuo, Pin-chia. China: New Age and New Outlook. N.Y.: Knopf,
C 1956. 231 pp. 56-5605.
Hucker, 935; JAS, 11/56; Library Journal, 2/1/56; Pacific
Affairs, 9/56; TLS, 7/20/56

1335 Kuo, Ping-wen. The Chinese System of Public Education. N.Y.:
B Teachers College, Columbia University, 1915. 209 pp.
15-17201. o.p.
Hucker, 1914

0213 Kuo, T'ing-i, comp. Sino-Japanese Relations 1862-1927, a Check-
C list of the Chinese Foreign Ministry Archives. N.Y.: East
Asian Institute, Columbia University, 1965. 228 pp.
65-26953.

1917 Kurth, Julius. Die Geschichte des Japanischen Holzschnitts.
C Leipzig: Hiersemann, 1925-1929. 3 v. 31-32662.
Silberman, 782

1574 Kurzman, Dan. Kishi and Japan; The Search for the Sun. fore.
A by James A. Michener. N.Y.: Obolensky, 1960. 394 pp.
60-9041.
Sup. 63, 2886; Silberman, 586; JAS, 2/63; Library Journal,
11/15/60; Pacific Affairs, Fall/61

0159 Kuznets, Simon Smith, ed. Economic Growth: Brazil, India,
C Japan. Durham, N.C.: Duke University Press, 1955. 613 pp.
55-9491.
Silberman, 384; FEQ, 5/56; Am. Econ. R., 6/56; Am. Soc. R.,
8/56; Ann. Am. Acad., 11/56; Pacific Affairs, 9/56; TLS,
10/5/56

1181 Kwok, Danny Wynn Ye. Scientism in Chinese Thought, 1900-1950.
C New Haven, Conn.: Yale University Press, 1965. 231 pp.
(Yale Historical Publications, Miscellany, 82). 65-22330.
Choice, 7-8/66; JAS, 11/66; Library Journal, 12/1/65; TLS,
4/21/66

0082 Lach, Donald Frederick. Asia in the Making of Europe. Chicago:
A University of Chicago Press, 1965- 985 pp. 64-19848.
Sup. 65, 3048; JAS, 2/68; Library Journal, 1/15/65; TLS,
8/26/65

0624 La Fargue, Thomas Edward. China and the World War. Stanford,
C Calif.: Stanford University Press, 1937. 278 pp.
37-39237. o.p.
AHR, 7/38; Am. Pol. Sci. R., 6/38; JAOS, 9/38

1024 Lai, Ming. A History of Chinese Literature. N.Y.: Putnam,
C 1966 (orig. pub. by John Day, 1964). 439 pp. 64-20468 rev.
(R).
Choice, 11/65; JAS, 5/65; JAOS, 7-9/65; Library Journal,
10/1/64; TLS, 8/6/64

0785 Lall, Arthur. How Communist China Negotiates. N.Y.:
B Columbia University Press, 1968. 291 pp. 67-29051.
Choice, 10/68; China Q., 1-3/69; Library Journal, 3/15/68

0494 Lamb, Alastair. Britain and Chinese Central Asia; The Road to
A Lhasa, 1767 to 1905. N.Y.: Humanities, 1960. 387 pp.
61-1070.
Hucker, 678; JAS, 2/63

0495 Lamb, Alastair. British Missions to Cochin China: 1778-
C 1822. Kuala Lumpur: Printcraft, 1961. 248 pp. (Royal
Asiatic Society. Journal of the Malayan Branch, Singapore,
Vol. 34, Parts 3 and 4). Hand catalog.
Sup. 63, 2921; JAS, 11/62

0381 Lamb, Harold. Genghis Khan, the Emperor of All Men. N.Y.:
C Doubleday, 1952 (orig. pub. by McBride, 1927). 270 pp.
A58-9870. (R).
Hucker, 369

0625 Lampard, David. A Present from Peking. Garden City, N.Y.:
B Doubleday, 1965. 353 pp. 65-13097. o.p.

1863 Lancaster, Clay. The Japanese Influence in America. N.Y.:
B Walton H. Rawls, dist. by Twayne, 1963. 292 pp. 63-18860.

Choice, 3/64; JAS, 5/65; Library Journal, 2/15/64

0786   Landman, Lynn. Profile of Red China. N.Y.: Simon & Schuster,
C   1951. 245 pp. 51-5047. o.p. (M-University).
        Library Journal, 8/51

1918   Lane, Richard Douglas. Masters of the Japanese Print, Their
A   World and Their Work. Garden City, N.Y.: Doubleday, 1962.
        319 pp. 62-12098.
        JAS, 8/63; Japan Q., 4-6/63; JAOS, 10-12/62

1160   Lang, Olga. Pa Chin and His Writings; Chinese Youth Between
A   the Two Revolutions. Cambridge, Mass.: Harvard
        University Press, 1967. 402 pp. (Harvard East Asian
        Series, 28). 67-17314.
        Choice, 11/68; JAS, 5/68; AHR, 4/68; TLS, 2/29/68

1597   Langdon, Frank. Politics in Japan. Boston: Little, Brown,
B   1967. 290 pp. 66-28736.

1598   Langer, Paul Fritz. The Japanese Communists and Their Struggle
C   for Power. Santa Monica, Calif.: Rand Corporation, 1962.
        39 pp. 62-39667. o.p.

1243   Lankavatara-sutra. The Lankavatara Sutra; A Mahayana Text, Trans-
C   lated for the First Time from the Original Sanskrit by Dai-
        setz Teitaro Suzuki. N.Y.: Humanities, 1966 (orig. pub.
        by Routledge and Kegan Paul, 1956). 300 pp. 57-37460. (R).
        AUFS, 1575; Hucker, 1293; JAOS, 3/33

1224   Lao-tzu. Tao Teh Ching. tr. by John C. H. Wu. ed. by Paul
B   K. T. Sih. Jamaica, N.Y.: St. John's University Press,
        1961. 115 pp. 60-16884.

1225   Lao-tzu. Tao Te Ching, the Book of the Way and Its Virtue.
C   tr. from Chinese by J. J. L. Duyvendak. London: Murray,
        1954. 172 pp. 54-4621. o.p.
        AUFS, 646; Hucker, 1186

1226   Lao-tzu. Tao Te Ching, a New Translation by Ch'u Ta-Kao.
B   5th ed. London: Allen & Unwin, 1959. 95 pp. A60-1769.
        o.p.
        Hucker, 1187

1227   Lao-tzu. The Way and Its Power; A Study of the Tao Te Ching
B   and Its Place in Chinese Thought, by Arthur Waley. N.Y.:
        Macmillan, 1956 (orig. pub. by Allen & Unwin, 1934). 262 pp.
        58-5092. (R).
        AUFS, 647; Hucker, 1185

1228   Lao-tzu. The Way of Lao Tzu. (Tao-te ching). tr. by Wing-tsit
A   Chan. N.Y.: Bobbs-Merrill, 1963. 285 pp. 62-21266.

1835   Lassalle, Hugo. Zen Buddhismus. von Hugo M. Enomiya. Koln:
B   Bachem, 1966. 449 pp. 66-66205.

0126   Latourette, Kenneth Scott. The American Record in the Far
C   East, 1945-1951. N.Y.: Macmillan, 1952. 208 pp.
        52-12394. o.p.
        Hucker, 821; AHR, 4/53; Am. Pol. Sci. R., 4/53; Ann. Am.
        Acad., 4/53; Library Journal, 6/1/52; Pacific Affairs,
        4/53; Pol. Sci. Q., 6/53

0787   Latourette, Kenneth Scott. China. Englewood Cliffs, N.J.:
C   Prentice-Hall, 1964. 152 pp. (The Modern Nations in
        Historical Perspective). 64-23560.
        Choice, 2/65; JAS, 5/65; AHR, 10/65; Library Journal, 3/15/65

0318   Latourette, Kenneth Scott. The Chinese; Their History and
C   Culture. 4th ed. rev. N.Y.: Macmillan, 1964. 714 pp.
        64-17372.
        AUFS, 688; Hucker, 4; Choice, 1/65; JAS, 2/65

0342   Latourette, Kenneth Scott. The Development of China. 6th ed.,
C   rev. Boston: Houghton Mifflin, 1946. 343 pp. 46-4889.
        o.p. (M-University).

0183   Latourette, Kenneth Scott. The Great Century: In Africa
C   and Asia, A.D. 1800-A.D. 1914. N.Y.: Harper, 1940.
        (A History of the Expansion of Christianity, Vol. VI).
        37-20993. o.p.
        FEQ, 2/45; J. Religion, 7/41

0496   Latourette, Kenneth Scott. A History of Christian Missions in
B   China. N.Y.: Russell & Russell, 1967 (orig. pub. by Mac-
        millan, 1929). 930 pp. 66-24721. (R). (M-University).
        AUFS, 749; Hucker, 548; AHR, 7/29; J. Religion, 10/29;
        Pol. Sci. Q., 12/29

0626   Latourette, Kenneth Scott. The History of Early Relations
C   between the United States and China, 1784-1844. N.Y.: Kraus,
        1964 (orig. pub. by Yale University Press, 1917). 209 pp.
        (Transactions of the Connecticut Academy of Arts and
        Sciences, August, 1917). 65-1071. (R).

0627   Latourette, Kenneth Scott. A History of Modern China. Balti-
C   more: Penguin, 1954. 233 pp. 55-1351. o.p.
        Hucker, 722

0083   Latourette, Kenneth Scott. A Short History of the Far East.
C   4th ed. N.Y.: Macmillan, 1964. 776 pp. 64-14965.
        AUFS, 99; Choice, 9/64; FEQ, 2/47; Ann. Am. Acad., 9/46;
        Library Journal, 4/15/46

0628   Lattimore, Owen. The Making of Modern China, a Short History.
C   London: Allen & Unwin, 1945. 212 pp. 45-4334. o.p.
        FEQ, 11/44

0629   Lattimore, Owen. Manchuria; Cradle of Conflict. rev. ed.
B   N.Y.: Macmillan, 1935. 343 pp. 35-6659. o.p.
        AUFS, 4986; Am. Pol. Sci. R., 8/35

0059   Lattimore, Owen. The Situation in Asia. Boston: Little,
C   Brown, 1949. 244 pp. 49-2218. o.p.
        AUFS, 34; Am. Pol. Sci. R., 10/49

0060   Lattimore, Owen. Solution in Asia. Boston: Little, Brown,
C   1945. 214 pp. 45-1566. o.p.
        FEQ, 8/45; Pacific Affairs, 12/45

0497   Laufer, Berthold. Chinese Clay Figures. Chicago: Field Museum
C   of Natural History, 1914- (Publication 177). 15-8603.
        o.p.
        Hucker, 1910

1849   Laures, John. The Catholic Church in Japan; A Short History.
C   Rutland, Vt.: Tuttle, 1954. 252 pp. A55-7332.
        Silberman, 661; JAOS, 4-6/55; J. Religion, 7/55

1850   Laures, John. Kirishitan Bunko; A Manual of Books and Docu-
B   ments on the Early Christian Missions in Japan, (With
        First Supplement). Tokyo: Sophia University Press, 1940.
        344 pp. 50-47693.
        Silberman, 654; FEQ, 2/42, 2/49; Japan Q., 4-6/58

1461   Laures, John. Nobunaga und das Christentum. Tokyo: Sophia-
C   Universitat, 1950. 54 pp. (Monumenta Nipponica Monographs,
        No. 10). 51-28771.
        Silberman, 242

0630   League of Nations. Commission of Enquiry into the Sino-
B   Japanese Dispute. Report. 1932. 291 pp. 50-53932.
        AUFS, 838

1919   Ledoux, Louis Vernon. Japanese Prints, Buncho to Utamaro, in
C   the Collection of Louis V. Ledoux. N.Y.: Weyhe, 1948.
        192 pp. A50-9099. o.p.
        FEQ, 11/49; JAOS, 4-6/50

1920   Ledoux, Louis Vernon. Japanese Prints by Harunobu and Shunsho
C   in the Collection of Louis V. Ledoux. N.Y.: Wehye, 1945.
        152 pp. 45-7008. o.p.
        FEQ, 8/48; JAOS, 7-9/47

1921   Ledoux, Louis Vernon. Japanese Prints, Hokusai and Hiroshige,
C   in the Collection of Louis V. Ledoux. Princeton, N.J.:
        Princeton University Press, 1951. 51-12844. o.p.
        FEQ, 5/52; JAOS, 4-6/52

1922   Ledoux, Louis Vernon. Japanese Prints of the Primitive Period
C   in the Collection of Louis V. Ledoux. N.Y.: Weyhe, 1942.
        186 pp. 42-14640. o.p.
        JAOS, 7-9/47

1923   Ledoux, Louis Vernon. Japanese Prints, Sharaku to Toyokuni, in
C   the Collection of Louis V. Ledoux. Princeton, N.J.:
        Princeton University Press, 1950. unpaged. 50-6469. o.p.
        Silberman, 780; JAOS, 7-9/51

2045   Lee, Chong-sik. The Politics of Korean Nationalism. Berkeley:
A   University of California Press for the Center for Japanese
        Studies, 1963. 342 pp. 63-19029.
        Sup. 65, 3077; JAS, 5/64; Ann. Am. Acad., 7/64; Library
        Journal, 11/1/63; TLS, 3/2/64

2056   Lee, Peter H., comp. and tr. Anthology of Korean Poetry From
A   the Earliest Era to the Present. N.Y.: John Day, 1964.
        196 pp. (UNESCO Collection of Representative Works:
        Korean Series). 64-14198. o.p.
        Sup. 65, 3078; Choice, 10/64; JAS, 11/64; Library Journal,

2058 Lee, Peter H. Korean Literature: Topics and Themes. Tucson:
B   University of Arizona Press, 1965. 141 pp. (Associa-
      tion for Asian Studies, Monographs and Papers, XVI).
      64-19167.
      Choice, 10/65; JAS, 11/65

2107 Lee, Rose Hum. The Chinese in the United States of America.
B   N.Y.: Oxford, 1960. 465 pp. 60-3959. o.p.
      Am. J. Soc., 3/61; Am. Pol. Sci. R., 2/61, 3/61; Ann. Am.
      Acad., 3/61; China Q., 1-3/61; Pacific Affairs, Winter/61

1299 Lee, Sherman E. Chinese Landscape Painting. 2d ed. rev. Cleve-
B   land: Cleveland Museum of Art, dist. by Abrams, 1962. 169 pp.
      62-11141.

0187 Lee, Sherman E. A History of Far Eastern Art. N.Y.: Abrams,
A   1964. 527 pp. 64-9319/CD.
      Choice, 12/64; JAS, 5/66

1894 Lee, Sherman E. Japanese Decorative Style. Cleveland:
A   Cleveland Museum of Art, dist. by Abrams, 1961. 161 pp.
      61-9910.

1300 Lee, Sherman E. Streams and Mountains Without End; A Northern
C   Sung Handscroll and Its Significance in the History of Early
      Chinese Painting, by Sherman E. Lee and Wen Fong. Ascona:
      Artibus Asiae, 1955. 57 pp. (Supplementum XIV). A56-6593.
      Hucker, 1474; FEQ, 2/56

1265 Lee, Sherman E. and Wai-kam Ho. Chinese Art under the Mongols:
C   the Yuan Dynasty (1279-1368). Cleveland: Cleveland
      Museum of Art, 1968. 403 pp. 68-9276.

1207 Legge, James, ed. and tr. The Chinese Classics. tr. into Eng-
B   lish, with preliminary essays and explanatory notes. Hong
      Kong: Hong Kong University Press, 1960 (orig. pub. by
      Trubner, 1875-1909). 5 v. 61-4012. (R). (M-University).
      Hucker, 1530; JAS, 2/63

1381 Lehmann, Winfred Phillip. A Grammar of Formal Written Japan-
C   ese, by W. P. Lehmann and Lloyd Faust. Cambridge, Mass.:
      Harvard University Press, 1951. 153 pp. (Harvard-Yenching
      Institute Studies, V). 51-587 rev. o.p.
      Silberman, 128; FEQ, 11/51

2108 Leigh, Michael B. The Chinese Community of Sarawak; A Study
B   of Communal Relations. Singapore: Malaysia Publishing
      House for Dept. of History, University of Singapore,
      1964. 68 pp. (Singapore Studies on Malaysia, No. 6).
      SA66-7066.

0844 Leng, Shao-chuan. Justice in Communist China: a Survey
B   of the Judicial System of the Chinese People's Republic.
      Dobbs Ferry, N.Y.: Oceana, 1967. 196 pp. 67-14398.
      Choice, 11/68; Library Journal, 2/15/68

0845 Leng, Shao Chuan. Sun Yat-sen and Communism. by Shao Chuan
A   Leng and Norman D. Palmer. N.Y.: Praeger, 1961. 234 pp.
      60-16426. o.p.

1462 Lensen, George Alexander. The Russian Push Toward Japan;
B   Russo-Japanese Relations, 1697-1875. Princeton, N.J.:
      Princeton University Press, 1959. 533 pp. 59-9608.
      o.p. (M-University).
      Silberman, 302; JAS, 2/60; AHR, 3/60; Am. Pol. Sci. R.,
      12/59; Ann. Am. Acad., 1/60; Japan Q., 10-12/59; Pacific
      Affairs, 12/59

1463 Lensen, George Alexander. Russia's Japan Expedition of 1852
C   to 1855. Gainesville: University of Florida Press, 1955.
      208 pp. 55-8081. o.p.
      Silberman, 304; FEQ, 2/56

0498 Lensen, George Alexander. The Russo-Chinese War. Tallahassee,
B   Fla.: Diplomatic Press, 1967. 315 pp. 67-26314.
      Choice, 3/68; JAS, 5/68; Pacific Affairs, Spring/68

0631 Levenson, Joseph Richmond. Confucian China and Its Modern
A   Fate. Berkeley: University of California Press, 1958-1965.
      3 v. 58-2791 rev. 2.
      AUFS, 942; Hucker, 648; Choice, 5/66, 9/64; JAS, 5/59,
      5/66; AHR, 1/59, 4/65; Library Journal, 9/15/64, 3/15/65;
      TLS, 8/29/58, 8/26/65

0499 Levenson, Joseph Richmond. Liang Ch'i-ch'ao and the Mind of
A   Modern China. Cambridge, Mass.: Harvard University Press,
      1959. 256 pp. 53-5069.
      AUFS, 750; Hucker, 749; FEQ, 11/54

0632 Levi, Werner. Modern China's Foreign Policy. Minneapolis:
B   University of Minnesota Press, 1953. 399 pp. 53-10470.
      AUFS, 839; Hucker, 824; FEQ, 11/54; AHR, 10/54; Pacific
      Affasrs, 9/54

1638 Levine, Solomon Bernard. Industrial Relations in Postwar
B   Japan. Urbana: University of Illinois Press, 1958.
      200 pp. 58-9997.
      AUFS, 360; Silberman, 1589; JAS, 5/59; Am. Econ. R., 3/59;
      Am. Soc. R., 2/59; Ann. Am. Acad., 3/59; Japan Q., 10-12/58;
      J. Pol. Econ., 10/59; Library Journal, 8/58; Pacific Affairs,
      12/58

0909 Levy, Marion Joseph. The Family Revolution in Modern China.
A   N.Y.: Octagon, 1963 (orig. pub. by Harvard University
      Press, 1949). 390 pp. 63-20892. (R).
      AUFS, 840; Hucker, 2034; FEQ, 2/52; Am. Anthropologist,
      1/50; Pacific Affairs, 12/49

1336 Lewis, Ida Belle. The Education of Girls in China. N.Y.:
B   Teachers College, Columbia University, 1919. 92 pp.
      20-7788. o.p.
      Hucker, 2056

0846 Lewis, John Wilson. Chinese Communist Party Leadership and
B   the Succession of Mao Tse-tung; An Appraisal of Tensions.
      Washington: External Research Staff, U.S. Dept. of State,
      1964. 35 pp. NUC 64-47659. o.p.

0847 Lewis, John Wilson. Leadership in Communist China. Ithaca, N.Y.:
A   Cornell University Press, 1963. 305 pp. 63-12090.
      JAS, 11/65; Am. J. Soc., 3/64; Am. Pol. Sci. R., 12/63;
      Am. Soc. R., 2/65; China Q., 11-12/63; Pacific Affairs,
      Fall/64; Pol. Sci. Q., 6/65

0848 Lewis, John Wilson, ed. Major Doctrines of Communist China.
B   N.Y.: Norton, 1964. 343 pp. 64-10892.
      Sup. 65, 3100; Choice, 9/64; JAS, 2/65

0382 Li, Chi. The Beginnings of Chinese Civilization; Three Lec-
A   tures Illustrated with Finds at Anyang. Seattle: Uni-
      versity of Washington Press, 1957. 123 pp. 57-5285.
      Hucker, 159; JAS, 5/58; Am. Anthropologist, 4/58; JAOS,
      1-3/59; Library Journal, 6/15/57

0383 Li, Chi. The Formation of the Chinese People; An Anthropo-
A   logical Inquiry. Cambridge, Mass.: Harvard University
      Press, 1928. 283 pp. 28-22008.
      Hucker, 57

1208 Li, Chi. The Li Ki. tr. by James Legge. Delhi: Motilal Banar-
C   sidass, 1966 (orig. pub. by Clarendon, 1885). 2 v. (Sacred
      Books of the East, Vols. 27-28). 32-15906. (R).

0788 Li, Ch'i. Preliminary Study of Selected Terms. Berkeley:
B   East Asia Studies, Institute of International Studies, Uni-
      versity of California, 1956. 23 pp. 62-58111. o.p.

0500 Li, Chien-nung. The Political History of China, 1840-1928.
B   tr. and ed. by Ssu-yu Teng and Jeremy Ingalls. Stanford,
      Calif.: Stanford University Press, 1968 (orig. pub. by
      Van Nostrand, 1956). 545 pp. 67-26648. (R).
      Hucker, 604; AHR, 4/57; Am. Pol. Sci. R., 9/57; Library
      Journal, 9/15/56; Pacific Affairs, 6/57; TLS, 6/14/57

0384 Li, Chih-ch'ang. The Travels of an Alchemist; The Journey of
B   the Taoist, Ch'ang-ch'un, from China to the Hindukush at
      the Summons of Chingiz Khan, Recorded by his Disciple. tr.
      by Arthur Waley. London: Routledge, 1931. 166 pp. 31-31754.
      Hucker, 437

0890 Li, Choh-min. Economic Development of Communist China; An
A   Appraisal of the First Five Years of Industrialization.
      Berkeley: University of California Press, 1959. 284 pp.
      58-13330.
      AUFS, 943; Hucker, 2160; JAS, 2/60; Am. Econ. R., 9/59; Am.
      Pol. Sci. R., 9/59; Ann. Am. Acad., 9/59; Pacific Affairs,
      12/59

1301 Li, Chu-tsing. The Autumn Colors on the Ch'iao and Hua
C   Mountains; A Landscape by Chao Meng-fu. Ascona: Artibus
      Asiae, 1965. 109 pp. (Supplementum XXI). 66-4539.
      JAOS, 7-9/65

0319 Li, Dun Jen, comp. The Essence of Chinese Civilization.
C   Princeton, N.J.: Van Nostrand, 1967. 476 pp.
      67-25328.
      Choice, 9/68; JAS, 5/68

1087 Li, Fei-kan. Living Amongst Heroes. by Pa Chin (pseud.).
C   Peking: Foreign Languages Press, 1954. 132 pp. 57-35603.
     o.p.

1000 Li, Hsing-tao. The Circle of Chalk; A Play in Five Acts, Adapted
C   from Chinese by Klabund (pseud.). English version by James
     Laver. London: Heinemann, 1929. 107 pp. o.p.

1001 Li, Hsing-tao. The Story of the Circle of Chalk; A Drama
C   from the Old Chinese. tr. by Frances Hume from French
     of Stanislas Julien. London: Rodale, 1954. 124 pp.
     A55-8680. o.p.

0928 Li, Ju-chen. Flowers in the Mirror. tr. by Lin Tai-yi. Lon-
A   don: Peter Owen, 1965. 310 pp. NUC 66-71903.

1088 Li, Liu-ju. Sixty Stirring Years, a Novel in Three Volumes.
C   Peking: Foreign Languages Press, 1961- NUC 63-50932. o.p.

0965 Li, Po. The Works of Li Po, the Chinese Poet. Done into English
A   Verse by Shigeyoshi Obata. N.Y.: Paragon, 1964 (orig. pub.
     by Dutton, 1922). 236 pp. 65-26103. (R).
     Hucker, 1598

0324 Li, Ssu-Kuang. The Geology of China, by J. S. Lee. London:
C   Thomas Murby, 1939. 528 pp. 40-310. o.p.
     Hucker, 54

0343 Li, Tieh-tseng. The Historical Status of Tibet. N.Y.: King's
C   Crown, 1956. 312 pp. 55-10627. o.p.
     Hucker, 120; JAS, 5/57; AHR, 7/56; Ann. Am. Acad., 11/56;
     JAOS, 7-9/56; Library Journal, 11/1/56

0214 Li, Tien-yi. Chinese Fiction: a Bibliography of Books and Arti-
C   cles in Chinese and English. New Haven, Conn.: Far Eastern
     Publications, Yale University, 1968. 356 pp. 68-7553.

0215 Li, Tien-yi. The History of Chinese Literature: a Selected Bib-
A   liography. New Haven, Conn.: Far Eastern Publications, Yale
     University, 1968. 24 pp. NUC 69-2096.

0929 Li, Yu. Jou Pu Tuan; The Prayer Mat of Flesh. tr. by Richard
B   Martin from the German version by Franz Kuhn. N.Y.: Grove,
     1963. 376 pp. 63-9803. o.p.
     JAS, 2/64

0501 Liang, Fang-chung. The Single-wip Method (I-t'iao-pien fa) of
B   Taxation in China. tr. by Wang Yu-ch'uan. Cambridge,
     Mass.: Harvard University Press, 1956. 71 pp. 56-4991.
     o.p.
     Hucker, 448

1089 Liang, Pin. Keep the Red Flag Flying. tr. by Gladys
C   Yang. Peking: Foreign Languages Press, 1961. 528 pp.
     63-6530.

1229 Lieh-tzu. The Book of Lieh-tzu. A New Translation by A. C.
C   Graham. London: Murray, dist. by Paragon, 1961. 183 pp.
     (Wisdom of the East Series). 62-51659.
     Hucker, 1203; JAS, 11/61

1230 Lieh-tzu. Taoist Teachings from the Book of Lieh Tzu. tr.
C   from Chinese with intro. and notes by Lionel Giles. 2d ed.
     London: Murray, dist. by Paragon, 1947. 121 pp. (Wisdom
     of the East Series). CA14-275p.
     Hucker, 1204

1678 Lifton, Robert Jay. Death in Life; Survivors of Hiroshima.
C   N.Y.: Random House, 1968. 594 pp. 67-22658.
     Choice, 11/68; Library Journal, 1/15/68

0789 Lifton, Robert Jay. Thought Reform and the Psychology of Total-
A   ism; A Study of "Brainwashing" in China. N.Y.: Norton, 1961.
     510 pp. 61-5934.
     Hucker, 942; JAS, 8/61; Ann. Am. Acad., 5/61; Library
     Journal, 2/15/61; TLS, 8/11/61

0966 Lin, Pu. Lin Ho-ching. tr. and annotated by Max Perleberg.
C   Hong Kong: K. Weiss, 1952. 150 pp. 55-36458.

1002 Lin Yin Chi. Love Under the Willows; A Szechuan Opera. Liang
C   Shanpo and Chu Ying-tai. tr. by Yang Hsien-yi and Gladys
     Yang. Peking: Foreign Languages Press, 1956. 85 pp.
     57-41511.

1302 Lin, Yutang. The Chinese Theory of Art, Translations From the
B   Masters of Chinese Art. N.Y.: Putnam, 1967. 244 pp.
     67-21121.
     JAS, 2/68; Library Journal, 2/1/68; TLS, 11/16/67

0930 Lin, Yutang. Famous Chinese Short Stories Retold by Lin Yutang.
B   N.Y.: Washington Square, 1961 (orig. pub. by John Day, 1952).
     299 pp. NUC 63-26649. (R).
     Hucker, 1650; FEQ, 5/54

1025 Lin, Yutang. The Gay Genius; The Life and Times of Su Tung po.
C   N.Y.: John Day, 1947. 427 pp. 47-11617 rev. o.p.
     Hucker, 1603; FEQ, 5/48

1337 Lin, Yu-t'ang. A History of the Press and Public Opinion in
B   China. Chicago: University of Chicago Press, 1936. 179 pp.
     37-27194. o.p.
     Hucker, 114; Am. J. Soc., 11/37; Am. Pol. Sci. R., 6/37;
     TLS, 8/7/37

0931 Lin, Yutang, comp. and tr. The Importance of Understanding;
C   Translations from the Chinese. Cleveland: World, 1960.
     494 pp. 60-6690. o.p.
     Hucker, 1609; Library Journal, 3/15/60

0932 Lin, Yutang, tr. Widow, Nun and Courtesan; Three Novelettes
C   from the Chinese. N.Y.: John Day, 1951. 266 pp.
     51-10944 rev. 2. o.p.
     Hucker, 1710; Am. Soc. R., 11/51; Library Journal, 6/1/51

0175 Lin, Yutang, ed. The Wisdom of China and India. N.Y.:
C   Random House, 1942. 1104 pp. 42-50902. o.p.
     AUFS, 36; Hucker, 1057; FEQ, 5/43

0790 Lindsay, Michael. China and the Cold War; A Study in Interna-
B   tional Politics. Carlton: Melbourne, 1955. 286 pp.
     55-1680.
     AUFS, 945; Hucker, 984; FEQ, 8/56

1338 Lindsay, Michael. Notes on Educational Problems in Communist
A   China, 1941-47. N.Y.: International Secretariat, Insti-
     tute of Pacific Relations, 1950. 194 pp. 50-7573. o.p.

0633 Linebarger, Paul Myron Anthony. The China of Chiang K'ai-shek;
B   A Political Study. Boston: World Peace Foundation, 1941.
     449 pp. 41-11374. o.p. (M-University).
     AUFS, 844; Hucker, 783; FEQ, 11/41; Am. Pol. Sci. R., 12/41;
     Pacific Affairs, 12/41

0140 Linebarger, Paul Myron Anthony. Far Eastern Government and
C   Politics: China and Japan. 2d ed. Princeton, N.J.:
     Van Nostrand, 1956. 643 pp. 56-12290.
     AUFS, 101; Hucker, 622; Silberman, 564; FEQ, 5/55

0634 Linebarger, Paul Myron Anthony. Government in Republican China.
C   N.Y.: McGraw-Hill, 1938. 203 pp. 38-25848. o.p. (M-Uni-
     versity).
     Hucker, 1934; FEQ, 11/41; Am. Pol. Sci. R., 12/38

0635 Linebarger, Paul Myron Anthony. The Political Doctrines of Sun
C   Yat-sen; An Exposition of the San min chu i. Baltimore:
     Johns Hopkins Press, 1937. 278 pp. 37-12528.
     Hucker, 1929; AHR, 10/37; Am. Pol. Sci. R., 6/37; Ann.
     Am. Acad., 5/37; TLS, 5/8/37

0636 Linebarger, Paul Myron Anthony. Sun Yat Sen and the Chinese
C   Republic. N.Y.: Century, 1925. 371 pp. 25-4930. o.p.
     Hucker, 762

0385 Ling-hu, Te-fen. Accounts of Western Nations in the History
C   of the Northern Chou Dynasty. tr. and annotated by Roy
     Andrew Miller. Berkeley: University of California Press,
     1959. 83 pp. (Chinese Dynastic Histories Translations,
     No. 6). A59-9437.
     Hucker, 268; JAS, 8/60

0386 Ling-hu, Te-fen. Biography of Su Ch'o. tr. by Chauncy S. Good-
C   rich. 2d ed. rev. and enl. Berkeley: University of Cali-
     fornia Press, 1961. 116 pp. (Chinese Dynastic Histories
     Translations, No. 3). A53-9763 rev.
     Hucker, 266; FEQ, 5/54

1382 List of Japanese Economic and Business Periodicals in English.
B   Tokyo: Japan Economic Research Center, 1967.

0035 Literature East and West. v.1- 1954-
B

0637 Liu, Chih-pu. A Military History of Modern China, 1924-1949.
A   Princeton, N.J.: Princeton University Press, 1956. 312 pp.
     56-8386. o.p.
     AUFS, 846; JAS, 2/57; Library Journal, 8/56

1090 Liu, Ching. Wall of Bronze. tr. by Sidney Shapiro. Peking:
C   Foreign Languages Press, 1954. 283 pp. 55-38605.

0933　Liu, E. The Travels of Lao Ts'an. tr. from Chinese by Harold
A　Shadick. Ithaca, N.Y.: Cornell University Press, 1966
　　(orig. pub. in 1952). 277 pp. NUC 68-1914. (R).
　　AUFS, 1067; Hucker, 1704; Choice, 12/67

1231　Liu, Hsiang. Le Lie-sien Tchouan, Biographie Legendaires des
C　Immortels Taoistes de l'Antiquite. tr. and annotated by
　　Max Kaltenmark. Peking: Centre d'Etudes Sinologiques de
　　Pekin, 1953. 204 pp. o.p.
　　Hucker, 1214

1026　Liu, Hsieh. The Literary Mind and the Carving of Dragons; A
B　Study of Thought and Pattern in Chinese Literature. tr. by
　　Vincent Yu-chung Shih. N.Y.: Columbia University Press, 1959.
　　298 pp. 58-13768.
　　Hucker, 1610; JAS, 5/60; JAOS, 7-9/60; Library Journal,
　　4/15/59; Pacific Affairs, 9/59; TLS, 12/4/59

0387　Liu, James Tzu-chien. Ou-yang Hsiu, an Eleventh Century Neo-
A　Confucianist. Stanford, Calif.: Stanford University Press,
　　1967. 227 pp. 67-13660.

1027　Liu, Jo-yu. The Art of Chinese Poetry, by James J. Y. Liu.
A　Chicago: University of Chicago Press, 1962. 165 pp.
　　62-53199.
　　JAS, 2/64

1028　Liu, Jo-yu. The Chinese Knight-Errant, by James J. Y. Liu.
B　Chicago: University of Chicago Press, 1967. 242 pp.
　　66-14112.
　　Choice, 7-8/68; JAS, 5/68

1029　Liu, Jo-yu. Elizabethan and Yuan; A Brief Comparison of Some
C　Conventions in Poetic Drama, by James Liu. London: The
　　China Society, 1955. 12 pp. (China Society Occasional
　　Papers, 8).
　　Hucker, 1666

0638　Liu, Kwang-ching, ed. American Missionaries in China; Papers
B　from Harvard Seminars. Cambridge, Mass.: Harvard Univer-
　　sity Press, 1966. 310 pp. (Harvard East Asian Monographs,
　　21). 66-31266.
　　Choice, 4/67; JAS, 5/67

0639　Liu, Kwang-ching. Anglo-American Steamship Rivalry in China,
B　1862-1874. Cambridge, Mass.: Harvard University Press,
　　1962. 218 pp. (Harvard East Asian Series, 8). 62-9426.
　　Sup. 63, 2923; JAS, 11/62; AHR, 10/62; Pacific Affairs,
　　Fall/62

1091　Liu, Pai-yu. Flames Ahead. Peking: Foreign Languages Press,
C　1954. 166 pp. 57-34675.

1092　Liu, Pai-yu. Six A.M. and Other Stories. Peking: Foreign
C　Languages Press, 1953. 149 pp. 57-35388.

0849　Liu, Shao-ch'i. How to Be a Good Communist. 2d rev. ed.
C　Peking: Foreign Languages Press, 1952. 118 pp. 55-20000.
　　o.p.
　　Hucker, 1351

0791　Liu, Shao-t'ang. Out of Red China. tr. from Chinese by
C　Jack Chia and Henry Walter. N.Y.: Duell, Sloan & Pearce,
　　1953. 269 pp. 52-12620. o.p.
　　Library Journal, 2/1/53

0891　Liu, Ta-chun. China's Economic Stabilization and Reconstruc-
B　tion, by D. K. Lieu. New Brunswick, N.J.: Rutgers Uni-
　　versity Press, 1948. o.p.
　　Hucker, 2155; Am. Econ. R., 12/48; Pacific Affairs, 9/48

0640　Liu, Ta-Chung. The Economy of the Chinese Mainland: National
A　Income and Economic Development, 1933-1959. Princeton,
　　N.J.: Princeton University Press, 1965. 771 pp. 64-12223.
　　Choice, 7-8/65; JAS, 5/66; Am. Econ. R., 6/65; Ann. Am.
　　Acad., 7/65; J. Pol. Econ., 8/65; TLS, 6/24/65

1030　Liu, Ts'un-jen. The Authorship of the Feng Shen Yen i. Wies-
B　baden: Otto Harrassowitz, 1962. 326 pp. (Buddhist and
　　Taoist Influences on Chinese Novels, Vol. I). NUC
　　63-26810.

1031　Liu, Ts'un-jen. Wu Ch'eng-en, His Life and Career. Leiden:
C　Brill, 1967. 102 pp. (T'oung Pao offprint). 68-86791.

0388　Liu, Tzu-chien. Reform in Sung China; Wang An-shih (1021-
B　1086) and his New Policies. Cambridge, Mass.: Harvard
　　University Press, 1959. 140 pp. (Harvard East Asian
　　Series, 3). 59-9281.
　　Sup. 63, 2922; Hucker, 348; JAS, 11/62

0910　Liu, William Thomas, ed. Chinese Society Under Communism; A
B　Reader. N.Y.: Wiley, 1967. 496 pp. 66-29625.
　　Choice, 1/68; JAS, 11/67; Am. Soc. R., 10/67

1032　Liu, Wu-chi. An Introduction to Chinese Literature. Bloom-
A　ington: Indiana University Press, 1966. 321 pp. 66-12729.
　　Sup. 67, 3245; Choice, 5/67; JAS, 5/67; Library Journal,
　　7/66; TLS, 4/20/66

2089　Lo, Hsiang-lin. Hong Kong and Western Cultures. Honolulu:
B　East-West Center Press, 1964. 345 pp. 65-7535.
　　Choice, 9/65

0934　Lo, Kuan-chung. Romance of the Three Kingdoms. San Kuo Chih
A　Yen-i. tr. by C. H. Brewitt-Taylor. Rutland, Vt.: Tuttle,
　　1959. 2 v. 59-10407 rev. o.p.
　　Hucker, 1694

1639　Lockwood, William Wirt. The Economic Development of Japan:
A　Growth and Structural Change, 1868-1938. Princeton,
　　N.J.: Princeton University Press, 1954. 603 pp. 54-6077.
　　AUFS, 252; Silberman, 322; FEQ, 8/55; Am. Econ. R., 6/55;
　　Ann. Am. Acad., 5/55; Japan Q., 1-3/56; J. Pol. Econ.,
　　8/55; Pacific Affairs, 6/55; Pol. Sci. Q., 12/55; TLS,
　　4/29/55

1640　Lockwood, William Wirt, ed. The State and Economic Enterprise
A　in Japan; Essays in the Political Economy of Growth.
　　Princeton, N.J.: Princeton University Press, 1965. 753 pp.
　　(Studies in the Modernization of Japan, 2). 65-15386.
　　Choice, 2/66; JAS, 5/66; Ann. Am. Acad., 5/66; Library
　　Journal, 11/15/65

1303　Loehr, Max. Chinese Landscape Woodcuts; From an Imperial
C　Commentary to the Tenth-century Printed Edition of the
　　Buddhist Canon. Cambridge, Mass.: Harvard University
　　Press, 1968. 114 pp. 67-22868.
　　Choice, 11/68; Library Journal, 6/15/68

1286　Loehr, Max. Ritual Vessels of Bronze Age China. N.Y.: Asia
B　Society, dist. by New York Graphic, 1968. 183 pp.
　　68-30798.

0389　Loewe, Michael. Records of Han Administration. N.Y.:
C　Cambridge, 1967. 2 v. (University of Cambridge Oriental
　　Publications, 11 and 12). 67-28684.
　　Choice, 7-8/68; JAS, 11/68; Pacific Affairs, Summer/68;
　　TLS, 8/15/68

0641　Loh, Pichon Pei Yung, ed. The Kuomintang Debacle of 1949; Col-
B　lapse or Conquest? Boston: Heath, 1965. 114 pp. (Problems
　　in Asian Civilizations). 64-8154.
　　Choice, 11/65

0036　London. University. School of Oriental and African Studies.
C　Bulletin, v.1- 1917- (R-Kraus, M-IDC).
　　Hucker, 30

0015　London. University. School of Oriental and African Studies.
A　Handbook of Oriental History, by Members of the Dept. of
　　Oriental History, School of Oriental and African Studies,
　　University of London. London: Offices of the Royal Histori-
　　cal Society, 1963 (orig. pub. in 1951). 265 pp. 51-4902.
　　(R).
　　AUFS, 38

0006　London. University. School of Oriental and African Studies.
B　Library. Monthly List of Periodical Articles on the Far
　　East and South East Asia. London: 1954- 56-16909.
　　(R-Kraus).
　　Silberman, 26

0061　Low, Sir Francis. Struggle for Asia. N.Y.: Praeger, 1955.
C　239 pp. 55-11624. o.p.
　　JAS, 11/57

1033　Lu, Chi. The Art of Letters; Lu Chi's "Wen-fu" A.D. 302. tr.
B　by E. R. Hughes. Princeton, N.J.: Princeton University
　　Press, 1951. 261 pp. (Bollingen Series, Vol. 29). 51-13302.
　　Hucker, 1588

1093　Lu, Chu-kuo. The Battle of Samgkumryung. tr. by A. M.
C　Condron. Peking: Foreign Languages Press, 1961. 162 pp.
　　Hand catalog.

1529　Lu, David J. From the Marco Polo Bridge to Pearl Harbor,
B　Japan's Entry into World War II. fore. by Herbert Feis.
　　Washington: Public Affairs Press, 1961. 274 pp. 61-15692.
　　o.p.
　　Sup. 63, 2887; JAS, 8/62

0967 Lu, Yu. The Rapier of Lu, Patriot Poet of China. tr. and
C   biography by Clara M. Candlin. London: Murray, 1946. 68 pp.
       48-10659.
       Hucker, 1606

0935 Lung t'u Kung an. The Strange Cases of Magistrate Pao; Chinese
C   Tales of Crime and Detection. tr. from Chinese and retold
       by Leon Comber. Rutland, Vt.: Tuttle, 1964. 137 pp.
       64-19359.

0216 Lust, John. Index Sinicus; A Catalogue of Articles Relating
A   to China in Periodicals and Other Collective Publications,
       1920-1955. Cambridge: Heffer, 1964. 663 pp. 64-7164.
       JAS, 8/65

2051 Lyons, Gene Martin. Military Policy and Economic Aid; The
C   Korean Case, 1950-1953. Columbus: Ohio State University
       Press, 1961. 298 pp. 61-7301.
       Sup. 63, 2901; JAS, 8/62; AHR, 10/61; Am. Pol. Sci. R.,
       3/62

1094 Ma, Chia. Unfading Flowers. Peking: Foreign Languages
C   Press, 1961. 106 pp. NUC 63-42012.

1095 Ma, Feng. The Sun Has Risen. Peking: Foreign Languages
C   Press, 1961. 174 pp. NUC 63-42013.

1464 Macauley, Edward Yorke. With Perry in Japan; The Diary of
C   Edward Yorke McCauley. Princeton, N.J.: Princeton
       University Press, 1942. 124 pp. 43-1901. o.p. (M-Uni-
       versity).
       AHR, 7/43

0792 MacFarquhar, Roderick, ed. The Hundred Flowers Campaign and
A   the Chinese Intellectuals. epilogue by G. F. Hudson.
       N.Y.: Praeger, 1960. 324 pp. 60-10877. o.p.
       Sup. 61, 2803; Hucker, 941; JAS, 2/61; Ann. Am. Acad., 5/61;
       Library Journal, 9/1/60; Pacific Affairs, Spring/61; TLS,
       12/30/60

0968 Mackintosh, Duncan Robert, comp. A Collection of Chinese Lyrics;
B   Rendered into Verse by Alan Ayling from Translations of
       the Chinese. London: Routledge & Paul, 1965. 254 pp.
       66-2532.
       JAS, 5/67

0259 MacMurray, John Van Antwerp, ed. Treaties and Agreements With
C   and Concerning China. N.Y.: Oxford, 1921. 2 v. 21-8012.
       o.p.
       Hucker, 659, 827

0320 MacNair, Harley Farnsworth, ed. China. Berkeley: University
B   of California Press, 1946. 573 pp. A47-14. o.p.
       AUFS, 691; Hucker, 1; Library Journal, 10/15/46

0642 MacNair, Harley Farnsworth. China in Revolution; An Analysis
B   of Politics and Militarism under the Republic. N.Y.: Fertig,
       1968 (orig. pub. by University of Chicago Press, 1931).
       244 pp. 31-28310. (R).
       AUFS, 847; Hucker, 743; Am. Pol. Sci. R., 2/32

2096 MacNair, Harley Farnsworth. The Chinese Abroad, Their Position
B   and Protection; A Study in International Law and Relations.
       Shanghai: Commercial, 1924. 340 pp. 25-17605. o.p.

0502 MacNair, Harley Farnsworth, ed. Modern Chinese History; Selected
B   Readings. N.Y.: Paragon, 1967 (orig. pub. by Commercial
       Press, 1923). 910 pp. 67-29257. (R).
       Hucker, 658

0084 MacNair, Harley Farnsworth. Modern Far Eastern International
B   Relations. 2d ed. Princeton, N.J.: Van Nostrand, 1955.
       777 pp. 55-8831.
       AUFS, 104; Silberman, 330; FEQ, 8/51

0643 MacNair, Harley Farnsworth. The Real Conflict between China
B   and Japan; An Analysis of Opposing Ideologies. Chicago:
       University of Chicago Press, 1938. 215 pp. 38-27812. o.p.
       Hucker, 794

0141 Macridis, Roy C., ed. Modern Political Systems. Vol. II,
A   Asia. ed. by R. E. Ward and R. C. Macridis. Englewood
       Cliffs, N.J.: Prentice-Hall, 1963. 482 pp. 63-11095 rev.
       Sup. 65, 3053; JAS, 5/64

1864 Maeda, Yasuji. Japanese Decorative Design. Tokyo: Japan
B   Travel Bureau, 1960. 157 pp. (Tourist Library, N.S. 23).
       59-15732.
       Silberman, 857

0390 Mahler, Jane Gaston. The Westerners Among the Figurines of
C   the T'ang Dynasty in China. Rome: Instituto Italiano
       per il Medio ed Estremo Oriente, 1959. 204 pp. A60-3049.
       Hucker, 310; JAS, 5/60; JAOS, 7-9/59

0085 Maki, John McGilvrey, ed. Conflict and Tension in the Far East:
B   Key Documents, 1894-1960. Seattle: University of Washington
       Press, 1961. 245 pp. 61-17709.
       Sup. 63, 2872; JAS, 8/62

1599 Maki, John McGilvrey. Government and Politics in Japan; The
C   Road to Democracy. N.Y.: Praeger, 1962. 275 pp. 62-13735.
       Sup. 63, 2888; JAS, 11/62; Am. Pol. Sci. R., 3/63; Japan Q.,
       10-12/62; Library Journal, 7/62; Pacific Affairs, Winter/62-
       63; Pol. Sci. Q., 9/63

1530 Maki, John McGilvrey. Japanese Militarism, Its Cause and
B   Cure. N.Y.: Knopf, 1945. 258 pp. 45-3717. o.p.
       Silberman, 1362; FEQ, 11/45; Pacific Affairs, 12/45;
       Pol. Sci. Q., 12/45

0016 Maki, John McGilvrey, comp. Selected Documents, Far Eastern
B   International Relations (1689-1951). Seattle: University
       of Washington Press, 1951. 333 pp. A52-9869. o.p.
       Sup. 61, 2752; Hucker, 656; Silberman, 332

0325 Mallory, Walter Hampton. China: Land of Famine. N.Y.: American
B   Geographical Society, 1926. 199 pp. (Special Publication,
       6). 27-1575. o.p. (M-University).
       Hucker, 2201

1962 Malm, William P. Japanese Music and Musical Instruments.
A   Rutland, Vt.: Tuttle, 1959. 299 pp. 59-10411 rev.
       Sup. 61, 2772; Silberman, 1165; JAS, 5/60; Japan Q., 4-6/60;
       JAOS, 4-6/60; Library Journal, 12/1/59; Music Lib. Assn.
       Notes, 6/60

0503 Malone, Carroll Brown. History of the Peking Summer Palaces
C   under the Ch'ing Dynasty. N.Y.: Paragon, 1966 (orig. pub.
       by University of Illinois, 1934). 247 pp. 66-30338. (R).
       Hucker, 527; AHR, 4/35

0108 Malonzemoff, Andrew. Russian Far Eastern Policy, 1881-1904,
B   With Special Emphasis on the Causes of the Russo-Japanese
       War. Berkeley: University of California Press, 1958.
       358 pp. 58-12831. o.p.
       Hucker, 701; Silberman, 415; JAS, 5/59

2074 Mancall, Mark, ed. Formosa Today. N.Y.: Praeger, 1964.
A   171 pp. 64-13491.
       Choice, 10/64; Library Journal, 9/15/64; TLS, 1/14/65

1722 Man'yoshu. The Manyoshu; The Nippon Gakujutsu Shinkokai Trans-
A   lation of One Thousand Poems with the Texts in Romaji, with
       a New Foreword by Donald Keene. N.Y.: Columbia University
       Press, 1965 (orig. pub. by University of Chicago Press,
       1941). 502 pp. (Records of Civilization: Sources &
       Studies, LXX). 65-15376. (R).
       Choice, 11/65; Library Journal, 6/1/65

0850 Mao, Tse-tung. Basic Tactics. tr. with an intro. by Stuart R.
B   Schram. N.Y.: Praeger, 1966. 149 pp. 66-18912.
       Choice, 7-8/67; Am. Pol. Sci. R., 12/67; Library Journal,
       12/1/66

0851 Mao, Tse-tung. China's "New Democracy". N.Y.: New Century, 1945.
C   47 pp. 46-20896. o.p.
       Hucker, 891; FEQ, 11/50

0852 Mao, Tse-tung. The Political Thought of Mao Tse-tung, Anthology
A   by Stuart R. Schram. N.Y.: Praeger, 1963. 319 pp. (Praeger
       Publications in Russian History and World Communism, No. 134).
       63-18539.
       Choice, 3/64; JAS, 8/64; China Q., 1-3/65; Library Journal,
       12/1/63; TLS, 6/25/64

0853 Mao, Tse-tung. Quotations from Chairman Mao Tse-tung.
C   ed. and with an intro., essay and notes by Stuart R.
       Schram. N.Y.: Praeger, 1968. 182 pp. 68-20400.
       Choice, 10/68; Library Journal, 8/68; TLS, 8/15/68

0793 Mao, Tse-tung. Selected Works. N.Y.: International Publishers,
A   1954- 54-9751.
       Hucker, 868; JAS, 5/63; China Q., 7-9/62

0644 Mao's China; Party Reform Documents, 1942-44. tr. by Boyd
A   Compton. Seattle: University of Washington Press, 1952.
       278 pp. 51-12273.
       AUFS, 953; Hucker, 876; FEQ, 11/52; Pacific Affairs, 12/52

1034 March, Benjamin. Chinese Shadow-figure Plays and their Making.
C   Detroit: Puppetry Imprints, 1938. 57 pp. 38-19584. o.p.
     Hucker, 1674

1035 Margoulies, Georges. Evolution de la Prose Artistique Chi-
C   noise. Munchen: Encyclopadie-Verlag, 1929. 334 pp. 31-5098.

1036 Margoulies, Georges. Le "Fou" dans le Wen-siuan, Etude et
C   Textes. Paris: Geuthner, 1926. 138 pp. 33-34621.

1037 Margoulies, Georges. Histoire de La Litterature Chinoise:
C   Poesie. Paris: Payot, 1951. 417 pp. 52-27648.
     Hucker, 1559

1038 Margoulies, Georges. Histoire de la Litterature Chinoise:
C   Prose. Paris: Payot, 1949. 336 pp.

0344 Marsh, Robert Mortimer. The Mandarins; The Circulation of Elites
A   in China, 1600-1900. N.Y.: Free Press of Glencoe, 1961.
     300 pp. 60-10899.
     JAS, 8/62; JAOS, 4-6/62

1531 Marshall, Byron K. Capitalism and Nationalism in Prewar
B   Japan; The Ideology of the Business Elite, 1868-1941.
     Stanford, Calif.: Stanford University Press, 1967.
     163 pp. 67-26528.
     Choice, 9/68; JAS, 8/68; Library Journal, 12/1/67

2027 Marshall, Samuel Lyman Atwood. Pork Chop Hill; The American
C   Fighting Man in Action, Korea, Spring, 1953. N.Y.:
     Apollo, 1965 (orig. pub. by Morrow, 1956). 315 pp.
     56-9545. (R).

2028 Marshall, Samuel Lyman Atwood. The River and the Gauntlet;
B   Defeat of the Eighth Army by the Chinese Communist Forces,
     November, 1950, in the Battle of the Chongchon River,
     Korea. N.Y.: Morrow, 1953. 385 pp. 53-5337. o.p.
     Silberman, 1789; Library Journal, 5/1/53

1575 Martin, Edwin M. The Allied Occupation of Japan. Stanford,
C   Calif.: Stanford University Press, 1948. 155 pp.
     48-9639. o.p.
     Silberman, 556; FEQ, 8/49; Am. Econ. R., 12/49; Ann. Am.
     Acad., 3/49; Pacific Affairs, 6/49

0391 Martin, Henry Desmond. The Rise of Chingis Khan and His Conquest
B   of North China. Baltimore: Johns Hopkins Press, 1950.
     360 pp. 51-444. o.p. (M-University).
     AUFS, 711; Hucker, 364; AHR, 7/51

1984 Martin, Samuel Elmo. A Korean-English Dictionary. New Haven,
C   Conn.: Yale University Press, 1967. 1902 pp. (Yale
     Language Texts). 67-24503.
     Choice, 6/68; JAS, 8/68; Library Journal, 4/1/68

1600 Maruyama, Masao. Thought and Behaviour in Modern Japanese
B   Politics. ed. by Ivan Morris. N.Y.: Oxford, 1963.
     344 pp. 63-5967.
     Sup. 65, 3066; JAS, 11/64; AHR, 7/64; Ann. Am. Acad.,
     7/64; TLS, 9/13/63

0392 Maspero, Henri. La Chine Antique. new ed. Paris: Imprimerie
C   Nationale, 1955. 519 pp. 56-43490.
     Hucker, 167

0321 Maspero, Henri. Les Institutions de la Chine; Essai Historique.
B   Paris: Presses Universitaires, 1952. 174 pp. 54-2554.
     Hucker, 105; FEQ, 11/53

0393 Maspero, Henri. Melanges Posthumes sur les Religions et
C   l'Histoire de la Chine. Paris: Civilisations du Sud,
     S.A.E.P., 1950. 3 v. A51-4214.
     Hucker, 202; FEQ, 8/52

0127 Massachusetts Institute of Technology. Center for Inter-
C   national Studies. Essays on Communism in Asia, Papers
     from the CENIS China Project. Cambridge, Mass.: M.I.T.,
     1955. 56-46285. o.p.

0260 Mathews, Robert Henry. Mathews' Chinese-English Dictionary. rev.
A   ed. Cambridge, Mass.: Harvard University Press for Harvard-
     Yenching Institute, 1944. 186 pp. A43-2019 rev. 2.
     Hucker, 84

1723 Matsuo, Basho. The Narrow Road to the Deep North, and Other
A   Travel Sketches. tr. by Nobuyuki Yuasa. Baltimore: Penguin,
     1966. 167 pp. (Penguin Classics). 67-71320.
     Choice, 7-8/67; Japan Q., 4-6/67

0645 Maugham, William Somerset. On a Chinese Screen. London:
B   Heinemann, 1953. 237 pp. 22-19940.

1532 Maxon, Yale Candee. Control of Japanese Foreign Policy,
C   a Study of Civil-Military Rivalry, s930-1945. Berkeley:
     University of California Press, 1957. 286 pp. A57-9540.
     o.p.
     AUFS, 257; Silberman, 441; JAS, 2/58; AHR, 1/58; Ann. Am.
     Acad., 7/58; Pacific Affairs, 6/58

0504 Mayers, William Frederick. The Chinese Government. A Manual of
C   Chinese Titles, Categorically Arranged and Explained, with
     an Index. 3d ed. rev. by G. M. H. Playfair. Taipai:
     Ch'eng-wen Publishing Co., dist. by Chinese Materials and
     Research Aids Service Center, 1966 (orig. pub. by Kelly &
     Walsh, 1897). 196 pp. Hand catalog. (R).
     Hucker, 542

0345 McAleavy, Henry. The Modern History of China. N.Y.:
B   Praeger, 1967. 392 pp. (Praeger Asia-Africa
     Series). 66-18911.
     Choice, 5/68; Library Journal, 10/15/67; TLS, 11/9/67

0646 McCormick, Thomas J. China Market: America's Quest for
B   Informal Empire 1893-1901. Chicago: Quadrangle, 1967.
     241 pp. 67-21637.
     Choice, 4/68; JAS, 5/68; J. Am. Hist., 3/68

2063 McCune, Evelyn. The Arts of Korea; An Illustrated History.
B   Rutland, Vt.: Tuttle, 1962. 452 pp. 61-11122.
     Sup. 63, 2902; JAS, 8/62; Library Journal, 2/1/62; TLS,
     9/21/62

2029 McCune, George MacAfee. Korea Today. Cambridge, Mass.: Harvard
A   University Press, 1950. 372 pp. 50-8875. o.p.
     AUFS, 556; Silberman, 1889; FEQ, 8/51; Am. Pol. Sci. R.,
     12/50; Library Journal, 8/50; Pol. Sci. Q., 12/50

2015 McCune, George MacAfee, ed. Korean-American Relations; Documents
B   Pertaining to the Far Eastern Diplomacy of the United
     States. Berkeley: University of California Press,
     1951- 2 v. 51-1111.
     Silberman, 1812; JAS, 11/64; FEQ, 2/52; Am. Pol. Sci. R.,
     6/51

2001 McCune, Shannon Boyd-Bailey. Korea, Land of Broken Calm. Prince-
A   ton, N.J.: Van Nostrand, 1966. 221 pp. 66-16903.
     Sup. 67, 3231; JAS, 11/66

2006 McCune, Shannon Boyd-Bailey. Korea's Heritage; A Regional and
B   Social Geography. Rutland, Vt.: Tuttle, 1956. 250 pp.
     56-6807.
     AUFS, 558; Silberman, 1671; JAS, 2/57; Ann. Am. Acad.,
     7/57; Pacific Affairs, 12/56

0394 McGovern, William Montgomery. The Early Empires of Central Asia;
C   A Study of the Scythians and the Huns and the Part They Played
     in World History, with Special Reference to the Chinese
     Sources. Chapel Hill: University of North Carolina Press,
     1939. 529 pp. 39-6490.
     Hucker, 221; Am. Anthropologist, 1/40; AHR, 1/40

1765 McKinnon, Richard N., ed. The Heart is Alone; A Selection
C   of 20th Century Japanese Short Stories. Tokyo: Hokuseido,
     1957. 171 pp. 57-14222.
     AUFS, 473; Silberman, 958; JAS, 8/58

0647 McLane, Charles B. Soviet Policy and the Chinese Communists,
A   1931-1946. N.Y.: Columbia University Press, 1958. 310 pp.
     58-11903. o.p.
     Hucker, 874; AHR, 7/59; Ann. Am. Acad., 5/59; Library
     Journal, 10/1/58

1533 McLaren, Walter Wallace. A Political History of Japan during
B   the Meiji Era, 1867-1912. N.Y.: Russell & Russell, 1966
     (orig. pub. by Scribner's, 1916). 379 pp. 65-17910. (R).
     (M-University).
     AUFS, 258; Silberman, 353; TLS, 8/3/16

1601 McNelly, Theodore. Contemporary Government of Japan. Boston:
C   Houghton Mifflin, 1963. 228 pp. 63-3353.
     Sup. 63, 2889; JAS, 2/64

2030 Meade, Edward Grant. American Military Government in Korea.
C   N.Y.: King's Crown, 1951. 281 pp. 51-9103. o.p.
     AUFS, 559; Silberman, 1776; FEQ, 8/51; Am. Soc. R., 6/51;
     Ann. Am. Acad., 5/51; Pacific Affairs, 9/51; Pol. Sci. Q.,
     12/51

0505 Meadows, Thomas Taylor. The Chinese and Their Rebellions,
A   Viewed in Connection with Their National Philosophy,
     Ethics, Legislation, and Administration. To Which is Added

an Essay on Civilization and Its Present State in the East
and West. Stanford, Calif.: Academic Reprints, 1953.
656 pp. 54-2175. o.p.
Hucker, 625

1534 Mears, Helen. Mirror for Americans: Japan. Boston: Hough-
C ton Mifflin, 1948. 329 pp. 48-8353. o.p.
Library Journal, 8/48; TLS, 12/25/48

0794 Mehnert, Klaus. Peking and Moscow. tr. from the German by
B Leila Vennewitz. N.Y.: Putnam, 1963. 522 pp. 63-16176.
Sup. 65, 5802; JAS, 5/63; China Q., 10-12/64; Library
Journal, 11/15/63; TLS, 5/21/64

1259 Mei, Yi-pao. Motse, the Neglected Rival of Confucius. London:
C A. Probsthain, 1934. 222 pp. 35-10340. o.p.
Hucker, 1220

2065 Meinecke, Charlotte Drummond. Education in Korea. Seoul:
C Ministry of Education, Republic of Korea, 1958. 70 pp.
59-32817.
Silberman, 1906

0795 Meisner, Maurice J. Li Ta-chao and the Origins of Chinese
A Marxism. Cambridge, Mass.: Harvard University Press,
1967. 326 pp. (Harvard East Asian Series, 27). 67-10904.
Choice, 1/68; JAS, 2/68; AHR, 12/67; Library Journal, 3/1/67;
Pacific Affairs, Spring/68; TLS, 1/18/68

1209 Mencius: Mencius. A New Translation Arranged and Annotated for
B the General Reader by W. A. C. H. Dobson. Toronto: Uni-
versity of Toronto Press, 1963. 215 pp. 63-23889.
JAS, 5/64; JAOS, 9-12/63

0796 Mende, Tibor. China and Her Shadow. London: Thames & Hud-
B son, 1961. 360 pp. 62-1393. o.p.

1576 Mendel, Douglas Heusted. The Japanese People and Foreign
C Policy; A Study of Public Opinion in Post-Treaty Japan.
fore. by Edwin O. Reischauer. Berkeley: University of California Press, 1961. 269 pp. 61-14553. o.p.
Sup. 63, 2890; JAS, 8/62; Japan Q., 7-9/62

0648 Meng, S. M. The Tsungli Yamen: Its Organization and Functions.
B Cambridge, Mass.: Harvard University Press, 1962. 146 pp.
(Harvard East Asian Monographs). 62-53393.
Sup. 63, 2925

0395 Menzel, Johanna Margarete, ed. The Chinese Civil Service; Career
A Open to Talent? Boston: Heath, 1963. 110 pp. 63-12327.
JAS, 11/64

0346 Meskill, John Thomas, ed. The Pattern of Chinese History;
A Cycles, Development, or Stagnation? Boston: Heath, 1965.
108 pp. (Problems in Asian Civilization). 65-17466.
Choice, 1/68

0396 Meskill, John Thomas. Wang An-shih, Practical Reformer? Bos-
A ton: Heath, 1963. 99 pp. 63-12328.
JAS, 11/64

0086 Michael, Franz H. The Far East in the Modern World. N.Y.:
B Holt, 1956. 724 pp. 55-6036.
AUFS, 105; Silberman, 324; JAS, 2/57; Pacific Affairs,
6/57; TLS, 4/5/57

0506 Michael, Franz H. The Origin of Manchu Rule in China; Frontier
A and Bureaucracy as Interacting Forces in the Chinese
Empire. N.Y.: Octagon, 1965 (orig. pub. by Johns Hopkins
Press, 1942). 127 pp. 65-25880. (R).
AUFS, 754; Hucker, 509; FEQ, 5/43; Am. Pol. Sci. R., 6/42;
Ann. Am. Acad., 7/42; Pacific Affairs, 9/42

0649 Michael, Franz H. The Taiping Rebellion; History and Documents.
A Vol. I: History. Seattle: University of Washington Press,
1966. 244 pp. (University of Washington Publications on
Asia). 66-13538.
Sup. 67, 3246; Choice, 9/66; JAS, 5/67; AHR, 4/67;
Library Journal, 6/15/66; Pacific Affairs, Spring-Summer/66;
Pol. Sci. Q., 9/67

0911 Michigan. University. Center for Chinese Studies. Occasional
C Papers. The Cultural Revolution: 1967 in Review. by Carl
Riskin, Michael Oksenberg, Robert Scalapino, and Ezra Vogel.
Ann Arbor: Center for Chinese Studies, University of Mich-
igan, 1968- (Papers in Chinese Studies, No. 2, July, 1968).

1408 Michigan. University. Center for Japanese Studies. Occa-
C sional Papers. Ann Arbor, Mich.: Center for Japanese
Studies, 1951- 54-33454.

Silberman, 28

1937 Miki, Fumio. Haniwa, the Clay Sculpture of Protohistoric
C Japan. Rutland, Vt.: Tuttle, 1960. 160 pp. 60-9286.
Silberman, 745; JAS, 2/61; Japan Q., 1-3/61; JAOS, 1-3/61;
Library Journal, 8/60

0650 Miles, Milton E. A Different Kind of War: the Little-known
C Story of the Combined Guerilla Forces Created in China
by the U.S. Navy and the Chinese During World War II,
as prepared by Hawthorne Daniel from the original manuscript. fore. by Arleigh Burke. Garden City, N.Y.:
Doubleday, 1967. 629 pp. 67-10399.
Choice, 9/68; JAS, 2/69; Library Journal, 10/15/67

1602 Miller, Frank O. Minobe Tatsukichi, Interpreter of Constitu-
C tionalism in Japan. Berkeley: University of California
Press, 1965. 392 pp. (Publications for the Center for
Japanese and Korean Studies). 64-18644.
Choice, 11/65; JAS, 2/66; AHR, 1/66; Am. Pol. Sci. R.,
3/66; Ann. Am. Acad., 11/65; TLS, 1/20/66

1895 Miller, Roy Andrew. Japanese Ceramics. N.Y.: Crown, 1962.
A 19 pp. 62-1506.
Silberman, 843; Japan Q., 10-12/60; JAOS, 4-6/61; Library
Journal, 8/60

1383 Miller, Roy Andrew. The Japanese Language. Chicago:
A University of Chicago Press, 1967. 428 pp. 67-16777.
JAS, 11/68

0171 Milton, Daniel L., ed. A Treasury of Modern Asian Stories.
B N.Y.: New American Library, 1961. 237 pp. 61-9137.
Hucker, 1744

1896 Minamoto, Hoshu. An Illustrated History of Japanese Art.
C Kyoto: K. Hoshino, 1935. 264 pp. 36-9490.

1724 Miner, Earl Roy. An Introduction to Japanese Court Poetry.
A Stanford, Calif.: Stanford University Press, 1968. 173 pp.
68-17138.

1897 Minnich, Helen Benton. Japanese Costume and the Makers of Its
C Elegant Tradition. Rutland, Vt.: Tuttle, 1963. 374 pp.
62-15063.
JAS, 5/64; Japan Q., 1-3/64; JAOS, 10-12/66

1096 Mirages and Sea-Markets, a Collection of Modern Chinese Essays.
C Peking: Foreign Languages Press, 1962. 122 pp. NUC 63-28310.

1679 Mishima, Sumio (Seo). The Broader Way; A Woman's Life in the
C New Japan. N.Y.: John Day, 1953. 247 pp. 53-6588. o.p.
Silberman, 1407; Library Journal, 5/15/53

1766 Mishima, Yukio, pseud. Confessions of a Mask. tr. by Mere-
B dith Weatherby. Norfolk, Conn.: New Directions, 1958.
255 pp. 58-12637.
AUFS, 474; Silberman, 1014; JAS, 2/59

1767 Mishima, Yukio, pseud. Death in Midsummer, and Other Stories.
B N.Y.: New Directions, 1966. 181 pp. 66-17819.
Choice, 1/67; Library Journal, 4/1/66; TLS, 4/20/67

1799 Mishima, Yukio, pseud. Five Modern No Plays. tr. from
A Japanese by Donald Keene. N.Y.: Knopf, 1957. 198 pp.
57-8684 rev.
AUFS, 510; Silberman, 1152; JAS, 5/58

1800 Mishima, Yukio, pseud. Madame de Sade. tr. by Donald Keene.
B N.Y.: Grove, 1967. 108 pp. 67-19616.
Choice, 4/68; Library Journal, 8/67

1768 Mishima, Yukio, pseud. The Sound of Waves. tr. by Meredith
B Weatherby. N.Y.: Knopf, 1956. 182 pp. 56-8911.
Silberman, 1013; Library Journal, 8/56

1769 Mishima, Yukio, pseud. The Temple of the Golden Pavilion.
B tr. by Ivan Morris. N.Y.: Knopf, 1959. 262 pp. 59-7222.
AUFS, 476; Silberman, 1015; Library Journal, 5/15/59

1801 Mishima, Yukio, pseud. Twilight Sunflower; A Play in Four Acts.
C tr. by Shigeho Shinozaki and A. Warren Virgil. Tokyo:
Hokuseido, 1958. 143 pp. Hand catalog.
Silberman, 1154

0651 Misselwitz, Henry Francis. The Dragon Stirs; An Intimate
C Sketch-Book of China's Kuomintang Revolution, 1927-29.
N.Y.: Harbinger, 1941. 293 pp. 41-11787. o.p.
Hucker, 784

1680 Mitchell, Richard H. The Korean Minority in Japan. Berkeley:
B   University of California Press, 1967. 186 pp. 67-18074.
      Choice, 6/68; Ann. Am. Acad., 7/68; Pacific Affairs,
      Summer/68

1898 Mitsuoka, Tadanari. Ceramic Art of Japan. Tokyo: Japan
B   Travel Bureau, 1949. 190 pp. (Tourist Library, 8).
      A51-3512.
      Silberman, 845

1851 Miura, Isshu. Zen Dust; The History of the Koan and Koan Study
C   in Rinzai (Lin-Chi) Zen. by Isshu Miura and Ruth Fuller
      Sasaki. with background notes, descriptive bibliography,
      genealogical charts, maps and reproductions of drawings
      by Haskuin. N.Y.: Harcourt, Brace & World, 1967. 574 pp.
      66-10044.
      JAS, 11/67

1924 Miyagawa, Torao. Modern Japanese Painting; An Art in Transi-
C   tion. Palo Alto, Calif.: Kodansha, 1967. 131 pp. 67-16770.
      Choice, 9/67; Library Journal, 9/15/67

1695 Miyamori, Asataro, ed. and tr. Masterpieces of Japanese Poetry,
C   Ancient and Modern. 2d ed. Tokyo: Taiseido Shobo, 1956.
      2 v. in 1. 37-29969 rev.
      AUFS, 420; Silberman, 1037

1182 Mo, Ti. The Ethical and Political Works of Motse. tr. from
C   original Chinese by Yi-Pao Mei. London: A. Probsthain, 1929.
      275 pp. 30-4133. o.p.
      AUFS, 600; Hucker, 1221

0037 Modern Asian Studies. v.1- 1967-
A

2060 Moffett, Samuel Hugh. The Christians of Korea. N.Y.: Friend-
C   ship Press, 1962. 174 pp. 62-17527.

1161 Monsterleet, Jean. Sommets de la Litterature Chinoise Con-
C   temporaine. Paris: Domat, 1953. 167 pp. 53-33054.

1398 Monumenta Nipponica. Tokyo: Sophia University, 1938-1943,
B   1951-
      Silberman, 34

0293 Monumenta Serica; Journal of Oriental Studies. v.1- 1935-
C   (R-Johnson, M-IDC).
      Hucker, 33

0164 Moore, Barrington. Social Origins of Dictatorship and Democ-
A   racy; Lord and Peasant in the Making of the Modern World.
      Boston: Beacon, 1966. 559 pp. 66-23782.
      Choice, 1/67; JAS, 2/68; AHR, 7/67; Am. Pol. Sci. R., 9/67;
      Am. Soc. R., 10/67; Library Journal, 10/15/66; Pol. Sci. Q.,
      12/67; TLS, 12/21/67

1535 Moore, Frederick. With Japan's Leaders; An Intimate Record
C   of Fourteen Years as Counsellor to the Japanese Govern-
      ment, ending December 7, 1941. N.Y.: Scribner's, 1942.
      365 pp. 42-17502. o.p.
      FEQ, 5/43

0109 Moore, Harriet Lucy. Soviet Far Eastern Policy, 1931-1945.
B   Princeton, N.J.: Princeton University Press, 1945.
      284 pp. A45-5523. o.p. (M-University).
      AUFS, 4989; Silberman, 489; FEQ, 5/46; Library Journal,
      9/15/45

0797 Moraes, Francis Robert. Report on Mao's China. N.Y.: Mac-
B   millan, 1953. 212 pp. 53-9391. o.p.
      AUFS, 954; Hucker, 965; Am. Pol. Sci. R., 9/53; Ann. Am.
      Acad., 11/53; Library Journal, 6/15/53; Pacific Affairs,
      9/53

0798 Moraes, Francis Robert. The Revolt in Tibet. N.Y.: Mac-
C   millan, 1960. 223 pp. 60-6644.
      JAS, 11/60; Am. Pol. Sci. R., 12/60; Ann. Am. Acad.,
      9/60; Library Journal, 1/1/60; TLS, 3/25/60

0062 Moraes, Francis Robert. Yonder One World; A Study of Asia and
C   the West. N.Y.: Macmillan, 1958. 209 pp. 58-6962.
      JAS, 5/59; Library Journal, 4/15/58

1770 Mori, Ogai. The Wild Geese. tr. by Kingo Ochiai and Sanford
B   Goldstein. Rutland, Vt.: Tuttle, 1959. 119 pp. 59-14087.
      Sup. 61, 2775; JAS, 8/60; JAOS, 4-6/60

1771 Mori, Rintaro. Sansho-Dayu, by Ogai Mori (pseud.). tr. by
C   Tsutomi Fukuda. Tokyo: Hokuseido, 1952. 72 pp.
      FEQ, 11/54

0128 Morley, James William. Japan and Korea: America's Allies in the
A   Pacific. N.Y.: Walker, 1965. 152 pp. 64-23055.
      Choice, 4/66; JAS, 8/66; Ann. Am. Acad., 9/66; Library
      Journal, 11/15/65

1536 Morley, James William. The Japanese Thrust Into Siberia, 1918.
B   N.Y.: Columbia University Press, 1957. 395 pp. (Studies
      of the Russian Institute). 57-5805. o.p.
      AUFS, 4839; Silberman, 493; JAS, 5/58; AHR, 4/58; Am. Pol.
      Sci. R., 4/58

1384 Morris, Ivan I. Dictionary of Selected Forms in Classical
C   Japanese Literature. N.Y.: Columbia University Press,
      1966. 155 pp. 66-13020.
      Choice, 10/67; JAS, 11/66

1772 Morris, Ivan I., ed. Modern Japanese Stories: an Anthology.
A   London: Eyre & Spottiswoode, dist. by Lawrence Verry, 1965
      (orig. pub. in 1961). 528 pp. (UNESCO Collection of Rep-
      resentative Works: Japanese Series). 61-11971. (R).
      Sup. 63, 2891; Choice, 5/66; JAS, 8/62; JAOS, 4-6/62

1603 Morris, Ivan I. Nationalism and the Right Wing in Japan; A
C   Study of Post-war Trends. N.Y.: Oxford for the Royal Insti-
      tute of International Affairs, 1960. 476 pp. 60-2705.
      Sup. 61, 2773; Silberman, 1357; JAS, 11/60; AHR, 1/61;
      Am. Pol. Sci. R., 12/60; Ann. Am. Acad., 1/61; Japan Q.,
      10-12/60; Pacific Affairs, 9/60; Pol. Sci. Q., 9/61;
      TLS, 8/5/60

1465 Morris, Ivan I. The World of the Shining Prince; Court Life in
A   Ancient Japan. N.Y.: Knopf, 1964. 336 pp. 64-12310.
      Sup. 65, 3067; Choice, 11/64; Japan Q., 1-3/65; Library
      Journal, 9/1/64

0507 Morse, Hosea Ballou. The Chronicles of the East India Company,
B   Trading to China, 1635-1834. Taipei: Chinese Materials
      and Research Aids Service Center (orig. pub. by Clarendon,
      1926-29). 5 v. 26-9732. (R).
      Hucker, 560; Am. Econ. R., 12/26; AHR, 10/26

0110 Morse, Hosea Ballou. Far Eastern International Relations. N.Y.:
A   Russell & Russell, 1967 (orig. pub. by Houghton Mifflin,
      1931). 2 v. 67-15998. (R).
      AUFS, 107; AHR, 1/32

0508 Morse, Hosea Ballou. The International Relations of the Chinese
B   Empire. Taipei: Chinese Materials and Research Aids Ser-
      vice Center, 1966 (orig. pub. by Longmans, Green, 1910-
      18). 3 v. 11-2033. (R).
      AUFS, 755; Hucker, 662

0509 Morse, Hosea Ballou. The Trade and Administration of Chinese
C   Empire. Taipei: Ch'eng-wen Publishing Co., dist. by
      Chinese Materials and Research Aids Service Center, 1966
      (orig. pub. by Longmans, Green, 1920). 451 pp. NUC 67-43061.
      (R).
      Hucker, 667

0854 Moseley, George, ed. and tr. The Party and the National Ques-
B   tion in China. Cambridge, Mass.: M.I.T. Press, 1966. 186 pp.
      66-27573.
      Choice, 7-8/67

0217 Mote, Frederick W. Japanese Sponsored Governments in China,
C   1937-1945: an Annotated Bibliography Compiled from Materials
      in the Chinese Collection of the Hoover Library. Stanford,
      Calif.: Stanford University Press, 1954. 68 pp. (Biblio-
      graphical Series, 3). 55-854. o.p. (M-University).

1039 Mote, Frederick W. The Poet Kao Ch'i, 1336-1374. Princeton,
A   N.J.: Princeton University Press, 1962. 261 pp. 62-7411.
      JAOS, 10-12/62

0261 Moule, Arthur Christopher. The Rulers of China, 221 B.C.-A.D.
B   1949; Chronological Tables. With an Introductory Section
      on the Earlier Rulers c. 2100-249 B.C. by W. Perceval
      Yetts. N.Y.: Praeger, 1957. 131 pp. 57-11146. o.p.
      Hucker, 93; JAS, 11/58

0855 Mu, Fu-sheng, pseud. The Wilting of the Hundred Flowers; The
C   Chinese Intelligensia Under Mao. N.Y.: Praeger, 1963.
      324 pp. (Praeger Publications in Russian History and World
      Communism, No. 122). 63-9812.
      JAS, 8/63; Am. Pol. Sci. R., 9/63; Ann. Am. Acad., 11/63;
      China Q., 4-6/63; Library Journal, 3/15/63; TLS, 5/17/63

0176 Muller, F. Max, ed. Sacred Books of the East. Varanasi:
C   Chowkhamba Sanskrit Studies Office, dist. by Lawrence Verry,
      1965-66 (orig. pub. by Clarendon, 1879). 50 v. (R).
      Hucker, 1112

1899 Munsterberg, Hugo. The Arts of Japan; An Illustrated History.
B   Rutland, Vt.: Tuttle, 1957. 201 pp. 56-13414.
      Silberman, 723; JAS, 2/58; Japan Q., 4-6/63; Library
      Journal, 7/57

1865 Munsterberg, Hugo. The Folk Arts of Japan. Rutland, Vt.:
C   Tuttle, 1958. 168 pp. 58-7496.
      AUFS, 393; Silberman, 831; Japan Q., 7-9/58; JAOS, 10-12/58;
      Library Journal, 7/58

0195 Munsterberg, Hugo. The Landscape Painting of China and Japan.
A   Rutland, Vt.: Tuttle, 1955. 144 pp. 55-10622 rev.
      Silberman, 753; FEQ, 5/56

0188 Munsterberg, Hugo. Zen & Oriental Art. Rutland, Vt.:
B   Tuttle, 1965. 158 pp. 65-17589.
      Choice, 12/65; JAS, 5/66

1824 Muraoka, Tsunetsuga. Studies in Shinto Thought. tr. by Delmer
B   Brown and James Araki. Tokyo: Japanese Ministry of Educa-
      tion, 1964. 264 pp. NUC 65-10734.

1706 Murasaki Shikibu. The Tale of Genji: a Novel in Six Parts.
A   tr. from Japanese by Arthur Waley. Boston: Houghton Mif-
      flin, 1935. 2 v. 36-27029. o.p.
      AUFS, 439; Silberman, 895

1420 Murdoch, James. A History of Japan. N.Y.: Ungar, 1964 (orig.
B   pub. by Routledge, 1903-26). 3 v. in 6. 64-15695. (R).
      AUFS, 167; Silberman, 155; Choice, 4/65

0652 Murphey, Rhoads. Shanghai, Key to Modern China. Cambridge,
B   Mass.: Harvard University Press, 1953. 232 pp. 53-5073.
      o.p.
      AUFS, 852; FEQ, 11/54

1802 Mushakoji, Saneatsu. The Passion, by S. Mushakoji and Three
C   Other Japanese Plays. Honolulu: Oriental Literature
      Society, University of Hawaii, 1933. 178 pp. 36-543. o.p.
      Silberman, 1158

0167 The Mythology of All Races. Vol. 8: Chinese and Japanese. ed.
C   by Louis Herbert Gray and George Foot Moore. Boston:
      Marshall Jones, 1916-32. 17-26477. o.p.
      Hucker, 150

1466 Nachod, Oskar. Die Beziehungen der Niederlandischen Ostin-
B   dischen Kompagnie zu Japan im Siebzehenten Jahrhundert.
      Leipzig: R. Friese, 1897. 444 pp. 38-11905. o.p.
      Silberman, 291

1366 Nachod, Oskar. Bibliographie von Japan, 1906-1926 (-1938-1943).
C   Leipzig: K. W. Hiersmann, 1928- 29-4184 rev. 2.
      Silberman, 21, 22

1367 Nachod, Oskar. Bibliography of the Japanese Empire, 1906-1926.
C   Leipzig: K. W. Hiersemann, 1928. 2 v. 29-4185. o.p.
      Silberman, 23

1537 Najita, Tetsuo. Hara Kei in the Politics of Compromise,
C   1905-1915. Cambridge, Mass.: Harvard University
      Press, 1967. 314 pp. (Harvard East Asian Series,
      31). 67-27090.
      Choice, 5/68; JAS, 5/68

0177 Nakamura, Hajime. Ways of Thinking of Eastern Peoples,
C   India, China, Tibet, Japan. rev., tr., and ed. by Philip
      P. Wiener. Honolulu: East-West Center Press, 1964.
      712 pp. 64-63438.
      Sup. 65, 3049; Choice, 9/65

1641 Nakamura, James I. Agricultural Production and the Economic
C   Development of Japan, 1873-1922. Princeton, N.J.: Prince-
      ton University Press, 1966. 257 pp. (Studies of the East
      Asian Institute, Columbia University). 66-11975.
      Choice, 5/67; Am. Econ. R., 9/67; Pacific Affairs, Spring-
      Summer/67

1681 Nakane, Chie. Kinship and Economic Organization in Rural
B   Japan. N.Y.: Humanities, 1967. 203 pp. 66-10915.

1737 Namiki, Gohei. Kanjincho; A Japanese Kabuki Play. by A. C.
C   Scott. N.Y.: Samuel French, 1968 (orig. pub. in Tokyo, 1953).
      50 pp. 55-57023. (R).

1925 Narazaki, Muneshige. The Japanese Print; Its Evolution and
A   Essence. Palo Alto, Calif.: Kodansha, 1966. 274 pp.
      66-12551.

0856 National Council of the Churches of Christ in the U.S.A.
C   Division of Foreign Missions. Far Eastern Office. Docu-
      ments of the Three-Self Movement; Source Materials for
      the Study of the Protestant Church in Communist China.
      Francis Jones, consultant and ed. N.Y.: National Council,
      1963. 209 pp. o.p.
      JAS, 8/64; China Q., 10-12/64

0294 National Palace Museum Quarterly. v.1- 1966-
C

1773 Natsume, Soseki. Botchan (Master Darling). tr. by Yasotaro
C   Morri. Rutland, Vt.: Tuttle, 1968 (orig. pub. in 1922).
      188 pp. 68-11974. (R).
      Choice, 1/69; Silberman, 1025

1774 Natsume, Soseki. Kokoro, a Novel. tr. by Edwin McClellan.
A   Chicago: Regnery, 1957. 248 pp. 57-10097.
      AUFS, 479; Silberman, 1024; JAS, 8/58

1775 Natsume, Soseki. Kusamakura and Buncho. tr. by Umeji Sasaki.
C   Tokyo: Iwanami-shoten, 1927. 276 pp.

1776 Natsume, Soseki. Ten Nights' Dreams and Our Cat's Grave. tr.
C   by Sankichi Hata and Dofu Shirai. Tokyo: Tokyo News
      Service, 1949. 112 pp. 57-19173.

1777 Natsume, Soseki. Within My Glass Doors. tr. by Iwao Matsuhara
C   and E. T. Iglehart. Tokyo: Shinseido, 1928. 154 pp.
      52-50336.

1358 Needham, Joseph. Chinese Astronomy and the Jesuit Mission:
A   an Encounter of Cultures. London: China Society, 1958.
      20 pp. 60-2893.
      Hucker, 1380

1359 Needham, Joseph. The Development of Iron and Steel Technology
A   in China. London: The Newcomen Society for the Study of
      History of Engineering and Technology, the Science Museum,
      1958. 76 pp. 59-1313.
      Hucker, 1361

1360 Needham, Joseph. Science and Civilisation in China. Cam-
A   bridge: University, 1954- 54-4723.
      AUFS, 693; Hucker, 136; Choice, 4/66; JAS, 11/59; FEQ, 8/55;
      AHR, 4/60, 1/63; Library Journal, 9/1/54, 5/1/66; Pacific
      Affairs, Fall/63; TLS, 10/15/54, 2/10/66

0347 Needham, Joseph. Time and Eastern Man. London: Royal Anthro-
B   pological Institute of Great Britain and Ireland, 1965.
      52 pp. 65-29667.
      JAS, 2/66

1385 Nelson, Andrew Nathaniel. The Modern Reader's Japanese-
B   English Character Dictionary. 2d rev. ed. Rutland,
      Vt.: Tuttle, 1966. 1108 pp. Hand catalog.
      JAS, 2/63; Japan Q., 4-6/62; JAOS, 4-6/62

2010 Nelson, Melvin Frederick. Korea and the Old Orders in Eastern
B   Asia. N.Y.: Russell & Russell, 1967 (orig. pub. by Louisiana
      State University Press, 1945). 326 pp. 66-27132. (R).
      AUFS, 561; Silberman, 1806; FEQ, 5/46; AHR, 10/45; Am. Pol.
      Sci. R., 8/45; Ann. Am. Acad., 11/45

1133 New Chinese Poetry. tr. by Yu Kwang-chung. Taipei: Heritage
C   Press, 1960. 94 pp. Hand catalog.
      JAS, 11/61

1097 A New Home and Other Stories, by Contemporary Chinese Writers.
C   Peking: Foreign Languages Press, 1955. 166 pp. Hand
      catalog. o.p.

1949 New York. Museum of Modern Art. The Architecture of Japan.
C   by Arthur Drexler. N.Y.: 1955. 286 pp. 55-5987. o.p.
      Japan Q., 4-6/57; Library Journal, 3/1/56

2109 Newell, William Hare. Treacherous River: a Study of Rural
A   Chinese in North Malaya. Kuala Lumpur: University of
      Malaya Press, dist. by Oxford, 1962. 233 pp. 63-2972.
      JAS, 11/65

1866 Newsom, Samuel. A Thousand Years of Japanese Gardens. 4th ed.
B   Tokyo: Tokyo News Service, 1959. 318 pp.
      Silberman, 829

1642 Nihon Ginko. Tokeikyoku. Hundred-Year Statistics of the Japa-
A   nese Economy (with two supplements). Tokyo: Statistics
      Dept., Bank of Japan, 1966. 616 pp. NUC 68-60340.

1368 Nihon PEN Kurabu. Japanese Literature in European Languages,
A   a Bibliography. Tokyo: Kasai, 1957. 69 pp. 61-32222.

Silberman, 865

1435 Nihongi; Chronicles of Japan from the Earliest Times to
B   A.D. 697. tr. from original Chinese and Japanese by
     W. G. Aston. London: Allen & Unwin, 1956. 443 pp.
     A56-5065.
     Silberman, 192; Japan Q., 1-3/57

0653 Ning, Lao T'ai-t'ai. A Daughter of Han; The Autobiography of
B   a Chinese Working Woman, by Ida Pruitt. Stanford, Calif.:
     Stanford University Press, 1967 (orig. pub. by Yale Uni-
     versity Press, 1945). 254 pp. 68-10633. (R).
     Hucker, 2055; Choice, 12/68; FEQ, 5/46; Library Journal,
     11/1/45

1797 Ninomiya, Takamichi, ed. The Poetry of Living Japan; An
A   Anthology. N.Y.: Grove, 1957. 104 pp. 58-12186. o.p.
     AUFS, 480; Silberman, 1080

1738 Nippon Gakujutsu Shinkokai. Dai 17 Sho (Nihon Koten Hon'yaku)
A   Iinkai. Japanese Noh Drama; Ten Plays Selected and Trans-
     lated from the Japanese. Tokyo: Nippon Gakujutsu Shin-
     kokai, 1955-1960. 3 v. 60-21422.
     Silberman, 1122

1538 Nish, Ian Hill. The Anglo-Japanese Alliance; The Diplomacy
B   of Two Island Empires, 1894-1907. London: Athlone, 1966.
     420 pp. (University of London Historical Studies, 18).
     66-73701.
     Sup. 67, 3221; Choice, 1/67; JAS, 11/67; AHR, 1/67;
     Japan Q., 1-3/67; Pacific Affairs, Spring-Summer/66

1682 Nishikiori, Hideo. Togo-mura, a Village in Northern Japan.
C   tr. by Toshio Sano, annotated by John Embree. N.Y.: Inter-
     national Secretariat, Institute of Pacific Relations, 1945.
     114 pp. A47-934. o.p.

1210 Nivison, David S., ed. Confucianism in Action. contrib. by
B   William Theodore De Bary and others. Stanford, Calif.:
     Stanford University Press, 1969 (orig. pub. in 1959).
     390 pp. (Studies in the Civilizations of Eastern Asia).
     59-7433. (R).
     Sup. 61, 2804; Hucker, 1098; JAS, 8/60; AHR, 4/60; Ann. Am.
     Acad., 1/60; Library Journal, 6/15/59; Pacific Affairs, 3/60

1183 Nivison, David S. The Life and Thought of Chang Hsueh-ch'eng
B   (1738-1801). Stanford, Calif.: Stanford University
     Press, 1966. 336 pp. (Studies in Civilization of Eastern
     Asia). 65-13112.
     Choice, 9/66; JAS, 11/67; JAOS, 10-12/67; Library Journal,
     11/15/65; TLS, 9/22/66

1938 Noguchi, Isamu. A Sculptor's World. fore. by R. Buckminster
A   Fuller. N.Y.: Harper & Row, 1968. 259 pp. 67-22505.
     Choice, 12/68; Library Journal, 6/1/68

1778 Noma, Hiroshi. Zone of Emptiness. tr. from French by Bernard
C   Frechtman. Cleveland: World, 1956. 317 pp. 56-9260. o.p.
     AUFS, 483; Library Journal, 9/1/56

1900 Noma, Seiroku. The Arts of Japan, Ancient and Medieval. tr.
A   and adapt. by John Rosenfield. Palo Alto, Calif.: Kodansha,
     1965. 236 pp. 65-19186.
     Choice, 6/66; JAS, 11/66; Library Journal, 12/1/65

1939 Noma, Seiroku. Japanese Sculpture. Tokyo: Board of Tourist
B   Industry, Japanese Government Railways, 1939. 99 pp.
     (Tourist Library, 29). 40-9656.
     Silberman, 740

1867 Noma, Seiroku. Masks. English adaptation by Merideth Weatherby.
C   Rutland, Vt.: Tuttle, 1957. unpaged. 57-8793.
     Silberman, 854

1683 Norbeck, Edward. Changing Japan. N.Y.: Holt, Rinehart &
B   Winston, 1965. 82 pp. 65-23200.
     JAS, 8/66

1684 Norbeck, Edward. Takashima, a Japanese Fishing Community.
B   Salt Lake City: University of Utah Press, 1954. 231 pp.
     54-3502. o.p.
     Silberman, 1411; FEQ, 11/54

1539 Norman, E. Herbert. Japan's Emergence as a Modern State;
A   Political and Economic Problems of the Meji Period.
     N.Y.: International Secretariat, Institute of Pacific
     Relations, 1940. 254 pp. 40-8128. o.p.
     AUFS, 264; Silberman, 336; FEQ, 8/43; Am. Econ. R., 9/40;
     Am. Pol. Sci. R., 8/40; Ann. Am. Acad., 10/40

1540 Norman, E. Herbert. Soldier and Peasant in Japan: the Origins
C   of Conscription. Vancouver: University of British Columbia
     Press, 1965 (orig. pub. by Institute of Pacific Relations,
     1943). 76 pp. NUC 67-46889. (R).
     Silberman, 393

0295 North China Herald. 1850-1941. (M-Microphoto).
C

0654 North, Robert Carver. Chinese Communism. N.Y.: McGraw-Hill,
B   1966. 256 pp. (World University Library). 64-66180.
     Choice, 11/66

0655 North, Robert Carver. Kuomintang and Chinese Communist Elites.
B   Stanford, Calif.: Stanford University Press, 1952.
     130 pp. 52-3689. o.p.
     Hucker, 775; FEQ, 5/53; AHR, 4/53; Am. Soc. R., 8/53;
     Pacific Affairs, 6/53

0656 North, Robert Carver. M. N. Roy's Mission to China; The Com-
B   munist-Kuomintang Split of 1927. tr. by Helen I. Powers.
     Berkeley: University of California Press, 1963. 399 pp.
     63-21387.
     China Q., 7-9/68; Pacific Affairs, Spring/64; Pol. Sci. Q.,
     6/64

0657 North, Robert Carver. Moscow and Chinese Communists. 2d ed.
A   Stanford, Calif.: Stanford University Press, 1963. 310 pp.
     62-18742.
     AUFS, 957; Hucker, 869; FEQ, 5/54; Am. Pol. Sci. R., 6/63;
     Library Journal, 4/1/63; Pol. Sci. Q., 3/64

1339 Nunn, Godfrey Raymond. Publishing in Mainland China. Cam-
A   bridge, Mass.: M.I.T. Press, 1966. 83 pp. (Report No. 4).
     66-17756.
     JAS, 2/67

1779 Oe, Kenzaburo. A Personal Matter. N.Y.: Grove, 1968. 214 pp.
B   68-22007.
     Library Journal, 7/68

1643 Ogura, Takekazu, ed. Agricultural Development in Modern Japan.
A   Tokyo: Japan FAO Association, 1963. 688 pp. 65-77317.

1846 Ogyu, Sorai. The Political Writings of Ogyu Sorai. by J. R.
C   McEwan. London: Cambridge, 1962. 153 pp. (Cambridge
     University Oriental Publication, No. 7). 62-52873.
     Sup. 63, 2892; JAS, 5/63

1644 Ohara, Keiji, ed. Japanese Trade & Industry in the Meiji-Taisho
B   Era. tr. and adapted by Okata Tamotsu. Tokyo: Obunsha,
     1957. 566 pp. A59-8760 rev.
     Silberman, 383

1868 Oka, Hideyuki. How to Wrap Five Eggs; Japanese Design in
A   Traditional Packaging. fore. by George Nelson. tr. and
     adapted for Western Readers by Atsuko Nii and Ralph Fried-
     rich. N.Y.: Harper & Row, 1967. 203 pp. 67-19619.
     Choice, 7-8/68

1901 Okada, Yuzuru. Netsuke, a Miniature Art of Japan. Tokyo:
B   Japan Travel Bureau, 1951. 212 pp. (Tourist Library,
     N.S. 14). A52-9342.
     Silberman, 850

1818 Okakura, Kakuzo. The Book of Tea. intro. and notes by E. F.
B   Bleiler. N.Y.: Dover, 1965 (orig. pub. in 1906). 76 pp.
     56-13134. (R).
     Silberman, 862

1869 Okakura, Kakuzo. The Ideals of the East, with Special Refer-
C   ence to the Art of Japan. London: Murray, 1903. 244 pp.
     3-11515. o.p.

1645 Okawa, Kazushi. The Growth Rate of the Japanese Economy Since
B   1878. Tokyo: Kinokuniya, 1957. 250 pp. (Hitotsubashi
     University, Institute of Economic Research, Series 1).
     A59-3538.
     Silberman, 1490

1748 Okazaki, Yoshie, comp. Japanese Literature in the Meiji Era.
C   tr. by V. H. Viglielmo. Tokyo: Obunsha, 1955. 673 pp.
     (Japanese Culture in the Meiji Era, Vol. I). 56-22381.
     Silberman, 935

1725 Okuma, Kotomichi. A Grass Path, Selected Poems from Sokeishu.
C   tr. by Yukuo Uyehara and Marjorie Sinclair. Honolulu:
     University of Hawaii Press, 1955. 72 pp. 55-10495.
     Silberman, 1077; Japan Q., 7-9/56

1541 Okuma, Shigenobu, comp. Fifty Years of New Japan. 2d ed.
B   London: Smith Elder & Co., 1909. 2 v. 20-7617. o.p.
         AUFS, 268; Silberman, 362; AHR, 7/10

0397 Olschki, Leonardo. Marco Polo's Asia; An Introduction to his
B   "Description of the World" called "Il Milione". Berkeley:
         University of California Press, 1960. 459 pp. 60-8315.
         Hucker, 410; AHR, 7/61; Ann. Am. Acad., 3/61; JAOS, 4-6/65;
         Pacific Affairs, Fall/61

0398 Olschki, Leonardo. Marco Polo's Precursors, with a Map of Asia.
B   Baltimore: Johns Hopkins Press, 1943. 100 pp. 43-8440. o.p.
         Hucker, 395; FEQ, 11/47; AHR, 1/44; Geog. R., 1/44

1409 Olson, Lawrence Alexander. Dimensions of Japan; A Collection
B   of Reports Written for the American Universities Field Staff.
         N.Y.: American Universities Field Staff, 1963. 403 pp.
         63-14762.
         Sup. 63, 2893; JAS, 8/65; Am. Anthropologist, 2/64;
         Am. Pol. Sci. R., 3/64; Am. Soc. R., 6/64; Japan Q.,
         7-9/64; Library Journal, 8/63

1707 Omori, Annie Shepley, tr. Diaries of Court Ladies of Old Japan.
C   Boston: Houghton Mifflin, 1920. 200 pp. 21-128. o.p.
         AUFS, 441; Silberman, 890

1542 Omura, Bunji. The Last Genro, Prince Saionji, the Man Who
C   Westernized Japan. Philadelphia: Lippincott, 1938.
         442 pp. 38-7536. o.p.
         AHR, 1/39; Am. J. Soc., 9/38; Am. Pol. Sci. R., 12/38;
         Pacific Affairs, 12/38

1739 O'Neill, P. G. Early No Drama: Its Background, Character, and
C   Development, 1300-1450. London: Lund Humphries, 1959.
         223 pp. 59-31584.
         Silberman, 1112; JAS, 5/60; Japan Q., 7-9/59

1740 O'Neill, P. G. A Guide to No. 2d ed. Tokyo: Hinoki Shoten,
C   1960. 229 pp. NUC 63-52409.
         Silberman, 1113

1825 Ono, Motonori. Shinto: the Kami Way. Tokyo: Bridgway, dist.
B   by Tuttle, 1962. 116 pp. 61-14033.
         Sup. 63, 2894; JAS, 5/62

1780 Ooka, Shohei. Fires on the Plain. tr. from Japanese by
B   Ivan Morris. N.Y.: Knopf, 1957. 246 pp. 57-5651. o.p.
         AUFS, 484; Silberman, 1030; Library Journal, 7/57; TLS,
         4/12/57

0038 Oriens, v.1- 1948-
C   Hucker, 37

0039 Oriens Extremus; Zeitschrift fur Sprache, Kunst und Kulture
C   der Laender des Fernen Ostens, v.1- 1954-
         Hucker, 36; Silberman, 38

1410 Orient/West. The Japanese Image. ed. by Maurice Schneps and
C   Alvin D. Coox. Philadelphia: Orient/West, 1965. 381 pp.
         65-6136. o.p.
         JAS, 8/66

0040 Oriental Art. v.1-3. 1948-1951. n.s.v.1- 1955-
C

0041 Oriental Ceramic Society. Transactions. London: 1921-
C

1399 Oriental Economist. Tokyo: Oriental Economist, 1934-
C   Silberman, 43

1340 Orleans, Leo A. Professional Manpower and Education in Com-
A   munist China. Washington: Government Printing Office,
         1961. 260 pp. 61-61233. o.p.
         Hucker, 2229; JAS, 2/62; China Q., 10-12/61

1781 Osaragi, Jiro, pseud. Homecoming. tr. from Japanese by Brewster
B   Horwitz. N.Y.: Knopf, 1955. 303 pp. 54-12040.
         AUFS, 482; Silberman, 1028; Japan Q., 10-12/55; Library
         Journal, 12/1/54; TLS, 9/9/55

2002 Osgood, Cornelius. The Koreans and Their Culture. N.Y.:
B   Ronald, 1951. 387 pp. 51-271.
         AUFS, 563; Silberman, 1616; Am. Anthropologist, 7/51;
         AHR, 7/51; Am. Soc. R., 6/51; Ann. Am. Acad., 9/51; JAOS,
         10-12/51; Library Journal, 2/15/51; Pacific Affairs, 9/51

0399 Ou-yang, Hsiu. Biography of Huang Ch'ao. tr. and annotated
C   by Howard S. Levy. 2d ed. rev. and enl. Berkeley: Univer-
         sity of California Press, 1961. 153 pp. (Chinese Dynas-
         tic Histories Translations, No. 5). NUC 64-11480.

Hucker, 322; FEQ, 8/55; JAOS, 7-9/55

1543 Oya, Soichi, ed. Japan's Longest Day. comp. by Pacific War
C   Research Society. Palo Alto, Calif.: Kodansha, 1968.
         339 pp. 68-17573.
         Choice, 11/68

0042 Pacific Affairs, v.1- 1926- (1926-28 as Institute of
A   Pacific Relations News Bulletin).
         AUFS, 44; Hucker, 26; Silberman, 33

0043 Pacific Historical Review. v.1- 1932-
B

1577 Packard, George R. Protest in Tokyo; The Security Treaty Crisis
B   of 1960. Princeton, N.J.: Princeton University Press, 1966.
         423 pp. 65-17156.
         Sup. 67, 3222; Choice, 10/67; JAS, 11/66; Am. Pol. Sci. R.,
         6/67; Ann. Am. Acad., 12/66; Library Journal, 9/66;
         Pol. Sci. Q., 6/67

2057 Pai, Inez (Kong), ed. and tr. The Ever White Mountain; Korean
B   Lyrics in the Classical Sijo Form. Rutland, Vt.: Tuttle,
         1965. 175 pp. 65-26821.
         Choice, 4/66; JAS, 11/66

1098 Pai, Wei. The Chus Reach Heaven. tr. by Yang Hsien-yi and
C   Gladys Yang. Peking: Foreign Languages Press, 1954.
         108 pp. 55-3971.

2031 Paige, Glenn D. The Korean People's Democratic Republic.
B   Stanford, Calif.: Hoover Institution on War, Revolution,
         and Peace, 1966. 60 pp. 65-27783.
         JAS, 2/67

1870 Paine, Robert Treat. The Art and Architecture of Japan. Balti-
A   more: Penguin, 1955. 316 pp. 55-12839.
         AUFS, 399; Silberman, 721; FEQ, 5/56; Library Journal,
         1/1/56; TLS, 1/27/56

2046 Pak, Chong-hui. Our Nation's Path; Ideology of Social Recon-
C   struction. Seoul: Dong-a, 1962. 172 pp. NUC 63-35548.

2061 Palmer, Spencer John. Korea and Christianity; The Problem
C   of Identification and Tradition. Seoul: Hollym Corpora-
         tion, 1967. 174 pp. NUC 68-60983.

0400 Pan, Ku. Food and Money in Ancient China. tr. and annotated
B   by Nancy Lee Swann. Princeton, N.J.: Princeton University
         Press, 1950. 482 pp. 50-7084. o.p. (M-University).
         Hucker, 172; FEQ, 5/51

0401 Pan, Ku. The History of the Former Han Dynasty: A Critical Trans-
C   lation with annotations by Homer H. Dubs. N.Y.: American
         Council of Learned Societies, dist. by Columbia University
         Press, 1964 (orig. pub. by Waverly, 1938-). 43-46839 rev.
         (R).
         Hucker, 187; JAS, 11/58; FEQ, 11/44

0402 Pan, Ku. Wang Mang; A Translation of the Official Account
B   of His Rise to Power as Given in the History of the
         Former Han Dynasty. intro. and notes by Clyde Bailey
         Sargent. Shanghai: Graphic Art Book Company, 1947. 206 pp.
         A49-7492. o.p.
         Hucker, 220; FEQ, 2/52

0799 Panikkar, Kavalam Madhava. In Two Chinas, Memoirs of a Diplo-
C   mat. London: Allen & Unwin, 1955. 183 pp. 55-4527. o.p.
         Hucker, 970

1386 Papinot, Edmond. Historical and Geographical Dictionary
B   of Japan. N.Y.: Ungar, 1964 (orig. pub. by Sansaisha,
         1910). 2 v. 64-25236. (R).
         Choice, 4/65

0510 Parsons, James B. A Preliminary Analysis of the Ming
C   Dynasty Bureaucracy. Kyoto: Kansai Asiatic Society, 1959.
         16 pp. (Occasional Papers of the Kansai Asiatic Society,
         VII). Hand catalog.
         Hucker, 1848

1544 Paske-Smith, Montague. Western Barbarians in Japan and
B   Formasa in Tokugawa Days, 1603-1868. N.Y.: Paragon,
         1968 (orig. pub. by Thompson, 1930). 431 pp. 68-30741.
         (R).
         Silberman, 297

1976 Passin, Herbert. Society and Education in Japan. N.Y.: Bureau
A   of Publications, Teachers College, Columbia University, 1965.
         347 pp. (Studies of the East Asian Institute, Columbia Uni-

versity). 65-19168.
Sup. 67, 3223; Choice, 9/65; JAS, 5/66

1646 Patrick, Hugh T. Monetary Policy and Central Banking in
B   Contemporary Japan. Bombay: University of Bombay Press,
     1962. 219 pp. (Series in Monetary and International Eco-
     nomics, No. 5). SA64-1456.
     JAS, 11/64

1134 Payne, Pierre Stephen Robert, ed. Contemporary Chinese Poetry,
C   an Anthology. London: Routledge, 1947. 168 pp.
     A48-4463. o.p. (M-University).
     Hucker, 1747

0800 Payne, Pierre Stephen Robert. Mao Tse-tung, Ruler of Red
B   China. N.Y.: Schuman, 1950. 303 pp. 50-10288. o.p.
     Hucker, 863; Library Journal, 9/15/60

0129 Payne, Pierre Stephen Robert. Red Storm over Asia. N.Y.:
B   Macmillan, 1951. 309 pp. 51-2375. o.p.
     FEQ, 5/52; Library Journal, 3/15/51

0130 Payne, Pierre Stephen Robert. The Revolt of Asia. N.Y.:
C   John Day, 1947. 305 pp. 47-31380. o.p.
     Library Journal, 9/15/47

0969 Payne, Pierre Stephen Robert. The White Pony; An Anthology
B   of Chinese Poetry from the Earliest Times to the Present
     Day. newly tr. N.Y.: New American Library, 1960 (orig.
     pub. by John Day, 1947). 320 pp. 47-6700. (R).
     Hucker, 1560; Library Journal, 12/1/47

1341 Peake, Cyrus. Nationalism and Education in Modern China. N.Y.:
A   Columbia University Press, 1932. 240 pp. 32-26886. o.p.

0007 Pearson, James Douglas. Oriental and Asian Bibliography, an
B   Introduction with Some Reference to Africa. Hamden, Conn.:
     Archon, 1966. 261 pp. 66-1006.
     Choice, 11/66; JAS, 2/67; Library Journal, 6/1/66

0658 Peck, Graham. Two Kinds of Time; Illustrated by the Author.
A   Boston: Houghton Mifflin, 1950. 725 pp. 50-10600. o.p.
     AUFS, 855; Hucker, 802; FEQ, 8/51

0087 Peffer, Nathaniel. The Far East, a Modern History. Ann
B   Arbor: University of Michigan Press, 1958. 489 pp.
     58-62522.
     AUFS, 109; Silberman, 325; JAS, 8/59; AHR, 4/59; Ann. Am.
     Acad., 5/59; Library Journal, 10/1/58; Pacific Affairs,
     12/59; TLS, 7/10/59

0296 Peking Review. v.1- 1958-
B

0511 Pelcovits, Nathan Albert. Old China Hands and the Foreign
A   Office. N.Y.: Octagon, 1967 (orig. pub. by American Insti-
     tute of Pacific Relations, 1948). 349 pp. 78-76003. (R).
     AUFS, 756; Hucker, 677; AHR, 10/48; Am. Pol. Sci. R., 4/48;
     Ann. Am. Acad., 5/48; FEQ, 8/48; Pacific Affairs, 9/48

0262 Perleberg, Max. Who's Who in Modern China. Hong Kong: Ye
B   Olde Printerie, 1954. 428 pp. 54-19583.
     Hucker, 716

1467 Perry, Matthew Calbraith. Narrative of the Expedition of an
A   American Squadron to the China Seas and Japan, Performed in
     the Years 1852, 1853, and 1854, Under the Command of
     Commodore M. C. Perry, U.S. Navy, by Order of the Government
     of the United States. ed. by Francis L. Hawks. N.Y.: AMS,
     1967 (orig. pub. by Nicholson, 1856). 3 v. 1-4228. (R).
     Silberman, 307

0063 Peterson, Alexander Duncan Campbell. The Far East, a Social
C   Geography. London: Duckworth, 1949. 336 pp. 50-717.

0044 Philosophy East and West. v.1- 1951- (R-Johnson).
B   FEQ, 5/45

1963 Piggott, Sir Francis Taylor. The Music and Musical Instruments
C   of Japan. 2d ed. Yokohama: Kelly & Walsh, 1909. 196 pp.
     10-20826. o.p.
     Silberman, 1167

1545 Pittau, Joseph. Political Thought in Early Meiji Japan,
C   1868-1889. Cambridge, Mass.: Harvard University Press,
     1967. 250 pp. (Harvard East Asian Series, 24).
     65-22065.
     Sup. 67, 3225; Choice, 10/67; JAS, 11/67; Japan Q., 10-12/67;
     JAOS, 10-12/67; Library Journal, 12/15/66

1685 Plath, David William. The After Hours; Modern Japan and the
A   Search for Enjoyment. Berkeley: University of California
     Press, 1964. 222 pp. 64-16133.
     Sup. 65, 3070; Choice, 9/64; JAS, 5/65; Ann. Am. Acad.,
     11/64; Japan Q., 10-12/64; Library Journal, 8/64

2032 Poats, Rutherford M. Decision in Korea. N.Y.: McBride,
C   1954. 340 pp. 54-7378. o.p.
     AUFS, 564; Silberman, 1786; Library Journal, 6/1/54

1604 Political Handbook of Japan. Tokyo: Tokyo News Service, 1949-
C   50-2733.
     Silberman, 1194a

0857 The Politics of the Chinese Red Army; A Translation of the Bulle-
B   tin of Activities of the People's Liberation Army. ed. by
     J. C. Cheng, with the collaboration of C. Han and others.
     Stanford, Calif.: Hoover Institution on War, Revolution, and
     Peace, 1966. 776 pp. 65-28426.
     JAS, 2/67; Library Journal, 6/1/66

0801 Portisch, Hugo. Red China Today. tr. from German by H. von
C   Koschembahr. Chicago: Quadrangle, 1966. 383 pp. 66-11872.
     Choice, 11/66; Ann. Am. Acad., 11/66; Library Journal,
     5/15/66

2003 Portway, Donald. Korea; Land of the Morning Calm. London:
C   Harrap, 1953. 187 pp. A54-1865. o.p.
     AUFS, 565

1826 Posonby-Fane, Richard Arthur Brabazon. Visiting Famous Shinto
C   Shrines in Japan. Kyoto: The Ponsonby Memorial Society, 1964.
     439 pp. 66-32263.
     JAS, 5/66

2092 Potter, Jack M. Capitalism and the Chinese Peasant: Social
B   and Economic Change in a Hong Kong Village. Berkeley:
     University of California Press, 1968. 215 pp. 68-10688.
     JAS, 11/68

0659 Powell, John Benjamin. My Twenty-five Years in China. N.Y.:
C   Macmillan, 1945. 436 pp. 45-9203. o.p.
     Hucker, 734; FEQ, 5/46

0858 Powell, Ralph L. Politico-Military Relationships in Communist
B   China. Washington: External Research Staff, U.S. Dept. of
     State, 1963. 21 pp. 64-60730. o.p.

0512 Powell, Ralph L. The Rise of Chinese Military Power, 1895-
A   1912. Princeton, N.J.: Princeton University Press, 1955.
     383 pp. 55-6247. o.p.
     Hucker, 647; AHR, 1/56; Ann. Am. Acad., 3/56; Library
     Journal, 8/55

0660 Price, Ernest Batson. The Russo-Japanese Treaties of 1907-
B   1916 concerning Manchuria and Mongolia. Baltimore: Johns
     Hopkins Press, 1933. 164 pp. 33-20423. o.p. (M-Uni-
     versity).
     AUFS, 1230; Am. Pol. Sci. R., 10/33; Pol. Sci. Q., 12/33

0802 Princeton University Conference. The United States and Communist
B   China. Papers Delivered at the Sixty-ninth Meeting of
     the Princeton University Conference Feb. 25-26, 1965.
     ed. by William W. Lockwood. Princeton, N.J.: 1965. 71 pp.
     65-5991. o.p.
     JAS, 8/66

1314 Prip-Moller, Johannes. Chinese Buddhist Monasteries; Their
C   Plan and Its Function as a Setting for Buddhist Monastic
     Life. 2d ed. N.Y.: Oxford, 1967. 396 pp. 68-2487.
     JAS, 11/68

1162 Prusek, Jaroslav. Die Literatur Des Befreiten China und
C   Ihre Volkstraditionen. tr. by Pavel Eisner und Ubers von
     Wilhelm Gampert. Prague: Artia, 1955. 736 pp. 56-3856.

1163 Prusek, Jaroslav, ed. Studies in Modern Chinese Literature.
C   Berlin: Akademie-Verlag, 1964. 179 pp. NUC 66-2065.
     JAS, 5/66

0936 P'u, Sung-ling. Strange Stories from a Chinese Studio. tr. and
B   annotated by Herbert A. Giles. 3d ed. rev. Shanghai:
     Kelly & Walsh, 1916. 488 pp. 24-18340 rev. o.p.
     AUFS, 1073; Hucker, 1651

0403 Pulleyblank, E. G. The Background of the Rebellion of An Lu-shan.
B   N.Y.: Oxford, 1955. 264 pp. A58-1352.
     Hucker, 279; FEQ, 11/55; JAOS, 7-9/55

2097 Purcell, Victor William Williams Saunders. The Chinese in South-
A   east Asia. 2d ed. N.Y.: Oxford, 1965. 623 pp. 65-4234.

Hucker, 118; FEQ, 2/52

1342 Purcell, Victor William Williams Saunders. Problems of Chinese
B   Education. London: Kegan Paul, Trench, Trubner, 1936.
      261 pp. 37-3092. o.p.
      Hucker, 1939

2102 Pye, Lucian W. Guerilla Communism in Malaya; Its Social and
A   Political Meaning. Princeton, N.J.: Princeton Univer-
      sity Press, 1956. 369 pp. 56-10827.
      AUFS, 1429; Ann. Am. Acad., 5/57

0859 Pye, Lucian W. The Spirit of Chinese Politics; A Psycho-
B   cultural Study of the Authority Crisis in Political
      Development. Cambridge, Mass.: M.I.T. Press, 1968.
      255 pp. 68-14451.
      Choice, 12/68; China Q., 1-3/69; Library Journal, 8/68

0008 Quarterly Check-list of Oriental Studies. v.1- Darien,
C   Conn.: American Bibliographic Service, 1959- 65-45222.
      Hucker, 21; Silberman, 25

0348 Quigley, Harold Scott. China's Politics in Perspective. Minne-
B   apolis: University of Minnesota Press, 1962. 266 pp.
      62-13606. o.p.
      Sup. 63, 2926; JAS, 11/62; China Q., 4-6/63; Library Journal,
      4/1/62

0111 Quigley, Harold Scott. Far Eastern War, 1937-1941. Boston:
C   World Peace Foundation, 1942. 369 pp. 42-14269. o.p.
      (M-University).
      Hucker, 795; Silberman, 498; FEQ, 2/43; Am. Pol. Sci. R.,
      10/42; Ann. Am. Acad., 11/42; Pacific Affairs, 9/42

1605 Quigley, Harold Scott. Japanese Government and Politics; An
C   Introductory Study. N.Y.: Century, 1932. 442 pp.
      32-30112. o.p.
      Silberman, 585; Am. Pol. Sci. R., 2/33; Ann. Am. Acad.,
      3/33

1606 Quigley, Harold Scott. The New Japan, Government and Politics.
C   Minneapolis: University of Minnesota Press, 1956. 456 pp.
      55-11708.
      Silberman, 564; FEQ, 8/56; AHR, 7/56; Am. Pol. Sci. R., 9/56;
      Ann. Am. Acad., 9/56; Japan Q., 7-9/56; Library Journal,
      1/15/56

1902 Rague, Beatrix Von. Geschichte Der Japanischen Lackkunst.
C   Berlin: De Gruyter, 1967. 380 pp. NUC 67-55214.

2090 Rand, Christopher. Hong Kong, the Island Between. N.Y.:
B   Knopf, 1952. 244 pp. 52-10942. o.p.
      AUFS, 960; Library Journal, 9/15/52

0661 Rankin, Karl Lott. China Assignment. Seattle: University
B   of Washington Press, 1964. 343 pp. 64-20488.
      Choice, 12/64; JAS, 5/65; J. Am. Hist., 6/65; Library
      Journal, 12/15/64

0803 Rasmussen, Albert Henry. China Trader. N.Y.: Crowell, 1954.
C   274 pp. 54-5530. o.p. (M-University).
      TLS, 8/13/54

0404 Ratchnevsky, Paul. Essai sur la Codification et la Legislation
C   a l'Epoque des Yuan. Paris: Leroux, 1937. 41-36376.
      Hucker, 415

0513 Rawlinson, John L. China's Struggle for Naval Development,
B   1839-1895. Cambridge, Mass.: Harvard University Press,
      1967. 318 pp. (Harvard East Asian Series, 25). 66-10127.
      Choice, 7-8/67; JAS, 11/67; AHR, 12/67; JAOS, 10-12/67

2033 Rees, David. Korea: the Limited War. N.Y.: St. Martin's,
C   1964. 511 pp. 64-14946.
      Sup. 65, 3079; Choice, 7-8/64; Library Journal, 5/15/64;
      TLS, 4/23/64

2047 Reeve, W. D. The Republic of Korea, a Political and Economic
A   Study. N.Y.: Oxford, 1963. 197 pp. 63-25579.
      JAS, 8/64

1099 Registration and Other Stories, by Contemporary Chinese Writers.
C   Peking: Foreign Languages Press, 1956. 210 pp. Hand cata-
      log. o.p.

1244 Reichelt, Karl Ludvig. Truth and Tradition in Chinese Buddhism;
B   A Study of Chinese Mahayana Buddhism. tr. from Norwegian by
      Kathrina Van Wagenen Bugge. Shanghai: Commercial Press,
      1927. 330 pp. 28-8949. o.p.
      Hucker, 1258

0514 Reichwein, Adolf. China and Europe: Intellectual and Artistic
A   Contacts in the Eighteenth Century. tr. by J. C. Powell.
      N.Y.: Barnes & Noble, 1968 (orig. pub. by Knopf, 1925).
      174 pp. 25-9577. (R).
      Hucker, 574   s

1320 Reinhard, Kurt. Chinesische Musik. Eisenach und Kassel:
C   Erich Roth, 1956. 246 pp. 57-17248.
      Hucker, 1774

0662 Reinsch, Paul Samuel. An American Diplomat in China. N.Y.:
B   Paragon, 1967 (orig. pub. by Doubleday, 1922). 396 pp.
      NUC 68-1766. (R).
      Am. Pol. Sci. R., 8/22; Ann. Am. Acad., 5/22

0064 Reischauer, Edwin Oldfather. Beyond Vietnam: the United States
B   and Asia. N.Y.: Knopf, 1967. 242 pp. 67-25614.
      Choice, 4/68; Library Journal, 10/15/67; TLS, 11/17/67

0405 Reischauer, Edwin Oldfather. Ennin's Travels in T'ang China.
A   N.Y.: Ronald, 1955. 341 pp. 55-6273.
      Hucker, 280; Silberman, 633; FEQ, 11/55; Ann. Am. Acad.,
      11/55; Library Journal, 6/15/55; Pacific Affairs, 12/55

0088 Reischauer, Edwin Oldfather. A History of East Asian Civili-
A   zation. Boston: Houghton Mifflin, 1960- 2 v. 60-4269.
      Sup. 61, 2753; Sup. 65, 3054; Hucker, 98; Silberman, 156;
      Choice, 5/65; JAS, 8/61, 11/65; AHR, 1/61; Ann. Am. Acad.,
      11/61; JAOS, 1-3/63, 4-6/66; Library Journal, 6/15/65;
      TLS, 8/18/61

1421 Reischauer, Edwin Oldfather. Japan, Past and Present.
A   3d ed. rev. N.Y.: Knopf, 1964. 323 pp. 64-12896.
      AUFS, 169; Silberman, 149; Choice, 5/64; FEQ, 8/53

1708 Reischauer, Edwin Oldfather, ed. and tr. Translations from
B   Early Japanese Literature. Cambridge, Mass.: Harvard Uni-
      versity Press for Harvard-Yenching Institute, 1951. 467 pp.
      51-10360.
      AUFS, 443; Silberman, 904; FEQ, 8/52

1578 Reischauer, Edwin Oldfather. The United States and Japan.
A   3d ed. Cambridge, Mass.: Harvard University Press,
      1965. 396 pp. (American Foreign Policy Library). 64-8057.
      AUFS, 369; Silberman, 3; Choice, 9/65; Japan Q., 4-6/58;
      Library Journal, 3/15/65

1436 Reischauer, Robert Karl. Early Japanese History, c.40 B.C.-
B   A.D. 1167. Gloucester, Mass.: Peter Smith, 1967 (orig.
      pub. by Princeton University Press, 1937). 2 v. 67-8701.
      (R).
      Silberman, 187; JAOS, 3/39; TLS, 1/1/38

1546 Reischauer, Robert Karl. Japan, Government-Politics.
C   N.Y.: Nelson, 1939. 221 pp. 39-3379. o.p.
      AUFS, 274; Silberman, 1189; Am. Pol. Sci. R., 12/39;
      Pol. Sci. Q., 6/39

0663 Remer, Charles Frederick. The Foreign Trade of China. Taipei:
C   Ch'eng-wen Publishing Co., dist. by Chinese Materials
      and Research Aids Service Center, 1967 (orig. pub. by
      Commercial, 1926). 269 pp. Hand catalog. (R). (M-Uni-
      versity).

0664 Remer, Charles Frederick. Readings in Economics for China,
C   Selected Materials with Explanatory Introductions. Shang-
      hai: Commercial, 1926. 685 pp. Agr 23-917. o.p.

0045 Revue des Arts Asiatiques, v.1-13. 1924-42.
B

0218 Revue Bibliographique de Sinologie. 1- Paris: Mouton, 1955-
B   58-23000.
      Hucker, 20

0970 Rexroth, Kenneth. One Hundred Poems from the Chinese. N.Y.:
C   New Directions, 1956. 159 pp. 56-13351.
      Hucker, 1577; JAS, 8/58

1726 Rexroth, Kenneth. One Hundred Poems from the Japanese.
C   N.Y.: New Directions, 1955. 143 pp. 56-2557.
      FEQ, 5/56; Japan Q., 10-12/56

0219 Rhoads, Edward J. M. The Chinese Red Army, 1927-1963; An Anno-
A   tated Bibliography. Cambridge, Mass.: Harvard University
      Press, 1964. 188 pp. (Harvard East Asian Monographs, No.
      16). 65-1422.
      Choice, 7-8/65; JAS, 11/65

0515 Ricci, Matteo. China in the Sixteenth Century: the Journals of
B   Matthew Ricci, 1583-1610. tr. from Latin by Louis J.
     Gallagher. N.Y.: Random House, 1953. 616 pp. 53-9708.
     o.p.
     Hucker, 546

1211 Richards, Ivor Armstrong. Mencius on the Mind; Experiments in
B   Multiple Definition. London: Paul, Trench, Trubner, 1932.
     131 pp. 32-21317.
     Hucker, 1128; JAOS, 9/33

0665 Richardson, Hugh Edward. A Short History of Tibet. N.Y.:
A   Dutton, 1962. 308 pp. 61-6023.
     JAS, 2/63; Library Journal, 8/62; TLS, 12/21/62

1977 Richie, Donald. The Films of Akira Kurosawa. Berkeley:
A   University of California Press, 1965. 218 pp. 65-26695.
     Choice, 4/66; Library Journal, 1/15/65; TLS, 2/24/66

0804 Rickett, Allyn. Prisoners of Liberation. N.Y.: Cameron, 1957.
B   288 pp. 57-13896. o.p.
     AUFS, 963; Hucker, 968; JAS, 2/58

2034 Ridgway, Matthew B. The Korean War: How We Met the Challenge,
A   How All-out Asian War Was Averted, Why MacArthur Was
     Dismissed, Why Today's War Objectives Must be Limited.
     Garden City, N.Y.: Doubleday, 1967. 291 pp. 67-11172.
     Choice, 4/68; Library Journal, 9/15/67

1686 Riesman, David. Conversations in Japan; Modernization, Politics,
A   and Culture. by David Riesman and Evelyn Thompson Riesman.
     N.Y.: Basic Books, 1967. 371 pp. 67-17861.
     Choice, 1/68; Library Journal, 6/15/67

0666 Rigg, Robert B. Red China's Fighting Hordes, a Realistic Account
C   of the Chinese Communist Army by a U.S. Army Officer. Har-
     risburg, Pa.: Military Service Publishing Co., 1951. 378 pp.
     51-14765 rev. o.p.
     Hucker, 1960; Pacific Affairs, 12/52

2075 Riggs, Fred Warren. Formosa under Chinese Nationalist Rule.
C   N.Y.: Macmillan, 1952. 195 pp. 52-3209. o.p.
     AUFS, 864; Hucker, 850; FEQ, 5/53; Am. Pol. Sci. R., 12/52;
     Ann. Am. Acad., 1/53; Pacific Affairs, 6/53

2035 Riley, John W. The Reds Take a City; The Communist Occupa-
B   tion of Seoul, with Eyewitness Accounts. tr. by Hugh
     Heung-wu Cynn. New Brunswick, N.J.: Rutgers University
     Press, 1951. 210 pp. 51-13868. o.p.
     Silberman, 1788

1926 Robertson, Ronald G. Contemporary Printmaking in Japan.
B   N.Y.: Crown, 1965. 120 pp. 65-24320.
     Choice, 9/66; Library Journal, 2/15/66

1871 Robinson, Basil William. A Primer of Japanese Sword Blades.
C   N.Y.: Paragon, 1965 (orig. pub. by Dyer, 1955). 95 pp.
     59-21053. (R).
     Silberman, 851

0077 Robinson, Harry. Monsoon Asia; A Geographical Survey. N.Y.:
B   Praeger, 1967. 561 pp. 67-24687.
     Choice, 11/68; JAS, 8/68; Library Journal, 2/1/68; Pacific
     Affairs, Fall/68

1245 Robinson, Richard H., tr. Chinese Buddhist Verse. N.Y.: Para-
C   gon, 1966 (orig. pub. by Grove, 1954). 85 pp. 55-25496.
     (R).
     AUFS, 665; Hucker, 1297

1246 Robinson, Richard H. Early Madhyamika in India and China.
C   Madison: University of Wisconsin Press, 1967. 347 pp.
     66-22853.

2011 Rockhill, William Woodville. China's Intercourse with Korea
C   from the XVth Century to 1895. New Hyde Park, N.Y.: Uni-
     versity Books, 1966 (orig. pub. by Luzac, 1905). 60 pp.
     6-7316. (R). (M-University).
     Silberman, 1742

1468 Rogers, Philip George. The First Englishman in Japan; The Story
C   of Will Adams. London: Harvill, 1956. 143 pp. 56-58999.
     o.p.
     Silberman, 296; JAS, 2/58; Japan Q., 1-3/57

0667 Romanus, Charles F. Stilwell's Command Problems. Washington:
A   Office of Chief of Military History, Dept. of the Army,
     1956. 518 pp. 55-60004. o.p.
     JAS, 2/58

0668 Romanus, Charles F. Stilwell's Mission to China. Washington:
A   Office of Chief of Military History, Dept. of the Army,
     1953. 441 pp. 53-60349. o.p.
     Hucker, 817; FEQ, 11/53

0669 Romanus, Charles F. Time Runs Out in CBI. Washington: Office
A   of Chief of Military History, Dept. of the Army, 1959.
     428 pp. 59-60003. o.p.
     JAS, 8/60

0065 Romein, Jan Marius. The Asian Century, a History of Modern
A   Nationalism in Asia. tr. by R. T. Clark. Berkeley:
     University of California Press, 1962. 448 pp. 62-51755.
     Sup. 63, 2874; JAS, 5/65; AHR, 10/63; Ann. Am. Acad., 11/63;
     Pacific Affairs, Fall/63; Pol. Sci. Q., 12/63

1387 Rose-Innes, Arthur. Beginners' Dictionary of Chinese-Japa-
C   nese Characters, with Common Abbreviations, Variants and
     Numerous Compounds. 4th ed. rev. Tokyo: Meisei Sha, 1959.
     507 pp. Hand catalog.
     AUFS, 413; Silberman, 108

1927 Rosenfield, John M. Japanese Arts of the Heian Period:
A   794-1185. N.Y.: Asia Society, dist. by New York Graphic,
     1967. 135 pp. 67-22187.
     Choice, 7-8/68; Library Journal, 4/1/68

0670 Rosinger, Lawrence Kaelter. China's Wartime Politics, 1937-1944.
B   Princeton, N.J.: Princeton University Press, 1945. 133 pp.
     45-10186. o.p.
     Hucker, 807; FEQ, 2/45; Am. Pol. Sci. R., 2/45; Ann. Am.
     Acad., 3/45; Pol. Sci. Q., 3/45

0066 Rosinger, Lawrence Kaelter. The State of Asia, a Contemporary
C   Survey. N.Y.: Knopf, 1951. 522 pp. 51-11245. o.p.
     AUFS, 51; FEQ, 2/52; Library Journal, 7/51

1647 Rosovsky, Henry. Capital Formation in Japan, 1868-1940.
A   N.Y.: Free Press of Glencoe, 1961. 358 pp. 61-12874.
     Sup. 63, 2895; JAS, 11/62

0516 Rosso, Antonio Sisto. Apostolic Legations to China of the
C   Eighteenth Century. South Pasadena, Calif.: P. D. and Ione
     Perkins, 1948. 502 pp. 49-25178. o.p.
     Hucker, 552; FEQ, 2/52

0805 Rostow, Walt Whitman. The Prospects for Communist China. Cam-
C   bridge, Mass.: Technology Press of M.I.T., 1954. 379 pp.
     54-13288.
     AUFS, 964; Hucker, 931; FEQ, 5/55; Am. Econ. R., 6/55; Am.
     Soc. R., 6/55; Ann. Am. Acad., 5/55; Pacific Affairs, 6/55;
     TLS, 4/29/55

0517 Rowbotham, Arnold Horrex. Missionary and Mandarin, the
A   Jesuits at the Court of China. N.Y.: Russell & Russell,
     1966 (orig. pub. by University of California Press, 1942).
     374 pp. 66-13253. (R).
     AUFS, 759; Hucker, 1307; FEQ, 5/43

0671 Rowe, David Nelson. China among the Powers. N.Y.: Harcourt,
B   Brace, 1945. 205 pp. 45-1826. o.p.
     Hucker, 806; FEQ, 8/45; Ann. Am. Acad., 7/45; Pol. Sci. Q.,
     6/45

0672 Rowe, David Nelson. Modern China, a Brief History. Prince-
C   ton, N.J.: Van Nostrand, 1959. 192 pp. 59-15095.
     Hucker, 724; China Q., 7-9/60

0196 Rowland, Benjamin. Art in East and West; An Introduction Through
B   Comparisons. Cambridge, Mass.: Harvard University Press,
     1954. 144 pp. 54-9777.
     Hucker, 1479; Library Journal, 4/1/55

0189 Rowland, Benjamin. The Harvard Outline and Reading Lists
C   for Oriental Art. rev. ed. Cambridge, Mass.: Harvard
     University Press, 1958. 74 pp. 58-13770.
     Silberman, 711; JAOS, 4-6/53

1304 Rowley, George. Principles of Chinese Painting. 2d ed. Prince-
A   ton, N.J.: Princeton University Press, 1959. 85 pp. 60-325.
     Hucker, 1472; FEQ, 2/48

0806 Roy, Manabendra Nath. Revolution and Counter-Revolution in
C   China. Calcutta: National Book Agency (orig. pub. by Renais-
     sance, 1946). 689 pp. 50-1167. (R).
     Hucker, 888

0046 Royal Asiatic Society of Great Britain and Ireland. Journal.
B   v.1-20. 1834-1863. n.s.v.1-21. 1864-1889. s.3 v.1-
     1889- (R-Kraus).
     Hucker, 44

1992 Royal Asiatic Society of Great Britain and Ireland. Korea
B   Branch. Transactions. Seoul: The Society, 1900- (R-Kraus,
      M-Microphoto).
      Silbsrman, 1646

0297 Royal Asiatic Society of Great Britain and Ireland. North
B   China Branch Journal, v.1-2. 1858-1860. n.s.v.1-
      1864- (R-Kraus, M-IDC, M-Research Publications).
      Hucker, 41

1287 Rudolph, Richard C. Han Tomb Art of West China: a Collection of
C   First- and Second-Century Reliefs by Richard C. Rudolph in
      collaboration with Wen Yu. Berkeley: University of Cali-
      fornia Press, 1951. 67 pp. 51-11148. o.p.
      Hucker, 1447; FEQ, 2/52

0673 Rue, John E. Mao Tse-tung in Opposition, 1927-1935. Stanford,
A   Calif.: Stanford University Press, 1966. 387 pp. 66-15302.
      Sup. 67, 3248; Choice, 5/67; JAS, 8/67; AHR, 7/67; Library
      Journal, 12/1/66; Pol. Sci. Q., 12/67

0674 Russell, Edward Frederick Langley Russell. Knights of the Bush-
B   ido, the Shocking History of Japanese War Atrocities. N.Y.:
      Dutton, 1958. 334 pp. 58-9587.
      TLS, 9/12/58

2004 Rutt, Richard. Korean Works and Days: Notes from the Diary
A   of a Country Priest. Rutland, Vt.: Tuttle, 1964. 231 pp.
      63-15271.
      Sup. 65, 3080; Choice, 10/64; Japan Q., 1-3/65

0406 Ruysbroek, Willem Van, 13th Century. The Journey of William
B   of Rubruck to the Eastern Parts of the World, 1253-55, as
      Narrated by Himself, with Two Accounts of the Earlier Jour-
      ney of John of Pian de Carpine. tr. by William W. Rockhill.
      Lichtenstein: Kraus, 1966 (orig. pub. by Hakluyt Society,
      1900). 304 pp. 1-9024. (R).
      Hucker, 402

1782 Ryan, Marleigh Grayer. Japan's First Modern Novel: Ukigumo
A   of Futabatei Shimei. N.Y.: Columbia University Press,
      1967. 381 pp. (UNESCO Collection of Representative Works).
      67-15896.
      Choice, 3/68; JAS, 5/68

1247 Saddharmapundarika. The Lotus of the Wonderful Law; or, The
B   Lotus Gospel, by W. E. Soothill. Oxford: Clarendon, 1930.
      275 pp. 30-31901. o.p. (M-University).
      Hucker, 1292; JAOS, 6/31; TLS, 7/17/30

1872 Sadler, Arthur Lindsay. Cha-no-yu, the Japanese Tea Ceremony.
C   Rutland, Vt.: Tuttle, 1963 (orig. pub. by Kegan, Paul,
      Trench and Trubner, 1934). 245 pp. 62-19787. (R).
      Silberman, 864; Japan Q., 10-12/63

1469 Sadler, Arthur Lindsay. The Maker of Modern Japan; The Life
B   of Tokugawa Ieyasu. London: Allen & Unwin, 1937. 429 pp.
      37-7531.
      Silberman, 235; FEQ, 8/42

1950 Sadler, Arthur Lindsay. A Short History of Japanese Archi-
A   tecture. Rutland, Vt.: Tuttle, 1962. 160 pp. 62-21539.

1903 Sagara, Tokuzo. Japanese Fine Arts. 4th ed. Tokyo: Japan
B   Travel Bureau, 1958. 249 pp. (Tourist Library, N.S. 9).
      58-12786.
      Silberman, 726

1741 Sakanishi, Shio, tr. Japanese Folk-plays: the Ink-Smeared Lady
A   and Other Kyooen. Rutland, Vt.: Tuttle, 1960. 150 pp.
      (UNESCO Collection of Representative Works: Japanese Series).
      60-1954.
      JAS, 11/60; Japan Q., 7-9/60

1742 Sakanishi, Shio, tr. Kyogen; Comic Interludes of Japan.
B   Boston: Marshall Jones, 1938. 150 pp. 38-16902. o.p.
      AUFS, 517; Silberman, 1128; JAOS, 3/39

1305 Sakanishi, Shio, tr. The Spirit of the Brush, Being the Out-
C   look of Chinese Painters on Nature, from Eastern China
      to Five Dynasties, A.D. 317-960. N.Y.: Grove, 1939.
      108 pp. 39-8538 rev. o.p.
      Hucker, 1490

1266 Salmony, Alfred. Antler and Tongue; An Essay on Ancient Chi-
C   nese Symbolism and Its Implications. Ascona: Artibus Asiae,
      1954. 57 pp. (Artibus Asiae Supplementum XIII). 55-1320.
      Hucker, 1510

1904 Sanders, Herbert H. The World of Japanese Ceramics. Palo Alto,
C   Calif.: Kodansha, 1967. 267 pp. 67-16771.

1388 Sansom, George Bailey. An Historical Grammar of Japanese.
B   Oxford: Clarendon, 1928. 347 pp. 28-23697.
      Silberman, 127

1422 Sansom, Sir George Bailey. A History of Japan. Stanford,
A   Calif.: Stanford University Press, 1958-63. (Studies
      in the Civilization of Eastern Asia). 3 v. 58-11694.
      Sup. 61, 2777; Sup. 65, 3071; AUFS, 204; Hucker, 306;
      Silberman, 147, 148; JAS, 8/59, 8/64; AHR, 7/59, 1/62, 7/64;
      Ann. Am. Acad, 5/64; Japan Q., 10-12/59, 1-3/62, 10-12/64;
      JAOS, 1-3/59, 9-12/61; Library Journal, 10/15/63; TLS,
      4/24/59, 10/13/61, 8/6/64

1423 Sansom, Sir George Bailey. Japan, a Short Cultural History.
A   rev. ed. N.Y.: Appleton-Century, 1943. 554 pp. 43-18417.
      AUFS, 170; Hucker, 132; Silberman, 146; Pacific Affairs, 6/44

1424 Sansom, Sir George Bailey. Japan in World History. N.Y.:
C   International Secretariat, Institute of Pacific Relations,
      1951. 94 pp. 51-13888. o.p.
      Silberman, 153; AHR, 7/52; Pacific Affairs, 6/52; TLS,
      12/21/51

1425 Sansom, Sir George Bailey. The Western World and Japan, a Study
A   in the Interaction of European and Asiatic Cultures. N.Y.:
      Knopf, 1950. 504 pp. 50-5199.
      AUFS, 172; Hucker, 559; Silberman, 278; FEQ, 5/51; AHR,
      7/50; Am. Pol. Sci. R., 8/50; Ann. Am. Acad., 9/50; JAOS,
      7-9/50; Library Journal, 2/1/50; TLS, 10/27/50

1212 Sargent, Galen Eugene. Tchou Hi contre le Bouddhisme. Paris:
C   Imprimerie Nationale, 1955. 158 pp.
      Hucker, 1152

1873 Sato, Shozo. The Art of Arranging Flowers; A Complete Guide
B   to Japanese Ikebana. N.Y.: Abrams, 1966. 366 pp.
      65-20323.
      Choice, 7-8/67; Library Journal, 1/15/67

1547 Satow, Sir Ernest Mason. A Diplomat in Japan; The Inner
B   History of the Critical Years in the Evolution of Japan
      When the Ports were Opened and the Monarchy Restored...
      London: Seeley, Service, 1921. 427 pp. 21-8608. o.p.
      Silberman, 411

0112 Satow, Sir Ernest Mason. Korea and Manchuria Between Russia
C   and Japan, 1895-1904; The Observations of Sir Ernest Satow,
      British Minister to Japan (1895-1900) and China (1900-
      1906). sel. and ed. with an historical intro. by George
      A. Lensen. Tallahassee, Fla.: Diplomatic Press, 1966.
      296 pp. 66-17316.
      Choice, 11/66; JAS, 8/66; AHR, 1/67; Japan Q., 10-12/66;
      Pacific Affairs, Spring-Summer/66

1836 Saunders, Ernest Dale. Buddhism in Japan, With an Outline
C   of Its Origins in India. Philadelphia: University of
      Pennsylvania Press, 1964. 328 pp. 64-10900.
      Sup. 65, 3072; Choice, 4/65; JAS, 5/65

0675 Scalapino, Robert A. The Chinese Anarchist Movement. Berke-
A   ley: Center for Chinese Studies, Institute of International
      Studies, University of California, 1961. 81 pp. A63-86 rev.
      o.p. (M-University).
      JAS, 11/61

1548 Scalapino, Robert A. Democracy and the Party Movement in
A   Prewar Japan, the Failure of the First Attempt. Berkeley:
      University of California Press, 1953. 471 pp. 53-10608.
      AUFS, 279; Silberman, 320; AHR, 4/54; Ann. Am. Acad., 1/54;
      Pacific Affairs, 12/53; Pol. Sci. Q., 6/54

1607 Scalapino, Robert A. The Japanese Communist Movement,
B   1920-1966. Berkeley: University of California Press,
      1967. 412 pp. 67-14443.
      Sup. 67, 3226; Choice, 10/67; JAS, 2/68; Library Journal,
      3/15/67

2036 Scalapino, Robert A., ed. North Korea Today. N.Y.: Praeger,
A   1963. 141 pp. 63-20152.
      Sup. 65, 3081; JAS, 5/64; Am. Pol. Sci. R., 6/64; Library
      Journal, 12/1/63; TLS, 4/6/64

1608 Scalapino, Robert A. Parties and Politics in Contemporary Japan.
A   Berkeley: University of California Press, 1962. 190 pp.
      61-14279.
      Sup. 63, 2896; JAS, 11/62; Am. Pol. Sci. R., 9/62; Japan
      Q., 10-12/62; Library Journal, 1/1/62

0407 Schafer, Edward H. Ancient China. by Edward H. Schafer and
C   the editors of Time-Life Books. N.Y.: Time-Life Books,
     dist. by Silver Burdett, 1967. 191 pp. (Great Ages of
     Man). 67-30847.
     Choice, 7-8/68; Library Journal, 4/15/68

0408 Schafer, Edward H. The Empire of Min. Rutland, Vt.: Tuttle
B   for Harvard-Yenching Institute, 1954. 146 pp. 59-34309.
     Hucker, 329; FEQ, 8/55; JAOS, 1-3/56

0409 Schafer, Edward H. Golden Peaches of Samarkand; A Study of
A   T'ang Exotics. Berkeley: University of California Press,
     1963. 399 pp. 63-8922.
     JAS, 2/64; JAOS, 4-6/65; Library Journal, 5/1/63; Pacific
     Affairs, Fall/63

0410 Schafer, Edward H. The Vermillion Bird; T'ang Images of the
A   South. Berkeley: University of California Press, 1967.
     380 pp. 67-10463.
     Choice, 3/68; JAS, 5/68; Library Journal, 9/1/67

0676 Schiffrin, Harold Z. Sun Yat-sen and the Origins of the Chinese
A   Revolution. Berkeley: University of California Press, 1968.
     412 pp. 68-26530.

0807 Schram, Stuart. Mao Tse-tung. N.Y.: Simon & Schuster,
A   1967. 351 pp. 67-12918.
     Choice, 10/67; China Q., 7-9/68; Library Journal, 5/1/67;
     TLS, 10/12/67

1549 Schroeder, Paul W. The Axis Alliance and Japanese-American
B   Relations, 1941. Ithaca, N.Y.: Cornell University Press
     for American Historical Association, 1958. 246 pp.
     58-2112.
     Silberman, 515; AHR, 10/58; Am. Pol. Sci. R., 12/59;
     Ann. Am. Acad., 7/58

1648 Schumpeter, Elizabeth Boody, ed. The Industrialization of Japan
C   and Manchoukuo, 1930-1940: Population, Raw Materials and
     Industry. N.Y.: Macmillan, 1940. 944 pp. 40-35446. o.p.
     Am. Econ. R., 3/41; Ann. Am. Acad., 5/41; Pacific Affairs,
     6/41

0808 Schurmann, Herbert Franz, comp. The China Reader: Communist
B   China. N.Y.: Random House, 1967. 667 pp. 66-21489.
     Choice, 1/68; JAS, 2/68

0411 Schurmann, Herbert Franz, comp. The China Reader: Imperial
B   China. N.Y.: Random House, 1967. 322 pp. 66-21489.
     Choice, 1/68; JAS, 2/68; Library Journal, 2/1/67, 11/15/67

0677 Schurmann, Herbert Franz, comp. The China Reader: Republican
B   China. N.Y.: Random House, 1967. 394 pp. 66-21489.
     Choice, 1/68; JAS, 2/68

0860 Schurmann, Herbert Franz. Ideology and Organization in Communist
A   China. Berkeley: University of California Press, 1966.
     540 pp. 66-15324.
     Sup. 67, 3249; Choice, 2/67; JAS, 2/67; Am. Pol. Sci. R.,
     3/67; Library Journal, 5/15/66; Pol. Sci. Q., 12/67

1411 Schwantes, Robert S. Japanese and Americans, a Century
B   of Cultural Relations. N.Y.: Harper for Council on Foreign
     Relations, 1955. 380 pp. 55-7220. o.p.
     AUFS, 281; Silberman, 430; FEQ, 5/56; Japan Q., 1-3/57;
     Library Journal, 8/55

0809 Schwartz, Benjamin Isadore. Chinese Communism and the Rise of
A   Mao. Cambridge, Mass.: Harvard University Press, 1951.
     258 pp. 51-12067.
     AUFS, 968; Hucker, 870; FEQ, 8/52; Am. Soc. R., 12/51; Ann.
     Am. Acad., 3/52; J. Pol. Econ., 3/52; Library Journal, 8/51

1213 Schwartz, Benjamin Isadore. In Search of Wealth and Power:
B   Yen Fu and the West. Cambridge, Mass.: Harvard Univer-
     sity Press, 1964. 298 pp. (Harvard East Asian Series,
     16). 64-16069.
     Sup. 65, 3105; Choice, 7-8/64; JAS, 11/64; Am. Pol. Sci. R.,
     3/65; JAOS, 7-9/65; Library Journal, 7/64; Pacific Affairs,
     Spring/65; Pol. Sci. Q., 12/65; TLS, 11/26/64

1164 Schyns, Joseph. 1500 Chinese Novels and Plays. Kentfield,
C   Calif.: Gregg International, 1965 (orig. pub. in Peking,
     1948). 546 pp. NUC 66-92546. (R).
     Hucker, 1722

1964 Scott, Adolf Clarence. The Kabuki Theatre of Japan. N.Y.:
B   Collier, 1966 (orig. pub. by Macmillan, 1955). 317 pp.
     NUC 67-62445. (R).
     Silberman, 1134; Library Journal, 2/1/56; TLS, 9/23/55

1040 Scott, Adolphe Clarence. The Classical Theatre of China. N.Y.:
A   Macmillan, 1957. 250 pp. o.p.
     AUFS, 1134; Hucker, 1661; JAS, 2/58; TLS, 5/10/57

1041 Scott, Adolphe Clarence. An Introduction to the Chinese Thea-
C   tre. Singapore: Donald Moore, 1958. 92 pp. NUC 64-44435.

1165 Scott, Adolphe Clarence. Literature and the Arts in Twentieth
A   Century China. Gloucester, Mass.: Peter Smith, 1968 (orig.
     pub. by Doubleday, 1963). 212 pp. 68-3339. (R).

1166 Scott, Adolphe Clarence. Mei Lan-fang, Leader of the Pear Gar-
B   den. N.Y.: Oxford, 1959. 139 pp. 60-16031.
     Hucker, 1721; JAS, 5/61

1965 Scott, Adolphe Clarence. The Puppet Theatre of Japan. Rutland,
C   Vt.: Tuttle, 1963. 173 pp. 63-21179.
     Choice, 3/64; JAS, 2/65; JAOS, 7-9/64

1003 Scott, Adolphe Clarence, ed. Traditional Chinese Plays: Ssu Lang
A   Visits His Mother; Ssu lang t'an mu. The Butterfly Dream; Hu
     tieh meng. Madison: University of Wisconsin Press, 1967.
     165 pp. 66-22854.
     Library Journal, 4/1/67; TLS, 9/28/67

0678 Scott, Robert Lee. Flying Tiger: Chennault of China. Gar-
C   den City, N.Y.: Doubleday, 1959. 285 pp. 59-7000.
     AUFS, 869; Library Journal, 2/1/59

1579 Sebald, William Joseph. With MacArthur in Japan; A Personal
C   History of the Occupation. N.Y.: Norton, 1965. 318 pp.
     64-23883.
     Choice, 9/65; Library Journal, 6/1/65

0190 Seckel, Dietrich. The Art of Buddhism. tr. by Ann E. Kemp.
C   N.Y.: Crown, 1964. 331 pp. (Art of the World). 64-23800.
     Choice, 4/65; JAS, 5/67; Library Journal, 2/15/65; TLS,
     6/10/65

1928 Seckel, Dietrich. Emakimono, the Art of the Japanese Painted
A   Hand Scroll. N.Y.: Pantheon, 1959. 238 pp. 59-4934.
     Silberman, 761; Library Journal, 1/1/60; TLS, 2/19/60

1743 Segawa, Joko. Genyadana; A Japanese Kabuki Play. by A. C.
B   Scott. Tokyo: Hokuseido, 1953. 52 pp. 53-11699.

1709 Sei Shonagon. The Pillowbook of Sei Shonagon. tr. by Ivan
A   Morris. N.Y.: Columbia University Press, 1967. 2 v.
     (UNESCO Collection of Representative Works). 67-24962.
     Choice, 4/69; JAS, 11/68; Library Journal, 1/1/68

1783 Seidensticker, Edward G. Kafu the Scribbler; The Life and
A   Writings of Nagai Kafu, 1879-1959. Stanford, Calif.:
     Stanford University Press, 1965. 360 pp. 65-21492.
     Choice, 9/66; JAS, 11/66; Japan Q., 4-6/66; Library Journal,
     12/1/65

1951 Seike, Kiyoshi. Contemporary Japanese Houses. Palo Alto,
A   Calif.: Kodansha, 1964. 205 pp. 64-25254.

1649 Seki, Keizo. The Cotton Industry of Japan. Tokyo: Japan
C   Society for the Promotion of Science, 1956. 417 pp.
     57-27081.

0679 Selle, Earl Albert. Donald of China. N.Y.: Harper, 1948.
B   374 pp. 48-5343. o.p. (M-University).
     Hucker, 780; Pacific Affairs, 9/48

0017 Sellman, Roger Raymond. An Outline Atlas of Eastern History.
A   London: Arnold, 1954. 63 pp. Map 54-1526. o.p.
     AUFS, 54; Hucker, 96

0518 Serruys, Henry. Sino-Jurced Relations During the Yung-lo
C   Period 1403-1424. Wiesbaden: Otto Harrassowitz, 1955.
     118 pp. 56-38257. o.p.
     Hucker, 498

0861 Serruys, Paul Leo Mary. Survey of the Chinese Language Reform
B   and the Anti-Illiteracy Movement in Communist China. Berke-
     ley: Center for Chinese Studies, Institute of International
     Studies, University of California, 1962. 208 pp. (Studies
     in Chinese Communist Terminology, No. 8). 62-63221. o.p.
     (M-University).
     China Q., 4-6/63

0326 Shabad, Theodore. China's Changing Map; A Political and
B   Economic Geography of the Chinese People's Republic.
     N.Y.: Praeger, 1956. 295 pp. 55-11530. o.p.
     AUFS, 970; Hucker, 47; JAS, 11/57; Ann. Am. Acad., 9/56;
     Library Journal, 7/56; TLS, 11/2/56

0298 Shanghai Evening Post and Mercury. 1931-35-
C

0810 Shao, Leng Chuan. Japan and Communist China. Kyoto: 1959.
B   130 pp. Hand catalog.

1929 Sharaku, Toshusai. Sharaku, by Juzo Suzuki. tr. by John
B   Bestor. Palo Alto, Calif.: Kodansha, 1968. 96 pp.
      (Masterworks of Ukiyo-e, Vol. 2). 68-13740.
      Choice, 12/68; Library Journal, 7/68

0680 Sharman, Lyon. Sun Yat-Sen, His Life and Its Meaning; A
A   Critical Biography. Stanford, Calif.: Stanford Univer-
      sity Press, 1968 (orig. pub. by John Day, 1934). 418 pp.
      68-17141. (R).
      AUFS, 871; Hucker, 759

1966 Shaver, Ruth M. Kabuki Costume. Rutland, Vt.: Tuttle, 1966.
C   396 pp. 66-15266.
      Choice, 4/67; Library Journal, 12/1/66

0182 Shcherbatskoi, Fedor Ippolitovich. The Conception of Buddhist
C   Nirvana, by Th. Stcherbatsky. The Hague: Mouton, 1965
      (orig. pub. by Publishing Office of the Academy of Science
      of the U.S.S.R., 1927). 246 pp. 65-6423. (R). (M-Uni-
      versity).

1470 Sheldon, Charles David. The Rise of the Merchant Class in
B   Tokugawa Japan, 1600-1868; An Introductory Survey. Locust
      Valley, N.Y.: Augustin, 1958. 205 pp. (Association for
      Asian Studies, Monographs and Papers, V). A59-8765.
      AUFS, 205; Silberman, 261; JAS, 8/59

0937 Shen, Fu. Chapters from a Floating Life; The Autobiography of
C   a Chinese Artist. tr. from Chinese by Shirley M. Black.
      London: Oxford, 1960. 108 pp. 60-4904. o.p.
      Hucker, 1711

2083 Shen, Tsung-han. Agricultural Development on Taiwan Since
A   World War II. Ithaca, N.Y.: Cornell University Press,
      1964. 399 pp. 64-18144.
      Choice, 7-8/65; JAS, 2/66

0892 Shen, Tsung-han. Agricultural Resources of China. Ithaca,
A   N.Y.: Cornell University Press, 1951. 407 pp. 51-7098.
      Hucker, 2198; FEQ, 5/52

1100 Shen, Ts'ung-wen. The Chinese Earth; Stories. tr. by Ching
C   Ti and Robert Payne. London: Allen & Unwin, 1947. 289 pp.
      56-43546. o.p.

1139 Shen, Tuan-hsien. The Test, a Play in Five Acts. tr. by Ying
C   Yu. Peking: Foreign Languages Press, 1956. 107 pp. Hand
      catalog.

1101 Shen, Yen-ping. Midnight by Mao Tun (pseud.). tr. by Hsu
A   Meng-hsiung. Peking: Foreign Languages Press, 1957.
      524 pp. 58-22593. o.p.
      AUFS, 1117

1102 Shen, Yen-ping. Spring Silkworms and Other Stories, by Mao
C   Tun (pseud.). tr. by Sidney Shapiro. Peking: Foreign Lan-
      guages Press, 1956. 278 pp. 57-34699. o.p.

0113 Shepherd, Jack. Australia's Interests and Policies in the
C   Far East. N.Y.: Institute of Pacific Relations, 1939.
      212 pp. 39-33667. o.p. (M-University).
      AUFS, 112

0681 Sheridan, James E. Chinese Warlord; The Career of Feng
A   Yu-hsiang. Stanford, Calif.: Stanford University Press,
      1966. 386 pp. 65-18978.
      Choice, 12/66; AHR, 7/67; Library Journal, 4/1/66; TLS,
      4/13/67

0811 Sherwani, Latif Ahmed. India, China, and Pakistan. Karachi:
C   Council for Pakistan Studies, 1967. 140 pp. SA68-657.

1550 Shibusawa, Keizo, ed. Japanese Life and Culture in the Meiji
C   Era. tr. by Charles Terry. Tokyo: Obunsha, 1958. 397 pp.
      (Japanese Culture in the Meiji Era, Vol. V). 59-52562.
      Silberman, 1367

1551 Shigemitsu, Mamoru. Japan and Her Destiny; My Struggle
A   for Peace. tr. by Oswald White. N.Y.: Dutton, 1958.
      392 pp. 57-5005. o.p.
      Silberman, 478; JAS, 2/61; Library Journal, 7/58;
      Pol. Sci. Q., 12/58; TLS, 6/6/58

0971 Shih Ching. The Book of Odes. Chinese text, transcription and
C   tr. by Bernhard Karlgren. Stockholm: Museum of Far Eastern

Antiquities, 1950. 270 pp. 52-65061.
      AUFS, 1074; Hucker, 1537

0972 Shih Ching. The Book of Songs. tr. from Chinese by Arthur
A   Waley. N.Y.: Grove, 1960. 358 pp. 60-6341. o.p.
      AUFS, 1075; Hucker, 1536

0973 Shih Ching. The Confucian Odes, the Classic Anthology Defined
C   by Confucius. tr. by Ezra Pound. N.Y.: J. Laughlin, 1959
      (orig. pub. by Harvard University Press, 1954). 223 pp.
      (New Directions Paperback, 81). 59-13170. (R).
      Hucker, 1538; FEQ, 2/55

0519 Shih, Vincent Yu-chung. The Taiping Ideology; Its Sources,
B   Interpretations, and Influences. Seattle: University
      of Washington Press, 1967. 553 pp. (Far Eastern and
      Russian Institute Publications on Asia, 15). 66-19571.
      Choice, 6/68; JAS, 8/68; Library Journal, 4/15/68; TLS,
      8/22/68

1471 Shinoda, Minoru. The Founding of the Kamakura Shogunate,
B   1180-1185, With Selected Translations from the Azuma Kagami.
      N.Y.: Columbia University Press, 1960. 385 pp. (Columbia
      University Records of Civilization: Sources and Studies,
      No. 57). 59-10433.
      Sup. 61, 2779; Silberman, 218; JAS, 11/60; AHR, 7/60;
      Ann. Am. Acad., 9/60; Library Journal, 2/1/60; Pacific
      Affairs, Summer/61; TLS, 1/27/61

1650 Shinohara, Miyohei. Growth and Cycles in the Japanese Eco-
B   nomy. Tokyo: Kinokuniya, 1962. 349 pp. 63-58420.

1687 Shiso no Kagaku Kenkyukai. Japanese Popular Culture; Studies
B   in Mass Communications and Cultural Change Made at the
      Institute of the Science of Thought, Japan. Rutland, Vt.:
      Tuttle, 1959. 223 pp. 58-5088.
      Silberman, 1405

1214 Shryock, John Knight. The Origin and Development of the State
C   Cult of Confucius; An Introductory Study. N.Y.: Paragon,
      1966 (orig. pub. by Century, 1932). 298 pp. 66-21765. (R).
      Hucker, 1168; Am. Pol. Sci. R., 8/32; J. Philosophy, 11/10/32

1103 Shu, Ch'ing-ch'un. City of Cats. by Lao sheh. tr. by James
C   E. Dew. Ann Arbor: Center for Chinese Studies, University
      of Michigan, 1964. 64 pp. (Occasional Papers No. 3).
      64-63813. o.p.

1104 Shu, Ch'ing-ch'un. Divorce. tr. by Evan King. St. Peters-
B   burg, Fla.: King Publications, 1948. 444 pp. 48-18747 rev.

1105 Shu, Ch'ing-ch'un. Dragon Beard Ditch; A Play in Three Acts, by
C   Lao Sheh (pseud.). tr. by Liao Hung-ying. Peking: Foreign
      Languages Press, 1956. 97 pp. 61-46449.

1106 Shu, Ch'ing-ch'un. The Drum Singers. tr. from Chinese by
A   Helena Kuo. N.Y.: Harcourt, Brace, 1952. 283 pp. 52-6438.
      FEQ, 11/52; Library Journal, 3/1/52

1107 Shu, Ch'ing-ch'un (Lau Shaw, pseud.). Heavensent. London:
B   Dent, 1951. 284 pp. o.p.

1108 Shu, Ch'ing-ch'un. The Quest for Love of Lao Lee. tr. by
B   Helen Kuo. N.Y.: Reynal & Hitchcock, 1948. 306 pp.
      48-9236. o.p.

1109 Shu, Ch'ing-ch'un. Rickshaw Boy, by Lau Shaw (pseud.). tr.
A   from Chinese by Evan King, pseud. Garden City, N.Y.: Sun
      Dial, 1946. 315 pp. 47-2841 rev. o.p.
      AUFS, 1120; Hucker, 1754; FEQ, 5/46; Library Journal, 7/45

1110 Shu, Ch'ing-ch'un. The Yellow Storm by Lau Shaw (pseud.).
B   tr. from Chinese by Ida Pruitt. N.Y.: Harcourt, Brace,
      1951. 533 pp. 51-9088. o.p.
      AUFS, 1121; Hucker, 1755; Library Journal, 2/1/51; TLS,
      10/26/51

0938 Shui Hu Ch'uan. All Men are Brothers. tr. from Chinese
A   by Pearl S. Buck. N.Y.: John Day, 1968 (orig. pub. by
      Grove, 1957). 2 v. 57-8648. (R).
      AUFS, 1076; Hucker, 1695

0939 Shui Hu Ch'uan. Water Margin, written by Shih Nai-an. tr.
C   by J. H. Jackson. N.Y.: Paragon, 1968 (orig. pub. in
      Shanghai, 1937). 2 v. 67-31568. (R).
      Hucker, 1696

1837 Shunjo. Honen, the Buddhist Saint; His Life and Teaching. tr.
C   by Harper Havelock Coates and Ryugaku Ishizuka. Kyoto: Soci-

ety for Publication of Sacred Books of the World, 1949. 5 v.
49-29237.
AUFS, 145; Silberman, 636

1267 Sickman, Laurence C. The Art and Architecture of China. by
A Laurence Sickman and Alexander Soper. Baltimore: Penguin,
1956. 334 pp. 56-1125.
AUFS, 1018; Hucker, 1394; JAS, 11/56; Library Journal,
4/1/56

0009 Silberman, Bernard S. Japan and Korea, a Critical Bibliogra-
A phy. Tucson: University of Arizona Press, 1962. 120 pp.
62-11821.
JAS, 5/63

1688 Silberman, Bernard S., ed. Japanese Character and Culture;
A A Book of Selected Readings. Tucson: University of
Arizona Press, 1962. 421 pp. 61-63840.
JAS, 2/63; Am. Anthropologist, 4/63; Am. Pol. Sci. R.,
3/63; Japan Q., 7-9/63; Pacific Affairs, Fall/63

0349 Silverberg, Robert. The Great Wall of China. Philadelphia:
C Chilton, 1965. 232 pp. 65-15940.
Choice, 1/66; Library Journal, 7/65

0142 Silvert, Kalman H., ed. Discussion at Bellagio; The Political
B Alternatives of Development. N.Y.: American Universities
Field Staff, 1964. 191 pp. 64-25830.
Sup. 65, 4566; Choice, 5/65

0412 Sino-Iranica. Sino-Iranica; Chinese Contributions to the History
C of Civilization in Ancient Iran, with Special Reference to
the History of Cultivated Plants and Products. N.Y.: Kraus,
1967 (orig. pub. in Chicago, 1919 as Field Museum of Natural History Publication, 201). 445 pp. 68-4203. (R).
Hucker, 2209

0299 Sinologica, v.1- 1947-
B Hucker, 34

1306 Siren, Osvald. The Chinese on the Art of Painting: Translations
C and Comments. N.Y.: Schocken, 1963 (orig. pub. by Vetch,
1936). 261 pp. 63-20262. (R).
Hucker, 1492; JAOS, 12/36

1307 Siren, Osvald. Chinese Painting: Leading Masters and Principles.
B N.Y.: Ronald, 1956- A57-1105.
AUFS, 1020; Hucker, 1466

1312 Siren, Osvald. Chinese Sculpture from the Fifth to the Four-
B teenth Century; Over 900 Specimens in Stone, Bronze, Lacquer
and Wood, Principally from Northern China. London: Benn,
1925. 4 v. 25-17954. o.p.
Hucker, 1456

1315 Siren, Osvald. Gardens of China. N.Y.: Ronald, 1949. 141 pp.
B Agr 49-79.
Hucker, 1501; FEQ, 8/50; JAOS, 10-12/51; Library Journal,
9/15/49

0220 Skachkov, P. E., comp. Bibliografia Kitain. Moscow: Isda-
C tel'stvo Vostochnoi Literatury, 1960. 691 pp.

2110 Skinner, George William. Chinese Society in Thailand: an Ana-
C lytical History. Ithaca, N.Y.: Cornell University Press,
1957. 459 pp. 57-3051.
AUFS, 1373; Hucker, 2097; Ann. Am. Acad., 11/57; Library
Journal, 10/1/57

2111 Skinner, George William. Leadership and Power in the Chinese
B Community of Thailand. Ithaca, N.Y.: Cornell University
Press for Association for Asian Studies, 1958. 363 pp.
(Association for Asian Studies, Monographs and Papers,
III). 58-1987.
AUFS, 1374; Hucker, 2098; JAS, 11/58; AHR, 1/59; Am. J. Soc.,
7/59; Ann. Am. Acad., 7/58

0893 Sladkovskii, M. I. History of Economic Relations Between
C Russia and China. tr. by M. Roublev. Sinological editor:
G. Grause. N.Y.: Daniel Davey, 1967. 299 pp. (Israel
Program for Scientific Translations). 67-7663.
Choice, 4/68; Am. Econ. R., 3/68

0682 Smedley, Agnes. Battle Hymn of China. N.Y.: Knopf, 1943.
C 528 pp. 43-12192. o.p.
Hucker, 899; FEQ, 5/44; Library Journal, 8/43

0683 Smedley, Agnes. China Fights Back; An American Woman with
C the Eighth Route Army. N.Y.: Vanguard, 1938. 282 pp.
38-27564. o.p.

0684 Smedley, Agnes. The Great Road; The Life and Times of Chu
A Teh. N.Y.: Monthly Review Press, 1956. 461 pp. 56-11272.
AUFS, s73; Hucker, 864; JAS, 8/57; Pacific Affairs, 6/57

0940 Smith, Arthur Henderson. Proverbs and Common Sayings from the
C Chinese, Together with Much Related and Unrelated Matter,
Interspersed with Observations on Chinese Things in General.
N.Y.: Dover, 1965 (orig. pub. by American Presbyterian
Mission Press, 1914). 374 pp. 64-18446. (R).
Choice, 6/66; JAS, 8/66

1472 Smith, Thomas Carlyle. The Agrarian Origins of Modern Japan.
A Stanford, Calif.: Stanford University Press, 1959. 250 pp.
59-7429.
Silberman, 259; JAS, 11/59; Am. Anthropologist, 12/59; Am.
Econ. R., 3/60; AHR, 7/60; Ann. Am. Acad., 11/59; Geog. R.,
7/60; Japan Q., 7-9/60; Library Journal, 5/15/59; Pacific
Affairs, 3/60; Pol. Sci. Q., 12/60

1552 Smith, Thomas Carlyle. Political Change and Industrial Develop-
B ment in Japan: Government Enterprise, 1868-1880. Stanford,
Calif.: Stanford University Press, 1955. 126 pp.
55-6687.
AUFS, 283; Silberman, 386; FEQ, 5/56; AHR, 4/56; Library
Journal, 6/15/56; Pacific Affairs, 3/56

1847 Smith, Warren W. Confucianism in Modern Japan; A Study of
C Conservatism in Japanese Intellectual History. Tokyo:
Hokuseido, 1959. 285 pp. 60-137.
Sup. 61, 2780; Silberman, 678; JAS, 11/60

1361 Snapper, Isidore. Chinese Lessons to Western Medicine; A Con-
C tribution to Geographical Medicine from the Clinics of
Peiping Union Medical College. 2d ed. N.Y.: Grune &
Stratton, 1965 (orig. pub. by Interscience Publications,
1941). 416 pp. 64-7771. (R).
Hucker, 1376

2076 Sneider, Vern J. A Pail of Oysters. N.Y.: Putnam, 1953.
B 311 pp. 52-13648. o.p.

0685 Snow, Edgar. Far Eastern Front. N.Y.: Smith & Haas, 1933.
B 336 pp. 33-27375. o.p.

1111 Snow, Edgar, ed. Living China, Modern Chinese Short Stories.
B N.Y.: Reynal & Hitchcock, 1937. 360 pp. o.p.
AUFS, 1122; Hucker, 1749; Pacific Affairs, 3/37; TLS, 11/21/36

0812 Snow, Edgar. The Other Side of the River, Red China Today.
A N.Y.: Random House, 1962. 810 pp. 61-6243.
JAS, 8/63; Ann. Am. Acad., 9/63; China Q., 4-6/63; Library
Journal, 5/15/63; Pacific Affairs, Summer/63; Pol. Sci. Q.,
12/63; TLS, 5/17/63

0686 Snow, Edgar. Random Notes on Red China (1936-1945). Cam-
B bridge, Mass.: Harvard University Press, 1957. 148 pp.
58-146. o.p.
JAS, 11/58

0687 Snow, Edgar. Red Star over China. 1st rev. and enl. ed. N.Y.:
A Grove, 1968. 543 pp. 68-17724.
AUFS, 975; Choice, 11/68; Hucker, 778; Library Journal, 7/68

0813 Snow, Helen (Foster). The Chinese Labor Movement by Nym
B Wales, pseud. N.Y.: John Day, 1945. 235 pp. 45-146. o.p.
Hucker, 2066; FEQ, 11/45

0688 Snow, Helen (Foster). Inside Red China. N.Y.: Doubleday,
B Doran, 1939. 356 pp. 39-27102 rev. o.p.

0814 Snow, Helen (Foster). Red Dust; Autobiographies of the Chi-
A nese Communists, As Told to Nym Wales, pseud. Stanford,
Calif.: Stanford University Press, 1952. 238 pp.
52-5970. o.p.
Hucker, 867; FEQ, 11/52; Ann. Am. Acad., 7/52

0689 Snow, Helen (Foster). Women in Modern China. The Hague: Mouton,
B 1967. 264 pp. 67-18165.
China Q., 1-3/68

1417 Society of Japanese Regional Geography. Regional Geography
C of Japan. Tokyo: Society of Japanese Regional Geography,
1957. 6 v.
Silberman, 76

1184 Soothill, William Edward. The Three Religions of China; Lectures
B Delivered at Oxford. 3d ed. N.Y.: Oxford, 1930. 271 pp.
24-13494. o.p.
AUFS, 604; Hucker, 1052

1952 Soper, Alexander Coburn. The Evolution of Buddhist Architecture
C   in Japan. Princeton, N.J.: Princeton University Press,
     1942. 330 pp. (Monographs in Art and Archaeologys 22).
     42-24943. o.p. (M-University).
     Silberman, 810

1268 Soper, Alexander Coburn. Literary Evidence for Early Buddhist
C   Art in China. Ascona: Artibus Asiae, 1959. 296 pp. (Sup-
     plementum XIX). A59-4696.
     Hucker, 1408

1321 Soulie, Charles George. Theatre et Musique Modernes en Chine,
B   Avec une Etude Technique de la Musique Chinoise et Trans-
     cription pour Piano par Andre Gailhard. Paris: Geuthner,
     1926. 195 pp. 28-24553.
     Hucker, 1779

0300 The South China Morning Post. Hong Kong. 1881-
C   (M-Microphoto).

0815 Soviet and Chinese Communism; Similarities and Differences.
C   ed. by Donald W. Treadgold. Seattle: University of Washing-
     ton Press, 1967. 452 pp. 66-19575.
     Choice, 9/67; AHR, 12/67

1848 Spae, Joseph John. Ito Jinsai, a Philosopher, Educator
C   and Sinologist of the Tokugawa Period. N.Y.: Paragon,
     1965 (orig. pub. by Catholic University, Peking, 1948).
     278 pp. A48-5462. (R).
     AUFS, 155; Silberman, 684

0520 Spector, Stanley. Li Hung-chang and the Huai Army; A Study
A   in Nineteenth-Century Chinese Regionalism. intro. by
     Franz Michael. Seattle: University of Washington Press,
     1964. 359 pp. (Washington University Publications on
     Asia). 64-11052.
     Sup. 65, 3106; JAS, 2/66; AHR, 7/65; Library Journal,
     9/15/64

1269 Speiser, Werner. The Art of China: Spirit and Society. tr. by
B   George Lawrence. N.Y.: Crown, 1961. 256 pp. 61-10700.

0521 Spence, Jonathan D. Ts'ao Yin and the K'ang-hsi Emperor;
A   Bondservant and Master. New Haven, Conn.: Yale Univer-
     sity Press, 1966. 329 pp. (Yale Historical Publications
     Miscellany, 85). 66-21537.
     Choice, 7-8/67; JAS, 8/68; AHR, 7/67; Library Journal,
     11/15/66; TLS, 3/16/67

0413 Ssu-ma, Ch'ien. Les Memoires Historiques de Se-ma Ts'ien.
C   tr. and annotated by Edouard Chavannes. Paris: Leroux for
     Societe Asiatique, 1895-1905. 5 v. in 6. 21-17126 rev.
     Hucker, 196

0414 Ssu-ma, Ch'ien. Records of the Grand Historian of China. tr.
B   from the Shih chi of Ssu-ma Ch'ien by Burton Watson. N.Y.:
     Columbia University Press, 1961. 2 v. (Records of Civili-
     zation: Sources and Guides, No. 65). 60-13348.
     Hucker, 188; JAS, 2/63; AHR, 7/62; Ann. Am. Acad., 5/62

0415 Ssu-ma, Ch'ien. Statesman, Patriot, and General in Ancient
B   China; Three Shih Chi Biographies of the Ch'in Dynasty (255-
     206 B.C.). tr. by Derk Bodde. N.Y.: Kraus, 1957 (orig.
     pub. by American Oriental Society, 1940). 75 pp. 40-11696.
     (R). (M-University).
     Hucker, 184

0416 Ssu-ma, Kuang. The Chronicle of The Three Kingdoms (220-265).
C   Chapters 69-78 from the Tzu Chih T'ung Chien. Cambridge,
     Mass.: Harvard University Press, 1952- (Harvard-Yenching
     Institute Studies, VI). 52-677.
     JAS, 5/66; FEQ, 11/52; JAOS, 4-6/66

1215 Ssu shu. The Four Books: Confucian Analects, The Great Learning,
A   The Doctrine of the Mean, and The Works of Mencius. tr.
     by James Legge. N.Y.: Paragon, 1966 (orig. dist. by P. D.
     and Ione Perkins, 1930). 1014 pp. 66-16894. (R).

0078 Stamp, Laurence Dudley. Asia; A Regional and Economic Geog-
B   raphy. 11th ed. N.Y.: Dutton, 1962. 730 pp. 62-5766.
     AUFS, 56; Hucker, 51; Silberman, 83

0522 Stanley, Charles Johnson. Late Ch'ing Finance: Hu Kuang-yung
B   as an Innovator. Cambridge, Mass.: Harvard University
     Press, 1961. 117 pp. 62-1254. o.p.
     JAS, 8/62

1473 Statler, Oliver. Japanese Inn. N.Y.: Random House, 1961.
C   365 pp. 61-6236.

Sup. 61, 2781; Japan Q., 7-9/61; Library Journal, 3/1/61;
Pacific Affairs, Summer/62; TLS, 2/9/62

1930 Statler, Oliver. Modern Japanese Prints: an Art Reborn.
A   Rutland, Vt.: Tuttle, 1956. 209 pp. 56-6810.
     AUFS, 400; Silberman, 786; JAS, 5/57; Japan Q., 4-6/57;
     Library Journal, 11/1/56

0816 Steele, Archibald Trojan. The American People and China. N.Y.:
B   McGraw-Hill, 1966. 325 pp. (The United States and China
     in World Affairs). 65-28736.
     Choice, 6/66; JAS, 5/67; AHR, 10/66; Ann. Am. Acad., 11/66;
     Library Journal, 11/15/66

0690 Stein, Guenther. The Challenge of Red China. N.Y.: McGraw-
C   Hill, 1945. 490 pp. 45-8957. o.p.
     Hucker, 895; Library Journal, 10/15/45

0817 Steiner, H. Arthur, ed. Chinese Communism in Action. Los
C   Angeles: Political Science 159, University of California,
     1953. 3 v. 54-185. o.p.

0818 Steiner, H. Arthur. The International Position of Communist
C   China, Political and Ideological Directions of Foreign Policy.
     Thirteenth Conference, Institute of Pacific Relations, Lahore,
     Pakistan, February, 1958. N.Y.: Institute of Pacific Rela-
     tions, 1958. 42 pp. 58-3925. o.p.
     Hucker, 979

1609 Steiner, Kurt. Local Government in Japan. Stanford, Calif.:
B   Stanford University Press, 1965. 564 pp. 64-17005.
     Choice, 12/65; JAS, 8/66; AHR, 7/66; Am. Pol. Sci. R.,
     12/65; Japan Q., 1-3/66; Library Journal, 5/1/65; Pol.
     Sci. Q., 6/66

1931 Stern, Harold P. Masters of the Japanese Print; Ukiyoe Hanga.
A   N.Y.: Abrams, 1969. 323 pp. 69-12794.

2112 Stewart, Watt. Chinese Bondage in Peru; A History of the
A   Chinese Coolie in Peru, 1849-1874. Durham, N.C.: Duke
     University Press, 1951. 247 pp. 51-10928. o.p.
     FEQ, 2/52

0691 Stilwell, Joseph Warren. The Stilwell Papers. ed. by Theo-
A   dore H. White. N.Y.: Sloane Associates, 1948. 357 pp.
     48-6966. o.p.
     AUFS, 875; Hucker, 816; Library Journal, 4/15/48

0114 Stimson, Henry Lewis. The Far Eastern Crisis; Recollections and
B   Observations. N.Y.: Harper for Council on Foreign Rela-
     tions, 1936. 293 pp. 36-20072. o.p. (M-University).
     Silberman, 521; TLS, 9/26/36

0047 Stockholm. Ostasiatiska Samlingarna Bulletin, v.1-
C   1929-
     Hucker, 42

1112 Stories of the Chinese People's Volunteers. tr. by the Teachers
C   of the English Faculty of the Foreign Languages Depart-
     ment of Futan University. Peking: Foreign Languages Press,
     1960. 258 pp. Hand catalog.

1553 Storry, Richard. The Double Patriots, a Study of Japanese
B   Nationalism. Boston: Houghton Mifflin, 1957. 335 pp.
     57-9520. o.p.
     AUFS, 284; Silberman, 374; Japan Q., 1-3/58

1554 Storry, Richard. A History of Modern Japan. N.Y.: Barnes &
C   Noble, 1962. 287 pp. 60-4354.
     Sup. 61, 2782; Silberman, 318; JAS, 5/61; Japan Q., 1-3/61;
     Library Journal, 2/15/58; Pacific Affairs, 9/58; TLS,
     10/11/57

1474 Straelen, Henricus van. Yoshida Shoin, Forerunner of the
C   Meiji Restoration; A Biographical Study. Leiden: Brill,
     1952. 149 pp. (T'oung Pao Monograph, No. 2). 52-12675.
     Silberman, 285

0067 Strausz-Hupe, Robert. American-Asian Tensions. N.Y.: Praeger,
C   1956. 239 pp. 56-10497 rev. o.p.
     JAS, 8/57; Am. Pol. Sci. R., 6/57; Am. Soc. R., 4/57;
     Ann. Am. Acad., 7/57; Library Journal, 6/15/56

0692 Stuart, John Leighton. Fifty Years in China; The Memoirs of
B   John Leighton Stuart, Missionary and Ambassador. N.Y.:
     Random House, 1954. 346 pp. 54-7808. o.p.
     Hucker, 733; Library Journal, 10/15/54

0018 Stucki, Curtis W. American Doctoral Dissertations on Asia,
A   1933-June, 1966, Including Appendix of Master's Theses at

Cornell University, 1933-June, 1968. Ithaca, N.Y.: Southeast Asia Program, Dept. of Far Eastern Studies, Cornell University, 1968. 304 pp. (Data Paper No. 71). 64-2901. (M-University).
Hucker, 23

0068 Studies on Asia. Lincoln: University of Nebraska Press, Vol.
B   I- 1960- 60-15432.
      Sup. 63, 2875; Choice, 6/66

0974 Su, Shih. Selections from the Works of Su Tung-p'o (A.D. 1036-
C   1101). tr. by Cyril Drummond Le Gros Clark. London:
      Cape, 1931. 180 pp. 32-23257. o.p.
      Hucker, 1604

0975 Su, Shih. Su Tung-P'o, Selections from a Sung Dynasty Poet.
A   tr. with intro. by Burton Watson. N.Y.: Columbia University
      Press, 1965. 139 pp. (UNESCO Collection of Representative
      Works: Chinese Series). 65-13619.
      Sup. 65, 3107; Choice, 11/65; JAS, 11/66; JAOS, 4-6/66;
      Library Journal, 2/1/65; TLS, 5/19/66

0976 Su Tung-p'o. The Prose-Poetry of Su Tung-p'o; Being Transla-
B   tions into English...with Introductory Essays, Notes and
      Commentaries by Cyril Drummond Le Gros Clark. N.Y.:
      Paragon, 1964 (orig. pub. by Kegan Paul, 1935). 280 pp.
      NUC 65-61237. (R).
      Hucker, 1605; JAOS, 3/36

0693 Sues, Ilona Ralf. Shark's Fins and Millet. Boston: Little,
C   Brown, 1944. 331 pp. 44-187. o.p.
      Hucker, 736; Am. J. Soc., 9/44; Pacific Affairs, 12/44

1555 Sugimoto, Etsu Inagaki. A Daughter of the Samurai; How a
C   Daughter of Feudal Japan, Living Hundreds of Years in One
      Generation, Became a Modern American. Rutland, Vt.:
      Tuttle, 1966 (orig. pub. by Doubleday, 1926). 314 pp.
      66-15849. (R).
      AUFS, 285; Choice, 4/67

2016 Suh, Dae-Sook. The Korean Communist Movement, 1918-1948.
A   Princeton, N.J.: Princeton Universtity Press, 1967. 406 pp.
      66-17711.
      Choice, 10/67; JAS, 2/68; AHR, 10/67; Am. Pol. Sci. R.,
      12/67; Library Journal, 3/15/67

0819 Suigo, Carlo. In the Land of Mao Tse-tung. tr. from Ital-
C   ian by Muriel Currey. ed. by Clifford Witting. London:
      Allen & Unwin, 1953. 311 pp. A55-2811. o.p.

1308 Sullivan, Michael. The Birth of Landscape Painting in China.
C   Berkeley: University of California Press, 1962. 213 pp.
      60-16863.
      JAS, 8/63; JAOS, 4-6/62; Library Journal, 5/1/62; TLS,
      6/29/62

1270 Sullivan, Michael. Chinese Art in the Twentieth Century.
B   Berkeley: University of California Press, 1959. 110 pp.
      59-16314. o.p.
      Hucker, 1414; JAS, 5/60

1271 Sullivan, Michael. An Introduction to Chinese Art. Berkeley:
B   University of California Press, 1961. 223 pp. 61-3831.
      o.p.
      Hucker, 1398; JAS, 2/62; JAOS, 1-3/62

1272 Sullivan, Michael. A Short History of Chinese Art. Berkeley:
A   University of California Press, 1967. 279 pp. 67-21260.
      Choice, 4/68; JAS, 5/68

1651 Sumiya, Mikio. Social Impact of Industrialization in Japan.
C   Tokyo: Japan National Commission for UNESCO, 1963.
      278 pp. NUC 66-62270.

0221 Sun, I-tu (Jen). Bibliography on Chinese Social History; A
B   Selected and Critical List of Chinese Periodical Sources, by
      E-tu Zen Sun and John de Francis. New Haven, Conn.: Institute
      of Far Eastern Languages, Yale University, 1952. 150 pp.
      53-780. o.p.
      Hucker, 116; FEQ, 2/54; JAOS, 10-12/53

0523 Sun, I-tu (Jen). Chinese Railways and British Interests, 1898-
C   1911, by E-tu Zen Sun. N.Y.: King's Crown, 1954. 230 pp.
      54-12129 rev. o.p.
      Hucker, 676; FEQ, 8/55; AHR, 4/55; Ann. Am. Acad., 5/55

0524 Sun Tzu. The Art of War; The Oldest Military Treatise in the
C   World. Taipei: Literature House, dist. by Chinese Materials
      and Research Aids Service Center, 1964 (orig. pub. by Luzac,
      1910). 204 pp. Hand catalog. (R).

Hucker, 1899

0694 Sun, Yat-sen. San Min Chu I, the Three Principles of the
B   People. tr. by Frank W. Price. Nanking: Ministry of
      Information, 1947. 317 pp. A49-5367. o.p.
      AUFS, 882; Hucker, 764

1978 Supreme Commander for the Allied Forces. Civil Information
B   and Education Section. Education in the New Japan.
      Tokyo: General Headquarters, Supreme Commander for the
      Allied Powers, Civil Information and Education Section,
      Education Division, 1948. 2 v. 48-4912. o.p.
      Silberman, 1473

1610 Supreme Commander for the Allied Powers. Government Section.
B   Political Reorientation of Japan, September 1945 to
      September 1948; Report. St. Clair Shores, Mich.: Scholarly
      Press (orig. pub. by Government Printing Office, 1949).
      2 v. 50-60501. (R).
      AUFS, 374; Silberman, 562

1248 Surangamasutra. The Surangama Sutra (Ieng Yen Ching); Chinese
C   Rendering by Master Paramiti of Central North India at
      Chih Chih Monastery, Canton, China, A.D. 705. tr. by
      Upasaka Lu K'uan Yu (Charles Luk). N.Y.: Hillary House,
      1966. 262 pp. 66-70040.
      Choice, 4/67; JAS, 5/67

1838 Suzuki, Daisetz Teitaro. Essays in Zen Buddhism, First
C   Series. N.Y.: Grove, 1961 (orig. pub. by Harper, 1949).
      383 pp. 50-13886. (R).
      AUFS, 147; Silberman, 646

1839 Suzuki, Daisetz Teitaro. Essays in Zen Buddhism, Second
C   Series. London: Rider, 1958. 326 pp. Hand catalog. o.p.
      AUFS, 147; Silberman, 647; JAOS, 6/34

1840 Suzuki, Daisetz Teitaro. Essays in Zen Buddhism, Third
C   Series. London: Luzac, 1934. 350 pp. 35-2983. o.p.
      AUFS, 147; Silberman, 648

1841 Suzuki, Daisetz Teitaro. The Training of the Zen Buddhist
C   Monk. New Hyde Park, N.Y.: University Books, 1965 (orig.
      pub. by Eastern Buddhist Society, 1934). 161 pp.
      65-23523. (R).
      Choice, 5/66; JAOS, 12/37

1842 Suzuki, Daisetz Teitaro. Zen and Japanese Culture. rev. and
C   and enl. 2d ed. Princeton, N.J.: Princeton University Press,
      1959. 478 pp. (Bollingen Series, Vol. 64). 58-12174.
      Silberman, 643; J. Religion, 4/60; TLS, 3/15/60

0417 Swann, Nancy Lee. Pan Chao: Foremost Woman Scholar of China,
B   1st Century A.D.; Background, Ancestory, Life and Writ-
      ings of the Most Celebrated Chinese Woman of Letters.
      N.Y.: Russell & Russell, 1968 (orig. pub. by Century, 1932).
      179 pp. 68-10946. (R).
      Hucker, 201

1309 Swann, Peter C. Chinese Painting. N.Y.: Universe Books, 1958.
B   153 pp. 58-11096. o.p.
      Hucker, 1470; JAS, 5/60; Library Journal, 12/1/58; TLS,
      3/13/59

1905 Swann, Peter C. An Introduction to the Arts of Japan. N.Y.:
B   Praeger, 1958. 220 pp. 58-12088. o.p.
      Silberman, 722; JAS, 8/60; JAOS, 5-6/67; Library Journal,
      12/15/58; TLS, 9/5/58

0165 Swarup, Ram. Communism and Peasantry, Implications of Col-
C   lectivist Agriculture for Asian Countries. Calcutta:
      Prachi Prakashan, 1954. 194 pp. 55-31858. o.p.
      Sup. 61, 2754

0695 Swarup, Shanti. A Study of the Chinese Communist Movement.
B   N.Y.: Oxford, 1966. 289 pp. 66-71987.
      Choice, 12/66; JAS, 11/67; Pol. Sci. Q., 12/67; TLS, 4/11/66

0820 Swearingen, Arthur Rodger. Soviet and Chinese Communist Power
C   in the World Today. N.Y.: Basic Books, 1966. 127 pp.
      66-29266.
      Choice, 5/67; Library Journal, 12/1/66

1611 Swearingen, Rodger. Red Flag in Japan; International Commu-
C   nism in Action, 1919-1951. Cambridge, Mass.: Harvard Uni-
      versity Press, 1952. 276 pp. 52-6434. o.p.
      Silberman, 443; FEQ, 5/53; Am. Pol. Sci. R., 12/52; Ann.
      Am. Acad., 11/52; Library Journal, 7/52; Pacific Affairs,
      9/53; Pol. Sci. Q., 12/53; TLS, 1/30/53

2093 Szczepanik, Edward F. The Economic Growth of Hong Kong. London:
A   Oxford for Royal Institute of International Affairs, 1960
     (orig. pub. in 1958). 186 pp. 61-1573. (R).
     JAS, 5/60

1310 Sze, Mai-Mai. The Tao of Painting, a Study of the Ritual Dis-
B   position of Chinese Painting. 2d ed. Princeton, N.J.:
     Princeton University Press, 1963. 587 pp. (Bollingen
     Series, Vol. 49). 64-2864.
     Hucker, 1471; Library Journal, 5/1/57

1216 Ta hsueh. The Great Learning & the Mean-in-Action. tr. from
B   Chinese by E. R. Hughes. N.Y.: Dutton, 1943. 176 pp.
     43-1988. o.p.
     AUFS, 641

1652 Taeuber, Irene Barnes. The Population of Japan. Princeton,
C   N.J.: Princeton University Press, 1958. 461 pp. 58-7122.
     Silberman, 266; JAS, 5/59; Am. Anthropologist, 4/59; Am.
     J. Soc., 11/59; Am. Soc. R., 6/59; Ann. Am. Acad., 6/59;
     Geog. R., 4/59; Japan Q., 1-3/59; Library Journal, 8/58

1167 Tagore, Amitendranath. Literary Debates in Modern China,
B   1918-1937. Tokyo: Centre for East Asian Cultural Studies,
     1967. 280 pp. (East Asian Cultural Studies Series,
     No. 11). NUC 68-69915.
     JAS, 5/68

0131 Tai, Sheng-yu. Peking, Moscow, and the Communist Parties of
B   Colonial Asia. Cambridge, Mass.: Center for International
     Studies, M.I.T., 1954. 167 pp. 55-32094. o.p.

1710 Taiheike. The Taiheki: a Chronicle of Medieval Japan. tr.
B   with intro. and notes by Helen Craig McCulloch. N.Y.:
     Columbia University Press, 1959. 401 pp. (Columbia Uni-
     versity Records of Civilization: Sources and Studies, No.
     59). 59-6662.
     Silberman, 909; JAS, 5/60; JAOS, 4-6/59; Library Journal,
     4/15/59; Pacific Affairs, 12/59; TLS, 3/15/60

1843 Takakusu, Junjiro. The Essentials of Buddhist Philosophy. ed.
B   by W. T. Chan and Charles A. Moore. 2d ed. Honolulu: Uni-
     versity of Hawaii Press, 1949. 221 pp. A51-1982. o.p.
     (M-University).
     Hucker, 1240; JAOS, 1-3/50

1426 Takekoshi, Yosaburo. The Economic Aspects of the History
A   of the Civilization of Japan. London: Dawsons, dist. by
     Paragon, 1967 (orig. pub. by Macmillan, 1930). 3 v.
     68-96138. (R).
     Silberman, 277; AHR, 4/31

1556 Takeuchi, Tatsuji. War and Diplomacy in the Japanese
B   Empire. N.Y.: Russell & Russell, 1966 (orig. pub. by
     Doubleday, Doran, 1935). 505 pp. 66-27158. (R).
     AUFS, 288; Silberman, 399; Am. Pol. Sci. R., 8/36; TLS,
     4/25/36

1784 Takeyama, Michio. Harp of Burma. tr. by Howard Hibbett.
B   Rutland, Vt.: Tuttle, 1966. 132 pp. (UNESCO Collection
     of Contemporary Works/Library of Japanese Literature).
     66-20570.
     Choice, 5/67

1427 Takizawa, Matsuyo. The Penetration of Money Economy in Japan
C   and Its Effects upon Social and Political Institutions.
     N.Y.: AMS, 1968 (orig. pub. by Columbia University Press,
     1927). 159 pp. 68-54302. (R).
     Silberman, 274

0525 T'an, Ch'un-lin. The Boxer Catastrophe, by Chester C. Tan.
A   N.Y.: Octagon, 1967 (orig. pub. by Columbia University
     Press, 1955). 276 pp. 66-18057. (R). (M-University).
     Hucker, 653; JAS, 2/57; AHR, 4/56; Ann. Am. Acad., 3/56;
     Library Journal, 3/6/56; Pacific Affairs, 9/56

2113 Tan, Giok-lan. The Chinese of Sukabumi: a Study in Social
B   and Cultural Accommodation. Ithaca, N.Y.: Modern Indo-
     nesia Project, Southeast Asia Program, Dept. of Asian
     Studies, Cornell University, 1963. 314 pp. (Modern
     Indonesia Project, Monograph Series). NUC 64-42481.
     JAS, 8/64

1967 Tanabe, Hisao. Japanese Music. 2d ed. Tokyo: Kokusai Bunka
B   Shinkokai, 1959. 74 pp. Hand catalog.

1557 Tanaka, Giichi. Japan's Dream of World Empire; The Tanaka
C   Memorial. N.Y.: Harper, 1942. 118 pp. 42-3102. o.p.

0696 T'ang, Leang-li. The Inner History of the Chinese Revolution.
B   London: Routledge, 1930. 391 pp. 30-27099. o.p.

Ann. Am. Acad., 11/30

0821 Tang, Peter S. H. Communist China Today. 2d ed. rev. and enl.
C   Washington: Research Institute on the Sino-Soviet Bloc,
     1961. 61-18067. o.p.
     Hucker, 934; JAS, 11/58, 8/62; China Q., 4-6/63

0697 Tang, Peter S. H. Russian and Soviet Policy in Manchuria
B   and Outer Mongolia, 1911-1931. Durham, N.C.: Duke Uni-
     versity Press, 1959. 494 pp. 59-7084.
     Hucker, 841

0977 T'ang-shih san-pai shou. The Jade Mountain; A Chinese Anthology,
A   Being Three Hundred Poems of the T'ang Dynasty, 618-906.
     tr. by Witter Bynner from the texts of Kiang Kang-hu.
     Garden City, N.Y.: Doubleday, 1964 (orig. pub. by Knopf,
     1929). 238 pp. 64-4615. (R).
     AUFS, 1080; Hucker, 1554; Choice, 12/64

1785 Tanizaki, Jun'ichiro. Ashikari and the Story of Shunkin;
B   Modern Japanese Novels. tr. from Japanese by Roy Humpher-
     son and Hajime Okita. Tokyo: Hokuseido, 1936. 172 pp.
     38-2496 rev.
     AUFS, 487

1786 Tanizaki, Jun'ichiro. Diary of a Mad Old Man. tr. from Jap-
B   anese by Howard Hibbett. N.Y.: Knopf, 1965. 177 pp.
     65-11115.
     Choice, 11/65; Library Journal, 8/65

1787 Tanizaki, Jun'ichiro. The Makioka Sisters. tr. from Japanese
A   by Edward G. Seidensticker. N.Y.: Knopf, 1957. 530 pp.
     57-10311.
     AUFS, 488; Silberman, 1031; JAS, 8/58; Library Journal,
     9/15/57

1788 Tanizaki, Jun'ichiro. Seven Japanese Tales. tr. from Japanese
A   by Howard Hibbett. N.Y.: Knopf, 1963. 298 pp. 62-15574.
     Library Journal, 7/63; TLS, 5/5/64

1789 Tanizaki, Jun'ichiro. Some Prefer Nettles. tr. from Japanese
B   by Edward G. Seidensticker. N.Y.: Knopf, 1955. 202 pp.
     55-5616.
     AUFS, 489; Silberman, 1032; Japan Q., 10-12/55; Library
     Journal, 4/1/55

0978 T'ao, Ch'ien. Poems. tr. by Lily Pao-hu Chang and Mar-
B   jorie Sinclair. Honolulu: University of Hawaii Press,
     1953. 133 pp. 53-8575. o.p.
     Hucker, 1592

0979 T'ao, Ch'ien. T'ao the Hermit; Sixty Poems. tr. by William
B   Acker. N.Y.: Thames & Hudson, 1952. 157 pp. 53-3610.
     o.p.
     AUFS, 1083; Hucker, 1591; TLS, 7/25/52

1558 Tasaki, Hanama. Long the Imperial Way. Boston: Houghton
B   Mifflin, 1949. 372 pp. 50-3997. o.p.
     Library Journal, 6/15/50

1874 Tatsui, Matsunosuke. Japanese Gardens. N.Y.: Japan Publica-
B   tions Trading Co., 19- (Tourist Library, N.S. 5).
     62-13698.
     Silberman, 828

1953 Taut, Bruno. Houses and People of Japan. 2d ed. Tokyo:
C   Sanseido, 1958. 326 pp. Hand catalog.
     Silberman, 822

0698 Tawney, Richard Henry. Land and Labour in China. N.Y.: Octagon,
C   1964 (orig. pub. by Allen & Unwin, 1932). 207 pp. 64-16384.
     (R).
     AUFS, 886; Hucker, 2126; Geog. R., 7/33; J. Pol. Econ., 10/33

0699 Taylor, George E. The Struggle for North China. N.Y.: Inter-
A   national Secretariat, Institute of Pacific Relations, 1940.
     250 pp. 41-51528. o.p.
     AUFS, 887; Hucker, 792; FEQ, 5/42; Am. Pol. Sci. R., 6/41;
     Ann. Am. Acad., 5/41; Pacific Affairs, 6/41

1875 Tea Cult of Japan, prepared by Y. Fukukita. Tokyo: Japan Travel
A   Bureau, 1934- (Tourist Library, N.S. 4). 59-13187 rev.
     Silberman, 863

1042 Teele, Roy Earl. Through a Glass Darkly; A Study of English
C   Translations of Chinese Poetry. Ann Arbor: 1949. 173 pp.
     A50-323. o.p.
     Hucker, 1558

0418 Teggart, Frederick John. Rome and China; A Study of Correla-
A   tions in Historical Events. Berkeley: University of
     California Press, 1939. 283 pp. 40-86. o.p.
     Hucker, 235; FEQ, 8/42

0222 Teng, Ssu-Yu. An Annotated Bibliography of Selected Chinese
B   Reference Works. rev. ed. Cambridge, Mass.: Harvard Uni-
     versity Press, 1950. 326 pp. (Harvard-Yenching Institute
     Studies, II). 50-11027.
     Sup. 61, 2805; Hucker, 1616

0526 Teng, Ssu-yu. Chang Hsi and the Treaty of Nanking, 1842. Chi-
B   cago: University of Chicago Press, 1944. 119 pp. A45-937.
     o.p.
     Hucker, 671; FEQ, 2/52; AHR, 10/45

0527 Teng, Ssu-yu. China's Response to the West; A Documentary
A   Survey, 1839-1923. Cambridge, Mass.: Harvard University
     Press in cooperation with Institute of Pacific Relations,
     1954. 296 pp. 53-5061 rev.
     Hucker, 607; FEQ, 8/55; Library Journal, 3/15/54

0528 Teng, Ssu-yu. New Light on the History of the Taiping Rebel-
B   lion. N.Y.: Russell & Russell, 1966 (orig. pub. by
     Harvard University Press, 1950). 132 pp. 66-13241. (R).
     Hucker, 618; FEQ, 8/51; AHR, 10/50; Am. Pol. Sci. R., 9/50;
     Pacific Affairs, 6/50

0529 Teng, Ssu-yu. The Nien Army and their Guerilla Warfare, 1851-
A   1868. N.Y.: Humanities, 1961. 254 pp. Hand catalog.
     JAS, 5/62; JAOS, 10-12/62

0263 Teng, Ssu-yu. Research Guide for China's Response to the
B   West; A Documentary Survey, 1839-1923. by Teng Ssu-yu
     and John K. Fairbank. N.Y.: Atheneum, 1963 (orig. pub.
     by Harvard University Press, 1954). 84 pp. NUC 63-59347.
     (R).
     FEQ, 8/55

0143 Tewksbury, Donald George, ed. Source Book on Far Eastern
C   Political Ideologies. N.Y.: Institute of Pacific Relations,
     1952- 53-24605. o.p.
     AUFS, 116

1232 The Texts of Taoism. tr. by James Legge. N.Y.: Julian Press,
C   1959. 790 pp. 58-14214. o.p.
     Hucker, 1184

1043 Thiele, Margaret Rossiter. None But the Nightingale, an Intro-
C   duction to Chinese Literature. Rutland, Vt.: Tuttle, 1967.
     159 pp. 67-20950.
     Choice, 7-8/68; Pacific Affairs, Spring/68

0822 Thomas, S. B. Communist China and Her Neighbors. Toronto:
C   Canadian Institute of International Affairs, 1955. 16 pp.
     55-3250. o.p. (M-University).
     Hucker, 985

0862 Thomas, S. B. Government and Administration in Communist
C   China. rev. 2d ed. N.Y.: International Secretariat, Insti-
     tute of Pacific Relations, 1955. 196 pp. A55-8710. o.p.
     AUFS, 988; Hucker, 1944; FEQ, 8/55

0160 Thompson, Warren Simpson. Population and Progress in the Far
C   East. Chicago: University of Chicago Press, 1959. 443 pp.
     59-10428.
     Hucker, 2192; Silberman, 1611; JAS, 2/60; Am. Anthropologist,
     6/60; Am. Econ. R., 3/60; Am. Soc. R., 2/60; Ann. Am. Acad.,
     11/59; Library Journal, 5/15/59; Pol. Sci. Q., 12/60

0069 Thomson, Ian. The Rise of Modern Asia. N.Y.: Pitman, 1958.
B   265 pp. 58-6406. o.p.
     Library Journal, 4/1/58; TLS, 2/7/58

1140 Tien, Han. Kuan Han-ching: a Play. Peking: Foreign Languages
C   Press, 1961. 134 pp. Hand catalog.

1141 Tien, Han, ed. The White Snake, a Peking Opera. tr. by
C   Yang Hsien-yi and Gladys Yang. Peking: Foreign Languages
     Press, 1957. 79 pp. Hand catalog. o.p.

0863 Tiewes, Frederick C. Provincial Party Personnel in Mainland
A   China, 1950-1966. N.Y.: East Asian Institute, Columbia
     University, 1967. 114 pp. 66-30799.
     Choice, 1/68; JAS, 11/67

1168 Ting, I. A Short History of Modern Chinese Literature by Ting
C   Yi. Peking: Foreign Languages Press, 1959. 310 pp.
     60-31434. o.p.
     Hucker, 1741

0980 Ting, Walasse, comp. Chinese Moonlight: 63 Poems by 33 Poets.
C   tr. and recomposed by Walasse Ting. Copenhagen: Permild
     and Rosengreen, dist. by Wittenborn, 1967. 71 pp. 67-21795.

0144 Tinker, Hugh. Ballot Box and Bayonet; People and Government
B   in Emergent Asian Countries. N.Y.: Oxford, 1964. 126 pp.
     (Chatham House Essays, 5). 64-5587.
     Choice, 11/64; JAS, 5/65

1932 Toda, Kenji. Japanese Scroll Painting. Chicago: University
C   of Chicago Press, 1935. 167 pp. 35-4632. o.p.
     Silberman, 763

1559 Togo, Shigenori. The Cause of Japan. tr. and ed. by Togo
B   Fumihiko and Ben Bruce Blakeney. N.Y.: Simon & Schuster,
     1956. 372 pp. 56-9916. o.p.
     AUFS, 319; Silberman, 479; JAS, 8/57; Japan Q., 4-6/57;
     Library Journal, 9/15/56

1653 Tohata, Seiichi, comp. The Modernization of Japan. Tokyo:
B   Institute of Asian Economic Affairs, 1966- 68-1427.
     JAS, 11/66

1790 Tokutomi, Kenjiro. Nami-ko, a Realistic Novel. tr. from
C   Japanese by Sakae Shioya and E. F. Edgett. Boston:
     Turner, 1904. 314 pp. 4-7710. o.p. (M-University).

1876 Tokyo. National Museum. Pageant of Japanese Art. Tokyo:
A   Toto Bunka, 1952-54. 6 v. 57-29427.
     AUFS, 403; Silberman, 733

0048 Tokyo. Oriental Library (Toyo Bunko). Publications. Series B.
C   Research Department Memoirs. no.1- 1926- (M-IDC).
     Hucker, 43

1654 Tokyo Keizai Kenkyu Senta. Postwar Economic Growth in Japan;
A   Selected Papers of the First Conference of the Tokyo
     Economic Research Center. ed. by Ryutaro Komiya. Berke-
     ley: University of California Press, 1966. 260 pp. 66-22705.
     JAS, 6/67

0700 Toland, John. The Flying Tigers. N.Y.: Random House, 1963.
C   170 pp. (Landmarks Books, 105). 63-18286.
     Library Journal, 1/15/64

1560 Tolischus, Otto David. Tokyo Record. N.Y.: Reynal & Hitchcock,
C   1943. 462 pp. 43-3080. o.p.
     FEQ, 8/43; Pacific Affairs, 9/43; TLS, 7/24/43

0115 Tompkins, Pauline. American-Russian Relations in the Far
C   East. N.Y.: Macmillan, 1949. 426 pp. 49-48919. o.p.
     FEQ, 2/51; AHR, 7/50; Am. Pol. Sci. R., 9/50; Ann. Am.
     Acad., 3/50; Pacific Affairs, 6/50

0701 Tong, Hollington Kong. Chiang Kai-Shek, Soldier and Statesman,
B   Authorized Biography. Shanghai: China Publishing, 1937.
     2 v. 38-32771. o.p.

0702 Tong, Te-kong. United States Diplomacy in China, 1844-60.
B   Seattle: University of Washington Press, 1964. 332 pp.
     64-11051.
     Choice, 2/65; JAS, 2/65; AHR, 4/65; Library Journal, 9/15/64

1475 Totman, Conrad D. Politics in the Tokugawa Bakufu,
C   1600-1843. Cambridge, Mass.: Harvard University
     Press, 1967. 346 pp. (Harvard East Asian Series,
     30). 67-22873.
     Choice, 10/68; JAS, 11/68

1561 Totten, George Oakley, ed. Democracy in Prewar Japan; Ground-
B   work or Facade? Boston: Heath, 1965. 107 pp. (Problems in
     Asian Civilization). 65-19459.
     Choice, 11/66

1612 Totten, George Oakley. The Social Democratic Movement in
C   Pre-war Japan. New Haven, Conn.: Yale University Press,
     1966. 455 pp. (Studies on Japan's Social Democratic
     Parties, Vol. I). 66-12515 rev.
     Sup. 67, 3227; Choice, 10/67; JAS, 2/68; AHR, 4/67; Library
     Journal, 10/1/67

0301 T'oung Pao ou Archives Concernant l'Histoire, les Langues, la
B   Geographie et l'Ethnographie de l'Asie Orientale. v.1-10.
     1890-1899. Series 2, v.1- 1900- (M-IDC).
     Hucker, 29

0864 Townsend, James Roger. Political Participation in Communist
A   China. Berkeley: University of California Press, 1967.
     233 pp. 67-11422.
     Choice, 10/67; JAS, 2/68; Library Journal, 3/1/67

0070 Toynbee, Arnold J. The World and the West. N.Y.: Oxford,
A   1953. 99 pp. 53-5911.
    AUFS, 60; AHR, 10/53; Am. Soc. R., 8/53; Ann. Am. Acad.,
    5/53; Library Journal, 5/15/53

0116 Treat, Payson Jackson. The Far East, a Political and Dip-
C   lomatic History. rev. ed. N.Y.: Harper, 1935. 563 pp.
    35-13968. o.p.
    AUFS, 120

0327 Tregear, Thomas R. A Geography of China. Chicago: Aldine, 1966.
A   342 pp. 65-26752/CD.
    Sup. 67, 3252; Choice, 5/67; JAS, 11/66; JAOS, 4-6/66;
    Library Journal, 4/15/66

0981 Trevelyan, Robert Calverley, ed. From the Chinese. Oxford:
C   Clarendon, 1945. 92 pp. A46-622. o.p.

1418 Trewartha, Glenn Thomas. Japan, a Physical, Cultural and Regional
A   Geography. Madison: University of Wisconsin Press, 1965.
    652 pp. 65-11200.
    Silberman, 75; Choice, 11/65; FEQ, 8/45

0703 Trotskii, Lev. Problems of the Chinese Revolution. tr. by
C   Max Schachtman. 2d ed. N.Y.: Paragon, 1962 (orig. pub. by
    Pioneer, 1932). 432 pp. A63-5007. (R).
    JAS, 11/66

1343 Tsang, Chiu-sam. Society, Schools and Progress in China. N.Y.:
A   Pergamon, 1968. 333 pp. 68-21109.

0941 Ts'ao, Chan. Dream of the Red Chamber. by Tsao Hsueh-chin.
A   with a continuation by Kao Ou. tr. from Chinese by
    Chi-chen Wang. N.Y.: Twayne, 1958. 574 pp. 58-1761.
    AUFS, 1084; Hucker, 1702; JAS, 5/59; Library Journal, 5/15/58

0942 Ts'ao, Chan. Dream of the Red Chamber. Hung Lou Meng. A
A   Chinese Novel of the Early Ching Period. tr. from Chinese
    by Franz Kuhn. tr. from German by Florence and Isabel
    McHugh. N.Y.: Pantheon, 1958. 582 pp. 58-6097. o.p.
    Hucker, 1703; JAS, 5/59

1142 Tsogtnarin. Golden Eagle. Translation of Chin Ying, a Play.
C   Peking: Foreign Languages Press, 1961. 100 pp. NUC 64-46554.

0704 Tsou, Tang. America's Failure in China: 1941-50. Chicago: Uni-
A   versity of Chicago Press, 1963. 614 pp. 63-13072.
    Sup. 65, 3108; JAS, 2/64; AHR, 1/64; Am. Pol. Sci. R., 3/64;
    China Q., 4-6/64; Pol. Sci. Q., 12/64

1476 Tsuchiya, Takao. An Economic History of Japan. tr. by Michi-
C   taro Shidehara. rev. by Neil Skene Smith. Tokyo: Asiatic
    Society of Japan, 1937. 269 pp. AC38-2554.
    AUFS, 208; Silberman, 229

1877 Tsuda, Noritake. Handbook of Japanese Art. Tokyo: Sanseido,
B   1935. 525 pp. 36-20290.
    Silberman, 732

1477 Tsukahira, Toshio George. Feudal Control in Tokugawa Japan;
C   The Sankin Kotai System. Cambridge, Mass.: Harvard
    University Press, 1966. 228 pp. 67-3532.
    Sup. 67, 3228; JAS, 5/67

1613 Tsukahira, Toshio George. The Postwar Evolution of Communist
C   Strategy in Japan. Cambridge, Mass.: Center for International
    Studies, M.I.T., 1954. 89 pp. 55-32093. o.p.

1614 Tsuneishi, Warren Michio. Japanese Political Style; An Intro-
B   duction to the Government and Politics of Modern Japan.
    N.Y.: Harper & Row, 1966. 226 pp. (Harper's Comparative
    Government Series). 66-11467 rev.
    Choice, 10/67

1428 Tsunoda, Ryusaku, tr. Japan in the Chinese Dynastic Histories:
C   Later Han through Ming Dynasties. ed. by L. Carrington Good-
    rich. South Pasadena, Calif.: P. D. and Ione Perkins,
    1951. 187 pp. 53-67. o.p.
    Hucker, 133; Silberman, 196

1412 Tsunoda, Ryusaku, ed. Sources of the Japanese Tradition.
A   N.Y.: Columbia University Press, 1958. 928 pp. 58-7167.
    AUFS, 175; Silberman, 152; JAS, 2/59; Ann. Am. Acad., 1/59;
    Japan Q., 1-3/59; JAOS, 10-12/59; Library Journal, 7/58;
    Pacific Affairs, 3/59

0982 Tu, Fu. Selected Poems. comp. by Feng Chih. tr. by Rewi Alley.
C   Peking: Foreign Languages Press, 1962. 178 pp. NUC 63-
    63022. o.p.

0983 Tu, Fu. Tu Fu, the Autobiography of a Chinese Poet, A.D.
C   712-770. tr. by Florence Ayscough. Boston: Houghton
    Mifflin, 1929-34. 2 v. 29-29750 rev. o.p.

1113 Tu, P'eng-ch'eng. Defend Yenan! tr. by Sidney Shapiro.
C   Peking: Foreign Languages Press, 1958. 404 pp. Hand
    catalog. o.p.

1114 Tu, P'eng-ch'eng. In Days of Peace. Peking: Foreign Lan-
C   guages Press, 1962. 219 pp. NUC 63-76507.

1143 Tuan, Cheng-pin. Taming the Dragon and the Tiger; A Play in
C   Six Scenes. by Tuan Cheng-pin and Tu Shih-tsun. tr. by
    A. C. Barnes. Peking: Foreign Languages Press, 1961.
    106 pp. Hand catalog.

0984 Tun-huang Manuscripts. English. Ballads and Stories from Tun-
A   huang; An Anthology, by Arthur Waley. London: Allen &
    Unwin, 1960. 273 pp. 61-4417.
    JAS, 5/62

1260 Tun, Li-ch'en. Annual Customs and Festivals in Peking As Recorded
C   in the Yen-ching Sui-shih-chi. tr. and annotated by Derk
    Bodde. 2d ed. rev. Hong Kong: Hong Kong University Press,
    dist. by Oxford, 1965 (orig. pub. by Vetch, 1936). 147 pp.
    65-8424. (R). (M-University).
    Hucker, 1076

1344 Tung, Chi-ping and Humphrey Evans. The Thought Revolution.
C   N.Y.: Coward-McCann, 1966. 254 pp. 66-13121.
    JAS, 2/68

0419 Twitchett, Denis Crispin. Financial Administration under the
B   T'ang Dynasty. Cambridge: University, 1963. 373 pp.
    63-3532.
    JAS, 2/64; JAOS, 1-3/64

2068 Tzu Yu Chung-Kuo Chih Kung Yeh. (Industry of Free China).
C   v.1- 1954-
    Hucker, 2180

2094 Uchida, Naosaku. The Overseas Chinese; A Bibliographical Essay
A   Based on the Resources of the Hoover Institution. Stan-
    ford, Calif.: Hoover Institution on War, Revolution, and
    Peace, 1959. 134 pp. (Bibliographical Series, 7). 60-1670.
    o.p.

1413 Ueda, Makoto. Literary and Art Theories in Japan. Cleve-
B   land, Ohio: Case Western Reserve University Press, 1967.
    274 pp. 67-14521.
    Choice, 7-8/68; JAS, 8/68; Library Journal, 3/1/68

1805 Ueda, Makoto. Zeami, Basho, Yeats, Pound: a Study in Japanese
C   and English Poetics. The Hague: Mouton, 1965. 165 pp.
    (Studies in General and Comparative Literature, I). 65-28168.

1878 Ueno, Naoteur, ed. Japanese Arts and Crafts in the Meiji Era.
C   English adaptation by Richard Lane. Tokyo: Pan-Pacific
    Press, 1958. 224 pp. (Japanese Culture in the Meiji Era,
    Vol. VIII). 59-52560.
    Silberman, 725

0302 Union Research Institute, Hong Kong. Communist China Prob-
B   lem Research Series. no. 1- 1953-

0049 United Asia, v.1- 1948-
C   AUFS, 61

0161 United Nations. Bureau of Social Affairs. The Population of
B   Asia and the Far East, 1950-1980. N.Y.: United Nations
    Dept. of Economic and Social Affairs, 1959. 110 pp.
    (Population Studies, No. 31). 60-1676. o.p.
    Hucker, 2189; JAS, 11/60

2037 United Nations Command. Military Armistice in Korea and
C   Temporary Supplementary Agreement, Signed at Panmunjon,
    Korea, July 27, 1958, Entered into Force July 27, 1953.
    Washington: Government Printing Office, 1953. 127 pp.
    54-61053. o.p.
    Silberman, 1795

0050 United Nations. Economic Commission for Asia and the Far
C   East. Economic Bulletin for Asia and the Far East. v.1-
    1950- (R-Johnson).
    FEQ, 11/52

0162 United Nations. Economic Commission for Asia and the Far
C   East. Economic Survey of Asia and the Far East. N.Y.:
    United Nations, 1947- 49-48996 rev. 2.
    AUFS, 62; Hucker, 2157; FEQ, 2/52, 5/52, 11/53, 11/54

2052   United Nations. Food and Agricultural Organization. Rehabil-
B   itation and Development of Agriculture, Forestry and Fish-
       eries in South Korea. Report prepared for the United
       Nations Korean Reconstruction Agency by a Mission selected
       by the Food and Agricultural Organization of the United
       Nations. N.Y.: Columbia University Press, 1954. 428 pp.
       54-11917. o.p.
       Silberman, 1926

1933   United Nations. UNESCO. Japan: Ancient Buddhist Paintings.
C   intro. by Takaaki Matsushita. Greenwich, Conn.: New York
       Graphic, 1959. 21 pp. (UNESCO World Art Series, 11).
       60-1597.

2066   United Nations. UNESCO-UNKRA Educational Planning Mission to
C   Korea. Rebuilding Education in the Republic of Korea;
       Report. Paris: UNESCO, 1954. 221 pp. 54-14822. o.p.
       Silberman, 1909

0823   U.S. Congress. Senate Committee on Foreign Relations. China,
C   Vietnam, and the United States; Highlights of the Hear-
       ings of the Senate Foreign Relations Committee. Washing-
       ton: Public Affairs Press, 1966. 218 pp. 66-25442. o.p.
       Sup. 67, 3253; Choice, 4/67; Library Journal, 10/15/66

0303   U.S. Consulate General. Hong Kong. Current Background, v.1-
B   1950-
       Hucker, 906

0304   U.S. Consulate General. Hong Kong. Index to Survey of Mainland
A   Magazines. no. 1- 1956-

0305   U.S. Consulate General. Hong Kong. Review of the Hong Kong
A   Chinese Press. no. 1-53/1961. 1947-1961.

0306   U.S. Consulate General. Hong Kong. Selections from China
A   Mainland Magazines. no. 1- 1955-

0307   U.S. Consulate General. Hong Kong. Survey of China Main-
A   land Press. no. 1- 1950-

0223   U.S. Department of the Army. Office of Military History. Guide
B   to Japanese Monographs and Japanese Studies on Manchuria,
       1945-1960. Washington: Office of Chief of Military History,
       Dept. of the Army, 1962. 282 pp. o.p.

0705   U.S. Department of State. The China White Paper, August, 1949.
B   Stanford, Calif.: Stanford University Press, 1967 (orig.
       pub. by U. S. Dept. of State, 1949 under title United States
       Relations with China, with Special Reference to the Period,
       1944-1949). 1079 pp. 67-26650. (R).
       AUFS, 993; Hucker, 820; Choice, 4/68; FEQ, 11/50

1655   U.S. Department of State. Mission on Japanese Combines. Report
B   of Mission on Japanese Combines. Part I, Analytical and Tech-
       nical Data, Report to Department of State and War Dept., Mar.
       1946. (Dept. of State Publication 2628/Far Eastern Ser-
       ies 14). o.p.
       Silberman, 463

2038   U.S. Department of State. Office of Public Affairs. Korea,
C   1945 to 1948; A Report on Political Developments and Eco-
       nomic Resources with Selected Documents. Washington: Dept.
       of State, 1948. 124 pp. 48-47165. o.p.
       Silberman, 1777

1580   U.S. Department of State. Treaty of Peace with Japan.
C   Signed at San Francisco, September 8, 1951, Proclaimed by
       President of the U.S., April 28, 1952. Washington:
       Dept. of State, 1952. (Department of State Publication
       4613. Treaties and Other International Acts Series, 2490).
       o.p.
       Silberman, 580

0264   U.S. Library of Congress. Orientalia Division. Eminent Chinese
A   of the Ch'ing Period (1644-1912). Taipei: Chinese Materials
       and Research Aids Service Center, 1966 (orig. pub. by
       Government Printing Office, 1943-44). 2 v. 64-53640. (R).
       Hucker, 508; FEQ, 8/44

1983   U.S. Library of Congress. Reference Department. Korea: an
B   Annotated Bibliography. Washington: Library of Congress,
       1950. 3 v. 50-62963 rev. o.p.
       Silberman, 1625

0224   U.S. Library of Congress. Science and Technology Division.
A   Chinese Scientific and Technical Serials Publications in
       the Collections of the Library of Congress. rev. ed. Wash-
       ington: Library of Congress, 1961. 107 pp. 62-60011. o.p.

2084   U.S. Mutual Security Mission to China. Economic Progress of
C   Free China, 1951-1958. Taipei: 1958. 83 pp. 58-62448.
       o.p.
       Hucker, 2182

2085   U.S. Mutual Security Mission to China. Urban and Industrial
C   Taiwan, Crowded and Resourceful, by Arthur F. Raper.
       Taipei: 1954. 370 pp. 55-60504.
       Hucker, 2185

1345   U.S. Office of Education. Basic Principles Underlying the
A   Chinese Communist Approach to Education, by Chester Cheng.
       Washington: U.S. Office of Education, 1961. 24 pp. (Infor-
       mation on Education Around the World Series, No. 51).

1656   U.S. Strategic Bombing Survey. The Effects of Strategic
C   Bombing on Japan's War Economy. Washington: Over-All Eco-
       nomics Effect Division, 1946. 244 pp. 47-32980. o.p.

0706   Utley, Freda. The China Story. Chicago: Regnery, 1951.
C   274 pp. 51-3311.
       Hucker, 822; FEQ, 5/52; Ann. Am. Acad., 11/51; Library
       Journal, 5/15/51; Pacific Affairs, 9/51

1562   Utley, Freda. Japan's Feet of Clay. N.Y.: Norton, 1937.
C   393 pp. 37-27234. o.p.
       Am. Econ. R., 9/37; Pacific Affairs, 3/37; TLS, 11/28/36

1615   Uyehara, Cecil H. and others. Comparative Platforms of Japanese
C   Major Parties: Social Democratic Party of Japan Reunified
       on October 13, 1955; Japan Liberal Democratic Party, Re-
       sulting from a Merger on November 15, 1955. Boston:
       Fletcher School of Law and Diplomacy, 1955. 65 pp. o.p.
       Silberman, 1352; FEQ, 8/56

0824   Van der Sprenkel, Otto P. N. B., ed. New China; Three Views, by
B   Otto B. Van der Sprenkel, Robert Guillain and Michael Lindsay.
       London: Turnstile, 1950. 241 pp. 51-2194. o.p.
       AUFS, 994; Hucker, 978; FEQ, 11/51; Library Journal,
       3/1/51; TLS, 12/15/50

0707   Van Slyke, Lyman P. Enemies and Friends; The United Front
A   in Chinese Communist History. Stanford, Calif.: Stan-
       ford University Press, 1967. 330 pp. 67-26531.
       Choice, 6/68; JAS, 8/68; AHR, 6/68

0708   Varg, Paul. The Making of a Myth: the United States and
A   China, 1897-1912. East Lansing: Michigan State Univer-
       sity Press, 1968. 184 pp. 68-20411.
       Choice, 11/68; JAS, 2/69; Library Journal, 10/1/68

1478   Varley, H. Paul. The Onin War; History of Its Origins and
B   Background with a Selective Translation of The Chronicle
       of Onin. N.Y.: Columbia University Press, 1967. 238 pp.
       (Studies in Oriental Culture, 1). 66-14595.
       Sup. 67, 3229; Choice, 11/67; JAS, 8/68; AHR, 10/67; Ann.
       Am. Acad., 11/67; Library Journal, 1/1/67

1414   Varley, H. Paul. A Syllabus of Japanese Civilization. N.Y.:
A   Columbia University Press, 1968. 98 pp. (Companion to
       Asian Studies/Committee on Oriental Studies). 68-55815.

1249   Vasu-bandhau. Vijnaptimatratasiddhi, la Siddhi de Hiuan-Tsang.
C   tr. and annotated by Louis de La Vallee Poussin. Paris:
       Geuthner, 1928-1929. 2 v. 32-34323.

1250   Vasu-bandhu. Un Systeme de Philosophie Bouddhique. Materiaux
C   pour L'Etude du Systeme Vijnaptimatra by Sylvain Levi. Paris:
       Champion, 1932. 206 pp.

1251   Vasu-bandhu. Wei Shih Er shih Lun or the Treatise in Twenty
C   Stanzas on Representation-Only, by Vasubandhu. tr. from
       the Chinese version of Hsuan Tsang, Tripitaka Master of
       the T'ang Dynasty, by Clarence H. Hamilton. N.Y.: Kraus,
       1966 (orig. pub. by American Oriental Society, 1938).
       82 pp. 39-16886. (R). (M-University).

2039   Vatcher, William H. Panmunjom; The Story of the Korean
B   Military Armistice Negotiations. N.Y.: Praeger, 1958.
       322 pp. 58-7887. o.p.
       JAS, 11/58; AHR, 1/59; Ann. Am. Acad., 7/58

0145   Vinacke, Harold Monk. Far Eastern Politics in the Postwar
C   Period. N.Y.: Appleton-Century-Crofts, 1956. 497 pp.
       55-10400.
       AUFS, 121; AHR, 10/56; Ann. Am. Acad., 7/56

0132   Vinacke, Harold Monk. A History of the Far East in Modern
B   Times. 6th ed. N.Y.: Appleton-Century-Crofts, 1959.
       877 pp. 59-7077.
       AUFS, 122; Silberman, 328; FEQ, 5/42

0133 Vinacke, Harold Monk. The United States and the Far East,
B 1945-1951. Stanford, Calif.: Stanford University Press,
1952. 144 pp. 52-1172. o.p. (M-University).
AUFS, 123; AHR, 10/52; Am. Pol. Sci. R., 6/52; Ann.
Am. Acad., 7/52

1273 Vincent, Irene (Vongehr). The Sacred Oasis; Caves of the
B Thousand Buddhas, Tun Huang. Chicago: University of
Chicago Press, 1953. 114 pp. Λ53-5284. o.p.
Hucker, 1483; TLS, 2/26/54

1844 Visser, Marinus Willem de. Ancient Buddhism in Japan; Sutras
C and Ceremonies in Use in the Seventh and Eighth Centuries
A.D. and their History in Later Times. Leiden: Brill,
1935. 2 v. 39-3106.
Silberman, 632

0420 Vladimirtsov, Boris Iakovlevich. The Life of Chingis-Khan. tr.
B from Russian by Prince D. S. Mirsky. London: Routledge,
1930. 172 pp. 30-31732. o.p.
Hucker, 366

0421 Vladimirtsov, Boris Iakovlevich. La Regime Social des Mongols;
C La Feodalisme Nomade. tr. by Michel Carsow. Paris: Maison-
neuve, 1948. 291 pp. 50-14455.
Hucker, 370

1689 Vogel, Ezra F. Japan's New Middle Class; The Salary Man and
A His Family in a Tokyo Suburb. Berkeley: University
of California Press, 1963. 299 pp. 63-21263.
JAS, 11/64; Am. Anthropologist, 8/64; Ann. Am. Acad.,
11/64; Library Journal, 10/1/63

1616 Von Mehren, Arthur Taylor, ed. Law in Japan; The Legal Order in
C a Changing Society. Cambridge, Mass.: Harvard University
Press, 1963. 706 pp. 62-19226.
Sup. 65, 3073; JAS, 8/64; Am. Pol. Sci. R., 6/64; Japan
Q., 7-9/64; Library Journal, 11/15/63

2055 Voorhees, Melvin B. Korean Tales. N.Y.: Simon & Schuster,
C 1952. 209 pp. 52-13787. o.p.

0530 Wakeman, Frederic E. Strangers at the Gate; Social Disorder
A in South China, 1839-1861. Berkeley: University of California
Press, 1966. 276 pp. (Center for Chinese Studies).
66-25349.
Choice, 7-8/67; JAS, 8/67; AHR, 10/67; Library Journal,
1/1/67

0985 Waley, Arthur, tr. Chinese Poems, Selected from 170 Chinese
A Poems, More Translations from the Chinese, The Temple
and The Book of Songs. London: Allen & Unwin, 1946.
213 pp. 47-5287.
AUFS, 1087

1311 Waley, Arthur. An Introduction to the Study of Chinese Paint-
B ing. N.Y.: Grove, 1958. 261 pp. 58-6228. o.p.
AUFS, 1022; Hucker, 1469

1727 Waley, Arthur. Japanese Poetry; The 'Uta'. London: Lund,
B Humphries, 1956. 110 pp. Hand catalog.
AUFS, 447; Silberman, 1043

1044 Waley, Arthur. The Life and Times of Po Chu-i, 772-846 A.D.
A N.Y.: Hillary House, 1951 (orig. pub. by Allen & Unwin,
1949). 238 pp. 52-55888. (R).
AUFS, 1088; Hucker, 1601; FEQ, 8/51; TLS, 1/20/50

0986 Waley, Arthur, tr. More Translations from the Chinese.
B N.Y.: Knopf, 1937. 144 pp. 19-17614. o.p.

1744 Waley, Arthur. The No Plays of Japan. N.Y.: Grove, 1957
A (orig. pub. by Knopf, 1922). 319 pp. 57-7376. (R).
AUFS, 520; Silberman, 1121

0531 Waley, Arthur. The Opium War through Chinese Eyes. Stanford,
B Calif.: Stanford University Press, 1968 (orig. pub. by
Allen & Unwin, 1958). 257 pp. 68-12334. (R).
Hucker, 669; JAS, 11/59; AHR, 1/60; Ann. Am. Acad., 11/59;
Library Journal, 5/1/59; TLS, 3/20/59

1045 Waley, Arthur. The Poetry and Career of Li Po, 701-162 A.D.
A N.Y.: Hillary House, 1958 (orig. pub. in 1950). 123 pp.
51-13161. (R).
AUFS, 1090; Hucker, 1597

0987 Waley, Arthur. The Real Tripitaka, and Other Pieces. London:
C Allen & Unwin, 1952. 291 pp. 55-18728.
Hucker, 1658

0988 Waley, Arthur, tr. The Temple, and Other Poems. N.Y.:
B Knopf, 1923. 150 pp. 23-17912. o.p.
AUFS, 1092; Hucker, 1551

1185 Waley, Arthur. Three Ways of Thought in Ancient China. Gar-
B den City, N.Y.: Doubleday, 1956. 216 pp. 56-5973.
AUFS, 607; Hucker, 1132; JAOS, 3/41

0989 Walcy, Arthur, tr. Translations from the Chinese. N.Y.:
B Knopf, 1941. 325 pp. 41-4061.
Hucker, 1561

1046 Waley, Arthur. Yuan Mei, Eighteenth Century Chinese Poet.
A N.Y.: Macmillan, 1957. 227 pp. 57-13771.
AUFS, 1094; Hucker, 1607; JAS, 2/60; JAOS, 7-9/57; TLS,
2/22/57

0894 Walker, Kenneth Richard. Planning in Chinese Agriculture;
C Socialisation and the Private Sector, 1956-1962. Chicago:
Aldine, 1965. 109 pp. 65-16721.
Choice, 4/66; JAS, 8/66; Am. Econ. R., 6/66; Ann. Am.
Acad., 5/66; J. Pol. Econ., 6/66

0825 Walker, Richard Louis. China under Communism, the First
C Five Years. New Haven, Conn.: Yale University Press, dist.
by Lawrence Verry, 1955. 403 pp. 55-6422.
AUFS, 995; Hucker, 927; FEQ, 2/56; Library JOurnal, 6/15/55

0532 Walker, Richard Louis, ed. China and the West: Cultural Col-
C lision; Selected Documents. New Haven, Conn.: Far Eastern
Publications, Yale University, 1956. 254 pp. 56-58515.
o.p.
Hucker, 657

0422 Walker, Richard Louis. The Multi-state System of Ancient China.
B Hamden, Conn.: Shoe String Press, 1954. 135 pp. 54-7778.
o.p.
Hucker, 164; AHR, 10/54; Am. Pol. Sci. R., 6/54; JAOS,
10-12/54

0225 Walker, Richard Louis. Western Language Periodicals on China; A
B Selective List. New Haven, Conn.: Institute of Far Eastern
Languages, Yale University, 1949. 3030 pp. 49-3650. o.p.

1144 Wan, Chia-pao. Bright Skies, by Tsao Yu, pseud. tr. by Cheng
B Pei-chi. Peking: Foreign Languages Press, 1960. 127 pp.
Hand catalog.

1145 Wan, Chia-pao. Sunrise; A Play in Four Acts. tr. by A. C.
B Barnes. Peking: Foreign Languages Press, 1960. 189 pp.
Hand catalog. o.p.

1146 Wan, Chia-pao. Thunderstorm; A Play by Tsao Yu. tr. by Wang
B Tso-liang and A. C. Barnes. 2d ed. Peking: Foreign Languages Press, 1964. 164 pp. NUC 66-91168. o.p.

1217 Wang, Ch'ang-chih. La Philosophie Morale de Wang Yang-ming...
C par Wang Tch'ang-tche. Paris: Geuthner, 1936. 217 pp.
(Varietes Sinologiques, 63). 42-43210.
Hucker, 1162

1135 Wang, Chao-ming. Poems of Wang Ching-wei. tr. by Seyuan
C Shu. London: Allen & Unwin, 1938. 96 pp. 39-757. o.p.

1115 Wang, Chi-chen, tr. Contemporary Chinese Stories. N.Y.:
A Columbia University Press, 1944. 242 pp. A44-726 rev.
o.p.
AUFS, 1124; Hucker, 1745; FEQ, 8/44; Library Journal,
11/15/43

1116 Wang, Chi-chen, ed. Stories of China at War. N.Y.: Columbia
B University Press, 1947. 158 pp. A47-1034. o.p.
Hucker, 1746; Library Journal, 12/15/46

0943 Wang, Chi-chen, tr. Traditional Chinese Tales. N.Y.: Colum-
B bia University Press, 1944. 225 pp. A44-727 rev. o.p.
(M-University).
AUFS, 1095; Hucker, 1649; FEQ, 8/44; Library Journal, 11/15/43

1362 Wang, Chi-min. History of Chinese Medicine; Being a Chronicle
C of Medical Happenings in China from Ancient Times to the
Present Period, by K. Chimin Wong and Wu Lien-teh. 2d ed.
Shanghai: National Quarantine Service, 1936. 906 pp.
37-34871. o.p.
Hucker, 1372

1261 Wang, Ch'ung. Lun-heng. tr. from Chinese and annotated by
C Alfred Forke. 2d ed. N.Y.: Paragon, 1962 (orig. pub. by
Luzac, 1907). 2 v. 63-411. (R).

0423 Wang, Gungwu. The Structure of Power in North China during
B the Five Dynasties. Stanford, Calif.: Stanford University
Press, 1968 (orig. pub. by University of Malaya Press,
1963). 257 pp. SA64-2651. (R).
JAS, 5/65

1117 Wang, Huo. Chieh Chen-Kuo, Guerilla Hero and Coal Miner.
C Peking: Foreign Languages Press, 1961. 122 pp.

0090 Wang, I-t'ung. Official Relations between China and Japan,
B 1368-1549, by Wang Yi-t'ung. Cambridge, Mass.: Harvard
University Press, 1953. 128 pp. (Harvard-Yenching Insti-
tute Studies, IX). 53-5062. o.p.
Hucker, 490; Silberman, 228; FEQ, 5/54; JAOS, 7-9/64

1004 Wang Pao-ch'uan. Lady Precious Stream; An Old Chinese Play Done
A into English According to Its Traditional Style by S. I.
Hsiung. London: Methuen, 1934. 168 pp.
35-11934.
Hucker, 1678

1218 Wang, Shou-jen. Instructions for Practical Living and Other
A Neo-Confucian Writings, by Wang Yang-ming. tr. by Wing-
tsit Chan. N.Y.: Columbia University Press, 1963. 358 pp.
62-16688.
JAS, 11/64

0990 Wang, Wei. Poems. tr. by Chang Yin-nan and Lewis C. Walmsley.
B Rutland, Vt.: Tuttle, 1958. 159 pp. 58-7723. o.p.
Hucker, 1596; JAS, 5/59

1118 Wang, Wen-shih. The Night of the Snowstorm. Peking: Foreign
C Languages Press, 1961. 222 pp. Hand catalog. o.p.

0709 Wang, Yi Chu. Chinese Intellectuals and the West, 1872-
A 1949. Chapel Hill: University of North Carolina Press,
1966. 557 pp. 66-10207.
Choice, 1/67; JAS, 11/66; AHR, 10/66; Ann. Am. Acad., 11/66;
J. Am. Hist., 12/66; Library Journal, 3/1/66; Pacific
Affairs, Spring-Summer/67; Pol. Sci. Q., 6/67; TLS, 12/1/66

1119 Wang, Yuan-chien. An Ordinary Labourer. Peking: Foreign
C Languages Press, 1961. 183 pp. 64-33730.

1617 Ward, Robert Edward. Five Studies in Japanese Politics. Ann
B Arbor: University of Michigan Press, 1957. 121 pp. 57-63486.
o.p.
JAS, 5/58

1618 Ward, Robert Edward. Japan's Political System. Englewood Cliffs,
A N.J.: Prentice-Hall, 1967. 126 pp. (Comparative Asian
Governments). 67-20230.
Choice, 2/68; JAS, 2/68

1619 Ward, Robert Edward. Political Development in Modern Japan.
C Princeton, N.J.: Princeton University Press, 1968.
637 pp. 66-14309.
JAS, 2/69

1563 Ward, Robert Spencer. Asia for the Asiatics? The Techniques of
C Japanese Occupation. Chicago: University of Chicago
Press, 1945. 204 pp. A45-3653. o.p.
Silberman, 549; FEQ, 5/46; Am. Pol. Sci. R., 10/45; Ann. Am.
Acad., 11/45; Pacific Affairs, 12/45

1879 Warner, Langdon. The Enduring Art of Japan. Cambridge,
C Mass.: Harvard University Press, 1952. 113 pp. 52-8220.
AUFS, 406; Silberman, 724; FEQ, 11/53

1940 Warner, Langdon. Japanese Sculpture of the Suiko Period.
C intro. by Lorraine d'O Warner. New Haven, Conn.: Yale
University Press, 1923. 80 pp. 24-2015. o.p.
Silberman, 744

1941 Warner, Langdon. Japanese Sculpture of the Tempyo Period;
C Masterpieces of the Eighth Century. ed. and arr. by James
Marshall Plumer. Cambridge, Mass.: Harvard University
Press, 1964. 217 pp. 64-23111.
Silberman, 742; Choice, 2/65; Art. Bul., 6/65; JAOS, 8-9/61;
Library Journal, 12/15/64; TLS, 6/10/65

1934 Waterhouse, David B. Harunobu and His Age; The Development of
C Colour Printing in Japan. London: The Trustees of the
British Museum, 1964. 326 pp. 65-28917.
JAS, 5/65; JAOS, 7-9/65

1047 Watson, Burton. Early Chinese Literature. N.Y.: Columbia
A University Press, 1962. 304 pp. 62-17552.

0424 Watson, Burton. Ssu-ma Ch'ien, Grand Historian of China.
A N.Y.: Columbia University Press, 1958. 276 pp. 57-13030.
Hucker, 190; Library Journal, 5/15/58; TLS, 9/26/58

1288 Watson, William. Ancient Chinese Bronzes. London: Faber
B & Faber, 1962. 117 pp. Hand catalog.
JAS, 11/63

1274 Watson, William. China Before the Han Dynasty. N.Y.: Praeger,
C 1962. 264 pp. 61-14105.
TLS, 9/21/62

0425 Watson, William. Early Civilization in China. N.Y.: McGraw-
A Hill, 1966. 143 pp. (Library of the Early Civilizations).
66-16974.
Choice, 2/67; Library Journal, 9/15/66; Pacific Affairs,
Fall-Winter/66-67

1942 Watson, William. Sculpture of Japan, From the Fifth to the
A Fifteenth Century. London: Studio, 1959. 216 pp. 60-41576.
o.p.
Silberman, 738; Library Journal, 4/1/60; TLS, 2/19/60

1415 Webb, Herschel. An Introduction to Japan. 2d ed. N.Y.: Colum-
B bia University Press, 1957. 130 pp. 54-12312.
AUFS, 176; Silberman, 2; JAS, 2/58; Library Journal, 2/15/55;
Pacific Affairs, 12/55

1479 Webb, Herschel. The Japanese Imperial Institution in the
B Tokugawa Period. N.Y.: Columbia University Press, 1968.
296 pp. (East Asian Institute, Columbia University).
68-11912.
Choice, 12/68

1389 Webb, Herschel. Research in Japanese Sources, a Guide. N.Y.:
C Columbia University Press for East Asian Institute, 1965.
170 pp. 64-21202.
Sup. 65, 3074; Choice, 7-8/65; JAS, 8/65; Library Journal,
1/1/65

1186 Weber, Max. The Religion of China: Confucianism and Taoism.
A tr. and ed. by Hans H. Gerth. with an intro. by C. K. Yang.
N.Y.: Macmillan, 1964. 308 pp. 64-9025.
AUFS, 609; Hucker, 1106; JAS, 5/65; FEQ, 5/52

2017 Weems, Benjamin B. Reform, Rebellion, and the Heavenly Way.
B Tucson: University of Arizona Press, 1964. 122 pp. (Association for Asian Studies, Monographs and Papers, XV).
64-17267.
Sup. 65, 3082; Choice, 4/65; JAS, 5/65

0710 Wehrle, Edmund S. Britain, China, and the Antimissionary
C Riots, 1891-1900. Minneapolis: University of Minnesota
Press, 1966. 223 pp. 66-15064.
Choice, 11/66; JAS, 11/66; AHR, 10/66; Ann. Am. Acad., 9/66;
Library Journal, 11/15/65

0711 Wei, Wen-ch'i. China and Soviet Russia. Princeton, N.J.: Van
B Nostrand, 1956. 379 pp. 56-9014. o.p.
Hucker, 838; JAS, 11/57; AHR, 4/57; Am. Pol. Sci. R., 9/57;
Ann. Am. Acad., 3/57; Library Journal, 5/1/56; TLS, 4/5/57

1233 Welch, Holmes. The Parting of the Way; Lao Tzu and the Taoist
C Movement. Boston: Beacon, 1957. 204 pp. 57-7729.
AUFS, 652; Hucker, 1176; JAS, 11/58; Am. Soc. R., 8/57

0170 Wells, Henry Willis. The Classical Drama of the Orient. N.Y.:
B Asia Publishing House, 1965. 348 pp. 66-75404.

1048 Wen-lin; Studies in the Chinese Humanities. ed. by Chow Tse-
C tsung. Madison: University of Wisconsin Press, 1968.
325 pp. 67-20756.
JAS, 5/69

0265 Werner, Edward Theodore Chalmers. A Dictionary of Chinese
B Mythology. Shanghai: Kelly & Walsh, 1932. 627 pp.
33-18090. o.p.
Hucker, 1086

0944 Werner, Edward Theodore Chalmers. Myths and Legends of China.
C N.Y.: Brentano, 1922. 453 pp. 23-5292. o.p.
Hucker, 1085

1564 White, John Albert. The Diplomacy of the Russo-Japanese War.
C Princeton, N.J.: Princeton University Press, 1964. 410 pp.
63-23417.
Sup. 65, 3075; Choice, 1/65; JAS, 11/65; AHR, 7/65

0712 White, Theodore Harold. The Mountain Road. N.Y.: Sloane Assoc-
B   iates, 1958. 347 pp. 58-6394. o.p.
     Library Journal, 5/15/58

0713 White, Theodore Harold. Thunder Out of China. N.Y.: Apollo
A   (orig. pub. by Sloane Associates, 1946). 331 pp. 46-11919.
     (R).
     AUFS, 891; Hucker, 799

1262 White, William Charles. Chinese Jews; A Compilation of Matters
C   Relating to the Jews of K'ai-feng Fu. 2d ed. N.Y.: Paragon,
     1966 (orig. pub. by University of Toronto Press, 1942).
     625 pp. 66-31664. (R).
     Sup. 67, 3255; Hucker, 1301; JAOS, 10-12/67

2040 White, William Lindsay. Back Down the Ridge. N.Y.: Harcourt,
B   Brace, 1953. 182 pp. 53-5642. o.p.

1690 Whitehill, Arthur Murray. The Other Worker; A Comparative Study
B   of Industrial Relations in the United States and Japan. by
     Arthur M. Whitehill and Shin-Ichi Takezawa. Honolulu:
     East-West Center Press, 1968. 481 pp. 67-21409.
     Choice, 4/69

0826 Whiting, Allen Suess. China Crosses the Yalu; The Decision
B   to Enter the Korean War. Stanford, Calif.: Stanford Uni-
     versity Press, 1969 (orig. pub. by Macmillan, 1960). 219 pp.
     (Rand Series). 68-13744. (R).
     Hucker, 949; JAS, 5/61; AHR, 7/61; Am. Pol. Sci. R., 3/61;
     Ann. Am. Acad., 5/61; China Q., 1-3/62; Library Journal,
     10/15/60; Pacific Affairs, Fall/61; TLS, 6/23/61

0714 Whiting, Allen Suess. Sinkiang: Pawn or Pivot? East Lansing:
B   Michigan State University Press, 1958. 314 pp. 58-11509.
     Hucker, 840; JAS, 8/59; AHR, 1/60; Am. Pol. Sci. R., 6/59;
     Ann. Am. Acad., 5/59; Pacific Affairs, 12/59; TLS, 8/7/59

0715 Whiting, Allen Suess. Soviet Policies in China, 1917-1924.
A   Stanford, Calif.: Stanford University Press, 1968 (orig.
     pub. by Columbia University Press, 1954). 350 pp.
     68-12355. (R).
     AUFS, 892; Hucker, 880; FEQ, 8/55; AHR, 7/55; Ann. Am. Acad.,
     9/55; Pacific Affairs, 9/55

1979 Whittemore, Edward P. The Press in Japan Today, a Case Study.
B   Columbia: University of South Carolina Press, 1961.
     91 pp. (Institute of International Studies. Studies
     in International Affairs, No. 1). 61-64390. o.p.
     Sup. 63, 2898; JAS, 8/62; Japan Q., 4-6/62

0266 Who's Who in China. 6th ed. Shanghai: 1919-1951. 51-1089.
B

2114 Wickberg, Edgar. The Chinese in Philippine Life, 1850-1898.
A   New Haven, Conn: Yale University Press, 1965. 280 pp.
     65-22475.
     Sup. 67, 3270; Choice, 1/66; JAS, 5/66; AHR, 4/66; Library
     Journal, 8/65

0163 Wickizer, Vernon Dale. The Rice Economy of Monsoon Asia.
C   Stanford, Calif.: Food Research Institute in cooperation
     with the International Secretariat, Institute of Pacific
     Relations, 1941. 358 pp. (Grain Economics Series, 3).
     42-355. o.p.
     Hucker, 2203; FEQ, 8/42

0716 Wieger, Leon, ed. and tr. Chine Modern...par le p. Leon Wieger.
B   Hien-hien: Imprimiere Editions, 1920-32. 10 v. 32-17022.
     o.p.

0717 Wilbur, Clarence Martin, ed. Documents on Communism, Nationalism,
B   and Soviet Advisers on China, 1918-1927; Papers Seized in
     the Peking Raid. N.Y.: Columbia University Press, 1956.
     617 pp. 56-6813. o.p.
     AUFS, 996; Hucker, 875; JAS, 11/57

1581 Wildes, Harry Emerson. Typhoon in Tokyo; The Occupation and Its
B   Aftermath. N.Y.: Macmillan, 1954. 356 pp. 54-10175. o.p.
     Silberman, 555; FEQ, 11/54; Ann. Am. Acad., 11/54

1219 Wilhelm, Hellmut. Change; Eight Lectures on the I Ching. tr.
C   from German by Cary F. Baynes. Princeton, N.J.: Princeton
     University Press, 1960. 111 pp. (Bollingen Series, Vol.
     62). 60-11791.
     Hucker, 1532; JAS, 8/61; JAOS, 1-3/61

1691 Wilkinson, Thomas Oberson. The Urbanization of Japanese
B   Labor 1868-1955. Amherst: University of Massachusetts
     Press, 1965. 243 pp. 65-26242.
     JAS, 8/66

1275 Willetts, William. Foundations of Chinese Art from Neolithic
A   Pottery to Modern Architecture. N.Y.: McGraw-Hill, 1965.
     456 pp. 64-66127.
     Library Journal, 10/15/65

0267 Williams, Charles Alfred Speed. Encyclopedia of Chinese Sym-
B   bolism and Art Motives; An Alphabetical Compendium of Leg-
     ends and Beliefs as Reflected in the Manners and Customs
     of the Chinese Throughout History. intro. by Kazimitsu
     W. Kato. N.Y.: Julian Press, 1960 (orig. pub. by Kelly &
     Walsh, 1932 under the title Outlines of Chinese Symbolism
     and Art Motives). 468 pp. 60-15987. (R).
     Hucker, 1508

2100 Williams, Lea E. Overseas Chinese Nationalism, the Genesis
B   of the Pan-Chinese Movement in Indonesia, 1900-1916.
     Glencoe, Ill.: Free Press, 1960. 235 pp. 60-9582.
     Hucker, 2103

0533 Williams, Samuel Wells. The Middle Kingdom; A Survey of the
B   Geography, Government, Literature, Social Life, Arts, and
     History of the Chinese Empire and Its Inhabitants.
     N.Y.: Paragon, 1966 (orig. pub. by Scribner's, 1883).
     2 v. 66-16895. (R). (M-University).
     Hucker, 10

0426 Williamson, Henry R. Wang An Shih...a Chinese Statesman and
C   Educationalist of the Sung Dynasty. London: A. Probsthain,
     1935-37. 2 v. 35-13711 rev. o.p.
     Hucker, 347; FEQ, 11/41; JAOS, 12/37

1582 Willoughby, Charles Andrew. MacArthur, 1941-1951. N.Y.:
C   McGraw-Hill, 1954. 441 pp. 54-11277. o.p.
     Silberman, 535

1346 Wilson, John Tuzo. One Chinese Moon. N.Y.: Hill & Wang, 1959.
B   274 pp. 59-14657. o.p.

1565 Wilson, Robert Arden. Genesis of the Meiji Government in Japan,
B   1868-1871. Berkeley: University of California Press, 1957.
     149 pp. (University of California Publications in History,
     Vol. 56). A58-9047. o.p.
     Silberman, 367; JAS, 11/59

1049 Wimsatt, Genevieve Blanche. Chinese Shadow Shows. Cambridge,
C   Mass.: Harvard University Press, 1936. 68 pp. 37-4449.
     o.p.
     Hucker, 1673

1050 Wimsatt, Genevieve Blanche. Selling Wilted Peonies; Biography
C   and Songs of Yu Hsuan-chi, T'ang Poetess. N.Y.: Columbia
     University Press, 1936. 119 pp. 37-1811 rev. o.p.
     JAOS, 6/37

0718 Winfield, Gerald Freeman. China, the Land and the People.
C   N.Y.: Sloane Associates in cooperation with American Insti-
     tute of Pacific Relations, 1948. 437 pp. 48-9514. o.p.
     Hucker, 2203; FEQ, 5/49; Library Journal, 12/15/48

0019 Wint, Guy, ed. Asia; A Handbook. N.Y.: Praeger, 1966.
B   856 pp. 65-13263.
     Sup. 67, 3207; Library Journal, 6/15/66; Pacific Affairs,
     Fall-Winter/66-67; TLS, 7/7/66

0117 Wint, Guy. The British in Asia. rev. ed. N.Y.: Institute
B   of Pacific Relations, 1954. 244 pp. 56-32415. o.p.
     AUFS, 63

0827 Wint, Guy. Common Sense About China. N.Y.: Macmillan, 1960.
A   176 pp. 60-15049.
     Sup. 61, 2807; Hucker, 922; JAS, 5/61; China Q., 7-9/60;
     Library Journal, 10/15/60; Pacific Affairs, Winter/61;
     TLS, 2/2/60

0719 Wint, Guy. Dragon and Sickle; How the Communist Revolution Hap-
C   pened in China. N.Y.: Praeger, 1959. 107 pp. 59-7728. o.p.
     JAS, 8/60

0071 Wint, Guy. Spotlight on Asia. Baltimore: Penguin, 1955.
B   221 pp. 59-7728. o.p.
     Pacific Affairs, 12/60; TLS, 4/17/59

0197 Winter, Henry James Jacques. Eastern Science; An Outline of
B   Its Scope and Contribution. London: Murray, dist. by
     Paragon, 1952. (Wisdom of the East Series). 52-10111.
     Hucker, 1367

0427 Wittfogel, Karl August. History of Chinese Society: Liao
B   (907-1125). Philadelphia: American Philosophical Society,
     1949. 725 pp. (Transactions of the American Philosophical
     Society, n.s., XXXVI). 49-8472. o.p.

Hucker, 355; FEQ, 5/50

0072 Wittfogel, Karl August. Oriental Despotism, a Comparative Study
A   of Total Power. New Haven, Conn.: Yale University Press,
     1957. 556 pp. 56-10873.
     AUFS, 65; Hucker, 1791; Am. Anthropologist, 6/57; JAOS,
     1-3/61; Library Journal, 4/1/57

1566 Wohlstetter, Roberta. Pearl Harbor; Warning and Decision.
B   Stanford, Calif.: Stanford University Press, 1962.
     426 pp. 62-15966.
     AHR, 1/63; Library Journal, 9/1/62; Pacific Affairs,
     Winter/62-63; TLS, 2/15/63

2087 Wolf, Margery. The House of Lim: a Study of a Chinese Farm
A   Family. N.Y.: Appleton-Century-Crofts, 1968. 147 pp.
     68-11211.
     Choice, 3/69; JAS, 11/68

1252 Wright, Arthur F. Buddhism in Chinese History. Stanford,
B   Calif.: Stanford University Press, 1959. 144 pp. 59-7432.
     AUFS, 671; Hucker, 1249; JAS, 11/59; JAOS, 10-12/59

1220 Wright, Arthur F., ed. The Confucian Persuasion. contrib. by
B   James Cahill and others. Stanford, Calif.: Stanford Uni-
     versity Press, 1969 (orig. pub. in 1960). 390 pp. (Studies
     in the Civilizations of Eastern Asia). 60-8561. (R).
     Sup. 61, 2808; Hucker, 1097; JAS, 5/61; JAOS, 4-6/62

1187 Wright, Arthur F., ed. Studies in Chinese Thought. Chicago:
B   University of Chicago Press, 1953. 317 pp. 53-13533.
     AUFS, 612; Hucker, 1064; FEQ, 5/55; AHR, 7/54; Ann. Am.
     Acad., 7/54

0534 Wright, Mary Clabaugh. The Last Stand of Chinese Conserva-
A   tism; The T'ung-chih Restoration, 1862-1874. Stanford,
     Calif.: Stanford University Press, 1957. 426 pp. 57-5946.
     AUFS, 767; Hucker, 617; JAS, 5/58; AHR, 1/58; Am. Pol. Sci.
     R., 3/58; JAOS, 7-9/58; Library Journal, 3/1/57; Pacific
     Affairs, 3/58; TLS, 4/25/58

0535 Wright, Stanley Fowler. Hart and the Chinese Customs. Belfast:
B   Mullan, 1950. 949 pp. 51-2518.
     Hucker, 673; FEQ, 8/52

0536 Wu, Ai-ch'en. China and the Soviet Union; A Study of Sino-
B   Soviet Relations. Port Washington, N.Y.: Kennikat, 1968
     (orig. pub. by John Day, 1950). 434 pp. 67-29610. (R).
     Hucker, 703; AHR, 7/51; Pacific Affairs, 3/51; TLS,
     12/22/50

0945 Wu, Ching-tzu. The Scholars. tr. by Yang Hsien-yi and
A   Gladys Yang. Peking: Foreign Languages Press, 1957.
     721 pp. A58-4116. o.p.
     Hucker, 1698

0865 Wu, Chun-hsi. Dollars Dependents and Dogma; Overseas Chinese
B   Remittances to Communist China. intro. by C. F. Remer.
     Stanford, Calif.: Hoover Institution on War, Revolution,
     and Peace, 1967. 231 pp. 67-24368.
     JAS, 8/68; China Q., 7-9/68

1120 Wu, Hung-tsao. New Chinese Writing. Taipei: Heritage Press,
C   1962. 170 pp.

0720 Wu, Lien-te. Plague Fighter; The Autobiography of a Modern
B   Chinese Physician. Cambridge: Heffer, 1959. 667 pp.
     59-1837.
     JAS, 11/59

1051 Wu, Shih-ch'ang. On the Red Chamber Dream; A Critical Study
C   of Two Annotated Manuscripts of the XVIIIth Century.
     Oxford: Clarendon, 1961. 391 pp. 61-1936.
     JAS, 11/61; JAOS, 1-3/62

0946 Wu tse tien ssu ta chian. Dee Goong An. Three Murder Cases
C   Solved by Judge Dee, an Old Chinese Detective Novel Trans-
     lated from the Original Chinese with Introduction and Notes,
     by R. H. van Gulik. Tokyo: Toppan Printing Co., 1949.
     237 pp. 57-17542.

0226 Wu, Wen-chin. Leaders of Twentieth Century China; An Annotated
C   Bibliography of Selected Chinese Biographical Works in
     the Hoover Library. Stanford, Calif.: Stanford University
     Press, 1956. 106 pp. (Bibliographical Series, 4).
     56-13811. o.p.

0895 Wu, Yuan-li. An Economic Survey of Communist China. N.Y.:
B   Bookman, 1956. 566 pp. 56-13636.
     Hucker, 2164; JAS, 11/56; Am. Econ. R., 12/56; Ann. Am.

Acad., 9/56; Geog. R., 10/56; Library Journal, 3/15/56;
Pol. Sci. Q., 12/56; TLS, 7/27/56

0896 Wu, Yuan-Li. The Economy of Communist China; An Introduction.
B   N.Y.: Praeger, 1965. 225 pp. 65-18082.
     Choice, 2/66; JAS, 8/66; Am. Econ. R., 6/66; Ann. Am. Acad.,
     5/66; TLS, 7/28/66

1052 Wylie, Alexander. Notes on Chinese Literature: With Introduc-
C   tory Remarks on the Progressive Advancement of the Art;
     And a List of Translations from the Chinese into Various
     European Languages. 2d ed. N.Y.: Paragon, 1964 (orig.
     pub. by Presbyterian Mission, 1922). 307 pp. 64-18442.
     (R).
     JAS, 2/65

0721 Yakhontoff, Victor A. The Chinese Soviets. N.Y.: Coward-
C   McCann, 1934. 296 pp. 34-25723. o.p. (M-University).
     Hucker, 890

1880 Yamada, Chisaburoh, ed. Decorative Arts of Japan. Tokyo: Ko-
A   dansha, dist. by Japan Publications Trading Co., 1964.
     262 pp. 63-22011.
     Choice, 11/65; Library Journal, 9/15/64; TLS, 12/23/65

1881 Yamada, Tokubei. Japanese Dolls. 2d ed. Tokyo: Japan Travel
B   Bureau, 1959. 190 pp. (Tourist Library, N.S. 17).
     59-13186.
     Silberman, 856

1429 Yamagiwa, Joseph Koshimi, ed. Readings in Japanese History.
C   Ann Arbor: University of Michigan Press, 1966. 2 v.
     66-31440.
     JAS, 5/67

1803 Yamamoto, Yuzo. Three Plays. tr. from Japanese by Glenn
C   W. Shaw. Tokyo: Hokuseido, 1935. 358 pp. 36-4894.
     Silberman, 1155

1657 Yamamura, Kozo. Economic Policy in Postwar Japan; Growth vs
C   Economic Democracy. Berkeley: University of California
     Press, 1967. 226 pp. (Center for Japanese and Korean
     Studies). 67-29726.
     Choice, 12/68; JAS, 11/68; Am. Econ. R., 9/68; Library
     Journal, 12/1/67; Pacific Affairs, Fall/68

1658 Yamanaka, Tokutaro, comp. Small Business in Japan. Tokyo:
B   Japan Times, 1960. 368 pp. 61-4047.

1430 Yanaga, Chitoshi. Japan since Perry. Hamden, Conn.: Archon,
B   1966 (orig. pub. by McGraw-Hill, 1949). 723 pp.
     66-16779. (R).
     AUFS, 300; Silberman, 316; FEQ, 11/50; AHR, 4/50; Ann. Am.
     Acad., 1/50; JAOS, 7-9/50; Pacific Affairs, 12/49

1567 Yanagida, Kunio, ed. Japanese Manners & Customs in the Meiji
C   Era. tr. by Charles S. Terry. Tokyo: Obunsha, 1957.
     335 pp. (Japanese Culture in the Meiji Era, Vol. IV).
     A59-8764.
     Silberman, 1368

1882 Yanagisawa, Soen. Tray Landscapes (Bonkei and Bonseki). rev. ed.
B   N.Y.: Japan Publications Trading Co., 1964. 193 pp.
     (Tourist Library, N.S. 19). 56-1256.
     Silberman, 835; JAS, 2/58

0912 Yang, Ch'ing-k'un. The Chinese Family in the Communist Revo-
B   lution. fore. by Talcott Parsons. Cambridge, Mass.: M.I.T.
     Press (orig. pub. by Harvard University Press, 1959).
     246 pp. 59-14897. (R).
     Sup. 61, 2809; Hucker, 2033; Am. Soc. R., 12/60; Library
     Journal, 1/1/60; Pacific Affairs, 9/60

1188 Yang, Ch'ing-k'un. Religion in Chinese Society; A Study of Con-
A   temporary Social Functions of Religion and Some of Their
     Historical Factors. Berkeley: University of California
     Press, 1961. 473 pp. 61-7520
     JAS, 8/62

0947 Yang, Hsien-i, tr. The Courtesan's Jewel Box; Chinese Stories
A   of the Xth-XVIIth Centuries. Peking: Foreign Languages
     Press, 1957. 553 pp. 57-41973. o.p.
     AUFS, 1100; JAS, 5/59

1005 Yang, Hsien-i. The Fisherman's Revenge; A Peking Opera. tr.
C   by Yang Hsien-yi and Gladys Yang. Peking: Foreign Languages
     Press, 1956. 53 pp. Hand catalog.

0948 Yang, Hsien-i, tr. The Man Who Sold a Ghost; Chinese Tales of
C   the 3rd-6th Centuries. Peking: Foreign Languages Press,

1958. 162 pp. Hand catalog. o.p.

0949 Yang, Hsien-i. Stories About Not Being Afraid of Ghosts. Pe-
C   king: Foreign Languages Press, 1961. 89 pp. Hand cata-
      log. o.p.

1121 Yang, I. The Bright Future. tr. by Tang Sheng. Peking:
C   Foreign Languages Press, 1958. 105 pp. Hand catalog.

1122 Yang, I. Uncle Kao, by Ouyang Shan (pseud.). tr. by Kuo Mei-
C   hua. Peking: Foreign Languages Press, 1957. 296 pp.
      57-48991.

1169 Yang, I-fan. The Case of Hu Feng. Hong Kong: Union Research
C   Institute, 1956. 169 pp. 57-35727.
      Hucker, 1740

1985 Yang, Key Paik. Reference Guide to Korean Materials, 1945-1959.
B   Washington: 1960. 131 pp. 60-50260. o.p.

0428 Yang, Lien-sheng. Money and Credit in China; A Short History.
C   Cambridge, Mass.: Harvard University Press, 1952. 143 pp.
      52-5413.
      Hucker, 2264; FEQ, 11/53; JAOS, 7-9/53; Pacific Affairs, 6/53

0350 Yang, Lien-sheng. Studies in Chinese Institutional History.
B   Cambridge, Mass.: Harvard University Press, 1961. 299 pp.
      (Harvard-Yenching Institute Studies, XX). 61-8844.
      Hucker, 107; JAS, 2/62

0351 Yang, Lien-sheng. Topics in Chinese History. Cambridge,
B   Mass.: Harvard University Press, 1950. 57 pp. (Harvard-
      Yenching Institute Studies, IV). 50-10183. o.p. (M-Uni-
      versity).
      Hucker, 97; JAOS, 1-3/51

1123 Yang, Shuo. A Thousand Miles of Lovely Land. tr. by Yuan
C   Ko-chia. Peking: Foreign Languages Press, 1957. 236 pp.
      57-40848. o.p.

0227 Yang, Winston L. Y. A Bibliography of the Chinese Language.
A   N.Y.: American Association of Teachers of Chinese Lan-
      guage and Culture, dist. by Paragon, 1966. 171 pp.
      66-27975.
      JAS, 5/67

1906 Yashiro, Yukio, ed. Art Treasures of Japan. Tokyo: Koku-
C   sai Bunka Shinkokai, 1960. 2 v. 63-2165.
      Japan Q., 1-3/61

1907 Yashiro, Yukio. 2000 Years of Japanese Art. ed. by Peter
B   C. Swann. N.Y.: Abrams, 1958. 268 pp. 58-13478.
      AUFS, 407; Silberman, 735; Japan Q., 7-9/59; TLS, 4/17/59

1728 Yasuda, Kenneth. The Japanese Haiku, Its Essential Nature,
C   History, and Possibilities in English with Selected Examples.
      Rutland, Vt.: Tuttle, 1958. 232 pp. 57-8795.
      Silberman, 1061; JAS, 8/58; Japan Q., 4-6/58

1437 Yasumaro. Translation of "Ko-ji-ki"....or "Records of Ancient
B   Matters", by Basil Hall Chamberlain. 2d ed. with annota-
      tions by W. G. Aston. New Hyde Park, N.Y.: University
      Books, 1966 (orig. pub. by J. L. Thompson, 1932). 495 pp.
      33-20689. (R).
      Silberman, 193

1124 Yeh, Chun-chan, tr. Three Seasons and Other Stories. Lon-
C   don: Staples Press, 1947. 136 pp. Hand catalog. o.p.

1125 Yeh, Shao-chun. Schoolmaster Ni Huan-chih; Novel. tr. by A. C.
B   Barnes. Peking: Foreign Languages Press, 1958. 383 pp.
      59-31782. o.p.

0950 Yen, Hui-ch'ing, comp. and tr. Stories of Old China. tr. by
C   W. W. Yeng. Shanghai: New Art and Literature Publishing
      House, 1958. 178 pp. NUC 63-39119.

1347 Yen, Maria, pseud. The Umbrella Garden; A Picture of Student
C   Life in Red China. adapted from Chinese by Maria Yen
      with Richard M. McCarthy. N.Y.: Macmillan, 1954. 268 pp.
      54-12389. o.p.
      AUFS, 1000; Hucker, 964; FEQ, 5/55

0537 Yen, Sophia Su-fei. Taiwan in China's Foreign Relations,
B   1836-1874. Hamden, Conn.: Shoe String Press, 1965. 404 pp.
      65-7577.
      Choice, 11/65; JAS, 5/66

2005 Yi, Miryok. The Yalu Flows, a Korean Childhood. tr. by H. A.
C   Hammelmann. East Lansing: Michigan State University Press,

1956. 149 pp. 56-12105.
Silberman, 1902; JAS, 5/57; TLS, 8/6/54

1798 Yosano, Akiko. Tangled Hair; Translated from the Works of the
B   Poet Akiko Yosano, by Shio Sakanishi. Boston: Marshall
      Jones, 1935. 71 pp. 36-137. o.p. (M-University).
      AUFS, 493

1711 Yoshida, Kenko. Essays in Idleness; The Tsurezuregusa of
A   Kenko. tr. by Donald Keene. N.Y.: Columbia University
      Press, 1967. 213 pp. (Columbia College Program of
      Translations from the Oriental Classics/Records of
      Civilization: Sources and Studies, LXXVIII). 67-23566.
      Choice, 7-8/68; JAS, 5/69

1431 Yoshida, Shigeru. Japan's Decisive Century, 1867-1967.
B   N.Y.: Praeger, 1967. 110 pp. 67-22296.
      Choice, 7-8/68; Library Journal, 7/67; TLS, 8/1/68

1935 Yoshida, Toshi. Japanese Print-Making; A Handbook of Traditional
A   & Modern Techniques. Rutland, Vt.: Tuttle, 1966. 176 pp.
      66-20674.
      Choice, 7-8/67; Library Journal, 1/15/67

1568 Yoshihashi, Takehiko. Conspiracy at Mukden; The Rise of the
C   Japanese Military. New Haven, Conn.: Yale University Press,
      1963. 274 pp. 63-17025.
      Sup. 65, 3076; JAS, 8/64; AHR, 7/64; Am. Pol. Sci. R., 9/64;
      Japan Q., 10-12/64; Library Journal, 3/15/64; TLS, 6/18/64

1791 Yoshikawa, Eiji. The Heike Story. tr. from Japanese by
C   Fuki Wooyenaka Uramatsu. N.Y.: Knopf, 1956. 626 pp.
      56-5778. o.p.
      Silberman, 1035; Japan Q., 4-6/57; Library Journal, 11/1/56

1053 Yoshikawa, Kojiro. An Introduction to Sung Poetry. tr. by
A   Burton Watson. Cambridge, Mass.: Harvard University
      Press, 1967. 191 pp. 67-14347.
      Choice, 2/68; JAS, 5/68; TLS, 1/4/68

1569 Young, Arthur Morgan. Imperial Japan, 1926-1938. N.Y.: Morrow,
B   1938. 328 pp. 38-27898. o.p.
      AUFS, 301; Silberman, 438

1570 Young, Arthur Morgan. Japan in Recent Times, 1912-1926. N.Y.:
C   Morrow, 1929. 347 pp. 29-26885. o.p. (M-University).
      AUFS, 302; Silberman, 437

0722 Young, Arthur Nichols. China and the Helping Hand, 1937-1945.
A   Cambridge, Mass.: Harvard University Press, 1963. 502 pp.
      (Harvard East Asian Series, 12). 63-20774.
      Choice, 3/64; JAS, 8/64; Ann. Am. Acad., 11/64; Library
      Journal, 12/1/63

0723 Young, Arthur Nichols. China's Wartime Finance and Inflation,
A   1937-1945. Cambridge, Mass.: Harvard University Press,
      1965. 421 pp. (Harvard East Asian Series, 20). 65-22049.
      Choice, 11/66; JAS, 8/66; Am. Econ. R., 12/66; AHR, 7/66;
      J. Pol. Econ., 6/66; Library Journal, 11/1/65

1126 The Young Coal-Miner and Other Stories, by Contemporary Chinese
C   Writers. Peking: Foreign Languages Press, 1958. 176 pp.
      59-24097. o.p.

0828 Young, Kenneth Todd. Negotiating with the Chinese Communists:
C   the United States Experience, 1953-1967. N.Y.: McGraw-
      Hill for Council on Foreign Relations, 1968. 461 pp.
      (United States and China in World Affairs/Council on For-
      eign Relations). 67-28088.
      Choice, 10/68; JAS, 2/69; Library Journal, 1/1/68

0724 Yu, George T. Party Politics in Republican China; The Kuo-
A   mintang, 1912-1924. Berkeley: University of California
      Press, 1966. 203 pp. 66-13089.
      Choice, 11/66; JAS, 8/67; AHR, 4/67; Am. Pol. Sci. R., 12/66;
      Ann. Am. Acad., 1/67; Library Journal, 5/15/66; Pacific
      Affairs, Spring-Summer/66; Pol. Sci. Q., 6/67

1127 Yu, Ho-lin. Harvest, by Yeh Tzu (pseud.). tr. by Tang Sheng
C   and Ma Ching-chun. Peking: Foreign Languages Press, 1960.
      183 pp. 61-28139.

2041 Yu, Hon. Study of North Korea. Seoul: Research Institute
C   of Internal and External Affairs, 1966. 317 pp. 68-44186.

1348 Yu, Te-chi. Mass Persuasion in Communist China, by Frederick
A   T. C. Yu. N.Y.: Praeger, 1964. 186 pp. (Praeger Publica-
      tions in Russian History and World Communism, 145). 64-13389.
      Choice, 7-8/64; Ann. Am. Acad., 1/65; Library Journal,
      5/1/64; Pol. Sci. Q., 9/65

0429   Yu, Ying-shih.   Trade and Expansion in Han China; A Study
C   in the Structure of Sino-barbarian Economic Relations.
         Berkeley: University of California Press, 1967.   251 pp.
         67-12492.
         Choice, 3/68; JAS, 5/68

1128   Yuan, Chia-hua, ed. and tr.   Contemporary Chinese Short Stories.
B   N.Y.: Carrington, 1946.   169 pp.   A48-5659.   o.p.

0228   Yuan, T'ung-li.   China in Western Literature; A Continuation of
B   Cordier's Bibliotheca Sinica.   New Haven, Conn.: Far East-
         ern Publications, Yale University, 1958.   802 pp.   58-59833.
         Hucker, 15; JAS, 8/59

0229   Yuan, T'ung-li.   Economic and Social Development of Modern
B   China: a Bibliographical Guide.   New Haven, Conn.: Human
         Relations Area Files, 1956.   130 pp.   57-92.   o.p.
         Hucker, 1972

0230   Yuan, T'ung-li.   Russian Works on China, 1918-1958; A Selected
B   Bibliography.   Tokyo: 1959.   388-430 pp.   (Monumenta Serica,
         Vol. 18).   60-4119.   o.p.

0538   Yule, Sir Henry, ed. and tr.   Cathay and the Way Thither; Being
C   a Collection of Medieval Notices of China.   new ed., rev. by
         Henri Cordier.   Taipei: Ch'eng-wen Publishing Co., dist. by
         Chinese Materials and Research Aids Service Center, 1966
         (orig. pub. by Hakluyt Society, 1913-16).   4 v. in 2.
         5-40435.   (R).
         Hucker, 135

0539   Yung, Wing.   My Life in China and America.   N.Y.: Holt, 1909.
B   286 pp.   9-31843.   o.p.
         Hucker, 696; Ann. Am. Acad., 5/10

0829   Zagoria, Donald S.   The Sino-Soviet Conflict, 1956-1961.
A   Princeton, N.J.: Princeton University Press, 1962.   484 pp.
         62-10890.
         Sup. 63, 2930; JAS, 11/62; AHR, 10/62; Am. Pol. Sci. R.,
         9/62; Ann. Am. Acad., 1/63; China Q., 7-9/63; Library
         Journal, 3/1/62; Pacific Affairs, Spring/63; Pol. Sci. Q.,
         9/62; TLS, 8/24/62

1349   Zi, Etienne.   Pratique des Examens Litteraires en Chine.
C   Shanghai: Mission Catholique, 1894.   (Varietes Sino-
         logiques, 5).   50-42950.   o.p.
         Hucker, 1840

0073   Zinkin, Maurice.   Asia and the West.   new and rev. ed.   N.Y.:
B   International Secretariat, Institute of Pacific Relations,
         1953.   304 pp.   A54-8866.   o.p.
         FEQ, 11/52; Am. Pol. Sci. R., 9/53; Am. Soc. R., 8/52;
         Ann. Am. Acad., 11/53; J. Pol. Econ., 8/52; Pacific Affairs,
         6/52

1712   Zolbrod, Leon M.   Takizawa Bakin.   N.Y.: Twayne, 1967.   162 pp.
C   (Twayne World Authors Series).   67-12269.
         JAS, 8/68; Library Journal, 1/1/68; Pacific Affairs, Summer/68

0725   Zolotow, Maurice.   Maurice William and Sun Yat-sen.   London:
B   Hale, 1948.   128 pp.   49-24346.   o.p.

1054   Zucker, Adolf Eduard.   The Chinese Theater.   Boston: Little,
C   Brown, 1925.   234 pp.   25-23016.   o.p.
         AUFS, 1137; Hucker, 1664

Addresses of Microform Companies

IDC, Inter Documentation Company, AG, Postrasse 9, Zug, Switzerland

Microphoto Division, Bell & Howell Company, 1700 Shaw Avenue, Cleveland, Ohio 44112

Research Publications Inc., 254 College Street, New Haven, Conn. 06510

University Microfilms, Ann Arbor, Mich, 48106

IDC, Rijnsburgerweg 177, Leiden, Netherlands

A Note on the Foreign Area Materials Center

The State Education Department in New York is actively concerned with strengthening opportunities and resources for international and comparative studies in the schools, colleges, and universities of New York, as well as with related activities in educational exchange and overseas service. Emphasis is being placed on the peoples, cultures, and contemporary institutions of those areas traditionally neglected in American education—namely, Asia, Africa, Latin America, Russia and Eastern Europe. Also emphasized are comparative studies which reflect recent scholarship in the social sciences and humanities and which explore significant aspects of American society in relation to developments elsewhere in the world.

Recent efforts of the Department in international studies include faculty fellowships and seminars; and programs of independent reading and seminar discussion, summer institutes, and other opportunities for secondary school teachers; consultant services to schools, colleges, and universities in developing foreign area studies; and experimental programs in the study of critical languages in schools and colleges, summer field work overseas for students and teachers, and the like.

As a further extension of these efforts, the State Education Department established, in December, 1963, the Foreign Area Materials Center. In March, 1967, because of increasing interest in the Center's work from institutions outside New York State, the National Council of Associations for International Studies, a group of eleven regional college associations and consortia, was established and has become an active sponsor of the Center's work. The Center, which is located in New York City, is concerned with the development of materials useful in teaching about foreign areas, mainly at the undergraduate level.

Types of materials which have been produced or are in preparation include color slides in South Asian studies, reproductions of museum materials from India, reviews of documentary films, computerized bibliographies for college libraries, and experimental teaching materials. The Center provides liaison with publishers and other organizations producing materials useful in undergraduate instruction and is particularly concerned with out-of-print books and other needs of college libraries. These activities are being supported by grants from foundation sources, the United States government, and the National Council of Associations for International Studies.

The Center also distributes various types of syllabi and reprints, bibliographies and similar materials to college faculty members offering courses related to the Center's main areas of interest—Asia, Africa, Latin America, Russia and Eastern Europe. A list of materials is available on request.

The Foreign Area Materials Center is under the direction of Ward Morehouse, Director, and Authur Osteen, Associate Director, Center for International Programs and Comparative Studies. The Manager of the Foreign Area Materials Center in New York City is Miss Edith Ehrman.

Correspondence regarding any of the activities mentioned above and requests for materials should be directed to the Foreign Area Materials (11 West 42nd Street, New York, 10036). Correspondence concerning other aspects of the Department's programs in foreign area studies and related international activities should be sent to the Director, Center for International Programs and Comparative Studies, University of the State of New York, State Education Department, Albany, N. Y. 12224.

Some Publications of the Foreign Area Materials Center

Occasional Publications Series

Ward Morehouse, editor, Foreign Area Studies and the College Library. 1964. (FAMC Occasional Publication No.1). $2.00.

L. A. Peter Gosling, Maps, Atlases and Gazetteers for Asian Studies: A Critical Guide. 1965. (FAMC Occasional Publication No. 2). $2.00

Patrick Wilson, Science in South Asia, Past & Present: A Preliminary Bibliography. 1966. (FAMC Occasional Publication No. 3). $2.00

Ward Morehouse, editor, The Comparative Approach to Area Studies and the Disciplines: Problems of Teaching and Research on Asia. 1967. (FAMC Occasional Publication No. 4). $2.00

Lyman Legters, Language and Area Studies: A Bibliography. 1967. (FAMC Occasional Publication No. 5). $2.00

George Fischer, American Research on Soviet Society. 1967. (FAMC Occasional Publication No. 6). $2.00.

Theodore Herman, editor. The Geography of China: A Selected and Annotated Bibliography. 1967. (FAMC Occasional Publication No. 7). $2.00.

Ward Morehouse, editor, Understanding Science and Technology in India and Pakistan. 1967. (FAMC Occasional Publication No. 8). $2.00.

Winston L. Y. Yang and Teresa S. Yang, editors, Asian Resources in American Libraries. 1968. (FAMC Occasional Publication No. 9). $3.00.

East Asia: A Bibliography for Undergraduate Libraries. 1969. (FAMC Occasional Publication No. 10). $8.95

South Asia: A Bibliography for Undergraduate Libraries. 1969. (FAMC Occasional Publication No. 11). $8.95

Africa south of the Sahara: A Bibliography for Undergraduate Libraries. 1969. (FAMC Occasional Publication No. 12). $8.95

Checklists of Paperbound Books

Cynthia T. Morehouse, compiler, Paperbound Books on Asia. 1966. $1.50.

Paul Rosenblum, compiler, Checklist of Paperbound Books on Africa. 1968. $1.00.

Sherman D. Spector and Lyman Legters, compilers, <u>Checklist of Paperbound Books on Russia and East Europe</u>. 1966. $1.00.

<u>Other Materials</u>

A number of syllabi, course outlines and teaching notes, bibliographies, and other materials are also available from the Foreign Area Materials Center. A list of these materials will be sent on request.

<u>Minimum order, $2.00; all orders must be prepaid</u>. Checks should be drawn to <u>The University of the State of New York</u>.

Foreign Area Materials Center, University of the State of New York, State Education Department, 11 West 42nd Street, New York, N. Y. 10036.